A Practical Guide to FDA's Food and Drug Law and Regulation

Fourth Edition

Edited by Kenneth R. Piña and Wayne L. Pines

ISBN 978-1-935065-53-1

FDLI

1155 15th Street NW
Ste. 800
Washington, D.C. 20005
Tel: (202) 371-1420; Fax: (202) 371-0649
www.fdli.org

Contents

Introduction

Since publication of the third edition of *A Practical Guide to Food and Drug Law and Regulation* there have been many changes to the laws and regulations that govern the development, marketing and sale of food, medical products and cosmetics. An entire new category has been added: tobacco. The goal of this fourth edition is to provide an up-to-date primer that continues to explain these laws and regulations in simple, non-technical terms.

It is hard for us, the editors, to believe that this text is now in its fourth edition! We are gratified that so many people have found the text to be useful. The idea for this book originated more than 15 years ago, when Ken was teaching the food and drug law course for the Temple University School of Pharmacy's Graduate Studies Program for Quality Assurance and Regulatory Affairs. He noted that existing books on food and drug law were written in the "case law" format commonly used to teach law students, or were written for audiences with pre-existing knowledge of the Food and Drug Administration (FDA) laws. What was needed was a practical legal/regulatory primer that was substantive but that could also be readily understood by a wide range of persons with an interest in FDA-related laws and regulations.

The Food and Drug Law Institute (FDLI) welcomed the idea for such a text and suggested that Ken work with Wayne to develop the book. Wayne, a non-lawyer with extensive FDA regulatory experience, embraced the idea and joined Ken as co-editor. We were on our way!

Since the first edition was published, this book has become a popular, basic resource both academically and within regulated industries. It is now used as a standard textbook in a number of established law school food and drug law courses, is used frequently to teach graduate-level regulatory courses, is a common reference text in many life science companies, and has been cited as a reference in judicial opinions (including a U.S. Supreme Court Opinion). For many entering the FDA regulatory world, it is their first primer on the laws and regulations that govern the development, marketing and sale of food, medical products and cosmetics.

The intended readers of this book include students in law schools and in other professional schools, plus professionals who work for regulated companies and in related fields. Their commonality is that they want and need to understand how the laws and regulations that guide FDA's activities work and they need the information to be provided in practical, real-world terms.

This fourth edition stays true to our original goal. The format is structured so as to provide a natural progression from subject to subject, so that it is useful not only as a resource but also as a teaching tool. Each chapter has been updated so as to reflect the most current status of relevant laws and regulations.

We continue to be very grateful to the chapter authors. Each of them is a recognized leader in their field, with extremely hectic schedules, yet they have kindly dedicated substantial time and energy not just to their original authorship, but to updating their chapters, for some three times now. They continue to provide not just their practical knowledge but their valuable insights. We would also like to thank the team at FDLI, who assisted in making sure this fourth edition became a reality. Finally, we acknowledge and thank our families, who supported this effort with patience and love.

We hope that this volume serves as a valuable introduction to the Food, Drug and Cosmetic Act—what the law says and how it and its implementing regulations really work.

Kenneth R. Piña
kpina@corerisksltd.com

Wayne L. Pines
wpines@apcoworldwide.com

About the Editors

Kenneth R. Piña, J.D., R.Ph.

Kenneth R. Piña is a founding Principal of Core Risks Ltd. LLC (CRL), a global provider of Compliance and Risk Solution services to the Life Science industry. Mr. Piña's practice focuses upon the development and maintenance of corporate compliance and ethics training programs, critical Enterprise Risk Assessments, the development of Corporate Crisis Management plans and infrastructure, and neutral fact-finding capabilities for sensitive internal investigations involving compliance-related claims. Mr. Piña also serves as an arbitrator in complex life science/pharmaceutical and commercial disputes.

Prior to joining CRL, Mr. Piña was the Senior Vice President, Chief Legal Officer and Secretary of Henkel Corporation, a consumer product and specialty chemical company. Before joining Henkel, Mr. Piña served as Vice President, General Counsel and Secretary of Rhone-Poulenc Rorer Pharmaceuticals Inc.

Mr. Piña received his Juris Doctorate from the Dickinson School of Law, The Pennsylvania State University, where he was named a Food and Drug Law Institute Scholar and also received the American Jurisprudence Award in Food and Drug law. He is also a graduate of the Rutgers University College of Pharmacy. Mr. Piña is active in numerous professional and charitable organizations and received a Presidential Call to Service Award in 2010 for his volunteer leadership efforts with the American Red Cross.

Wayne L. Pines

Wayne L. Pines is President of Health Care and Regulatory Services at APCO Worldwide in Washington, D.C. He is an international consultant on FDA-related issues, specializing in crisis management, drug/device approvals, advertising and promotion issues, advisory committee preparation, and media outreach.

A graduate of Rutgers University, Mr. Pines served as Director of Consumer Education, Chief of Press Relations, and Associate Commissioner for Public Affairs at FDA. He has written or edited a dozen books, including *How to Work with the FDA*; *FDA: a Century of Consumer Protection*; two books on risk management, three books on crisis management, and the *FDA Advertising and Promotion Manual*. He has chaired since their inception in the late 1980s the annual promotion/advertising education conferences for both the Food and Drug Law Institute and the Drug Information Association, and is a frequent speaker at other conferences.

Mr. Pines is a director and served as founding President of the Alliance for a Stronger FDA. He also is a director and former Chairman of the MedStar Health Research Institute. He serves on the boards of other organizations. His awards include the FDA Award of Merit twice, the Public Health Service Superior Service Award and the FDA Alumnus of the Year award.

Chapter 1

Overview of the U.S. Legal System

Edward P. Richards, III, J.D., M.P.H., Louisiana State University Law Center, Baton Rouge, LA

Key Points

- The Constitution is the fundamental source of U.S. law.
- The Constitution divides legal powers between the states and the federal government.
- The federal government is divided into three parts to create checks and balances on its power.
- The Supreme Court ensures that other branches of the government do not violate the Constitution.
- Agencies are created by Congress and overseen by the President.
- Federal agencies such as the Food and Drug Administration (FDA) are in the executive branch of the federal government.
- FDA may only regulate products that affect interstate commerce.
- The courts defer to agency decisions.
- Agencies may take emergency actions to protect the public health and safety.
- Formal agency regulations are subject to public notice and comment.

INTRODUCTION

The food, drug and medical devices industries are unique in their breadth and complexity, and their Intimate impact on individual lives. They are heavily regulated by state and federal government agencies to ensure that the public is protected from unsafe goods and from intentional contamination. This chapter introduces the basic structure and process of the legal system as it affects food, drug and medical device regulation.

FEDERALISM

The American legal system is a federal system, with powers divided between the states and the central government. The sharing of power between state and federal governments, and the primacy of the federal government's powers, are key characteristics of the American legal system. This system was shaped by the Revolutionary War. Each of the 13 original colonies had an independent government that was overseen by England. Communications were slow, and England's concerns generally were limited to taxes and keeping the exports and imports flowing. The colonies had some freedom to govern themselves in domestic matters. With the Declaration of Independence, they became separate nations with complete control over their legal affairs. When they joined together under the Articles of Confederation to fight the war, none was willing to give up control of its government to a central authority. The result was a weak federation that almost lost the war because it could not raise troops and supplies.

The drafters of the Constitution wanted to assure that the United States would present a unified face to the world and would be able to defend itself in future conflicts. The federal government was given the sole power to deal with foreign governments. This includes the power of Congress to declare war, and the President's broad national security powers to counter both foreign and domestic threats to the nation. Conflicts between the states led the drafters to give the federal government primary authority over interstate commerce to prevent trade wars between the states that would interfere with the interests of the nation. The states retained the powers that were not given to the federal government. These included the public health and safety powers. The Supremacy Clause of the Constitution allows Congress to preempt state regulation in areas where the states and the federal government share legal authority.

The Supremacy Clause of the Constitution allows Congress to preempt state regulation in areas where the states and the federal government share legal authority.

The powers of the federal government were constrained by the Bill of Rights, a series of 10 amendments to the Constitution that protect individual liberty. Constitutional amendments adopted after the Civil War banned slavery and gave the federal government additional powers to protect individual rights from state abuses. These amendments provided the legal authority to extend the Bill of Rights protections to actions by state governments, which was done by the Supreme Court over the next 100 years.

Federal Commerce Powers

The import and export of foods, drugs and medical devices is regulated through treaties with other countries and statutes passed by Congress. Unless specifically authorized by Congress, states have no role in the regulation of foreign trade. At the federal level, domestic food and drug law is authorized through the Commerce Clause of the Constitution. States may not pass laws that attempt to limit interstate commerce by favoring in-state businesses. Thus, state laws that banned milk from out-of-state dairies were held unconstitutional because they interfered with interstate commerce in their attempts to protect local businesses. State consumer protection laws, such as those requiring the inspection of imported milk and banning the import of contaminated milk, are constitutional, provided they also apply to milk produced within the state.

The breadth of federal power to regulate interstate commerce is defined by Congress, subject to limits imposed by the Supreme Court. Generally speaking, anything that moves between the states, any business that uses raw materials that come from out of state or any business that affects interstate commerce is subject to regulation under the Commerce Clause. The Civil Rights Act uses this broad definition of interstate commerce, and a court found that a barbecue restaurant whose only customers were local in-state residents was involved in interstate commerce because it bought condiments that originated outside the state.

The Food and Drug Administration's (FDA's) regulatory authority traditionally has been limited to products, or products for which at least some ingredients travel in interstate commerce. Thus, a pharmaceutical firm that wants to market a new drug must have FDA approval before it can be advertised or shipped in interstate commerce. While some states require FDA approval for drugs sold within the state, there are states that permit the sale and use of non-FDA approved drugs. As long as these drugs are made wholly within the state and used only by physicians in the same state, FDA has no authority to ban the use of the drug. This is a congressional, rather than a constitutional, limit. Congress could allow FDA to use the broad definition of interstate commerce and regulate all drug sales and also the practice of medicine. The Drug Enforcement Administration can prosecute the manufacture and use of drugs used only intrastate, even if, as in the case of medical marijuana, the state has approved the sale of the drug.

The Police and National Security Powers

Police power is the right to protect against threats to the public health and safety. It is the state equivalent of the federal national security powers to protect the state itself. Both are fundamental to government. The police power predates police forces and was historically more about public health. In the colonial period, police power was used to control nuisances, such as tanneries that fouled the air and water in towns, to prevent the sale of bad food and to quarantine persons who were infected with communicable diseases. The police power was left to the states in the Constitution, although the federal government can wield what looks like the same power for domestic threats through the Commerce Clause. If the threat has national security implications, such as bioterrorism, the President can exercise broad authority through his or her national security powers.

Police power is the right to protect against threats to the public health and safety.

For food, drug and medical device law and regulation, the important federal powers are the right to regulate interstate and international commerce; the important state power is the police power to protect the public health and safety.

Food, drug and medical device regulation is a federal health and safety function, as are environmental protection laws and workplace safety laws. The states have companion laws in most of these areas, plus local public health enforcement such as restaurant inspections, communicable disease control and drinking water sanitation. The courts usually find that true public health and safety concerns take priority over individual rights. For example, persons with dangerous communicable diseases, such as tuberculosis, can be isolated until they are no longer infectious and thus pose no threat to the community. Persons exposed to a dangerous disease such as smallpox can be quarantined until it is clear that they are not infected. As long as the confinement is to protect the public against future harm and not to punish the individual for past acts, it may be done as a civil law matter without giving the individual criminal law protections.

After the attacks on the United States on September 11, 2001, Congress passed laws dealing with the prevention and mitigation of bioterrorism acts, which also include powers to respond to threats such as pandemic influenza. These allow the emergency use of drugs and vaccines that are not FDA approved. They also provide comprehensive immunity from damage claims for manufacturers and persons administering these measures under a presidential emergency or national security directive.

Federal Preemption of State Law

Since food and drug law implicates both interstate commerce and local public health and safety, the states and the federal government share regulatory power in many areas. Areas of shared power require national businesses to deal with 50 state governments and with the federal government. As long as the laws do not conflict, each can be enforced by the appropriate level of government. If they do conflict, the Constitution provides that federal law preempts the conflicting state regulation. This conflict can arise because the federal law *explicitly* states that it is taking away the states' power to regulate. For example, federal law specifies the necessary labeling for hearing aids and limits what additional requirements a state may impose without FDA permission. When Massachusetts passed a law requiring more information on hearing aid labels, a federal court barred enforcement of the law.

Federal law can *implicitly* preempt a state's right to regulate if the federal government so completely controls the area there is no room for state regulation. The federal government regulates use of the electromagnetic spectrum for communications such as broadcast television, radio and cell phones. These are intrinsically interstate activities because electronic signals do not respect state lines. These regulations cover all aspects of broadcast communication, leaving no room for state regulation.

In some cases, federal law also preempts private lawsuits brought under state law. The Cigarette Labeling and Advertising Act (Cigarette Labeling Act) provided that states cannot require more or different health warnings on a cigarette package than those required by federal law. The Supreme Court found that this preempted state court lawsuits by smokers who claimed that the cigarettes were defective because the packages did not carry adequate warnings. Federal law also preempts certain lawsuits alleging vaccine-related injuries, substituting an administrative compensation fund for possible state tort recoveries. FDA regulation of drugs does not provide any preemption of state tort law claims, but the Medical Device Amendments of 1976 do preempt claims against medical device manufacturers for aspects of devices that have been comprehensively regulated by FDA. Compensation for persons injured by defective prescription drugs is determined by state law, which differs substantially among the states. While Congress could preempt state tort claims for drugs under the same logic as for medical devices, it has not done so.

Limits to Federal Power

While federal power under the Commerce Clause is very broad, there are limits to Congress commandeering state governments to enforce federal laws. The states have to obey federal law themselves, but the Supreme Court has limited the extent to which Congress can force states to use their own resources to enforce federal law. Despite this ruling, legislation passed after the terrorist attacks on September 11, 2001, and the Hurricane Katrina disaster gives the President broad emergency authority and the National Response Plan anticipates that state and local authorities will follow orders from the President.

While federal power under the Commerce Clause is very broad, there are limits to Congress commandeering state governments to enforce federal laws.

If Congress wants the states to follow federal guidance or enforce federal laws, it can avoid questions of constitutional limits by giving states financial incentives to do its bidding. When Congress wanted the states to pass laws requiring people in cars to wear seatbelts, it told the states to pass seatbelt laws or lose some of their federal highway construction money. The Medicaid program is a state-federal partnership in which the federal government controls actions of state personnel through contractual restrictions on the federal matching money. The Centers for Disease Control and Prevention uses grant funding to impose some uniformity on state public health programs such as childhood vaccination requirements and communicable disease reporting. The federal government has historically used the power of the purse much more than legal coercion to impose uniform standards on the states.

SEPARATION OF POWERS

The Constitution divides the federal government into three branches: the legislative (Congress), the executive (President) and the judicial (Supreme Court). These divisions are intended to act as checks and balances to prevent any branch from dominating the government. The states have basically the same organizational structure, although some states make one branch of the government much stronger than the others. This chapter focuses on the federal system, which is most important to FDA law.

The Constitution divides the federal government into three branches: the legislative (Congress), the executive (President) and the judicial (Supreme Court).

The Legislative Branch

Congress has two houses: the Senate and the House of Representatives. These houses have different procedural rules and their members serve terms of different lengths. Congress is the only branch of government that can authorize the spending of government funds and the imposition of taxes.

Each proposed law (bill) must be passed by both houses of Congress and signed by the President. The President can veto legislation, and Congress can override a presidential veto only by a two-thirds majority vote. The President can propose legislation, and does so each year when he or she presents the proposed budget. Ultimately, however, it is Congress that passes laws. To keep Congress from becoming too powerful, the Constitution gave the power to enforce the laws to the President.

The Executive Branch

The President is head of the executive branch and is charged with enforcing the laws passed by Congress. The President has two areas of power: domestic and international. In domestic affairs, most of the President's power comes from laws passed by Congress, such as the Federal Food, Drug, and Cosmetic Act (FDCA). These laws constrain domestic action to areas specifically approved by Congress, although the President does have some flexibility to respond to emergencies. Enforcement is carried out through various agencies, including FDA. The Constitution grants the President broad powers over international affairs, including international trade, foreign policy and national security. These powers are subject to only limited review by Congress and the courts.

The Judicial Branch

The judicial branch consists of the Supreme Court, the courts of appeal (circuit courts) and the district (local) federal courts. The district courts hold trials for federal criminal cases, decide disputes arising under federal law or the Constitution and hear cases involving citizens of different states under "diversity jurisdiction." The courts of appeal do not conduct trials but review the trial records from the district courts. Since many agency actions generate a record like a trial, Congress often provides that these agency actions be reviewed directly by the court of appeals. When a case is heard on appeal, the court does not collect new evidence or hear the testimony of the witnesses; it only considers the record generated at the district court or administrative level.

Cases before the Supreme Court are one of four types: 1) cases involving one state suing another; 2) cases that arise from courts of appeal rulings; 3) cases reviewing state court decisions involving questions of federal law or rights under the Constitution; and 4) cases where Congress has given "original jurisdiction" to the Supreme Court. The Supreme Court ensures that federal laws are given the same meaning by all courts of appeal, it resolves conflicts between state and federal laws, and it determines if state or federal laws impermissibly infringe on rights guaranteed by the Constitution. If the Supreme Court determines that a state law, federal law or administrative regulation, such as an FDA rule, conflicts with the Constitution, it will strike the law down so that it may no longer be enforced.

How the Courts Work

When most people think of law, they think of the courtroom. While most law and law practice does not happen in the courtroom, it is important to understand how the courts work because the courtroom is where disputes, both private and governmental, end up if they cannot be resolved in any other way.

The U.S. litigation system has three key characteristics: 1) it is a common law system, meaning that judges rely on the opinions of other judges; 2) it is an adversarial system (i.e., it is driven by the litigants rather than the judges); and 3) it is divided into civil and criminal law, with the greatest legal protections reserved for persons accused of a crime and at risk of imprisonment or execution.

Characteristics of the U.S. litigation system:
- *a common law system*
- *an adversarial system*
- *divided into civil and criminal law*

Understanding the Common Law

England is a common law country. As a consequence, so were the original British colonies in America. Common law means that the law evolves through judges applying the law to specific cases and writing opinions about how the law applies in those cases. The laws they apply may be from earlier court decisions enforcing even earlier traditions, or they may apply statutes passed by legislatures. Cases still arise that involve rules laid down in cases decided more than 200 years ago. Each case decided by a common law court becomes a precedent, or guideline, for subsequent decisions involving similar disputes. The Constitution accepted most of the English common law that was in force when it was written.

The evolution of the law on the preemption of state tort claims against medical device manufacturers is a good example of how the common law system functions. The Medical Device Amendments of 1976 (MDA) gave FDA the authority to regulate sale of medical devices. Congress wanted to assure uniform standards for medical devices so the MDA contains language that the states cannot impose additional standards on medical devices. In an early case under the MDA, the court ruled that state regulation of hearing aids was preempted by the MDA because it conflicted with federal regulations. This was a simple application of the law to a direct regulatory conflict.

In 1992, the United States Supreme Court ruled that the Cigarette Labeling Act preempted state tort claims against tobacco companies, holding that tort claims were a form of state regulation. Since the language in the Cigarette Labeling Act was similar to the MDA, defendants in tort cases involving medical devices began to argue that the MDA preempted these tort claims. Some federal courts accepted this argument, and some rejected it. In 1996, the United States Supreme Court reviewed the law to resolve these conflicting opinions. The court found that there could be preemption, but only if FDA really regulated the device, rather than just letting it be sold because it was like a device already on the market. This led to a second wave of cases with conflicting decisions over how much oversight FDA had to have over the device before preemption was triggered. The United States Supreme Court further clarified the law by finding preemption in a case decided in 2008.

The value of a common law system is that the law can be adapted to situations that were not contemplated by the legislature.

The value of a common law system is that the law can be adapted to situations that were not contemplated by the legislature. There are two disadvantages. First, the law will often be unclear for years, with the outcome of cases depending on which court decides them. Second, the court will only resolve the issues before it, so even the 2008 case on the MDA, decided more than 30 years after the passage of the MDA, still leaves some preemption issues unresolved.

The Adversarial System

The U.S. judicial system uses an adversarial model in which the judge acts as an impartial referee to ensure that the case is presented properly to jurors but does not assist the parties in developing their cases (although, in some instances, cases can be decided by the judge without a jury). In private litigation, the plaintiff—the person who brings the litigation—hires a lawyer to file a complaint against the defendant. The defendant then hires a lawyer to oppose the plaintiff's charges and to bring any possible counterclaims against the plaintiff. In criminal cases and in agency enforcement actions, it is the government who brings the proceedings against the defendant. There are some federal statutes, such as the False Claims Act, that allow a private person to bring a civil action on behalf of the government and share in any recovery as an incentive to vindicate the government's interest. A few states allow private citizens to bring criminal actions in very limited circumstances.

The U.S. judicial system uses an adversarial model in which the judge acts as an impartial referee to ensure that the case is presented properly to jurors but does not assist the parties in developing their cases (although, in some instances, cases can be decided by the judge without a jury).

The courts protect against bias by excluding judges or jurors who have a relationship with the plaintiff or the defendant or are familiar with the factual issues in the case. Each side presents its case to the court or the jury, and the opposing side tries to discredit it. Lawyers must be truthful in what they say, but have no duty to volunteer information, even if not doing so misleads the judge or jury. If the case involves scientific or medical matters, each side will present experts who testify to why the facts support their client's case. Because neither the jurors nor the judge are knowledgeable about the specific facts being litigated, they have to decide which expert to trust based on credentials and demeanor. The great strength of the jury system is that it allows citizens to control the power of the government in criminal cases and to resolve difficult policy problems when these involve only the parties to the case. The great weakness of the jury system is that it cannot deal with complex scientific issues and it cannot balance the rights of persons not involved in the case. For example, in product liability cases involving persons claiming to have been injured by pharmaceuticals, the jury has no way to balance the interests of the injured person against those who may be denied access to the drug if the litigation is successful.

Criminal Law

The United States has two types of law, civil law and criminal law. The key distinction between civil and criminal law is that criminal laws punish for past conduct and can use imprisonment or execution. A law that imposes a five-year prison sentence for selling adulterated drugs would be a criminal law. (There are also criminal laws that punish with a fine.) Mental health commitment laws and communicable disease isolation and quarantine laws are not criminal laws, even if they require the person to be locked up. Their purpose is to protect the person or the public from future injury, not to punish for past conduct.

Criminal laws are enforced by the government in its own name. In the federal system, only the Department of Justice (DOJ) can bring criminal cases; for example, *United States v. Leichter*, in which Leichter was prosecuted for defrauding FDA. Because the federal and state governments are so powerful, the Constitution provides special protections for criminal defendants: criminal defendants have a right to: 1) free legal counsel if they are indigent, 2) a jury trial, 3) not be forced to testify against themselves, 4) refuse to talk to the police, 5) be free from unreasonable searches and seizures and 6) force the government to prove its case beyond a reasonable doubt.

The Constitution bars laws that criminalize actions that happened before the law was passed (ex post facto law) and laws that declare a person to be a criminal without a trial (a bill of attainder). If the jury finds the defendant not guilty, the same government cannot try the defendant again for the same crime (no double jeopardy). This does not, however, bar another government from prosecuting the defendant. Thus, it is not unusual to see the federal government retry a defendant who has been acquitted by a jury in state court. The second prosecution will be for a federal crime, such as the federal law prohibiting violations of civil rights.

Criminal prosecutions can be devastating to a legitimate business, even if the business is ultimately found not guilty. The publicity can hurt the value of the stock, the company records may be seized as evidence and individual employees may have to hire lawyers because their interests are different from the company's. Criminal defense is very expensive, and is not covered by most insurance policies. A regulated industry may be forced to give up its operating license if indicted. The draconian consequences allow the government to use the threat of criminal prosecution to persuade a company to settle, rather than fight, civil regulatory charges.

Civil Law

Civil lawsuits can be brought by the government or by private citizens.

Civil lawsuits can be brought by the government or by private citizens. Government agencies use civil litigation to enforce regulatory rulings and statutes. Private civil litigation includes business disputes over private law matters, such as compliance with contracts, ownership of property and tort claims for compensation for personal injuries. Private plaintiffs can sue FDA to enjoin it from enforcing questionable statutes or regulations.

In most civil cases, there is no right to government-supplied counsel and the defendant can be forced to testify. The case need only be proved by a preponderance (>50 percent) of the evidence, which is much lower than the "beyond a reasonable doubt" standard used in criminal cases. The more the case resembles a criminal law case, however, the more protections to which the defendant is entitled. Thus, while a case to institutionalize a person who is dangerous because of mental illness is a civil case, the defendant may be entitled to a lawyer and a higher standard of proof than in a proceeding to collect money.

Civil lawsuits called injunctions ask the court to order the defendant to stop doing something illegal, such as selling unpasteurized milk. If the defendant disobeys the injunction, the court may hold the defendant in contempt of court and impose a fine or imprisonment. FDA can also bring a civil seizure or embargo action to take possession or forbid the sale of goods. These are very powerful measures in the food and drug industry, where seized or embargoed inventory can go out of date faster than the defendant can get a trial to contest the court's order. The agency has great leverage to negotiate a settlement if the defendant has 1,000 tons of fresh fruit that cannot be moved off a ship.

Tort Damage Claims

Simple tort lawsuits generally are based on negligence, which means proving that the defendant did not act as a reasonable person and thus exposed the plaintiff to unnecessary risk. An example would be a diagnostic laboratory that improperly read a lab test and thus delayed a patient's diagnosis of cancer. To win a negligence case, the plaintiff must show what a reasonable laboratory would have done, how the defendant laboratory failed to meet this standard and that this failure caused plaintiffs' harm. This generally requires a lot of information from the defendant, which is obtained by court orders in a process called "discovery."

The most expensive tort lawsuits are brought against product manufacturers under the theory of strict liability. All states have adopted some form of strict liability, which requires that, to recover, an injured person show that the product was defective and unreasonably dangerous and that it was the cause of his or her injury. Unlike a negligence lawsuit, the plaintiff does not need to prove that the defendant acted "unreasonably." Thus, even if the defendant was more careful than other manufacturers and the plaintiff cannot show that the defendant could have prevented the injury, the plaintiff still can recover. For example, assume that after a drug has been on the market for three years, some patients begin to show serious liver damage. The evidence shows that this could not have been detected during clinical testing because it was either too rare or required a cofactor that could not have been anticipated during the clinical trial. Under the theory of strict (products) liability, the manufacturer could be held liable to the patients for their injuries.

Personal injury lawsuits generally are based on negligence, which means proving that the defendant did not act as a reasonable person and thus exposed the plaintiff to unnecessary risk.

FDA can be sued for negligence causing personal injury under the Federal Tort Claims Act (FTCA). The FTCA allows ordinary negligence actions, such as suing FDA for failing to test and detect a dangerous batch of polio vaccine when its regulations required testing every batch of vaccine. Unlike private tort actions, however, if the plaintiff is injured because of an intentional policy choice, the agency is not liable. For example, the government tested atomic weapons in the western desert, knowing that this would put local residents at risk. When these residents sued, the case was eventually dismissed because the injuries were the result of a policy decision, rather than negligence. Agencies cannot be sued when regulatory decisions reduce or destroy the value of regulated products, such as when FDA pulls a drug from the market.

Discovery

Discovery is the process for obtaining information in legal proceedings.

Discovery is the process for obtaining information in legal proceedings. Discovery is used in civil and criminal litigation, and in administrative proceedings. There are three types of discovery: 1) depositions, where the witness answers questions in person and the answers are recorded by a court reporter or by video tape; 2) interrogatories, which are written questions that are served on a party to a lawsuit and filled out with the help of the party's lawyer; and 3) subpoenas, which are legal orders to produce documents or other physical evidence, such as a batch of allegedly contaminated drugs. As companies have moved to electronic communications and document storage, the courts have extended discovery rules to electronic records and e-mail. Discovery of electronic records ("e-discovery") poses new legal and practical issues. It is easier for parties to convince the court to grant very broad discovery orders when the data can be delivered on a small portable hard drive, rather than as truckloads of paper records.

Discovery is the most time-consuming and expensive part of litigation. For example, in a product liability lawsuit over the side effects of a new drug, a plaintiff will want copies of all the documents that contain any information about the drug, including the thousands of pages contained within the new drug application submitted to FDA. These will be reviewed carefully for comments by researchers or others that might indicate that the company knew of the problem or structured the research in ways that would minimize discovery of side effects. The plaintiff also would want to depose the senior executives of the company.

Privileged Information

U.S. law recognizes several circumstances where information is privileged from discovery, particularly in criminal trials. Traditional common law privileges protect information that a priest gets in confession, communications between spouses, and communications to a person's attorney. There are also statutory privileges, such as the physician-patient privilege, and restrictions on the discovery of drug and alcohol abuse treatment records. Statutory privileges usually contain exceptions, and even the attorney-client privilege does not protect information about future crimes or conspiracies with the attorney to commit crimes.

U.S. law recognizes several circumstances where information is privileged from discovery.

The attorney-client privilege protects information a client tells his or her attorney. It does not protect documents or other materials that the client gives the attorney, unless these were protected already under a different privilege. If the client tells the same information to a non-attorney, such as a co-worker, then the information can be obtained by deposing the co-worker. If the attorney is the corporation's employee, the attorney-client privilege runs to the corporation, not to any employees or corporate officers who may talk to the attorney. If there is a conflict between the corporation's interests and employee's interests, the attorney must choose to protect the corporation. Thus, in criminal cases, employees being investigated need to retain their own attorneys.

The work that the attorney does for the client is also protected through the attorney work product doctrine. It applies to work done for the client in anticipation of litigation, meaning that it is not available if the attorney is acting as a business advisor rather than as legal counsel. This doctrine protects information, such as accident investigation reports, if they are done under the supervision of the attorney. It also protects the legal research done by the attorney. The protection is not absolute, however. A court can order the discovery of attorney work product if necessary to ensure fairness in the case. For example, assume that the attorney has an engineer test a medical device that was involved in an accident. The test destroys the device, making the engineer's report the only evidence of performance of the device. Even though the report was prepared at the instruction and under the supervision of an attorney, the court could allow discovery of the report.

THE ADMINISTRATIVE LAW SYSTEM

Most food, drug and medical device law is administrative law enforced by executive branch agencies, primarily FDA. In the United States, administrative law dates back to sanitary commissions and other citizens' boards in the colonial period. The growth of federal agencies reflects the growth of federal government after World War II. Administrative law is civil law, although agencies can refer cases to the DOJ or state prosecutors if they find criminal activity. The agencies that conduct administrative practice are diverse, ranging in size and power from the Department of Health and Human Services (HHS), which has a budget exceeding many small states, to specialized state agencies that have very small budgets and no full-time staff.

Creating Agencies

Congress creates agencies and gives them power through laws called "enabling legislation," which specifies what the agency is to do, how the agency is structured and its budget.

Congress creates agencies and gives them power through laws called "enabling legislation," which specifies what the agency is to do, how the agency is structured and its budget. Once an agency is established, Congress can modify or expand its duties with subsequent legislation; for example, FDA was given authority to regulate medical devices by amendments that were made in 1976 to its enabling legislation. Congress also controls agency action through setting the agency's budget, which can include specific limits on money for each agency activity. Congress may not directly interfere with agency management.

The heads of most agencies and their top administrators, such as FDA's Commissioner of Food and Drugs, are officers of the United States. The Constitution requires that these officials be appointed by the President and confirmed by the Senate. The President is free to replace them with new appointees at will. This allows the President to set agency policy through his political appointments.

Some agencies, such as the Securities and Exchange Commission (SEC) and the Federal Trade Commission (FTC), are governed by appointed boards whose members have staggered terms. The President can replace board members only when their terms expire. These are called independent agencies. A newly elected President will not be able to change the governance of an independent agency by replacing the board with his or her own appointments. This gives the agency greater political independence. Congress creates independent agencies when it is wants to insulate an agency that is charged with politically sensitive enforcement.

Deference to Agency Expertise

Agencies occupy a privileged legal position because courts generally defer to agency decisions, as long as the agency is acting within the legal authority it was given by Congress in its enabling legislation. The courts recognize that there are many regulatory matters that can be resolved only through expert decision-making because they turn on highly technical issues, they demand quick action, or some combination of both. In a classic case, the owners of a freezer plant attacked the right of a public health agency to seize and destroy thousands of pounds of chickens that had thawed when the refrigeration failed. The court ruled that the agency was justified in seizing and destroying the chicken without first having a court hearing because of the potential threat to the public.

This deference to agency decision making gives agencies flexibility in responding to problems. If a foodborne illness like listeriosis breaks out because of problems with cheese made from unpasteurized milk, health agencies can institute control measures much faster than Congress or the state legislatures could pass specific laws on the subject. The agency also has the freedom to modify its strategies as it learns more about a problem.

Deference to Agency Expertise
Agencies occupy a privileged legal position because courts generally defer to agency decisions, as long as the agency is acting within the legal authority it was given by Congress in its enabling legislation.

ADMINISTRATIVE PROCEDURE

While agencies may act quickly and with little oversight during emergencies, they are more limited in their actions that deal with routine matters. Federal agencies are governed by the Administrative Procedure Act (APA), and each state has a comparable set of rules for its agencies. The APA establishes the basic framework for making regulations (rules), conducting adjudications (hearings and trials) and for challenging agency actions in court. Congress may supersede the APA and specify different procedures in the agency's enabling act.

Rulemaking

A federal agency can do only what Congress gives it the power to do in its enabling legislation. In many cases, however, that enabling legislation is broad and general. This gives the agency flexibility, and makes it difficult to know how to comply with the law. Agencies can write regulations to provide industries and individuals with more detailed legal standards than are in the general enabling legislation. The APA and an agency's enabling legislation specify the process for promulgating regulations. Properly promulgated regulations have the same force as a law passed by Congress. Like statutes, regulations control future conduct and apply to everyone.

Rulemaking
FDA must follow a defined process before it can release a new rule. In addition, it must first publish the proposed regulation in the Federal Register.

For example, a rule might define how many insect parts are allowed in a pound of butter. FDA would publish its proposed regulation in the *Federal Register*, which is a compilation of the federal notices, including proposed and final rules, by agencies. This notice could exceed 100 pages. All interested persons, which might include butter and cookie makers as well as cookie eaters, are given 90 days to comment on the rule. If the proposed rule allows three insect parts per pound, the butter industry might complain that reducing insect parts to less than 20 per pound would increase the cost of butter. A public interest group might comment that there should be no insect parts in butter and, if there are, they should appear on the label so consumers know what they are buying.

FDA must review the responses to the proposed regulation, and in some cases Congress may require it to hold public hearings to get more input. It then decides whether it wants to change the regulation. In this case, assume it decides to raise the level to five parts per pound. It then publishes in the *Federal Register* a final rule with this standard. The final rule will include a summary of the comments FDA received and explanations of why it did or did not follow them. In this case, the agency would say that it was persuaded that three would be too expensive, but that 20 was too many and indicated filthy conditions. It also would say that it is too expensive to ban insect parts, and because they do not carry disease, putting insect parts on the label would give consumers the wrong impression that the butter was unsafe.

When the final rule goes into effect, it is published as part of a series of books called the *Code of Federal Regulations* (C.F.R.). A food manufacturer who wants to start producing butter could look in Title 21 of the C.F.R., where the FDA regulations are codified. Agencies also can publish informal guides for the industries they regulate. While these do not have the same legal standing as regulations that were subject to notice-and-comment in the *Federal Register*, they are very useful guides to agency practice. FDA publishes both notice-and-comment regulations and more informal guidelines to help industry comply with its requirements.

Administrative Searches

The Right to Inspect
FDA inspectors may visit regulated facilities to check for violations without a search warrant.

When a party to a lawsuit wants discovery, it must file its request with the court. The opposing party can contest the request and the court will have a hearing to determine if the request must be complied with or if it will be quashed (denied). When the government wants to enter the premises of a business to collect evidence for a criminal case, it must get a search warrant from a judge. The warrant must show that there is probable cause to believe that specific evidence of a known crime will be found on the premises to be searched. In contrast, an administrative search warrant, say to look for fire code violations, need only show the legal authority to do a search and the general area to be searched. It need not be based on any specific information about the premises to be searched.

Regulated industries must consent to allow warrantless searches and to comply with reporting requirements as a condition of licensure or permitting. Thus, a drug company has to allow an FDA inspector onto its manufacturing site to check for current good manufacturing practices (cGMPs) because the permit to produce drugs includes the right to inspect. If the company refuses and demands that the agency get a search warrant, the agency can revoke its permit to make drugs at the facility while it seeks the warrant.

Information collected during administrative searches can be used for regulatory actions, but there are limits on how it can be used in criminal prosecutions.
If FDA believes that a criminal prosecution is possible, it will refer the case to
the DOJ so the prosecutors can determine if a probable cause criminal warrant
should be used, rather than an administrative warrant, or a warrantless search.

Adjudications

Statutes and regulations set the standards. Adjudications are used to determine
facts about specific businesses or individuals. Adjudications take many forms.
Some look like trials. The new drug application process is a form of adjudication.
An inspection of a manufacturing facility for GMP violations is also a form of
adjudication—it determines whether the facility is meeting the standards. No
matter the form, the primary difference between an adjudication and a civil trial
is that adjudications are inquisitorial, not adversary proceedings.

Unlike the previously discussed adversarial system, where the judge is just
a referee without knowledge of the subject matter, the inquisitorial judge is
knowledgeable and is often an expert. The judges who conduct adjudications
that look like hearings or trials are call administrative law judges (ALJs). Agency
hearings do not have juries. The ALJ will question witnesses and the parties
before the agency to fully develop the facts. Often the ALJ is the representative
of agency, so the ALJ is acting as both judge and prosecutor. At the end of the
adjudication, the ALJ will issue a recommended opinion. The agency may adopt
this as the final decision or modify it.

Most agency proceedings are less formal than civil trials. The regulated parties talk directly to relevant agency staff, who is usually encouraged to help
the regulated party prepare their case or comply with the regulation. While
live witness testimony is permitted, agencies generally prefer written reports
from experts because they are easier to evaluate than live testimony. In agency
practice the lawyers and their clients will deal with the same agency personnel
on many different matters. The agency will know whether they are credible and
will act accordingly. Parties that have a reputation for cutting corners will be
regulated more closely.

Judicial Review of Agency Actions

In situations where an agency believes a public health and safety risk is imminent, it can act without first going to court. In a classic case from 1908, a health
agency seized chicken from a freezer plant that had experienced a power
failure. The agency did not have a court order and was sued for unconstitution-
ally seizing the property. The court ruled that the seizure was proper, given the

*In situations where an
agency believes a public
health and safety risk is
imminent, it can act without
first going to court.*

imminent threat to the public health and that the defendant's due process right was satisfied by a post-seizure hearing. If the agency was found to have acted without proper authority or justification, it can be ordered to pay for damages.

The U.S. Supreme Court has ruled that in reviewing the order of a public health agency, the courts should not second-guess the underlying scientific basis of the agency's decision: "It is not for the courts to determine which scientific view is correct in ruling upon whether the police power has been properly exercised. The judicial function is exhausted with the discovery that the relation between means and end is not wholly vain and fanciful, an illusory pretense." To successfully attack an agency's expert decision making, it must be shown that the agency acted "arbitrarily or capriciously," which means that the agency acted without a rational basis for its decision. To defeat such a challenge, the agency must present a proper record explaining the factual and legal basis for its actions.

The courts do not defer to agencies' interpretation of laws because that is the area of the courts' expertise. However, if the law is subject to more than one interpretation—very frequently the case—the courts will defer to the agency's choice of interpretation, as long as it is reasonable. Thus, an early case under the Clean Air Act found that the act directed the Environmental Protection Agency to control air pollution. But since the act did not specify the details of how to do it, it was the agency's decision, not the courts, in how to implement the law. The court found that substituting its decision for the agency would undermine separation of powers because agency policy is an executive branch function. In contrast, when FDA tried to regulate tobacco, the Supreme Court found that while the FDCA could be interpreted to allow tobacco regulation, it was clear from the history of FDA that Congress did not intend FDA to regulate tobacco. Congress had to pass new legislation to allow tobacco regulation by FDA.

In rare cases, courts will review an agency's failure to act.

In rare cases, the courts will also review an agency's failure to act. In one case, the Secretary of the Department of Health and Human Services refused to promulgate a rule banning the interstate shipment of unpasteurized milk. A public interest group sued the agency, arguing that such a rule was necessary to protect the public's health. The agency record showed that FDA scientists had built an overwhelming record that unpasteurized milk posed a threat to the public health. The court found that the Secretary was acting arbitrarily and capriciously in refusing to promulgate the rule, and ordered her do so.

Summary

Food, drug and medical device regulation can be understood only in the larger context of the U.S. legal system. FDA regulation is administrative law, governed by the APA and statutes passed by Congress. FDA is under executive branch control through the presidential appointment of the Commissioner and ongoing White House oversight. FDA can bring civil enforcement actions and can refer cases to the DOJ for criminal prosecution. Any industry regulated by FDA must be familiar with the statutes and the specific regulations promulgated by FDA governing their industry. Failure to follow these regulations can result in seizures, closing of facilities, and civil and criminal penalties.

Food, drug and medical device regulation can be understood only in the larger context of the U.S. legal system.

Chapter 2

U.S. Food and Drug Law and FDA— A Historical Background

*Paul Hyman, Hyman, Phelps & McNamara, PC, Washington, D.C.**

Key Points

- Food and drug law dates back to the beginning of commerce, arising with laws to protect consumers of food from false weights and measures.
- U.S. food and drug law derives primarily from British food laws adopted by the colonies and the states after the Revolutionary War.
- Until the mid-19th century, almost all food and drug regulation occurred at the local level, reflecting the prevailing pattern of commerce.
- With regional and national expansion of food distribution, the states became more involved; the few federal laws focused primarily on imports, taxes and duties rather than consumer protection.
- The Vaccine Act of 1902 marked the federal government's venture into domestic drug regulation, and included premarket approval.
- The Food and Drugs Act of 1906, the first comprehensive federal law regulating foods and drugs, was strictly an enforcement statute, designed to punish violations.
- A tragedy involving a new dosage form of a sulfa drug, Elixir Sulfanilamide, which contained an unlabeled solvent and killed almost 100 people, helped induce Congress to enact the Federal Food, Drug, and Cosmetic Act of 1938 (FDCA), the basic law today.
- In addition to strengthening enforcement and federal jurisdiction, the 1938 act included government premarket clearance of drugs for safety.
- The FDCA has been amended numerous times, strengthening the regulation of drugs, food and color additives, and medical devices, adding user fees and, more recently, promoting the availability of generic drugs, new therapeutic agents, nutrition information for foods, and dietary supplements, regulating tobacco products and enhancing food safety.
- The Food and Drug Administration (FDA), which enforces the FDCA, is the oldest federal regulatory agency, beginning in 1848 as the Agricultural Division of the Patent Office, subsequently becoming part of the U.S. Department of Agriculture; the Federal Security Agency; the Department of Health, Education and Welfare; and now the Department of Health and Human Services, but lacking a statutory existence until 1988.

* The author gratefully acknowledges the invaluable assistance of Riëtte van Laack, Kurt R. Karst, Cassandra A. Soltis and David B. Clissold in the update of this chapter.

INTRODUCTION

The basic statute under which the federal government regulates food, drugs, medical devices, cosmetics and, most recently, tobacco products is the Federal Food, Drug, and Cosmetic Act of 1938 (FDCA). The history of food and drug regulation, however, goes back virtually to the beginning of recorded history, or at least since such products were offered for sale to consumers. Moreover, that history did not stop with the 1938 act. There have been numerous amendments to the statute, both expanding and contracting its reach, as well as court decisions that have changed the interpretation of the statutory language in ways that frequently have surprised the law's congressional proponents, government regulators, regulated industry and consumers.

ROOTS OF FOOD AND DRUG LAW AND REGULATION

The development of food and drug law can be said to have paralleled the development of civilization.

The development of food and drug law can be said to have paralleled the development of civilization. Laws to protect consumers from adulterated food products and from false weights and measures date back at least to biblical times and can be found in all civilizations. Until relatively recent times, and the development of analytical chemistry and the beginnings of modern medicine, the regulation of food encompassed drugs as well. With the development of "consumer" products, early civilizations had to take steps to protect consumers who, like today's consumers, could not readily protect themselves from fraudulent practices. Early regulations can be found in the Code of Hammurabi in the 18th century B.C., and in early Chinese and Indian laws.

The Greeks and Romans enacted increasingly complicated food laws, addressing adulteration of staples such as wine, wheat, flour and bread. In Rome, the sale of watered, flavored and colored wines; the use of false weights and measures; and other fraudulent practices could give rise to a private right of action or to a civil crime punishable by condemnation to the mines or temporary exile. Thus, the Romans did not rely entirely on the doctrine of *caveat emptor* ("buyer beware") to regulate foods.

In the Middle Ages, following the Crusades, certain regulatory functions, particularly with respect to short weights and measures, were the responsibility of mercantile guilds. For instance, the Pepperers Guild was appointed custodian of official weight standards in the 13th century by King Henry III of England and its members became the first public food inspectors in England.

Concern over inadequate policing by these private, commercial interests eventually led to the enactment of local ordinances or state laws to regulate sales of particular commodities. Laws in England and the Continent regulated the quality of bread, wine, beer, ale, meat, fish, honey, spices, butter, milk and water. Punishment for violations of these laws could range from public humiliation to fines to corporal or even capital punishment.

During the 16th and 17th centuries, colonial expansion brought more exotic goods—such as chocolate, tea, coffee and sugar—to Europe. The substitution of cheaper ingredients and other fraudulent practices became more sophisticated and more widespread. The ability of regulatory officials to detect these adulterated foods was limited, although many ordinances and laws were enacted to try to prevent these practices. It was only with the development of the science of chemistry, however, that modern food and drug regulation could begin to develop. By the middle of the 19th century, the advance of analytical chemistry and the use of the microscope to analyze foods led at last to broad food and drug laws in Europe and the United States.

The American colonies followed English legal precedents for food regulation, but the early laws and ordinances primarily were intended to protect trade in the colonies. Independence did not change this legal tradition. Most states, like Virginia, formally adopted all of the English common law. Massachusetts enacted its own food adulteration law as early as 1785, again modeled on British regulations. Throughout the 19th century and into the 20th century, the United States was influenced most strongly by British law and regulation.

In the 1800s, Great Britain and other European countries began to update their laws to protect the public from unsafe and fraudulently presented foods and drugs. Their laws shifted from protection of revenue to protection of consumers as more fraud and adulteration were recognized and the public demanded better protection.

In 1820, a German chemist working in London, Frederick Accum, published *A Treatise on Adulteration of Food and Culinary Poisons*, which described the fraudulent adulteration of bread, beer, wine, liquor, tea, coffee, cream, confectionery, vinegar, mustard, pepper, cheese, olive oil and pickles. Accum bravely identified merchants who were selling adulterated foods and drugs. His book also discussed various methods available to detect these frauds.

1820
Frederick Accum, a German chemist working in London, publishes A Treatise on Adulteration of Food and Culinary Poisons.

As exposed by Accum and others, adulteration of food and drugs was widespread. Candy was colored with highly toxic mineral pigments such as compounds of lead, arsenic, copper, mercury and chromium. "Rock-and-rye" candy, popular among children, was made of glucose, flour and fusel oil. Coffee was regularly adulterated with chicory, as well as roasted ox or horse liver. Tea was adulterated with copper arsenite, lead chromate and indigo.

Dr. A.H. Hassall, an English physician, performed microscopic analyses on common food adulterations that were published in the medical journal *The Lancet*, and then republished in a book in 1855. Like Accum, Dr. Hassall's articles identified merchants responsible for the adulterations, and they received much public attention. In analyses of many samples of foods such as coffee, bread, flour, milk and tea, Dr. Hassall found most to be adulterated with cheaper food ingredients and such extraneous materials as metals, colors, shells, husks, sand and grit.

In response to public pressure, in 1860 the English Parliament enacted the first general food law in England, the Adulteration of Food and Drink Act. This legislation was extended to medicines in 1868 and 1872. In 1875, these acts were replaced by the Sale of Food and Drugs Act.

In the United States, until the middle of the 19th century, most food and drug regulation was carried out on a local level, reflecting the type of commerce prevalent at that time. As with other commerce, however, food distribution expanded regionally and nationally, and the states became more involved. By 1900, almost every state had some type of food and drug law in place.

Federal legislation through the 19th century focused on foreign commerce. Thus, in 1848, Congress passed the Drug Importation Act that ordered U.S. Customs to prevent entry of foreign adulterated drugs. The law's primary purpose was to levy taxes and duties on imported articles, and to protect U.S. industry. Protecting consumers was of secondary importance. Other laws enacted during the latter half of the 19th century included the Tea Acts of 1883 and 1897, the Oleomargarine Act of 1886 and the Filled Cheese Act of 1896. All were enforced by the Treasury Department and had similar commercial purposes.

1850

Lemuel Shattuck attributes a decrease in average life expectancy to adulterated food and drugs, and he recommends establishing boards of health to counter the problems.

Accum's treatise had raised public concern in the United States, as well as in Europe, about food adulteration. Several similar investigations in the United States added to this concern. Among these was a report by Lemuel Shattuck in 1850 that showed that average life expectancy had decreased in Boston from 27.85 years to 21.43 years and in New York from 26.15 years to 19.69 years between the years 1810 to 1820, and 1840 to 1845. He attributed this in part to adulterated food and drugs and recommended establishing boards of health to counter the problems.

Findings of this type helped put pressure on Congress to pass federal legislation. Many scientists, journalists and social reformers joined the effort. Dr.

Harvey W. Wiley, who became the Chief Chemist of the U.S. Department of Agriculture (USDA) (the forerunner of Commissioner of Food and Drugs) in 1883, took an aggressive public role in exposing food adulteration and demanding a federal response. Some industry leaders also spoke out on the need for federal regulation, based both on their concerns over lax enforcement and on the difficulties of complying with the patchwork of state and local laws. More than 100 food and drug bills were introduced in Congress, unsuccessfully save one, from the 1880s to 1906.

The one federal law enacted in that period was the Virus Act of 1902 (subsequently known as the Biologics Control Act), which was intended to ensure purity and safety of therapeutic serums, vaccines, toxins, anti-toxins and similar products used to prevent, treat or cure diseases in humans. Vaccines had long been widely accepted in the United States, but regulation of their safety and purity was left to the states. The direct impetus for the 1902 federal law arose from two tragedies that occurred in 1901: one involving contaminated smallpox vaccine that caused an outbreak of tetanus in Camden, New Jersey; the other involving diphtheria antitoxin contaminated with tetanus in St. Louis, Missouri. These incidents convinced Congress that federal action was necessary to protect the public from contaminated products. Ironically, vaccines originally were regulated by the Vaccines Act of 1813, apparently the first federal regulatory law, but that law was repealed in 1822 after similar incidents of contaminated batches occurred.

The 1902 act for the first time required government premarket approval of a product. Biologics manufacturers were required to obtain both product and establishment licenses. The act also, for the first time, authorized federal agents (from the Treasury Department) to inspect biologics establishments. Enforcement of the human biologics law subsequently was transferred to the National Institutes of Health and became the Food and Drug Administration's (FDA's) responsibility in 1972. Animal biologics are still regulated by USDA.

THE FOOD AND DRUGS ACT OF 1906

The pressure on Congress to enact federal legislation from Dr. Wiley and others was heightened around the turn of the century by public opinion whipped up by "muckrakers," "investigative reporters" who exposed food and drug adulteration, consumer fraud and other social issues. Probably the most influential was Upton Sinclair, whose 1906 novel *The Jungle* dramatically portrayed food adulteration in the meat industry as part of his description of the exploitation of workers and the poor in Chicago. In response, President Theodore Roosevelt

1906
The original Food and Drugs Act is passed by Congress and signed by President Theodore Roosevelt. It prohibits interstate commerce in misbranded and adulterated foods, drinks and drugs.

sent his own representatives to Chicago who confirmed the abominable conditions. President Roosevelt then added his support for federal legislation.

On June 30, 1906, both the Food and Drugs Act (often called the "Pure Food and Drugs Act") and the Meat Inspection Act were signed into law. The former was enforced by the predecessor to today's FDA. The latter was, and remains, the jurisdiction of the USDA, continuing the historic split in regulatory authority between the two agencies and the corresponding segments of the food industry.

The 1906 act was the first comprehensive U.S. legislation relating to foods and drugs. It was designed as an "enforcement" statute intended to punish violations by criminal prosecution or by seizure of the offending goods. In concise and simple terms, the 1906 act commanded the federal government to ferret out adulterated and misbranded foods and drugs in interstate commerce. The government was not authorized to establish industry-wide standards or broad rules to protect the public health or to approve any products before they could be marketed.

The 1906 act commanded the federal government to ferret out adulterated and misbranded foods and drugs in interstate commerce but it did not authorize the government to establish industry-wide standards or broad rules to protect the public health.

Section 2 of the 1906 act prohibited the interstate shipment, including import from and export to a foreign country, of any adulterated or misbranded food or drug. The person who delivered a violative product *and* the person who subsequently delivered such an article "in original unbroken packages" were guilty of a misdemeanor and subject to a fine of up to $200. A subsequent offense was punishable by either or both a $300 fine and one year in prison. A dealer who could show a "guaranty" from a U.S. supplier to the effect that the article was not adulterated or misbranded would be exempt from prosecution (section 9 of the 1906 act).

Section 6 of the 1906 act defined "drug" to include "all medicines and preparations recognized in the United States Pharmacopoeia (USP) or National Formulary (NF) for internal or external use, and any substance or mixture of substances intended to be used for the cure, mitigation, or prevention of disease of either man or animals." The act provided that a drug was "adulterated" if: 1) the drug failed to meet the standards of "strength, quality, or purity" as prescribed by the USP or the NF, unless the drug's container "plainly stated" a different standard of purity; or 2) the drug failed to meet its own labeled strength or purity (section 7 of the 1906 act).

Section 6 of the 1906 act also defined "food" to include "all articles used for food, drink, confectionary or condiment by man or other animals, whether simple, mixed, or compound." A food was adulterated:

First. If any substance has been mixed and packed with it so as to reduce or lower or injuriously affect its quality or strength.

Second. If any substance has been substituted wholly or in part for the article.

Third. If any valuable constituent of the article has been wholly or in part abstracted.

Fourth. If it be mixed, colored, powdered, coated, or stained in a manner whereby damage or inferiority is concealed.

Fifth. If it contain any added poisonous or other added deleterious ingredient which may render such article injurious to health. . . .

Sixth. If it consists in whole or in part of a filthy, decomposed, or putrid animal or vegetable substance, or any portion of an animal unfit for food, whether manufactured or not, or if it is the product of a diseased animal, or one that has died otherwise than by slaughter.

The statute further declared confectionary to be adulterated if it contained certain minerals, poisonous color or flavor, other ingredients harmful to health, "spirituous liquor" or narcotic drugs (section 7 of the 1906 act).

The 1906 act also listed several acts that would constitute "misbranding" as to both food and drugs. In particular, any drug, food or food ingredient "the package or label of which shall bear any statement, design, or device regarding such article [or its components] which shall be false or misleading in any particular" would be misbranded (section 8 of the 1906 act). A drug could also be misbranded if: 1) it was an imitation of or was offered for sale under the name of another drug; 2) the original contents were replaced by other materials; or 3) the package label failed to state "the quantity or proportion of any alcohol, morphine, opium, cocaine, heroine, alpha or beta eucaine, chloroform, cannabis indica, chloral hydrate, or acetanilide" or any derivatives of those substances. A food could be misbranded for the same conditions and also if the package contained: 1) an inaccurate quantity of contents statement or 2) a false statement about the food's ingredients.

"Misbranded" as defined in the 1906 act:
In particular, any drug, food, or food ingredient "the package or label of which shall bear any statement, design, or device regarding such article [or its components] which shall be false or misleading in any particular" would be misbranded.

An adulterated or misbranded article in interstate commerce, or still "unloaded, unsold, or in original unbroken packages," could be seized and condemned by a U.S. district court (section 10 of the 1906 act). The procedures were to conform to admiralty proceedings except that either the claimant of the article or the government could demand a jury trial.

The act was administered jointly under "uniform rules and regulations" established by the Secretaries of Agriculture, Commerce and Treasury, including "collection and examination of specimens of foods and drugs" (section 3 of the 1906 act). The Secretaries established a committee to draw up rules and regulations for enforcement of the law. The committee included Dr. Wiley, Chief of the USDA Bureau of Chemistry, which was primarily responsible for the enforcement of the act. The bureau, in particular, examined samples and, if they appeared to be violative, notified and provided the party from whom the samples were obtained an opportunity to be heard. "[I]f it appears that any of the provisions of [the 1906] Act have been violated," the Secretary of Agriculture certified the matter to the appropriate U.S. District Attorney for formal action in the federal district court (sections 4 and 5 of the 1906 act).

A controversy soon arose over whether a drug label was "false or misleading in any particular" if it contained unproved therapeutic claims.

A controversy soon arose over whether a drug label was "false or misleading in any particular" if it contained unproved therapeutic claims. The Supreme Court, in *United States v. Johnson*, 211 U.S. 488 (1911), held that "Cancerine tablets," offered as part of "Dr. Johnson's Mild Combination Treatment for Cancer, Tumor and Other Chronic Diseases," were not misbranded because the statute prohibited only misleading statements about the ingredients of a drug, not about the drug's effectiveness.

Congress reacted in 1912 with the Sherley Amendment, which expanded the definition of misbranding for drugs to include "any statement, design, or device regarding the curative or therapeutic effect of such article or [its components], which is false and fraudulent." Significantly, the government still had the burden of proving fraudulent intent.

There were only five other amendments to the 1906 act before it was replaced by the FDCA in 1938:

- The Net Weight Amendment of 1913 required the quantity of a packaged food's contents to be plainly and conspicuously marked on the outer package in terms of weight, measure or numerical count.

- The Kenyon Amendment of 1919 overturned an adverse administrative decision by defining the word "package," as used in the act, to include "wrapped meats inclosed [sic] in papers."

- In 1923 Congress responded to requests from the dairy industry to provide the first standard definition of a food product in "An Act to Define Butter and to Provide a Standard Therefore."

♦ At the urging of the canned foods industry, Congress passed the McNary-Napes Amendment in 1930, authorizing the Secretary of Agriculture to establish standards of quality, condition and fill of container for each class of canned foods.

♦ In 1934 Congress implemented the Shrimp Inspection Amendment, which authorized the Secretary of Agriculture to create a voluntary seafood inspection program that would allow a participant to market its shrimp as "USDA Approved."

Five amendments to the 1906 act:
- *The Net Weight Amendment*
- *The Kenyon Amendment*
- *Butter Amendment*
- *McNary-Napes Amendment*
- *Shrimp Inspection Amendment*

The Bureau of Chemistry and others quickly recognized deficiencies in the 1906 act. Among other things, the bureau was concerned that the law did not reach dangerous cosmetics and medical devices. The bureau also was concerned that the 1906 act did not extend to fraudulent statements made in food and drug advertising, as opposed to package labels. Although the bureau and other critics initially believed amendments to the existing statute would remedy the 1906 act's failings, they came to the conclusion over time that a completely new statute would be necessary.

THE FEDERAL FOOD, DRUG, AND COSMETIC ACT

In the 1920s and early 1930s, consumers were exposed to increasing numbers of processed and manufactured foods, drugs, cosmetics and medical devices. Occasionally, these new products had tragic consequences. For example, a depilatory known as "Koremlu Cream," advertised as a cosmetic, contained thallium acetate that caused severe injury to unsuspecting users. Various "slenderizing" compounds, containing powerful pharmacologic agents, could not be regulated as drugs under the 1906 act because obesity was not recognized as a disease. These products were outside the scope of the 1906 act and the government had no means to remove them from the market.

In another notorious example, "Radiothor" was labeled accurately as "radium-containing water." Because that statement was true and the label made no fraudulent therapeutic claims, the government could not take action against the manufacturer. The agency could only warn consumers not to use "Radiothor," even as people were dying from radiation poisoning.

Further, the 1906 act prohibited fraudulent advertising only if attached to, or packaged with, the product. Thus, both consumers and honest manufacturers were susceptible to the deceptive advertising practices of the unscrupulous producer (and the 1906 act provided for only the mildest criminal penalties).

1938

The FDCA was passed by Congress, containing new provisions:

- *Extending control to cosmetics and therapeutic devices.*
- *Requiring new drugs to be shown safe before marketing—starting a new system of drug regulation.*
- *Eliminating the Sherley Amendment requirement to prove intent to defraud in drug misbranding cases.*
- *Providing that safe tolerances be set for unavoidable poisonous substances.*
- *Authorizing standards of identity, quality and fill-of-container for foods.*
- *Authorizing factory inspections.*
- *Adding the remedy of court injunctions to the previous penalties of seizures and prosecutions.*

By 1933, critics of the 1906 act included consumer advocates, politicians, reporters and other commentators, as well as officials of FDA (the bureau became FDA in 1930).

Rexford G. Tugwell, who became Assistant Secretary of Agriculture in 1933 under President Franklin D. Roosevelt, assembled a committee of FDA officials, USDA attorneys and several administrative law professors. Their objective was the complete overhaul of the 1906 act. These efforts resulted in a bill introduced by Senator Copeland of New York in 1933 as S. 1944.

Consistent with New Deal political theory, the bill would have increased greatly FDA's regulation of the food and drug industries. Most contentious was a provision that authorized the Secretary of Agriculture to issue any regulations deemed necessary to enforce the law. (It was generally understood that the Secretary would delegate all authority to FDA to enforce the law unless the law specifically barred such delegation.) The regulations would have the force and effect of law. The Secretary also would have the authority to set the procedures for issuing regulations.

Jurisdiction over medical devices would be established by including them in the definition of "drug." Cosmetics, previously subject to little regulation, would be brought within the jurisdiction of FDA. Factories that manufactured or processed foods, drugs or cosmetics, and warehouses that stored such goods would be subject to inspection. FDA also by regulation could require permits for manufacturing, processing and packaging facilities. False advertising of regulated products would also be prohibited.

S. 1944 would have expanded greatly the criteria for "adulterated" or "misbranded" foods, drugs, cosmetics or devices. For example, in response to various "quack" remedies then on the market, a drug would be adulterated if dangerous when used according to its labeling and misbranded if it claimed to have an effect that general medical opinion did not support. Food would be misbranded if it failed to meet standards of quality, standards of identity and standards of package fill that the Secretary was to promulgate by regulation. Adulterated or misbranded goods in interstate commerce were subject to seizure, and any person (including corporate officers) responsible for introducing or receiving such goods could be subject to criminal liability. Significantly, the bill established a strict liability standard; a "knowing" violation of these provisions was not necessary (although more severe penalties applied if a person acted with scienter). In addition, the Secretary was authorized to use "publicity" when necessary to protect the public health or prevent consumer fraud.

S. 1944 sparked a five-year legislative battle that reflected, in large part, the ongoing debate over the rise in administrative autonomy under the New Deal. Critics focused on the broad discretionary authority vested in the Secretary of Agriculture and the lack of procedural safeguards to prevent misuse of power. Although the Secretary was authorized to issue many regulations only after "notice and hearing," the Secretary also was given the authority to define "notice" and "hearing" by regulation. Moreover, any findings of fact after such a hearing were deemed to be conclusively established for purposes of judicial review. The false advertising provisions were another major target of criticism. Both advertisers and publishers believed that the definition of false advertising was too vague and the penalties for publishing such advertising were too severe.

S. 1944, introduced in 1933 by Senator Copeland, sparked a five-year legislative battle that reflected the ongoing debate over the rise in administrative autonomy under the New Deal.

As a result, S. 1944 was revised over successive years in attempts to agree with the objectives of the affected industries. The first revision (S. 2000), submitted to the Senate in 1934, attempted to enhance procedural safeguards by establishing two five-member advisory panels, the Committee on Public Health and the Committee on Food. A majority vote of the appropriate committee was required before FDA could propose a regulation. After a hearing, another majority vote was required before FDA could issue the regulation. The bill also gave jurisdiction to the U.S. district courts to enjoin the enforcement of any regulation that would cause substantial harm to the petitioner "if it is shown that the regulation is unreasonable, arbitrary, or capricious, or not in accordance with the law." "False advertising" was required to be "false or misleading in any particular relevant to the purposes" of the act. The bill died in committee, but was amended and resurfaced in the same session as S. 2800.

In a concession to the publishing industry, S. 2800 modified some provisions relating to advertising and specifically exempted publishers from liability for false advertisements. To deflect criticism that the government was attempting to regulate the practice of medicine, the bill contained an explicit statement to the contrary. A drug was still considered misbranded, however, if the labeling contained the name of a disease for which the drug was not a cure, as supported by "substantial medical opinion" or "demonstrable scientific facts." The Senate Committee on Commerce held hearings on S. 2800 and, after further modification, reported it favorably to the Senate but Congress adjourned without action on the bill.

Senator Copeland persisted, and in 1935 he introduced a new bill, S. 5. This bill retained the Committee on Food and the Committee on Public Health and granted them broader authority to formulate and issue regulations. The bill authorized the Secretary to appoint additional advisory committees to include representatives of the food, drug, cosmetic and advertising industries and consumers in the regulatory process. S. 5 eliminated the provision granting the

Secretary conclusive power with respect to questions of fact and transferred this to the judicial system. Judicial authority to review regulations was made explicit. FDA was given jurisdiction over false advertising. The bill passed in the Senate.

In the House of Representatives, a subcommittee of the Committee on Interstate and Foreign Commerce held hearings on S. 5 and competing legislation sponsored in the House. In May 1936, this subcommittee agreed to a bill. Among other things, this bill granted sole authority for enforcing the false advertising prohibitions to the Federal Trade Commission (FTC). The House bill eliminated the Committees on Public Health and Food and the advisory committees. Rulemaking authority was transferred back to the Secretary, with some restrictions.

The bill passed the House and went to conference. However, neither side would yield on the issue of which agency should control advertising, and the bill failed again.

In January 1937, Senator Copeland reintroduced S. 5 in another attempt to achieve a food and drug bill. To address one of the advertising issues, the bill would use injunctions, rather than criminal sanctions, to enforce the prohibition of advertising that was "false or misleading in any particular." Further, the "particulars" that a court could enjoin were enumerated, including statements regarding the identity, strength, quality, purity, safety, dietary, curative, therapeutic or beneficial effects of a food, drug, device or cosmetic. Jurisdiction over advertising was placed in FDA on the theory that advertising was an extension of labeling. The FTC would retain jurisdiction over advertising that was an unfair method of competition. With several other amendments (including a separate definition for "device"), the Senate passed S. 5 and the bill was referred to the House Committee on Interstate and Foreign Commerce.

The Elixir Sulfanilamide tragedy led to passage of the 1938 law.

While the bill was in the House committee, a drug manufacturer released a product labeled "Elixir Sulfanilamide," a new dosage form of a sulfa drug. Before the elixir was marketed, the manufacturer tested the product for flavor, but not for safety. One ingredient in the elixir, which was not listed on the label, was diethylene glycol, a solvent used to prepare the elixir. Almost 100 people died from ingesting the drug. FDA immediately initiated a recall, but could base its actions only on a technical violation of the 1906 act: "elixir" could be used only to describe a solution that contained alcohol; as Elixir Sulfanilamide did not contain alcohol, it was misbranded. The manufacturer's failure to test the drug for safety or to list a lethal ingredient on the label did not violate the 1906 act.

This tragedy reinvigorated the efforts to enact a food and drug bill. In addition, the jurisdictional controversy over advertising was resolved early in 1938 by the Wheeler-Lea Amendments to the Federal Trade Commission Act, which gave the FTC jurisdiction over false advertising of food, drugs, devices and cosmetics as an unfair or deceptive trade practice. The House committee amended S. 5 to specify that foods, drugs, devices or cosmetics were misbranded if the labeling was false or misleading in any particular. The committee added a list of factors that would be considered to decide whether labeling was misleading, including representations or suggestions of fact and the omission of any material facts. This provision was intended to prevent manufacturers of drugs and devices from making false effectiveness claims. The bill, however, deleted the provision that deemed a drug misbranded if scientific opinion did not support a labeling claim of efficacy.

As a response to the Elixir Sulfanilamide tragedy, the committee added a provision to S. 5 that defined "new drugs" and required manufacturers to apply to FDA before a new drug could be marketed. As part of the application, the manufacturer had to test the new drug for safety and submit full reports of the investigations conducted to establish safety to FDA for review. If FDA did not act within 60 days, the manufacturer could market the drug. If FDA questioned an application's assertion of safety, the agency could initiate a hearing. Whether by oversight or intention, devices were not subject to premarket safety review.

To facilitate judicial oversight of administrative action, an administrative hearing was required before FDA could issue many regulations. The Secretary could issue, modify or repeal a proposed regulation only on evidence of record at the hearing. The bill required that the Secretary publicize detailed findings of fact before taking action. Within 90 days after a regulation issued, individuals or businesses could challenge the regulation in any district court. If challenged, the Secretary was required to furnish a certified copy of the administrative record. The court could then review the agency's findings of fact and, in appropriate circumstances, could supplement the record with additional evidence.

The Senate disagreed with some of these amendments and another conference committee was convened. The committee decided that judicial review would be more consistent and less burdensome to the agency if it were conducted in the circuit courts of appeal. Further, to the extent that evidence outside the administrative record was to be taken, it would be done in a proceeding before the Secretary. Other amendments clarified certain labeling provisions. Both houses then approved the bill, and President Roosevelt signed the FDCA on June 25, 1938.

President Roosevelt signed the FDCA on June 25, 1938.

Structure of the Federal Food, Drug, and Cosmetic Act of 1938

The Federal Food, Drug, and Cosmetic Act of 1938
The FDCA remains the basic law governing food and drug regulation.

As enacted, the FDCA is divided into 10 chapters. While each chapter will be explained in greater detail later in this text, the following brief summary of each chapter's subject matter should prove beneficial at this juncture.

Chapter I is the short title of the act. Chapter II provides definitions of important terms.

Chapter III sets forth the prohibited acts and penalties. In particular, section 301 states that "The following acts *and the causing thereof* are hereby prohibited" (emphasis added), thus including aiding and abetting. Among other things, the act prohibits the "adulteration" or "misbranding" of food, drugs, devices, tobacco products and cosmetics in interstate commerce, or the introduction or delivery for introduction of adulterated or misbranded goods into interstate commerce.

The FDCA also established, for the first time, jurisdiction in the district courts to restrain violations of the act by injunction. A violation of any of the prohibited acts in section 301 can be prosecuted as a misdemeanor under a strict liability standard, applicable to both companies and individuals. The Supreme Court upheld this standard in *United States v. Dotterweich*, 320 U.S. 277 (1943), and in *United States v. Park*, 421 U.S. 658 (1975). As in the 1906 act, a person could avoid criminal penalties by showing a supplier's guaranty. The act also provides the accused an opportunity to present oral or written views to FDA before the agency reports the case to the U.S. Attorney for prosecution. The Supreme Court in *Dotterweich*, however, held that failure to provide that opportunity does not preclude prosecution. In addition, the Secretary is authorized to enforce "minor" violations of the act by means of "written notice or warning." All formal enforcement proceedings are brought by the government, meaning that FDA must act through the Department of Justice (DOJ).

As in the 1906 act, violative articles are subject to seizure and condemnation in the district courts. Multiple seizures are authorized for adulterated products, unapproved new drugs or products previously adjudicated as misbranded.

Chapter IV addresses regulation of foods. The Secretary is authorized to promulgate regulations establishing standards of identity, quality and fill of containers for foods. In a concession to the agricultural and dairy industries, most fresh or dried fruits and vegetables, as well as butter, are exempt from these regulations. An adulterated food is defined as a food that contains any "poisonous or deleterious substance," or any "filthy, putrid, or decomposed substance," or that was prepared, packaged, or stored "under unsanitary conditions." Food is also adulterated if missing a "valuable constituent," or if any substance has been added to increase its bulk or make it appear to be of greater value (known as "economic adulteration").

Food is deemed misbranded, among other things, if its labeling is "false or misleading in any particular," if it is an imitation of another food (unless clearly labeled as an imitation) or if it does not meet FDA regulations setting standards of identity, quality or container fill. Foods for special dietary use must comply with FDA regulations.

The act also provides for FDA to impose emergency permit controls by regulation, requiring a permit to manufacture certain foods where microbial contamination cannot be readily controlled after the fact. FDA is also authorized to set tolerances for poisonous or deleterious substances that cannot be avoided by good manufacturing practices.

Drugs and devices are the subject of Chapter V. A drug or device is deemed adulterated if it is unsafe or unsanitary. Drugs that fall below the standards of strength and purity established in specified official references (unless clearly labeled as such) or that do not meet the standards of strength or purity represented on the label also are adulterated.

A drug or device is misbranded, among other reasons, if its labeling is "false or misleading in any particular"; fails to identify the manufacturer, packer or distributor; lacks a statement of net contents; does not list the common name of the drug and every active ingredient; does not contain "adequate directions for use" and "adequate warnings"; or is dangerous to health when used according to the labeling.

"New drugs" cannot be introduced into interstate commerce unless an application has been filed with the Secretary that includes reports showing that the new drug is safe for use. The application becomes effective in 60 days unless FDA notifies the applicant to the contrary. An opportunity for hearing is provided, and the applicant can appeal an adverse decision to a federal district court. Drugs for investigational purposes are exempted from these requirements.

Chapter VI describes the adulteration and misbranding provisions for cosmetics and is the shortest chapter. A cosmetic is adulterated if it:

Food is deemed misbranded if its labeling is "false or misleading in any particular," if it is an imitation of another food (unless clearly labeled as an imitation), or if it does not meet FDA regulations setting standards of identity, quality or container fill.

"Misbranded" as defined in the 1938 act:
A drug or device is misbranded, among other reasons, if its labeling is "false or misleading in any particular"; fails to identify the manufacturer, packer or distributor; lacks a statement of net contents; does not list the common name of the drug and every active ingredient; does not contain "adequate directions for use" and "adequate warnings"; or is dangerous to health when used according to the labeling.

♦ contains any "poisonous or deleterious substance which may render it injurious to users" when used as directed (except that a coal tar hair dye is exempt if it bears a label warning);

♦ is or contains any "filthy, putrid, or decomposed substance";

♦ was "prepared, packaged or held under unsanitary conditions" and became contaminated or rendered injurious to health;

♦ has a poisonous or deleterious container; or except for a hair dye, contains an unapproved color or one from an uncertified batch.

FDA is authorized to list and batch certify harmless colors.

A cosmetic is misbranded if its labeling is "false or misleading in any particular," fails to list the manufacturer and quantity of contents on any package label, lacks prominence and conspicuousness for required label statements, or is in a misleading container. FDA is authorized to exempt cosmetics shipped in bulk to be labeled or repacked elsewhere.

Administrative provisions are the subject of Chapter VII. Section 701(a) authorizes FDA "to promulgate regulations for the efficient enforcement of this Act." No procedures are specified. More formal rulemaking procedures are set out for regulations to implement such rules as food standards; standards of strength, purity and quality for noncompendial drugs; and listing of habit-forming drugs. FDA must offer an opportunity for hearing and the agency's decision must be based on "substantial evidence of record at the hearing." Within 90 days, any adversely affected party can appeal the order to an appropriate circuit court of appeals.

FDA's principal enforcement tool is the establishment inspection.

Chapter VII also spells out the authority and limits of FDA's principal enforcement tool, the establishment inspection. It authorizes the agency to:

♦ Use its own or state agents to conduct examinations and investigations.

♦ Take samples of foods, drugs, cosmetics or tobacco products. (This is stated in a backhanded way in section 702(b), which requires FDA to give a portion of the sample to the owner "where a sample . . . is collected for analysis.")

♦ Review and copy records of interstate shipment in the possession of a carrier or the recipient of a food, drug, device, cosmetic or tobacco product. Refusal of a written request is unlawful, but FDA may not use evidence so obtained in a criminal action against the person who provided the evidence.

♦ Enter and inspect, "at reasonable times," any factory, warehouse, establishment or vehicle where food, drugs, devices, cosmetics or tobacco products are produced, packed or held for introduction into interstate commerce, or after such introduction. FDA inspectors must first obtain permission, but refusal is a prohibited act. The inspection may extend to the facilities, vehicle, equipment, finished and unfinished materials, container, labeling and, with the exception of cosmetics, all records except for financial data, nontechnical or nonpertinent professional personnel data, or research unrelated to product approvals and other reporting requirements.

♦ Publish reports of formal actions under the act and disseminate information where FDA believes there is an imminent danger to health or "gross" consumer deception.

Chapter VIII governs imports and exports of products. The Secretary of the Treasury is ordered to deliver samples of food, drugs, devices, cosmetics or tobacco products offered for import as requested by the Secretary of Agriculture. Section 801 states: "If it appears from the examination of such samples or otherwise that" the products violate the FDCA, such products may be refused admission. The refused article must be exported or destroyed. Significantly, no direct right to judicial review is provided.

Articles intended for export are exempt from the adulteration or misbranding provisions of the act only if they comply with the foreign purchaser's specifications, do not violate foreign law, are labeled on the shipping package for export only and have not been offered in domestic commerce. Unapproved new drugs cannot be exported.

Chapter IX, added in 2009 by the Family Smoking Prevention and Tobacco Control Act, authorizes FDA to set performance standards for tobacco products, require the disclosure of tobacco product ingredients and regulate "modified risk" tobacco products.

Chapter IX, added in 2009 by the Family Smoking Prevention and Tobacco Control Act (with the previous Chapter IX renumbered to Chapter X), authorizes FDA to set performance standards for tobacco products, require the disclosure of tobacco product ingredients and regulate "modified risk" tobacco products. In addition, FDA can restrict tobacco sales, distribution and marketing, and can require stronger health warnings on packaging and in advertisements. The Tobacco Products Scientific Advisory Committee is established, charged with making recommendations regarding the use of menthol in cigarettes, dissolvable tobacco products and other issues.

Finally, Chapter X exempts meat and meat food products, biologics and certain other products from the provisions of the act because they are governed by other statutes. It also specifies the "mission" of FDA and formally exempts the practice of medicine from FDA's authority, among other things.

AMENDMENTS TO THE FDCA

There have been numerous amendments of the FDCA since 1938, but there has been no overhaul of the entire regulatory scheme comparable to the 1938 act's relationship to the 1906 act.

Since 1938, there have been numerous amendments of the FDCA; however, there has been no general overhaul of the entire regulatory scheme comparable to the 1938 act's relationship to the 1906 act. Early amendments primarily were aimed at overcoming omissions and shortcomings in the law, often following court decisions. These statutes generally broadened FDA's regulatory authority and left implementation largely to FDA. More recent amendments have required FDA to focus on commercial and economic issues, frequently specifying precisely how and when FDA must implement the FDCA. In 1997 and 2007, Congress enacted laws that represented the most comprehensive efforts to "reform" the agency and improve regulation of all products since 1938.

Significant Amendments from 1938 to 1962

Scientific developments, as well as the demands of World War II, led to a number of new laws directed at specific drugs. In December 1941, Congress amended the FDCA to require batch certification of the strength, quality and purity of insulin in order "to adequately ensure safety and efficacy of use." Congress was persuaded of the need to ensure uniformity among batches because of the difficulties in making this drug. Significantly, this law gave FDA, for the first time, specific authority to regulate the efficacy of a particular drug.

Batch certification subsequently was required for penicillin (1945); streptomycin (1947); aureomycin, chloramphenicol and bacitracin (1949); and all antibiotics (1962). By 1982, however, FDA was convinced that the quality of these drugs was now adequate to permit them to be regulated the same as other new drugs, and the agency ceased requiring batch certification in most instances. These provisions on batch certification of insulin and antibiotics were repealed in the Food and Drug Administration Modernization Act of 1997, Pub. L. No. 105-115, § 125, 111 Stat. 2325.

In 1948, after an appellate court held that the FDCA did not reach products after shipment in interstate commerce, Congress amended the FDCA to hold expressly that a product may be in violation of the act while "held for sale (whether or not the first sale) after shipment in interstate commerce." This brought local warehouses and retailers within FDA's jurisdiction.

◆ The Durham-Humphrey Amendment

In 1951, in the Durham-Humphrey Amendment, Congress for the first time defined prescription drugs for purposes of FDA regulation. Prescription and over-the-counter (OTC) status previously were determined by state law or by industry, although FDA had used the misbranding provision requiring "adequate directions for use" to impose prescription limits on some drugs. As amended, the FDCA defines a prescription drug to include habit-forming drugs; drugs that are dangerous for use except under the supervision of a (state) licensed practitioner because of their "toxicity or other potentiality for harmful effect,. . . method of use, or the collateral measures necessary to [their] use"; and those that are limited to prescription dispensing by approved new drug applications (NDAs). OTC drugs are not defined but comprise all those drugs that do not meet the prescription drug criteria.

For several years, FDA used this definition (as well as the misbranding and new drug provisions) to prohibit sales of stimulant, depressant and hallucinogenic drugs, which, unlike narcotics, were not subject to specific laws outlawing their abuse. During the 1950s and 1960s, FDA criminally prosecuted manufacturers, distributors, importers, physicians, truck stop operators and others engaged in the illicit diversion of these drugs. In the late 1960s, FDA prosecuted a few students for distribution of LSD and other hallucinogens. Congress subsequently passed several controlled substances laws that ultimately were transferred to DOJ and are now enforced by the Drug Enforcement Administration (DEA).

In 1953, after a court restricted FDA's inspectional authority, Congress amended section 704 of the act to make clear that FDA had the right to inspect without the permission of the owner or operator of the establishment.

In 1954, and again in 1958, Congress attended to problems relating to chemical contamination of foods. In 1954, Congress set tolerances for pesticide chemicals in or on raw agricultural commodities, including a complex premarket approval system based on a demonstration of safety for use of pesticides in foods intended for human use (FDCA §§ 201(q), (r), 402(a)(2), 408). Authority for establishing the tolerances subsequently was transferred to the Environmental Protection Agency, with FDA retaining the authority to proceed against foods that contain unapproved or unsafe levels of pesticides.

♦ The Food Additives Amendment of 1958

Congress subsequently enacted the Food Additives Amendment of 1958, which gave FDA authority to require premarket approval for safety of components added to foods (FDCA §§ 201(s), (t), 402(a)(2), 409). This followed several years of hearings on the appropriate regulatory mechanism to ensure the safety of food ingredients.

Under this law, a food additive is defined as any substance intended or reasonably expected to become a food component or to affect a food's characteristics

1951
The Durham-Humphrey Amendment
The Durham-Humphrey Amendment defines the kinds of drugs that cannot be safely used without medical supervision and restricts their sale to prescription by a licensed practitioner.

that is "not generally recognized [by] qualified experts" as safe (GRAS) for its intended use based on "scientific procedures" or, for substances marketed prior to 1958, based on experience from common use in food (FDCA § 201(s)). A food additive is deemed unsafe unless FDA has reviewed data proving its safety and issued a regulation allowing its use. Human safety data is not required. The law established formal rulemaking procedures for the process.

1958
Food Additives
Amendment
The Food Additives Amendment required manufacturers of new food additives to establish safety. The Delaney Provision prohibits the approval of any food additive shown to induce cancer in humans or animals.

In addition, the law contains an anticancer provision, known as the Delaney Clause after its leading sponsor, Representative James Delaney (D-NY), which prohibits approval of any food additive that has been "found to induce cancer when ingested by man or animal" or found to induce cancer in appropriate tests. As analytic testing has advanced, this "one molecule" approach has affected several widely used food components, such as the artificial sweeteners cyclamate and saccharin and the preservative nitrite. On two occasions, Congress has taken steps to exempt specific substances from the Delaney Clause. In 1962, the FDCA was amended to exempt ingredients of animal feeds (primarily diethylstilbestrol) if no residue is found in edible portions of the animal. In the Saccharin Study and Labeling Act of 1977, Congress put a moratorium on FDA action to ban saccharin, but required labeling of products containing the sweetener. That act was repealed in December 2000. The Delaney Clause was modified in 1996 with respect to pesticides but otherwise remains in place.

♦ The Color Additive Amendments of 1960

Congress enacted the Color Additive Amendments of 1960 to regulate colors added to foods, drugs or cosmetics separately from the Food Additives Amendment. A color additive is defined in the amendment as a dye, pigment or other coloring agent that "is capable (alone or through reaction with other substance) of imparting color" when added to a food, drug, cosmetic or the human body. Unlike food additives, the definition of color additives does not contain any grandfather protection for a GRAS color. FDA can approve a color for one use and not others. For example, some colors are approved for external use; some are approved for use everywhere but around the eye.

1960
Color Additive
Amendments
The Color Additive Amendments required manufacturers to establish the safety of color additives in foods, drugs and cosmetics.

Like food additives, color additives are unsafe unless used in compliance with a regulation issued by FDA. The color also must be "listed" in the FDA regulation for specific uses, and must be batch certified or exempted by FDA regulation. FDA previously had established a provisional listing of "harmless" coal tar colors based on the 1938 act. FDA was authorized to continue this "provisional listing of commercially established colors" for 30 months. The provisional listing, however, lasted until 1981, and several colors still are provisionally regarded as safe by FDA pending receipt of further data.

The amendment also contains a Delaney Clause that prohibits FDA from approving any color additive found to induce cancer when ingested by man or animal, or found to induce cancer "after tests which are appropriate for the evaluation of the safety of additives for use in food." The prohibition thus is slightly narrower than the similar provision for food additives.

1962
Drug Amendments
Thalidomide tragedy leads to passage of major amendment to the law. Since 1962, drugs must be proven effective as well as safe.

◆ The 1962 Drug Amendments

In the late 1950s, Senator Estes Kefauver began a series of investigations of the drug industry for antitrust and price-fixing violations. In the midst of these investigations, there was, as in 1938, a public health tragedy that convinced Congress to enact legislation to protect the public. The incident involved thalidomide, a tranquilizer that was available in the United States only as an investigational drug, but was commercially marketed in other countries. The drug was found to cause birth defects in children whose mothers took the drug during their pregnancy. As a result of the thalidomide tragedy, Congress reexamined the new drug approval process. This led to enactment of the Drug Amendments of 1962, the most comprehensive revision of the drug regulatory law since 1938.

Ironically, although thalidomide raised drug safety concerns, the most significant change brought about by the 1962 Drug Amendments was the added requirement to prove *effectiveness* to obtain premarket approval of a new drug. The definition of "new drug" also was amended to include a drug that was not generally recognized by qualified experts as "safe and effective" for its labeled use (FDCA § 201(p)(1)).

In addition, the drug approval provisions were changed substantially:

◆ FDA now must affirmatively approve a product before it can be marketed;

◆ FDA can deny approval for false or misleading labeling;

◆ there must be "substantial evidence" of efficacy, "consisting of adequate and well-controlled investigations, including clinical investigations, by experts qualified by scientific training and experience to evaluate the effectiveness of the drug involved";

◆ new record and reporting requirements were added;

◆ the investigational new drug exemption authority was broadened to authorize FDA to issue regulations to require reports of preclinical tests, investigator agreements, informed consent and other records and reports; and

◆ the Secretary of the Department of Health and Human Services (HHS), but not FDA, can suspend the NDA immediately if there is an imminent hazard to health.

The 1962 Drug Amendments also broadened FDA's regulatory authority over all drugs in several respects, authorizing:

♦ good manufacturing practice regulations for all drugs,

♦ increased authority over antibiotics,

♦ mandatory use of the generic name in drug labeling,

♦ inspection authority over prescription drug records,

♦ mandatory inspection of drug establishments every two years,

♦ annual drug establishment registration,

♦ regulation of prescription drug advertising and

♦ a requirement to prove the efficacy of all new drugs approved from 1938 to 1962.

Considerable emphasis was placed on regulation in the decade and a half following the Drug Amendments of 1962, but the types of legislation affecting FDA were unusually varied.

Legislation From 1962 to 1976

In the decade and a half following the Drug Amendments of 1962, there was considerable emphasis on regulation, but the types of legislation affecting FDA were unusually varied. For example, Congress passed the Drug Abuse Control Amendments of 1965, authorizing FDA to act against depressant, stimulant and hallucinogenic drugs, which previously had been regulated only as adulterated, misbranded or unapproved new drugs under the FDCA. The statute added felony penalties for selling such drugs, including counterfeit drugs, and authorized FDA personnel enforcing the law to carry firearms, execute and serve search and arrest warrants, seize products under court order, and arrest an individual who violated the law in the investigator's presence or where there was probable cause to believe that the individual had committed or was committing a felony.

FDA established the Bureau of Drug Abuse Control (BDAC), recruiting those FDA inspectors who enjoyed such activity, as well as law enforcement personnel from other federal and state agencies. BDAC was transferred to DOJ in 1968 as part of the Bureau of Narcotics and Dangerous Drugs and, more recently, to DEA.

♦ The Child Protection Act

In 1966, the Federal Hazardous Substances Labeling Act was modified by the Child Protection Act to ban hazardous toys and other articles, broadening FDA's jurisdiction over products not covered by the FDCA. In 1972, jurisdiction was transferred to the newly created Consumer Product Safety Commission (CPSC).

◆ The Fair Packaging and Labeling Act

The Fair Packaging and Labeling Act (FPLA) also was passed that year, requiring truthful and informative labeling for all consumer products in interstate commerce. FDA shared jurisdiction with the FTC, focusing on foods, drugs, cosmetics and medical devices. FDA used the FPLA to require cosmetics to bear ingredient labeling. Both the FDCA and the FPLA were amended by the Poison Prevention Packaging Act of 1970, which required child-resistant packaging for household substances that could be hazardous to children. CPSC now enforces that act.

◆ The Animal Drug Amendments of 1968

In the Animal Drug Amendments of 1968, Congress established procedures for approving new animal drugs and animal feed containing new animal drugs. This included the certification of antibiotics intended for use in animals.

◆ The Radiation Control for Health and Safety Act

That same year, Congress passed the Radiation Control for Health and Safety Act, which was intended to protect the public from unnecessary exposure to radiation from electronic products. The law authorizes FDA to set standards for emissions for such products as microwave ovens, X- ray machines, color televisions and cathode ray tubes for computers. Civil penalties may be imposed for noncompliance and, since 1990, the criminal penalties applicable to devices under the FDCA apply as well to radiologic products. The act originally was enforced by the Bureau of Radiological Health, a division of the Public Health Service. In 1971, that bureau was transferred to FDA where it ultimately was merged with the Bureau of Devices to become today's Center for Devices and Radiological Health. The law itself was added to the FDCA.

◆ The Drug Listing Act

In 1972, Congress enacted the Drug Listing Act requiring that all marketed drugs be listed with FDA when a company first registers, and that the lists be updated each June and December. The listing must include all labeling and representative advertisements for prescription drugs, and labels, package inserts and representative labeling for OTC drugs. Like establishment registration, listing does not involve FDA approval, although FDA occasionally does respond to a listing by questioning whether a product is a new drug.

1966
Fair Packaging and Labeling Act
The Fair Packaging and Labeling Act requires all consumer products in interstate commerce to be honestly and informatively labeled, with FDA enforcing provisions on foods, drugs, cosmetics and medical devices.

The Medical Device Amendments of 1976

Under the 1938 act, FDA's authority to regulate medical devices was limited to action against adulterated or misbranded devices. FDA could not review or approve medical devices to confirm that they were safe and effective before they could be distributed commercially. FDA reacted by trying to regulate devices as drugs whenever possible in order to obtain the premarket approval authority that existed for new drugs. Thus, FDA regulated absorbable sutures and injectable liquid silicone as drugs, although they were chemically inert.

After the 1962 Drug Amendments, greater attention was given to regulation of devices. This came from industry, health professionals, some patient groups and even Congress. Concerns arose over the dangers of some devices, such as the Dalkon Shield, an intra-uterine device that was associated with a number of injuries to women.

In response to these pressures, in 1969 the Secretary of Health, Education and Welfare appointed a departmental study group on medical devices, chaired by Dr. Theodore Cooper, director of the National Heart and Lung Institute. The Cooper Committee issued a report in 1970, which concluded that greater device regulation was needed, but should not follow the drug regulatory scheme. The report recommended, among other things, nongovernmental expert reviews and varying degrees of regulation based on risks of different types of devices. The Cooper Committee report was influential in shaping the Medical Device Amendments of 1976 (MDA), the first comprehensive federal regulatory framework for medical devices in the United States.

Among other things, the MDA revised the definition of "device" to distinguish it from "drug," thereby clarifying some of the confusion that existed in the 1938 act. Specifically, a "device" is intended for the same therapeutic use as a drug, but is

> ... an instrument, apparatus, implement, machine, contrivance, implant, in vitro reagent, or other similar or related article... which does not achieve its primary intended purposes through chemical action within or on the body of man or other animals and which is not dependent upon being metabolized for the achievement of its primary intended purpose [FDCA § 201(h)].

Devices that previously had been regulated as drugs were to be returned to device status as "transitional devices."

The MDA established a comprehensive system for classifying and clearing medical devices, based on risk, for introduction in interstate commerce. The

1976
Medical Device Amendments
The Medical Device Amendments were passed to ensure the safety and effectiveness of medical devices, including diagnostic products. The amendments require manufacturers to register with FDA and follow quality control procedures. Some products must have premarket approval by FDA; others must meet performance standards before marketing.

MDA distinguished between devices on the market before and after enactment of the 1976 law (i.e., "pre-amendment" or "predicate" devices, and "post-enactment" or "post-amendment" devices). Any device not marketed before the enactment date is automatically placed in the highest risk class of devices (Class III) unless it is "substantially equivalent" to a predicate device already on the market and classified at a lower risk to the public health. To enable FDA to determine if such substantial equivalence exists, the MDA added section 510(k), which requires a person who proposes to market such a device to notify FDA at least 90 days in advance of introduction of the device (commonly referred to as "the 510(k)"). A Class III device requires premarket approval, similar to new drug approval. Class I devices are regulated by general controls. Class II devices may require performance standards.

FDA also was given broad regulatory powers by the MDA, including the authority to:

♦ require registration of device establishments and listings of device products;

♦ prescribe good manufacturing practice regulations;

♦ ban worthless or dangerous products;

♦ require notification, repair, replacement and/or refund for defective devices;

♦ require records and reports on devices;

♦ define by regulation "restricted devices," which go beyond prescription devices and for which FDA may inspect records;

♦ detain suspected violative devices for 20 days pending the filing of a formal action; and

♦ recall dangerous devices.

The MDA elevated the importance of device regulation within FDA, and reflected the increasing significance of devices in medical practice.

Several of these powers are unique to device regulation.

The MDA elevated the importance of device regulation within FDA, and reflected the increasing significance of devices in medical practice.

Legislation from 1977 to Present

♦ The Orphan Drug Act

In 1982, after much lobbying by patient groups and some manufacturers, Congress concluded that the pharmaceutical industry was not sufficiently committed to the development of drugs to treat rare diseases. Because of the limited market for such drugs, and because patents for them often had expired, manufacturers could not expect to recoup their research and development costs through sales. In 1983 Congress responded with a package of economic incentives embodied in the Orphan Drug Act.

The act applies to drugs "for a rare disease or condition," which initially was defined as one that "occurs so infrequently in the U.S. that there is no reasonable expectation" of recovering development costs. This definition proved unworkable and the act was amended in 1985 to include diseases that affect fewer than 200,000 people in the United States. Sponsors of orphan drugs qualify for tax credits to offset their research costs and may be eligible for FDA research grants. Most important, the sponsor is granted seven years of "market exclusivity," which prevents FDA from approving a competitor's version of the identical drug for the same disease. This is separate from any patent protection and has been a major economic benefit for some companies.

1984
Drug Price Competition and Patent Term Restoration Act
This act expedites the availability of less costly generic drugs by permitting FDA to approve applications to market generic versions of brand-name drugs without repeating the research done to prove them safe and effective. At the same time, the brand-name companies can apply for up to five years longer patent protection for the medicines they developed to make up for time lost while their products were going through FDA's approval process.

♦ The Drug Price Competition and Patent Term Restoration Act

Several factors during the 1970s and early 1980s led Congress to address more broadly competitive issues in the drug market. These included concerns over the cost of drugs to patients, the development of the generic drug industry, the increasing number of important drugs whose patents were due to expire and the need to encourage pharmaceutical research. These factors led to the Drug Price Competition and Patent Term Restoration Act of 1984, commonly called Waxman-Hatch after its two principal sponsors, Representative Henry Waxman (D-CA) and Senator Orrin Hatch (R-UT). The act was designed as a compromise to promote competition by encouraging the development of low-cost generic drugs, and to encourage research by granting certain competitive benefits to innovators.

The act requires FDA to approve generic drugs that are shown to be "bioequivalent" to a previously approved drug that is "listed" in an FDA publication, without requiring new proof of safety or effectiveness. By filing this "abbreviated" new drug application (ANDA), the generic manufacturer is spared the cost of conducting clinical studies and can offer the product to consumers at a reduced price.

In return, the act grants brand-name manufacturers two important benefits to encourage drug research. The first is the opportunity to extend the patent term to make up for time lost while a drug is undergoing development and FDA review. The second benefit is a period of "market exclusivity" granted to a sponsor that develops a new chemical entity or a new use for a previously approved drug. For a new chemical entity, the act grants five years of exclusivity against approval of an ANDA or other application that lacks clinical data. For a new use for a previously approved drug, in a new full NDA or a supplement that contains clinical tests "essential" to approval, the act grants three years of exclusivity against an ANDA. FDA also must honor a patent and withhold approval of a generic drug until the patent expires or is held invalid by a court.

The Waxman-Hatch Act has resulted in an explosion of generic drug approvals. There also have been a number of lawsuits brought to interpret some of its provisions. The act was followed by FDA's worst scandal, involving bribes to FDA generic drug staff and submission of false information in several ANDAs.

♦ The Generic Animal Drug and Patent Term Restoration Act

In 1988, Congress passed the Generic Animal Drug and Patent Term Restoration Act, extending to veterinary products the same benefits given to human drugs under the Waxman-Hatch Act. Companies are authorized to produce and sell generic versions of animal drugs using abbreviated new animal drug applications for previously approved drugs based on evidence demonstrating their safety and efficacy.

1987
Prescription Drug
Marketing Act
Addressed the unacceptable risks associated with counterfeit, adulterated, misbranded, subpotent or expired drugs.

♦ The Prescription Drug Marketing Act of 1987

In the mid-1980s, Congress became concerned about diverted or counterfeit drugs in the marketplace. The response was the Prescription Drug Marketing Act of 1987 (PDMA), which was intended to address "an unacceptable risk that counterfeit, adulterated, misbranded, subpotent, or expired drugs will be sold to American consumers." In addition to attempting to regulate diversion of legitimate prescription drugs and counterfeits in domestic commerce, the law prohibits the re-import of exported drugs as U.S. goods returned except to the original manufacturer or for emergency use.

The PDMA bans the sale or purchase of or trade in prescription drug samples and establishes comprehensive storage, handling and recordkeeping requirements for such samples. The PDMA also prohibits, with certain exceptions, the resale of prescription drugs purchased by hospitals, healthcare entities and charitable institutions, and regulates prescription drug wholesale distributors by requiring states to license them in accordance with federal guidelines. Manufacturers must report loss or theft of samples and the conviction of their sales representatives for illegal diversion. There is a substantial civil penalty for a manufacturer's failure to take appropriate steps to prevent diversion (up to $1,000,000 per violation after two convictions of the firm's representatives). There is also a bounty for whistle-blowers of one-half the criminal fine, up to $125,000.

♦ Safe Medical Devices Act of 1990

The Safe Medical Devices Act of 1990 (SMDA) was the first major revision of the medical device requirements of 1976. The SMDA increases FDA's regulatory authority over the medical device industry, particularly in the areas of post-marketing requirements and the premarket notification and approval process. The SMDA was particularly intended to expedite device premarket clearances and approvals by shifting some of FDA's emphasis from premarket reviews to postmarket regulation and surveillance.

The SMDA defines substantial equivalence, essentially codifying FDA's substantial equivalence decision-making structure. Under the SMDA, to determine that a device is substantially equivalent (and therefore, subject to 510(k) clearance), FDA must find that it has the same intended use as the predicate device. The SMDA gives FDA authority to order special controls for Class II devices beyond the performance standards allowed under the MDA, including postmarket surveillance, patient registry, development and dissemination of guidelines, and other appropriate actions deemed necessary by FDA. The SMDA also includes provisions enabling FDA to implement postmarket surveillance, civil penalties, temporary suspension of premarket approval (PMA) applications, required reports of removals and corrections, user and distributor reporting, and medical device tracking. Perhaps the most important postmarketing provision is the requirement of notification to FDA and the manufacturer of all incidents that contribute to serious injury, death or illness that may have been associated with the use of a medical device. Under the SMDA, anyone who is aware of or has knowledge of an incident that reasonably suggests that a medical device has caused or contributed to the death, serious injury or serious illness of a patient, visitor or staff member of a healthcare facility must report the incident to FDA.

♦ The Generic Drug Enforcement Act of 1992

1992

Generic Drug Enforcement Act

The Generic Drug Enforcement Act imposes debarment and other penalties for illegal acts involving approval of abbreviated new drug applications.

In 1992, following a notorious scandal in which officials of FDA's Generic Drugs Division were convicted of taking bribes and a number of generic drug industry personnel were convicted of bribing FDA officials or submitting false data to the agency, Congress enacted the Generic Drug Enforcement Act (GDEA). The act authorizes FDA to "debar" firms and individuals convicted of felonies in connection with the drug approval process from participating in that process for periods ranging from one to 10 years for firms and as long as lifetime for individuals. Despite its name, the law applies to both generic and brand-name drug companies. FDA also can bar a "high managerial agent" who had actual knowledge of a violation, and failed to take steps to report or prevent the violation. FDA can temporarily deny approval of an ANDA submitted by a person under criminal investigation for bribery or false statements.

The GDEA also imposes civil penalties for false statements, bribes, destruction of documents, failure to disclose a required material fact, obstruction of an investigation, use of a debarred person to help prepare a drug application, or work on an application by a debarred person. The fines are severe: up to $250,000 per violation for an individual and $1,000,000 for others. The penalty can be levied by FDA via an administrative proceeding or through a court proceeding brought by DOJ. In either case, there is a right of appeal. Informants are entitled to an award of the lesser of $250,000 or one-half the penalty collected.

♦ The Prescription Drug User Fee Act of 1992

As FDA became more engrossed in approving generic drugs, the research-based industry began to push Congress to give FDA more resources to review full NDAs. The political and economic climate, however, was not conducive to enlarging the budget of any government agency. Instead, there developed a philosophy of applying marketplace principles to government activity. In particular, the administration and Congress began to look to the beneficiaries of government services to pay for those services rather than putting a greater burden on taxpayers.

1992
Prescription Drug User Fee Act
PDUFA adds more resources to FDA's review process for drugs and biologics.

The Prescription Drug User Fee Act of 1992 (PDUFA) established requirements for drug and biologics manufacturers to pay fees for applications and supplements that require FDA to review clinical studies. These user fees are intended to enable FDA to hire more reviewers to assess the clinical studies in these applications. In return, FDA pledged (but was not statutorily committed) to speed up the review of NDAs. The act also included annual establishment fees and annual product fees for companies with approved NDAs. The PDUFA was scheduled to expire on September 30, 1997, but was extended by the FDAMA of 1997.

♦ The Nutrition Labeling and Education Act of 1990

In the mid- to late-1980s, increased consumer interest and advances in studies of nutrition and health led some major food companies to begin to experiment with nutritional claims in advertising and labeling. In particular, one manufacturer launched a labeling and advertising program for cereal that claimed the product could be useful in a high-fiber diet to help prevent cancer. The claim had been reviewed and approved by the National Cancer Institute and the FTC. FDA was more critical but ultimately took no regulatory action.

1990
Nutrition Labeling and Education Act
Health claims on foods are regulated under the Nutrition Labeling and Education Act of 1990.

Congress also became interested in this subject, enacting the Nutrition Labeling and Education Act of 1990 (NLEA), the first comprehensive revision of the food labeling requirements of the FDCA since 1938. Building on FDA's much earlier voluntary nutrition labeling requirements and more recent proposals to permit health claims for food products, the NLEA ordered FDA to encourage the food industry to "assist consumers in maintaining healthy dietary practices." Among other things, the NLEA provides for mandatory nutrition labeling in a uniform format, including serving size, number of servings per container and the nutrition content of the food per serving based on a common household measure.

The NLEA authorized, for the first time, the use of a "health claim" in food labeling. This is a claim "that characterizes the relationship of [a] nutrient . . . to a disease or a health-related condition." Such health claims were permitted only in compliance with FDA regulations. Congress, however, ordered FDA to consider issuing regulations pertaining to the relationship of calcium and osteoporosis, fiber and cancer, lipids and cardiovascular disease, lipids and cancer, sodium and hypertension, fiber and cardiovascular disease, folic acid and neural tube defects, antioxidant vitamins and cancer, zinc and immune function in the elderly, and omega-3 fatty acids and heart disease. Regulations must be based on "significant agreement" of qualified experts that "the totality of publicly available scientific evidence" supports the claims.

The NLEA imposed federal preemption for any food labeling requirements mandated by the FDCA, preempting any state regulation not identical to the FDA requirements. This does not apply to actions against false or misleading labeling or to food advertising.

1994

Dietary Supplement Health and Education Act

Addresses the regulation of dietary supplements by exempting them from some regulatory requirements.

♦ The Dietary Supplement Health and Education Act of 1994

Manufacturers of dietary supplements and other "health foods" felt that the NLEA did not address adequately their interests. After considerable lobbying and a great deal of grass-roots support, Congress was persuaded to enact the Dietary Supplement Health and Education Act of 1994 (DSHEA). In doing so, Congress expressly recognized, defined and allowed specific claims for dietary supplements, exempting them from some regulatory requirements applicable to other foods.

Among other things, the DSHEA provides a definition of dietary supplement that includes vitamins; minerals; herbs or other botanicals; amino acids; dietary substances used by man to supplement the diet by increasing the total dietary intake; and any concentrate, metabolite, constituent, extract or combination of any of these ingredients. The law expressly states that such dietary supplements are foods. Dietary supplements are exempt from the "food additive" provisions of the law, thus placing the burden on FDA to demonstrate that dietary supplements are unsafe. New dietary ingredients, not marketed in the United States before October 15, 1994, must contain only ingredients that have been used in the food supply before that time, or have a history of use elsewhere or other evidence of safety.

The DSHEA also permits dissemination of published scientific information and labeling statements pertaining to nutritional claims for dietary supplements, subject to certain specified conditions. FDA was required to issue regulations for nutrition labeling for dietary supplements and for good manufacturing practices (GMPs) for these products, which are required to be modeled after FDA's food GMPs.

The DSHEA also established a Commission on Dietary Supplement Labels and an Office of Dietary Supplements within the National Institutes of Health to study label claims for dietary supplements and report to the President and Congress with recommendations for legislation and changes in regulations. The office was created to study the potential role of dietary supplements as part of the effort to improve U.S. healthcare, and to promote scientific study of dietary supplements to maintain health, prevent chronic disease and for other health-related conditions.

In November 1997, the commission issued its report, which included several recommendations to FDA for distinguishing unauthorized disease claims from permissible claims that describe the effect of a dietary supplement on the structure or function of the body ("structure-function" claims). The commission's report served as a basis for FDA's final rule in January 2000 regarding permissible label claims for dietary supplements.

♦ Export Reform and Enhancement Act of 1996

The Export Reform and Enhancement Act of 1996 (EREA) amended the FDCA to alter FDA's role in regulating the trade of drugs, biologics and medical devices, and eased import and export restrictions on drugs and medical devices. Under the EREA, manufacturers may export both approved and unapproved medical products to certain foreign countries, and may import the components and raw materials necessary to manufacture products intended for export.

♦ The Food and Drug Administration Modernization Act of 1997

Over the years, FDA's regulatory role has expanded considerably from that of removing unsafe or misbranded products from the marketplace, to determining whether drugs and medical devices are safe and effective for their intended use. Critics, including members of Congress, industry, patient groups and others, became convinced that FDA's ability to accomplish the duties embodied in this expanded role had not kept pace with the agency's statutory

1997
Food and Drug Administration Modernization Act
FDAMA, enacted in 1997, broadened FDA's authority and reformed several areas of regulation.

responsibilities, resulting in an overly burdensome and inefficient regulatory system. The requirements for the clinical testing and premarket review of new products had become increasingly complex, time-consuming and costly, with the result that patients had been denied timely access to safe and useful drugs and medical devices.

The Food and Drug Administration Modernization Act of 1997 (FDAMA) is the culmination of a comprehensive legislative reform effort designed to stream-line regulatory procedures within FDA and to improve the regulation of drugs, medical devices and foods. Passed with wide bipartisan support, the legislation is the broadest amendment of the basic law since 1938. The FDAMA is principal-ly designed to ensure the timely availability of safe and effective drugs, biolog-ics and medical devices by expediting the premarket review process for new products, while maintaining FDA's "gold standard" for product approval.

Building on the reauthorization of the Prescription Drug User Fee Act of 1992 (PDUFA I) for five more years, the FDAMA improves FDA's public accountability, requires an FDA mission statement to define the scope of the agency's regula-tory responsibilities, and requires FDA to publish a compliance plan, in consulta-tion with appropriate scientific and academic experts, healthcare professionals, representatives of patient and consumer advocacy groups, and the regulated industry. This is intended to eliminate backlogs in the drug and medical device approval process and ensure the timely review of applications. As part of the agency's new mission statement, FDA must promptly and efficiently review clinical research and take appropriate action on the marketing of regulated products so that innovation and product availability are not impeded or discouraged.

The FDAMA included a unique provision, which amended the FDCA to encourage drug manufacturers to study their drugs in pediatric populations.

The FDAMA included a unique provision, which amended the FDCA to encour-age drug manufacturers to study their drugs in pediatric populations. This new provision grants the sponsor of a pending or approved NDA for a drug with current exclusivity under the Waxman-Hatch Act or the Orphan Drug Amend-ments an extra six months of market exclusivity for performing certain studies in pediatric populations. Pediatric exclusivity attaches to an active moiety and not to a specific drug product, allowing a manufacturer's entire product line containing the active moiety to receive six months of additional market protec-tion. Although this authorization was subject to a sunset provision on January 1, 2002, Congress has reauthorized the provision in 2002 and 2007, and its current sunset date is October 1, 2012.

The FDAMA also creates a statutory fast-track approval process for drugs for serious or life-threatening diseases and conditions (based on existing FDA regulations), establishes a data bank of information on clinical trials for such conditions (with the help of the National Institutes of Health), authorizes the use of expert scientific panels to review clinical investigations of drugs, and expands the rights of drug and device manufacturers to disseminate treatment information.

The FDAMA also broadened FDA's authority over OTC drugs by extending the agency's inspection authority over OTC drug records to the same extent allowed for prescription drugs. Ingredient labeling requirements are also expanded to include inactive ingredients. The FDAMA preempts labeling for OTC drugs (and cosmetics) from state regulation where federal requirements are in place.

The FDAMA reforms the regulation of medical devices with regard to the review of applications, standards and data requirements. For example, the law mandates priority review for breakthrough technologies in medical devices and grants FDA the authority to contract with outside scientific experts to review medical device applications.

The FDAMA provides streamlined procedures and greater flexibility in FDA regulations regarding nutrient content and health claims for foods. Such claims may be permitted on food labels, without the need for FDA to issue a regulation, if a scientific body of the U.S. government has published an authoritative statement endorsing the claim. The law also establishes a "notification" procedure for the marketing of indirect food additives.

The FDAMA provides streamlined procedures and greater flexibility in FDA regulations regarding nutrient content and health claims for foods.

♦ Fiscal Year 2001 Agricultural Appropriations—Drug Import Provisions

The Fiscal Year 2001 Agricultural Appropriations, Pub. L. 106-387 (Oct. 28, 2000), included two provisions that amend the FDCA to allow the importation of prescription drugs into the United States from foreign countries. The Medicine Equity and Drug Safety Act of 2000 (MEDS Act) allows wholesalers and pharmacists to import prescription drugs from specified foreign countries, provided certain documentation and testing information, to be defined in FDA regulations, is included with the drugs. The Prescription Drug Import Fairness Act of 2000 prevents FDA from issuing warning notices to individuals, not in the business of importing drugs, who import drugs for personal use. The purpose was to try to lower the costs of prescription drugs in the United States. However, on December 26, 2000, the outgoing Secretary of the Department of Health and Human Services declined to implement the MEDS Act, and this decision was reaffirmed by the new Secretary of the Department of Health and Human Services on July 9, 2001.

◆ Best Pharmaceuticals for Children Act

The Best Pharmaceuticals for Children Act, Pub. L. No. 107-109 (Jan. 4, 2002), *inter alia,* renewed FDA's authority to grant six months of exclusivity for pediatric studies; eliminated the user fee waiver for pediatric use supplements; gave priority review status for pediatric supplements; and authorized government contracts for pediatric studies of drugs that lack patent protection or marketing exclusivity. The law also allowed ANDAs for generic drugs with added pediatric information. In addition, the law directed the Secretary of the Department of Health and Human Services to establish an Office of Pediatric Therapeutics within the FDA Commissioner's office to coordinate all FDA pediatric activities.

◆ The Bioterrorism Act

BIOHAZARD

In June 2002, the Public Health Security and Bioterrorism Preparedness and Response Act of 2002 (Pub. L. No. 107-188) (Bioterrorism Act) amended the FDCA and the Public Health Service Act to increase the capacity of government at all levels to detect and respond effectively to public health emergencies related to bioterrorist attacks. Among other things, the Bioterrorism Act provided for accelerated approval, licensing or clearance, as a "priority countermeasure," for a drug, biologic product, medical device, vaccine, vaccine adjuvant, antiviral or diagnostic test, intended to treat, identify or prevent infections or diagnose conditions caused by biological agents or toxins. The act required the creation of a national database of biological agents and toxins that could pose a severe threat to human, animal or plant health; development of security safeguards and mandatory registration for the possession, use or transfer of such agents and toxins; and inspections, with limited exceptions for clinical or diagnostic laboratories and certain investigational, approved or licensed products. Prescription drug user fees were extended through the year 2007 with only minor changes.

The Bioterrorism Act also provides for:
- *maintenance of certain manufacturing and shipping records*
- *administrative detention of adulterated foods*
- *pre-importation notifications*
- *prohibition against port shopping*
- *debarment for repeated violations*

Most importantly, the Bioterrorism Act granted FDA significant new authority with respect to foods, including dietary supplements and animal feeds. Domestic and foreign facilities that manufacture, process, pack or hold food for U.S. consumption must register with FDA. Inspections are permitted upon "a reasonable belief that a food article is adulterated and presents a threat of serious adverse health consequences or death to humans or animals." The Bioterrorism Act also provides for maintenance of certain manufacturing and shipping records; administrative detention of adulterated foods; pre-importation notifications; prohibition against port shopping; and debarment for repeated violations.

The existing "import for export" requirements were broadened to include submission of information and data upon importation of drug components, device components or accessories, food additives, color additives and dietary supplements (including those in bulk form) that are intended for further processing or incorporation into a regulated product and for subsequent export.

♦ **Medical Device User Fee and Modernization Act of 2002**

Following the trend to seek user fees from regulated industry, the Medical Device User Fee and Modernization Act of 2002, Pub. L. No. 107-250 (Oct. 26, 2002) (MDUFMA), was enacted to amend the FDCA to subject medical device manufacturers to medical device user fees for certain applications, reports, application supplements and submissions sent to FDA for evaluation. The law also established certain performance goals for FDA to meet. In addition, the law included provisions for device establishment inspections by accredited third parties, established new regulatory requirements for reprocessed single-use devices and provided for modular (i.e., discrete sections) review of PMAs.

Following the trend to seek user fees from regulated industry, the Medical Device User Fee and Modernization Act of 2002 was enacted to amend the FDCA to subject medical device manufacturers to medical device user fees.

♦ **Rare Diseases Orphan Product Development Act of 2002**

Stating its concerns over 25 million Americans suffering from more than 6,000 rare diseases, and recognizing the role of the National Organization for Rare Diseases, Congress passed the Rare Diseases Orphan Product Development Act of 2002, Pub. L. No. 107-281 (Nov. 6, 2002), to amend the Orphan Drug Act by reauthorizing the Orphan Products Research Grant program to authorize appropriations for Fiscal Years 2002-2006 for grants and contracts for the development of orphan drugs. Fiscal Year 2003-2006 appropriations were set at $25 million per year.

♦ **Animal Drug User Fee Act of 2003**

Congress added user fees for veterinary products in the Animal Drug User Fee Act of 2003, Pub. L. No. 107-130 (Nov. 18, 2003), directing FDA to assess and collect user fees for animal drug applications. The law was scheduled to sunset at the end of Fiscal Year 2008, but was reauthorized and extended until 2013. Animal Drug User Fee Amendments of 2008, Pub. L. No. 110-316, § 108, 122 Stat. 3515.

♦ **Medicare Prescription Drug, Improvement, and Modernization Act of 2003**

Title XI of the Medicare Prescription Drug, Improvement, and Modernization Act of 2003, Pub. L. No. 108-173 (Dec. 8, 2003), titled "Access to Affordable

Title XI of the Medicare Prescription Drug, Improvement, and Modernization Act of 2003 is the culmination of several years of congressional attempts to reduce the cost of drug products to consumers.

Pharmaceuticals," is the culmination of several years of congressional attempts to reduce the cost of drug products to consumers. To accomplish this goal, the changes in Title XI target two issues: generic drug approvals (including government review of marketing agreements between companies) and the importation of prescription drugs from Canada into the United States. The generic drug revisions in the law primarily amend provisions of the FDCA that were added in 1984 by the Drug Price Competition and Patent Term Restoration Act.

The provisions on importation of prescription drugs from Canada recognized that Americans increasingly have sought to purchase drugs from Canada and other foreign countries. This law authorized importation from Canada, under specific conditions, if the Secretary of the Department of Health and Human Services certifies to Congress that the imports will not pose any additional risk to the public health and will result in a significant savings to American consumers. To date, the Secretary has declined to provide such certification.

♦ Pediatric Research Equity Act of 2003

To encourage drug research for pediatric use, Congress enacted the Pediatric Research Equity Act of 2003, Pub. L. No. 107-155 (Dec. 3, 2003), amending the FDCA to require that applications for a new active ingredient, new indication, new dosage form, new dosing regimen or new route of administration for drugs and biological products include a pediatric assessment (unless waived or deferred), and that sponsors of marketed drugs and biologics conduct such an assessment by a specified date (unless waived) under certain circumstances. This law essentially codified FDA's 1998 "Regulations Requiring Manufacturers to Assess the Safety and Effectiveness of New Drugs and Biological Products in Pediatric Patients" (commonly referred to as the "Pediatric Rule"), which had been invalidated by a federal district court for exceeding FDA's authority under the act.

♦ Minor Use and Minor Species Animal Health Act of 2004

Concerned over lack of animal drugs for marginal uses, Congress enacted the Minor Use and Minor Species Animal Health Act of 2004, Title I of Pub. L. No. 108-282 (Aug. 2, 2004), to encourage the development of new animal drugs intended for a minor use (i.e., an indication that occurs infrequently in a few animals, or in limited geographic areas, and in a small number of animals annually) or for a use in a minor species (i.e., other than cattle, horses, swine, chickens, turkeys, dogs and cats). It provides a conditional approval mechanism under which existing safety requirements must be met but the effectiveness standard is "a reasonable expectation of effectiveness" rather than "substantial evidence of effectiveness." In addition, a sponsor of a new animal drug for a minor use or use in a minor species may petition FDA to declare its product a "designated new animal drug," similar to the status of human drugs under the Orphan Drug Act.

◆ Food Allergen Labeling and Consumer Protection Act of 2004

In Title II of Pub. L. No. 108-282, Congress enacted the Food Allergen Labeling and Consumer Protection Act of 2004, requiring food labels to declare any major food allergen present. The major food allergens are milk; eggs; fish; crustacean shellfish; tree nuts (e.g., almonds, pecans or walnuts); wheat; peanuts; and soybeans, as well as any protein derived from those allergens, unless it is a "highly refined oil." Tree nuts, fish and crustacean shellfish must be identified by specific type or species.

◆ Anabolic Steroid Control Act of 2004

Congress enacted the Anabolic Steroid Control Act of 2004, Pub. L. No. 108-358 (Oct. 22, 2004), to address the abuse of steroids by professional athletes and the widespread use of steroids and steroid precursors among students. The act amended the Controlled Substances Act in several ways, including revising the definition of "anabolic steroid" to eliminate the requirement that the substance promote muscle growth. The act also expanded the list of substances regulated as controlled substances to 59 steroids, including active steroids and steroid precursors.

The Anabolic Steroid Control Act of 2004 addresses the abuse of steroids by professional athletes and the widespread use of steroids and steroid precursors among students.

◆ Project BioShield Act of 2004

Passed largely in response to the terrorist attacks in the fall of 2001, the Project BioShield Act of 2004, Pub. L. No. 108-276 (July 21, 2004), provides industry with incentives to develop new chemical, biological, radiological and nuclear medical countermeasures. The act also grants FDA the authority to allow the interim emergency use of investigational drugs, biological products, and devices to respond to domestic emergencies.

◆ Medical Device User Fee Stabilization Act of 2005

Congress revisited the medical device user fees established in the Medical Device User Fee Stabilization Act of 2005, Pub. L. No. 109-43 (Aug. 1, 2005). Among other things, the law set the premarket approval application fees for Fiscal Years 2006 and 2007, increased the annual gross receipts or sales threshold below which businesses are eligible for reduced user fees or a user fee waiver, and added a provision holding any reprocessed single-use device to be misbranded unless it identifies the manufacturer.

♦ Regulation of Contact Lenses as Medical Devices (2005)

Congress amended the FDCA to deem all contact lenses to be medical devices.

Because FDA had previously regulated some non-corrective, decorative contact lenses as cosmetics, Congress amended the FDCA to deem all contact lenses to be medical devices in this very succinct statute, Pub. L. No. 109-96 (Nov. 9, 2005).

♦ Stem Cell Therapeutic and Research Act of 2005

The Stem Cell Therapeutic and Research Act of 2005, Pub. L. No. 109-129 (Dec. 26, 2005), provides "for the collection and maintenance of human cord blood stem cells for the treatment of patients and research." It amended the Public Health Service Act to authorize the C.W. Bill Young Cell Transplantation Program, which is intended to increase "the number of transplants for recipients suitably matched to biologically unrelated donors of bone marrow and cord blood."

♦ Sanitary Food Transportation Act of 2005

Title VII, section 7201 of Pub. L. No. 109-59, the Sanitary Food Transportation Act of 2005, authorizes FDA to promulgate regulations establishing sanitary food transportation practices, including sanitation, packaging, recordkeeping and isolation, among other things. In addition, FDA is to issue regulations specifying those nonfood products that may not be shipped with food products. To date, FDA has not issued such regulations.

♦ Pandemic and All-Hazards Preparedness Act of 2006

To address some of the shortcomings of the BioShield Act of 2004, Congress enacted the Pandemic and All-Hazards Preparedness Act of 2006, Pub. L. No. 109-417 (Dec. 19, 2006). Among other things, the act requires FDA to establish a team of manufacturing and regulatory experts to provide chemical, biological, radiological and nuclear countermeasure manufacturers with technical assistance and it allows HHS to convene meetings with industry under specified circumstances that would otherwise violate federal antitrust laws.

♦ Dietary Supplement and Nonprescription Drug Consumer Protection Act of 2006

The Dietary Supplement and Nonprescription Drug Consumer Protection Act of 2006, Pub. L. No. 109-462 (Dec. 22, 2006), requires manufacturers, packers or distributors of dietary supplements and OTC drugs to submit to FDA all serious adverse event reports associated with the use of their products in the United States. The act also requires dietary supplements and OTC drugs to bear either a domestic telephone number or domestic street address where consumers can call or write to report serious adverse events.

♦ Food and Drug Administration Amendments Act of 2007

In what has been described as the broadest amendment of the FDCA in recent memory, the Food and Drug Administration Amendments Act of 2007, Pub. L. No. 110-85 (Sept. 27, 2007) (FDAAA), reauthorized and amended several drug and medical device statutory provisions that were scheduled to sunset, provided FDA with new funding and drug safety oversight responsibility, and addressed *virtually all* regulated product categories. The law includes 11 titles, the first five of which reauthorize drug and medical device user fee and pediatric-related programs through Fiscal Year 2012, including PDUFA, MDUFMA, the Best Pharmaceuticals for Children Act and the Pediatric Research Equity Act. Title III also amends the FDCA to provide new incentives to medical device manufacturers to develop devices for pediatric patients and to give FDA new authority to review and regulate such devices. Titles VI-VIII establish a new private-public partnership intended to modernize medical product development and enhance product safety, amend the FDCA with respect to certain conflict of interest issues among FDA advisory committee members, and establish databases for clinical trial registries and results.

Title IX, perhaps the farthest-reaching provision of the law, includes various programs intended to improve the postmarket safety of drugs, including giving FDA the authority to impose risk evaluation and mitigation strategies. Title IX modifies the citizen petition process with respect to petitions having the potential to delay approval of generic drug products. The section also prohibits the sale of any food that contains an approved drug, an approved biological product, or a "drug [or biological product] for which substantial clinical investigations have been instituted and for which the existence of such investigations has been made public," unless the food containing the drug or biologic had been marketed prior to such approval or testing. This provision, in particular, might have a significant impact on the development of functional food ingredients.

Title X concerns food safety, requiring the creation of a reportable food registry for foods "for which there is a reasonable probability that the use of, or exposure to, such article of food will cause serious adverse health consequences or death to humans or animals." Title X also includes a provision requiring FDA to establish ingredient and processing standards and definitions for pet food and update standards for the labeling of pet food. FDA must also establish early warning and surveillance and notification systems "to identify adulteration of the pet food supply and outbreaks of illness associated with pet food." Finally, Title XI includes several miscellaneous provisions intended, among other things, to improve antibiotic access and innovation.

The Food and Drug Administration Amendments Act of 2007 reauthorized and amended several drug and medical device statutory provisions that were scheduled to sunset, provided FDA with new funding and drug safety oversight responsibility and addressed virtually all regulated product categories.

♦ **Animal Drug User Fee Amendments of 2008/Animal Generic Drug User Fee Act of 2008**

In a single piece of legislation, Congress enacted the Animal Drug User Fee Amendments of 2008, which amend and reauthorize the Animal Drug User Fee Act of 2003 (ADUFA I) through Fiscal Year 2013, and the Animal Generic Drug User Fee Act of 2008 (AGDUFA). To support FDA's continuing efforts to address antimicrobial resistance, ADUFA II requires that animal drug sponsors submit annual reports to FDA on certain products containing antimicrobial active ingredients and for FDA to make summaries of these reports available to the public.

AGDUFA establishes a user fee for generic new animal drugs, including abbreviated application, product and sponsor fees.

The legislation also includes technical corrections to FDAAA, in particular, to clarify that consideration of a citizen petition seeking to delay generic approval must be "separate and apart from review and approval of any application."

♦ **Patient Protection and Affordable Care Act**

The Patient Protection and Affordable Care Act signed into law by President Barack Obama on March 23, 2010, includes some provisions concerning the FDCA, affecting both drugs and food.

The broad healthcare reform law, the Patient Protection and Affordable Care Act (PPACA), signed into law by President Barack Obama on March 23, 2010, while focusing primarily on healthcare and insurance industries, the medical community and healthcare consumers, includes some provisions concerning the FDCA, affecting both drugs and food.

With respect to drugs, PPACA amended the FDCA to permit FDA to approve an abbreviated new drug application (ANDA) notwithstanding certain changes in the labeling of the reference listed drug (RLD) approved within 60 days of the anticipated ANDA approval. Changes to "Warnings" in the RLD are excepted, and FDA may decide against the ANDA approval for safety reasons. The ANDA applicant must agree to submit revised labeling quickly. This amendment essentially creates an exception, albeit limited, to the requirement that labeling for a generic drug be identical to that of the RLD.

PPACA also creates a new pathway for the approval of applications for biological products shown to be biosimilar to or interchangeable with a licensed reference product. It amends the FDCA to make user fees under PDUFA applicable to biosimilar and interchangeable biological products.

For foods, PPACA amends the FDCA to require restaurants and similar retail food establishments with 20 or more locations doing business under the same name and offering substantially the same menu items to disclose on menus and menu boards the calorie content for standard menu items and information on suggested daily caloric intake. The establishments must also make other nutrition information, e.g., sodium and sugar content per serving, available on the premises. An owner or operator of 20 or more vending machines also must disclose calorie content for the products, unless a prospective buyer, before purchase, can examine the nutrition facts panel or, at the point of purchase, obtain nutritional information about the products. FDA must issue regulations implementing the new law. Those regulations preempt state requirements that are not identical to the federal laws, but states may impose non-identical menu-labeling requirements for restaurateurs and vending machine operators not subject to the law unless they choose to subject themselves to the federal requirements.

◆ The Family Smoking Prevention and Tobacco Control Act

Ending a contentious legal and political battle and radically changing the relationship between the federal government and the tobacco industry, the Family Smoking Prevention and Tobacco Control Act (FSPTCA) (Pub. L. No. 111-131), enacted on June 22, 2009, provides FDA with regulatory authority over almost every aspect of tobacco products. The new law specifically applies to cigarettes, cigarette tobacco, roll-your-own tobacco and smokeless tobacco. FDA has the authority to apply the law to other tobacco products by regulation. The law does not apply to producers of tobacco leaves, including "tobacco warehouses."

Ending a contentious legal and political battle and radically changing the relationship between the federal government and the tobacco industry, the Family Smoking Prevention and Tobacco Control Act provides FDA with regulatory authority over almost every aspect of tobacco products.

Following the basic structure of the FDCA, the FSPTCA provides essential definitions, establishes the conditions that cause tobacco products to be adulterated or misbranded, and establishes a comprehensive statutory framework for FDA's oversight of tobacco products. FSPTCA adds a new Chapter IX to the FDCA, causing old Chapter IX to be renumbered as Chapter X.

Significant provisions of the FSPTCA include the requirement for FDA premarket review of new products, authority for FDA to subject advertising for modified risk products (those marketed as being less harmful) to premarket approval, and mandatory annual registration for any owner or operator of a domestic establishment engaged in the manufacture, preparation, compounding or processing of tobacco products. Owners or operators must also submit a list of all products they manufacture, prepare or process, as well as labeling of certain products. Manufacturers and importers of tobacco products must submit "health information" about their current and future tobacco products. The FSPTCA gives FDA the authority to require reports on adverse events, corrective actions and product removals.

Although the FSPTCA does not authorize FDA to ban certain tobacco products (including cigarettes), it does provide FDA with authority to establish tobacco product standards and to impose restrictions on promotion and distribution of tobacco products. Several provisions aim at reducing smoking by youth (e.g., prohibition of all flavors, herbs, or spices (except menthol) in cigarettes). In addition, tobacco products introduced after February 15, 2007, are subject to premarket review modeled after the process for medical devices. This gives tobacco products already on the market as of February 15, 2007 ("grandfathered products") a distinct advantage over products introduced after that date ("new tobacco products").

♦ Food Safety Modernization Act

The FDA Food Safety Modernization Act is the most significant update of U.S. food safety laws since the 1938 original enactment of the FDCA.

The FDA Food Safety Modernization Act (FSMA), signed into law on January 4, 2011, is the most significant update of U.S. food safety laws since the 1938 original enactment of the FDCA. Spurred by *Escherichia coli* and *Salmonella* outbreaks, FSMA provides FDA with more power to recall tainted products, strengthen inspections of food and produce processors, and require tougher standards for keeping food safe.

The three main goals of FSMA are to: 1) shift the emphasis from response to prevention, 2) improve the government's capacity to detect and respond to food safety problems and 3) address the challenge posed by the nation's increased reliance on food imports.

FSMA provides FDA with a legislative mandate to require comprehensive, science-based preventive controls across the food supply and to establish science-based minimum standards for the safe production and harvesting of fruits and vegetables. Food facilities will be required to implement a written preventive control plan, monitor the performance of those controls and take specified corrective actions when necessary. FSMA enhances FDA's authority to inspect food establishment records, imposes biennial food facility registration, authorizes FDA to impose requirements to protect against intentional adulteration, and authorizes the collection of re-inspection fees, among other things.

FSMA also increases FDA's capacity to detect and respond to food safety problems. It mandates increased frequency of inspections, provides for accreditation of food-testing laboratories, mandates the collection of information on food traceability, confers mandatory recall authority on FDA, greatly enhances FDA's administrative detention authority and amends the reportable food registry to require grocery stores to notify consumers.

Another focus area of FSMA is the safety of imported food, providing FDA with new tools to ensure that imported foods meet U.S. standards and are safe. Among other things, FSMA requires importers to verify that the food they import meets certain legal requirements, gives FDA the authority to require certification that an imported food complies with the FDCA, directs FDA to implement a voluntary qualified importer program to speed the importation process and provides for accreditation of third-party auditors.

The addition of whistle-blower protections for food facility employees to the FDCA provides an extra incentive for food facilities to comply with the law.

FSMA requires FDA to undertake more than a dozen rulemakings and issue at least 10 guidance documents, as well as prepare a host of reports, plans, strategies, standards, notices and other tasks. Thus, implementation of the legislation likely will take several years.

The History of the Food and Drug Administration

FDA is the oldest federal regulatory agency, dating back to its initial establishment in 1848 as the Agricultural Division of the Patent Office. The agency has had several, essentially accumulating, roles. For its first six decades, it was a scientific and technical advisor to other agencies. It added a law enforcement function in 1906. In 1938, the agency was given responsibility for approving the marketing of new drugs, and that premarket licensing function has been broadened by subsequent legislation. Today the agency is regarded as a science-based law enforcement agency responsible for ensuring safe foods and cosmetics, and safe and effective drugs and medical devices in the U.S. marketplace.

FDA is the oldest federal regulatory agency, dating back to its initial establishment in 1848 as the Agricultural Division of the Patent Office.

More than half of FDA's existence was spent in the USDA, beginning with the transfer of the Agricultural Division to USDA upon the department's creation in 1862. The division's chemical laboratory became known as the USDA Chemical Division. The agency became the Division of Chemistry in 1890 and the Bureau of Chemistry in 1901. Until 1906, the agency had no statutory enforcement duties but primarily provided information and advice to other USDA offices and other agencies, such as the Treasury Department, responsible for enforcing the few relevant federal laws during that time.

Although there were six Commissioners of the agency from 1862 to 1883, it was the seventh Commissioner, Harvey W. Wiley, MD, who is generally acknowledged as the "father of the FDA." Dr. Wiley strengthened and trans-formed the staff of the division into an advocacy organization and, ultimately, a law enforcement agency. He crusaded for the creation of a national food and drug law, and was credited with a major role in the passage of the 1906 act. Po-litical and personal differences with his superiors, however, led to the establish-ment of a three-person Board of Food and Drug Inspection, including Dr. Wiley, to approve all legal actions recommended by the bureau. Dr. Wiley frequently was outvoted, and he ultimately resigned under pressure in 1912.

For the next 53 years, until 1965, FDA was directed by career employees, only a few of whom were physicians. Moreover, there were only seven Commissioners or top officials of FDA from 1883 to 1965. Since then, there have been 14 Com-missioners in slightly more than 45 years, all but two (Dr. Herbert Ley, 1968-1969, and Dr. Lester Crawford, July-September 2005) of whom had never previously worked for the agency.

When the 1906 act passed, the Bureau of Chemistry had six field laboratories (San Francisco, New York, Boston, Philadelphia, Chicago and New Orleans). Seventeen more were opened from 1907 to 1911. The agency's budget in that period was less than $1,000,000, and the agency employed fewer than 100 people.

In 1914, the agency's second "modern" commissioner, Dr. Carl Alsberg, re-organized the agency. He established the Division of Food Control and del-egated control of the field laboratories, which were reduced from 23 to 16 to save money, to three food and drug inspection districts (Eastern, Central and Western). This decentralized the agency's inspection activities and joined the enforcement functions more closely with the scientific functions, and remained the basic organization for the agency until 1948.

FDA did not officially exist by statute until the Food and Drug Administration Act of 1988.

In 1927, the agricultural research and the enforcement functions of the Bureau of Chemistry were separated, with the latter becoming the Food, Drug, and Insecti-cide Administration (FDIA). The Drug Control Laboratory, which was responsible for surveillance of proprietary drugs, was included in the FDIA. In 1930, the FDIA became the Food and Drug Administration, although the agency did not of-ficially exist by statute until the Food and Drug Administration Act of 1988.

FDA remained a part of USDA until 1940 when it was transferred to the Fed-eral Security Agency, which also included such agencies as the Public Health Service, the Office of Education, the Civilian Conservation Corps and the Social Security Administration. The move was in part due to the differing missions and inherent conflict between FDA and its parent, USDA. At the same time, the head of FDA became known as the Commissioner of Food and Drugs, the present title of the post, although no commission existed. The Federal Security Agency became the Department of Health, Education and Welfare in 1953, and subsequently HHS in 1979, when a separate Department of Education was established.

In 1948, due to concerns over lack of uniformity and efficiency among the three operating districts, the agency was reorganized to centralize authority in Washington, D.C. Commissioner Paul B. Dunbar, whose career with the agency dated to 1907, dismantled the three districts, moving many of the staff to Washington D.C. to join the divisions of Field Operations, Regulatory Management and Program Research. The 16 field stations became district offices and reported directly to the Commissioner. There were some morale and related problems, as the districts had developed different enforcement styles over the years.

In 1963, following several years of increasing statutory authority and wider jurisdiction, a tripling of the agency's enforcement budget, and two citizen advisory committee reports (in 1955 and 1962), then Commissioner George P. Larrick reorganized the agency to try to emphasize scientific research, education and voluntary compliance. He added a Bureau of Education and Voluntary Compliance, and divided the previously existing scientific bureau into the Bureau of Scientific Research and the Bureau of Scientific Standards and Evaluation. These three bureaus joined the Bureau of Medicine and the Bureau of Regulatory Compliance.

Despite this reorganization, congressional criticism led, in 1966, to the appointment of the first outsider, and the first physician in more than 40 years, as the Commissioner of Food and Drugs, Dr. James L. Goddard. Dr. Goddard came from the Communicable Disease Center of the Public Health Service, and had a reputation as a reformer and aggressive regulator. He was given a mandate to reform FDA. In 1966, he extensively reorganized FDA, essentially reversing the 1963 changes. Among other things, the two separate science bureaus were recombined as the Bureau of Science and the district offices reported directly to the Commissioner rather than the Bureau of Regulatory Compliance. A new Bureau of Drug Abuse Control was added, following the Drug Abuse Control Amendments of 1965. (This was transferred to the Department of Justice in 1968.) In addition, the Bureau of Veterinary Medicine was created.

Congressional criticism led, in 1966, to the appointment of the first outsider, and the first physician in more than 40 years, as the Commissioner of Food and Drugs.

Dr. Goddard's brief stay (less than two and one-half years) marked the beginning of what has been called the period of often "short-term," outsider Commissioners. Since then, FDA has had 13 Commissioners: Herbert Ley Jr., MD (7/1/1968–12/12/1969), Charles Edwards, MD (12/13/1969–3/15/1973), Alexander M. Schmidt, MD (7/20/1973–11/30/1976), Donald Kennedy, PhD (4/4/1977–6/30/1979), Jere E. Goyan, PhD (10/21/1979–1/20/1981), Arthur Hull Hayes Jr., MD

(4/13/1981–9/11/1983), Frank E. Young, MD (7/15/1984–12/17/1989), David A. Kessler, MD (11/8/1990–2/28/1997), Jane E. Henney, MD (1/17/1999–1/19/2001), Mark B. McClellan, MD, PhD (11/14/2002–3/26/2004), Lester M. Crawford, DVM, PhD (7/18/2005–9/23/2005), Andrew C. von Eschenbach, MD (12/13/2006–1/20/2009) and Margaret Hamburg, MD (5/18/2009 to present). Most of these 13 Commissioners were appointed from outside the agency, and most were physicians. At times, the post of Commissioner was vacant and temporarily filled by an acting Commissioner. (Full biographies of all FDA Commissioners since Harvey W. Wiley, MD are available on FDA's website at http://www.fda.gov/oc/commissioners/default.htm.)

In addition, more professionals began to join the agency in positions of authority, often as political appointees. There also has been increasing scrutiny and involvement in FDA's activities by Congress, its parent department and the White House.

In 1968, FDA was placed by the Department of Health, Education and Welfare under the Public Health Service, then combined with other agencies in the new Consumer Protection and Environmental Health Service (CPEHS). This placed another official above the Commissioner, but CPEHS was abolished less than two years later and FDA again became part of the Public Health Service.

Reorganization

FDA's current structure stems from the 1970s reorganization along product lines. The products regulated by FDA account for some 25 cents of every dollar spent by U.S. consumers.

FDA was reorganized in 1970, with the regulatory and voluntary compliance bureaus combined into the Bureau of Compliance and with the establishment of 10 Regional Food and Drug Directors, paralleling the department regional structure. The agency also reorganized along product lines, establishing a Bureau of Drugs and a Bureau of Foods, Pesticides, and Product Safety. Almost 30 years later, FDA still follows that basic organization, although the bureaus have all become centers with the following names: the Center for Drug Evaluation and Research, the Center for Biologics Evaluation and Research, the Center for Devices and Radiological Health, the Center for Food Safety and Applied Nutrition, and the Center for Veterinary Medicine. Each center has undergone its own changes and reorganizations, but the general organization remains the same.

On August 19, 2009, FDA established its first new center in several years, the Center for Tobacco Products, to implement the newly enacted Family Smoking Prevention and Tobacco Control Act.

Over the years, FDA has had to contend with tight budgets and battles with Congress and other agencies over resources and authority. FDA has grown from a budget of some $12,000 in 1890 to a proposed budget of more than $2.71 billion for Fiscal Year 2012, and from a handful of employees to more than 911,000 employees. The products regulated by FDA account for some 25 cents of every dollar spent by U.S. consumers. The agency has an immense, if often unsung, effect on the economy and the public's health, safety and well being.

Chapter 3

The Philosophy of Food and Drug Law

Richard M. Cooper, Williams & Connolly LLP, Washington, D.C.

Key Points

- Food and drug law is primarily about physical things.
- The overriding purpose of the Federal Food, Drug, and Cosmetic Act (FDCA) is to protect the consuming public.
- As new risks have been recognized, the FDCA has been amended to make it more protective.
- Expansion of Food and Drug Administration (FDA) authority has coincided with expansion of administrative tools throughout the federal government.
- There has been a substantial transfer of power from the courts to FDA.
- FDA has been, and will continue to be, a scientific regulatory agency that protects the public from unsafe or ineffective medical products.
- The review process must be rigorous enough to ensure that new products meet the statutory standards.
- FDA technically does not regulate the practice of medicine; however, its regulations do bear directly on physicians conducting FDA-regulated clinical investigations.
- Consumers now have greater opportunity and necessity to make informed decisions about matters that affect their own health.
- FDA is accountable to the Department of Health and Human Services, the Office of Management and Budget, the President, Congress, and the courts, as well as practically to the scientific and medical communities, the press and the public.
- FDA takes an expansive view of its mission and authority.
- FDA is increasingly facing issues raised by international trade in the categories of products it regulates.

INTRODUCTION

Food and drug law is primarily about physical things—foods, drugs (including biological products such as blood and vaccines), medical devices, cosmetics, tobacco products and radiation-emitting products. It is only secondarily about the companies and people who manufacture, distribute, sell and prescribe those things.

This focus on things is reflected in many aspects of the law and practice under it. The main segments of the governing statute—the Federal Food, Drug, and Cosmetic Act (FDCA)—are organized by type of product: food (Chapter IV); drugs, devices and electronic products (Chapter V); cosmetics (Chapter VI); and tobacco products (Chapter IX). The agency that administers the statute—the Food and Drug Administration (FDA)—is also organized by product type. Its main operating units include the Center for Food Safety and Applied Nutrition (which also regulates cosmetics), the Center for Drug Evaluation and Research, the Center for Biologics Evaluation and Research, the Center for Devices and Radiological Health, the Center for Veterinary Medicine (which regulates foods and drugs for animals) and the Center for Tobacco Products.

Principal types of FDCA
violations:
- *"adulterated" products*
- *"misbranded" products*
- *products marketed*
  without required FDA
  approval

In general, the principal types of violation of the statute are defined so as to make a product "adulterated" or "misbranded" or marketed without a required FDA permission for marketing. In identifying a violation by a company or individual, it generally (although not universally) is necessary to identify a product that violates the statute in one of those three ways.

When the government goes to court under the FDCA, the remedy it often seeks is a seizure and condemnation of a product it claims is in violation of the statute or an injunction against shipment of one or more products in interstate commerce. Indeed, the official legal title of such a seizure action is of the form, "United States v. [an estimated number of units of a particular kind of product]." In such a case, the units of the product literally are the defendants. Anyone who claims to own them may enter the lawsuit to defend on their behalf; but, if no one does, the government wins by default, and the products generally are condemned and destroyed.

The reason for this primary focus on things is that the overriding purpose of the FDCA is to protect the consuming public from regulated products that are unsafe (food, drugs, devices, cosmetics, radiation-emitting products), ineffective (drugs and devices), or deceptively or otherwise inadequately labeled (food, drugs, devices and cosmetics). The general standard applicable to tobacco products is that their marketing be appropriate for protection of the public health (and that they be properly labeled). Where a product is violative, FDA's first objective is to protect the public from the product, itself, by bringing about its removal from commerce. Accordingly, the most common informal remedy for a violative product is a recall, which is a more or less voluntary alternative to a seizure by the government.

In some cases, FDA, acting through the Department of Justice (DOJ), may pursue an additional objective. It may seek to prevent future violations through an injunction against those likely to cause a violation in the future. In addition or in the alternative, it may seek punishment of companies and individuals for past violations, through criminal prosecution in the courts or an administrative proceeding for civil penalties.

The FDCA's main judicial remedies—seizure, injunction and criminal prosecution—are very forceful. Upon the filing of a complaint for seizure by DOJ—before any defense is presented—the products proceeded against are legally seized by U.S. Marshals; and, in general, they are released from seizure only if a claimant appears, and the government fails to persuade the court that the products are violative of the FDCA. If the government obtains an injunction, it generally shuts down a manufacturing facility unless and until FDA is satisfied that the facility can manufacture products that comply with the statute. A company or an individual can be convicted of a misdemeanor (an offense punishable by fine and imprisonment for not more than one year) under the FDCA merely for causing or being responsible for the shipment of a product in violation of the FDCA—even without an intent to violate the statute, and even without knowledge that a violation was occurring. Where there is intent to defraud, a violation may be treated, under the FDCA or the general criminal law, as a felony (which is punishable by a higher fine and longer term of imprisonment).

A company or an individual can be convicted of a misdemeanor under the FDCA merely for causing or being responsible for the shipment of a product in violation of the act—even without an intent to violate the statute, and even without knowledge that a violation was occurring.

The law's enforcement scheme is so severe because its purposes, as the Supreme Court put it in 1943, "touch phases of the lives and health of people which, in the circumstances of modern industrialism, are largely beyond self-protection." In explaining why the FDCA imposes strict misdemeanor liability on individuals involved in violations, the Supreme Court stated in 1975 that the FDCA "imposes not only a positive duty to seek out and remedy violations when they occur but also, and primarily, a duty to implement measures that will insure that violations will not occur. The requirements of foresight and vigilance imposed on responsible corporate agents are beyond question demanding, and perhaps onerous, but they are no more stringent than the public has a right to expect . . . ."

This overriding concern to protect the public is, of course, also fully reflected in the statutory standards applicable to regulated products. For example, a food additive may be approved only if its sponsor affirmatively shows that there is a reasonable certainty that it will not harm any consumers. In general, the sponsor of a new drug or medical device must affirmatively show that its product is effective for some appropriate medical use, and that the benefits provided by that effectiveness outweigh the risks to health presented by the product. Where there are reasonable scientific or medical doubts about whether these standards have been met, the product is not approved.

Food and drug law, however, was not always this protective. As new risks to the public health have been recognized, Congress has amended the law scores of times to make it more protective.

The first general federal food and drug statute, the Pure Food and Drugs Act of 1906, was much simpler than today's law. It applied only to foods and drugs, and did not require any governmental review of any such product before it was put onto the market. If a product was marketed in violation of the statute, the government had to find out about it and bring a court action against the product or against those who were marketing it. Over time, it became clear that the scope of the statute was too narrow, and that the statutory scheme did not adequately protect the public.

The FDCA was enacted in 1938. It extended food and drug law coverage to medical devices and cosmetics. It also established a mechanism for FDA to regulate research on drugs, and required FDA review of new drugs to ensure that they were safe before they could be marketed. This "premarket review" was limited to safety, and did not apply to devices, cosmetics or foods (except that FDA was authorized to impose a permit requirement on certain classes of foods that can present a severe risk to health if not processed properly). The 1938 act also gave FDA authority to inspect establishments where regulated products are manufactured, processed, packed or held.

The philosophy of premarket review is simple: to the extent reasonably possible, the most significant benefits and risks of a product should be identified and assessed before the product is marketed.

Although the original FDCA was a marked improvement over the 1906 statute, it, too, proved deficient in protecting the public. Consequently, the statute has been strengthened by a series of amendments, among the most important of which were these: premarket review for safety was extended to food additives (1958) and color additives (1960); premarket review of drugs was extended to effectiveness as well as safety (1962); premarket review for safety and effectiveness and FDA regulation of research were extended to devices (1976). Numerous other aspects of FDA regulation have been strengthened in other amendments, including enactments to strengthen FDA's ability to prepare for and respond to bioterrorism and other emergencies. In 2009, Congress amended the FDCA and other statutes to give FDA jurisdiction over tobacco products.

The philosophy of premarket review is simple: to the extent reasonably possible, the most significant benefits and risks of a product should be identified and assessed before the product is marketed. If the risks are not justified, the product should not be marketed. If the risks are justified only if the product is used in accordance with certain conditions, or if certain conditions can reduce even the justified risks, those conditions should be identified and disclosed.

The extension of the premarket review requirements from 1958 to 1976 coincided with a vast expansion throughout the federal government of the use of administrative tools rather than court actions to impose regulatory requirements. Prior to this change in method of governing, FDA had established new interpretations of the statutory standards for regulated products principally through judicial opinions in court actions. Through the DOJ, FDA would file court actions against regulated products and marketers of such products; it would argue in court that the general words of the statute should be interpreted to impose particular detailed requirements, and that those requirements had been violated; and generally the courts would accept FDA's interpretations and embody them in judicial opinions, on which FDA could rely in later cases. Manufacturers and other marketers interested in learning what the applicable requirements were would consult the statute and the judicial decisions interpreting it. FDA supplemented these sources principally with so-called "trade correspondence" and announcements.

There has been a substantial transfer of power from the courts to FDA. The courts, however, still have the final say on the validity of regulatory requirements. In practice the courts defer to FDA's views most of the time.

Through its new premarket approval authority and the use of rulemaking (the issuance of regulations of general applicability) and administrative adjudication (the deciding of individual cases in administrative rather than judicial proceedings), FDA developed much more efficient ways (faster, less expensive, more systematic, more coherent, more within the agency's control) to establish binding regulatory requirements. Thus, today, the court cases FDA initiates serve principally not to create new regulatory requirements but rather to enforce regulatory requirements already established through administrative means. Consequently, during the last 50 years there has been not only a large increase in regulatory requirements but also a substantial transfer of power over such requirements from the federal courts to FDA. The courts still have the final say on the validity of regulatory requirements, but in practice the courts defer to FDA's views most of the time. Today, someone seeking to learn the requirements applicable to a particular product would consult the statute, the regulations in Title 21 of the *Code of Federal Regulations*, regulations not yet codified and other issuances in the *Federal Register*, FDA guidance documents, letters, speeches, congressional testimony and judicial decisions.

Premarket review and the increased use of administrative techniques to establish regulatory requirements and policy have substantially changed the nature of food and drug law and FDA. In its early years, FDA was essentially a law enforcement agency. The operating units that are now called "centers" were then called "bureaus." Science in the agency was a handmaiden to enforcement: its role was to identify problems in the marketplace, and help the agency react to the problems and win in court.

More recently, currently, and for the foreseeable future, FDA has been, is and will continue to be essentially a scientific regulatory agency. It protects the public health principally by screening out unsafe or otherwise inadequate products in premarket review, and by establishing, on the basis of scientific knowledge, general regulatory requirements for the design, manufacture, testing, labeling and, in limited circumstances, advertising, of marketed products. The vast bulk of public protection is achieved through these *preventive* activities. They are backed up, of course, by the agency's continued ability and willingness to react to violations by having DOJ file court actions against violative products and those who market them. Thus, today, court enforcement is a handmaiden to scientific regulation.

FDA is a scientific regulatory agency.

This change in the nature of FDA's role has created or sharpened a number of issues central to the philosophy of food and drug regulation, including these:

♦ the general relationship between FDA and the industries it regulates, the agency's roles with respect to health promotion and health protection, and the relative importance of enforcement and voluntary compliance;

♦ the relation between FDA's regulation of medical products (drugs and devices) and the practice of medicine and related professions;

♦ the relation between FDA's regulation of medical products and reimbursement for those products under federal healthcare programs (and private health insurance programs);

♦ the extent to which FDA should or, as a practical matter, must rely on consumers to protect their own health, and the role of FDA's regulation of product labeling in that connection;

♦ with its greatly increased regulatory authority, to whom and through what means FDA is ultimately accountable;

♦ in what ways, and to what extent, FDA should adapt its regulatory role to the international market, particularly the increasing volumes of imported products subject to FDA's jurisdiction;

♦ how FDA will be able to maintain protection of the public during what is likely to be a prolonged period of stringency in the federal budget; and

♦ to what extent FDA's activities should be paid for by special fees from the firms FDA regulates rather than by revenues from taxation of the general population.

The remainder of this chapter will address these issues.

THE TENSION BETWEEN PREVENTION OF HARM AND PROMOTION OF BENEFIT

Public health is improved when safe and effective drugs and devices are made available and when those that are unsafe or ineffective are kept off the market. Clearly, it is part of FDA's mission to protect the public from medical products that are unsafe or ineffective. Under legislation enacted in 1997, it is also part of the agency's mission to "promote public health by promptly and efficiently reviewing clinical research and taking appropriate action on the marketing of regulated products in a timely manner." How should FDA harmonize those objectives? To what extent and in what ways should FDA's premarket review of new drugs and devices be made more searching, more detailed and more deliberate in order to detect inadequacies that would make a product unsafe or ineffective or to develop additional information that would make product use more safe or more effective; and to what extent and in what ways should FDA review be simplified, streamlined and speeded up in order to ease entry to the market for products that may improve health? More generally, should FDA's relationship with the research-based corporations that develop new drugs and devices be at arm's length and hierarchical (regulator/regulated firm) or should there be a significant cooperative and collegial element?

> **FDA's Mission:**
> *"promote public health by promptly and efficiently reviewing clinical research and taking appropriate action on the marketing of regulated products in a timely manner."*

Plainly, there are no simple answers. In our free enterprise system, although much basic research is sponsored by government, most new medical technologies and the products that embody them are developed by private firms operating for profit. Under the FDCA, the responsibility for testing new products also rests with private firms, not with FDA. FDA's role is to review proposed new products on the basis of information on safety and effectiveness developed and presented by private firms that have a financial interest in marketing the products, and to determine on the basis of that information (and general scientific and medical knowledge) whether the products meet statutory requirements for marketing.

The review process must be rigorous enough to ensure that new products meet the statutory standards, and that the information submitted is sufficient to make possible the writing of adequate directions for prescribing and use. The review process must not be so demanding, however, that the availability of good products is unduly delayed.

Similarly, FDA must not abdicate its regulatory role, its responsibility to ensure that no product is approved unless it satisfies the statutory standards, or its legal duty to review all products independently, objectively and impartially. These objectives might be compromised if FDA reviewers became too deeply involved in product development or interacted too collegially with employees of private firms, so that they came to have an emotional stake in product approval. The development of beneficial products will be hindered, however, if FDA reviewers do not work collaboratively with knowledgeable counterpart physicians, scientists, engineers and statisticians at private companies to develop appropriate test protocols and criteria for review, to identify appropriate medical uses for new products, and to draft maximally useful guidance for prescribing physicians.

FDA and AIDS: AIDS caused FDA to establish a trade-off between current patients and future patients.

A striking example of an adjustment in the review process in response to urgent need was FDA's reaction to acquired immunodeficiency syndrome (AIDS). Under political pressure for rapid development and approval of drugs to treat persons infected with human immunodeficiency virus (HIV), the agency adopted an actively cooperative role, adopted lenient interpretations of the statutory criteria, drastically reduced its normal demands for test data and greatly streamlined its review process. The result was swift market entry of any drug that appeared beneficial in the treatment of AIDS. The cost of this success was, in most cases, a lack of the usual quantity and quality of data to support solid conclusions about the detailed benefits and risks presented by particular products and to provide the basis for adequate directions to physicians for use of the products. This overall approach involved a trade-off between the interests of current patients and those of future patients. Because, at the time, there was no effective treatment and the disease was considered fatal in all cases, this was a fully understandable but nevertheless difficult trade-off.

In the area of enforcement, FDA necessarily is a cop; but it cannot, itself, continuously patrol every factory, whether in the United States or abroad, where the products it regulates are made, or test the actual quality of every unit of every such product that is on the market in the United States. Thus, the agency has had to develop strategies that maximize the effectiveness of its limited resources in inducing compliance by regulated firms. The agency has had to blend elements of strict enforcement with technical assistance in the form of guidelines, development of consensus implementation standards, and random and for-cause inspections and sampling of products.

For example, FDA regulations require that foods, drugs and devices be manufactured in accordance with "current good manufacturing practices." The regulations set forth only very general standards, such as that buildings and facilities shall be clean and sanitary, equipment shall be suitable for its purposes, and employees shall be adequately qualified and trained. Introduction into commerce of a product made in violation of these requirements is technically unlawful. Detailed elaborations of the general requirements in the regulations are set forth in guidance documents created by FDA, in consensus documents developed by experts from FDA and the regulated industries, and in a substantial literature developed by private experts. Additional elaboration is set forth in documents resulting from FDA compliance and enforcement activities— reports of violations observed during FDA inspections, FDA Warning Letters, and judicial decisions resulting from court cases initiated by FDA.

Of course, to some extent, an additional incentive for compliance is provided by the state law of products liability. Where a consumer claims to have been harmed by an FDA-regulated product, violation of an FDA requirement generally may be considered as evidence that the product was defective and that its manufacturer was negligent.

FDA's control over warnings and other information in drug and device labeling and other regulatory decisions the agency makes can have a significant effect on products liability litigation. Issues have been raised as to whether, and if so how, FDA should take account of this effect in carrying out its regulatory responsibilities; and as to whether FDA approval of certain aspects of a product and the product's compliance with the conditions for FDA approval should preempt the imposition of products liability on a theory that such approval and compliance were insufficient under state law.

FDA's control over warnings and other information in drug and device labeling and other regulatory decisions the agency makes can have a significant effect on products liability litigation.

In the past, the agency generally attempted to be neutral as between injured plaintiffs and defendant manufacturers, and regarded products liability as a useful adjunct to regulation, and therefore generally opposed arguments that its regulatory requirements preempt different or additional requirements under state law. During the administration of President George W. Bush, the agency asserted that certain aspects of its regulation of medical products do preempt different or additional state law requirements. Moreover, concerns about liability have contributed to a recognized insufficiency of medical products in certain categories (e.g., drugs to treat illnesses in pregnant women, products for neonates and contraceptives). There is ongoing debate about what degree of preemption best serves the public health in the long term.

FDA AND THE PRACTICE OF MEDICINE

Although FDA's product-approval decisions and other regulatory actions have a large effect on healthcare, FDA technically does not regulate the practice of medicine, nursing, pharmacy or the other healing professions, except when they conduct clinical trials within FDA's jurisdiction and when they become involved in the manufacture, distribution or promotion of products within that

FDA technically does not regulate the practice of medicine.

jurisdiction. Outside those exceptions, the healthcare professions are regulated by the states.

FDA's regulations bear directly on physicians and nurses when they conduct FDA-regulated clinical investigations to develop information for product approval. In general, when a physician's relationship with a patient is also that of a scientific investigator with a research subject, FDA's role is to protect the rights and welfare of the subject by ensuring that risks to the subject have been reduced to the practical minimum and that the subject's informed consent to participation in the investigation has been properly obtained, to ensure that the remaining risks entailed by use of an investigational drug or device are justified by the likelihood that the investigation will yield useful scientific data, and to ensure that the investigational product is not used outside the investigational protocol.

Use of an approved drug or device by a healthcare professional treating a patient is outside FDA's jurisdiction. When FDA approves a drug or device, it approves it for use only in specific medical circumstances (e.g., to treat certain diseases or other bodily conditions [called "indications"], in certain patient populations). The manufacturer of an approved product may advertise and promote it only for use in the circumstances specified in the labeling FDA has approved (or, in the case of some devices, cleared). Physicians and others authorized by state law to prescribe medical products, however, may prescribe the product for any indication or other circumstance they choose (e.g., for the FDA-approved indication but for a patient population different from the one for which FDA approved the indication, or for a different indication altogether), subject only to the requirements of state law with respect to medical licensure and malpractice.

Many products develop medically accepted indications that are outside the FDA-approved indications; some unapproved indications may even become the standard of care.

Over time, many products develop medically accepted indications or uses in patient populations that are outside the FDA-approved or FDA-cleared indications; some unapproved indications and other uses may even become the standard of care. Unless a manufacturer submits to FDA data adequate to support approval of an additional indication or use, it will remain unapproved. Consequently, it commonly occurs that a drug or device has a medically significant indication or other use outside its approved or cleared indications, but the product's manufacturer is prohibited from recommending or promoting, or providing guidance for, that indication or use to physicians and other healthcare providers (except in response to an unsolicited inquiry by a provider to the manufacturer). Organizations that are independent of the manufacturer are not subject to any such prohibition, and are free to meet any marketplace need for information about unapproved indications and other uses of FDA-regulated products.

Manufacturers have nevertheless objected to this restriction on their free-dom to disseminate information about their products. Historically, FDA has responded that, if manufacturers were free to disseminate information about unapproved uses, they would have much less incentive to seek FDA approval of additional indications and to develop the scientific data required for such approval. Thus, on this issue, our society's general commitment to free competi-tive dissemination of truthful information collides with FDA's role as approver of new drugs and devices and reviewer of manufacturers' statements in the marketplace about their FDA-regulated products. A limited compromise of the competing views was included in FDA reform legislation enacted in 1997, but has now expired. In a document published in the *Federal Register* in January 2009, near the end of the Bush administration, FDA endorsed (with certain con-ditions) dissemination by manufacturers of reprints of medical journal articles and medical and scientific publications relating to unapproved uses of their approved or cleared medical products. The debate, however, persists.

Historically, FDA has responded that, if manufacturers were free to disseminate information about unapproved uses, they would have much less incentive to seek FDA approval of additional indications and to develop the scientific data required for such approval.

The issue extends beyond purely medical information. As economic consid-erations have come explicitly to play a much larger role in decisions about healthcare, and as important elements of healthcare decision making have shifted from individual physicians to managed care organizations and third-party payers, the demand for economic information about the performance of drugs and medical devices also has increased. The managed care organizations and third-party payers want to know not only whether a drug or device is safe and effective and for which indications in which patient populations, but also whether it is cost-effective as compared to alternative products and other treat-ments (such as surgery).

When manufacturers undertake to provide such information, should it have to be approved by FDA before the manufacturers can disseminate it? Even if the recipients are sophisticated organizations? Is such a role for FDA an appropriate or an inappropriate extension of its existing role as reviewer of information on product safety and effectiveness?

FDA's current position is that such information, when disseminated by regu-lated firms, is subject to its jurisdiction and to the FDCA's standards for scientific validity. The studies that are needed to satisfy those standards are expensive and time-consuming. Plainly, there is a trade-off between the availability of information from regulated firms and its quality: if only high-quality and costly information may be disseminated by such firms, they will provide less informa-tion. Where manufacturers do not provide information, decision makers who would benefit from such information will have to turn to whatever information may be available from other sources or do without. It is a fair question whether,

It is a fair question whether FDA has made the optimal trade-off between availability and quality of medical-economic information from regulated firms.

in the circumstances, FDA has made the optimal trade-off between availability and quality of medical-economic information from regulated firms.

THE RESPONSIBILITIES OF CONSUMERS

As a result of vastly increased knowledge in the health-related sciences and changes in the healthcare delivery system, consumers now have greater opportunity and necessity than in recent decades to make informed decisions about matters that affect their own health. These changes are most clearly reflected by the labeling of foods and over-the-counter (OTC) drugs.

As to both types of products, FDA has implemented a philosophy of encouraging competition in product innovation by increasing manufacturers' communications about their products to consumers. The result has been a plethora of new products in food stores and drug stores, and new claims and information on product labels and in advertisements. Congress has particularly encouraged this development with respect to foods.

FDA encourages competition in product innovation.

Increased scientific understanding of human nutrition and of the role of diet in general health has led to fundamental revision of food labels, so as to provide increased information to consumers, and incentives to food processors to produce more healthful foods. Food labels now contain more easily usable information about the nutrient content of foods and, as permitted by FDA pursuant to statutory criteria, claims about the relationship between particular food products and specific diseases.

FDA's strategy in overseeing food labels is to enable consumers to make informed choices in the construction of a healthful overall diet. One might ask, however, how well such a strategy actually serves a population that includes many people who never see such information (in institutions where meals are served—schools, nursing homes, prisons, etc.), who cannot understand or use such information (because, e.g., their language is other than English, or they are functionally illiterate or innumerate) or simply do not have, or do not spend, the time and energy to use it.

In recent years, many medically significant drugs have been switched by FDA from prescription to OTC status. Pharmaceutical manufacturers seek such switches when they see attractive marketing opportunities for OTC sales (e.g., after profits from prescription sales have been reduced by generic competition). Such switches make drugs more accessible to consumers and reduce the overall cost of using them by eliminating the requirement of contact with a physician.

They also shift the cost of the drugs from the healthcare system to the drugs' users because most insurance and other third-party-payer systems that cover prescription drugs do not also cover OTC drugs.

Even where consumers do consult a physician, they are more likely now than in the past to use an OTC rather than a prescription drug. Because managed care systems generally do not cover OTC drugs, the systems have a financial incentive to induce their physicians to direct patients to OTC, rather than prescription, drugs when suitable OTC drugs are available; and the widening range of OTC drugs available expands the opportunities for physicians to do so. Thus, FDA policy combines with the incentives facing pharmaceutical manufacturers and managed care systems to lead to greater usage of OTC drugs.

Increased societal reliance on OTC drugs means increased reliance on consumers to deal with their own medical needs: increased consumer autonomy, but also increased consumer responsibility. The economics of healthcare drives in this direction, as, perhaps, does the demand of sophisticated consumers. There are important issues of how far and how fast the shift from prescription to OTC should go, and as to what extent, and at what cost, society can or should protect those who cannot cope with the increased personal responsibility.

FDA ACCOUNTABILITY

FDA is accountable to:
- *executive branch Public Health Service*
- *Congress*
- *the courts*
- *scientific and medical communities*

In making decisions critical to the health of the American people, to whom is FDA accountable? Within the government, FDA is triply accountable.

First, it is part of the Public Health Service in the Department of Health and Human Services (HHS), and thus part of the executive branch. The agency and its head, the Commissioner of Food and Drugs, are answerable to the Secretary of Health and Human Services, the Office of Management and Budget and, ultimately, the President. The agency's major regulatory and personnel decisions, budget, congressional testimony and legislative proposals all are reviewable by one or more of these officials or offices.

Second, the agency is overseen by Congress. The Senate Committee on Health, Education, Labor and Pensions and the House Committee on Energy and Commerce have jurisdiction over the FDCA and other statutes that FDA administers; authorize the agency's budget; and conduct frequent hearings (in the House, through the Subcommittee on Oversight and Investigations and the Subcommittee on Health) on the agency's performance. Because FDA originated as the Bureau of Chemistry in the Department of Agriculture (before it was transferred to what is now HHS), however, FDA's appropriations are determined by agricultural subcommittees of the Appropriations Committees in the House and Senate. Thus, those committees, too, have a continuing interest in FDA, which is reflected in FDA's annual appropriations hearings. From time to time, other Senate and House committees also take an interest in FDA.

Regulated firms, public interest groups and others dissatisfied with an FDA action (or inaction) can seek recourse in the courts.

Third, FDA is overseen by the courts. The agency's enforcement program is conducted mostly in the courts, although in recent years Congress has given it increased authority to impose civil monetary penalties administratively. Regulated firms, public interest groups and others dissatisfied with an FDA action (or inaction) can seek recourse in the courts. Because FDA can appear in court only through the DOJ, that department can also impose some check on the agency.

As a practical matter, FDA is also accountable to the scientific and medical communities, and particularly to their academic components. Most of the principal decision makers at FDA are physicians or scientists, to whom the respect of their professional peers is of great importance. Particularly when FDA makes decisions about cutting-edge technologies or other matters at the scientific frontier (as it often does), the agency's decision makers want to make decisions that will be respected as sensible in the relevant scientific and medical disciplines. Routinely, the agency, when faced with such a decision, formally seeks the advice of one of its advisory committees, which are composed principally of leading academic physicians and scientists. FDA generally follows their advice.

Like all government agencies, FDA is also accountable to public opinion, as shaped by the press. The agency's relations with all the constituencies with which it deals—regulated firms, trade associations, federal and state governmental bodies, scientific and medical groups, organizations representing patients, public interest groups and others—are all influenced significantly by the agency's standing with the public.

Nevertheless, in a large and critical part of its work—review of new products—FDA is largely insulated from effective outside oversight. Such reviews are based on trade secret data generally not otherwise disclosed elsewhere, except to similar regulatory bodies in other countries. The reviews are highly technical, require highly specialized competence in several disciplines, and are extremely labor-intensive. Probably no other governmental institution currently is equipped to oversee the quality of FDA's performance of this distinctive function on an ongoing basis.

Because, over time, FDA's new-product decisions are critical to the fate of many regulated firms, they are extremely reluctant to challenge any particular FDA product-review decision in another forum. Resort to the courts to challenge an

FDA denial of approval of a new product is particularly unappealing for several reasons:

♦ the technical nature of the subject matter;

♦ prevailing doctrines of administrative law, which lead to deference to administrative agencies on scientific and technical matters;

♦ the institutional limits on the judiciary, which is not well equipped to make ultimate judgments about scientific and technical matters (as distinct from ascertaining the status of scientific opinion); and

♦ the unattractiveness of trying to market a product that FDA has initially refused to approve.

The result is a limited, but important, area in which the exercise of governmental power is, to a considerable extent, unaccountable.

FDA is held accountable, however, on infrequent occasions when the press or a segment of the public takes a particularly strong interest in a pending review of a proposed new product or when a past approval of a product has turned out to be a serious mistake. In such circumstances, extraordinary public attention focuses on FDA's decision-making process, and the agency is called to public account for its decision.

FDA is held accountable, however, on infrequent occasions when the press or a segment of the public takes a particularly strong interest in a pending review of a proposed new product or when a past approval of a product has turned out to be a serious mistake.

For example, organized groups representing patients, such as those with the AIDS virus or Alzheimer's disease, have brought public pressure on FDA to approve proposed new drugs. News media sometimes have championed particular drugs or devices. When an approved product has turned out to be much more harmful than was anticipated when FDA approved it, FDA has been called before a congressional committee to explain its decision.

These two types of scenarios create conflicting pressures on FDA. The agency may be subjected to public pressure to hasten the approval of an apparently promising new product, but the agency knows it is likely to be criticized severely if its approval turns out to have been a mistake. Few products, however, attract public support before approval, and few FDA approvals turn out to have been mistaken. In the general run of decision making about approvals of new products—including decisions about what indications and claims for a product will be permitted and how other information will be presented in the product's official labeling—FDA is largely unaccountable as a practical matter.

Ultimately, FDA's accountability is a function not only of how other governmental bodies and other constituencies view the agency, but also of other, competing demands on the attention and resources of those to whom FDA is accountable. The variability in effective oversight of the agency presents a persistent philosophical issue for FDA: what should be its basic stance toward the statute it administers? Should FDA officials view the statute as a set of detailed instructions from Congress to be carried out in a manner as faithful as possible to what congressional drafters presumably intended? Or should the statute be viewed as basically a set of authorities for FDA to use to advance its views of what promotes the public health, through whatever means FDA can use without being overridden by some governmental body or group to which the agency is formally accountable?

For example, if the agency views a particular statutory limitation on its authority as reflecting a congressional compromise inimical to the public health, should the agency respect the limitation faithfully or seek ways to evade it through other statutorily permitted means? To what extent should the agency seek to expand its powers in the face of inertia or distraction in other centers of power? To what extent should the agency be creative and aggressive in asserting its power to advance policies it considers beneficial to the public health? Alternatively, should the agency seek to discern and carry out the policy preferences of its political superiors in the executive branch and of Congress? In sum, what is the appropriate role of a subordinate agency entrusted with a mission to protect the public health?

FDA takes an expansive view of its mission and its authorities.

Over the decades, different FDA decision makers have responded differently to this set of issues. In general, the agency has taken an expansive view of its mission and its authorities, and has used its statutory tools aggressively to advance its institutional views of what is good for the public health. The most striking example was FDA's assertion of jurisdiction over tobacco products without an express delegation of statutory authority—an assertion of authority that the Supreme Court held to be invalid, but that later led to the enactment of legislation giving the agency that authority.

FDA IN THE INTERNATIONAL COMMUNITY

Before the advent of what today is called "the global economy," FDA's concerns were focused almost entirely on protecting consumers in the United States. FDA viewed itself as having only limited responsibility toward consumers abroad, and only a limited role in facilitating the marketing of American products abroad. The agency also devoted relatively little effort to monitoring imports. Amendments to the FDCA and globalization have required FDA to rethink the proper role of the American national food and drug regulator in the international economy.

What is America's responsibility with respect to FDA-regulated products exported from this country to a foreign country? Should the United States be an international nanny? Should its attitude toward foreign consumers be "let the buying country beware"? Should its role be something in between—and, if so, what? Does it matter whether the importing country does or does not have its own sophisticated regulatory system? Does it matter whether products exported from the United States may be re-exported from the original import-ing country to a third country? (If the products are re-exported back to the United States, that clearly is a matter of legitimate FDA concern.) If the United States does have some responsibility toward consumers in foreign countries, does it follow that the very same standards of safety, effectiveness, labeling and product quality that apply to domestically distributed products should also ap-ply to exported products, even when they are going to countries that are very different in population characteristics, healthcare systems, healthcare needs and general economic level? If different standards should apply, what are they, how should they be ascertained, and what degree of deference should FDA give to the views of governments in the importing countries? What level of FDA effort and resources should FDA allocate to reviewing products to be exported, under any standard? To these difficult questions, there are no simple, obviously correct answers.

What is America's responsibility with respect to FDA-regulated products exported from this country to a foreign country?

In general, FDA would prefer that American firms not export products within its jurisdiction whose safety and effectiveness for the ultimate consumers have not been demonstrated. FDA recognizes, however, that standards of safety and effectiveness appropriate for the affluent United States, with its sophisticated healthcare system, may not be appropriate for countries that are much poorer and have only rudimentary healthcare systems. Moreover, FDA owes respect to the authority and responsibility of foreign governments to decide what products may be marketed to their own people. In addition, the limitations on FDA's resources and the undesirability of driving export manufacturing facilities abroad constrain FDA's ability to act, and the willingness of Congress to have FDA act, as the protector of all the world's consumers.

The increasing dependence of the United States on imports of medical prod-ucts and foods and, since 9/11, concerns about bioterrorism have raised serious issues about FDA's ability to protect American consumers from products that are fraudulent or adulterated, have been tampered with or are otherwise defective. Plainly, in cooperation with Congress and through agreements with foreign governments, FDA will have to upgrade its programs for protection against unlawful imports. This effort will, of course, require the allocation of sig-nificantly increased resources, as well as the development and implementation of significantly improved monitoring and inspection systems. Congressional en-actments have increased FDA's responsibilities in these areas, yet Congress has been unwilling to provide FDA the resources it needs for inspection programs adequate to provide confidence in the quality of imported products within FDA's jurisdiction. This serious problem is likely to persist and to increase as imports of FDA-regulated products increase and the stringency of federal budgets for regulatory programs becomes more severe.

To facilitate the international movement of foods, drugs and devices, FDA has made a major effort to harmonize its regulatory requirements and standards with those of counterpart agencies in other countries. A host of issues relate to the extent to which FDA should compromise with foreign regulators in order to promote international uniformity in data development to support the approval of new products, product labeling, manufacturing systems and practices, factory inspection standards and other matters. A further issue relates to the level of effort and resources that FDA should devote to assisting U.S. manufacturers to meet importation requirements of foreign governments.

How FDA Should Be Funded

An issue that arose in the 1990s and continues to be the subject of debate is whether, and if so to what extent, the activities of FDA should be funded by "user fees" from regulated firms.

Finally, an issue that arose in the 1990s and continues to be the subject of debate is whether, and if so to what extent, the activities of FDA should be funded by "user fees" from regulated firms rather than from the federal government's general revenues (collected principally from taxpayers). Plainly, from the perspective of the national budget and the interest of taxpayers, any shift of the burden of payment to regulated firms is desirable. Does such a shift, however, raise legitimate concerns?

Is product review (or inspection of a manufacturing facility) properly viewed as a service provided by FDA to regulated firms, for which it is appropriate that those firms pay a fee? Were not the systems of product review and factory inspection established for the benefit of the public rather than the regulated firms, even though regulated firms benefit generally from the existence of regulatory systems that give the public confidence in the safety and quality (and, as relevant, effectiveness) of their products? Are there likely to be adverse practical consequences of re-conceptualizing product review as a service to regulated firms?

If regulated firms are paying for a particular FDA activity (e.g., review of applications for approval of new drugs), is there a risk that the fact of payment by the firms will affect the performance of the function and the interaction between the agency personnel performing it and the personnel of the paying firms? Over time, might the firms become more assertive in their dealings with the agency, and might FDA personnel feel that they "owe" the paying firms more? If such consequences do occur, are they necessarily undesirable?

Is there a risk that particular FDA functions paid for by regulated firms will receive disproportionate financial support as compared to agency functions funded by the taxpayers, so that, over time, an imbalance will occur between, e.g., product review (paid for by firms) and enforcement (paid for by the taxpayers)? Has such an imbalance already occurred, and with undesirable consequences? Can the political process, including congressional oversight and the appropriations process, be relied on to maintain a reasonable balance?

If FDA functions are paid for by private firms rather than from the public treasury, is there a risk that there will be a natural bureaucratic tendency for the firm-supported functions (and FDA jobs) to proliferate unnecessarily? Or can it reasonably be expected that firms and their trade associations will have sufficient political capital with Congress and the administration to maintain checks on such a development?

These questions raise fundamental issues about the principles underlying the regulatory system FDA administers. The risks just described are real; but it is also undeniable that the political system has been unwilling to provide, from general revenues, an adequate level of resources for timely FDA reviews of new products and inspections of factories, and that the additional resources from user fees can accelerate product reviews and approvals and increase factory inspections, to the general benefit of the public. Whether the advantages of this approach outweigh the disadvantages over the long term will depend principally on the quality of FDA management and the ability of outside constituencies (principally Congress and the news media) to find an effective way to monitor the quality of FDA's performance despite the relative imperviousness of FDA product reviews to public scrutiny. As funding of FDA by user fees extends beyond particular product reviews and types of inspections to other functions, these concerns and the need for effective management and oversight of FDA will increase.

The political system has been unwilling to provide, from general revenues, an adequate level of resources for timely FDA reviews of new products.

CONCLUSION

Food and drug law is a fascinating microcosm of old and new issues in political and social philosophy, including many facets of social justice among different groups affected by regulatory decisions. These issues influence day-to-day administration of the law and the large controversies that erupt from time to time.

Chapter 4

The Food and Drug Administration— How It Is Organized and Works

Fred H. Degnan, King & Spalding, Washington, D.C.

Key Points

- Although the Food and Drug Administration (FDA) is not an independent agency, it makes every effort to operate as if it were one. It is unique among its sister agencies within the Department of Health and Human Services (HHS) because of the variety of products and scientific issues it confronts and because of the extensive regulatory and enforcement authority it wields, not to mention the latitude it has been given to police the domestic and international commerce of the products it regulates.

- The agency's evolution from a small bureau in the U.S. Department of Agriculture in 1906 to a very visible and active component of HHS reveals the development of a highly specialized agency that can adapt and adjust to increased regulatory burdens.

- The fundamental structure and organization of FDA for decades has remained unchanged: the Office of the Commissioner, substantive centers and field offices form the nucleus of agency activity and initiatives. Always a national presence, the agency now has a global face as well with offices in key overseas regions.

- Because of the complexity, variety and importance of the issues within its responsibilities, FDA has been forced to lead the way in developing and employing regulatory tools, such as rulemaking and advisory committees, and has forged generally strong collaborative working arrangements with sister agencies and state authorities. As a result, the agency has enhanced its ability to function efficiently and in a substantively and scientifically sound way.

INTRODUCTION

Although perhaps the most visible and well-known of all public health organizations, the U.S. Food and Drug Administration (FDA) is not an independent agency. Rather, it is a component of the U.S. Department of Health and Human Services (HHS).

Moreover, and perhaps even more surprising, only very limited statutory authority (e.g., authority with respect to dispute resolution regarding the timeliness of agency review of drug, device or biological combination product applications) is directly vested in the Commissioner of Food and Drugs. The governing core legislation, the Federal Food, Drug, and Cosmetic Act (FDCA), is designed to be administered almost exclusively by the Secretary of Health and Human Services. In fact, until 1988, the Commissioner, for all practical purposes, served at the pleasure of the Secretary. The FDCA was modified in 1988 to require that the Commissioner be appointed by the President and confirmed by the Senate. Although now in a more favorable political position, the Commissioner, nevertheless, remains answerable to the Secretary of Health and Human Services, as well as to others in the political system.

The routine administration of the FDCA is conducted by FDA.

Notwithstanding the language of the FDCA, the Secretary has delegated the majority of authority under the act to the Commissioner. In turn, the Commissioner has re-delegated the bulk of the authority received from the Secretary to the Directors of FDA's Centers and regional offices. Delegations and re-delegations under the act can be found in Part 5 of FDA's regulations (21 C.F.R. §§ 5.10, 5.20). Thus, as a practical matter, the routine administration of the FDCA is conducted by FDA. The Secretary, however, has not delegated—and, in fact, has specifically reserved—the authority to approve FDA regulations that present significant public issues involving the quality, availability, marketing or cost of foods, drugs, cosmetics, medical devices, biologics or any other article subject to regulation by FDA. This hierarchy is important to understanding the role of various parts of the government in highly visible and important FDA activities.

FDA is unique among its sister agencies within HHS because of the variety of products and scientific issues it confronts, because of the extensive regulatory and enforcement authority it wields and due to the latitude it has been given to police the domestic and international commerce of the products it regulates. In large part because of the complexity, variety and importance of the issues within its responsibility, FDA frequently has restructured itself in an effort to enhance its efficiency. And, to be successful in its public health mission, the agency has led the way in developing and employing regulatory tools such as rulemaking and advisory committees, and has forged generally strong, collaborative working arrangements with sister agencies and state authorities. In the process, the agency attempts to maintain a workable balance with Congress and its overseers in the executive branch, HHS, and the Office of Management and Budget (OMB).

Because the volume of imported food and medical products is ever increasing, FDA has in recent years dramatically expanded its overseas presence. The agency has established offices in China, India, Africa and Europe in an effort to provide greater access for FDA inspections and to improve understanding and cooperation between FDA and foreign manufacturers as well as between FDA and foreign counterpart regulatory agencies.

How FDA Is Organized: Headquarters and the Field

In 1906 the Bureau of Chemistry of the U.S. Department of Agriculture (USDA), FDA's first lineal ancestor, faced real challenges. At issue was how best to regulate the safety and labeling of foods and drugs in interstate commerce. Right from the start there was recognition that such regulation, to be effective, required not only policy guidance and decision making from a central organization (the Bureau of Chemistry), but also a strong presence throughout the diverse regions of the United States. As a result, "field" laboratories in New York, Boston, Philadelphia, Chicago, New Orleans and San Francisco were established to provide critical reports and information needed to enforce what were viewed as the sweeping provisions of the Pure Food and Drugs Act of 1906.

With the passage of time, the complexity of the challenges confronting FDA has increased dramatically. The agency's regulatory authority extends far beyond the food and drug products subject to the 1906 act. Moreover, whereas the tasks and responsibilities that faced the Bureau of Chemistry in 1906 centered primarily around ensuring against the adulteration and misbranding of food and drugs, the tasks and responsibilities confronting the agency today include the development of scientific and regulatory policy; the expert and prompt scientific review of premarket applications; the comprehensive investigation of an array of diverse manufacturers; the even-handed enforcement of statutory prohibitions and standards; the security of regulated products from tampering and terrorist activity; and the coordination of international policies and regulation to foster trade, yet protect domestic consumers from harmful or bogus products.

The fundamental structure of the agency continues to embrace the concept of a national headquarters for policy and decision making and an extensive, professional field force throughout the country to provide informed, consistent public health decision making and regulatory enforcement.

The agency's structure must accommodate these diverse and broad-ranging initiatives and goals. Although restructuring, or at least tinkering with existing structures, has occurred frequently, the fundamental structure of the agency continues to embrace the concept of a national headquarters for policy and decision making and an extensive, professional field force throughout the country to provide informed, consistent public health decision making and regulatory enforcement.

Headquarters: The Office of the Commissioner

FDA is a highly centralized administrative agency. The Office of the Commissioner is structured with the goal of coordinating agency enforcement activity and public policy and ensuring consistency of approach between various agency components in their interpretation of scientific understanding, application of regulatory requirements, and exercise of discretion and judgment. See Figure 1. Simply put, the Office of the Commissioner is involved in every significant agency activity.

Figure 1

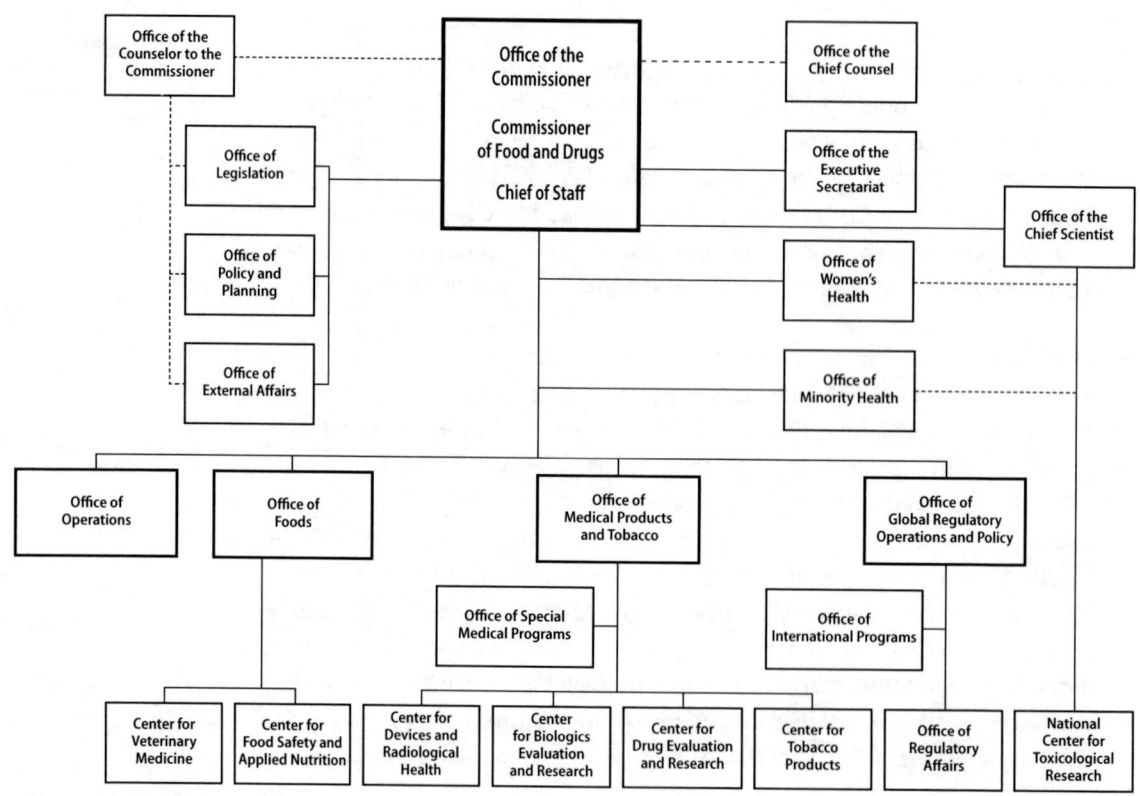

It is not uncommon for the Commissioner's office to be reorganized to reflect a particular administration's or a particular Commissioner's perception of the agency and preferred way of conducting business. The office was most recently reorganized in July 2011. The restructuring included reshaping the Office to allow it to better support the agency's core scientific and regulatory functions. To this end, the Commissioner established four "directorates" to report on and oversee the agency's core functions and responsibilities. The concept behind the restructuring is to unite programs that share common regulatory and scientific foundations. The substantive areas of focus for the four directorates are medical and tobacco products, globalization and import safety, foods and administrative functions. The directorates will be headed, respectively, by the Deputy Commissioner for Medical Products and Tobacco, the Deputy Commissioner for Global Regulatory Operations and Policy, the Deputy Commissioner for Foods and the Chief Operating Officer. The changes reflect the importance of Commissioner-level oversight of the agency's regulation of drugs, medical devices, tobacco and foods, of the agency's efforts with respect to enforcement and globalization, and of the practical reality that such regulation requires critical decision making with respect to the use of available resources.

The new structure has resulted in a shift in the reporting lines of authority and reduced the number of offices in the Office of the Commissioner that report directly to the Commissioner. Now, for example, the Offices of Legislation, Crisis Management, Counterterrorism, and Science and Health Coordination no longer report to the Commissioner but rather to a designated deputy commissioner.

The reorganization appears to leave untouched the direct access to the Commissioner on the part of the agency's substantive centers and its Office of Regulatory Affairs (ORA), the office that coordinates FDA's enforcement activities nationwide. The role of the deputy position for medical products and tobacco, like that of the similar position for foods, is described as "both an advocate and a support for Center directors." FDA centers conduct the bulk of FDA's scientific and regulatory evaluations and interpret and apply FDA's statutory authority over food, drugs, cosmetics, devices and radiological products. The centers are: the Center for Biologics Evaluation and Research (CBER), the Center for Devices and Radiological Health (CDRH), the Center for Veterinary Medicine (CVM), the Center for Drug Evaluation and Research (CDER), the Center for Food Safety and Applied Nutrition (CFSAN) and the Center for Tobacco Products (CTP). Enhancing the communication lines between the Office of the Commissioner and the centers helps ensure that scientific issues are fully aired and understood.

FDA's six centers:
- *Center for Biologics Evaluation and Research (CBER)*
- *Center for Devices and Radiological Health (CDRH)*
- *Center for Drug Evaluation and Research (CDER)*
- *Center for Food Safety and Applied Nutrition (CFSAN)*
- *Center for Tobacco Products (CTP)*
- *Center for Veterinary Medicine (CVM)*

A Closer Look at the Operation of FDA's Six Substantive Centers

Each substantive center possesses the machinery of an administrative agency. Each center has a director and related hierarchy of managers. Moreover, each center has a focal point for policy guidance, programs and enforcement actions, as well as the necessary scientific capabilities to support policy and compliance activities.

Each center has a focal point for policy guidance, programs and enforcement actions, as well as the necessary scientific capabilities to support policy and compliance activities.

Consider, for example, CFSAN. Its offices include but are not limited to: the Office of Food Additive Safety, which provides a centralized coordinated focal point for food and color additive petition review; the Office of Food Defense, Communication and Emergency Response, which provides a single focus for all CFSAN programs affecting food security and protection; the Office of Management Systems, which focuses on administrative processes and the management of resources; and the Office of Regulatory Science, which provides centralized support throughout the center in specialty areas such as mathematics and statistics, pathology, physical chemical analysis, consumer studies, economics and epidemiology. The agency's other five centers are, generally, similarly structured.

Centers are active in responding to policies and programs suggested by the Office of Commissioner or the executive branch. Nonetheless, the mainstay of most Centers' initiatives involves reviewing premarket applications; developing scientific and regulatory policy in the form of guidance documents or regulations; proactively and reactively addressing issues of potential public health concern; preventing, intervening and responding to food-related risks; and ensuring compliance with the food adulteration and misbranding provisions of the FDCA. Thus, as a practical matter, the first stop in dealing with FDA is usually with the Center whose jurisdiction covers the substantive matter at issue. The Office of the Commissioner is unlikely to act in the absence of substantive input from a Center but, particularly in light of current restructuring in the Office of Commissioner, the Commissioner may, although rarely, disagree with a Center's science-based analysis of an issue.

"The Field"

Although the field offices report to the Office of the Commissioner, they have traditionally served—and continue to serve—rather specialized functions related to enforcement of the FDCA and its implementing regulations. The "field" is divided into five regions, each responsible for a distinct part of the country. There are more than 20 "district" offices and over 100 additional resident inspection posts within the regions. See Figure 2.

A regional field office is responsible for agency activities within its boundary. Its primary focus is to ensure that regulated industry within a given region complies with the laws and regulations enforced by the agency. Regional directors report to the Associate Commissioner of Regulatory Affairs who, in turn, reports to the Deputy Commissioner of Operations.

A regional field office is responsible for agency activities within its boundary.

The district offices, as well as the much smaller resident inspection posts, perform the nuts-and-bolts, hands-on work. They inspect the facilities in which regulated products are prepared, packed, manufactured, processed or held,

Figure 2

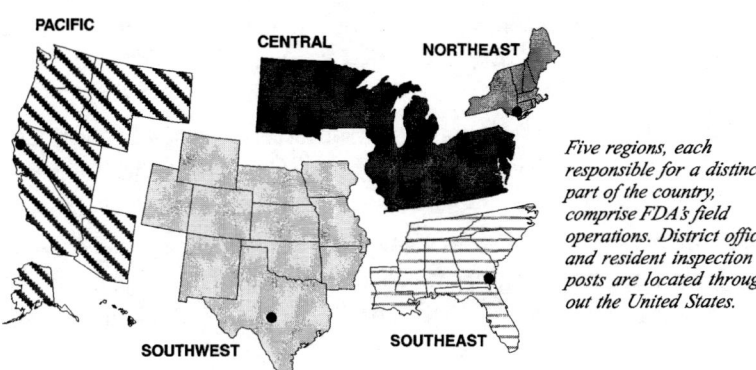

Five regions, each responsible for a distinct part of the country, comprise FDA's field operations. District offices and resident inspection posts are located throughout the United States.

and perform the initial task of evaluating compliance with agency criteria, standards and regulations. These offices also work cooperatively with state, local and other federal agencies; encourage local consumer protection programs in areas related to agency-enforced laws and regulations; and provide valuable consumer education.

Field offices are also an important source of information for headquarters. They are often the first to identify new or emerging problems and trends, future program needs and priorities. Moreover, they refine and improve existing analytical methodologies and explore and develop new monitoring systems (e.g., techniques to detect a specific contaminant in a food or drug product). The field offices also play a major role in managing product recalls, conducting follow-up checks to determine the effectiveness of a recall and preventing recurring violations of the FDCA. The field recommends legal action to headquarters and to the Office of the Chief Counsel or, as necessary, to the U.S. Attorney in its area. A key role for the field involves providing extensive factual and evidentiary support in civil or criminal proceedings.

The Office of the Chief Counsel

Although integral to the functioning of the agency, the Office of the Chief Counsel is not part of FDA. Rather the office is, technically, the Food and Drug Division of HHS's Office of General Counsel. Nevertheless, for all practical purposes, the Office of the Chief Counsel generally has served as FDA's law firm and the Chief Counsel as the Commissioner's lawyer. The Chief Counsel position is currently a career, as opposed to a political, post. The position, however, has on occasion in the past been a political position.

The Office of the Chief Counsel reviews and evaluates the propriety of proposed agency actions to enforce the FDCA, helps defend the agency in litigation,

Although integral to the functioning of the agency, the Office of the Chief Counsel is not part of FDA.

works closely with the centers in developing proposed and final regulations, and generally advises all components of the agency on the requirements of the law and the legal implications of an action or inaction.

The fundamental role of the Office of the Chief Counsel is to measure agency decision making by the prevailing legal standard.

Basically, the role the Office of the Chief Counsel serves in advising various components of the agency is to identify issues of law, policy and fact that are likely to arise in the context of a given initiative and assess the lawfulness of—or perhaps, more precisely, the probability that the agency will prevail in—such issues. Simply put, the fundamental role of the Office of the Chief Counsel is to measure agency decision making by the prevailing legal standard.

So. . . How Does It All Work? A Hypothetical

The interplay among the various components of FDA perhaps can be made more concrete by resort to a hypothetical. Assume a producer of fresh-cut and packaged salad greens fails to follow good agricultural or manufacturing practices in the production of a large lot of product. Assume further that the failure causes an indeterminable number of packages of salad greens to be contaminated with a potentially harmful microorganism. Packages from the lot of salad greens at issue are shipped to retail stores in three states. In time, a few people who have consumed salad greens from packages from the lot in question begin to suffer adverse reactions.

Working independently, two healthcare providers send stool specimens to different clinical laboratories for analysis. In both cases, a strain of *Escherichia coli (E. coli)* is isolated. Both laboratories send the *E. coli* strain to separate public health laboratories which perform DNA finger-printing and submit the pattern to pulse-field gel electrophoresis (PFGE). Additional people become ill and similar testing occurs.

Connecticut is the first state to identify a cluster of *E. coli* cases with matching PFGE patterns. Connecticut health authorities notify the Centers for Disease Control and Prevention (CDC). CDC looks for the strain in other reports of possible outbreaks and quickly confirms matching patterns in the two other states. CDC contacts FDA's Office of Crisis Management, which begins coordinating the agency's internal and external investigational, scientific and communication activities.

CFSAN, ORA, the Office of Public Affairs and the two district offices having jurisdiction in the respective states all become involved. CDC works with the states and FDA to create a standard questionnaire and to develop a process for identifying and reporting cases. Working in cooperation with CDC, FDA districts coordinate investigations to gather information related to the illnesses and identify the possible source of contamination. Meanwhile the Commissioner's office has been preparing for media, consumer and legislative inquiries and has designated an official in the Office of the Commissioner as the primary contact for CFSAN with respect to any new developments concerning the outbreaks.

CFSAN experts, working with CDC experts, identify an apparent association between a number of the outbreaks and consumption of the producer's salad greens. The applicable district office sends investigators to visit the producer's facility and inspect its records, equipment, processing line, and overall harvesting, shipping, cooling and related practices. While that inspection is going on, an FDA laboratory analyst identifies a strain of *E. coli* in one of the open packages of salad greens retrieved by an agency investigator from the home of one of the outbreak victims. The strain matches the infectious strain reported by the state public health laboratories.

Officials in CFSAN immediately contact the chief executive officer (CEO) of the producer, inform him or her of the confirmatory laboratory results, and request the CEO to cease production of product and to begin a recall of all salad green products currently marketed. The CEO requests a short time to consider the information. CFSAN officials consult with the Office of the Chief Counsel, which in turn advises that based on the facts at hand, the center is justified in immediately issuing a public alert on its own initiative and also, working through the FDA District Director in the district where the producer is located, to automatically detain the producer's salad greens in light of the credible evidence indicating that the food presents a threat of serious adverse health consequences. Notified of these developments, the CEO agrees to stop distribution and implement a recall immediately, accompanied by a press release. FDA investigators at the company's facility verify that the product was shipped to only three states and that, therefore, there is no need to alert public health counterparts in other states or in Canada and Mexico.

The immediate threat to health now avoided, officials in CFSAN and the Office of the Commissioner study the implications of the episode particularly in light of similar past episodes involving these products. Learnings from the episode may affect agency efforts to implement and enforce the preventive controls requirements of the Food Safety Modernization Act of 2011 and, accordingly, have the potential to influence agency rulemaking, guidance and enforcement activities.

Meanwhile, the district, in a follow-up inspection of the facility, finds evidence that the producer had reason to suspect the contamination of its products but opted to distribute them. Working closely with the Office of the Chief Counsel

This hypothetical, although bereft of specifics, nevertheless reveals the coordinated approach that FDA routinely applies in handling such public health issues.

and the Office of Criminal Investigations, the district helps develop a criminal action against the producer.

This hypothetical, although bereft of specifics, nevertheless reveals the coordinated approach that FDA routinely applies in handling such public health issues. Field, center, Commissioner's office and the Office of the Chief Counsel work together, combining their respective expertise to address not only the immediate problem but also long-term solutions to avoid or deter comparable threats to public health.

FDA's Administrative and Regulatory Tools and How It Uses Them

Rulemaking

Like all agencies, FDA has finite resources that force it to ask hard questions about the best way to regulate. Before 1970 most regulatory agencies like FDA answered the question in a traditional manner, emphasizing enforcement litigation against products, companies or individuals in violation of the FDCA. There is merit to this approach—particularly for FDA. Because FDA has broad litigation authority, the agency can rely on that authority to bring an array of regulatory actions. It can invoke, for example, the seizure provisions of the act to promptly and efficiently withdraw violative products from the marketplace. In addition, the agency has statutory authority to enjoin manufacturers from producing and marketing violative products. Moreover, FDA has broad authority to recommend that the Department of Justice (DOJ) criminally prosecute, either as a misdemeanor or felony, or both, individuals involved in the interstate commerce of violative products.

FDA pioneered rulemaking as a regulatory tool.

As a regulatory tool, however, there can be practical drawbacks to enforcement litigation. It is time-consuming and resource intensive. It is reactive to a situation or problem. It can encourage a "cop" mentality as opposed to an objective, fact-driven assessment of how best to accomplish statutory and regulatory goals.

By the 1970s the complex issues accompanying the variety of products and the distinctive manufacturing disciplines FDA was charged to police prodded the agency to consider, in addition to litigation, proactive means of encouraging and accomplishing compliance. The primary tool the agency chose for this purpose was "informal" rulemaking. In the process FDA "pioneered" rulemaking as a regulatory tool.

FDA's statutory authority to conduct rulemaking is found in sections 701(a) and 701(e) of the FDCA. Section 701(e) contains "formal" rulemaking authority—authority that involves issuing regulations on the basis of a rulemaking record that may be tested in a quasi-judicial administrative proceeding. Simply put, elaborate procedural safeguards are built into section 701(e) of the act—in fact, the provisions in section 701(e) may be the most elaborate rulemaking procedures under which any federal agency operates.

In stark contrast to section 701(e), section 701(a) is a model of brevity. It reads, in full, as follows: "The authority to promulgate regulations for the efficient enforcement of this Act, except as otherwise provided in this section, is hereby vested in the Secretary."

Under this authority, FDA recognized it could achieve compliance by publishing regulations prescribing how firms interested in being in compliance in the first place could so conform. For example, instead of relying exclusively on seizing misbranded products, the agency recognized that it could publish regulations prescribing how to label a product—e.g., how to name a product, how to craft a principal display panel, how to phrase declarations concerning net weight, sodium content, etc. Instead of relying exclusively on injunctions to force manufacturers to manufacture a food or drug in an appropriate manner, the agency could promulgate regulations containing basic procedures to follow in manufacturing such a product and which, if followed, would enhance the likelihood that a product would not be found to be adulterated or misbranded. Instead of case-by-case consideration of the procedures used by a new drug developer for evaluating data, the agency could issue regulations describing the attributes of a well-controlled investigation, identifying requirements for informed consent, oversight by Institutional Review Boards, etc.

FDA's concept of rulemaking as a regulatory tool was premised on the fundamental notion that regulated industries would, if not welcome, at least follow guidance as to how to manufacture and market compliant, nonviolative products. The notion that an aggressive regulatory agency could enhance its ability to protect the public health by issuing guidance-based regulations was novel in the 1970s. What made the use of rulemaking truly "pioneering," however, was the weight that courts accorded to the agency's regulations.

An agency can issue interpretative or substantive rules.

This is an especially critical point. There are basically two kinds of regulations that an administrative agency can issue. One is "interpretative," the other "substantive." Interpretative rules or regulations are, for purposes of this discussion, synonymous; they contain the agency's view of what the statute means. Enforcement, therefore, is hinged on whether the agency can establish that a particular statutory requirement has been violated. Although an interpretative rule may add persuasive insight to a court's interpretation of the statute, it lacks the force of law and courts are free to disagree with it. A substantive rule or regulation is quite different. It expands an existing substantive provision of law and specifies what that provision requires. If held to be a valid extension of the statutory scheme, a substantive regulation has the force and effect of law—thereby rendering an administrative agency, to an extent, a legislative power.

A string of court cases has recognized the substantive force of a regulation issued under section 701(a). The most notable of these is *Weinberger v. Hynson, Westcott & Dunning*, 412 U.S. 609 (1973), in which the Supreme Court upheld as substantive FDA's regulations defining the fundamental elements of what constitutes "substantial evidence" of effectiveness. By permitting FDA to adopt substantive rules delineating the contours of what constituted an adequate and well-controlled investigation, the court converted controversial questions of scientific fact that normally would be the subject of extensive litigation into the very narrow objective issue of whether a manufacturer complied with the regulation.

The validity of any FDA regulation may be tested in court.

The validity of any FDA regulation may be tested in court. In determining whether a regulation is appropriate, courts focus on whether the statutory scheme and the specific provisions cited by the agency justify the promulgation of the regulation. Such an inquiry focuses on not only the statutory purpose but also such practicalities as the types of enforcement problems that may be encountered and the type of supervision required to accomplish the goals of the FDCA. Moreover, a hallmark of any rulemaking is the "administrative record" compiled by the agency in support of the regulation. The administrative record includes comments received from the public on the agency's initial notice of its proposed regulation. In finalizing a rule, the agency must respond with a reasonable explanation as to why the regulation is legitimate, lawful and supported by the facts.

One of FDA's most creative exercises of its substantive rulemaking authority involved its efforts to regulate the nutrition labeling of food. The FDCA did not mention the word "nutrition" until the passage in 1990 of the Nutrition Labeling and Education Act (NLEA). Nevertheless, nearly 20 years earlier, FDA had embarked on rulemaking initiatives that specifically defined when nutrition food labeling would be necessary, the required format for such information and the criteria by which the adequacy of certain claims (e.g., "low sodium") would be judged. The promulgation of FDA's nutrition labeling regulations in the 1970s effectively prescribed—with the force and effect of law—how an entire industry had to label its products and formulate product claims. This type of rulemaking, as should be readily apparent, is far more efficient industry-wide as an enforcement tool than are individual lawsuits.

Today, FDA continues to rely on its substantive rulemaking authority. The internal process of issuing regulations is somewhat more cumbersome than it was in the 1970s. While the essential elements of informal notice and comment remain the same, the layers of review in the Office of the Commissioner, the Office of the Secretary of Health and Human Services, and OMB in the White House are more numerous. Moreover, concerns such as environmental impacts, economic burdens and paperwork reduction must now be taken into account in every major new regulatory proposal. Nevertheless, the point is as true today as it was decades ago: FDA's ability to issue substantive regulations has changed dramatically how it operates as an administrative agency.

Agency Guidance Documents

Although rulemaking in many ways remains the tool of choice to provide guidance to the regulated community and to gauge regulatory compliance, FDA more and more frequently today resorts to issuing less formal "guidance documents" to assist manufacturers in efficiently dealing with it on matters of mutual interest and concern. The purposes of such "guidance documents" are: 1) to provide assistance by clarifying requirements that have been imposed by Congress or issued by FDA in regulations, 2) to explain how compliance with those statutory and regulatory requirements may be achieved and 3) to outline specific review and enforcement approaches so as to ensure that the agency acts in an effective, fair and consistent manner.

Guidance documents are less formal and assist manufacturers by clarifying requirements, explaining compliance, and outlining specific review and enforcement approaches.

A guidance document, for example, may define what the agency considers to be the important characteristics of preclinical and clinical test procedures, manufacturing practices and scientific protocols. Other guidance documents explain FDA's views on how to comply with relevant statutes and regulations, and how to avoid enforcement actions. CFSAN, for example, has issued guidance documents on issues such as how to submit a food additive petition, the types of changes that constitute a "major change" in an infant formula and thus require documented premarket notification and—with the passage of the NLEA—how to avoid misbranding a product. One of the most successful guidance documents is the agency's "Questions and Answers" publication addressing some of the more common issues raised by the agency's implementation of the NLEA.

FDA distinguishes between "Level 1" and "Level 2" guidance documents. Level 1 guidance documents include documents that set forth initial interpretations of statutory or regulatory requirements, or set forth changes in interpretation or policy that are of more than a minor nature (including complex scientific issues or highly controversial issues). Level 2 guidance documents set forth existing practices or minor changes in the interpretation of a policy.

Before FDA prepares a draft of a Level 1 guidance document, the agency often seeks or accepts early input from individuals or groups outside the agency via public meetings and workshops. After FDA prepares a draft Level 1 guidance, the agency publishes a notice in the *Federal Register* announcing that the draft guidance is available and inviting comment on it. If it wishes, FDA may hold public meetings on the draft guidance or present it to an advisory committee for review. After receiving and reviewing comments, the agency will prepare the final version of the document and publish a notice in the *Federal Register* announcing that the guidance document is available.

No such procedures attend the issuance of a Level 2 guidance. FDA may post and immediately implement a Level 2 guidance document and may request and accept comment.

Guidance documents do not establish legally enforceable rights or responsibilities, and are not legally binding on the public or the agency.

Guidance documents do not establish legally enforceable rights or responsibilities, and are not legally binding on the public or the agency. Rather, they explain how the agency believes relevant statutes and regulations apply to certain regulated activities. Because a guidance document represents the agency's current thinking on a given subject, FDA has formally committed to ensure that its staff does not deviate from it unless there is an appropriate justification and "appropriate supervisory concurrence." Agency guidances are available by request or over the Internet. When dealing with a center on a particular issue, it is critical to ask whether a relevant guidance document exists.

In between regulations and guidance documents are "guidelines." For years, FDA relied on guidelines to refine and explain the principles and details in an existing regulation. Guidelines also have been used by the agency to lay out clinical test procedures, manufacturing practices, product standards, scientific protocols, ingredient specifications and other technical or policy criteria. Because, however, the agency's position has been that a guideline represents the formal position of FDA and obligates the agency to follow it, the agency in recent years has placed far more time and resources into the preparation of guidance documents that do not carry such obligatory force.

Meetings

FDA officials want the agency to be as "transparent" as practicable.

FDA officials want the agency to be as "transparent" as practicable. This posture clearly has evolved over the years as the agency broadened from mere enforcement to helping ensure maximum voluntary compliance on the part of industry. This is not to say that FDA is not an aggressive enforcer when the situation merits; it is. But, in recent years the agency has made real efforts to communicate guiding criteria and standards to help industry steer clear of conduct that could give rise to enforcement-related concerns. In addition to regulations and guidance documents, meetings and correspondence are valuable ways the agency attempts to respond to industry questions, issues and concerns. Meetings can be initiated either by industry or the agency. They may be private or public.

Before a meeting takes place, FDA generally wants the company or group to provide an agenda and a list of attendees. Minutes of every private meeting are prepared and placed on public review in the administrative file of the proceeding. Rather comprehensive regulations govern the conduct of any meeting with the agency. See 21 C.F.R. § 10.65.

Hearings

Another valuable regulatory tool is the administrative "hearing." FDA has extensive regulations governing the conduct of administrative hearings. Formal hearings involving the approval or withdrawal of a licensed product (e.g., under a drug, a food additive, etc.) are conducted generally like formal trials (formal evidentiary public hearings, 21 C.F.R. Part 12) or like scientific boards of inquiry (public hearings before a public board of inquiry, 21 C.F.R. Part 13). Traditionally, these hearings, like most any form of litigation, have been both time-consuming and resource intensive, and, as a result, have become increasingly rare as FDA and industry look to more efficient dispute resolution mechanisms.

Another valuable regulatory tool is the administrative "hearing."

Regulations also govern the procedures to be followed at hearings before the Commissioner or his or her delegate. Public hearings before the Commissioner have served, particularly in the last 15 years, to permit the agency to hear directly from public and industry sectors alike in various locations nationwide, and to collect informed scientific opinion regarding possible agency initiatives or requirements. In implementing the Nutrition Labeling and Education Act, for example, FDA held a series of nationwide hearings regarding the purpose of the food label, and the nature and extent of the nutrition information that should be required to appear on it. The agency also has held hearings on the risks presented by microbial contamination in the manufacture of food and possible procedures designed to prevent such contamination. This type of hearing provides a valuable mechanism for industry and the public to have input in agency policies and practices well before they have been decided.

AGENCY INTERACTION WITH OUTSIDE EXPERTS

Although FDA is a science-based organization possessing a great deal of expertise, outside expert advice has become increasingly critical to its decision making. In part, this is due to the fact that some of the laws administered by the agency (e.g., the Medical Device Amendments of 1976) require the use of outside expert advisory committees. But, in addition, the increasing complexity associated with advances in science and reduced internal resources for developing "in-house" expertise, creates the need to include advice from "outside" experts. This heightened role of outside experts seems likely to increase in the future.

Two key sets of regulations govern FDA's "advisory" committees.

Two key sets of regulations govern FDA's "advisory" committees. The General Services Administration has published regulations that apply to all government advisory committees. See 41 C.F.R. Parts 105-154. These regulations set forth basic policies and procedures regarding the establishment, operation, termination and control of advisory committees.

FDA's own regulations deal with basic administrative aspects that apply to the conduct of an advisory committee. See 21 C.F.R. Part 14. The regulations delineate meeting procedures: what portions of the committee proceedings can be "closed" to the public; the rules of general conduct for a hearing; the preparation of minutes and reports; the maintenance of transcripts; and the handling of public inquiries and requests for advisory committee recommendations. FDA's regulations require that members of an advisory committee must have diverse interests, education, training and experience. They also describe the procedures for nominating voting and nonvoting members to "technical" and "nontechnical" committees. FDA treats all of its current advisory committees as technical committees, which is important because technical committees may have consumer or industry members. In any event, however, only technical experts can serve as voting members. On technical committees, nonvoting members are meant to serve as liaisons between the groups or constituencies they represent and the committee.

The responsibilities and powers of nonvoting members and voting members are similar. The primary difference between them is that a nonvoting member may vote only on procedural matters, such as the adoption of rules or the approval of minutes and future meeting dates. Moreover, a nonvoting member who represents industry, for example, may have access to data and information that constitute a trade secret, or confidential or commercial financial information, only if that member has been appointed as a special government employee.

FDA pays its advisory committee members a fixed daily rate when the committee meets, and also reimburses for travel, food and lodging. While most members are physicians, committee memberships also generally include registered nurses, statisticians, epidemiologists, pharmacists and pharmacologists. In addition to the expert members, one consumer representative and usually one industry representative serve on each committee.

Professional members are recruited through notices published at least once a year in the *Federal Register* and through other means, such as contacting professional organizations and medical schools. Nominations are reviewed by FDA staff and the Commissioner of Food and Drugs. A list of candidates is then submitted to the Secretary of the Department of Health and Human Services for final selection. Committee chairpersons are appointed from among the nominees; they are not elected by their committees. Committee members are subject to federal laws that prohibit them from taking part in any official action in which they have a financial interest. Members must file financial disclosure forms and declare in advance of a meeting any conflict of interest that exists.

FDA'S STANDING ADVISORY COMMITTEES
Office of the Commissioner
Science Board
Risk Communication Advisory Committee
Pediatric Advisory Committee
Center for Biologics Evaluation and Research
Allergenic Products Advisory Committee
Cellular, Tissue, and Gene Therapies Advisory Committee
Blood Products Advisory Committee
Transmissible Spongiform Encephalopathies Advisory Committee
Vaccines and Related Biological Products Advisory Committee
Center for Drug Evaluation and Research
Anesthetic and Life Support Drugs Advisory Committee
Anti-Infective Drugs Advisory Committee
Antiviral Drugs Advisory Committee
Arthritis Drugs Advisory Committee
Cardiovascular and Renal Drugs Advisory Committee
Dermatologic and Ophthalmic Drugs Advisory Committee
Drug Safety and Risk Management Committee
Endocrinologic and Metabolic Drugs Advisory Committee
Gastrointestinal Drugs Advisory Committee

Nonprescription Drugs Advisory Committee
Oncologic Drugs Advisory Committee
Peripheral and Central Nervous System Drugs Advisory Committee
Pharmaceutical Science and Clinical Pharmacology Advisory Committee
Psychopharmacologic Drugs Advisory Committee
Pulmonary-Allergy Drugs Advisory Committee
Reproductive Health Drugs Advisory Committee
Center for Food Safety and Applied Nutrition
Food Advisory Committee
Center for Devices and Radiological Health
Device Good Manufacturing Practice (GMP) Advisory Committee
National Mammography Quality Assurance Advisory Committee
Medical Device Advisory Committee
– Anesthesiology and Respiratory Therapy Devices Panel
– Circulatory System Devices Panel
– Clinical Chemistry and Clinical Toxicology Devices Panel
– Dental Products Panel
– Ear, Nose, and Throat Devices Panel
– Gastroenterology and Urology Devices Panel
– General and Plastic Surgery Devices Panel
– General Hospital and Personal Use Devices Panel
– Hematology and Pathology Devices Panel
– Immunology Devices Panel
– Medical Devices Dispute Resolution Panel
– Microbiology Devices Panel
– Molecular and Clinical Genetics Panel
– Neurological Devices Panel
– Obstetrics and Gynecology Devices Panel
– Ophthalmic Devices Panel
– Orthopaedic and Rehabilitation Devices Panel
– Radiological Devices Panel
Technical Electronic Product Radiation Safety Standards Committee
Center for Tobacco Products
– Tobacco Products Scientific Advisory Committee
Center for Veterinary Medicine
Veterinary Medicine Advisory Committee

National Center for Toxicological Research
Special Studies Relating to the Possible Long-Term Health Effects of Phenoxyl Herbicides
Contaminants Committee (Ranch Hand Committee)
Science Advisory Board

The size of FDA committees ranges from nine to 15 members. The committees vary in the extent to which they are used. The average number of meetings per year per advisory committee is less than two, but that is misleading as one committee could have six meetings and another none.

Committee agendas are created by FDA staff. Most commonly, committees are asked to recommend whether a product should be approved. They also may be asked for advice on policy. A *Federal Register* notice announcing the meeting is published in advance of the date, along with the products or issues to be considered.

Companies prepare extensively to present to advisory committees because the outcome of the committee vote is extremely important to the fate of the product at issue.

Companies prepare extensively to present to advisory committees because the outcome of the committee vote is extremely important to the fate of the product at issue. In the case of a product review, usually both FDA and the manufacturer present their data or analysis. Any member of the public who has so requested also may make a presentation. The presentations, the committee's deliberations, and the final vote—in short, every aspect of the meeting—are on the record. A transcript of the record is made available.

Once a committee has voted and submitted its advice to FDA, the agency is free to follow, or not follow, the advice. In 2007, in an effort to maximize the integrity, consistency and utility of advisory committee voting results, FDA issued a guidance recommending that advisory committees adhere to a process of simultaneous voting in which all members vote at once. According to the guidance, the results of the vote should be announced immediately and how each voted should become part of the public administrative record.

In recent years, the integrity of advisory committees has become increasingly a matter of public focus and attention. The reason is obvious: in the wake of public concern over issues involving the safety of FDA-approved products (e.g., Vioxx), it is considered essential that the input from the agency's expert advisory committees help ensure the credibility of agency decision making. As a result, the disclosure of financial interest information has received legislative as well as agency attention. Effective in October 2007, section 712(c)(2) of the FDCA prohibits advisory committee members from participating in a committee matter if they or any immediate family members have a financial interest that could be affected by the advice proffered. Disqualification may be avoided

Advisory committee members are prohibited from participating in a committee matter if they or any immediate family members have a financial interest that could be affected by the advice proffered.

if FDA grants a waiver. Section 712 and 18 U.S.C. § 208 specify the circumstances under which FDA may grant participation. Section 712 of the FDCA also requires that FDA disclose on its website the type, nature and magnitude of the financial interests of each advisory committee member who has received a waiver.

Based on section 712, FDA issued a guidance detailing procedures for determining whether a conflict of interest exists and, as a result, the eligibility of a candidate to participate in an advisory committee's consideration of a particular matter. The guidance sets out a rather stringent policy for considering eligibility for participation than is permitted under the current legal authorities. Under the approach recommended in the guidance, a member possessing a conflict of interest may participate only in the narrowest of circumstances: where the potential conflict is minimal and the member's expertise is needed for the committee's deliberations.

Specifically, if an individual has a disqualifying financial interest, the combined value of which exceeds $50,000, the member "generally" would not be permitted to participate in an advisory committee meeting on the particular matter in which the conflict arises regardless of the need for the member's expertise. If the disqualifying financial interests are $50,000 or less, the member would be eligible to participate only if he or she meets the applicable statutory standard for participation—the need for his or her services outweighs the potential conflict. Third, if the standard for participation is met, the individual's participation is to be limited to nonvoting. Moreover, in cases where there may be a perception of a conflict of interest, FDA reserves the right to limit participation even though full participation would be permitted under the applicable laws.

In addition to standing advisory committees, FDA has submitted with some regularity over the last two decades projects or problems to outside experts for their consideration and recommended resolution. The agency on occasion has used such highly regarded bodies as the National Academy of Sciences, the National Research Council and the Life Sciences Research Office of the Federation of American Societies for Experimental Biology. Requests for such outside help, as well all the supporting, nonproprietary information reviewed by the outside group, and the final recommendations of such a group, are publicly available and open to public comment.

How FDA Deals and Interacts with Other Federal Agencies

Introduction

Although the laws that FDA administers provide generally comprehensive authority to regulate products, the agency's authority is not always exclusive. In some cases its jurisdiction may overlap with other federal agencies. In other cases, the agency's jurisdiction may simply be complementary. And, in still other cases, its statutory authority may conflict with that of other agencies.

Although these circumstances easily could lead to chaos, they have not. For decades, FDA has relied on agreements and memoranda of understanding (MOUs) to clarify regulatory responsibilities, areas of primary jurisdiction, reciprocal regulatory and information-based roles, and funding responsibilities with other agencies involved in aspects of food and drug regulation.

Agencies with which FDA works closely:
- *U.S. Department of Agriculture*
- *Environmental Protection Agency*
- *Federal Trade Commission*
- *Consumer Product Safety Commission*
- *Drug Enforcement Administration*
- *National Institute on Drug Abuse*
- *Department of State*
- *U.S. Customs Service*
- *Department of Justice*

U.S. Department of Agriculture

Historically, no agency is closer to FDA than USDA. As noted earlier, FDA's predecessor, the Bureau of Chemistry, originated in USDA and undertook its food and drug responsibilities upon enactment of the Pure Food and Drugs Act of 1906. Although the bureau eventually evolved into the Food and Drug Administration in 1930, it remained part of USDA until 1940. Thereupon, FDA became part of the Federal Security Agency which, in turn, became the Department of Health, Education and Welfare and then, as it is now, HHS.

USDA has broad authority over the food supply, including the inspection of meat and poultry and the labeling of food products containing meat or poultry.

USDA continues to have broad authority over the food supply, including the inspection of meat and poultry and the labeling of food products containing meat or poultry. USDA also inspects and grades fresh fruits, vegetables, and grains.

FDA and USDA have entered into scores of MOUs. For example, while FDA has broad authority over the safety and labeling of food, including fresh fruits and vegetables, USDA's Agricultural Marketing Service (AMS) carries out a number of functions designed to aid in the efficient marketing of agricultural products. AMS develops commercial grade standards and specifications for foods, and the rendering of inspection and grading services to producers, processors, shippers, buyers or other interested parties.

MOUs between the two agencies commit AMS to advising FDA of all the food processing and packaging plants operating under AMS supervision, and to report to FDA, for possible enforcement, any processor or packer that has not corrected objectionable conditions found to exist by FDA and who otherwise, based upon AMS's first-hand information, may not have the capability to consistently produce and market quality food. In turn, FDA agrees to work closely with AMS inspectors and cooperate with them in their efforts to grade and inspect produce. Similar agreements exist between FDA and USDA's Animal and Plant Health Inspection Service, Food Safety and Inspection Service (FSIS) and, concerning public education initiatives, the USDA itself.

FSIS and FDA also coordinate efforts in the meat and seafood industries to curtail the contamination of meat, poultry and fish products from harmful microorganisms. The agencies have worked extensively to develop consistent, forward-looking Hazard Analysis and Critical Control Point (HACCP) procedures designed to ensure the safest possible food supply. In accomplishing these ends, there has been a significant exchange between the agencies of scientific data and information, as well as expertise.

USDA, FDA and the Environmental Protection Agency (EPA) coordinate the agencies' respective regulatory authorities over products developed by plant biotechnology, and USDA and FDA coordinate their respective authorities with respect to products developed by animal biotechnology techniques. In 1986 the agencies established the Coordinated Framework for regulating genetically engineered organisms and products. This coordination has been essential in the overall efforts of the federal government to encourage new technologies while at the same time to ensure that every aspect of the use of such technology, from initial investigation to the ultimate production of a consumer product, is carefully and appropriately regulated.

In light of the numerous "overlapping" opportunities in the regulation of food, the notion of vesting one agency with all federal responsibility for food regulation has been considered frequently.

In light of the numerous "overlapping" opportunities in the regulation of food, the notion of vesting one agency with all federal responsibility for food regulation has been considered frequently. Regardless of how this organizational issue is eventually resolved, the cooperative efforts between FDA and USDA have unquestionably formed a foundation for meeting future regulatory challenges involving the evaluation of scientific data, the accommodation of new innovations and how the public health goals of the country's various food safety laws can be applied in a meaningful fashion.

To this end, key provisions of the Food Safety Modernization Act (FSMA) underscore the need for coordination and communication between FDA and USDA if nationwide, and in fact global, food safety concerns are addressed and the nation's infrastructure for assuring food safety is strengthened. FSMA calls for numerous collaborative efforts between FDA and USDA in order to ensure FDA's scope of regulation is as comprehensive and meaningful as possible. For example, section 418 of the FDCA now requires FDA to consult with USDA before conducting a study of the incidence of foodborne illness. Similarly, in section 419, FDA is instructed to coordinate with USDA prior to establishing science-based, minimum standards for the safe production and harvesting of produce. And, in furtherance of this purpose, FDA is to consult with USDA prior to establishing good agricultural practices and guidances with respect to the safe production of fresh fruits and vegetables. Section 420 provides that FDA must, upon consultation with USDA, promulgate regulations to protect against the intentional adulteration of food. Moreover, FDA must work with USDA to develop and submit to Congress a comprehensive "food defense" strategy to ensure an efficient response to agriculture and food emergencies. Clearly, a strong working relationship between FDA and USDA and information sharing, collaboration and meaningful communication between the two agencies are critical to the country's national and global goals of food safety.

EPA and Foods
Two EPA laws directly impact on the food supply: the Federal Insecticide, Fungicide, and Rodenticide Act (FIFRA) and the Safe Drinking Water Act (SDWA).

Environmental Protection Agency

EPA administers two laws that have direct impact on the food supply: the Federal Insecticide, Fungicide, and Rodenticide Act (FIFRA) and the Safe Drinking Water Act (SDWA). FIFRA governs the registration of pesticides. Without such registration, a pesticide cannot be sold lawfully for use in the United States. A major part of the registration process for food use pesticides involves tolerance setting, which is conducted under section 408 of the FDCA. EPA was vested with this tolerance-setting authority in 1970 pursuant to a reorganization plan. As a result, EPA determines the safety of pesticide residues in food, while FDA takes enforcement action under the FDCA for products violating the standards established by EPA.

Under the SDWA, EPA controls contaminants in drinking water that may have adverse effects on the public health. The SDWA gives exclusive control over the safety of public water to EPA. FDA, however, always has considered drinking water to be a food under section 201(f) of the FDCA. Through an MOU both parties agreed that the passage of the SDWA in 1974 implicitly repealed FDA's authority under the FDCA over water used for drinking purposes (although section 410 of the FDCA makes clear that FDA retains exclusive control over bottled drinking water). The MOU goes on to establish that EPA in essence controls all aspects related to the safety of water prior to the water coming out of a public tap, and that water used as an ingredient in food or in food processing remains subject to the FDCA.

FDA and EPA also share authority over chemical additives. The Toxic Substances Control Act (TSCA) gives EPA authority to regulate mixtures of chemical substances and articles containing such substances or mixtures. EPA can require testing of a chemical substance or a mixture based on possible unreasonable risk of injury to health or the environment. Under TSCA, for example, EPA regulates the addition of direct and indirect additives to drinking water. The agencies have agreed that the appropriate interpretation of TSCA excludes from the definition of "chemical substance" products regulated under the FDCA.

The commonality of safety concerns presented by the products regulated by each agency (the toxicity of pesticides, chemical substances and additives to food or water) has resulted in significant efforts between FDA and EPA to coordinate their scientific approaches to assessing the safety of such substances. MOUs provide general guidance and encouragement to the agencies in accomplishing such harmonization. Nevertheless, differences in opinion as to how most accurately to assess risks do exist between the two agencies. For example, only recently, after years of debate, FDA decided to accept EPA's use of "scaling factors" in extrapolating the results of data from laboratory animals to assess their significance and relevance to the health of people.

The Federal Trade Commission

FTC and FDA
FTC and FDA work together under a 1971 liaison agreement.

FDA and the Federal Trade Commission (FTC) possess concurrent jurisdiction over the labeling and advertising of foods, over-the-counter drugs, veterinary drugs and related products, and cosmetics. The two agencies have agreed that the FTC should exercise primary responsibility concerning the advertising of such products, and that FDA will do likewise for matters relating to product labeling. Accordingly, under the Federal Trade Commission Act (FTC Act), the FTC investigates and prosecutes "unfair methods of competition" including "unfair or deceptive practices" and "methods of competition." The FTC's goal is to protect consumers from unfair and deceptive advertising and marketing practices, and to prohibit unfair trade practices that could impact on competitive markets and business relationships. FDA's jurisdiction over product labeling is more consumer oriented, and is designed to ensure that products and all the printed graphic or related material that may accompany their sale do not mislead consumers and are presented in a truthful, unambiguous manner.

By virtue of a "liaison agreement" entered into in 1971, the agencies coordinate their activities, and share information and expertise. The arrangement, however, is complicated by the fact that substantiation requirements for labeling under the FDCA are more stringent than those for advertising under the FTC Act. Thus, on occasion, the FTC is placed in the position of appearing more lax in its enforcement posture when compared to FDA. The FTC's unique enforcement powers, however, which include adjudication by the five FTC commissioners as well as the ability to issue cease and desist orders enforceable by injunctive, civil penalty and criminal contempt proceedings, compensate for whatever lesser substantiation standard the agency may possess.

In many cases, the FTC's follow through in enforcing advertising is important, if not essential, to FDA initiatives over labeling. For example, FDA's comprehensive efforts to implement the NLEA and limit the type of health-related information that may be communicated about the relationship between a component of a diet and the prevention of a disease or health-related condition would be severely diluted if the FTC did not endorse a comparable regulatory philosophy with regard to the advertising of such food components. Working together on this issue the two agencies have developed a comprehensive approach to regulating and ensuring the comparability of health claims on food.

The FTC has also played an important role in helping FDA adapt to judicial precedent requiring FDA to consider the commercial speech implications of any regulatory effort with respect to product misbranding. The FTC's history of relying upon 1) consumer survey data to show that a given advertising claim has the potential to mislead and 2) disclaimers to cure any such potential has provided a helpful framework for FDA in considering enforcement and regulatory policy concerning the lawful contours of product promotion.

Consumer Product Safety Commission

The Consumer Product Safety Act protects the public from unreasonable risks of injury associated with consumer products. The Consumer Product Safety Commission (CPSC) was formally established in 1973. A major component was FDA's Bureau of Product Safety, established in the early 1960s to administer provisions of the Federal Hazardous Substances Act relating to the labeling of products presenting consumer hazards.

CPSC
FDA generally prevails in jurisdiction questions with CPSC.

In spite of, or perhaps because of, the etiology of CPSC, disputes arose quite early between the two agencies over jurisdictional points. Whereas FDA believed that a container having a food contact surface should be regulated by FDA as a "food additive" (i.e., because of the potential for migration of a component to the food), CPSC considered such an article within its jurisdiction as a consumer commodity. After much discussion, the agencies agreed to draw the jurisdictional line on the basis of whether an article could cause contamination or spoilage of food as a result of migrating to or otherwise becoming a component of food. Under this approach, home canning equipment that fails to provide a seal adequate to keep air from passing into stored food is regulated by CPSC, as are pressure cookers, slow cookers, refrigerators or freezers that fail to perform at proper temperatures thereby rendering food unfit to eat. A food container that presents the possibility of components migrating into the food itself (e.g., lead leeching from the soldered lining of a tin can into the food or beverage) would be regulated by FDA as a food contaminant or additive.

This focus on the "mechanical" versus "component" nature of a hazardous substance has come to form the fundamental distinction between CPSC and FDA jurisdiction. Thus, FDA retains its basic jurisdiction over foods, medical devices, drugs and cosmetics except in those cases where the container of such articles possesses a defect such as sharp edges or a propensity to explode or break. Such situations are regulated by CPSC.

Disputes between the two agencies continue on occasion, and are resolved either informally or through the somewhat time-consuming process of issuing an advisory opinion. In close-call situations, FDA generally prevails, perhaps because of its more efficient and successful track record in enforcement litigation.

The Drug Enforcement Administration, the National Institute on Drug Abuse and the U.S. Department of State

FDA, DEA, NIDA and DoS share in the federal regulation of drugs of abuse.

Federal regulation of drugs of abuse is a shared enterprise among four distinct entities: FDA, the Drug Enforcement Administration (DEA), National Institute on Drug Abuse (NIDA) and the U.S. Department of State (DoS). One area of joint enterprise is establishing "schedules" for drugs of abuse. The "schedules" establish the level of control in the manufacture, importing, prescribing or handling of drugs of abuse.

Acting on behalf of the Secretary of the Department of Health and Human Services, FDA has the authority to make domestic drug scheduling recommendations, which, in turn, determine the level of control that will accompany an addictive substance under the Controlled Substances Act. DEA, however, conducts the relevant scheduling proceedings and administers the scheduling, amendment or repeal of any domestic classification. NIDA, by formal agreement with FDA, provides FDA with recommendations and views regarding the addictive potential of a drug substance. FDA, DEA and DoS collaborate on issues relating to the administration of international treaties governing the scheduling and classification of narcotics and psychotropic drugs. FDA, NIDA and DEA also collaborate in administering provisions of the Narcotic Addict Treatment Act that establishes a basis for control of narcotic addict treatment programs to prevent the diversion of narcotic drugs, and to ensure proper treatment of narcotic addicts. All of these relationships are spelled out in MOUs.

Responsibility among the agencies in these areas is generally well defined. FDA and NIDA limit their focus to scientific factors relating to the safety, pharmacology and addiction potential. DEA implements the scientific findings of FDA and NIDA, and conducts comprehensive enforcement of the control, distribution and diversion of scheduled substances. In the context of narcotic addict treatment programs, including methadone, FDA and DEA work closely together, with FDA obtaining DEA approval prior to authorizing any treatment program. Both FDA and DEA maintain the authority to deny or revoke approval of a treatment program independent of each other.

U.S. Customs Service

Perhaps in no other area of food and drug regulation does FDA have broader authority than it does over imported products. FDA exercises that authority in conjunction and cooperation with the U.S. Customs Service. Section 801(a) of the FDCA permits FDA to refuse admission to an imported article if "it appears" that the article is in violation of the act. FDA has no burden to prove that a product for import actually violates the act. The fundamental test for refusal merely rests upon the "appearance" of a violation—a standard that, when considered literally, is impossible for the agency not to meet should it believe a product to be violative.

Perhaps in no other area of food and drug regulation does FDA have broader authority than it does over imported products.

Customs' authority over imports arises under the Tariff Act of 1930 as well as under section 801. Section 801 vests the Secretary of the Treasury with the authority to deliver samples of imported products to FDA for analysis. In actual practice, FDA personnel at most ports collect the samples, issue the appropriate notice of sampling and, where applicable, having determined that an article is in violation and may not be brought into compliance, issue a refusal notice. If FDA does not have the personnel to carry out these functions, Customs will do so in close cooperation with agency officials.

In 1979, Customs and FDA entered into an MOU formalizing this process, and delegating to FDA the authority to collect samples, issue notices of sampling and issue notices of refusal of admission. The MOU permits designation of FDA employees as Customs officers. If an importer wishes to recondition a violative product or to contest a refusal of admission, a bond must be filed. Only Customs can issue the bond. Although FDA can admit a product to import, Customs still must release the product for entry into the market.

Policing the safety of imported food is perhaps FDA's most daunting job. Currently, more than $65 billion worth of food products is imported annually. The sheer volume precludes inspection of every imported product and, as a practical matter, demands the cooperation FDA and the Customs Service has forged. The problems presented by potentially violative products being introduced through import regularly invite congressional scrutiny of FDA actions and consideration of ways, usually through greater resources, to augment FDA's and the Customs Service's abilities to protect the public from risks presented by imported products.

Notably, in 2002 Congress passed legislation designed to help reduce the ability of international terrorists to contaminate foods imported into the United States. The legislation requires food importers to provide FDA with advance notice of shipments of human and animal food imported or offered for import into the United States. This advance information permits FDA, in conjunction with U.S. Customs, to channel resources and target inspections—a necessity in light of the fact that every day FDA receives approximately 25,000 notifications with respect to incoming shipments of food. The legislation also authorizes FDA to ask Customs to institute a temporary hold for 24 hours on any food offered for import if FDA has credible evidence or information indicating that the food presents a threat of serious adverse harm and FDA is unable to immediately inspect or examine the food.

In sum, as a legal—and practical—matter, import issues demand daily cooperation between FDA and Customs. The case can be made that, in light of the volume of FDA-regulated products imported annually, coordination between the two agencies is more crucial to the public health than the coordination between FDA and any other agency.

Department of Justice

Going to Court
FDA cannot go to court itself; it is always represented by the Department of Justice.

FDA does not possess independent authority to represent itself in judicial proceedings. As is the case with most other federal agencies, FDA is represented in court by DOJ. DOJ's Office of Consumer Litigation is the primary overseer of agency-related litigation—litigation that may be either enforcement-based (i.e., brought by the government) or defensive in nature. Because of the frequent science-based expertise that comes into play in FDA-related litigation, DOJ has historically and continues to welcome participation by lawyers from FDA's Office of the Chief Counsel in the conduct of such litigation. Although occasionally characterized by differences in litigation strategy or assessments of legal empowerment, FDA and DOJ generally have worked well together in defending agency actions and in enforcing the provisions of the FDCA—as the agency's successful litigation track record bears out.

Centers for Disease Control and Prevention

FDA's sister agency, CDC, plays an important complementary and nonregulatory public health role.

Although FDA unquestionably has the lead responsibility within HHS for ensuring the safety of food and the safety and effectiveness of drugs and devices, FDA's sister agency, CDC, has an important complementary and nonregulatory public health role. As the lead federal agency for conducting disease surveillance, CDC monitors the occurrence of illness and outbreaks in the United States attributable to food and other FDA-regulated products. The disease surveillance systems coordinated by CDC constitute an essential information network for early warnings about dangers presented by regulated products.

With respect to food in particular, CDC's surveillance systems are helpful in measuring federal, state and local initiatives to reduce foodborne illness. Moreover, CDC's surveillance systems are critical indicators of new and changing patterns of foodborne illness. CDC, time and again, has been able to promptly alert FDA of products implicated in foodborne disease and has provided both agencies with expert scientific opinion on the effectiveness of foodborne disease prevention strategies.

Recognizing the unique expertise of CDC, FSMA provides explicit direction to CDC to take a lead role in food safety surveillance of foodborne illness outbreaks. Section 205(a) of FSMA defines "food-borne illness outbreak" in as broad terms as possible: "the occurrence of two or more cases of a similar illness resulting from the ingestion of a certain food." Paragraph (b) requires CDC to "enhance food-borne illness surveillance systems" and to improve the collection, analysis, reporting and usefulness of data on foodborne illnesses. As a practical matter, CDC has performed these functions for years without the specific authorization FSMA now provides. CDC is now statutorily empowered to take the lead in coordinating federal, state and local foodborne surveillance systems, including complaint systems, and increasing participation in national networks of public health and food regulatory agencies and laboratories. CDC is also required to facilitate the sharing of surveillance information, develop improved epidemiological tools, obtain quality exposure data and microbiological methods for classifying cases, augment such systems to improve attribution of a foodborne illness outbreak to a specific food, and expand the capacity of such systems to identify new or rarely documented cases of foodborne illness.

CDC's role in providing critical expertise with respect to disease control and prevention will only increase in the coming years. With that increased role, however, comes the potential for the two agencies to hold inconsistent or divergent positions. Ultimately, any FDA regulatory action based on a potential public health threat identified by CDC must be evaluated in light of the governing legal standards FDA is charged to enforce.

Because it is not a regulatory agency, however, CDC is unconstrained by statutory burdens of proof and is free to opine on the extent and severity of potential hazards it defines. Apparent, or real, conflicts between the two agencies can arise. Consider, for example, the use of the compound Bisphenol A (BPA) in plastic bottles. FDA initially advised that the food contact uses of BPA were "safe" within the meaning of existing regulatory standards. CDC, on the other hand, has taken the more aggressive public position that more study and investigation are needed to assess whether BPA, which may have hormone-like effects on the reproductive system, is not, in fact, injuring consumers. The extent to which the two agencies work together to harmonize discordant views and, where such views remain at odds, to help educate consumers as to why each view is responsibly held, is a coordination goal worthy of attention.

Other Agencies

Other agencies play critical roles in FDA's ability to efficiently exercise its jurisdiction. FDA has developed MOUs or agreements with these agencies to ensure cooperation, including the exchange of scientific information and investigative evidence. These other agencies and their areas of overlapping interests include: the Nuclear Regulatory Commission (licensing and regulation of the nuclear industry, and knowledge and information regarding radiation); the Federal Bureau of Investigation (Federal Anti-tampering Act implementation); the National Marine Fisheries Service (voluntary seafood inspection program); the Department of Homeland Security (bioterrorism concerns); and the Bureau of Alcohol, Tobacco and Firearms (the regulation of alcoholic beverages and tobacco).

FDA AND CONGRESS

For any federal agency, Congress basically has three distinct functions: legislative (the development, modification or repeal of legislation); oversight (overseeing how the agency is administering its legislative authority); and appropriations (funding agency programs).

Particularly within the last two decades, FDA has paid increasing attention to managing its relations with Congress.

Particularly within the last two decades, FDA has paid increasing attention to managing its relations with Congress. The Office of Legislative Affairs (OLA) in the Office of the Commissioner is the agency's primary liaison with Capitol Hill. OLA initiates, coordinates and provides in-depth analyses of agency legislative needs and prepares supporting documents and position papers not only for the Commissioner and agency officials but also for Congress and OMB. A large part of OLA activities also involves responding to congressional and legislative inquiries— inquiries that from time to time may involve sensitive correspondence critical of agency action or inaction. In cooperation with the FDA centers, OLA coordinates hearings before Congress and coordinates briefings with congressional members and staff.

FDA decisions affect, sometimes dramatically, discrete constituencies. As a result, FDA issues are often lightning rods for congressional attention. The resulting congressional oversight hearings can be contentious affairs that can affect the course of agency regulation and decision making. Saccharin, infant formulas, AIDS treatments, dietary supplements, the pace of product approvals, tobacco and numerous other issues have been the subject of high-publicity, high-profile and intense congressional scrutiny. FDA takes these encounters seriously and treats them with enormous care. A large part of FDA's role at any congressional hearing involves education—concise, clear explanations of the roles scientific data, public policy and legal requirements have in the melding of its positions, decisions and practices.

FDA issues are often lightning rods for congressional attention.

Several House and Senate committees have a degree of jurisdiction over FDA activity. As a vestige of FDA's days as part of USDA, the Agricultural Subcommittees of the House and Senate Appropriations Committees continue to review and determine FDA's annual appropriation. The agency's authorizing committees, however, are the House Committee on Energy and Commerce and the Senate Committee on Labor and Human Resources. The House Subcommittee on Oversight and Investigations and the Subcommittee on Health and the Environment traditionally have been very active in surveying and directing agency activity. Other committees with FDA-related responsibilities include, in the Senate, the Committee on Agriculture, Nutrition, and Forestry and the Committee on Governmental Affairs and, in the House of Representatives, the Committee on Agriculture, the Committee on Government Operations, the Committee on Merchant Marine and Fisheries, the Committee on Science, Space and Technology and the Committee on Small Business.

Another feature of FDA's congressional relations involves the Government Accountability Office (GAO), formerly known as the General Accounting Office. Since the early 1970s, GAO has been called upon by Congress to investigate and report back to Congress on an array of FDA-related matters. As a result, a significant part of FDA's congressional activity is spent in cooperation with GAO in its investigations. OLA coordinates agency responses and serves as the primary liaison with GAO.

FDA AND ITS RELATIONS WITH THE STATES

FDA's ability to efficiently regulate hinges to a certain extent on its relationship with state and local authorities. Although FDA possesses the lion's share of regulatory authority, states nevertheless play an important role in public health protection. Every state has a food and drug act, in most cases patterned quite closely upon the FDCA. Moreover, local authorities may have specific regulations or ordinances governing product labeling, weight, and related attributes.

Every state has a food and drug act, in most cases patterned quite closely upon the FDCA.

The Association of Food and Drug Officials of the United States and the Association of Official Analytical Chemists generally work closely with FDA to accomplish the public health protection goals of both the FDCA and its state counterparts. State food and drug officials often are trained by FDA and, in return, provide valuable service to FDA in enforcing provisions of the FDCA. In the food area, for example, an extensive array of model codes governing the sanitation of milk and other retail foods characterize the cooperation between FDA and state officials. In general, FDA prepares the model codes and ensures that they contain the latest and best scientifically based advice about food safety issues. The agency also helps implement the codes at the state level. These codes recognize that thousands of local and state agencies assume the frontline responsibility for inspecting and enforcing food safety laws.

In recent years FDA has intensified these initiatives with the development of a model Food Code designed to prevent foodborne illness. Although neither federal law nor federal regulation, the Food Code provides the states with FDA's best advice for a uniform system of regulation to ensure that food is safe and properly protected at the retail and food service level.

FDA's substantive licensing decisions concerning food additives, drugs and medical devices generally are deferred to by the states.

FDA's substantive licensing decisions concerning food additives, drugs and medical devices generally are deferred to by the states. From time to time a state (e.g., California, under its ballot referendum legislation Proposition 65) may wish to impose an additional requirement, such as a warning, on an FDA authorized product but this is rare.

Under the NLEA and the Safe Medical Device Amendments of 1990, FDA possesses express preemption authority over inconsistent state requirements. The agency also has extensive implied preemption authority under the Supremacy Clause and the Commerce Clause of the U.S. Constitution. The agency, however, rarely seeks to exercise its preemptive authority over state actions. The agency's policy regarding preemption reflects a general presumption against preemption, and favors working together with state authorities to make the state and federal schemes at issue consistent with one another. On occasion these efforts have not been successful and the agency has preempted with regular success, thereby rendering null and void inconsistent state requirements or activities (e.g., state efforts to regulate imitation food labeling in a manner inconsistent with FDA's nationwide efforts have been found, by two U.S. Courts of Appeals, to be preempted).

Part of FDA's deference to and willingness to work with states, and thereby avoid preemption, is grounded in the recognition that states provide FDA needed support in conducting regulated facility and manufacture inspections, in accomplishing significant product recalls and in collecting valuable enforcement- and compliance-related information (the nature and extent of these various state activities are contained in scores of MOUs with the agency). These examples of state assistance provide very real deterrents to actions by FDA—like preemption—that could be viewed as being meaningfully at odds with long-term federal and state relations.

FDA's International Relations

For years FDA has inspected foreign new drug manufacturers who wish to market their products in the United States, processed and granted approvals for the export of investigational new drugs, negotiated MOUs on regulatory matters and agreements with foreign governments, and conducted international training programs and conferences. Although FDA continues these important activities, its most fundamental international function today involves efforts to "harmonize" international enforcement and trade-related matters. The initial impetus for this focus arose from the Uruguay Round Agreement on Tariffs and Trade (also referred to as GATT), the Agreement on the Application of Sanitary and Phytosanitary Measures and the Agreement on Technical Barriers to Trade.

Recognizing the importance of assisting appropriate foreign governmental entities in understanding and implementing measures to provide for the safety of food regulated by FDA and exported by such country to the United States, Congress, in passing FSMA, required that FDA establish offices in foreign countries. In addition to envisioning the educational role such offices are to perform, Congress contemplated that the offices would also conduct "risk-based inspections" of imported foods and would support inspections by foreign government entities. The new requirement reinforced FDA's prior decision to expand its overseas presence in an effort to provide greater access for FDA inspections and for greater engagement with foreign industry and foreign counterpart agencies. FDA has opened offices in China, India, Latin America and Europe. Operating from its headquarters, FDA has also opened offices focused on Africa and the Middle East.

FDA's most fundamental international function today involves efforts to "harmonize" international enforcement and trade-related matters.

For years, FDA's Office of International Programs (OIP) has been the focal point for the agency's international efforts. OIP has been dedicated to achieving FDA's mission of ensuring the integrity of all imported regulated products by collaborating with international health and regulatory partners with respect to the proper operation of foreign facilities engaging in technical cooperation and training. Overseas presence not only helps achieve the goal of compliant imported regulated products but also builds stronger cooperative relationships .

As might be expected, FDA's international affairs staff in the Office of the Commissioner works closely with the Office of the U.S. Trade Representative and various trade groups in dealing with issues arising from these agreements. FDA also participates with the Codex Alimentarius Commission to develop international standards regarding the safety and sanitation of food. Moreover, FDA works closely with foreign governments to harmonize international technical requirements for pharmaceuticals and biologics, international vaccines, and cosmetics and veterinary drugs.

Although FDA activities in this area are largely overseen by the Office of the Commissioner, experts in each of the agency's centers are actively involved. Moreover, FDA publishes for comment in the *Federal Register* the procedures it proposes to follow and the criteria it believes appropriate on which to base harmonization decisions.

FDA AND THE EXECUTIVE BRANCH

FDA is a component of HHS. Thus, it is part of the executive branch. Accordingly, the agency's activities are not only subject to oversight from or by the Secretary of Health and Human Services but also from OMB. Thus, the agency's major regulatory initiatives and rulemaking proposals, legislative proposals, congressional appearances and testimony, and budgetary requests are subject to review, scrutiny and approval by OMB. OMB's oversight of FDA budget requests is not new, but OMB's oversight and review of agency rulemaking and related initiatives begun under the Carter administration in the late 1970s was increased under the Reagan administration, and continues through today.

The HHS Office of Inspector General has the authority to investigate fraud and "abuses" of FDA's substantive program authority.

One additional source of FDA oversight resides in the Inspector General (IG) of HHS. The IG has the authority to investigate fraud and "abuses" of FDA's substantive program authority. In the late 1980s and early 1990s the IG was involved in a number of issues concerning the agency, most notably a series of matters arising from the agency's administration of its generic drug approval program.

Conclusion

Over the years, the fundamental structure of FDA, however, has remained unchanged: the Office of the Commissioner, the substantive centers and the field offices form the nucleus of agency activity and initiatives. Relations with sister agencies are generally positive and based on years of collaboration and compromise, with only an occasional incident of controversy. The agency also has developed tools, such as rulemaking and advisory panels, to enhance its ability to function efficiently and in a substantively and scientifically sound way.

The agency's evolution from a small bureau in USDA to a very visible and active component of HHS reveals the development of a highly specialized agency that can adapt and adjust to increased regulatory burdens. By and large, the processes and structures put into place by both Congress and FDA have provided regulation that is commensurate with the risks to be prevented and the goals to be achieved.

Among the more intractable problems that confront the agency today is the issue of resources. The pressure placed upon an agency with as many public health responsibilities as FDA to address and resolve complex public health issues with ever diminishing resources is enormous. As a result, the agency's cooperative efforts with sister agencies, state authorities and international governments appear likely to increase over time. Moreover, reliance on outside expertise and substantive transparent efforts by industry at voluntary compliance are likely to be key components of any agency effort to continue to function effectively.

Among the more intractable problems that confront the agency today is the issue of resources.

Chapter 5

The Drugs/Biologics Approval Process

Geoffrey M. Levitt, Pfizer Inc, New York, NY

Key Points

- The new drug application (NDA) and biologics license application (BLA) processes follow a series of defined phases, including:
  1) preclinical investigation (laboratory and animal testing);
  2) clinical investigation (human testing);
  3) Food and Drug Administration (FDA) review of the application;
  4) postmarketing.
  Each of these phases involves varying levels of FDA oversight.

- At the preclinical phase, there is little direct FDA oversight. If proper practices and guidelines are not observed, however, the applicant's ability to use preclinical data in support of its application may be jeopardized.

- Clinical investigation is carried out under much closer FDA supervision. During this phase, the applicant must file an investigational new drug application (IND) with FDA before beginning new clinical studies, and must operate under rules and procedures designed to protect the rights and safety of human subjects. In addition, the applicant normally consults closely with FDA on the design of human studies (particularly in the later stages) with the goal of ensuring that the studies will support approval of its NDA or BLA.

- The FDA review phase is initiated by submission of the NDA or BLA. This phase is typically characterized by an ongoing dialogue between the applicant and FDA, wherein the applicant answers the agency's questions and tries to satisfy its concerns. If FDA concludes the drug is safe and effective for its intended use or uses, this phase culminates in approval; if not, the NDA or BLA may be denied (or more often, withdrawn for an overhaul).

- The abbreviated new drug application (ANDA) is an important variant of the NDA. With an ANDA, the applicant must pass all the same hurdles as for a full NDA, with one critical exception: the ANDA applicant does not have to demonstrate the safety and efficacy of its drug. Instead, the ANDA relies on the proven safety and efficacy of an already approved drug to which it refers (the "reference drug"). Therefore, the ANDA applicant, instead of showing safety and efficacy, must show that its drug will work the same in the body (i.e., will be "bioequivalent") to that reference drug.

* The author gratefully acknowledges the assistance of Natalie Zaidman of the Pfizer Legal Division in preparing this updated chapter.

Key Points, continued

- The biosimilar application is an analogous variant of the BLA. The biosimilar applicant must show that its product is "highly similar" to its reference approved biological product and that there are no "clinically meaningful differences" between the biosimilar and the reference product in terms of safety, purity or potency. In contrast to an ANDA, the standards for approval of a biosimilar are more flexible and rely more heavily on FDA's scientific judgment. As the biosimilars authority is still quite new, there is still a great deal of room for development of these standards in practice.

- There are various forms of exclusivity that are of concern to both NDA/ANDA and BLA/biosimilar applicants, including patent protection, statutory exclusivity, potential generic or biosimilar exclusivity for qualifying ANDA or biosimilar applicants, and orphan exclusivity.

- Various mechanisms exist for expedited availability of a drug or biologic, including treatment investigational new drug applications (under which an investigational product is distributed more widely than otherwise, and for more treatment-oriented purposes) and fast-track approval (under which a drug or biologic that shows potential to address unmet therapeutic needs for serious or life-threatening diseases is given priority treatment by FDA). These mechanisms are worth bearing in mind for the new drug or biologic applicant as a way of obtaining wider and/or faster access to the market.

INTRODUCTION

Before a new drug or biologic may be lawfully marketed in the United States, it must be approved by the Food and Drug Administration.

Before a new drug or biologic may be lawfully marketed in the United States, it must be approved by the Food and Drug Administration (FDA). In reality, there is not one single FDA approval framework that covers all drugs and biologics, but rather a set of distinct frameworks, each of which applies to a specific category of product. These include new drug approvals, abbreviated new drug approvals, the over-the-counter (OTC) review process, new animal drug approvals, abbreviated new animal drug approvals, biologics and biosimilars.

All these frameworks have some important elements in common, but also some key differences. The new drug approval process is, in many ways, the standard model and provides a basic framework for understanding the other processes.

FDA Drug Review: The New Drug Application

What Is a "Drug"? What Is a "New Drug"?

Under section 201(g)(1) of the Federal Food, Drug, and Cosmetic Act (FDCA), a "drug" includes: 1) articles recognized in the U.S. Pharmacopoeia, the U.S. Homeopathic Pharmacopoeia or the National Formulary; 2) articles "intended for use in the diagnosis, cure, mitigation, treatment, or prevention of disease"; 3) articles (other than food) "intended to affect the structure or any function of the body"; and 4) articles intended for use as a component of any of the above. "New drug," as defined in section 201(p) of the FDCA, means virtually any drug that first came onto the market, or is offered for entry onto the market, after the enactment of the act in 1938 (which includes the overwhelming majority of drugs in existence today), unless the drug is "generally recognized as safe and effective"—a category whose main practical importance is in the context of OTC drugs. A "new drug" must have an approved new drug application (NDA), or one of the recognized variants of an NDA, such as an abbreviated new drug application (ANDA), to be marketed lawfully in the United States.

Although the specifics of product development and FDA review may differ for each new drug product, the process of bringing a new compound onto the market generally follows a series of defined phases: preclinical investigation, clinical trials, submission and review of the NDA and postmarketing.

Preclinical Investigation

The first stage in a drug's regulatory life cycle is preclinical investigation. The basic goals of preclinical investigation are: 1) to identify the potential effects in the body of the chemical substance being investigated, through laboratory experimentation and animal testing; and 2) to gather enough evidence on the potential new drug to determine if it is reasonably safe to begin preliminary trials in humans.

The first stage in a drug's regulatory life cycle is preclinical investigation.

Unlike human clinical trials, prior notification to FDA is not required to begin a preclinical investigation, although the preclinical phase is subject to specific FDA regulations known as good laboratory practices (GLPs). Unapproved new drugs shipped interstate as part of a preclinical investigation are exempted from the FDCA's general prohibition on interstate shipments of unapproved drugs as long as the drugs are appropriately labeled and adequate records of shipment and receipt are maintained. FDA may, however, terminate a preclinical investigator's ability to ship unapproved drugs if it determines that continuing the investigation is unsafe or otherwise contrary to the public interest, or that the drugs are being used for purposes other than bona fide scientific investigation.

Direct FDA involvement in a preclinical investigation ordinarily comes at the conclusion of the investigation, when the agency reviews the investigational new drug application (IND) that the drug sponsor submits prior to beginning human clinical trials. FDA then evaluates the soundness of the data the sponsor has gathered through preclinical investigation, as well as the adequacy of the methods used to gather those data. The agency's evaluation focuses in particular on the preclinical data the sponsor relied on to reach the conclusion that it was reasonably safe to conduct the proposed human clinical investigations. This primarily involves data regarding what effects the drug actually has in the body (pharmacology) and how toxic it is at various possible dose levels (toxicology).

FDA's GLP regulations, which are codified in Part 58 of Title 21 of the Code of Federal Regulations (C.F.R.), govern the laboratory work and facilities associated with any nonclinical study intended to support a marketing application for an FDA-regulated product, including drugs and biologics. These regulations establish certain minimum requirements for different aspects of a testing laboratory's practices, subject the laboratory to FDA inspectional oversight and provide penalties for noncompliance.

The good laboratory practices regulations specify minimum standards in such areas as personnel, facilities, equipment and operations.

The GLP regulations specify minimum standards in such areas as personnel, facilities, equipment and operations. The regulations typically set these standards through procedural and structural safeguards, rather than through specific substantive requirements.

For example, in the area of personnel, the GLP regulations require that individuals involved in preclinical studies be sufficiently trained to conduct the study appropriately, but do not specify what such training must encompass. The personnel controls also require the designation of a study director to oversee, monitor and certify the study and require the establishment of a separate quality assurance unit charged with independently monitoring the progress and scientific soundness of any study. This quality assurance unit, among other tasks, must maintain copies of study schedules and written protocols; conduct periodic inspections to ensure compliance with all regulations and specifications; submit regular status reports to the management of the testing facility; and prepare and sign a written statement outlining quality assurance efforts, which is to be included in the final study report.

The GLP regulations also require facilities to be of suitable size and construction, including proper animal care facilities, as applicable. The regulations provide that any study to be submitted to FDA in support of an IND (or other official application) must be conducted with a detailed protocol specifying the study's objectives and methodologies, and that all relevant records and data from the study must be retained for specified periods. FDA may inspect any GLP-covered facility and its records to determine its compliance with applicable standards.

A testing facility's failure to conform to applicable GLP requirements can result in various sanctions. If the violation adversely affected the validity of a preclinical study and FDA considers lesser regulatory actions inadequate, the violation can result in the facility's being disqualified from carrying out any preclinical testing. In addition, any studies undertaken at a disqualified testing facility that are submitted in support of a subsequent product application may be excluded from consideration. FDA also may disregard a preclinical laboratory study done at a nonconforming facility, even if the nonconformance would not warrant disqualification of the facility. Exclusion of a preclinical study under either of these circumstances may lead, in extreme cases, to the termination or withdrawal of approval of the application.

A testing facility's failure to conform to applicable GLP requirements can result in various sanctions.

Although the direct burden of GLP compliance is on the testing facility, the GLP regulations create strong incentives for sponsors who plan to rely on preclinical studies for subsequent FDA applications to take an active role in overseeing those studies.

Clinical Investigation

The primary purpose of the preclinical investigation is to gather sufficient evidence about the proposed new drug to proceed to the next regulatory stage— testing the product in people. The primary goal of human clinical investigation, in turn, is to gather sufficient information about the safety and efficacy of the drug to support an NDA. In contrast to the preclinical stage, clinical trials involve much more active FDA oversight, designed both to protect the health and safety of the human test subjects and to ensure the integrity and usefulness of the clinical study data.

The Investigational New Drug Application

Unlike the preclinical stage, commencement of clinical trials requires formal notification to FDA. At least 30 days before the drug's sponsor wishes to begin such trials, the sponsor must submit an IND to the agency (basic IND requirements are set out at title 21 C.F.R. Part 312 and in section 505(i) of the FDCA). If FDA does not object to the IND within 30 days, it automatically becomes effective and clinical trials may begin. If FDA finds a problem with the application, however, it may impose a "clinical hold," barring commencement of the investigational studies proposed in the application until the problem is resolved to the agency's satisfaction.

The specific contents of an IND depend both on the nature of the drug and the scope of the proposed trials. All INDs, however, must include the following basic elements: 1) a detailed cover sheet; 2) a table of contents; 3) an introductory statement and general investigative plan; 4) an investigator's brochure, except in the case of sponsor-investigator INDs (i.e., where the investigator herself or himself is the sponsor); 5) a set of comprehensive investigative protocols; 6) information on the proposed drug's chemistry, manufacturing and controls; 7) pharmacology and toxicology information; 8) a summary of previous human experience with the drug; and 9) any additional information FDA deems necessary.

Thus, the IND covers two basic categories of information: information on the study drug itself, and information on the proposed clinical investigation. As to the study drug, the sponsor must provide the pharmacological and toxicological data upon which the sponsor concluded it was reasonably safe to propose clinical trials involving humans. The IND also must include information describing the manufacturing and control of the study drug, as well as comprehensive information on the drug's chemical composition, structural formula, proposed dosage form and proposed route of administration. Information on any prior human experience with the drug also is required, including any relevant foreign experience, as well as any history of the drug's being withdrawn from investigation or marketing.

An IND includes:
- *information on the study drug itself*
- *information on the proposed clinical investigation*

As to the information on the proposed investigation, the application must include proposed study protocols, with varying levels of detail depending on the phase of the clinical trial being undertaken. Generally, protocols must identify the objectives and purpose of the study, names and qualifications of investigators, patient selection criteria, study design and methodologies, and the study's measurement criteria, including clinical or laboratory monitoring. The IND also must identify the person(s) with overall responsibility for monitoring the study, as well as outside contract research organizations.

In addition, the application must include a detailed "investigative plan" addressing, among other things, the rationale behind the planned clinical research, an outline of the proposed approach, the types of clinical trials to be conducted, an estimate as to the number of patients involved and a discussion of any significant anticipated patient risks based on toxicological data. Further, the application must contain a commitment from the sponsor to conduct clinical trials under the supervision of an Institutional Review Board (IRB), and to follow all applicable rules and regulations, including those pertaining to informed consent.

Informed Consent and Institutional Review Boards

A fundamental goal of regulatory requirements for informed consent and review of clinical studies by IRBs is to ensure the protection of the rights and welfare of human subjects. FDA investigators regularly check for compliance with these regulations, and an institution or sponsor's noncompliance can result in the temporary suspension or formal termination of a clinical study, as well as other administrative sanctions or legal proceedings.

The thrust of the informed consent regulations, which are codified at 21 C.F.R. Part 50, is to ensure that patient participation in clinical trials is entirely voluntary and knowing. Potential participants in clinical trials must be informed adequately about risks, possible benefits and alternative courses of treatment *before* making the decision to participate in the experimental research. Such consent must be documented, and research subjects cannot be forced to waive any potential future claims for negligence against the study's investigator, sponsor or institution. Furthermore, when prisoners are used as research subjects, additional restrictions and requirements exist to ensure truly voluntary participation in light of the inherently more coercive prison environment.

Potential participants in clinical trials must be informed adequately about risks, possible benefits and alternative courses of treatment before making the decision to participate in the experimental research.

The regulations pertaining to IRBs, codified at 21 C.F.R. Part 56, require IRB oversight of a clinical study in order to ensure that the rights of the human test subjects are adequately protected, while, at the same time, rigorous scientific and medical standards are maintained. The IRB is essentially a committee designated by an institution (e.g., university medical center, contract research organization or hospital) to review biomedical research involving human subjects. The IRB must approve a proposed clinical study before the study can begin and must continue to monitor the research as it progresses. IRB approval of a proposed clinical study can be given only if certain conditions are met, including that the proposed research appropriately minimizes patient risks and that such risks are reasonable in relation to anticipated benefits.

The regulations also set up relatively detailed requirements for an IRB's internal "housekeeping." Thus, the IRB must establish written procedures detailing, among other things, its review processes and criteria, and its procedures designed to ensure the prompt reporting of changes in ongoing clinical research or in informed consent documents. Moreover, IRB members must come from sufficiently diverse disciplines to enable the IRB to review the study not only in terms of specific research issues but also in terms of the study's acceptability under community and legal standards, as well as professional conduct and practice norms. The IRB also must keep detailed records of its activities; those records are subject to FDA inspection.

The Phases of a Clinical Investigation

Clinical investigations are typically divided into three phases, which often overlap in practice.

Phase 1 studies ordinarily involve the initial administration of the drug to a small number (typically 20 to 80) of healthy test subjects or patients. Such studies are designed to determine the metabolism and pharmacologic actions of the drug in humans and the side effects associated with increasing doses, and, if possible, to gain early evidence on effectiveness. The drug's sponsor also must derive sufficient pharmacological data from Phase 1 trials to devise appropriate Phase 2 studies. In the case of more toxic drugs intended to treat serious or life-threatening conditions, such as many cancer drugs, Phase I trials may take place in patients with the target condition.

Clinical investigations are typically divided into three phases.

Phase 2 investigations involve an expanded patient group (up to several hundred patients) afflicted with the disease or condition being studied. The thrust of Phase 2 trials is to obtain evidence of the drug's effectiveness against the targeted disease, to explore further risk and side effect issues, and to confirm preliminary data regarding optimal dosage ranges. At the end of Phase 2 trials, the sponsor typically meets with FDA to discuss specific regulatory or scientific concerns the sponsor must address in designing and conducting its Phase 3 studies. While such conferences are technically optional, they are almost always advisable as they can provide an invaluable opportunity to address agency concerns that might otherwise impede review of the application.

The sponsor may request a formal meeting with responsible FDA officials to reach a binding agreement on the size or design of clinical or bioequivalence trials. After testing begins, such agreements may be changed only with the written consent of the sponsor or if the director of the responsible FDA division issues a written decision identifying a substantial scientific issue "essential to determining the safety or effectiveness of the drug" that would not otherwise have been addressed.

Phase 3 clinical trials may commence, with appropriate notification to FDA, once the drug's sponsor has gathered preliminary evidence that suggests the drug may be effective. Such studies may involve up to several thousand patients. They frequently take place at multiple locations and involve more clinical investigators than in earlier phases. The primary goal of a Phase 3 clinical trial, or "pivotal" trial, is to collect the data necessary to meet the safety and efficacy standards required for FDA approval.

Obligations of Clinical Sponsors and Investigators

Throughout all phases of a clinical investigation, both the sponsor of the study and the individual investigators have responsibilities and duties designed to ensure patient safety as well as the integrity and soundness of the data derived from the investigation. Noncompliance with these requirements may result in FDA regulatory actions including Warning Letters, exclusion of a disqualified investigator's study results, suspension of an IND or NDA predicated on discredited study data, or even civil or criminal proceedings.

The study sponsor is responsible for ensuring patient safety and appropriate scientific conduct, and has the primary responsibility to keep FDA informed of the progress of the study and of any significant safety-related events. The sponsor also bears responsibility for selecting appropriate investigators, ensuring adherence to proper protocols and practices, recordkeeping, and shipping and handling of investigational product. In addition, sponsors are responsible for compliance with regulations on informed consent and IRBs.

The rules regarding safety reporting requirements for human drugs and biologics being investigated under an IND were amended in 2010. Under these revised rules, the sponsor bears responsibility for reporting to FDA and to clinical investigators any reportable adverse safety event that occurs during clinical trials. If the adverse event suggests a serious hazard or side effect that has not been previously identified in the written investigative materials accompanying the study, the sponsor must report it to FDA and to investigators within 15 calendar days after the sponsor determines the event qualifies for reporting. A telephone report to the agency within seven calendar days of the sponsor's initial receipt of the information is required if an unexpectedly life-threatening or fatal event has occurred.

Under the Food and Drug Administration Amendments Act of 2007 (FDAAA), the sponsor is required to register on a public database certain summary information about controlled clinical trials, other than Phase I investigations, of products subject to FDA regulation. The sponsor is required to register such trials within 21 days after the first patient is enrolled in the trial. FDAAA also requires sponsors to submit basic results for these trials for posting on the same public database (www.ClinicalTrials.gov) within one year of the completion date of the trial. Sponsors are required to certify to FDA that they have complied with these requirements at the time they submit any "application" under section 505 of the FDCA (for drugs) or section 351 of the Public Health Service Act (for biologics). Per FDA Guidance issued in 2009, the certification requirement applies to various types of applications including INDs, NDAs, BLAs and efficacy supplements to approved NDAs and BLAs. FDAAA also provides for further expansion of the

Obligations of clinical sponsors:
- *ensuring patient safety*
- *ensuring appropriate scientific conduct*
- *keeping FDA informed*
- *selecting appropriate investigators*
- *adhering to proper protocols and practices*
- *recordkeeping*
- *shipping and handling of product*
- *reporting any adverse event*
- *obtaining valid informed consent*

database by regulation. Such regulations were to have issued by September 27, 2010 (i.e., by three years after the September 27, 2007, enactment date); however, as of this writing, that has not occurred.

Clinical investigators are required, among other things, to obtain valid informed consent from any participating subjects, to follow study protocols, to ensure that other study personnel follow the required protocols and to report significant adverse events. An investigator may be disqualified from conducting studies for repeated violations of the regulations, or may be subject to further administrative, civil or criminal proceedings. If an investigator disqualification occurs, the study's sponsor will be required to establish that the study's overall viability is not threatened by the investigator's misconduct. Investigator misconduct also may result in an FDA determination that the IND can no longer remain in effect, or, in extreme cases, that an NDA predicated upon the investigator's data must be withdrawn.

FDA Oversight: Clinical Holds

Through the imposition of a "clinical hold," FDA may forestall a proposed clinical investigation or suspend an existing one

Through the imposition of a "clinical hold," FDA may forestall a proposed clinical investigation or suspend an existing one. A clinical hold can be imposed for a number of reasons, including an unreasonable and significant risk to patients, the use of improperly qualified investigators, a deficient or disregarded investigative protocol, or any other serious deficiency in an IND or a particular clinical trial. FDA must communicate the imposition of a clinical hold by telephone or other form of rapid communication, and must provide the drug sponsor, within 30 days, with a written explanation of the basis for the clinical hold. As a general rule, until the agency's consent to lift a clinical hold is obtained, any clinical trial or trials subject to the hold cannot commence or resume. Under the Food and Drug Administration Modernization Act of 1997 (FDAMA), a sponsor faced with a clinical hold may submit a written request to FDA that the hold be removed. FDA must respond to such a request in writing within 30 days.

IND Withdrawal

As with the imposition of a clinical hold, FDA can halt further use or distribution of an investigational drug through withdrawal or suspension of an IND. Similar concerns, such as undue patient risk or serious deficiencies in the application or the clinical protocol, trigger both types of agency action, with withdrawal obviously reserved for the more serious cases.

Where the continuation of a clinical study poses, in FDA's judgment, an immediate and substantial danger to human subjects, the agency may order immediate termination of an IND, subject to possible reinstatement. Where no such immediate risk is present, however, if FDA proposes to withdraw an IND, the agency will notify the sponsor in writing and provide 30 days to submit any corrections or explanations. The sponsor's failure to respond within the specified time frame results in the termination of the IND. The sponsor, however, may request a formal hearing if FDA refuses to accept a submitted correction or explanation.

The New Drug Application: Standards and Procedures

Once Phase 3 clinical trials are completed, the applicant prepares to submit its NDA. This preparation process ordinarily includes a pre-NDA meeting with FDA staff, with the goal of helping to ensure that the application will contain all required data.

Contents of the New Drug Application

The regulatory requirements that govern the contents of an NDA, codified at 21 C.F.R. Part 314, are intended to give FDA enough information to make a meaningful evaluation of the drug. Specific NDA data requirements are lengthy and detailed, covering seven broad categories: 1) preclinical data, such as animal and laboratory studies, evaluating the drug's pharmacology and toxicology; 2) human pharmacokinetic and bioavailability data; 3) clinical data (i.e., data obtained from administering the drug to humans, which must include adequate tests to demonstrate that the drug is safe under the proposed conditions of use, as well as "substantial evidence" that the drug is effective under such proposed conditions); 4) a description of proposed methods by which the drug will be manufactured, processed and packed; 5) a description of the drug product and drug substance; 6) a list of each patent claiming the drug, drug product or method of use, or a statement that there are no relevant patents making such claims; and 7) the drug's proposed labeling. The applicant also must provide a summary of the application, concluding with a presentation of both the risks and benefits of the new drug. In addition, the NDA must contain various regulatory certifications covering such matters as financial ties between the sponsor and clinical investigators and compliance with clinical trial registry requirements.

Data requirements in a NDA cover seven broad categories.

Unless an application is publicly disclosed or acknowledged, FDA will keep the application's existence a secret until the agency sends an approval letter. Similarly, the contents of an application generally are kept secret until an approval letter is sent, even if the existence of the application is known. Following approval of the NDA, material in the application that contains trade secrets or confidential commercial information continues to be protected from disclosure, at least in theory. FDAAA added the requirement that FDA must publish on its website within 48 hours of approval of a new drug or biologic a summary review documenting conclusions about the drug from all reviewing disciplines, noting any critical issues or disagreements that arose during the review and how they were resolved. In addition, FDA must publish on its website, within 30 days of approval, the action package for approval of any new drug or biologic that is a new chemical entity; for any other new drug or biologic, the action package must be published within 30 days of receipt of the third Freedom of Information Act request for the package.

Risk Evaluation and Mitigation Strategy

FDA may require a sponsor to include a REMS in its NDA when the agency deems it "necessary to ensure that the benefits of the drug outweigh the risks of the drug."

An additional element that may be required as part of an NDA is the risk evaluation and mitigation strategy (REMS), as provided under the FDAAA. FDA may require a sponsor to include a REMS in its NDA when the agency deems it "necessary to ensure that the benefits of the drug outweigh the risks of the drug."

A REMS must contain, at a minimum, a timetable for submission to FDA by the sponsor of REMS assessments at set intervals (18 months, three years and in the seventh year after approval), subject to possible variations in frequency and possible elimination of the assessment requirement altogether if, after the initial three-year period, FDA determines that the drug's serious risks have been adequately identified and are being adequately managed (FDCA § 505-1(d)). A sponsor may also submit an assessment of an existing REMS to FDA at any time, along with a proposed modification of the REMS. In addition, a sponsor must submit a REMS assessment (which may include a proposal for modification of the strategy):

♦ when submitting a supplemental application for a prescription drug for a new indication;

♦ when specifically required under the REMS;

♦ as specified by FDA if the agency determines that new safety or efficacy information indicates that any REMS element should be modified or added; or

♦ within 15 days if the Secretary of the Department of Health and Human Services determines there may be cause to withdraw the drug's NDA under section 505(e) of the act.

In addition to the required periodic assessments, a REMS may also be required to provide for the distribution of a Medication Guide or a patient package insert to each patient when the drug is dispensed if FDA determines that such a requirement may help "mitigate a serious risk of the drug." A communication plan aimed at healthcare professionals may also be required if FDA determines that such a plan may support implementation of an element of the REMS.

A more stringent set of REMS elements may be required if FDA determines them necessary to "assure safe use of the drug, because of its inherent toxicity or potential harmfulness." These elements may require:

♦ that healthcare professionals who prescribe or dispense the drug have particular training or experience or are specially certified;

♦ that the drug be dispensed only in specified settings such as hospitals;

♦ that patient testing, monitoring and/or enrollment in a registry be required in connection with dispensing the drug.

A more stringent set of REMS elements may be required if FDA determines them necessary to "assure safe use of the drug, because of its inherent toxicity or potential harmfulness."

Whenever a REMS assessment is submitted, FDA must initiate discussion with the sponsor within 60 days, except for assessments required because the Secretary of the Department of Health and Human Services has determined there may be cause to withdraw the NDA, in which case such discussions must begin within 30 days after submission. For proposed REMS modifications submitted as part of an NDA or supplement, FDA must describe the final REMS or any modification to the REMS, as applicable, in the action letter on the application. For proposed REMS modifications submitted as part of a REMS assessment, FDA must describe the final REMS, in most cases, within 90 days of the beginning of the required discussions with the sponsor. Detailed dispute resolution processes apply if FDA and the sponsor disagree on a REMS or REMS modification.

Generic drugs referencing a drug approved with a REMS are subject to all elements of the REMS except the requirement to submit assessments and proposed modifications. For those REMS elements involving restrictions on distribution and use, the generic drug applicant and the reference drug applicant are to use a single, shared system, unless FDA determines that the burdens of such a system outweigh the benefits, or that any aspect of the REMS elements in question is patent-protected or proprietary and the ANDA applicant is not able to obtain a license. In this connection, the law prohibits an NDA sponsor from using any REMS element required to assure safe use in order to "block or delay" approval of an ANDA.

FDA will refuse to file an NDA if:

- *it is incomplete*
- *it is in improper form*
- *it omits critical data*
- *it fails to make required certifications*

Submitting and Filing the New Drug Application

When an NDA arrives at FDA, the agency considers it to be "received," not "filed." The application is considered "filed" only when formally accepted for review by FDA. The agency must determine whether or not to file an application within 60 days of its receipt. If no grounds for refusing to file the application exist, FDA must file it; the filing date will be 60 days after the date of receipt.

FDA will accept an application for filing only if it is sufficiently complete to permit a substantive review. FDA has the authority to refuse to file an application on several grounds, for example: 1) if the application is incomplete or in improper form, or omits data critical to assessing safety, efficacy or adequate directions for use; or 2) if the application fails to make required certifications regarding how the preclinical and clinical trials were conducted.

Although its refusal to file (RTF) authority sounds quite broad, FDA typically uses that authority only for obvious deficiencies in the application, not in cases that involve "matters of subtle judgment." The agency's RTF guidance document states: "It is important . . . that [RTF] be reserved for applications . . . plainly inadequate, non-reviewable without major repair, or that make review unreasonably difficult." Applications that contain deficiencies this severe will be subject to refusal, because FDA believes that accepting applications in need of extensive repair is unfair to new drug sponsors whose submissions were complete and properly formatted. (One notable exception to the normal requirement for a complete NDA submission is the category of "fast-track" drugs, discussed later in this chapter. FDAMA explicitly permits FDA to review applications for fast-track drugs on a "rolling" basis.)

There are three circumstances where FDA is especially likely to use its RTF power: 1) omission of a required section of the NDA, or presentation of a section in so haphazard a manner as to render it incomplete on its face; 2) clear failure to include evidence of effectiveness that can meet the statutory and regulatory standards; and 3) omission of critical data, information or analyses needed to evaluate safety and effectiveness, or to provide adequate directions for use. Because the agency's RTF power is discretionary, it can choose not to use this procedure for particularly critical drugs even if specific grounds for invoking it exist. In practice, potential RTF issues usually are addressed and resolved before the NDA is submitted. The pre-NDA meeting often provides a forum for this process. (Because the ANDA process does not typically involve pre-application meetings between the sponsor and FDA, RTFs are more common for ANDAs.)

If FDA chooses to use its RTF authority, it will notify the applicant, which can then request an informal conference. After the conference, the applicant can request that FDA file the application, with or without amendments to correct the deficiencies. The agency then will file the application "over protest." As a practical matter, however, an applicant has little or no incentive to ask the agency to do this. If FDA believes the application contains deficiencies egregious enough to warrant an RTF response, there is little chance of subsequent favorable FDA action on the application. Therefore, requests to file an application "over protest" are extremely rare.

Substantive Standards for Review

FDA reviewers must find that an application meets several substantive requirements before the agency will approve the NDA. The most basic requirement is that the drug be both "safe" and "effective." These words have specialized meanings in the new drug approval context.

"Safe" and "effective" have special meanings in the new drug approval context.

The FDCA, as enacted in 1938, did not require a sponsor to address efficacy as part of its application to market a new drug—only safety. The Drug Amendments of 1962 added the requirement that a new drug must be supported by "substantial evidence" that the drug will have the effect it purports to have under the indicated conditions of use. "Substantial evidence" is defined in the law as evidence from adequate and well-controlled clinical studies. Although FDA has traditionally required two independent pivotal studies to demonstrate efficacy, FDAMA provided that one "adequate and well-controlled" study accompanied by confirmatory evidence could constitute substantial evidence of effectiveness if FDA determines, "based on relevant science," that data from the study are sufficient to establish effectiveness.

In addition, a drug may not be approved unless there are "adequate tests by all methods reasonably applicable to show whether or not such drug is safe for use under the conditions prescribed, recommended, or suggested in the proposed labeling thereof." In applying this standard, FDA recognizes that there is no such thing as an absolutely safe drug; in addition to the benefits it provides, every drug will present some risks. Therefore, FDA's safety assessment requires consideration of a product's efficacy. As the agency said in its 1995 statement on the efficacy standard, "FDA weighs the product's demonstrated effectiveness against its risks to determine whether the benefits outweigh the risks." This risk/benefit analysis takes account of information such as the seriousness of the disease, the adequacy of any existing remedies, and adverse reaction and any other safety data.

In addition to evidence of safety and effectiveness, there also must be adequate manufacturing controls in place before FDA will approve a drug. In particular, the methods used in, and the controls and facilities used for, manufacturing, processing, packing and holding the drug substance and finished product must comply with FDA's current good manufacturing practice (cGMP) requirements, and must be adequate to maintain the drug's purity, quality, strength, identity and bioavailability. A pre-approval inspection of the applicant's facilities typically will be conducted to verify compliance with these requirements.

An additional prerequisite to approval is that the drug's labeling must meet applicable statutory and regulatory requirements. The labeling cannot be false or misleading, and must comply with general requirements concerning content and form, including such matters as presentation of clinical data, warnings, and dosage and administration information. The labeling review is usually the final step in the approval process.

Under the Pediatric Research Equity Act of 2003 (PREA) (as reauthorized by the FDAAA in 2007), an NDA or biologic license application (BLA) for a new drug or biologic must include an assessment of the safety and efficacy of the product in all relevant pediatric subpopulations (as defined by FDA in consultation with the sponsor), as well as data to support dosing and administration for each pediatric subpopulation for which the product is to be deemed safe and effective. These requirements may be deferred for various reasons, including an FDA finding that the product is ready for approval for use by adults before pediatric studies are complete. The requirement may also be waived partially or entirely on a variety of grounds, including that 1) the necessary studies are impossible or highly impractical; 2) there is evidence strongly suggesting that the product would be ineffective or unsafe in children; 3) the product does not represent a meaningful benefit over existing therapies for children and is not likely to be used in a substantial number of children; or 4) (for a partial waiver applicable to a specific age group) reasonable efforts to produce a pediatric formulation necessary for that age group have failed. FDA also has authority under PREA to require pediatric assessments for marketed products if FDA finds that 1) the product is used in a substantial number of children for the labeled indications and adequate pediatric labeling could confer a benefit on pediatric patients; 2) there is reason to believe the product would represent a meaningful therapeutic benefit over existing therapies for pediatric patients for one or more claimed indications; or 3) the absence of adequate pediatric labeling could pose a risk to pediatric patients.

Advisory Committees
Important issues raised by an NDA (or BLA) may be reviewed by FDA advisory committees made up of outside experts.

Advisory Committee Review

Although the primary review of an NDA is carried out by the appropriate division within the Center for Drug Evaluation and Research (CDER), FDA may also seek the advice of its expert advisory committees. These committees may review studies of the drug under consideration, as well as its proposed labeling, and provide recommendations on issues pertaining to approval of the drug. Each review division within CDER has access to one or more advisory committees. Advisory committees are composed primarily of prominent research and clinical specialists, but also must include a representative of consumer interests, a representative of the drug manufacturing industry not directly affected by the matter before the panel, and at least two specialists in the disease or condition for which the drug under review is to be indicated.

Advisory committees respond to specific questions posed by the agency regarding safety and efficacy, and evaluate whether additional studies are needed to support approval. FDA typically has been more likely to use advisory committee review if the new drug is particularly significant therapeutically, or if review of the drug involves evaluation of complex scientific data. The FDAAA now requires FDA to refer any BLA or any NDA for a new chemical entity to an advisory committee for review prior to approval or to summarize in the action letter why it did not do so. In addition to advisory committees, FDA also has discretion to consult outside expert reviewers from the scientific community. Advisory committee and outside review recommendations, however, are not binding on the agency. Under FDAMA, FDA must make a final decision on a matter reviewed by an advisory committee and notify the affected parties, or explain why no decision has been reached, within 90 days after the advisory committee's recommendation.

Advisory committees respond to specific questions posed by the agency regarding safety and efficacy, and evaluate whether additional studies are needed to support approval.

The New Drug Application: FDA Action and Time Frames

The FDCA provides that within 180 days after the filing of an NDA "or such additional period as may be agreed" between FDA and the applicant, FDA must either approve the application or give the applicant notice of an opportunity for a hearing as to whether the application is approvable (essentially, a procedural step required before FDA may formally reject an NDA). Because FDA rarely is in a position to reach a final yes-or-no decision on an NDA within 180 days after it is filed, the agency has created a procedural framework that allows it to engage in multiple rounds of review of an NDA that may stretch on much longer than 180 days without running afoul of the statutory deadline.

First, as described above, FDA has by regulation established a 60-day period following actual receipt of the NDA during which the agency decides if the application is sufficiently complete to allow it be "filed." Only after this determination is made does the statutory "filing clock" start to run.

While the filing step effectively extends the 180-day statutory deadline by 60 days, even this additional amount of time is usually insufficient for FDA to reach a final decision on an application. Accordingly, the primary mechanism by which FDA ensures itself the timing flexibility it needs to complete its review of an application without violating the statutory deadline is to rely on the "or such additional period as may be agreed" language of the statute to create a system in which the NDA applicant in effect agrees to allow the review of the application to continue until FDA is either ready to approve it or makes clear that the application is not approvable in its current form, in which case the applicant typically withdraws the application on its own. (Situations in which an applicant forces FDA to provide a formal hearing on approvability, as the statute contemplates, are quite rare.)

This mechanism in turn is premised on the concept of the review cycle, formerly referred to in FDA regulations as the "review clock." FDA regulations state that within 180 days of the receipt of an NDA, FDA will review it and send the applicant either an approval letter or a "complete response" letter describing the deficiencies that must be satisfactorily addressed before the application can be approved. This 180-day period is called the "initial review cycle." Significantly, however, the regulations also provide that the initial review cycle "may be adjusted by mutual agreement between FDA and an applicant or as . . . the result of a major amendment" (amendments to the NDA are discussed below).

A key vehicle for expressing applicants' agreement to extending the initial review cycle is FDA's performance goals under the Prescription Drug User Fee Act (PDUFA), which are negotiated between industry and FDA and formally presented to Congress. First enacted in 1992 with the intent of providing additional resources for FDA drug review and accelerating drug review times, PDUFA is reauthorized on a five-year cycle, with the most recent reauthorization taking place in 2007 as part of the FDAAA. PDUFA applies only to NDAs and BLAs, not to generic drug applications.

Under PDUFA, FDA collects a substantial user fee for each NDA (and BLA) it receives, with certain minor exceptions. In exchange, FDA commits to the PDUFA performance goals.

Under PDUFA, FDA collects a substantial user fee for each NDA (and BLA) it receives, with certain minor exceptions. In exchange, FDA commits to the PDUFA performance goals, which provide for specific review times for NDAs and BLAs. Though technically not legally binding, these performance goals represent FDA's side of a three-way bargain under which industry agrees to pay the user fees and Congress authorizes FDA to collect the fees and use them for drug reviews and related tasks. As such, the performance goals are taken very seriously by the agency.

In its PDUFA performance goals under the 2007 reauthorization, FDA committed to review and act on 90 percent of standard original NDA and BLA submissions (i.e., submissions for drugs similar to existing treatments) within 10 months of receipt, and 90 percent of priority original NDA and BLA submissions (i.e., submissions for drugs that represent significant advances over existing treatments) within six months of receipt. Thus, by signing on to the PDUFA performance goals, industry has effectively agreed to an extension of the initial review cycle for standard NDA and BLA applications from six months to 10 months.

As noted above, at the conclusion of the initial review cycle, FDA will send the applicant either an approval letter or a complete response letter. Because outright approval at the end of the initial review cycle is quite rare, in the vast majority of most cases the applicant will receive a complete response letter outlining the additional steps that need to taken before the application can be approved. Upon receipt of a complete response letter, the applicant must either resubmit the application, addressing the deficiencies noted in the letter; withdraw the application; or ask FDA to provide an opportunity for a hearing on the approvability of the application. Under FDA regulations, the applicant that receives a complete response letter automatically agrees to an extension of the statutory review deadline until it takes any of these actions. Failure to take any of the specified actions within one year after the issuance of a complete response letter will be considered a request by the applicant to withdraw the application, unless the applicant has requested an extension. If FDA considers the applicant's failure to take action within one year to be a request to withdraw the application, the agency will give the applicant written notice and a 30-day period in which to explain why the application should not be withdrawn and to request an extension of time to resubmit it.

Because outright approval at the end of the initial review cycle is quite rare, in the vast majority of most cases the applicant will receive a complete response letter outlining the additional steps that need to taken before the application can be approved.

Resubmissions of an application following receipt of a complete response letter fall into two categories. A Class 1 resubmission is one that contains relatively minor information such as final printed labeling, draft labeling, certain safety or stability updates, postmarketing study commitments, assay validation data, final release testing on lots used to support approval or minor re-analyses of previously submitted data. Under FDA's regulations a Class 1 resubmission constitutes an agreement by the applicant to start a new two-month review cycle beginning on the date FDA receives the resubmission. A Class 2 resubmission is one that includes any item not specified as part of a Class 1 resubmission, including any item that would require presentation to an advisory committee. A Class 2 resubmission constitutes an agreement by the applicant to start a new six-month review cycle beginning on the date FDA receives the resubmission.

Submission by the applicant of an amendment to a pending application can also affect the review timelines. If the applicant submits a "major amendment" within three months of the end of a review cycle, FDA's regulations state that this constitutes an agreement by the applicant to extend the review cycle by three months. Submission of a major amendment prior to that time will not extend the review cycle, although FDA may, at its discretion, defer review of such an amendment until the next review cycle. Submission of an amendment that is not major at any time during a review cycle will not extend the cycle, although FDA also may defer review of such an amendment to the next cycle. Although the prior version of FDA's regulations gave an example of a major amendment (an amendment that contains significant new data from a previously unreported study or detailed new analyses of previously submitted data), the agency explicitly refused to provide any definition, explanation or example of a major amendment in its current regulations, leaving itself with almost unrestricted discretion to define an amendment as major or not, and therefore with a maximum of control over the timing of NDA review.

The Postmarketing Period

An applicant's responsibilities with respect to its NDA do not cease upon approval. The postapproval stage brings with it its own set of obligations for the NDA holder. Of particular note, FDAAA gave expanded FDA powers over such areas as safety-related labeling changes and the conduct of postmarketing studies.

Changes Affecting an Approved Application

Changes affecting an approved drug are grouped into three categories, each of which carries different procedural requirements.

Changes affecting an approved drug are grouped into three categories, each of which carries different procedural requirements. For some changes, the sponsor must submit a supplement to its NDA, and FDA must approve that supplement, before the sponsor can implement the desired changes. This is a "prior approval" supplement. A second group of changes also requires supplementing the NDA, but the sponsor can implement the changes before FDA approves the supplement. These supplements are commonly referred to as "change being effected" supplements. A third category of changes need only be listed in the annual report that the sponsor must file with FDA concerning the drug covered by the NDA.

Prior approval supplements are required for any change to the drug or its manufacturing processes, equipment or facilities that has "a substantial potential to have an adverse effect" on the drug's identity, strength, quality, purity or potency as these factors may relate to its safety or effectiveness. On the manufacturing side, this may include changes in the drug's qualitative or quantitative formulation or approved specifications; changes that may affect the sterility assurance of the drug; and changes in the synthesis of the drug substance that may affect its impurity profile or its physical, chemical or biological properties. All changes in labeling—including new indications, dosing regimens, populations and the like—require a prior approval supplement, with limited exceptions that will be discussed below.

"Change being effected" supplements are utilized for changes with only a moderate potential for an adverse effect on the performance of the drug. These supplements fall into two subcategories. The first subcategory requires the sponsor to wait 30 days after submitting the supplement before starting distribution of the drug product incorporating the change in question—the so-called "CBE-30." CBE-30s are to be used, for instance, for a change in the drug's container-closure system that does not affect its quality, or for relaxation of an acceptance criterion or deletion of a test to comply with an official compendium that is consistent with FDA statutory and regulatory requirements. When an applicant submits a CBE-30, it may not distribute the drug incorporating the change in question if within the 30-day period following submission FDA informs it that the change requires prior approval or that required information is missing from the supplement. For the second subcategory of CBE changes, the applicant may begin distribution of the affected drug product immediately upon receipt by FDA of the supplement. These CBEs are often referred to as CBE-0s. CBE-0s may be used for changes involving addition to a specification or changes in methods or controls to provide increased assurance that the drug will have the characteristics it purports to possess, or a change in labeling that adds or strengthens a contraindication, warning, precaution or adverse reaction; adds or strengthens dosage and administration information to increase safe use of the product; or deletes false or misleading information.

"Change being effected" supplements are utilized for changes with only a moderate potential for an adverse effect on the performance of the drug.

Finally, changes in conditions with only a minimal potential for an adverse effect on the drug's performance need only be described in the annual report submitted by the applicant. Examples of such changes include editorial or minor changes in labeling, deletion or reduction of an ingredient that only affects the product's color, and changes in the drug's container size or shape without changes in the closure system (for nonsterile solid dosage forms).

Postmarketing Safety-Related Label Changes

A key FDAAA provision aimed at strengthening FDA's safety oversight powers provides FDA with new authority to compel a sponsor to make safety-related changes in drug labeling after approval of the drug. Under this new authority, if FDA becomes aware of "new safety information" about a serious drug risk that the agency believes should be included in the drug's labeling, the agency must promptly notify the sponsor. The sponsor then has 30 days to either submit a labeling supplement reflecting the new safety information or explain why it does not believe a labeling change is warranted. If the agency disagrees with the sponsor's conclusion, it must initiate discussions with the sponsor that may not take more than 30 days from the due date of the sponsor's response, unless extended by the agency. Within 15 days of the conclusion of these discussions, FDA may issue an order requiring the sponsor to make those labeling changes

FDA deems appropriate to address the new safety information. Violations of any of these requirements by the sponsor will subject the sponsor to misbranding charges and potential civil money penalties.

Adverse Reaction Reporting

"Adverse drug experiences" are somewhat circularly defined under FDA's regulations as any adverse events associated with the use of a drug in humans. An applicant holding an approved NDA must promptly review reports of adverse drug experiences associated with its drug, regardless of the source from which such reports are obtained. If a reaction is both serious (e.g., fatal, life threatening or permanently disabling) and unexpected (not listed in labeling, or differing from reactions listed in the labeling due to greater severity or specificity), it must be reported to FDA in an "alert report" within 15 calendar days of the applicant's receipt of the information. All adverse reactions that are not serious and unexpected must be reported at quarterly intervals for three years after an application is approved, and annually thereafter.

Withdrawal

Although FDA rarely invokes its statutory authority to withdraw NDAs, there are several circumstances under which it can initiate such action.

Withdrawal

Although FDA rarely invokes its statutory authority to withdraw NDAs, there are several circumstances under which it can initiate such action. As might be expected, the conditions that can trigger NDA withdrawal generally relate to serious problems with the drug or the application. For instance, FDA can withdraw an NDA if the drug is unsafe for use under the conditions of use for which the application was approved. Similarly, FDA can use its withdrawal authority if new clinical evidence shows that the drug is not safe under approved conditions, or if the drug is not effective. Additionally, FDA can seek withdrawal of an application if the drug's labeling is false or misleading, or if there are inadequate assurances that the drug's quality, strength and purity are as claimed. The agency also can withdraw an NDA if the sponsor fails to file required patent information in a timely manner, or if the NDA contains false statements of material fact.

If FDA seeks to withdraw an NDA, usually it must give the applicant notice and the opportunity for a hearing. If the drug in question presents an "imminent hazard," however, the Secretary of the Department of Health and Human Services can summarily suspend approval of the application and give the applicant the opportunity for an expedited hearing. The Secretary cannot delegate the authority to summarily suspend NDAs in this fashion, but can and has delegated to FDA the authority to hold the expedited hearing. In practice, FDA rarely invokes its authority to withdraw or summarily suspend NDAs.

Phase IV Studies

Although clinical studies are a prerequisite to approval, they also are performed after approval as "Phase IV" studies. Such studies can be designed to: 1) obtain additional safety data, 2) obtain additional efficacy data, 3) detect new uses for or abuses of a drug or 4) determine effectiveness for labeled indications under conditions of widespread usage.

There are at least two reasons FDA may be interested in Phase IV studies. First, such studies allow FDA to grant approval of a new drug on the condition that the applicant complete studies that shed additional light on the drug's safety and efficacy subsequent to approval. Phase IV studies also can be used to facilitate FDA's postapproval monitoring of an approved drug.

The FDAAA added to FDA's postmarketing study toolkit new authority to outright require a sponsor to complete a previously agreed postmarketing study or to impose a new requirement to conduct and complete a postmarketing study on a marketed drug either to 1) assess a known serious risk related to use of the drug; 2) assess signals of serious risk related to use of the drug; or 3) identify an unexpected serious risk when available data indicate the potential for such risk. This new authority comes with several restrictions, including that FDA may require a postmarketing study only if adverse event reporting and active surveillance would not be sufficient to fulfill the purpose of the study, and that the required study may take the form of a clinical trial only if a less burdensome kind of study (e.g., a patient registry or an epidemiological study) would not be adequate. Failure to comply with a postmarketing study requirement imposed under this new authority carries with it a potential misbranding charge and substantial civil monetary penalties.

> *Phase IV*
> *After a new drug is approved, FDA often requires additional studies to obtain more information.*

Marketing Protection

An issue virtually every drug sponsor faces at some point is what kind of market protection, if any, its product is eligible for, or, conversely, how its product can overcome a competitor's exclusivity in order to enter the market. There are three main statutory routes to securing market protection for qualifying new drug products outside of, or in addition to, standard patent protection: 1) the patent term extension provisions; 2) nonpatent statutory exclusivity provisions for new chemical entities and approvals requiring new clinical studies; and 3) nonpatent exclusivity for orphan drugs.

> *The three main statutory market protections are:*
> • *the patent extension provisions;*
> • *statutory exclusivity for new chemical entities and approvals requiring new clinical studies; and*
> • *exclusivity for orphan drugs.*

Patent Term Extension

The statutory patent term extension provision, codified at section 156 of Title 35 of the United States Code (U.S.C.), recognizes the reality that many pharmaceutical products receive patents long before they are approved for marketing. Because the premarketing regulatory review period may last for a large portion of the product's patent life, Congress amended the patent law as part of the 1984 amendments to the FDCA to allow extensions of a product's patent term in certain situations.

A drug is eligible for a patent term extension if its patent has not expired and has not been extended previously, and if the drug has been subject to a regulatory review period prior to commercial marketing or use. Only one patent per product is eligible for extension.

The length of the extension is based on the length of the regulatory review period. This includes a "testing period," which begins on the date the IND became effective and ends on the date the NDA was submitted, and an "approval period," which covers the time from the submission of the NDA to its approval. In determining the patent extension, each of these two periods will be reduced by: 1) any portion of the period that took place prior to the patent's issuance, and 2) any amount of time during which the applicant did not act with "due diligence" in pursuing regulatory review. After each component of the review period has been calculated and adjusted, the patent will be extended for one-half of the "testing" period and all of the "approval" period, up to a maximum of a five-year extension and a total of 14 years of extended patent life postapproval.

A drug patent owner seeking an extension must submit an application to the Commissioner of Patents and Trademarks within 60 days of receiving NDA approval. FDA assists the Patent and Trademark Office (PTO) in reviewing the application, because only FDA has the information necessary to calculate the regulatory review period and make the due diligence determination. At the end of the review process, the PTO issues or denies the extension.

Statutory Exclusivity for New Chemical Entities and Approvals Based on New Studies

In addition to patent term extension, the FDCA contains provisions that authorize various periods of statutory exclusivity independent of a product's patent status. The goal of these exclusivity provisions is to give innovator drug companies a monetary incentive to invest in the research and testing needed to develop new products, while simultaneously affording consumers broader access to drug products by making available generic products that rely on studies conducted by an innovator company.

Under the FDCA's exclusivity provisions, if an NDA is approved for a drug containing an active ingredient never before approved under an NDA (or "new chemical entity"), then no application for a generic drug that references the drug may be submitted for five years from the date of approval of the drug. Thus, the law in this situation effectively delays generic competition for five years from NDA approval plus the time it takes FDA to review and approve the first generic application. An exception to this five-year rule allows a generic applicant to submit its application beginning four years from the date of NDA approval if that applicant is challenging a patent covering the reference drug (such patent challenges are discussed in more detail below). Another form of statutory market protection is the three years of exclusivity for an NDA or NDA supplement for a previously approved active ingredient if the application contains reports of new clinical studies essential to approval. A second applicant who wishes to market its drug sooner than these exclusivity provisions allow can always do its own clinical studies and submit a full NDA for its version of the product, instead of a generic application, although in practice few companies choose this route because of the cost involved.

Orphan Drug Exclusivity

The goal of the Orphan Drug Act of 1983 was to motivate pharmaceutical manufacturers to develop and bring to market drugs for orphan diseases—that is, diseases thought to be too rare to attract the commercial interest of pharmaceutical manufacturers in the ordinary course of business. A "rare" disease is defined in the statute as any disease that affects fewer than 200,000 persons in the United States, or that affects more than 200,000 persons and for which there is no reasonable expectation that the manufacturer will recover from U.S. sales the cost of developing and making the drug available in the United States. Although the Orphan Drug Act created a series of incentives for manufacturers to develop drugs for these rare diseases—including FDA assistance with clinical protocols, available grant assistance for clinical development and a tax credit for a portion of research and development expenses—by far the most important incentive under this act is the seven-year market exclusivity awarded to the first applicant to obtain marketing approval of a designated orphan drug for a particular disease or condition. To obtain this exclusivity, the applicant must request orphan drug designation for the drug before the submission of the marketing application, and the drug must be so designated before approval of the application. Upon approval of the drug, and assuming that these conditions are met, FDA may not approve another sponsor's application for the same drug for the same disease or condition until seven years from the date of the first

Orphan Drugs

Orphan drugs are drugs for diseases that affect 200,000 people or less in the U.S., or that affect more than 200,000 persons and for which there is no reasonable expectation that the manufacturer will recover from U.S. sales the cost of developing and making the drug available in the U.S.

applicant's approval, unless: 1) the drug's orphan designation is revoked, 2) its marketing approval is withdrawn, 3) the orphan exclusivity holder consents to the approval of another applicant's product or 4) the orphan exclusivity holder is unable to assure the availability of a sufficient quantity of the drug.

FDA's orphan drug regulations also provide that a sponsor's drug will not be blocked by a previous sponsor's orphan exclusivity, even if the two sponsors' drugs otherwise would be considered structurally the same, if the second sponsor's drug is "clinically superior" to the first sponsor's drug. Clinical superiority may be shown by greater efficacy, greater safety or a major contribution to patient care.

Pediatric Exclusivity

Under the Best Pharmaceuticals for Children Act, patent terms, statutory exclusivities and orphan exclusivity are all eligible for a six-month extension (for an NDA-approved drug only) if the NDA sponsor completes a pediatric study for the drug in response to a written request from FDA.

Under the Best Pharmaceuticals for Children Act (BPCA), patent terms, statutory exclusivities and orphan exclusivity are all eligible for a six-month extension (for an NDA-approved drug only) if the NDA sponsor completes a pediatric study for the drug in response to a written request from FDA. Under the 2007 reauthorization of the BPCA contained in the FDAAA, FDA has 180 days to review studies submitted in response to a written request in order to determine whether the studies comply with the terms of the request, and that determination must be made no later than nine months prior to the expiration of any exclusivity the sponsor wishes to extend. Thus, in practice, a sponsor wishing to qualify for an extension of a particular exclusivity (patent, statutory or orphan) now must submit its pediatric studies in response to a written request not less than 15 months (180 days plus nine months) prior to the expiration of that exclusivity.

FDA REGULATION OF DRUGS: VARIATIONS ON THE STANDARD MODEL

Non-NDA Routes to Market: Historical Development

Meeting the safety and efficacy standards required to obtain approval of an NDA entails substantial expense, effort and expertise. These factors create significant barriers to market entry, a situation that, as in any area of economic activity, can lead to higher prices to consumers. This situation in turn sets up an inherent tension between maintaining the regulatory standards needed to protect the public health and safety, on the one hand, and mitigating the economic burdens imposed by drug prices, on the other. When the need to offer adequate financial incentives to induce companies to undertake the formidable task of new drug development is added to this mixture, the policy equation becomes complex indeed.

Since the passage of the FDCA in 1938, Congress and FDA have made periodic efforts to readjust the balance between each of these goals. Such efforts generally result in further moves to re-level the economic playing field.

"Not-New" Drugs

Before the enactment of the FDCA in 1938, there were no significant regulatory barriers to generic competition in the drug market. With the statutory establishment of the "new drug" category, however, a drug could not be marketed unless it was either "generally recognized as safe" or its NDA was allowed to become effective absent FDA disapproval, which was the standard approval process under the 1938 version of the act until the 1962 Drug Amendments added the requirement for affirmative FDA approval, as well as the substantive efficacy standard. This process was minimal by today's standards, but it was not cost-free, and as a result imposed certain barriers to entry.

Before the enactment of the FDCA in 1938, there were no significant regulatory barriers to generic competition in the drug market.

Thus, to facilitate generic competition for post-1938 drugs, FDA established an informal practice whereby, on request, it would inform an interested party whether a particular drug was generally recognized as safe, and consequently not a "new drug" subject to a premarket application. The factual basis for such a "general recognition" decision was typically a history of safe marketing of the pioneer version of the drug in the United States. This policy continued under the 1962 amendments (modified to consider general recognition of both safety and efficacy), but at a slower pace, until the practice was discontinued in 1968 and all such "not new drug" letters were formally revoked by the agency.

The Drug Efficacy Study Implementation Review

The 1962 Drug Amendments contained a provision for the retroactive evaluation of the efficacy of drugs approved as safe (or which had been subject to a "not new drug" letter) between 1938 and 1962. The Drug Efficacy Study Implementation (DESI) Review, established by FDA in 1968, designated the National Academy of Sciences/National Research Council to establish expert panels to review available data on all marketed post-1938 drugs, and to make recommendations as to their efficacy. FDA was then to act on those recommendations by withdrawing drugs found ineffective and by notifying potential generic manufacturers of what information would be required for approval of a generic version of a marketed drug (other than proof of safety and efficacy, which were deemed to have been established by the DESI Review panel).

The DESI Review examines all available data on drugs approved between 1938 and 1962 and makes recommendations as to their efficacy.

In response, the agency created a new form of NDA, the ANDA, for which approval was based on sameness of active ingredients and on bioequivalence rather than on safety and efficacy data. This ANDA process for DESI drugs later was codified by statute in the 1984 drug amendments.

The "Paper NDA" Policy

As the patent terms on post-1962 drugs began to expire in the 1970s and the early 1980s, it became evident that under existing law there were no feasible means to get competing versions of approved drugs on the market without costly and repetitive testing for safety and efficacy. Because such repeat testing would unnecessarily put more human test subjects at risk, and would waste scarce clinical and agency resources, FDA sought a way to expand the concept of the DESI Review and ANDA policy to generic versions of certain post-1962 drugs. The result was the "paper NDA" policy which, although short-lived, provides a historical and conceptual bridge between the "old drug" and "general recognition" bases for generic drug marketing and the modern statutory ANDA approval process.

The paper NDA policy permitted competing versions of approved new drugs to be approved based on the submission of publicly available reports of well-controlled studies demonstrating the drug's safety and efficacy. The policy was challenged and ultimately upheld in court (*Burroughs Wellcome Co. v. Schweiker*, 649 F.2d 221 (4th Cir. 1981)). Because adequate published studies documenting safety and efficacy were available for only a few post-1962 drugs, however, and because FDA review of such paper NDAs was not significantly easier than for full NDAs, the policy made only a marginal contribution to fostering generic competition. It survives today in modified form as the "505(b)(2)" application, discussed below.

Generic Drugs and the Abbreviated New Drug Application Process

Legislative Background

In the late 1970s and early 1980s Congress began to consider legislative options in response to the lack of a viable generic drug approval process for post-1962 drugs.

In the late 1970s and early 1980s Congress began to consider legislative options in response to the lack of a viable generic drug approval process for post-1962 drugs. During that time, other legislative efforts were underway to restore the part of drug patents' effective life lost due to increasingly lengthy FDA review times. In 1983, a patent term restoration bill was narrowly defeated in the House of Representatives, and it became apparent that neither an ANDA bill nor a patent term restoration bill could pass Congress independently. As a result, leaders of the generic and innovator sides of the pharmaceutical industry agreed to cooperate in crafting a bill incorporating both the ANDA mechanism sought by generic manufacturers, and patent restoration protections desired by research-based companies. The resulting legislation—the Drug Price Competition and Patent Term Restoration Act—was enacted in 1984.

The dual purposes of this legislation were to expedite the availability of safe and effective, but less expensive, generic versions of approved drugs, while simultaneously encouraging the costly research and development efforts that lead to the discovery of therapeutically important new drugs. The amendments created an abbreviated process whereby a generic company could gain approval of its version of a drug without repeating the expensive and lengthy clinical trials already performed for the drug. As previously discussed, innovator companies received restoration of patent rights to compensate for the time expended in the FDA review process, as well as nonpatent exclusivity for qualifying drug products.

The 1984 amendments also provided protection for the generic drug industry in the form of a provision establishing that it is not an act of patent infringement for a nonpatent holder to make, use or sell a patented drug during the term of the patent, as long as such activity is reasonably related to the contemplated submission of an application to FDA. This provision, which specifically overruled the early 1984 decision of the newly created Court of Appeals for the Federal Circuit in *Roche Prod., Inc. v. Bolar Pharmaceutical Co.* (733 F.2d 858 (Fed. Cir. 1984)), was necessary to allow generic applicants to have their ANDAs submitted and approved in time to begin marketing on the date of patent expiration. If the court's ruling had stood, development of ANDAs could not have begun until patent expiration. As a result, *de facto* market exclusivity would have extended well beyond the term of the patent. The protection provided by the statutory provision overruling the *Bolar* decision was counterbalanced by a provision allowing an innovator to sue an ANDA applicant upon submission of an ANDA challenging the innovator's patent.

The Statutory ANDA Requirements

The required contents of an ANDA are set forth in section 505(j) of the FDCA and in agency regulations (21 C.F.R. § 314.94). The statute requires that an ANDA contain:

♦ information showing that the proposed conditions of use for the drug have previously been approved for a drug that is listed by FDA as approved for safety and efficacy;

♦ proof that the active ingredient(s) are the same as in the listed drug;

- ♦ proof that the generic drug will use the same route of administration, dosage form and strength as the listed drug;

- ♦ proof that the generic drug is bioequivalent to the listed reference drug;

- ♦ information showing that the proposed generic labeling is the same as the labeling approved for the listed drug, except for differences related to an approved "suitability petition";

- ♦ the basic technical information required of a full NDA, including a list of components, statement of the composition of the drug, and description of the methods and facilities used in the production of the drug;

- ♦ samples of the generic product and proposed labeling; and

- ♦ a patent certification informing FDA of the patent status of the listed reference drug relied upon by the ANDA.

Although the statutory requirements for an ANDA appear relatively straightforward on their face, many of these requirements have been the basis of contentious administrative and judicial battles.

The Prior Approval and Current Listing Requirements

Two threshold requirements for a drug to be ANDA-eligible are: 1) that the drug's active ingredient has been approved already by FDA for the conditions of use proposed in the ANDA, and 2) that nothing has changed to call into question the basis of approval of the original drug's NDA.

The 1984 amendments require FDA to publish a monthly list of all approved drugs. That publication, commonly known as the *"Orange Book"* (officially titled *Approved Drug Products and Therapeutic Equivalence Evaluations*), serves as the crucial point of reference for many aspects of the ANDA process. In particular, an ANDA may only be submitted if the drug it copies is currently listed in the *Orange Book* as a "reference" listed drug. Such a listing signifies that the drug has been approved, and that as of the date of the *Orange Book* edition consulted, the drug has not been withdrawn from the market over issues of safety or efficacy. Although it is rare for approved drugs later to be found unsafe, an approved drug is on occasion withdrawn from the market voluntarily by the manufacturer. In such cases, FDA must make a determination of whether the drug was withdrawn for safety or effectiveness reasons 1) before approving any ANDA that refers to the listed drug, 2) if any ANDAs that reference the drug have already been approved or 3) if an interested person petitions FDA to make such a determination.

An ANDA may only be submitted if the drug it copies is currently listed in the Orange Book *as a "reference" listed drug.*

The other situation in which a current listing in the *Orange Book* is significant is when FDA withdraws approval of an NDA pursuant to FDCA section 505(e), as discussed above. This rare occurrence will prevent approval of any pending ANDA for the product and also will serve to withdraw approval of any existing approved ANDAs.

"Suitability Petitions" for Different Active Ingredient(s), Routes of Administration, Dosage Forms, and Strengths

Although a product approved under an ANDA presumptively must have the same active ingredient(s), route of administration, dosage form and strength as the listed drug it seeks to copy, the FDCA also permits generic products to incorporate differences from those requirements where such differences ultimately will not affect the safety and efficacy of the generic product. (The potential for approval of a generic drug with a different active ingredient from the reference drug only applies to a combination drug for which the generic applicant proposes to substitute a different active ingredient for one of the active ingredients in the reference drug.)

To market a generic product with any of these differences, however, the generic applicant must first submit, and FDA must approve, an ANDA "suitability petition." FDA is required to approve any such petition unless it finds that investigations must be conducted in order to demonstrate the safety and efficacy of the generic drug in question.

Bioequivalence

A primary requirement for approval of an ANDA is that the proposed generic drug be shown to be "bioequivalent" to the innovator drug it purports to copy. For generic products that meet the bioequivalence requirement, the FDCA allows the presumption that the generic version of the drug will be as safe and as effective as the original version.

A primary requirement for approval of an ANDA is that the proposed generic drug be shown to be "bioequivalent" to the innovator drug it purports to copy.

The core of the bioequivalence concept, as interpreted by FDA in regulations, is an "absence of a significant difference" in the extent to which, and the rate at which, two different drug products' active ingredients "become available at the site of drug action when administered at the same molar dose under similar conditions in an appropriately designed study." For the typical solid oral dosage form drug, this concept means that one version of the drug provides the same total and peak blood concentrations of the active ingredient as another version. FDA regulations and policy, however, provide a number of different methods for assessing bioequivalence.

FDA regulations require ANDAs to contain either 1) "evidence" of bioequivalence of the ANDA product to the listed reference drug, or 2) "information" showing bioequivalence that is sufficient to allow FDA to waive the "evidence" requirement. In practice, this means that an ANDA must contain either results of human studies showing bioequivalence, or other facts on which FDA can conclude that the ANDA product will be bioequivalent to its reference listed drug.

The regulations regarding "evidence" of bioequivalence specifically state that FDA may accept such evidence based on human (*in vivo*) testing, laboratory (*in vitro*) testing or both. Those regulations also set out, in rank order of acceptability, types of *in vivo* and *in vitro* tests that may be used to establish bioequivalence. Those tests include *in vivo* blood concentration tests, *in vitro* tests that have been correlated to such *in vivo* blood tests, urinary excretion tests, measurement of observable pharmacological effects over time, comparative clinical trials of safety and efficacy, FDA-accepted *in vitro* dissolution tests, or the catch-all "any other approach deemed adequate by FDA" to establish bioequivalence. Consistent with these options, the regulations permit FDA, "for good cause," to "waive a requirement for the submission of evidence of *in vivo* bioavailability if waiver is compatible with the public health."

Bioequivalence issues associated with generic versions of innovator drugs have created considerable debate and litigation between and among innovator and generic drug companies and FDA.

Bioequivalence issues associated with generic versions of innovator drugs have created considerable debate and litigation between and among innovator and generic drug companies and FDA. This debate has been particularly focused on drugs that are not "systemically effective"—that is, whose active moiety is not delivered to the site of drug action by systemic blood flow (e.g., drugs that are inhaled, topically applied or locally active in the gastrointestinal tract, such as antiparasitics).

Patent Certification

The final procedural requirement for an ANDA is a patent certification with respect to each patent that covers the reference listed drug the ANDA seeks to copy, or that claims a use for the listed drug. The statute sets out four types of certifications that can be made by a generic applicant in relation to a patent on the reference listed drug:

> (I) that information on the patent has not been filed with FDA by the patent owner;
> (II) that the patent already has expired;
> (III) a statement of the date on which the patent will expire; or
> (IV) that the patent is invalid or will not be infringed by the manufacture, use or sale of the generic applicant's drug.

FDA by regulation has expanded the paragraph IV certification to include an allegation of unenforceability as well as invalidity or non-infringement and has added a fifth type of certification: a statement that there are no patents that claim the listed drug. It is also possible for a generic applicant to "carve out" a listed method-of-use patent by stating that it is not seeking approval for the particular indication covered by that patent (the so-called "section viii statement," after the statutory subparagraph that addresses it).

It is possible for a generic applicant to "carve out" a listed method-of-use patent by stating that it is not seeking approval for the particular indication covered by that patent.

If a paragraph I or II certification, or a certification of no relevant patents, is filed, FDA may make approval of the ANDA effective immediately upon completion of its review. If a paragraph III certification is filed, the approval may be made effective on the patent expiration date specified in the ANDA, although a tentative approval may be issued before that time. If the ANDA contains a paragraph IV certification, however, a complex series of events will be triggered, the outcome of which will determine the effective date of approval of the ANDA.

This process begins when a generic company submits an ANDA containing a paragraph IV certification and, as required, notifies the patent owner and the NDA holder that it has submitted such a certification, which is done once FDA has formally accepted the ANDA for review (typically 30 to 60 days after the ANDA is initially submitted, unless the ANDA is refused for filing [see discussion above under "Submitting and Filing the New Drug Application"]). The notification must set forth in detail the factual and legal bases for the ANDA applicant's belief that the listed patent is invalid or will not be infringed by the ANDA applicant's drug.

After receiving this paragraph IV notification, the patent/NDA holder must evaluate the legal and factual arguments asserted by the ANDA applicant. If the patent/NDA holder so decides, it may file a lawsuit against the applicant for patent infringement. The lawsuit must be filed within 45 days of receipt of the paragraph IV notification, or FDA may make approval of the ANDA effective immediately upon the conclusion of the review process. If a lawsuit is brought, an automatic statutory injunction prohibits FDA from making approval of the ANDA effective for 30 months, unless the court rules in favor of the generic company prior to that time or unless the 30-month injunction is shortened or lengthened by the district court in response to undue delay by either party.

Filing a paragraph IV certification is an "artificial act" of patent infringement created by the 1984 amendments to allow the courts to decide whether the patent is valid, or if the proposed future manufacture and sale of the generic version would infringe the patent. Without making the paragraph IV certification itself an act of infringement, it was believed that the courts would be barred under the Constitution from issuing what would otherwise amount to an advisory opinion about potential future infringement by the generic competitor. Once a patent suit based on a paragraph IV certification is brought, the only issues to be decided are whether the proposed generic marketing of the drug will infringe the patent, or whether the patent is otherwise invalid or unenforceable.

Although a paragraph IV challenge is often costly and difficult, the 1984 amendments included an incentive for a generic company to bring such a challenge in the form of a 180-day delay in FDA approval of other companies' ANDAs to the benefit of a generic company that first challenges a listed drug patent.

Although a paragraph IV challenge is often costly and difficult, the 1984 amendments included an incentive for a generic company to bring such a challenge in the form of a 180-day delay in FDA approval of other companies' ANDAs to the benefit of a generic company that first challenges a listed drug patent. The original version of this incentive provision was ambiguous in several respects and gave rise to frequent litigation, creating uncertainty that seriously undermined its effectiveness. In December 2003 Congress amended the 180-day exclusivity provision, resolving a good deal of the previous uncertainty in favor of an approach aimed at balancing the exclusivity incentive with the interest of getting generic drugs onto the market more quickly and reliably. In particular, the December 2003 amendments established a mechanism whereby a first paragraph IV challenger could forfeit its right to the 180-day exclusivity under a variety of circumstances, including the failure to put its generic drug on the market within a specified period following approval.

The New "Paper NDA"—Section 505(b)(2) Applications

In addition to codifying procedures for ANDAs, the 1984 amendments also established a new category of NDA under section 505(b) of the FDCA—the "505(b)(2) application." This type of application, like the earlier paper NDA, provides for NDAs submitted by an applicant in reliance on safety and efficacy data supplied by another applicant, and to which the 505(b)(2) applicant has no right of reference. Unlike with the old paper NDA, however, the 505(b)(2) applicant is not restricted to reliance on published studies, but may also rely on previous FDA findings of safety and efficacy for another applicant's drug based on unpublished data in FDA's files that is no longer legally protected.

There are several scenarios where a 505(b)(2) application may come into play. One involves an applicant that seeks to market its version of an established drug for a new therapeutic indication or with some other modification requiring new clinical studies, and seeks to rely on relevant safety findings on the drug in a previously approved NDA. Another scenario is where an ANDA suitability petition for a significantly different version of an approved drug—such as a different dosage form or route of administration—is inappropriate because clinical studies are required, but prior studies on the original drug product are still relevant to showing the overall safety and efficacy of the new version of the drug.

The 505(b)(2) application also is similar to an ANDA in that the applicant is required to certify as to the patent status of the drug for which the referenced investigations were conducted, by stating either that the relevant patent information has not been filed by the original applicant (as evidenced by the lack of a listing in the *Orange Book*), that such patent has expired, the date on which the patent will expire, that there are no patents that cover the listed drug, or that the patent is invalid, unenforceable or will not be infringed by the manufacture, use or sale of the proposed 505(b)(2) drug. Also, as with ANDAs, the 505(b)(2) applicant who files a paragraph IV patent certification of invalidity or non-infringement must notify the patent holder, who then has 45 days to decide whether to sue the applicant for patent infringement and trigger an automatic 30-month statutory injunction while the courts decide the substantive patent issues involved. Unlike the ANDA situation, however, no 180-day exclusivity is available in connection with a 505(b)(2) application.

Over-the-Counter Drugs

The OTC Review

As noted above, in order to avoid regulation as a new drug, a drug ordinarily must be deemed generally recognized as safe and effective (GRAS/ GRAE). The test for general recognition of safety and effectiveness, as it has been applied by FDA and the courts, is a stringent one. In brief, it requires 1) that the drug be "generally recognized, among experts qualified by scientific training and experience to evaluate the safety and effectiveness of drugs, as safe and effective for use under the conditions prescribed, recommended, or suggested in the labeling thereof"; 2) that such general recognition be based on adequate published data demonstrating the drug's safety and efficacy (*Weinberger v. Bentex Pharm., Inc.*, 412 U.S. 645, 652 (1973)); and 3) that the drug have been used "to a material extent" and "for a material time" under the labeled conditions. The courts have stipulated that general recognition of effectiveness for an individual drug product must be supported by the same level of evidence as required for an NDA, including adequate and well-controlled investigations demonstrating efficacy (*Weinberger v. Hynson, Westcott & Dunning, Inc.*, 412 U.S. 609, 629-32 (1973)).

> *In order to avoid regulation as a new drug, a drug ordinarily must be deemed generally recognized as safe and effective.*

Although it is exceedingly difficult for a drug product to qualify as GRAS/GRAE on an individual basis, the GRAS/GRAE concept has provided FDA with a key legal tool to regulate over-the-counter (OTC) drugs, namely the OTC review. Starting in 1972, FDA instituted a system to review the safety and efficacy of active ingredients (as opposed to individual drug products) in each category of OTC drugs. For each such category, FDA issues a call-for-data notice that is published in the *Federal Register*. These notices ask manufacturers to submit clinical/marketing data for the individual active ingredients contained in their products.

The test for general recognition of safety and effectiveness requires:

- *that the drug be "generally recognized, among experts qualified by scientific training and experience to evaluate the safety and effectiveness of drugs, as safe and effective for use under the conditions prescribed, recommended, or suggested in the labeling thereof;"*
- *that such general recognition be based on adequate published data demonstrating the drug's safety and efficacy; and*
- *that the drug have been used "to a material extent" and "for a material time" under the labeled conditions.*

The agency then convenes expert advisory panels that are responsible for reviewing the data submissions for the active ingredients in each category.

Once each panel is finished with its review of the active ingredients and the submitted data, it is responsible for providing a final report to FDA. This report reviews each ingredient and places it into one of three categories. Category I ingredients are deemed GRAS/GRAE; Category II ingredients are considered either unsafe, ineffective or both; and Category III ingredients are viewed as having insufficient data to determine safety and/or efficacy. The report is published by FDA in the *Federal Register* as an advance notice of proposed rulemaking with an opportunity for public comment. FDA then reviews the report, takes into account any public comment and publishes in the *Federal Register* its interpretation of the report, sometimes disagreeing with the panel's interpretations and making changes as necessary. This action, which is also open for public comment, is referred to as the Tentative Final Monograph, and is technically a notice of proposed rulemaking.

FDA then undertakes a final review of the ingredients, again taking into account any public comments, which could include new or additional data. On this basis, the agency publishes in the *Federal Register* a rule establishing a Final Monograph. Following the effective date of the Final Monograph (usually a year after publication), continued marketing is permitted only for drug products with active ingredients, labeling claims, dosage strengths and other specified conditions included in the Final Monograph.

Occasionally, companies petition FDA to re-open or amend an OTC monograph, or FDA sees a need to re-open the review of a particular category of drugs. The agency will publish a notice in the *Federal Register* to that effect. This action is considered a proposed monograph amendment (technically a notice of proposed rulemaking) and is open for public comment. The review process then proceeds as explained above.

While most OTC drug categories have been finalized by FDA, the OTC Drug Review process technically remains open, with certain categories of drugs still under review. Until a Final Monograph is published in the *Federal Register* and takes effect, all products containing active ingredients under review in a particular category and meeting certain other conditions regarding labeling claims and other product attributes may continue to be marketed although FDA may take regulatory action against an individual ingredient or product over safety or efficacy issues.

Rx-to-OTC Switches

A rapidly increasing proportion of the OTC market is made up of products that originally were approved as prescription drugs and subsequently were switched to OTC status, a transition commonly referred to as an "Rx-to-OTC switch." There are three ways to accomplish such a switch. A drug manufacturer can supplement the drug's existing NDA; FDA may create or amend an OTC monograph; or the manufacturer may petition FDA to make the switch.

Currently, by far the most common way to accomplish the Rx-to-OTC switch is by supplementing the drug's NDA. This is in large part due to the opportunity this route affords the drug's sponsor to obtain marketing exclusivity for the switched product. In particular, if the Rx-to-OTC switch supplement involves a change to the drug that is supported by "new clinical investigations" that are "conducted or sponsored by [the applicant]" and are "essential to the [supplement's] approval," the applicant will gain three additional years of marketing exclusivity for the OTC product, as discussed above. There is no set formula for determining what kinds of changes will meet the exclusivity requirements; such changes can relate to such matters as active ingredient, dosage form, route of administration, conditions of use or dosing regimen.

Procedurally, an applicant seeking to switch a product must file a supplemental application to the drug's NDA and must include a statement explaining why its studies meet the requirements for exclusivity, as described above. Next, FDA will decide whether to approve the switch, and subsequently will make the exclusivity determination. Generic manufacturers of the switched product, however, may file citizen petitions or take other administrative or legal actions to encourage FDA to deny exclusivity. Conversely, a manufacturer who is unhappy with an agency denial of exclusivity may challenge that denial in court.

> *There are three ways to make an Rx-to-OTC switch:*
> - *the manufacturer supplements an existing NDA*
> - *FDA creates or amends an OTC monograph*
> - *the manufacturer can petition FDA for the switch*

Expedited Availability

As discussed above, one major response to concerns about drug approval delays has been the establishment of the user fee system. Separate and apart from that system, however, a number of special pathways have been created both by FDA and Congress to expedite the availability of drugs for seriously ill patients. This section provides a brief review of those pathways.

Treatment INDs

The treatment IND mechanism, established by regulation in 1987 and codified by FDAMA, allows an investigational drug to be provided outside controlled clinical trials to treat patients with serious or immediately life-threatening

The treatment IND mechanism, established by regulation in 1987 and codified by FDAMA, allows an investigational drug to be provided outside controlled clinical trials to treat patients with serious or immediately life-threatening diseases for which no comparable or satisfactory alternative therapy is available.

diseases for which no comparable or satisfactory alternative therapy is available. The standard for FDA clearance of a treatment IND for a "life-threatening disease" is whether the available scientific evidence, taken as a whole, provides a reasonable basis for concluding that the drug "may be effective for its intended use" and would not expose patients to an "unreasonable and significant risk of illness or injury." For a "serious" disease, the standard is whether there is "sufficient evidence of safety and effectiveness" to support treatment use. Most IND procedural requirements apply to treatment INDs, including informed consent requirements and prohibitions on pre-approval promotion or other commercialization of experimental treatments (although companies may charge patients enough to cover costs). In addition, the drug sponsor is expected to continue conventional clinical trials and to pursue marketing approval of the drug with "due diligence."

Individual Patient Access to Investigational Drugs for Serious Diseases

Under the expanded access mechanism established by FDAMA in 1997, a patient acting through a physician may request an investigational drug, and a manufacturer may provide such a drug, if the patient's physician determines that the patient has no comparable or satisfactory alternative therapy, and that the risk to the patient from the investigational drug is no greater than the risk from the disease or condition. For a drug to qualify for this mechanism, FDA must determine that there is sufficient evidence of safety and effectiveness to support its use and that provision of the investigational drug will not interfere with clinical investigations in support of marketing approval. In addition, the sponsor or clinical investigator must submit to FDA a protocol describing the use of the drug in a single patient or small group of patients.

Emergency Access

FDAMA also codified current regulations permitting the shipment of investigational new drugs for the diagnosis, monitoring or treatment of a serious condition or disease in emergency situations as determined by FDA.

Fast-Track Approval

Fast-track designation is available for drugs or biologics that demonstrate the potential to address unmet medical needs for serious or life-threatening conditions.

Under the fast-track authority established by FDAMA, fast-track designation is available for drugs or biologics that demonstrate the potential to address unmet medical needs for serious or life-threatening conditions.

The first step in the fast-track program is that the sponsor requests FDA to designate its drug as a fast-track product. If the drug is given fast-track status, the law permits approval based on evidence of the drug's effect on a "surrogate endpoint" that reasonably suggests clinical benefit, or on a clinical endpoint. Such approval may be conditioned on the completion of postmarketing, or Phase IV, clinical studies to verify and describe the drug's clinical benefit and to resolve remaining uncertainty about the surrogate endpoint or clinical endpoint on the basis of which the product was approved. Drugs and biologics approved under the fast-track procedure may also be subject to pre-dissemination review requirements for promotional labeling and advertising, and to a streamlined procedure for withdrawal of approval if, among other reasons, a postmarketing clinical study fails to verify clinical benefit. The law also provides that FDA may review marketing applications for fast-track products on a rolling basis (i.e., may begin review based on partial submissions); user fee deadlines, however, do not apply to such an application until it is complete.

The Combination Drug Policy

FDA's combination drug policy provides that:

> (a) Two or more drugs may be combined in a single dosage form when each component makes a contribution to the claimed effects and the dosage of each component (amount, frequency, duration) is such that the combination is safe and effective for a significant patient population requiring such concurrent therapy as defined in the labeling for the drug. Special cases of this general rule are where a component is added:
>
> (1) To enhance the safety or effectiveness of the principal active component; and
>
> (2) To minimize the potential for abuse of the principal active component.
>
> 21 C.F.R. § 300.50.

Although this regulation on its face reads as a permissive policy, it was actually promulgated to require additional evidence of efficacy for many fixed combination drug products already on the market. For an NDA for a combination drug containing two (or more) active ingredients, the combination policy means that evidence of safety and efficacy would be required not only for the drug as a whole, but also for each of the components. In other words, each component must be shown to contribute individually to the claimed overall effects of the product. This contribution, however, need not relate to efficacy—a component also may be added if it is shown to increase the safety of the other component or components. Of key importance under the combination drug policy is the principle that prior efficacy (or safety) results on individual active components cannot be extrapolated to a proposed combination drug; rather, that combination drug must undergo its own clinical investigations to demonstrate safety, efficacy and the contribution of the active components. Like many such principles in the drug approval setting, however, this one is not necessarily absolute, and FDA may exhibit more (or less) flexibility in individual cases.

Animal Drugs

Basic Elements

In broad outline, the approval process for animal drugs tracks that for human drugs.

In broad outline, the approval process for animal drugs tracks that for human drugs. Indeed, the legal definition of a "drug" itself includes articles "intended for use in the diagnosis, cure, mitigation, treatment, or prevention of disease *in man or other animals*" or "intended to affect the structure or any function of the body *of man or other animals*" (FDCA § 201(g)(1)(B), (C) (emphasis added)). Although the law provides separate definitions of a "new drug" requiring affirmative FDA approval for human drugs and animal drugs, respectively, these definitions are virtually identical in substance. The "new animal drug" definition, however, explicitly includes drugs intended for use in animal feed (but excludes the feed itself) (FDCA § 201(v)).

Like new drugs intended for use in humans, a new animal drug must ordinarily be investigated in preclinical and then clinical studies in order to gather evidence about its safety and efficacy. Clinical studies typically take place under the animal counterpart of an IND, the "Notice of Claimed Investigational Exemption for a New Animal Drug" (commonly referred to as an INAD), covered in 21 C.F.R. Part 511. The procedures and standards for the submission and FDA review of a new animal drug application (NADA) (codified in section 512 of the FDCA and 21 C.F.R. Part 514) are, in turn, very much like those for an NDA. In particular, a new animal drug must be shown to be safe and effective in order to obtain FDA approval. (One procedural difference between human and animal drug approvals is that all new animal drug approvals are published as regulations in the C.F.R.) Once the new animal drug is approved, proposed changes in the conditions of approval trigger the requirements of the supplemental NADA process, which are roughly similar to those of the supplemental NDA process.

In addition, although animal drugs were not included in the 1984 amendments that established the current patent term extension and generic drug approval provisions for human drugs, they were the subject of counterpart legislation four years later, in the form of the 1988 Generic Animal Drug and Patent Term Restoration Act (GAD-PTR Act). As the 1984 amendments had done for human drugs, the GAD-PTR Act established a framework in the area of animal drugs for patent term restoration, approval of generic products and exclusivity protection for innovator products.

Special Issues

Beneath the overall structural similarities between the approval processes for human and animal drugs, there are a few important differences in policy and approach, particularly with respect to drugs for use in food-producing animals. One such difference stems from the fact that such drugs are often administered in animal feed. In such cases FDA regulates not only the drug itself, but also the premixes and concentrates into which the drug is initially mixed (the so-called "Type A medicated articles" and "Type B medicated feeds") as well as the final medicated feed incorporating such concentrates to be fed to animals in the field (the so-called "Type C medicated feed") (21 C.F.R. Part 558). A drug intended for incorporation in animal feed may be lawfully shipped only to the holder of an approval for the medicated feed in question (FDCA § 512(a)). That feed, in turn, must be used in accordance with the conditions of its approval (FDCA § 512(m)).

In addition, as might be expected for drugs administered to food-producing animals, the safety of humans who may ultimately ingest products derived from such animals is an overriding concern. FDA accordingly oversees not only the safety and efficacy of such drugs in the animal "patients" themselves but also the possible health effects of potential residues of such drugs in meat, milk or other products of those animals. Of particular importance here is the FDCA's prohibition on the use of any cancer-causing compound in food animals, unless it can be determined by methods satisfactory to FDA that no residue of such compound will be found in food produced from such animals under conditions reasonably certain to be followed in practice (the so-called "DES proviso") (FDCA § 512(d)(1)(I); 21 C.F.R. Part 500, Subpart E).

FDA oversees not only the safety and efficacy of drugs administered for food-producing animals in the animal "patients" themselves but also the possible health effects of potential residues of such drugs in meat, milk or other products of those animals.

Animal Biologics

As in the human arena, biological products—that is, products produced from living beings, such as sera, antitoxins and the like—intended for therapeutic use in animals are subject to a separate legal and regulatory regime from that for drugs, under the 1913 Virus-Serum-Toxin Act (VST Act). Unlike human biologics, however, animal biologics are regulated not only under a separate legal regime but also by an altogether separate agency, the U.S. Department of Agriculture (USDA).

The VST Act made it illegal to ship from one state to another any virus, serum, toxin or analogous product intended for use in the treatment of domestic animals unless the product in question was prepared in accordance with regulations issued by USDA at an establishment holding a current license from USDA (21 U.S.C. § 151). On the basis of this rather sparse legislative statement, USDA has erected a system of licensing animal biologics and the establishments that produce them whose main substantive features parallel those of FDA animal drug regulation (this system is codified in 9 C.F.R. subch. E). New animal biologics must be supported by adequate showings of safety and efficacy in order to obtain approval, and are subject to more or less the same level of postapproval regulatory oversight as new animal drugs. One peculiarity in the animal biologics area is that the original language of the VST Act was read to exempt the preparation and shipment of animal biologics entirely within one state from USDA regulation. Congress filled this gap in 1985 when it amended the act to cover shipments of animal biologics "in or from the United States" (Pub. L. No. 99-198, 99 Stat. 1654).

BIOLOGICS

In simple terms, biological products (sometimes referred to as "biologics" or "biologicals") are medical products derived from living organisms.

In simple terms, biological products (sometimes referred to as "biologics" or "biologicals") are medical products derived from living organisms. Such products are regulated under section 351 of the PHSA (42 U.S.C. § 262), as well as under various provisions of the FDCA. Legally, biological products are defined under section 351 of the PHSA as including "a virus, therapeutic serum, toxin, antitoxin, vaccine, blood, blood component or derivative, allergenic product, or analogous product, or arsphenamine or derivatives of arsphenamine (or any other trivalent organic arsenic compound) applicable to the prevention, treatment, or cure of a disease or condition of human beings." To be lawfully marketed in interstate commerce, a biological product must be the subject of a biologics license, issued by FDA on the basis of a demonstration that the product is "safe, pure, and potent," and that the facility in which the product is manufactured meets standards to assure that it continues to be safe, pure and potent.

Originally, the regulatory scheme for biologics was quite distinct from that for nonbiologic drugs.

Originally, the regulatory scheme for biologics was quite distinct from that for nonbiologic drugs. The most prominent difference was that whereas drugs must obtain NDAs in order to be lawfully marketed, biological products were the subject of a bifurcated approval system under which a product had to obtain a product license, by means of a product license application (PLA), *and* the establishment where the product was manufactured had to obtain an establishment license, through an establishment license application (ELA), before the product could be lawfully marketed.

In 1997, however, FDAMA amended section 351 of the PHSA to establish the single biologics license in place of the former product and establishment licenses for all biological products. FDAMA also stipulated that the FDCA applies to a biological product, with the sole exception that a product for which a license has been approved under PHSA § 351 is not required to have an approved NDA. Finally, Congress stated directly in FDAMA that FDA "shall take measures to minimize differences in the review and approval" of new drugs and biologics. For most practical purposes, therefore, the regulation of human therapeutic biologics in both the pre-approval and postapproval periods is closely similar to that of new drugs.

Thus, as in the new drug model previously discussed, to gain marketing approval for a therapeutic biologic, the sponsor of that biologic must demonstrate its safety and efficacy for its recommended uses. Along the road to that approval, the IND requirements applicable to new drugs also apply to the investigation of therapeutic biologics. Similarly, in the postapproval world, biologics manufacturers must report adverse events under a scheme similar to that for drugs (21 C.F.R. Part 600, Subpart D).

Biosimilars

In March 2010—more than 25 years after the enactment of the law establishing the modern ANDA system for approval of generic drugs, and following a lengthy period of policy and legislative debate—Congress enacted the Biologics Price Competition and Innovation Act of 2009 (BPCIA), establishing a pathway for abbreviated approval of biologics, or so-called biosimilars. The BPCIA was part of a comprehensive package of healthcare reform legislation, the Patient Protection and Affordable Care Act. While the fundamental concept of creating an abbreviated approval pathway for subsequent-entry products is common to both ANDAs and biosimilars, the requirements for these two categories of products are fundamentally different in a number of respects, reflecting the scientific differences between drugs and biologics.

Application and Approval Requirements

The BPCIA amended section 351 of the PHSA by adding a new subsection (k) establishing requirements for biosimilar applications and approval. Under subsection (k), a biosimilar application must include information demonstrating that: 1) the biological product that is the subject of the application is "biosimilar" to a reference product; 2) the biosimilar product and reference product use the same mechanism(s) of action for the condition(s) of use prescribed, recommended or suggested in the proposed labeling, to the extent the mechanism(s) of action are known for the reference product; 3) the condition(s) of use prescribed, recommended or suggested in the labeling proposed for the biosimilar product have been previously approved for the reference product; 4) the biosimilar product has the same route of administration, dosage form and strength as the reference product; and 5) the facility in which the biosimilar product is manufactured, processed, packed or held meets standards designed to assure that the product continues to be safe, pure and potent.

FDA must license a biosimilar if: 1) the agency determines that the information in the application is sufficient to show that the biological product is biosimilar to (or, if sought by the applicant, interchangeable with) the reference product; and 2) the applicant or other appropriate person consents to inspection of the facility that is the subject of the application.

"Biosimilarity" means that the biological product in question is "highly similar" to the reference product "notwithstanding minor differences in clinically inactive components" and that there are no clinically meaningful differences between the biological product and the reference product in terms of safety, purity or potency.

For purposes of this statute, "biosimilarity" means that the biological product in question is "highly similar" to the reference product "notwithstanding minor differences in clinically inactive components" and that there are no clinically meaningful differences between the biological product and the reference product in terms of safety, purity or potency. The biosimilar application must establish biosimilarity on the basis of data from 1) analytical studies showing that the biosimilar and its reference product are "highly similar" notwithstanding minor differences in clinically inactive components, 2) animal studies, including an assessment of toxicity and 3) a clinical study or studies (including an assessment of immunogenicity and pharmacokinetics or pharmacodynamics) sufficient to show the safety, purity and potency of the proposed product for one or more "appropriate" conditions of use for which licensure is sought and for which the reference product is licensed. FDA may, however, waive any of these application requirements if it determines they are unnecessary for a finding of biosimilarity.

Interchangeability

A biosimilar applicant that wishes its product to be considered interchangeable with the reference product must separately seek and obtain an interchangeability determination from FDA.

While a generic drug approved under an ANDA is presumptively the "same" as, and therefore interchangeable with, its reference product, this is not the case for biosimilars. Rather, a biosimilar applicant that wishes its product to be considered interchangeable with the reference product must separately seek and obtain an interchangeability determination from FDA. The agency must reach such a determination if it finds that the information submitted in the application shows that: 1) the biological product is biosimilar to the reference product, and 2) the biological product can be expected to produce the same clinical result as the reference product in any given patient. If the product will be administered more than once to an individual, FDA must also find the risk in terms of safety or diminished efficacy of alternating or switching between the two products is not greater than the risk of using the reference product without such alternation or switching. A product that qualifies as interchangeable under the statute may be substituted for its reference product without the intervention of the prescriber.

As a counterpart of the 180-day exclusivity available to the first ANDA applicant to challenge a listed patent covering the reference drug, the first biosimilar product determined to be interchangeable with a particular reference product for any condition of use receives a period of exclusivity protection during which no other product may be deemed interchangeable to that reference product for any condition of use. The exclusivity period terminates on the earlier of: 1) one year after the first commercial marketing of the first interchangeable biosimilar product; 2) 18 months after either a final court decision on all patents in suit, or the dismissal with or without prejudice of an action brought by the reference product sponsor against the biosimilar applicant under the patent resolution provisions of the BPCIA (discussed below); 3) 42 months after approval of the first interchangeable biosimilar product, if the applicant has been sued under section 351(l)(6) and the litigation is still ongoing; or 4) 18 months after approval of the first interchangeable product, if the applicant has not been sued under section 351(l)(6). For this purpose "interchangeable" means that the biosimilar "may be substituted for the reference product without the intervention of the health care provider who prescribed the reference product."

Exclusivity

FDA may not make approval of a biosimilar application effective until 12 years after the date on which the reference product was first licensed. A biosimilar application may not be submitted until four years after the date on which the reference product was first licensed under section 351(a). A supplement to the reference product application is not eligible for these exclusivity periods, nor is a subsequent application filed by the same sponsor or a related entity for 1) a change (not including a structural modification) that results in a new indication, route of administration, dosing schedule, dosage form, delivery system, delivery device or strength, or 2) a structural modification that does not result in a change in safety, purity or potency. The available exclusivity periods may be extended by six months if the sponsor satisfies the statute's pediatric testing requirements. These requirements incorporate by reference the key provisions of the Best Pharmaceuticals for Children Act, which sets forth the basic scheme for pediatric exclusivity for new drugs (discussed above).

Patents

Under the BPCIA the reference product sponsor and biosimilar applicant privately exchange information about relevant patents as a prelude to possible patent infringement litigation.

In lieu of the *Orange Book* patent listing process under the Drug Price Competition and Patent Term Restoration legislation, under the BPCIA the reference product sponsor and biosimilar applicant privately exchange information about relevant patents as a prelude to possible patent infringement litigation. The statute's mechanism for resolving patent disputes may be altered by agreement between the parties.

Under the BPCIA mechanism, within 20 days after FDA notifies the biosimilar applicant that the application has been accepted for review, the applicant must send the reference product sponsor a copy of the application and information describing the processes used to manufacture the biosimilar. Outside counsel and one in-house counsel for the reference product sponsor are entitled to confidential access to the application and accompanying information, provided those attorneys do not engage in formal or informal patent prosecution related to the reference product.

Within 60 days after receiving this information, the reference product sponsor must provide the biosimilar applicant with a list of patents for which the sponsor believes it (or a patent owner that has granted it an exclusive license) could reasonably assert a claim of patent infringement, and must identify which patents it would be prepared to license to the applicant. Within 60 days of receiving this list, the biosimilar applicant may provide to the reference product sponsor its own list of patents for which it believes the reference product sponsor (or a patent owner that has granted it an exclusive license) could reasonably assert a claim of patent infringement. It must also provide, for each patent listed by the reference sponsor or itself, either: 1) a detailed statement that describes, on a claim-by-claim basis, the factual and legal basis of its opinion that the patent is invalid, unenforceable or will not be infringed by the commercial marketing of the biosimilar product; or 2) a statement that it does not intend to begin commercial marketing of its product until after expiry of the patent. The biosimilar applicant must also provide a response regarding each patent that the reference product sponsor has stated it is prepared to license to the applicant.

Not more than 60 days after receiving this information, the reference product sponsor must provide the biosimilar applicant with a detailed statement describing on a claim-by-claim basis, as to each patent that the biosimilar applicant claims to be not infringed, why the sponsor believes the patent will be infringed by the commercial marketing of the biosimilar, and, as to each patent the biosimilar applicant claims to be invalid and not enforceable, a response to the biosimilar applicant's claim.

Following these exchanges, the parties must engage in good faith negotiations to agree which patents will be the subject of an action for patent infringement pursuant to the expedited process provided in the statute. If the parties do not agree on such a list of patents within 15 days, the parties will simultaneously exchange lists of patents each believes should be the subject of a patent infringement action. (The reference sponsor's list may not contain more patents than the biosimilar applicant's list, except that if the biosimilar applicant does not list any patents the reference sponsor may list one.)

If the parties agree on a list of patents to be litigated, the reference product sponsor must bring the infringement action within 30 days after the agreement. If the parties do not agree, the reference product sponsor must bring an infringement action within 30 days after the exchange of lists as described above. Failure to adhere to these deadlines will limit the reference product sponsor's remedy to a reasonable royalty. Not more than 30 days after being served with a complaint in such an infringement action, the biosimilar applicant must provide a copy of the complaint to FDA, which will then publish notice of the complaint in the *Federal Register*.

If the parties agree on a list of patents to be litigated, the reference product sponsor must bring the infringement action within 30 days after the agreement.

- If the reference product sponsor should have included a patent in its initial list but failed to do in a timely fashion, the patent owner may not bring a patent infringement action with respect to the biosimilar.

- After the list of patents has been initally provided to the biosimilar applicant, a patent newly issued to or exclusively licensed by the reference product sponsor that the sponsor reasonably believes could be asserted in an infringement action must be provided to the biosmilar applicant in a supplement to the initial list not more than 30 days after the issuance or licensing.

- The biosimilar applicant must provide notice to the reference product sponsor not less than 180 days before the first commercial marketing of the biosimilar product. The reference product sponsor then may seek a preliminary injunction against the marketing of the biosimilar product until the court has reached a finding as to any patent that was in its initial list but not subject to expedited litigation under the statute.

Guidance Documents

Section 351(k) provides that FDA may issue general or specific guidance on the licensure of biosimilars. If the agency issues guidance, it must follow the requirements of section 701(h) of the FDCA (which addresses FDA's authority to issue nonbinding guidance documents generally), and must offer the public an opportunity to comment before finalizing the document. FDA must also establish a process for the public to provide input on priorities for issuing guidance.

FDA may issue general or specific guidance on the licensure of biosimilars.

Significantly, the issuance or non-issuance of guidance does not preclude the review of, or action on, an application submitted under section 351(k).

If FDA issues a product class-specific guidance, that guidance must include a description of the criteria FDA will use to determine whether a biological product is highly similar to a reference product in that product class, as well as the criteria, if available, that FDA will use to determine whether a biological product in that class meets the standards for interchangeability. FDA may indicate in a guidance that science and experience, as of the date of the guidance, do not allow approval of section 351(k) applications with respect to a particular product or product class, not including recombinant proteins.

In February 2012 FDA issued three general draft guidances on biosimilar product development. These draft guidances address a number of issues relating to biosimilar product development, including scientific and quality considerations in demonstrating biosimilarity to a reference product.

Case Studies

Case Study: Court Enforcement of FDA Approval Deadline

The futility of trying to enforce the statutory 180-day filing clock deadline in court seemed to have been confirmed by a 1991 case in which a disgruntled drug company, Barr Laboratories, Inc., sued FDA for not completing the review of its drug applications within the deadline. The court agreed that FDA's delay violated the statute, but refused to do anything about it on the ground that it was up to the agency, not the court, to set drug review priorities, and that to order FDA to meet the deadline on the plaintiff's applications would disadvantage other, equally worthy applicants. *In re Barr Lab., Inc.*, 930 F.2d 72 (D.C. Cir. 1991), *cert. denied*, 502 U.S. 906 (1991).

In 2005, however, a section 505(b)(2) NDA applicant challenged the conventional wisdom, with unexpected results. Sandoz, Inc. had submitted its NDA for the recombinant human growth hormone product Omnitrope in July 2003, relying in part on FDA's prior approval of Pfizer's recombinant human growth hormone product Genotropin. In April 2004, Pfizer objected to the Omnitrope application. In August 2004, FDA told Sandoz that although the agency had completed its review of Omnitrope, it was deferring a decision because of the application's "nature and complexity." *Sandoz v. Leavitt et al.*, Civ. No. 05-1810 (RMU), D.D.C. April 10, 2006, at 3.

In September 2005 Sandoz sued FDA, asserting that the agency had violated the statutory 180-day action deadline. FDA did not dispute that assertion, but argued that the statutory deadline was "aspirational" and had effectively been modified by the subsequent user fee action date structure agreed upon with Congress. The court brushed this defense aside and granted summary judgment for Sandoz, concluding that the statutory requirement was clear, unambiguous and unchanged, and that to hold otherwise would be to "accept governmental mediocrity and vitiate the statute's mandatory language." The court distinguished the *Barr* case on the grounds that FDA had approved a number of other subsequently filed NDAs, including 505(b)(2) NDAs, for both naturally sourced and recombinant biologic drugs since Sandoz had submitted its application, so that it was evident that ordering FDA action on Sandoz's NDA would not "directly bottleneck other NDAs." Further, with additional resources now available to FDA under PDUFA, the court felt the agency should be held to a higher standard. Accordingly, the court ordered FDA to comply with the statutory requirement and either approve the application or provide Sandoz with the required notice and opportunity for a hearing on the approvability of the application. To the surprise of some, FDA chose in response to approve Sandoz's application.

For better or worse, however, thus far the *Sandoz* case has led neither to a meaningful change of FDA's NDA review practices nor to a wholesale legal assault on those practices by drug sponsors. For one thing, the specific facts of the case are relatively unique, in particular FDA's written acknowledgement to the sponsor that it had completed its substantive review of the application but was nonetheless refusing to take final action, presumably at least in part because of Pfizer's objections, without any clear end in sight. This left FDA with a glaring legal vulnerability the agency would be unlikely to take on again. More broadly, under the user fee system, it remains the case that sponsors typically have much more to gain by working with FDA within the framework of their action dates to move the application forward than by taking the agency on in court. Nonetheless, the *Sandoz* case illustrates that there are limits to FDA's discretion under the user fee system and that the statutory filing clock deadline retains at least some life still.

Case Study: Early Access to Investigational Drugs

Evidently unsatisfied with the existing mechanisms for expedited availability of experimental drugs described above, the patient advocacy group Abigail Alliance sued FDA over the agency's refusal to allow dying patients unrestricted access to unapproved drugs. After an unexpected ruling by a panel of the D.C. Circuit Court of Appeals in 2006 that the Due Process Clause of the U.S. Constitution protects terminally ill patients' rights to have access to "potentially

The patient advocacy group Abigail Alliance sued FDA over the agency's refusal to allow dying patients unrestricted access to unapproved drugs.

life-saving" investigational drugs that have passed successfully through Phase I studies, FDA sought reconsideration by the full court. In August 2007 the court rejected the panel's conclusion and ruled that "there is no fundamental right . . . of access to experimental drugs for the terminally ill." *Abigail Alliance v. von Eschenbach*, 495 F.3d 695, 697 (D.C. Cir. 2007).

Case Study: Bioequivalence for Non-systemically Absorbed Drugs

As noted above, NDA sponsors have frequently challenged FDA's application of bioequivalence requirements to ANDAs referencing their products, particularly for non-systemically absorbed drugs that do not lend themselves to standard *in vivo* blood level testing to determine equivalence. A prominent early example of conflict over bioequivalence involved the asthma drug albuterol administered by metered dose inhaler (MDI). The NDA holder for the drug, Schering-Plough, submitted a petition to FDA arguing that the statutory bioequivalence requirement, which specifies only measurements of "rate and extent of absorption," categorically precluded FDA from approving any ANDAs for non-systemically absorbed drugs, including, of course, MDI albuterol. FDA denied the petition on the basis that the statute specifically contemplates determinations of bioequivalency based on evidence other than rate and extent of absorption. Schering-Plough then sued FDA in federal district court, but the court agreed with FDA's interpretation and dismissed the complaint. (*Schering Corp. v. Sullivan*, 782 F. Supp. 645, 647 (D.D.C. 1992), *vacated*, 995 F.2d 1103 (D.C. Cir. 1993).) On appeal, the substance of the district court's holding was affirmed. The appellate court stated that although the FDCA's definition of bioequivalence is "ambiguous," FDA's interpretation of that definition, on the basis of which the agency proposed to approve generic MDI albuterol products, was "reasonable." (*Schering Corp. v. FDA*, 51 F.3d 390, 400 (3d Cir. 1995), *cert. denied*, 116 S. Ct. 274 (1995).).

A more recent challenge to FDA's bioequivalence standards involving a variation on the standard approach was brought by ViroPharma Inc., holder of the NDA for vancomycin, a non-systemically absorbed drug to treat severe gastrointestinal (GI) infections. Citing FDA's response to a citizen petition filed by the sponsor of a different locally acting GI drug in which the agency stated that it could accept *in vitro* studies to show bioequivalence for such drugs, ViroPharma brought suit against FDA alleging that this agency response had effectively amended the bioequivalence regulations without the required notice-and-comment rulemaking. The district court dismissed ViroPharma's case on standing grounds, *ViroPharma Inc. v Hamburg*, 777 F. Supp. 140 (D.D.C. 2010), and so did not reach the question of regulatory interpretation posed by the plaintiff. At this writing, however, the case is on appeal and may yet provide a judicial read on the scope of FDA discretion to interpret its own bioequivalence regulations.

Chapter 6

A Pharmacovigilance Primer

Edward John Allera, Buchanan Ingersoll & Rooney PC, Washington, D.C.

Key Points

- Pharmacovigilance includes all activities directed toward detecting, assessing, understanding and preventing adverse events or other product-related problems.
- The regulatory framework for pharmacovigilance has been in place for decades, imposing postapproval requirements on all categories of drugs.
- Any adverse experience that is not listed on a drug's current label is considered an "unexpected" drug experience.
- There are five basic types of postmarketing reports, whose requirements are dictated by the seriousness of the adverse experience.
- Congress, in the Food and Drug Administration Amendments Act of 2007, created a statutory mechanism in recognition of the importance of pharmacovigilance: risk evaluation and mitigation strategy.
- Pharmacovigilance reporting requirements are designed to safeguard public health and safety by creating a system for improving the labeling of drug products.

INTRODUCTION

Pharmacovigilance encompasses all postapproval scientific and data-gathering activities relating to the detection, assessment, understanding and prevention of adverse events or any other product-related problems. Interestingly, no statutory definition of the practice exists under the Federal Food, Drug, and Cosmetic Act (FDCA) or the Food and Drug Administration's (FDA's) regulations. FDA has created the regulatory framework for pharmacovigilance indirectly under its authority to regulate all drug labeling as well as its authority to require maintenance of records for new drugs.

Pharmacovigilance has played a role in the safe use of pharmaceuticals for decades. For example, the declaration of phenformin as an "imminent hazard to health" in the 1970s was based on pharmacovigilance information. The role of pharmacovigilance has dramatically increased in recent years as public policy considerations, public perceptions and acceptance of risk have shifted.

It has long been accepted by FDA and industry that the risk analysis that occurs during the drug development process has to be thorough and rigorous. In recent years, there has been increased recognition of the need and importance of monitoring a drug's safety after approval, while in actual medical use. As a result, the discipline of pharmacovigilance has become increasingly central to the regulatory life cycle of drugs.

It is well recognized that not all safety concerns will be identified during the clinical trial process.

It is well recognized that not all safety concerns will be identified during the clinical trial process. Even drugs intended for chronic use are seldom tested in more than 3,000 to 5,000 patients prior to approval. In contrast, postapproval patient exposure to a new drug increases by orders of magnitude. Of particular concern are patients with co-morbid conditions and those who are taking other drugs.

Heavy publicity about postapproval adverse events allegedly associated with drugs such as Vioxx and Avandia have heightened both public and political awareness of the important role that pharmacovigilance plays in protecting public health. In the Food and Drug Administration Amendments Act of 2007 (FDAAA), Congress recognized the importance of pharmacovigilance and created a statutory mechanism—the risk evaluation and mitigation strategy—for increasing the scrutiny of safety for premarket approval and postmarket approval. This activity has also led to an increase in the amount of product liability litigation involving the safety of drugs. Further, the Centers for Medicare and Medicaid Services (CMS) has issued regulations to facilitate gathering data from the Medicare Part D drug program to aid, in part, pharmacovigilance. All of these factors magnify the importance of pharmacovigilance.

BACKGROUND

The regulatory framework for pharmacovigilance has been in place for decades. Specific FDA regulations impose postapproval pharmacovigilance requirements on all categories of drugs: grandfathered drugs (21 C.F.R. § 310.305); drugs approved under a new drug application (NDA) (21 C.F.R. § 314.80); drugs approved under an abbreviated new drug application (ANDA) (21 C.F.R. § 314.98); and biologics (21 C.F.R. § 600.80). Additional regulations exist for postapproval testing requirements (21 C.F.R. § 310.303), highlighting the need for congruency between the information gathered during the pre-approval phase with information collected postapproval. The symmetry of the pharmacovigilance process is further confirmed in 21 C.F.R. § 314.70(c)(6)(iii)(A) where supplemental applications are required to add or strengthen a contraindication, warning, precaution or adverse reaction. Supplements are subject to a 30-day pre-implementation FDA review and approval of the proposed language.

REPORTING REQUIREMENTS

Overview

Even before the current focus on pharmacovigilance, two principles for adverse event reporting were set forth in FDA's regulations: timeliness and accuracy. Each has weaknesses given the partially voluntary nature of the reporting system, the limitations on the data and clinical information available, and the need for data interpretation.

With regard to timing, the current environment of an ever-increasing number of reports to FDA, faster FDA review cycles for NDAs, more complex new drug submissions, and the greater use of drugs by an aging population has placed more pressure on FDA, and as a consequence, manufacturers, to develop sophisticated infrastructures that will help them to quickly and aggressively obtain and report adverse effects.

The accuracy of reporting, however, represents a unique challenge. The accurate interpretation of reported information can be difficult, especially considering the common usage of gross or crude terms, ranging from various lexicons to differences in human perception (i.e., different clinicians and patients may define specific adverse effects vastly differently).

Because crises involving drug safety always permit cynical hindsight and second-guessing of pharmacovigilance data, the timeliness of submitting adverse event reports to FDA is also critical. FDA has vast experience in adverse events, drug safety reports and safety evaluation not only concerning the drug in question, but also identical, similar and related drugs. This database affords FDA a perspective on risk that is unavailable to any single applicant because no single report or series of reports is dispositive; it is only a piece of the greater safety picture. For a manufacturer, not only is thorough and timely reporting of adverse events necessary but it is also important that it maintain an active dialogue with FDA about the reports, trends and any other data that may affect the labeling or status of the drug. Significantly, U.S. courts have viewed such collaborative efforts by manufacturers with FDA to be a basis for limiting product liability.

Definitions

FDA has developed a glossary of terms to deal with pharmacovigilance (21 C.F.R. §§ 310.305, 312.32, 314.80 and 600.80). An "adverse drug experience" is defined as any adverse event associated with the use of a drug in humans,

> *Even before the current focus on pharmacovigilance, two principles for adverse event reporting were set forth in FDA's regulations: timeliness and accuracy.*

whether or not drug related, in the course of professional practice, including intentional or unintentional overdosage, drug abuse, drug withdrawal or the failure of the drug to have its intended effect.

"Disability" is a substantial disruption in a person's ability to conduct normal life functions.

"Life-threatening" is an adverse drug experience that places the patient at the immediate risk of death, but does not include an adverse experience that, had it occurred in a more severe form, might have caused death.

A "serious adverse experience" is one occurring at any dose of a drug that results in death, a life-threatening experience, inpatient hospitalization or prolongation of an existing hospitalization, a persistent or significant disability or incapacity, or a congenital anomaly or birth defect. Other events that do not cause the foregoing are also deemed serious if they may jeopardize the patient and require medical or surgical intervention to prevent those events.

Any adverse experience that is not listed in the current labeling of the drug is regarded as an unexpected drug experience.

The role of labeling surfaces in the definition of unexpected drug experiences. Any adverse experience that is not listed in the current labeling of the drug is regarded as an unexpected drug experience. These include events that may be symptomatically and pathophysiologically related to an event listed in the labeling but differ due to greater severity or specificity. FDA interprets "unexpected" as relating to the actual observation rather than the theoretical pharmacological possibility.

For unapproved drugs, approved drugs and approved biologics these terms are considered to be identical, and reporting should be handled consistently. Attempts to create different systems within a company only increase the likelihood of failing to comply with FDA's regulations and expectations.

Reports

Five basic types of postmarketing reports exist, and their reporting requirements are dictated by the seriousness of the adverse experiences: 15-day Alert Reports, 15-day Follow-Up Reports, Periodic Adverse Experience Reports, Field Alerts and Annual Reports.

♦ 15-day "Alert Report"

An applicant is required to report each adverse drug experience that it becomes aware of that is both serious and unexpected, whether foreign or domestic, as soon as possible but not later than 15 calendar days from initial receipt of the information. For an unapproved drug, any person whose name appears on the label, whether as its manufacturer, packer or distributor, has the filing obligation. Thus, the obligation applies to any adverse reaction that does not appear on the label and is serious by virtue of either its increased severity or incidence. Information from scientific literature or from abroad is subject to the 15-day Alert reporting requirement if the information is found in scientific or medical journals as case reports or as the result of a clinical trial. A copy of the published article is to be filed with the report.

An applicant is required to report each adverse drug experience that it becomes aware of that is both serious and unexpected, whether foreign or domestic, as soon as possible but not later than 15 calendar days from initial receipt of the information.

These reports are designed to quickly provide FDA with relevant data from participants in the healthcare delivery system about a potentially adverse event related to a drug. The focus is on new or potentially new adverse experiences. While the adverse reports system in the United States has been termed voluntary in the general sense (healthcare providers and others in the healthcare distribution system), it is mandatory for drug applicants or persons whose names appear on the label.

♦ 15-day "Alert Report" Follow-Up

The obligation for follow-up falls directly on every person identified on the label of the drug product whether the holder of the approved application, the manufacturer, the packer or the distributor of either approved drugs or those drugs marketed without approvals. The reports must be prominently identified as to their content (e.g., "15-day Alert Report" or "15-day Alert Report Follow-Up"). The format for submission has historically been FDA Form 3500A, or a computer-generated version that provides an equivalent in all elements of data and is agreed to by FDA.

The holder of the application is obligated to conduct a comprehensive follow-up investigation. This point is critical. FDA's regulations impose an additional 15-calendar-day requirement on the report of new information or as requested by the agency. FDA's regulations require records of the steps taken in the investigation to be maintained even if no new information is detected. If new information is detected, it is subject to a new 15-day reporting requirement. Normally, however, FDA will be in contact with the company, and a thorough report will be prepared in accord with a time frame agreed to by the parties. Similar obligations apply to the manufacturer of the drug, whether approved or unapproved. To reduce duplicative reporting, companies listed on the labeling can fulfill their obligations by providing notice to the applicant or manufacturer within five calendar days of the receipt of the adverse experience. In the contemporary environment, there appears to be no restriction on persons listed on the label from fulfilling these obligations in lieu of the holder of the approval or the manufacturer.

Persons or companies included on the labeling who report the adverse experience to the manufacturer or holder of the approval must maintain records of their adverse experience reporting, including the following: the date the adverse event was reported to them; the date it was reported to its business cohort (e.g., the manufacturer); and the name and address of the applicant or manufacturer.

As expected, confusion often arises regarding who is responsible for reporting. This has occurred, in large part, as a result of pharmaceutical industry operations becoming more "virtual" in recent years. The subcontracting by pharmaceutical companies of key operations, such as manufacturing, distribution, marketing and recordkeeping, has become commonplace. While it is commonly recognized that such arrangements require the creation of defined contractual obligations, this does not always take place in practice, creating reporting vulnerabilities where there is the absence of precise delegation of responsibilities among the parties. Confusion can arise about fulfillment of the legal obligations under the FDCA, resulting not only in the failure to comply with obligations of the act but also the potential for substantive commercial liabilities among the parties. The specific issues associated with follow-up are discussed below because they are the basis for the Periodic Adverse Experience Reports.

As expected, confusion often arises regarding who is responsible for reporting. This has occurred, in large part, as a result of pharmaceutical industry operations having become more "virtual" in recent years.

♦ Periodic Adverse Experience Reports

For the first three years after approval of an application, the applicant must submit quarterly reports of all adverse events that do not fall within the 15-day Alert Reports (i.e., those reported adverse events that are already noted within the product labeling or are not deemed to be "serious and life threatening"). The reports must be filed within 30 days of the end of the quarter, and the annual report must be filed within 60 days of the date of the NDA or ANDA approval. The reports must contain a narrative summary and analysis of the available information, an analysis of the 15-day Alert Reports (which are to be fully referenced) and a description of any action taken by the manufacturer since its receipt of the most recent report of the adverse event.

Information from postmarketing studies, reports from the scientific literature and foreign marketing experience are exempt from the periodic reporting system. Should an applicant conclude, however, that an adverse event is associated with a recently approved drug being studied under a new investigational NDA, FDA regulations provide that the applicant should include this event in its periodic report but should also clearly mark this incident as being distinct from those experiences that are being spontaneously reported.

All submitted records must protect the privacy of the patients involved, and therefore should not include the specific names and addresses of the individual patients. Unique identifiers of no more than eight characters that are assigned by the reporter should be created. The applicant should also include the name of the reporter. Under FDA's regulations the names of the patients, healthcare professionals, hospitals and geographical identifiers are not publicly releasable.

Further, the agency has a regulation that states that the submission of a report does not necessarily reflect a conclusion by the filer or FDA that the report or information constitutes an admission that the drug has caused or contributed to an adverse event. The regulation leaves open the ability of the applicant or other filer to not admit or deny that any report constitutes an admission.

The submission of a report does not necessarily reflect a conclusion by the filer or FDA that the report or information constitutes an admission that the drug has caused or contributed to an adverse event.

Limitations exist with any reporting system—whether spontaneous, mandatory or voluntary—and FDA recognizes them: passivity, under reporting, variable quality and incompleteness, duplicate reporting and inability to determine accurately the incidence rate because the numerator is uncertain and the denominator must be projected. More than 90 percent of the adverse experience reports are manufacturer reports, and the majority of them are periodic reports, although the rate of 15-day reports is increasing. Fewer than 10 percent of the reports are direct reports from healthcare professionals.

Acknowledging these limitations, FDA has issued guidelines intended to improve both the accuracy and the consistency of adverse experience reporting, thus hoping to further improve the public health value of pharmacovigilance. Optimally, FDA prefers reports to contain a description of the adverse event or disease experience, including the time to onset of signs and symptoms. Suspected and concomitant therapy details should be provided, including the regimen. A listing of over-the-counter, nutrient supplement and discontinued medications that were being taken concomitantly should also be included in the description as well as, to the extent possible, patient characteristics. In essence, the agency is seeking important baseline patient information that is relevant to the detection and diagnosis of the adverse event, as well as the methods used in making the diagnosis and the clinical course of the event and outcome. Relevant therapeutic measures and laboratory data are also sought, both at baseline and during the event, if available. Any information about response to dechallenge or rechallenge should also be submitted.

FDA has developed principles to assess submitted reports. Some of the questions that it poses include: Did the event occur within an expected time frame? Was there an absence of symptoms prior to drug exposure? Was there a positive challenge or dechallenge? Is the event consistent with the pharmacological effect of the drug or the class of drugs administered? Was the event identified in clinical trials? Is there an absence of alternative explanations?

Currently, there is no internationally agreed-upon standard or criteria for assessing causality. Moreover, confounded cases are common, and it is rarely possible to know with a high level of certainty that a specific event was specifically caused solely by a drug product. Of critical importance, FDA does not presently recommend any specific categorization of causality, although commentators have used the categories of probable, possible and unlikely.

FDA does not presently recommend any specific categorization of causality, although commentators have used the categories of probable, possible and unlikely.

For both approved and unapproved drugs subject to the recordkeeping requirements, a 10-year requirement exists for maintaining raw material and records, although the periodic reporting requirement does not apply to unapproved drugs.

♦ Field Alerts

The notification may be provided by telephone or other method of rapid communication, and a prompt written follow-up is required that is plainly marked "NDA-Field Alert Report." These reports are filed directly with the local field office, and by regulation are applicable only to approved products. There is no specific requirement in FDA's regulations for manufacturers of unapproved drugs to make such filings.

These reports have the shortest time requirement—three days. The clock is normally considered to start after the completion of the investigations into the potential manufacturing deficiencies. For marketed approved applications, whether NDAs or ANDAs, Field Alerts can be the most critical filings. These reports normally concern manufacturing problems and they often relate to more imminent public health risks. Accordingly, many consider such filings an integral part of current good manufacturing practices (cGMPs) that are applicable to all drugs, whether approved or marketed without an approval. As previously noted, within three working days of the receipt of information about distributed drugs or drugs about to be distributed, the application holder is to notify the district office that is responsible for the manufacturing facility should it believe that or become aware that its drug product is mislabeled or adulterated; that the drug product's labeling is not correct; and/or that the drug product could be mistaken for and/or erroneously used in place of another product. Some specific types of circumstances that require notification within three days include bacterial contamination; significant chemical, physical or other change; deterioration in the distributed drug product; or any failure of one or more distributed batches to meet the specifications established for it in its applications.

◆ Annual Reports

Within 60 days of the anniversary date of the application's approval, the applicant is required to file an annual report with the FDA reviewing division that was responsible for its approval. Two copies are required, accompanied by a transmittal Form FDA 2252. The report is to contain a summary of all significant new information that might affect the safety, effectiveness or labeling of the drug product subject to the application. The description is to include any actions taken or that the applicant intends to take as a result of any new information gathered during the year (e.g., labeling changes, new studies). A description of steps taken to evaluate pediatric use of the product should also be included.

Drug advertisements and promotional labeling are subject to the annual report. Specimens of mailing pieces and other labeling or advertising devised for promotion of the drug product at the time of the initial submission of the labeling and at the time of the initial publication of the advertisement must be submitted.

Distribution data according to National Drug Code number, the number of units, and quantities distributed for domestic and foreign use are to be reported. Patient, professional and package inserts are to be supplied, including all text, tables, etc. A summary of any labeling changes should also be included. Also to be filed are chemistry, manufacturing and controls changes, but only for new information that may affect the agency's previous conclusions about the drug product's safety or effectiveness. Any change that does not require a supplemental filing should be included in the annual report. It should last be noted that electronic submissions are now available.

Clinical data submissions are essential. Published clinical trials of the drug, or abstracts that include trials on the safety and effectiveness of the drug, must be submitted. Clinical trials on new uses, biopharmaceutics studies, pharmacokinetics and clinical pharmacology studies must also be submitted. Reports of clinical experience pertinent to safety, such as epidemiologic studies or analyses of experience in monitored patients, must be filed whether they are conducted by the applicant or otherwise obtained by it. Summaries of completed unpublished clinical trials are to be filed. The status of postmarketing study commitments must be filed as well as a log of outstanding regulatory commitments.

The various pharmacovigilance reporting requirements are designed to safeguard public health and safety by creating a system for improving the labeling of drug products.

The various pharmacovigilance reporting requirements are designed to safeguard public health and safety by creating a system for improving the labeling of drug products. The annual report is the most comprehensive and lucid document intended for this purpose. Each report is designed to highlight the occurrence of new, unexpected adverse events or an increase in the incidence of adverse events. In contemporary terms, FDA's various pronouncements in speeches and guidelines define the mission of pharmacovigilance as to facilitate the safe and effective use of drug products by promptly gathering and evaluating drug safety data and identifying "safety signals" that in turn allow for the most accurate labeling of drug products and their safe use.

A "safety signal" is an apparent excess of adverse events that can be found in a single well-documented case report, preclinical findings or experience with other similar products in the drug's pharmacological class.

A safety signal is, simply stated, a key component of an effective risk management program. FDA uses the term to refer to a concern that needs to be further assessed when an excess number of adverse events is detected and potentially associated with the use of a specific drug product as compared to what one would expect based on the drug's current labeling. The importance of strong pharmacovigilance activities was underscored by Congress, which specifically created a statutory "signal of a serious risk" in the FDAAA. The term pharmacovigilance and related term "signal of a serious risk" are analogous to terms such as cGMPs and current Good Clinical Practices. The terms are not static. They are evolving and have the potential for retroactive application by adversaries attempting to prove that the labeling of the drug product failed to contain all the relevant information.

According to both contemporary guidance and FDAAA, a "safety signal" is an apparent excess of adverse events that can be found in a single well-documented case report, preclinical findings or experience with other similar products in the drug's pharmacological class. It can also come from literature or risk management programs. Such signals should be assessed in terms of magnitude, population at risk, changes in risk of time, biological plausibility and interactions.

FDA expects companies to develop and maintain effective pharmacovigilance signal detection and reporting systems. Generally, such systems search available case reports, adverse experience databases, the literature and FDA's adverse experience review system to look for product-related data. Data searches are often carried out using sophisticated database-mining systems, with updated coding terminology like that of the *Medical Dictionary for Regulatory Activities*. The goal is to identify potential product-event linkages that may be considered signals and calculate the rate of risk (i.e., the reporting rates versus the actual incidence rate). Effective risk management systems will not only help detect these signals but also help manage them and reduce the risks.

When a signal is detected, investigation is considered appropriate through observational studies, either randomized or nonrandomized. Types of nonrandomized studies include pharmacoepidemiologic studies, surveys and registries. Signals that may warrant further investigation include new unlabeled adverse events (especially if serious); an apparent increase in the severity of a labeled event; the occurrence of serious events presently thought to be rare; new interactions; identification of previously unrecognized at-risk populations; confusion about the product's name or use; or inadequacies that are detected relative to current risk minimization efforts.

FDA's policies relative to pharmacovigilance activities are constantly evolving to reflect changes in technology as well as the growing sophistication of drug products. In this regard, it is important to note that retrospective data reviews, as well as reviews of currently reported data, can both play an important role in drug product safety. Thus, manufacturers must constantly be evaluating available data, both old and new, to safeguard the public health. Such a landscape, especially where the guidelines are broad and constantly evolving, also represents a challenge to drug manufacturers, who can potentially face significant liability risks despite vigilant efforts to maintain effective pharmacovigilance programs.

Supplemental Applications—Closing the Loop

The goal of pharmacovigilance is to ensure that labeling of drug products is comprehensive and contains the most contemporary description of the drugs' safe and effective data. This allows the risks associated with the drugs' use to be intelligently weighed, and for physicians, healthcare providers and patients to make informed decisions about the drugs' usage. Based upon the information gathered by pharmacovigilance plans and submissions to FDA, informed decisions can be made about any changes necessary to the product's current labeling. The pharmacovigilance process is continuous, as is the need to improve the labeling of a product during its entire life cycle.

The pharmacovigilance process is continuous, as is the need to improve the labeling of a product during its entire life cycle.

It is unquestioned that the holder of an approved NDA must satisfy the fundamental requirements of pharmacovigilance. Until generic competition arrives, the holder of the approved application is the focal point of all the relevant data. Today, generic drug products constitute more than 60 percent of the drug units sold in the U.S. market. Once an ANDA is approved for a drug, generic penetration can reach 90 percent in just 90 days. After a period of years, the generic version unquestionably will become the market leader, and the evidence on the drug's use gleaned from the market for reporting may be primarily about generic versions of the drug. FDA's regulations setting forth obligations of holders of approved NDAs are incorporated by reference into the agency's regulations imposing obligations on holders of approved ANDAs (see 21 C.F.R. §§ 314.70 (c), 314.97 and 314.98). As the role of generic drugs grows, the obligations of the holders of approved ANDAs in the area of pharmacovigilance may increase dramatically. Holders of these approvals must be aware of the current and evolving environment.

If the pharmacovigilance data lead one or more holders of an approval to conclude that a labeling change may be appropriate, the critical question becomes the proper approach for implementing the change. Theoretically, FDA's regulations permit the holder of an approved application, either NDA or ANDA, to file a supplemental application to implement the change at least within 30 days to strengthen a contraindication, warning, precaution and adverse experience. That interpretation is often proffered in product liability litigation, and the failure of companies to implement the change is alleged to be negligence or a breach of the appropriate standard of care.

Recent case law has created some inconsistencies and issues between FDA regulation and product labeling based on pharmacovigilance that affect companies in the market. A series of cases in the last two years have established that although the holder of an approved new drug application generally may not modify a drug label without FDA approval, it nonetheless can unilaterally make certain post-NDA labeling changes in order to add or strengthen a warning to improve drug safety, without FDA approval of the change. The NDA holder is responsible for its label regardless of FDA's concerns, and bears responsibility for the content of its label at all times, even if FDA disagrees or cannot decide on the appropriate warning.

Changes to generic drug labels are permitted only when a generic drug manufacturer is attempting to match an updated brand-name label or to follow FDA's instructions.

Confusingly, this unilateral authority to effect labeling changes is not available to manufacturers of generic drug products. Because the listed drug product is the basis for generic drug approval, the generic drug's labeling must always be the same as that of its brand-name predecessor. Accordingly, changes to generic drug labels are permitted only when a generic drug manufacturer is attempting to match an updated brand-name label or to follow FDA's instructions. Unilateral labeling changes to strengthen a warning, and "Dear Doctor" letters containing any substantial new warning information are considered to be violations of a generic manufacturers' duty of "sameness."

The case law has not considered this issue when the generic is the market leader or when the holder of the reference listed drug surrenders its NDA and the only products on the market hold approved ANDAs. However, generic drug manufacturers have the option of proposing to FDA that stronger warning labels are needed. If a generic drug manufacturer believes new safety information should be added to a product's labeling, it should convey that to FDA, and the agency will determine whether the labeling for the generic and listed drugs should be revised. If it agrees that a label change is necessary, it can work with the brand-name manufacturer to create a new label for both the brand-name and generic drug. It is crucial, therefore, for generics manufacturers to keep an open line of communication with FDA at all times.

The most appropriate way for a company to protect itself is to maintain a dialogue with FDA on the issues associated with pharmacovigilance and to be as meticulous as possible in filing necessary reports. We are entering a new era when pharmacovigilance will be the foundation for improved drug product labeling and potential litigation. FDA, CMS and other agencies, such as the Veterans Administration, are committed to improving their skills in keeping electronic records in this area. In the current atmosphere the courts have been receptive to limiting liability when proper dialogue and diligent filing are followed. Following the principles that apply to pharmacovigilance is one step toward following the standards of care that are evolving in the industry.

The most appropriate way for a company to protect itself is to maintain a dialogue with FDA on the issues associated with pharmacovigilance and to be as meticulous as possible in filing necessary reports.

Chapter 7

The Medical Device Approval Process

Edward C. Wilson, Jr.* & Michael S. Heyl, Hogan Lovells US LLP, Washington, D.C.

Key Points

- Medical devices include thousands of healthcare products, from simple articles such as thermometers, tongue depressors and heating pads, to more complex products such as heart pacemakers, kidney dialysis machines and proton beam therapy systems.
- Medical device manufacturers generally must obtain clearance of a 510(k) premarket notification or approval of a premarket approval application (PMA) for any device they intend to commercially distribute for the first time in the United States, unless the device is exempt from such requirements.
- Medical devices are classified into one of three classes according to their level of risk, with Class I devices posing the least amount of risk and Class III devices generally posing the greatest risk.
- The 510(k) premarket notification process refers to section 510(k) of the Federal Food, Drug, and Cosmetic Act (FDCA), and is used for devices that are substantially equivalent to a legally marketed low to moderate risk device. The 510(k) premarket notification process is shorter than the PMA process because the Food and Drug Administration (FDA) usually requires less data and other information in 510(k) notifications in order to demonstrate that the device is substantially equivalent to a predicate device.
- High-risk devices and devices not found to be substantially equivalent to a legally marketed predicate device require approval of PMAs. The PMA process is lengthy because FDA generally requires clinical data demonstrating the safety and effectiveness of the device for its intended use.
- The FDCA permits device manufacturers to ship devices solely for investigational use without an approved PMA or cleared 510(k) notice if they meet the requirements of FDA's investigational device exemption (IDE) regulations.

OVERVIEW

The Food and Drug Administration's (FDA's) regulation of medical devices is extremely complex. As new technologies emerge, the challenges of determining how products will be regulated, and navigating the premarket clearance and approval process, is complicated and often daunting. Once products

* The authors would like to thank Kelliann H. Payne, Lina R. Kontos and Kristin M. Zielinski of Hogan Lovells US LLP for their valuable contributions to this chapter.

are cleared or approved to market, companies face rigorous regulatory requirements to keep them there. Until 1976, Congress had never enacted specific legislation governing the regulation of medical devices. Prior to that date, public protection from defective devices depended on FDA's enforcement of the limited provisions in the Federal Food, Drug, and Cosmetic Act of 1938 (FDCA) and on judicial interpretations that extended FDA's regulatory authority over drugs to devices. This combination of sources for the agency's authority proved cumbersome.

The Medical Device Amendments of 1976 expanded FDA's statutory authority over devices.

By the mid-1970s, it had become clear that, due to significant and rapid scientific advances, and because some unsafe, ineffective and even fraudulent devices were occasionally marketed, an increase in federal regulation was needed. In 1976, Congress passed the Medical Device Amendments (amendments) (Pub. L. No. 94-295, 90 Stat. 539), which vastly expanded FDA's statutory authority over devices. Since that time, Congress has enacted several pieces of legislation in an attempt to create a workable system to ensure the safety and effectiveness of medical devices. Among other things, congressional amendments to the FDCA have further expanded FDA's authority to clear or approve medical devices prior to marketing. For example, FDA is authorized to collect user fees from applicants of medical device submissions. Congressional amendments, however, also have required FDA to increase the transparency of the medical device clearance and approval process. In sum, FDA's medical premarket clearance and approval processes have evolved over time to a somewhat complicated set of regulatory requirements and FDA policies. The purpose of this chapter is to provide a practical summary and perspective to those premarket clearance and approval requirements that are applicable to most medical devices.

WHAT THE STATUTE AND REGULATIONS SAY

FDA defines the term "medical device" as:

> . . . an instrument, apparatus, implement, machine, contrivance, implant, in vitro reagent, or other similar or related article, including any component, part, or accessory, which is: (1) recognized in the official National Formulary, or the United States Pharmacopoeia, or any supplement to them, (2) intended for use in the diagnosis of disease or other conditions, or in the cure, mitigation, treatment, or prevention of disease, in man or other animals, or (3) intended to affect the structure or any function of the body of man or other animals, and which does not achieve its primary intended purposes through chemical action within or on the body of man or other animals and which is not dependent upon being metabolized for the achievement of its primary intended purposes.

In contrast, products that accomplish their principal objectives by chemical action or by being metabolized by the body are considered drugs. Examples of devices range from simple devices such as thermometers, tongue depressors, and heating pads, to more complex products such as intrauterine contraceptive devices, heart pacemakers, kidney dialysis machines and total hip replacements. It is not always easy to determine if a product would be considered by FDA to be a drug or a device and some products are considered "combination products"—meaning they are a combination of a device and a drug or a biologic.

CLASSIFICATION OF DEVICES

Generally, medical devices available on the market on or before May 28, 1976 (called "pre-amendment devices"), and devices similar to them, are distinguished from devices introduced after that date. Unless they are significantly modified, pre-amendment devices are permitted to remain on the market, pending final classification or other action by FDA, without any FDA review.

On the other hand, devices introduced after the enactment date are subject to a certain level of FDA review depending on the amount of control necessary to ensure their safety and effectiveness. Those medical devices are assigned to one of three regulatory classes based on the level of control necessary to ensure their safety and effectiveness. Thus, the most risk-laden medical devices require the highest level of government review and approval. For example, Class I devices are generally subject only to "general controls" because they are perceived as presenting the least potential harm to the user. Class II devices, on the other hand, are normally subject to general controls and "special controls," while Class III devices are the most regulated and generally require premarket approval in addition to these controls. Overall, FDA has established classifications for approximately 1,700 different types of devices and grouped them into 16 medical specialties, such as hematology, ophthalology, OB/GYN and general surgery.

Medical devices are assigned to one of three regulatory classes based on the level of control necessary to ensure their safety and effectiveness.

Class I devices include elastic bandages, examination gloves and certain hand-held surgical instruments, and, barring the exemptions discussed below, are subject only to general controls. These controls include requirements for facility registration and product listing with FDA; premarket notification (unless specifically exempt from those requirements); maintenance of records and filing reports with respect to device marketing experience; adherence to good manufacturing practices (GMPs), known as the Quality System Regulation (QSR) (unless exempt); and any distribution and use limitations FDA may impose. In addition, the general controls provide FDA with the authority to ban devices that present substantial deception or significant risks, as well as to detain devices that are alleged to violate the FDCA, pending legal action. Finally, FDA may require manufacturers to notify purchasers and users of devices that present unreasonable risks, and to impose corrective action in certain situations.

The Food and Drug Administration Modernization Act of 1997 (FDAMA) (Pub. L. No. 105-115, 111 Stat. 2296) exempted all Class I devices from FDA's premarket notification requirements except those that are intended for a use which is of substantial importance in preventing the impairment of human health or that present a potentially unreasonable risk of injury or illness (Class I reserved devices). Several dozen devices fall into the Class I reserved category, such as bloodbank supplies, keratomes, cannulas, cardiovascular surgical instruments and positron cameras. In addition, many Class I devices are exempt from the design control provisions of the QSR requirements. Still other Class I devices are exempt from most of the QSR requirements and some Class I devices are exempt from certain other QSR requirements.

Class II devices are those for which general controls alone are insufficient to ensure their safety and effectiveness. Class II devices are subject to both general and special controls (e.g., performance standards, postmarket surveillance, patient registries and FDA guidelines). Examples of Class II devices are powered wheelchairs, infusion pumps and surgical drapes.

A 510(k) is a process under which a manufacturer notifies FDA of its intent to market a device that is identical to, or substantially similar to, a marketed device.

Most Class II devices require 510(k) clearance. A 510(k) is a process under which the manufacturer notifies FDA of its intent to market a device that is substantially equivalent to a legally marketed device (see below). The manufacturer must submit data demonstrating the equivalence, and FDA clears for marketing devices that meet the criteria. Under FDAMA, however, FDA exempted some Class II devices from 510(k) requirements. FDA may continue to add additional Class II devices to the exemption list on its own initiative or in response to a petition from an interested person. It is important to note that there are certain limitations to the 510(k) exempt status of otherwise exempt Class I and Class II devices. The limitations to the exemption are included in the device classification provisions of the *Code of Federal Regulations* (C.F.R.).

Generally, Class III devices are those that must receive premarket approval by FDA to ensure their safety and effectiveness. They are life-sustaining, life-supporting and implantable devices, or new devices that have been found not to be substantially equivalent to legally marketed devices. In general, Class III devices require FDA approval of a premarket approval application (PMA) or a Product Development Protocol (discussed at the end of this chapter).

Examples of Class III devices that require a PMA are heart valves, silicone gel-filled breast implants, drug-eluting stents and certain bone growth stimulators. Class III devices that were on the market prior to May 28, 1976, may be marketed via the 510(k) notification route until FDA calls for PMAs for these devices by publishing a notice in the *Federal Register*.

Certain devices ordered by members of the health professions to conform to their special needs or to those of their patients are considered "custom devices." This term is distinguished from "customized" devices which, by their nature, are required to be customized to meet each individual's specific anatomical needs. Under section 520(g) of the FDCA, custom devices are exempt from registration and from otherwise applicable performance standards or premarket approval and clearance requirements. This exemption applies only to devices that are: 1) ordered by physicians or dentists for their own use or for a specific patient identified in the order, 2) not generally available in finished form and 3) not labeled or advertised for commercial distribution. In addition, custom devices must not be generally available to other licensed practitioners. Custom devices, although exempt from the 510(k) notification requirement, still must comply with all other general control requirements, including the QSR regulations; banned devices; restrictions on sale; and prohibitions against adulteration and misbranding. Traditionally, FDA has interpreted the term "custom device" very strictly so that many devices claimed to be "custom" by manufacturers have been determined not to be custom devices by FDA.

Custom devices are exempt from registration and from otherwise applicable performance standards or premarket approval and clearance requirements. However, strict requirements must be met for a device to be considered "custom."

Congress provided a mechanism for changing the classification of a device if new information emerges regarding its safety and effectiveness. FDA has reclassified hundreds of devices from either Class III to Class II or from Class II to Class I. As noted above, in most cases, FDA has exempted Class I devices from its 510(k) requirements and has also exempted some Class II devices. When FDA reclassifies a device, it reclassifies the "generic type" of device, not the specific device for which a reclassification petition was submitted. Thus, a manufacturer may expend significant resources preparing a reclassification petition and indirectly benefit competitors that manufacture devices within the same generic type.

FDA can also use its enforcement discretion in determining if certain devices require 510(k) clearance (e.g., convenience kits comprising legally marketed devices that are simply being assembled in kit form strictly for the "convenience" of the purchaser or user). Historically, convenience kits were the subject of 510(k) review. FDA determined, however, that under certain circumstances, premarket clearance for convenience kits is not necessary. Therefore, FDA published a list of generic types of convenience kits that are exempt from FDA's 510(k) requirements, but not exempt from the registration, listing, prohibition against misbranding and QSR regulations. To be subject to the policy, all components of the kit must be legally marketed (e.g., subject to a cleared 510(k) notification, exempt from FDA's premarket notification requirements or have pre-amendments status), and further processing of the kit cannot significantly affect the safety or effectiveness of the kit or its components.

The intended use of a device is also a significant factor in determining its classification.

The intended use of a device also is a significant factor in determining its classification. For example, lasers that are used for most dermatological and urological procedures are regulated as Class II devices. However, if the same laser (with certain modifications) is capable of performing ophthalmic procedures, such as LASIK, the device would be a Class III device and require PMA approval for that indication.

How does one determine under what classification a device falls? Part 800 of the C.F.R. identifies, describes and classifies hundreds of products by device type (e.g., ophthalmic devices are covered in 21 C.F.R. Part 886). If a device has the same intended use and meets the general description of the device described in the classification regulation, the "new" device will likely fall under that regulation.

If a "new" device is not classified, the sponsor should determine the regulatory pathway used by competitors with similar products. Certain information about cleared 510(k) notifications and approved PMAs is publicly available after FDA has taken final action on the submission. This information is helpful in determining how a device likely will be regulated by FDA.

Another means for determining the likely classification of a device is to have a pre-submission meeting with FDA to discuss the device's description, technological characteristics and intended uses. Alternatively, a person may submit a written request under section 513(g) of the FDCA that requires FDA to identify the classification of a device and applicable premarket requirements. In addition, under section 513(c) of the FDCA, any interested party may submit a citizen's petition requesting that FDA downclassify a Class III device to Class I or Class II, or upclassify a Class I device to Class II or III or a Class II device to Class III. FDA's guidance for submitting reclassification petitions explains the procedures and requirements for a reclassification petition and includes a Classification Questionnaire Form.[1] A person also may submit a 510(k) premarket notification for a device and see if FDA clears the submission or finds the device not substantially equivalent (NSE) to a predicate device. However, once an NSE determination is made, the company may need to submit a new 510(k) notice to the agency with additional data to support clearance or submit a *de novo* petition for downclassification (discussed in more detail below). If the agency does not agree that a device can be cleared to market via the 510(k) or *de novo* pathway, the agency will require the submission and approval of a PMA to market the device.

As mentioned above, a company that submits a 510(k) notice for an unclassified device, which is determined to be not substantially equivalent, and thus Class III because of the lack of a clear predicate device, can request immediate reclassification into Class I or II based upon the low level of risk of the device. This process is known as the *"de novo* review" process. The manufacturer's request for a *de novo* classification must be made within 30 days of receiving a not substantially equivalent determination. The request for *de novo* classification must describe the device and provide a detailed recommendation for classification. If FDA classifies the device into Class I or Class II, the product is then considered cleared and may be marketed. That newly classified device may also serve as a predicate device for substantial equivalence determinations for future devices. On the other hand, if the agency does keep the device in Class III, PMA approval for the device will be required before marketing. It is important to note that the agency has proposed another pathway for the *de novo* process, which would be initiated with a pre-*de novo* submission (PDS).

Where an unclassified device is determined to not be substantially equivalent, and thus Class III, a company can request reclassification based upon the low level of risk of the device.

The PDS submission would allow companies to engage in early discussions with the agency about the suitability of the device for *de novo* classification. Companies could then file a concurrent 510(k) notice with a *de novo* petition after this initial review if the device appears suitable for the *de novo* process. This preliminary interaction with the agency is designed to allow companies to obtain earlier feedback on the likely classification and the likely performance and/or clinical data necessary to support the *de novo* petition. Alternatively, under the draft guidance document, a company may continue to utilize the existing *de novo* pathway by choosing not to submit a PDS and instead submit a *de novo* petition within 30 days of receiving an NSE determination.[2]

MEDICAL DEVICE USER FEES

Under the Medical Device User Fee and Modernization Act of 2002 (MDUFMA), FDA established user fees for the review of certain premarket submissions. The revenue generated by those user fees is intended to provide financial stability for FDA's medical device review program in return for improved and predictable performance by the agency in the review of new marketing submissions. Under MDUFMA, user fees were required for the review of: premarket notifications (510(k)), PMA applications, biologic license applications (BLAs), premarket reports (PMRs), product development protocols (PDPs), panel-track PMA supplements, BLA efficacy supplements and real-time PMA supplements.

The Food and Drug Administration Amendments Act of 2007 (FDAAA), among other things, extended FDA's authority to collect user fees until 2012. FDAAA restructured the fee schedule to provide manufacturers with more predictability and stability in the payment of medical device user fees. FDAAA also added the user fee provisions to additional types of submissions. For example, FDA may collect user fees for: 30-day notices (for PMAs), PMA annual reports and 513(g) requests for designation. Fees also are required for initial and annual establishment registrations for each facility engaged in covered activities, such as manufacturing, importation, specification development and contract sterilization.

Revenues generated from FDA's user fee program are to be used to expedite the medical device review process in accordance with FDA performance goals. In consultation with industry, after FDAAA was enacted, the agency restructured its performance goal framework to emphasize deadlines for "final decisions" rather than the agency's previous incremental, or "cycle goals" scheme. The performance goal framework also encouraged a more informal, interactive process between FDA and the medical device industry. To this end, FDA published a guidance document on February 28, 2008, entitled "Interactive Review for Medical Device Submissions: 510(k)s, Original PMAs, PMA Supplements, Original BLAs, and BLA Supplements."[3] The purpose of the guidance document was to recommend an interactive premarket review process for submissions, designed to expedite FDA's review of device applications while continuing to assure device safety and effectiveness.

INVESTIGATIONAL DEVICE EXEMPTIONS

Purpose of an Investigational Device Exemption

An investigational device exemption allows an unapproved device to be shipped in interstate commerce for purposes of conducting supportive clinical research.

Devices used on human subjects to conduct investigations of the device's safety and effectiveness for a certain intended use not yet cleared or approved by the agency are considered "investigational devices" under section 520(g) of the FDCA. These devices have not been approved for commercial distribution by FDA for their investigational use. An investigational device exemption (IDE) allows an unapproved device to be shipped in interstate commerce for purposes of conducting clinical research that can be submitted in support of a 510(k) or PMA submission. Without this exemption, shipment of an unapproved device in interstate commerce would violate the FDCA. Notably, although an approved IDE application exempts a device from certain provisions of the FDCA, it does not exempt it from other federal, state or local regulations. For example, an investigational device that emits radiation may be subject to radiological health regulations, including product performance standards for equipment such as lasers and diagnostic x-rays. Investigational devices must also comply with FDA's advertising and labeling requirements regarding such devices.

Significant Risk and Nonsignificant Risk Devices

The IDE regulations describe two types of devices: 1) significant risk and 2) nonsignificant risk. The IDE regulation (21 C.F.R. § 812.3(m)) defines a significant risk device as an investigational device that: 1) is intended as an implant and presents a potential for serious risk to the health, safety or welfare of a subject; 2) is purported or represented to be for use in supporting or sustaining human life and presents a potential for serious risk to the health, safety or welfare of a subject; 3) is for a use of substantial importance in diagnosing, curing, mitigating or treating disease, or otherwise preventing impairment of human health and presents a potential for serious risk to the health, safety or welfare of a subject; or 4) otherwise presents a potential for serious risk to the health, safety or welfare of a subject. Some examples of significant risk studies include clinical trials on cardiac pacemaker/pulse generators; balloon dilation catheters for benign prostatic hyperplasia; implantable prostheses (ligament, tendon, hip, knee and finger); and intraocular lenses.

A nonsignificant risk device study is one that does not pose a significant risk to patients. Some examples of nonsignificant risk studies include clinical trials on daily wear contact lenses, denture repair kits and general urological catheters.

Studies of significant risk devices must meet all of the regulatory requirements set forth in 21 C.F.R. Part 812, including the requirements that the sponsor obtain approval from FDA of the IDE, and approval of the investigational plan from each participating Institutional Review Board (IRB) before commencing the study. If the investigation does not present a significant risk to the health of the patients, the sponsor may begin without obtaining FDA approval of the study (nonsignificant risk studies are "deemed" to have IDE approval by FDA), provided that each reviewing IRB agrees that the study poses a nonsignificant risk and approves the study. Informed consent must be obtained from each subject regardless of whether the investigation involves a significant or nonsignificant risk study device.

An assessment of whether a device study presents a nonsignificant risk is made initially by the sponsor. If the sponsor believes a study poses a nonsignificant risk, the sponsor provides the IRB with the study proposal, an explanation of why the study is a nonsignificant risk study and other supporting information (e.g., any reports of prior investigations). The sponsor or investigator must also advise the IRB whether the study subjects must undergo a procedure as part of the investigational study (e.g., a surgical procedure), so it can evaluate the potential harm that could be caused by the procedure in addition to the potential harm that could be caused by the device. In making this initial determination, a sponsor and IRB should consider FDA's guidance under "Information Sheet

A significant risk device:

1) *is intended as an implant and presents a potential for serious risk to the health, safety or welfare of a subject;*

2) *is purported or represented to be for use in supporting or sustaining human life and presents a potential for serious risk to the health, safety or welfare of a subject;*

3) *is for a use of substantial importance in diagnosing, curing, mitigating or treating disease, or otherwise preventing impairment of human health and presents a potential for serious risk to the health, safety or welfare of a subject; or*

4) *otherwise presents a potential for serious risk to the health, safety or welfare of a subject.*

Guidance For IRBs, Clinical Investigators, and Sponsors Significant Risk and Non-significant Risk Medical Device Studies" on the agency's website at http://www.fda.gov/ScienceResearch/SpecialTopics/RunningClinicalTrials/GuidancesInformationSheetsandNotices/ucm113709.htm.

Institutional Review Boards (IRBs)

An IRB must be assured that:

1) risks to subjects are minimized and are reasonable in relation to anticipated benefits and knowledge to be gained,

2) subject selection is equitable,

3) informed consent materials and procedures are adequate and

4) provisions for monitoring the study and protecting the privacy of subjects are acceptable.

IRBs are committees (independent or affiliated with medical institutions) that are composed of qualified experts who are tasked with reviewing and approving biomedical research, as well as continuing review of ongoing research, to assure the protection of the rights and welfare of human subjects. In deciding whether a study (whether nonsignificant risk or significant risk) is approvable, an IRB must be assured that: 1) risks to subjects are minimized and are reasonable in relation to anticipated benefits and knowledge to be gained, 2) subject selection is equitable, 3) informed consent materials and procedures are adequate, and 4) provisions for monitoring the study and protecting the privacy of subjects are acceptable. To ensure that the risks to the subjects are reasonable in relation to the anticipated benefits, the risks and benefits of the investigation are compared to the risks and benefits of alternative devices or procedures. If all reviewing IRBs agree that the study presents a nonsignificant risk and is approvable, the investigation may proceed without FDA approval of an IDE application. If any reviewing IRB determines that the study poses a significant risk, the sponsor must notify FDA that a significant risk determination has been made and an IDE application must be submitted to and approved by FDA before beginning the study. Moreover, at any time, FDA may overrule a nonsignificant risk determination by an IRB and require the sponsor to submit an IDE application to FDA for approval.

IDE Exempt Investigations

In general, clinical investigations of devices to support a market application are subject to the IDE requirements. There are, however, limited exemptions from the IDE regulations. For example, per 21 C.F.R. § 812.2(c), a diagnostic device that complies with the labeling requirements in 21 C.F.R. § 809.10(c) is exempt from the IDE regulations if the testing: 1) is noninvasive, 2) does not require an invasive sampling procedure that presents significant risk, 3) does not by design or intention introduce energy into a subject and 4) is not used as a diagnostic procedure without confirmation by another medically established diagnostic product or procedure. However, any such exempt studies also still must comply with FDA's IRB and informed consent requirements.

Certain other studies also are exempt from FDA's IDE regulations, including evaluation of a device for consumer product testing, a device that is legally marketed provided if it is used in accordance with its cleared labeling (or labeling in effect prior to May 28, 1976, for pre-amendments devices), and a custom device unless the device is being studied to determine its safety or effectiveness for commercial distribution.

Content of an IDE

Per 21 C.F.R. § 812.20(b) the sponsor of the proposed human clinical investigation that is not exempt per 21 C.F.R. § 812.2(c) must include the following information in an IDE application:

(1)   name and address of sponsor;

(2)   report of prior investigations, including published and unpublished information relevant to the evaluation of the safety and effectiveness of the device;

(3)   investigational plan, including a description of the objectives and duration of the study, analysis of risk, justification, patient population, monitoring procedures and the protocol;

(4)   device description and description of methods, facilities and controls for manufacturing;

(5)   example of investigator agreement;

(6)   certification that all investigators who will participate in the study have signed the investigator agreement;

(7)   names, addresses and chairpersons of IRBs;

(8)   participating institutions;

(9)   statement of noncommercialization;

(10) labeling; and

(11) informed consent materials.

An IDE application that does not contain all required information will be returned to the sponsor for revision before FDA begins a substantive review.

FDA's guidance document entitled "Center for Devices and Radiological Health's Investigational Device Exemption (IDE) Refuse to Accept Policy" dated June 30, 1996, includes an IDE "refuse to accept" checklist, which provides a listing of all the elements required in the IDE application. If an IDE application does not contain all of these elements, it will be returned to the sponsor for revision before FDA begins a substantive review.

IDE Review Process

FDA has 30 days to review the IDE application. Technically, an IDE application is considered approved 30 days after it has been received by FDA, unless FDA notifies the sponsor that the IDE is approved with conditions or disapproved prior to the 30 days. In practice, however, sponsors await an approval notification from FDA so as not to begin studies that might have to be stopped or modified a short time later. If FDA disapproves an IDE, the sponsor may respond to the deficiencies and/or request a regulatory hearing under 21 C.F.R. Part 16. If FDA approves the IDE with conditions, the sponsor has 45 days in which to address the conditions of approval.

Notably, sponsors of clinical studies of any Class III or any implantable device may submit an investigational plan (including the clinical protocol) to FDA for review, in order to reach agreement on the proposed plan. In practice, FDA also typically agrees to review investigational plans for Class I and II nonimplantable devices, and neither Blue Book Memorandum #D95-1 (Goals and Initiatives for the IDE Program) nor IDE Guidance #99-1 (Pre-IDE Program: Issues and Answers) make distinctions with respect to class or type of device. The plan can be submitted prior to the actual official submission of the IDE application or prior to seeking approval from an IRB to conduct a study. This IDE provision states that any agreement reached by the sponsor and FDA must be made part of the administrative record and may be changed only: 1) with the written agreement of the sponsor, or 2) pursuant to a decision made by the director of the office in which the device is reviewed that a substantial scientific issue essential to determining the safety or effectiveness of the device has been identified. Such a determination must be documented after providing the study sponsor with an opportunity for a meeting with the director during which the scientific issues involved are documented.

Informal, nonbinding guidance is also available via the pre-IDE process to allow the reviewing division to provide guidance and feedback on development of supporting preclinical data or the investigational plan for incorporation into the IDE application. These meetings can take many forms, including conference calls, video conference calls or face-to-face meetings.

IDE Supplements

Sponsors of significant risk studies are required to obtain approval of an IDE supplement before making a change in the investigational plan that may affect scientific soundness or the rights, safety or welfare of subjects.

Pursuant to FDA's IDE regulations, sponsors of significant risk studies are required to obtain approval of an IDE supplement before making a change in the investigational plan that may affect its scientific soundness or the rights, safety or welfare of subjects. Under section 201 of FDAMA, FDA was required to promulgate new regulations that allow study sponsors to make modifications to investigational devices and study protocols without submitting IDE supplements to FDA. The regulations set forth several specific changes that no longer require IDE supplements: 1) developmental changes in the device (including manufacturing changes) that do not constitute a significant change in design or basic principles of operation and that are made in response to information gathered during the course of investigation; and 2) changes or modifications to clinical protocols that do not affect: a) the validity of data or information resulting from the completion of an approved protocol, or the relationship of likely patient risk to benefit relied upon to approve a protocol; b) the scientific soundness of an investigational plan submitted in the IDE; or c) the rights, safety or welfare of the human subjects involved in the investigation.

Moreover, the IDE regulations state that these types of changes can be made if the sponsor of the study: 1) determines, on the basis of credible information, that the change or modification meets the specified criteria; and 2) submits to FDA, not later than five days after making the change or modification, a notice of the change or modification. The intent of this provision is to place the burden on the study sponsor to determine whether proposed changes necessitate the filing of an IDE supplement. Of course, FDA has the option to disagree with the sponsor's determination and can later require an IDE supplement at its discretion.

Investigational Device Labeling Requirements

Per 21 C.F.R. § 812.5, investigational devices are subject to specific labeling requirements. The labeling of investigational devices must include:

(1) name and place of business of the manufacturer, packer or distributor;
(2) the quantity of contents;
(3) the statement, "CAUTION—Investigational device. Limited by federal (or United States) law to investigational use";
(4) all relevant contraindications, hazards, adverse effects, interfering substances or devices, warnings and precautions;
(5) no false or misleading statements; and
(6) no representation that the device is safe or effective for the purposes for which it is being investigated.

There are specific labeling requirements for investigational devices.

Note that a manufacturer also may include a statement that the product has an approved IDE.

Sponsor and Investigator Responsibilities

Per the IDE regulations, sponsors of IDE investigations and the investigators participating in the IDE investigation have various responsibilities. Investigators are responsible for the following: 1) ensuring that the study is conducted according to investigational plan and applicable FDA regulations; 2) obtaining informed consent from study subjects; 3) supervising the use of the device; and 4) returning unused investigational devices to the sponsor or disposing of them as the sponsor directs. Sponsors are responsible for: 1) selecting qualified investigators and providing them with the information they need to conduct the study properly; 2) properly labeling the device; 3) obtaining IRB review and approval; 4) ensuring proper monitoring of the study; 5) investigating any unanticipated adverse events that occur during the study and taking appropriate action; and 6) informing FDA and IRBs about significant new information (21 C.F.R. § 812.40).

Sponsors and investigators have recordkeeping and reporting responsibilities.

In addition to the above responsibilities, both sponsors and investigators are subject to recordkeeping responsibilities. Per 21 C.F.R. § 812.140(a), investigators must keep records of: 1) correspondence with the sponsor, FDA, IRB, other investigators and monitors; 2) receipt and disposition of investigational devices; 3) study subjects' case history and exposure to the device; 4) documentation of informed consent; and 5) the protocol and any deviations. Sponsors are responsible for maintaining records of the following per 21 C.F.R. § 812.140(b): 1) correspondence with investigators, FDA, IRB, other sponsors and monitors; 2) shipment and disposition of investigational devices; 3) signed investigator statements; 4) name and address of each investigator; and 5) name and address of each IRB that has reviewed the study.

Finally, both sponsors and investigators are subject to reporting responsibilities. For investigators, per 21 C.F.R. § 812.150(a), the following must be reported: 1) unanticipated adverse effects reports (should be submitted to the sponsor and IRB of any unanticipated adverse device effect occurring during the study within 10 working days after the investigator first learns of the event); 2) deviations from the investigational plan or informed consent process; 3) progress reports (should be submitted to the sponsor and IRB, and the investigator should monitor progress reports on the study at regular intervals—at least yearly); and 4) final reports (should be submitted to the sponsor and IRB within three months of the end of the study).

Sponsors' reporting requirements include: 1) evaluating the reports of unanticipated adverse effects from the investigator and reporting results to FDA, all reviewing IRBs and participating investigators within 10 working days after sponsor first receives notice of the effect; 2) submitting a current investigator list to FDA every six months; 3) submitting progress reports at regular intervals (at least yearly) to all IRBs and, for a significant risk study, to FDA; 4) in the instance of IRB or FDA withdrawal of approval, notification of all reviewing IRBs and all participating investigators within five working days; and 5) for significant risk studies, notifying FDA of termination of the study within 30 days and submitting final reports to FDA, all reviewing IRBs and participating investigators within 30 days of the end of the study. For nonsignificant risk studies, a final report must only be submitted to all reviewing IRBs within six months of study termination (21 C.F.R. § 812.150(b)).

Disqualification of Investigators

Per 21 C.F.R. § 812.119, an investigator can be disqualified by FDA from performing clinical research for failure to comply with regulatory requirements, or for repeated or deliberate submission of false information to a sponsor. Should a study investigator be disqualified, FDA typically will examine the study data to determine whether it is reliable. If found unreliable, this can be a basis for withdrawing approval of the IDE or marketing application that included the unreliable data.

Registration Requirements for Clinical Trials

FDAAA established registration requirements for "applicable clinical trials." An applicable device clinical trial is defined as:

(1) "a prospective clinical study of health outcomes comparing an intervention with a device subject to [510(k), PMA and Humanitarian Device Exemptions premarket requirements] against a control in human subjects (other than a small clinical trial to determine the feasibility of a device, or a clinical trial to test prototype devices where the primary outcome measure relates to feasibility and not to health outcomes)"; and

(2) "a pediatric postmarket surveillance [requirement]."

"Applicable clinical trials" must meet registration requirements established by the Food and Drug Administration Amendments Act of 2007.

Thus, per FDAAA, it may be the case that a study being conducted under an approved IDE and even studies that have NSE designations must be registered with the ClinicalTrials.gov data bank.

To register a study, the following information is required, but is not limited to: the study title; a brief summary of the study written for the lay public; the study design; the primary purpose of the study; the study phase; the study type; the disease or condition being studied; the intervention name and type; the start date; the expected completion date; the sample size; and the primary and secondary endpoints. The sponsor also must provide recruitment information including: eligibility criteria; gender; age limits; policies on accepting healthy volunteers; recruitment status; and individual site status. In addition, contact information for the sponsor's facility, as well as certain administrative information (e.g., the unique protocol identification number, the name and contact information for the individual responsible for the study, etc.), must be provided.

FDAAA also requires that product submissions, including 510(k)s, PMAs and humanitarian device exemption applications, be accompanied by a certification that the applicant has complied with the clinical trial registration requirements. FDA has created a certification form, Form FDA 3674, which is available on FDA's website, in order to provide these certifications to the agency. Draft guidance is currently available on the ClinicalTrials.gov website to assist sponsors with the determination of whether its study meets the definition of an applicable trial and, therefore, is subject to the reporting requirements.

HUMANITARIAN DEVICE EXEMPTIONS

The humanitarian device exemption applies to devices that:

- *are designated to treat or diagnose a disease or condition that affects fewer than 4,000 persons per year,*
- *are not available otherwise and there is no comparable device available,*
- *do not expose patients to unreasonable or significant risk, and*
- *the benefits to health outweigh the risks.*

To encourage the discovery of devices that benefit a small number of patients in the United States, FDA may grant a humanitarian device exemption (HDE) from the effectiveness requirements of the FDCA after finding that: 1) the device is designated to treat or diagnose a disease or condition that affects fewer than 4,000 individuals per year; 2) the device is not available otherwise, and there is no comparable device available to treat or diagnose the disease or condition; 3) the device will not expose patients to unreasonable or significant risk; and 4) the benefits to health from its use outweigh the risks.

Two distinct steps are necessary to obtain approval to market a humanitarian device. First, the sponsor must submit a request to FDA's Office of Orphan Products Development (OOPD) seeking a determination that the disease or condition that the device is intended to treat or diagnose affects or is manifested in fewer than 4,000 individuals in the United States per year. This request for humanitarian use designation (HUD) should provide the following: 1) the precisely defined proposed indication(s) for use based upon current medical and scientific knowledge; 2) a brief description of the device, including illustrations and a discussion of its principle of operation; and 3) documentation, with authoritative references appended, of the target population demonstrating that the rare disease or condition affects or is manifested in fewer than 4,000 people in the United States per year. FDA must approve, disapprove, or return the HUD request for additional information within 45 days of the request.

Second, if OOPD determines that the device is eligible for a humanitarian designation, an HDE application must be submitted to the relevant center within FDA
(Center for Biologics Evaluation and Research, Center for Drug Evaluation and
Research, Center for Devices and Radiological Health). The application is similar
in both form and content to a PMA; however, it is not required to contain the
results of scientifically valid clinical investigations demonstrating that the device
is effective for its intended purpose. Importantly, FDA will only grant an HDE if
there are no other devices on the market to diagnose or treat the same condition or disease.

*FDA will only grant an
HDE if there are no other
devices on the market to
diagnose or treat the same
condition or disease.*

The HDE application must also estimate the number of patients who would
be required to generate data to support a full PMA, and an explanation of
why such a study is not feasible or why the cost of conducting such a study
could not reasonably be expected to be recovered. Such application must
also include a description of all pediatric subpopulations that suffer from the
disease or condition that the device seeks to address and the approximate
number of affected pediatric patients. Finally, as previously stated, all HDE applications must include certification that the applicant has complied with the
clinical trial registration requirements. FDA is required to send the applicant an
approval order, approvable letter or order denying approval within 75 days of
receipt of an HUD request accepted for filing and for which there were no major
amendments.

If the amount to be charged for the device is greater than $250, the application
also must contain a report by an independent certified public accountant or
attestation from a responsible individual in the organization verifying that the
amount charged does not exceed the costs of the device's research, development, fabrication and distribution. Manufacturers of pediatric devices receiving
an HDE, however, are permitted to sell their devices for a profit, provided that
the devices meet all other HDE requirements. Despite this, the number of pediatric devices distributed during a year may not exceed the annual distribution
number specified by FDA when the HDE was granted.

The use of an HUD must initially and continually be reviewed by an IRB. The IRB
does not, however, have to approve each use of an HUD, but rather the general
use of the HUD at the facility.

HDEs will be granted for an unlimited timeframe. Nevertheless, FDA may
require the sponsor of the HDE device to demonstrate continued compliance
with the HDE regulations if FDA believes that such a demonstration is necessary
to protect the public health, or if FDA has reason to believe that the criteria for
the HDE are no longer met. FDA can suspend or withdraw the HDE only after
providing the holder of the HDE an opportunity for an informal hearing.

510(k) PREMARKET NOTIFICATION PROCESS

Overview

The 510(k) process involves a comparison of a company's new device to one or more legally marketed devices (i.e., predicate device(s)). A predicate device is a legally marketed Class I or Class II device, or a Class III device for which PMAs are not yet required. According to FDA's regulations, a manufacturer is required to file an FDCA section 510(k) premarket notification prior to: 1) initial marketing of a device; 2) making a change or modification to a cleared device that could significantly affect the safety or effectiveness of the device; or 3) making a major change or modification to the intended use of its previously cleared device. The regulations require manufacturers to submit to FDA a 510(k) notification at least 90 days prior to the applicant's intended introduction into the market of a device that requires premarket clearance. A device that requires 510(k) clearance may not be marketed until the applicant receives an "order" from FDA, which states that the new device is substantially equivalent to a legally marketed predicate device (21 U.S.C. § 360(k)).

To be "substantially equivalent," a new device must have:
- *the same intended use as a predicate; and*
- *either the same technological characteristics as the predicate device or*
- *different technological characteristics, but the information submitted must not raise new questions of safety and effectiveness and must demonstrate substantial equivalence.*

For a new device to be found "substantially equivalent" to one or more legally marketed predicate devices, it must have 1) the same intended use as a predicate; and 2) either a) the same technological characteristics as the predicate device or b) different technological characteristics, but the information submitted must not raise new questions of safety and effectiveness and must demonstrate substantial equivalence. Technically, a device that is the subject of a 510(k) notification may have multiple predicate devices, as certain features of the device may be substantially equivalent to certain predicate devices, while other features may be substantially equivalent to other predicates (21 U.S.C. § 360c(1)(l)(a)). However, FDA recently has questioned the approach of using combination predicates to demonstrate substantial equivalence. FDA has developed a decision tree that facilitates making the substantial equivalence determination. With regard to 510(k) submissions, FDA is directed to limit its determination as to whether the product is substantially equivalent based on the device's proposed labeling included in the 510(k) filing. That said, FDA has questioned the clinical utility of certain devices reviewed under the 510(k) pathway when such utility is not clearly identified in the submitted labeling for review. As a potential mitigation to prevent cleared devices from being used outside the scope of the FDA-cleared indications for use, the agency has requested on occasion that companies place a black box warning on device labels to prevent specific off-label uses.

Initially, the agency required proof of equivalence to an actual pre-amendments device (i.e., one that was on the market prior to May 28, 1976). The Safe

Medical Devices Act of 1990 (SMDA) made it clear, however, that a post-amendments Class I or Class II device may be found substantially equivalent to any legally marketed Class I or Class II device or Class III device for which FDA has not yet called for PMAs. The predicate device, therefore, need not be a pre-amendments device, but it cannot be a device that was removed from the market by FDA or determined to be misbranded or adulterated by judicial order (21 U.S.C. § 360c(l)(2)).

Contents of a 510(k) Premarket Notification

The format and information required in a 510(k) premarket notification, outlined below, are specified in 21 C.F.R. §§ 807.87, 807.90, 807.92 and 807.93. The contents of a premarket notification include the following:

- **Device Name.** The device name, including both the trade or proprietary name and the classification name, must be included in a 510(k) premarket notification.

- **Identification.** The applicant's name and street address must be included in a 510(k) premarket notification.

- **Registration Number.** If applicable, the FDA establishment registration number of the owner or operator submitting the premarket notification should be included.

- **Classification.** The applicant should include the class of the device (i.e., Class I, II or III). If known, include the appropriate classification panel.

- **Description.** The 510(k) notification should include a physical description of the new device, together with an explanation of its intended use, principles of operation, power source, composition and other information necessary to understand the device.

- **Substantial Equivalence Comparison.** Applicants should attempt to make a comparison of the new device to its predicate as easy as possible for the FDA reviewer. The 510(k) notification should, therefore, include a discussion of the similarities and differences between the device and its predicate device(s), and should make use of comparative tables whenever possible.

- **Software.** Applications for computerized devices must follow the appropriate CDRH guidance.[4]

- **Standards.** The applicant should identify any mandatory or voluntary standards met by the device.

- **Performance.** Performance data are often needed to help demonstrate that the proposed device is as safe and effective as the predicate device.

Applicants should attempt to make a comparison of the new device to its predicate as easy as possible for the FDA reviewer.

♦ **Biocompatibility.** Submissions for devices that directly contact the body must include a description of the characteristics of their materials. This description should compare the device to its predicate in sufficient detail to determine biocompatibility, as well as the kind of tests needed to determine biocompatibility. Any material differences between the new device and the claimed predicate device must be stated explicitly, but it is just as important to state whether the materials comprising the two devices are identical. Manufacturers need to provide biocompatibility test data for any materials found in the new device that are not present in the predicate device.

♦ **Sterility.** Submissions for devices that are labeled sterile must cite their sterilization method as well as the method used to validate the sterilization cycle and the sterility assurance level that the validated method ensures.

♦ **Labeling.** Although applicants may submit drafts of their device labeling, the submission should be representative of the final version.

♦ **Class III Certification and Summary.** All 510(k) submissions for Class III devices must have a special added certification statement by which the applicant must certify in its 510(k) premarket notification that it has searched for all available information relative to that device's safety and effectiveness, and the 510(k) notification must include citations to any adverse safety and effectiveness data.

♦ **510(k) Summary or Statement.** A premarket notification must include either a summary of the 510(k) safety and effectiveness information upon which the substantial equivalence determination is based or a statement that this information will be made available by the 510(k) applicant to any person within 30 days of a written request.

♦ **Truthful and Accuracy Statement.** All 510(k) applicants must include a statement certifying that all information in the application is truthful and accurate and that no material fact has been omitted.

In addition, ODE has issued many device-specific guidance documents that contain requirements for data and information to be submitted with the 510(k). The data and information may include engineering testing data, information regarding applicable national and international standards, and/or human clinical data. These documents are posted on FDA's website, which should be consulted frequently as documents are added and removed from the site as necessary.

510(k) Premarket Notifications Supported with Clinical Data

Those 510(k)s that include clinical information in order to demonstrate substantial equivalence have been referred to as "hybrid 510(k)s" or "mini-PMAs."[5] More and more premarket notifications are required to contain clinical data to support a device clearance. In sum, 510(k)s supported with clinical data are becoming commonplace. For such submissions, FDA requires that the 510(k) notification be supported by clinical data demonstrating equivalence of the new device to its predicate device(s) and/or the current standard of care. The data collected is intended to validate that any technological differences between the device under consideration and the predicate device(s) and/or standard of care do not raise any new questions of safety and efficacy.

In most cases in which a PMA or 510(k) includes clinical data, FDA requires study sponsors to either disclose certain financial interests of the clinical investigators or certify that the clinical investigators do not hold any disclosable financial interests. Under FDAAA, any 510(k) that contains clinical data must be accompanied by a certification that the applicant has complied with the clinical trial registration requirements.

Device Modifications

One of the most difficult decisions for 510(k) holders is when to submit a new premarket notification for changes that the holder intends to make to one of its legally marketed devices. As stated above, FDA's regulations require that a new 510(k) notification be cleared by FDA before the holder makes a change or modification to the device that "could significantly affect the safety or effectiveness of the device, e.g., a significant change or modification in design, material, chemical composition, energy source, or manufacturing process"; or makes a major change or modification in the intended use of the device.[6] FDA has disseminated a recently revised draft guidance document to assist manufacturers in determining which modifications require the submission of new 510(k) notices.[7] When finalized, this draft guidance document will replace the agency's 1997 guidance document that addressed modifications to cleared devices.[8]

The basic framework of the 2011 draft guidance document is very similar to the 1997 guidance and does not appear to significantly alter the type of analysis that FDA expects manufacturers to conduct in response to a device change.

Although the 510(k) holder is responsible for making the initial determination as to whether a change or modification could significantly affect safety or effectiveness, FDA may second-guess the company's decisions. If FDA disagrees with the company's decision not to file a new 510(k) notification for a device modification or change, the agency may make the company file a 510(k) notification and discontinue marketing the device while the 510(k) is pending. The agency may also take enforcement action against the company. As a practical matter, however, if the company has made a good faith effort to document the reasons that it did not submit a new 510(k) for the device change, if the reasons appear genuine and there are no demonstrated safety problems with the modified device, FDA may use its enforcement discretion to allow the company to continue marketing the device while the new 510(k) notification is pending.

"The New 510(k) Paradigm"

To streamline the evaluation of 510(k)s, FDA developed "The New 510(k) Paradigm" (March 20, 1998), which offered manufacturers three alternative approaches for seeking 510(k) clearance.[9] The paradigm retained the traditional methods of demonstrating substantial equivalence (through adequate device descriptions, appropriate preclinical testing and, occasionally, clinical trials). In addition, under the 510(k) Paradigm, the device manufacturer has the option of submitting a "Special 510(k)" for certain types of device modifications or an "Abbreviated 510(k)."

Under the Special 510(k): Device Modification option, a manufacturer that intends to modify its own legally marketed cleared device may conduct the necessary verification and validation activities to demonstrate that the design outputs of the modified device meet the design input requirements. Special 510(k)s are usually processed by the ODE within 30 days of receipt. Modifications that affect the intended use or alter the basic fundamental scientific technology of the device are not eligible for this alternate type of submission, but may be eligible for the proposed Abbreviated 510(k) route as described below.

While not frequently utilized, device manufacturers may submit an Abbreviated 510(k) when: 1) a device-specific guidance document exists; 2) a special control has been established; or 3) FDA has recognized a relevant consensus standard. Abbreviated 510(k)s include summary information that describes how special controls have been used to address the risks associated with the device type and a declaration of conformity with any relevant recognized standards, if applicable.

Review Process

FDA responds to a 510(k) notification in one of three ways. FDA can: 1) decide that a device is substantially equivalent to a legally marketed device that does not require premarket approval; 2) decide that it is not substantially equivalent (NSE); or 3) notify the applicant that additional information is required to determine whether the device is, in fact, substantially equivalent. A decision by FDA that a device is substantially equivalent to a predicate device gives the 510(k) holder the right to commercially market it in the United States. A finding that a device is not substantially equivalent to the predicate device means that FDA needs additional data to determine the device to be substantially equivalent or it is a "new" Class III device, thus requiring approval of a PMA before being marketed (unless FDA downclassifies the entire device category from Class III to either Class I or Class II or clears the device through the *de novo* classification process described above). It generally takes four to 12 months from the time of submission to obtain 510(k) premarket clearance, but the process can take longer if FDA requires additional information. There are no assurances that FDA will ultimately clear the 510(k).

In making a request for information, FDA is directed to consider the "least burdensome means of demonstrating substantial equivalence." In a guidance document, FDA defined the least burdensome concept as "a successful means of addressing a premarket issue that involves the most appropriate investment of time, effort, and resources on the part of industry and FDA."[10] FDA has also developed a number of principles for applying the least burdensome concept, which may serve as useful starting points in discussions with reviewers. First, information unrelated to the regulatory decision should not be part of the decision-making process. Second, alternative approaches to all regulatory issues should be considered to optimize time, effort and resources. Third, all reasonable mechanisms to lessen review times should be used. While it is often advisable to at least raise with FDA least burdensome arguments, the agency ultimately determines what amount and type of data and information are necessary to support marketing applications.

Although FDA's response to applications under section 510(k) establishes, for all practical purposes, whether a particular device can be marketed without a PMA, FDA does not "approve" a premarket notification in the same way that it approves a PMA. FDA's response to section 510(k) notifications makes clear that its findings under this provision extend only to whether a device is substantially equivalent to a predicate device and not whether if it is safe and effective for its intended use(s).

If FDA determines that a device is not substantially equivalent, the applicant may:

♦ resubmit another 510(k) with new data,

♦ request a Class I or II designation through the *de novo* process,

♦ file a reclassification petition,

♦ submit a premarket approval application (PMA), or

♦ appeal the NSE determination to the CDRH ombudsman.

> *In making a request for information, FDA is directed to consider the "least burdensome means of demonstrating substantial equivalence."*

Third-Party Review

FDA-accredited third parties can conduct initial review of 510(k)s for low-to-moderate risk devices.

On August 1, 1996, FDA began a voluntary Third-party Review Pilot Program for selected medical device 510(k)s to 1) provide manufacturers of eligible devices with an alternative 510(k) review process that could yield more rapid marketing clearance decisions; and 2) enable FDA to use its scientific review resources for higher-risk devices, while maintaining confidence in the review by third parties of low-to-moderate risk devices.

In 1997, with the passage of FDAMA, Congress codified and expanded the pilot program. FDAMA directed FDA to accredit third parties (Accredited Persons) in the private sector to conduct the initial review of 510(k)s for low-to-moderate risk devices; specified that an Accredited Person may not review any Class III device, "Class II devices that are permanently implantable, life-supporting, or life-sustaining," or Class II devices for which clinical data are required; and set limits on the number of Class II devices that may be ineligible for Accredited Person review because clinical data are required. In early 2001, FDA clarified that all Class I devices and all Class II devices that are not permanently implantable, life sustaining or require clinical data are eligible for third-party review. It is important to note that in 2008 60 percent of all 510(k) submissions were eligible for third-party review but only 8 percent of 510(k)s were cleared via this pathway.

Within 30 days of receiving the written classification and substantial equivalence recommendation from the accredited party, FDA must make its decision as to whether the device is substantially equivalent. If the agency does not adopt the recommendation of the accredited party, FDA must provide the 510(k) applicant and the reviewer a statement explaining in detail its reasons.

EVALUATING THE 510(K) PATHWAY

Although the current 510(k) pathway provides FDA with the flexibility to tailor the premarket review process to address the specific characteristics of the device under review, over the past few years, industry, consumers, healthcare providers, as well as FDA staff and Congress have questioned whether the 510(k) process functions as initially intended. Consumer advocacy groups have characterized the 510(k) pathway as a "fast-track process" and have expressed concern that the process allows devices with unproven safety and effectiveness onto the market. In addition, FDA staff has raised concerns regarding the pathway's effectiveness and implementation. Meanwhile, industry has complained that increased scrutiny by some reviewers at FDA is hindering medical device development.

In response to the concerns raised by industry, consumers, FDA staff and increasing congressional pressure, CDRH commissioned evaluations of the 510(k) process to evaluate how well the process was facilitating innovation and assuring that medical devices are safe and effective. The evaluations were conducted by the 510(k) Working Group and the Task Force of the Utilization of Science in Regulatory Decision Making with each group issuing preliminary reports. The 510(k) Working Group issued a report that evaluated how well the current 510(k) pathway is meeting its public health goals of facilitating innovation and assuring that medical devices are safe and effective.[11] The Task Force of the Utilization of Science in Regulatory Decision Making addressed how CDRH can better incorporate new science into its regulatory decision-making in a separate report.[12]

In response to the concerns raised by industry, consumers, FDA staff and increasing congressional pressure, CDRH commissioned evaluations of the 510(k) process to evaluate how well the process was facilitating innovation and assuring that medical devices are safe and effective.

These preliminary reports from the 510(k) Working Group and the Task Force of the Utilization of Science in Regulatory Decision Making outlined 55 recommendations for improving the 510(k) program. In follow-up to public comments received on the proposed 55 recommendations, CDRH announced a plan for implementing 25 initiatives to improve the 510(k) process in 2011.[13] Of the 25 initiatives proposed by FDA for implementation during 2011, the following are likely to have the most impact on the medical device industry: 1) streamlining the *de novo* classification process via a draft guidance (as discussed earlier); 2) providing additional guidance on pre-submission communications; 3) issuance of new draft guidance regarding modifications to 510(k) devices (as discussed earlier); 4) providing additional guidance on the use of multiple predicates to establish substantial equivalence; 5) establishment of a Center Science Council to oversee development of a procedure for responding to new scientific information and periodically audit 510(k) decisions; 6) issuance of additional guidance on clinical data requirements; 7) establishment of a network of external experts; and 8) providing notice to industry when FDA has modified the regulatory expectations for devices based on new scientific evidence.

In addition to the internal reports cited above, the Institute of Medicine (IOM) also evaluated the 510(k) program and issued a report on its findings.[14] The IOM found that the current 510(k) process is flawed based on its legislative foundation. Rather than continuing to modify the 35-year-old 510(k) process, the IOM concludes that FDA's finite resources would be better invested in developing an integrated premarket and postmarket regulatory framework that provides a reasonable assurance of safety and effectiveness throughout the device life cycle. This recommendation was extremely disappointing to industry and CDRH has stated that the 510(k) process should not be eliminated. As indicated above, CDRH has begun to implement recommendations from the agency's internal 510(k) Working Group and Task Force of the Utilization of Science in Regulatory Decision Making and plans to continue modernization of the 510(k) pathway.

The progress of the proposed 510(k) pathway initiatives can be tracked on FDA's website.

PMA Approval Process

A PMA differs significantly from a 510(k) premarket notification in the amount of information that must be submitted to FDA.

An approved PMA is, in effect, a license granted to the applicant to market a particular medical device. Under section 515 of the FDCA, a PMA must be filed if a proposed device is not substantially equivalent to a legally marketed Class I or Class II device, or if it is a pre-amendments Class III device for which FDA has called for PMAs.

A PMA differs significantly from a 510(k) premarket notification in the amount of information (particularly clinical data) that must be submitted to FDA. In contrast to 510(k) notices, which must demonstrate that the new device is "substantially equivalent" to a predicate device, a PMA must be supported by valid scientific evidence to demonstrate the "safety and effectiveness" of the device for its intended use. PMAs typically include the results of extensive clinical trials, bench tests, laboratory studies, animal studies and references to any standards relevant to a device's safety or effectiveness. The PMA also must contain a complete description of the device and its components; a detailed description of the methods, facilities and controls used to manufacture the device; the proposed labeling and advertising literature; and any training materials. In addition, all published and unpublished literature concerning the prior use of the product must be included, as well as a bibliography of all published reports that were not submitted and were known to the applicant concerning the device's safety and effectiveness. The review time for a PMA is significantly longer than for 510(k) notifications.

The following table summarizes the major distinctions between 510(k) notices and PMAs.

	510(k) Premarket Notification	Premarket Approval (PMA)
Devices Subject to Requirement	Few Class I, most Class II and some Class III pre-amendments devices*	All Class III post-amendments devices and some Class III pre-amendments devices
Clinical Data Requirements	Most are not supported by clinical data; Hybrid 510(k) notifications include clinical data	Clinical studies almost always required to support submission
Evidence of Safety and Efficacy Required	Information and data to support the "substantial equivalence" of the device to a legally marketed predicate device	Clinical data and/or scientific evidence supporting "safety and efficacy" claims
Marketing Rights	No exclusivity	Like a Product License
Average FDA Review Time[15]	63 FDA days (ODE) (09 FY) 98 total days (ODE) (09 FY)	225 FDA days (ODE) (08 FY) 284 total days (ODE) (08 FY)
Regulations on Device Changes	Must file new 510(k) if the change "could significantly affect" the safety or efficacy of the device or a major change to the intended use of the device	Must file a new PMA, some form of PMA supplement, or annual report depending on the nature and effect of change on the safety and effectiveness of the device
Advisory Panel Review	No Advisory Panel Review for almost all 510(k) devices	Advisory Panel Review for some but not all PMAs. Generally, no Advisory Panel Review for PMA Supplements

* FDA is in the process of reviewing and classifying all remaining categories of Class III pre-amendments devices, after which submission of a 510(k) notice will no longer be an option to market a Class III device.

FDA's Least Burdensome Approach policies also apply to PMAs. However, as with the least burdensome requirements for 510(k)s, while it is often advisable to at least raise with FDA least burdensome arguments, the agency ultimately determines what amount and type of data and information are necessary to support marketing applications.

FDA ultimately determines what amount and type of data and information are necessary to support marketing applications.

Contents of a PMA

The format and information required in a PMA are outlined in 21 C.F.R. § 814.20:

- The name and address of the applicant.
- A table of contents that specifies the volume and page number for each item referred to in the table. A PMA shall include separate sections on nonclinical laboratory studies and on clinical investigations involving human subjects.
- A summary in sufficient detail that the reader may gain a general under-standing of the data and information in the application. The summary shall contain the following information:
    - *Indications for use.* A general description of the disease or condition the device will diagnose, treat, prevent, cure or mitigate, including a description of the patient population for which the device is intended.
    - *Device description.* An explanation of how the device functions, the basic scientific concepts that form the basis for the device, and the significant physical and performance characteristics of the device. A brief description of the manufacturing process should be included if it will significantly enhance the reader's understanding of the device. The generic name of the device as well as any proprietary name or trade name should be included.
    - *Alternative practices and procedures.* A description of existing alternative practices or procedures for diagnosing, treating, preventing, curing or mitigating the disease or condition for which the device is intended.
    - *Marketing history.* A brief description of the foreign and U.S. marketing history, if any, of the device, including a list of all countries in which the device has been marketed and a list of all countries in which the device has been withdrawn from marketing for any reason related to the safety or effectiveness of the device. The description shall include the history of the marketing of the device by the applicant and, if known, the history of the marketing of the device by any other person.
    - *Summary of studies.* An abstract of any information or report described in the PMA under paragraph (b)(8)(ii) of this section and a summary of the results of technical data submitted under paragraph (b)(6) of this section. Such summary shall include a description of the objective of the study; a description of the experimental design of the study; a brief description of how the data were collected and analyzed; and a brief description of the results, whether positive, negative or inconclusive.

This section shall include the following:

♦ A summary of the nonclinical laboratory studies submitted in the application;

♦ A summary of the clinical investigations involving human subjects submitted in the application including a discussion of subject selection and exclusion criteria, study population, study period, safety and effectiveness data, adverse reactions and complications, patient discontinuation, patient complaints, device failures and replacements, results of statistical analyses of the clinical investigations, contraindications and precautions for use of the device, and other information from the clinical investigations as appropriate (any investigation conducted under an IDE shall be identified as such).

♦ *Conclusions drawn from the studies.* A discussion demonstrating that the data and information in the application constitute valid scientific evidence within the meaning of 21 C.F.R. § 860.7 and provide reasonable assurance that the device is safe and effective for its intended use. A concluding discussion shall present benefit and risk considerations related to the device including a discussion of any adverse effects of the device on health and any proposed additional studies or surveillance the applicant intends to conduct following approval of the PMA.

♦ A complete description of:

♦ The device, including pictorial representations;

♦ Each of the functional components or ingredients of the device if the device consists of more than one physical component or ingredient;

♦ The properties of the device relevant to the diagnosis, treatment, prevention, cure or mitigation of a disease or condition;

♦ The principles of operation of the device; and

♦ The methods used in, and the facilities and controls used for, the manufacture, processing, packing, storage and, where appropriate, installation of the device, in sufficient detail so that a person generally familiar with current good manufacturing practice can make a knowledgeable judgment about the quality control used in the manufacture of the device.

♦ Reference to any performance standard under section 514 of the act or the Radiation Control for Health and Safety Act of 1968 (42 U.S.C. 263b et seq.) in effect or proposed at the time of the submission and to any voluntary standard that is relevant to any aspect of the safety or effectiveness of the device and that is known to or that should reasonably be known to the applicant. The applicant shall—

- ◆ Provide adequate information to demonstrate how the device meets, or justify any deviation from, any performance standard established under section 514 of the act or under the Radiation Control for Health and Safety Act, and
- ◆ Explain any deviation from a voluntary standard.
- ◆ The following technical sections which shall contain data and information in sufficient detail to permit FDA to determine whether to approve or deny approval of the application:
  - ◆ A section containing results of the nonclinical laboratory studies with the device including microbiological, toxicological, immunological, biocompatibility, stress, wear, shelf life and other laboratory or animal tests as appropriate.
  - ◆ A section containing results of the clinical investigations involving human subjects with the device including clinical protocols, number of investigators and subjects per investigator, subject selection and exclusion criteria, study population, study period, safety and effectiveness data, adverse reactions and complications, patient discontinuation, patient complaints, device failures and replacements, tabulations of data from all individual subject report forms and copies of such forms for each subject who died during a clinical investigation or who did not complete the investigation, results of statistical analyses of the clinical investigations, device failures and replacements, contraindications and precautions for use of the device, and any other appropriate information from the clinical investigations. Any investigation conducted under an IDE shall be identified as such. Information on clinical investigations involving human subjects shall include the following:
    - ◆ A statement with respect to each study that it either was conducted in compliance with the institutional review board regulations in 21 C.F.R. Part 56, or was not subject to the regulations under 21 C.F.R. §§ 56.104 or 56.105, and that it was conducted in compliance with the informed consent regulations in 21 C.F.R. Part 50; or if the study was not conducted in compliance with those regulations, a brief statement of the reason for the noncompliance.
    - ◆ A statement that each study was conducted in compliance with 21 C.F.R. Part 812 concerning sponsors of clinical investigations and clinical investigators, or if the study was not conducted in compliance with those regulations, a brief statement of the reason for the noncompliance.
- ◆ For a PMA supported solely by data from one investigation, a justification showing that data and other information from a single investigator are sufficient to demonstrate the safety and effectiveness of the device and to ensure reproducibility of test results.

- The following:
  - A bibliography of all published reports not submitted under this section, whether adverse or supportive, known to or that should reasonably be known to the applicant and that concern the safety or effectiveness of the device.
  - An identification, discussion and analysis of any other data, information or report relevant to an evaluation of the safety and effectiveness of the device known to or that should reasonably be known to the applicant from any source, foreign or domestic, including information derived from investigations other than those proposed in the application and from commercial marketing experience.
  - Copies of such published reports or unpublished information in the possession of or reasonably obtainable by the applicant if an FDA advisory committee or FDA requests.
- One or more samples of the device and its components, if requested by FDA. If it is impractical to submit a requested sample of the device, the applicant shall name the location at which FDA may examine and test one or more devices.
- Copies of all proposed labeling for the device. Such labeling may include, e.g., instructions for installation and any information, literature or advertising that constitutes labeling under section 201(m) of the act.
- An environmental assessment. However, PMAs are categorically excluded from requiring an environmental assessment (EA) or environmental impact statement (EIS) if the device is of the same type and for the same use as a previously approved device (21 C.F.R. § 25.34(d)). For these types of products, sponsors must include a statement requesting a categorical exclusion in the PMA application.
- A financial certification or disclosure statement or both as required by 21 C.F.R. Part 54.
- Such other information as FDA may request. If necessary, FDA will obtain the concurrence of the appropriate FDA advisory committee before requesting additional information.

Review Process

Upon receipt of a PMA, FDA makes a threshold determination as to whether it is sufficiently complete to permit a substantive review. If so, FDA will accept the application for filing. Once accepted, FDA begins an in-depth review of the submission. FDA often asks for more information or clarification of information already provided in the application, which extends the review period. Additionally, if FDA determines that additional clinical trials are necessary, the PMA review may be delayed for the additional period of time required to conduct the studies and to submit the results in an amendment to the pending PMA.

FDA often asks for more information or clarification of information already provided in the application, which extends the review period.

In 1998, the Center for Devices and Radiological Health (CDRH) implemented a "modular approach" for PMA submissions to expedite the PMA review process. Instead of waiting for all sections to be complete, the modular approach allows sponsors to submit parts of their application as soon as they are ready for filing. CDRH and the sponsor must come to a mutual agreement as to which elements will be included in each module. This approach opens communications between the sponsor and CDRH at every step in the application process.

At some point during the review period, FDA usually convenes an advisory committee (typically a panel of clinicians) to evaluate the application and to recommend whether FDA should approve the device. FDA is not bound by the recommendation of the advisory panel. During the PMA review process, FDA will inspect the manufacturer's facilities to ensure compliance with applicable QSR requirements. In addition, FDA will also conduct a Bioresearch Monitoring audit of clinical data, if applicable.

If FDA's evaluations of the PMA, the manufacturing facilities and the integrity of the clinical data are favorable, FDA may issue either an approval letter or an "approvable" letter, which contains a number of conditions that must be met in order to secure final PMA approval. When and if the manufacturer satisfies those conditions, FDA will issue an approval letter authorizing commercial marketing of the device for specific indications. If FDA's evaluation of the PMA or the manufacturing facilities is not favorable, FDA will deny approval of the application or issue a "non-approvable" letter, which identifies the major deficiencies with the PMA that must be resolved before the application is approved.

Postapproval Requirements

Since 1986, FDA has had the authority to impose postmarket approval requirements on any device requiring premarket approval. These requirements could be imposed in the following ways: 1) in the order approving a PMA; 2) by regulation at the time FDA approved the PMA; and 3) by regulation subsequent to FDA's approval of the PMA. Postapproval requirements may include the following as a condition of a device's approval:

♦ Restriction of the device's sale, distribution, or use;

♦ Continuing evaluation and periodic reporting on the device's safety, effectiveness and reliability;

♦ The inclusion, in the labeling of a device and in the advertising of any restricted device, of warnings, hazards or precautions important for the device's safe and effective use;

♦ The inclusion of identification codes on the device or its labeling or, for an implanted device, on cards given to patients;

In 1998, CDRH implemented a "modular approach" for PMA submissions to expedite the PMA review process.

- Maintenance of records that will enable the applicant to submit to FDA information needed to trace patients;

- Maintenance of records for specified periods of time and organization and indexing of records into identifiable files to enable FDA to determine whether there is reasonable assurance of the device's continued safety and effectiveness;

- At specified intervals, submission of periodic reports containing required information;

- Batch testing of the device; and

- Any other requirements determined by FDA to be necessary to provide reasonable assurance, or continued reasonable assurance, of the device's safety and effectiveness.

A sponsor must also grant FDA access to records and reports, and permit authorized FDA employees to copy and verify such records and reports. It must also permit FDA to inspect, at a reasonable time and in a reasonable manner, all manufacturing facilities to verify that the device is being manufactured, stored, labeled, and shipped under approved conditions. The failure to comply with any postapproval requirement constitutes grounds for withdrawing a PMA's approval.

Postmarket Surveillance Studies

Recognizing that FDA's PMA review process cannot be expected to identify all possible problems with a device, Congress provided in the SMDA that FDA must impose additional postmarket surveillance (PMS) requirements in certain cases (i.e., in the form of postmarketing studies) and that it had the discretion to impose such requirements in other cases. The Medical Device Amendments of 1992 (the MDA 1992) further amended the FDCA to provide the following:

- That a company's failure to comply with the PMS requirements is a prohibited act, subject to criminal and civil penalties; and

- A device for which required PMS is not carried out is misbranded and subject to seizure.

Under section 522 of the FDCA (21 U.S.C. § 360l), as amended by MDA 1992 (Pub. L. No. 102-300), FDA was required to impose PMS requirements on certain devices (mandatory surveillance), and was allowed to impose PMS requirements on any other device for which the agency decides that studies must be conducted to protect the public health or to provide safety and effectiveness data (discretionary surveillance). Under FDAMA, however, FDA is no longer required to mandate that manufacturers of high-risk devices conduct PMS studies.

Recognizing that FDA's PMA review process cannot be expected to identify all possible problems with a device, Congress provided in the SMDA that FDA must impose additional postmarket surveillance requirements in certain cases and that it had the discretion to impose such requirements in other cases.

Instead, FDA may order PMS studies for the following types of Class II and Class III devices: 1) devices whose failure would be reasonably likely to have a serious adverse consequence; or 2) devices intended to be implanted in the human body for more than one year; or 3) devices intended to be life-sustaining or life-supporting devices used outside a device user facility.

Upon receiving a PMS order, the manufacturers must, within 30 days of receipt, submit a surveillance plan. FDA is then given 60 days to evaluate the qualifications of the person designated to conduct the surveillance and determine whether the plan will result in the collection of useful data. The duration of any agency-required study may not exceed 36 months. Any longer study must be mutually agreed upon by the manufacturer and FDA. If no such agreement can be reached, the dispute resolution process in section 404 of FDAMA is followed.

In the PMA approval letter (or in the substantial equivalence order for 510(k) notifications), FDA will notify the manufacturers that it is required to conduct PMS studies. However, manufacturers may be alerted to the need for PMS studies in the PMA "approvable" letter (and in the case of 510(k) notifications, in correspondence shortly after the 510(k) notification is submitted).

Device Modifications

Approval of a PMA supplement is required before making a change that affects the safety or effectiveness of the device. Supplements to a PMA often require the submission of the same type of information required for an initial PMA, except that the supplement generally is limited to the information needed to support the safety and effectiveness of the proposed modification, or clarify safety and effectiveness of an existing device (i.e., new adverse event information, higher than predicted failure rates, etc.). The regulations identify types of changes that require the submission of a PMA supplement if the change affects safety or effectiveness. These include 1) new indications for use of the device; 2) labeling changes; 3) the use of a different facility or establishment to manufacture, process or package the device; 4) changes in manufacturing facilities, methods or quality control procedures; 5) changes in sterilization procedures; 6) changes in packaging; 7) changes in the performance or design specifications, circuits, components, ingredients, principle of operation or physical layout of the device; and 8) extension of the expiration date of the device based on data obtained under a new or revised stability or sterility testing protocol that has not been approved by FDA. Many of these changes, such as a change in the manufacturing site, are presumed to affect safety and efficacy and require a PMA supplement.

Types of changes that require a PMA supplement submission:

1) new indications for use of the device;

2) labeling changes;

3) the use of a different facility or establishment to manufacture, process or package the device;

4) changes in manufacturing facilities, methods or quality control procedures;

5) changes in sterilization procedures;

6) changes in packaging;

7) changes in the performance or design specifications, circuits, components, ingredients, principle of operation or physical layout of the device; and

8) extension of the expiration date of the device based on data obtained under a new or revised stability or sterility testing protocol that has not been approved by FDA.

Additionally, when a PMA supplement is required for an incremental change to the design of a device that affects safety and effectiveness, the PMA supplement must be approved by FDA if 1) nonclinical data demonstrate that the design modification creates the intended additional capacity, function or performance of the device; and 2) clinical data from the approved PMA application and any supplement provide a reasonable assurance of safety and effectiveness of the modified device. FDA is allowed to require, when necessary, additional clinical data to evaluate the design modification of the device to provide a reasonable assurance of safety and effectiveness.

There are several types of submissions that may be used to obtain FDA approval for a modification to a PMA device. These include: a new PMA; a traditional PMA Supplement; a 30-day notice; a Special PMA Supplement for Changes Being Effected; or a PMA Manufacturing Site Change Supplement. FDA has disseminated a guidance document to assist manufacturers in determining which type of PMA Supplement is required for various types of device modifications.[16]

PMA Annual Reports

FDA requires that the PMA holder report a change for which a PMA supplement is not required in a periodic (annual) report. This change may be made before it is reported to FDA. FDA guidance on PMA changes also allows manufacturers to make certain very minor changes to their approved devices by simply documenting the change information in the firm's files. As a practical matter, most companies include in their annual reports at least general information about all changes that have been made to the device that have not been the subject of an approved supplement in order to put FDA on notice of the changes.

Annual reports must also contain a bibliography and a summary of unpublished reports of data from any clinical investigations or nonclinical laboratory studies involving the device or related devices and any reports in the scientific literature concerning the device. The annual report should summarize information pertaining to the original PMA, as well as any subsequent PMA supplements and should include all postapproval reports for PMA supplements. The annual report should also describe any adverse device effects.

When a PMA supplement is required for an incremental change to the design of a device that affects safety and effectiveness, the PMA supplement must be approved by FDA if:

1) nonclinical data demonstrate that the design modification creates the intended additional capacity, function or performance of the device; and

2) clinical data from the approved PMA application and any supplement provide a reasonable assurance of safety and effectiveness of the modified device.

The PDP Is an Alternative to the PMA Process

An alternative to the PMA process is the Product Development Protocol (PDP) (FDCA § 515(f)), though it is rarely used.

Under 21 C.F.R. § 814.19, a device with a completed PDP will be considered to have an approved PMA. The PDP procedure is optional; FDA cannot require a sponsor to use the PDP process for determining market approval. The major distinguishing feature of a PDP from a PMA approach is FDA's early involvement at the design or preclinical testing phase. Thus, the PDP approach involves a close relationship between FDA and the sponsor in designing appropriate preclinical tests and clinical investigations to establish the safety and effectiveness of the device. The requirements for proof of safety and effectiveness are no less stringent under a PDP than they are under a PMA; thus, the PDP process offers little advantage if the device already has undergone considerable design investigation and evaluation. Historically, the PDP rarely has proven to be feasible for a manufacturer and to be overly demanding of FDA's resources.

Radiological Health

The Electronic Product Radiation Control provisions of the FDCA, which are set forth in sections 531 through 542 (originally enacted as the Radiation Control for Health and Safety Act of 1968 and incorporated into the FDCA by the SMDA) give FDA responsibility for all *medical* and *nonmedical* electronic products that emit any ionizing or nonionizing electromagnetic or particulate radiation or any sonic, infrasonic or ultrasonic wave. FDA's implementing regulations are codified in 21 C.F.R. Parts 1000 through 1299. These regulations set forth the following three types of requirements: 1) performance standards, 2) reporting requirements and 3) labeling. Such products must comply with all of the applicable requirements unless they are exempted from certain requirements by regulation.

FDA has issued radiation performance standards intended to control unnecessary human exposure to potential hazardous ionizing and non-ionizing radiation and to ensure the safe and effective use of such radiation. Performance studies apply to products such as television receivers and diagnostic x-ray systems.

Manufacturers must submit product reports (including supplements and abbreviated reports), annual reports and notices of defect or noncompliance. Manufacturers must document any actual or possible unexpected exposure during manufacturing, testing or use of any electronic product in the appropriate report or notice.

Electronic products subject to a standard must bear label(s) identifying the name and address of the manufacturer, the date of manufacture and the manufacturer's statement that the product complies with the Department of Health and Human Service's radiation standards or similar language.

FDA has made available product-specific guidance documents and information packages to assist manufacturers in meeting the reporting requirements for radiation-emitting products. If the product is a medical device, these requirements are in addition to any premarketing or postmarketing requirements that apply to the device.

CONCLUSION

FDA's regulations on devices are quite extensive and often complex. This chapter summarizes FDA's premarket requirements for devices. It does not address postmarketing requirements, including QSR compliance, medical device reporting, tracking or product recalls. It is also certainly not an exhaustive account of what is necessary to comply with all of the premarket device requirements. Nonetheless, it highlights the basic requirements for marketing devices in the United States.

Endnotes

1. Center for Devices and Radiological Health, Food and Drug Administration, Guidance: Changes in Device Classification (Feb. 1997).
2. Office of Device Evaluation, Center for Devices and Radiological Health, Food and Drug Administration, Draft Guidance for Industry and Food and Drug Administration Staff - De Novo Classification Process (Evaluation of Automatic Class III Designation) (Oct. 3, 2011).
3. Center for Devices and Radiological Health and Center for Biologics Evaluation and Research, Food and Drug Administration, Interactive Review for Medical Device Submissions: 510(k)s, Original PMAs, PMA Supplements, Original BLAs, and BLA Supplements (Feb. 28, 2008).
4. Office of Device Evaluation, Center for Devices and Radiological Health, Food and Drug Administration, "Guidance for the Content of Premarket Submissions for Software Contained in Medical Devices" (May 11, 2005).
5. If information concerning similarity to a predicate device must be obtained through a clinical trial, the trial is subject to the requirement of the IDE regulation, 21 C.F.R. § 812.22.
6. 21 C.F.R. § 807.81(a)(3)(i).
7. Office of Device Evaluation, Center for Devices and Radiological Health, Food and Drug Administration, "Draft Guidance for Industry and FDA Staff – 510(k) Device Modifications: Deciding When to Submit a 510(k) for a Change to an Existing Device" (July 27, 2011).
8. Office of Device Evaluation, Center for Devices and Radiological Health, Food and Drug Administration, "Guidance for Industry and FDA Staff – 510(k) Device Modification: Deciding When to Submit a 510(k) for a Change to an Existing Device" (Jan. 10, 1997).

9. Office of Device Evaluation, Center for Devices and Radiological Health, Food and Drug Administration, "The New 510(k) Paradigm— Alternate Approaches to Demonstrating Substantial Equivalence in Premarket Notifications—Final Guidance" (Mar. 20, 1998).

10. *See* Office of Device Evaluation, Center for Devices and Radiological Health, Food and Drug Administration, "The Least Burdensome Provisions of the FDA Modernization Act of 1997: Concept and Principles; Final Guidance for FDA and Industry" (Oct. 4, 2002).

11. Center for Devices and Radiological Health, Food and Drug Administration, 510(k) Working Group Preliminary Report and Recommendations, Aug. 2010.

12. Center for Devices and Radiological Health, Food and Drug Administration, Task Force of the Utilization of Science in Regulatory Decision Making Preliminary Report and Recommendations (Aug. 2010).

13. Center for Devices and Radiological Health, Food and Drug Administration, "510(k) and Science Report Recommendations: Summary and Overview Comments and Next Steps" (Jan. 19, 2011).

14. INSTITUTE OF MEDICINE, MEDICAL DEVICES AND THE PUBLIC'S HEALTH: THE FDA 510(k) CLEARANCE PROCESS AT 35 YEARS (July 29, 2011).

15. U.S. FOOD AND DRUG ADMINISTRATION, OFFICE OF DEVICE EVALUATION, ANNUAL REPORT, FISCAL YEAR 2009 at 5-9.

16. Office of Device Evaluation, Center for Devices and Radiological Health, Food and Drug Administration, "Guidance for Industry and FDA Staff—Modifications to Devices Subject to Premarket Approval (PMA)—The PMA Supplement Decision-Making Process" (Dec. 11, 2008).

Chapter 8

Combination Products

Suzanne O'Shea, Faegre Baker Daniels, Indianapolis, IN

Key Points

- A combination product comprises two or more different types of regulated components. It can be a drug/device, a biologic/device, a drug/biologic or a drug/device/biologic.
- The Safe Medical Devices Act of 1990 directs the Food and Drug Administration (FDA) to assign review of a combination product to an agency center based on the product's primary mode of action, the single mode of action that provides the most important therapeutic effect of the combination product.
- A sponsor of a combination product can submit a request for designation where the jurisdiction of the reviewing center is unclear or in dispute.
- FDA has issued proposed rules on good manufacturing practices and postmarket safety reporting for combination products.
- FDA has issued draft guidance documents that describe how the agency classifies products as drugs or devices.

WHAT THE STATUTE AND REGULATIONS SAY

A combination product is one that has multiple characteristics. It could be a drug/device, a biologic/device, a drug/biologic or a drug/device/biologic.

Products that combine two products of the same type are not regarded as combination products. For example, a fixed combination drug product comprising two or more drug ingredients in a single dosage unit is not a combination product. Similarly, products comprising two or more devices, or two or more biological products, are not combination products. Products comprising a drug and a cosmetic, or a drug and a dietary supplement, are also not considered combination products, although they raise some of the same issues as combination products.

The Safe Medical Devices Act of 1990 addresses the threshold combination product issue: when a product comprises more than one type of product, which FDA center will review and regulate it?

The first statutory reference to combination products occurred in the Safe Medical Devices Act of 1990. The statute addresses the threshold combination product issue: when a product comprises more than one type of product, which center within the Food and Drug Administration (FDA) will review and regulate it? The statute directs the agency to assign combination products to an agency center for review based on the product's primary mode of action (PMOA), but significantly contains no definition of "combination products" or PMOA:

> The Secretary shall designate a component of the Food and Drug Administration to regulate products that constitute a combination of a drug, device, or biological product. The Secretary shall determine the primary mode of action of the combination product. If the Secretary determines that the primary mode of action is that of—
>
> (A) a drug (other than a biological product), the persons charged with premarket review of drugs shall have primary jurisdiction,
>
> (B) a device, the persons charged with premarket review of devices shall have primary jurisdiction, or
>
> (C) a biological product, the persons charged with premarket review of biological products shall have primary jurisdiction.
>
> FDCA § 503(g); 21 U.S.C. § 353(g)

Regulations issued shortly thereafter included the following definition(s) of combination products:

◆ A product comprising two or more regulated components—i.e., drug/device, biologic/device, drug/biologic or drug/device/biologic—that are physically, chemically or otherwise combined or mixed and produced as a single entity (21 C.F.R. § 3.2(e)(1)). Examples include drug-coated stents, an implantable replacement joint coated with a growth factor and a monoclonal antibody with a therapeutic drug attached.

◆ Two or more separate products packaged together in a single package or as a unit and comprising drug and device products, device and biological products, or biological and drug products (21 C.F.R. § 3.2(e)(2)). An example would be a kit containing a drug and a device applicator.

◆ A drug, device or biological product packaged separately that according to its investigational plan or proposed labeling is intended for use only with an approved individually specified drug, device or biological product where both are required to achieve the intended use, indication, or effect and where upon approval of the proposed product the labeling of the approved product would need to be changed (e.g., to reflect a change in intended use, dosage form, strength, route of administration or significant change in dose) (21 C.F.R. § 3.2(e)(3)). An investigational device intended to deliver an already approved drug product in a new way for a new use would fit this definition.

♦ Any investigational drug, device or biological product packaged separately that according to its proposed labeling is for use only with another individually specified investigational drug, device or biological product where both are required to achieve the intended use, indication or effect (21 C.F.R. § 3.2(e)(4)). An investigational device intended to deliver an investigational new drug would be deemed a "combination product" under this definition.

The statute does not address the statutory provisions under which a combination product is to be regulated. In practice, combination products are almost always regulated under the type of application ordinarily submitted to the center with jurisdiction over the product. In other words, combination products assigned to the Center for Drug Evaluation and Research (CDER) are ordinarily reviewed under the new drug provisions of the Federal Food, Drug, and Cosmetic Act (FDCA); combination products assigned to the Center for Devices and Radiological Health are ordinarily reviewed under the device provisions; while combination products assigned to the Center for Biologics Evaluation and Research (CBER) are ordinarily reviewed under the licensing provisions of the Public Health Service Act or the device provisions of the FDCA.

Combination products are almost always regulated under the type of application ordinarily submitted to the center with jurisdiction over the product.

An exception to the above is FDA's final rule "Regulations Restricting the Sale and Distribution of Cigarettes and Smokeless Tobacco to Protect Children and Adolescents." FDA asserted that it had the discretion to choose the premarket approval authority for combination products that provides the best public health protection (61 Fed. Reg. 44,395, 44,402 (Aug. 28, 1996)). In practice, combination products are almost always reviewed under the premarket approval authority ordinarily used by the lead reviewing center.

PRIMARY MODE OF ACTION AND ASSIGNMENT OF A LEAD AGENCY CENTER

Intercenter Agreements

In 1991, CBER, CDER and CDRH entered into three Intercenter Agreements (ICAs): a CBER–CDER Intercenter Agreement, a CBER–CDRH Intercenter Agreement and a CDER–CDRH Intercenter Agreement. Although they differ in content, format and scope, the ICAs share the common purpose of explaining how various categories of both combination and single-entity medical products were classified and assigned at the time the agreements were written in 1991. The ICAs constitute guidance that is not binding on the public or the agency.

The usefulness of Intercenter Agreements (ICAs) is becoming increasingly limited as new products are developed that were not envisioned when the ICAs were established.

At the time the ICAs were written, they were the major jurisdictional statements issued by the agency, but their usefulness is becoming increasingly limited as new products are developed that were not envisioned when the ICAs were established. Since 1991, FDA has continued to classify and assign many new products not specifically covered by the ICAs. The body of jurisdictional decisions has therefore grown significantly, and over time, the ICAs have become incomplete statements.

In 2006, the agency published a *Federal Register* notice in which it concluded that while the CDER–CDRH and CBER–CDRH ICAs continue to provide useful nonbinding guidance about the assignment and classification of products, the CBER–CDER ICA was rendered almost completely out of date by the transfer of many therapeutic biological products from CBER to CDER in 2003. For these reasons, the agency proposed to continue the CDER–CDRH and the CBER–CDRH ICAs in effect, and to rescind the CBER–CDER ICA. As of the writing of this chapter, this proposal had not been finalized.[1]

Primary Mode of Action

As noted above, the FDCA requires that combination products be assigned to an agency center on the basis of the product's PMOA, but does not include a definition of PMOA. In 2005, FDA amended the combination product regulations to include a definition of PMOA.

The amended regulations begin by defining mode of action as "the means by which a product achieves an intended therapeutic effect or action. For purposes of this definition, 'therapeutic' action or effect includes any effect or action of the combination product intended to diagnose, cure, mitigate, treat, or prevent disease, or affect the structure or any function of the body" (21 C.F.R. § 3.2(k)).

PMOA is defined as "the single mode of action of a combination product that provides the most important therapeutic action of the combination product. The most important therapeutic action is the mode of action expected to make the greatest contribution to the overall intended therapeutic effects of the combination product" (21 C.F.R. § 3.2(m)).

In many cases, this definition suffices to determine a combination product's PMOA. The preamble to the final rule provides several examples, including a drug-coated vascular stent. A vascular stent provides a mechanical scaffold to keep a blood vessel open while the drug is slowly released from the stent to prevent the buildup of new tissue that would re-occlude the artery. This product has two modes of action—the device mode of action contributed by the stent and the drug mode of action contributed by the drug coating. The stent itself provides the most important therapeutic effect of the product, while the drug augments the effectiveness of the stent. Accordingly, drug-coated stents are generally assigned to CDRH for review and regulation under the device provisions of the act.

In contrast, a drug-eluting disc, which is surgically implanted and contains a drug that is slowly released for prolonged, local delivery of chemotherapeutic agents to a tumor site, also has device and drug modes of action. In this case, however, the chemotherapeutic drug makes the most important contribution to the therapeutic effect of the product. Products like this are assigned to CDER for review and regulation under the new drug provisions of the FDCA.

In some cases, FDA has not been able to determine which component makes the major therapeutic contribution to the product. For example, consider a contact lens that corrects vision and also contains a drug that will be delivered from the lens to treat glaucoma. This hypothetical product has both drug and device modes of action, but the two modes of action are independent of one another, and neither appears to be subordinate to the other. In cases like this, where it is impossible to say that one component provides the most important therapeutic action of the product, the agency follows an assignment algorithm set out in the regulations.

Where it is impossible to say that one component provides the most important therapeutic action of the product, FDA follows an assignment algorithm set out in the regulations.

The first step of the algorithm is to determine whether one agency center regulates other combination products presenting similar questions of safety and effectiveness with regard to the combination product as a whole. In this case, CDER regulates glaucoma drugs presenting questions of safety and effectiveness similar to those presented by the drug in the combination product, and CDRH regulates devices presenting questions of safety and effectiveness similar to those presented by the contact lens in the combination product but neither agency center regulates combination products that present questions similar to those presented by both the contact lens and the glaucoma drug.

When no agency center regulates combination products presenting questions of safety and effectiveness with regard to the combination product as a whole, the agency proceeds to the second step of the algorithm; the agency considers which center has the most expertise related to the most significant safety and effectiveness questions presented by the combination product. In this case, the most significant safety and effectiveness questions are related to the characterization, manufacturing and clinical performance of the drug component, while the safety and effectiveness questions raised by the vision-correcting contact lens are considered more routine. As a result, the corrective contact lens with a glaucoma drug product would be assigned to CDER for review. If a second manufacturer were to submit a marketing application for a similar product, the similar product would be subsequently assigned to CDER under the first step of the algorithm. (21 C.F.R. § 3.4(b).)

REQUESTS FOR DESIGNATION

A request for designation (RFD) is the formal process by which a sponsor of a combination product requests that the agency assign a combination product to a center for review when it is unclear or in dispute as to which center has jurisdiction over the product. An RFD is limited to 15 pages, and contains summary information about the product and its intended use. FDA recommends that an RFD be submitted as soon as sponsors have enough information about the product to enable FDA to make a decision.

A request for designation is a formal process by which the sponsor of a combination product requests that FDA assign the product to a center for review when it is unclear or disputed as to which center has jurisdiction over the product.

An RFD is also to contain the sponsor's assessment of the modes of action of the components of the combination product, as well as the sponsor's description of the product's PMOA. Sponsors may include data on these points if it is useful to the determination of the product's modes of action and PMOA. The sponsor is also given the opportunity to recommend which center should have jurisdiction over the product.

By statute, the agency is allowed 60 days to respond to RFDs. The agency's decision is in the form of a designation letter. Decisions made in an RFD letter are unique in two respects. First, the agency may change these decisions without the consent of the sponsor only to protect the public health or for other compelling reasons. Second, if the agency does not issue a designation letter in response to an RFD within the 60-day time period, the sponsor's recommendation as to assignment of the product takes effect. The agency rarely, if ever, fails to issue an RFD letter within the 60-day time frame.[2]

Consults and Collaboration

Even though one agency center is designated as the lead, the other center will likely be involved in the review. In general, participation by the other relevant agency center is either a consultative review or a collaborative review. The RFD designation letter will state the role of the other center.

A consult occurs when one center requests advice from another center on a specific question or issue. A collaboration occurs when two or more centers have primary review responsibilities, generally for a defined portion of a submission. Regulatory and scientific decisions will be made by the management of each center for that portion of the review assigned to it, including the decision to approve or refuse to approve the product.

FDA has issued a Standard Operating Procedure (SOP) for the Intercenter Consultative/Collaborative Review Process.[3] The objective of this SOP is to improve intercenter communication on combination products, as well as the timeliness and consistency of intercenter consultative and collaborative reviews.

A frequent concern about consults and collaborations is that they will slow down the review process. To allay such concerns, the SOP states that "all consulted and collaborating reviewers should be held accountable and receive credit for thorough and timely expert reviews and advice. Every effort should be made to meet the due date identified by the request originator." The SOP also stresses the importance of frequent, ongoing communication between the primary reviewer and the consulting or collaborative reviewer.

POSTMARKET SAFETY REPORTING

On October 1, 2009, the FDA issued a proposed rule that includes a new set of regulations (to be contained in 21 C.F.R. Part 4) covering the reporting of adverse events for combination products.[4] During the development of this proposed rule, FDA reviewed postmarketing safety rules governing each type of product that could be contained in a combination product: drugs (21 C.F.R. Parts 310 and 314), biological products (21 C.F.R. Parts 600 and 606) and devices (21 C.F.R. Part 803). According to the preamble to the proposed rule, FDA concluded as a result of this review that each set of regulations contains many substantially similar requirements as well as certain important differences.

On October 1, 2009, FDA issued a proposed rule that includes a new set of regulations covering the reporting of adverse events for combination products.

The postmarket safety rules that are unique to a particular type of constituent part include:

- 5-day report when remedial action is required to prevent an unreasonable risk of substantial harm to public health by a medical device (21 C.F.R. 803.53(a));

- 30-day device malfunction report (21 C.F.R. 803.20(b)(3)(ii));

- 15-day "Alert Report" for Drugs and Biological Products (21 C.F.R. §§ 314.80(c)(1) and (e), and 600.80(c)(1) and (e));

- 3-day Field Alert to report certain problems with drugs in distribution (21 C.F.R. 314.81(b)(1)); and

- 7-day Expedited Blood Fatality Report (21 C.F.R. § 606.170).

Under the proposed rule, reporters would follow the postmarketing safety reporting regulations associated with the type of marketing application used to approve or clear the combination product, supplemented as necessary with any of the required reports listed above.

When considering whether a report is required under the set of regulations pertaining to the marketing application under which the combination product was approved or cleared, the combination product as a whole should be considered.[5] When determining whether an additional report must be filed, only the constituent part to which the regulation applies should be considered.[6]

The preamble to the proposed rule states that FDA does not expect or desire that reporters submit duplicate reports.

The preamble to the proposed rule states that FDA does not expect or desire that reporters submit duplicate reports.[7] Reports other than those associated with the type of marketing application under which the combination product is reviewed are to be submitted only when such report is required at an earlier date than the report associated with the marketing application.

For example, adverse events occurring from use of a drug–device combination product approved under a new drug application would be reported according to the requirements contained in 21 C.F.R. §§ 314.80 (15-day alert).[8] In addition to the reporting requirements found in 21 C.F.R. Part 314, reporters would also be required to consider whether a five-day report or a 30-day device malfunction report is also required. If a 30-day device malfunction report is required, it would not need to be submitted because the 15-day alert would have already been submitted. On the other hand, if a five-day remedial action report is required in this case, that report should be submitted within the regulatory time frame. Although the proposed rule does not appear to address the issue, presumably, the five-day remedial action report and the 15-day alert could be combined into one report and submitted at the same time. The proposed rule states that submissions should be made using the submission method and timeframes identified in the regulations for the combination product or constituent part.[9]

According to the Proposed Rule, the lead center within FDA will have responsibility for reviewing all postmarket safety reports received. The lead center will be required to consult with the other agency center as necessary.
FDA received numerous comments on the proposed rule. At the time of this writing, the framework for the final rule is not known.

Until the final rule is published, reporters may voluntarily follow the procedure outlined in the Proposed Rule or they may consult a concept paper on the Office of Combination Products (OCP) website.[10] The concept paper and the Proposed Rule are very similar.

Good Manufacturing Practices

On September 23, 2009, FDA issued a proposed rule on current good manufacturing practices (cGMPs) for combination products.[11] The proposal sets forth a new set of regulations, also to be contained in 21 C.F.R. Part 4. As of this writing FDA had not issued a final regulation covering the application of cGMPs (including 21 C.F.R. Parts 210 and 211 for drugs and biological products and Quality System Regulations (QSRs) for devices, 21 C.F.R. Part 820).[12]

cGMPs and QSRs are intended to ensure that drugs; biological products; human cells, tissues, and cellular and tissue-based products; and devices are made properly. Each set of regulations, however, is somewhat different because each is tailored to the characteristics of the types of products for which they were designed. Each set of regulations contains certain express or specific requirements that may be only generally expressed in the other set of regulations. For example, the cGMP regulations for drugs and biological products specifically require calculation of yield and stability while QSRs contain more general design validation provisions. Similarly, QSRs have detailed Corrective and Preventive Action (CAPA) provisions, while cGMPs contain more general production record requirements.

Current good manufacturing practices and Quality System Regulations are intended to ensure that drugs; biological products; human cells, tissues, and cellular and tissue-based products; and devices are made properly.

Under the proposed rule, each drug, biological product or device constituent part of a combination product, taken individually, is subject only to its governing cGMP regulations until it is actually combined with another type of constituent part to form a combination product. For example, when the constituent parts of a combination product are separately marketed, such as a new device intended for use with an individually specified, already approved drug product marketed by a different manufacturer, the device constituent part would be subject only to the QSRs, while the drug constituent part would be subject only to the cGMP regulations. Once the constituent parts are combined, each constituent part is still subject to its own cGMP regulations, which means that the combination product as a whole may be subject to more than one set of cGMP regulations.[13]

However, for single-entity and co-packaged combination products, the proposed rule would allow manufacturers to demonstrate compliance with cGMP requirements by implementing and complying with either the drug cGMPs or the QS regulation, rather than both, under certain conditions. These conditions include demonstrating that the cGMP operating system complies with specified provisions from the other of these two sets of regulations.[14]

For single-entity and co-packaged combination products, the proposed rule would allow manufacturers to demonstrate compliance with cGMP requirements by implementing and complying with either the drug cGMPs or the QS regulation, rather than both, under certain conditions.

More specifically, if a single-entity or co-packaged combination product includes both a drug and a device and the cGMP operating system is shown to comply with the drug cGMP regulations at 21 C.F.R. parts 210 and 211, the system would also have to be shown to comply with the additional specific provisions of the QS regulation, but not necessarily the entire device QS regulation. Similarly, if the manufacturer opts to comply with device QS regulation, it must be supplemented with specific drug cGMP regulations once the constituent parts of the combination product are combined.

The following chart identifies provisions of the cGMP and QSRs that should supplement a manufacturer's quality system (either drug cGMPs or device QS regulations).

Current Good Manufacturing Practice Provisions to Consider During and After Joining Together Co-Packaged and Single-Entity Combination Products[15]

If The Operating Manufacturing Control System Is Part 820 (QS Regulation), carefully consider these specific cGMP requirements:		If the Operating Manufacturing Control System Is Part 210/211 (cGMP Regulation), carefully consider these specific QS requirements:	
Regulation	**Title**	**Regulation**	**Title**
§ 211.84	Testing and approval or rejection of components, drug product containers, and closures	§ 820.20	Management responsibility
§ 211.103	Calculation of yield	§ 820.30	Design controls
§ 211.132	Tamper-evident packaging for OTC drugs	§ 820.50	Purchasing controls
§ 211.137	Expiration dating	§ 820.100	Corrective and preventative action
§ 211.165	Testing and release for distribution	§ 820.170	Installation
§ 211.166	Stability testing	§ 820.200	Servicing
§ 211.167	Special testing requirements		
§ 211.170	Reserve samples		

FDA recommends that manufacturers present information to the agency during the development phase about how they intend to achieve compliance with both sets of regulations during and after joining the constituent parts together of proposed combination products that will have constituent parts that are physically, chemically or otherwise combined, or that will be co-packaged. For example, FDA recommends that a pre-investigational new drug (pre-IND) or pre-investigational device exemption (pre-IDE) meeting include a discussion of the sponsor's implementation of cGMPs, including consideration of risks of the combination product, its technology and any anticipated postmarket development and postapproval changes. FDA recommends that the sponsor include all critical manufacturers in these discussions and include information on critical steps that may be conducted at source/contract firms and any special testing. FDA's OCP is available as a resource to sponsors in the resolution of cGMP concerns.[16]

At the time of this writing, FDA had not finalized the Proposed Rule for current Good Manufacturing Practices for Combination Products. Manufacturers may voluntarily follow the proposed rule or consult a Draft Guidance Document on the OCP website.[17] The Draft Guidance sets forth an approach to current Good Manufacturing Practices for Combination Products that is very similar to the proposed rule.

Draft Guidance Documents

In July 2011, the OCP issued two draft guidance documents:

♦ "Classification of Products as Drugs and Devices and Additional Product Classification Issues,"[18] and

♦ "Interpretation of the Term "Chemical Action" in the Definition of Device Under Section 201(h) of the Federal Food, Drug, and Cosmetic Act."[19]

These guidance documents provide additional information on how FDA will classify products, or constituent parts of combination products, as drugs or devices.[20] Thus, they do not affect how FDA will review and regulate products once it has determined they meet the definition of a combination product. A discussion of these guidance documents has been included in this chapter because the documents were issued by the OCP.

These guidance documents quickly provoked strong negative reaction. In particular, several comments noted a concern that FDA would re-classify previously classified devices as drugs. A number of commentators argued that FDA must go through notice-and-comment rulemaking before implementing changes of this nature. At the time of this writing, it is not known whether FDA will finalize these guidance documents.

Number of Applications

According to FDA regulations, "the designation of one agency component as having primary jurisdiction for the premarket review and regulation of a combination product does not preclude . . . in appropriate cases, the requirement by FDA of separate applications." (21 C.F.R. § 3.4(c).) This regulation suggests that most of the time combination products will be reviewed and regulated under one application.

While a combination product is assigned to an agency center based on the product's primary mode of action, the PMOA does not automatically determine the type of marketing application that will be used.

FDA has also issued a concept paper intended to clarify the number of marketing applications necessary for approval or clearance of a combination product.[21] According to the concept paper, while a combination product is assigned to an agency center based on the product's primary mode of action, the PMOA does not automatically determine the type of marketing application that will be used. Depending on the type of product, approval or clearance could be obtained either through a single marketing application, or through separate marketing applications for the individual constituent parts of the combination product.

For most combination products, a single marketing application should be sufficient to ensure product safety and effectiveness. FDA review of a combination product under a single application addresses the combination product as a whole and its constituent parts.

Although two applications for a combination product have rarely been required, the concept paper notes that there are some circumstances in which two applications could be necessary to ensure safety or effectiveness of the combination product. According to the concept paper, two applications might be required in the following circumstances:

♦ when the constituent parts are separate and complex products;

♦ when one constituent part has uses beyond the combination product;

♦ when a biologics license application for further manufacture is appropriate to ensure the identity, safety, purity and potency of certain biological products when the product as a whole is being regulated under the drug or device provisions;

♦ to effect labeling revisions for a constituent part that is already approved for uses that do not include the proposed combination product indication;

♦ to maintain regulatory consistency.

Additionally FDA, under some circumstances, may accept two applications from the manufacturer when one would suffice to ensure the safety and effectiveness of the product. FDA recognizes that certain regulatory mechanisms (such as new drug exclusivity or orphan drug benefits) are associated only with certain types of marketing applications and that sponsors may wish to derive specific benefits that accrue under a particular application. In addition, when two manufacturers are involved in the development and manufacture of a combination product, each manufacturer may prefer its own application. The concept paper requests stakeholder perspectives on appropriate FDA responses when sponsors desire to have multiple applications.

User Fees

Congress first authorized FDA to collect fees from companies that manufacture drugs and biological products under the Prescription Drug User Fee Act of 1992 (PDUFA), and from companies that manufacture devices under the Medical

Although two applications for a combination product have rarely been required, there are some circumstances in which two applications could be necessary to ensure safety or effectiveness of the combination product.

Device User Fee and Modernization Act of 2002 (MDUFMA). FDA has issued a guidance describing the assessment of user fees for combination products.[22]

In general, combination products reviewed under one application will be subject to the user fees associated with that type of application. For example, a biologic/device or a drug/device combination product for which a device premarket approval (PMA) application is required would be subject to the PMA fee under MDUFMA.

In instances where one application would suffice but the sponsor(s) elect to submit two applications covering the constituent parts of a combination product, FDA believes that the user fees associated with both applications should be payable. Although sponsors may still be eligible for fee waivers or reductions, FDA assesses the two fees because review of two applications when one would suffice places an extra burden on FDA resources.

On the other hand, when FDA requires two applications for a combination product, sponsors are encouraged to consider submitting a request for user fee waiver or reduction. In particular, according to the guidance, FDA will look closely at whether a PDUFA "barrier to innovation" waiver may be applicable to reduce the additional fee burden associated with FDA's requirement for two marketing applications.

Both PDUFA and MDUFMA provide waivers or reductions of fees associated with the submission of applications by small businesses, although the eligibility standards and amount of the fee waiver or reduction differ. Sponsors of combination products requiring two applications should consider applying for the small business waiver or reduction under PDUFA and/or MDUFMA if they meet the qualification criteria.

Other than certain specific situations, such as marketing applications submitted by small businesses, standard MDFUMA fees are required for nearly all device-marketing applications. In contrast, PDUFA provides for waivers or reduction of fees where:

♦ Such waiver is necessary to protect the public health.

♦ The assessment of the fee would present a significant barrier to innovation because of limited resources or other circumstances.

♦ The fees to be paid by such person will exceed the anticipated present and future costs incurred by the Secretary in conducting the process for the review of human drug applications for such person.

A combination product that incorporates cutting-edge, innovative technology that holds promise for advancing patient care may also be eligible for waiver or a reduction of fees as FDA believes that assessment of two marketing application fees could represent a significant barrier to its development. To be eligible for the "innovative combination product" waiver under PDUFA's "barrier to innovation because of . . . other circumstances" provision, FDA considers the following factors:

♦ the combination product as a whole is innovative;

♦ FDA is requiring two fee-bearing marketing applications for the product;

♦ the applications request approval only of the two components of the combination product for use together (i.e., neither application includes an independent use for that constituent part of the combination product); and

♦ the applicant does not qualify for a small business waiver or have limited resources.

FDA considers the following factors in determining whether a combination product is innovative for purposes of the waiver application:

♦ the product addresses an unmet medical need in the treatment, diagnosis or prevention of disease and therefore provides significant, meaningful advantage over alternatives;

♦ factors such as whether one of the two applications includes a new molecular entity, has been designated as a priority drug, is eligible for expedited device review or has been granted fast-track status; and

♦ the existence of treatment alternatives (which would weigh against deciding that a product is innovative).

For innovative combination products requiring two applications, FDA would expect to reduce PDUFA fees as follows in appropriate situations:

♦ For products requiring a MDUFMA application and a PDUFA application, FDA would expect to reduce the PDUFA fee by the amount of the MDUFMA fee. Thus a sponsor would pay the full MDUFMA fee associated with the MDUFMA application, and a PDUFA fee reduced by the amount of the MDUFMA fee. The total amount paid would be the equivalent of one PDUFA fee.

♦ For products requiring two PDUFA applications (for combination products comprising a drug constituent part and a biological product constituent part), FDA would expect to reduce each PDUFA fee by half. In such a case, the total amount paid would be equivalent to one PDUFA fee.

A combination product that incorporates cutting-edge, innovative technology that holds promise for advancing patient care may be eligible for waiver or a reduction of fees as FDA believes that assessment of two marketing application fees could represent a significant barrier to its development.

According to the guidance, the "innovative combination product" waiver provides for a possible waiver only of application fees; the waiver is not applicable to annual product and establishment fees. FDA reviews requests for waivers of product and establishment fees, as well as requests for waivers or reductions of application fees not qualifying for the "innovative combination product" waiver, under criteria applicable to both combination and noncombination products.

FDA's Office of Combination Products

Immediately following formal creation of the combination products category in 1990, the task of designating a lead agency center for review and regulation of combination products was assigned to the Office of the Chief Mediator and Ombudsman in the Office of the Commissioner. Over the years, a number of concerns have been raised about combination products, including concerns about the consistency, predictability and transparency of the assignment process; issues related to the management of the review process when two or more FDA centers had review responsibilities for a combination product; and lack of clarity about the postmarket regulatory controls applicable to combination products.

The Medical Device User Fee and Modernization Act of 2002 gives FDA's Office of Combination Products broad responsibilities covering the regulatory life cycle of combination products.

FDA's OCP was established on December 24, 2002, as required by MDUFMA, to address such concerns. The law gives OCP broad responsibilities covering the regulatory life cycle of combination products. As outlined in MDUFMA, the responsibilities of OCP include:

♦ assigning an FDA center to have primary jurisdiction for review of a combination product;

♦ ensuring timely and effective premarket review of combination products by overseeing reviews involving more than one agency center;

♦ ensuring consistency and appropriateness of postmarket regulation of combination products;

♦ resolving disputes regarding the timeliness of premarket review of combination products;

♦ updating agreements, guidance documents or practices specific to the assignment of combination products; and

♦ submitting annual reports to Congress on the office's activities and impact.

By most accounts, OCP has been successful in meeting these objectives.[23] In particular, the annual report to Congress provides a great deal of detail about the activities of the OCP.

Endnotes

1. The most recent information relative to these ICAs is available at www.fda.gov/oc/combination/intercenter.html.
2. Additional details about RFDs can be found in 21 C.F.R. §§ 3.7 – 3.9, and in a guidance document issued by the Office of Combination Products, "How to Write a Request for Designation (RFD)" *available at* http://www.fda.gov/CombinationProducts/default.htm.
3. Available at www.fda.gov/oc/ombudsman/intercentersop.pdf.
4. 74 Fed. Reg. 50,744 (Oct. 1, 2009).
5. Proposed 21 C.F.R. 4.103(a).
6. Proposed 21 C.F.R. 4.103(b).
7. 74 Fed. Reg. 50,744, 50,749 (Oct. 1, 2009).
8. The need to submit reports under 314.81, 314.98 and 314.540 should also be considered.
9. Proposed 21 C.F.R. 4.105(b).
10. http://www.fda.gov/downloads/CombinationProducts/RequestsforComment/UCM108195.pdf.
11. 74 Fed. Reg. 48,423 (Sept. 23, 2009).
12. For the most up-to-date information, see www.fda.gov/oc/combination/OCLove1dft.html.
13. Proposed 21 C.F.R. 4.4(a).
14. Proposed 21 C.F.R. 4.4(b).
15. Proposed 21 C.F.R. 4.4(b).
16. "Draft Guidance: Current Good Manufacturing Practice for Combination Products," http://www.fda.gov/RegulatoryInformation/Guidances/ucm126198.htm.
17. http://www.fda.gov/RegulatoryInformation/Guidances/ucm126198.htm.
18. http://www.fda.gov/RegulatoryInformation/Guidances/ucm258946.htm.
19. http://www.fda.gov/RegulatoryInformation/Guidances/ucm259059.htm.
20. The OCP has responsibility for classifying products as drugs, devices, biological products, or combination products under 21 C.F.R.
21. See www.fda.gov/oc/combination/singlesepconpaper.html.
22. See www.fda.gov/oc/combination/userfees.html.
23. For further information, please see the OCP website at www.fda.gov/oc/combination.

Chapter 9

The Cosmetics Regulatory Process

Elizabeth H. Anderson and Thomas F. Myers, The Personal Care Products Council, Washington, D.C.

Key Points

- The Federal Food, Drug, and Cosmetic Act (FDCA) defines cosmetics as articles applied to the human body to cleanse, beautify, promote attractiveness and alter the appearance, etc.
- The FDCA prohibits "adulterated" cosmetics, which includes not only contaminated ingredients or packaging, but also use of unapproved color additives or banned ingredients.
- The FDCA prohibits "misbranding," which includes false or misleading labeling by claims about the product, inaccurate labeling such as net content declaration, having a misleading container size or amount and other violations.
- Cosmetics are not subject to premarket approval by the Food and Drug Administration (FDA), but the product and ingredients must be tested for safety. If the manufacturer cannot substantiate safety, a warning is required.
- Color additives are the only cosmetic ingredients that must be pre-approved ("listed") by FDA. Color additives are subject to the Delaney Clause, which bars using any color shown to cause cancer "in man or animal."
- Coal tar hair dyes are subject to special regulatory requirements.
- FDA monitors compliance through random inspections of cosmetic facilities.
- The cosmetic industry has several self-regulatory programs to work with FDA in assuring ingredient and product safety.
- The "intended use" doctrine states that cosmetic or drug status is determined by claims about the intended use of the product.
- Cosmetic product labeling is governed by the FDCA and the Fair Packaging and Labeling Act (FPLA). Cosmetic labels must state the statement of identity, net contents, ingredients, any required warning and other information.

WHAT THE LAW AND REGULATIONS SAY

Under the Federal Food, Drug, and Cosmetic Act (FDCA), the standards governing cosmetics differ significantly from those governing food, medical devices, drugs or tobacco products largely because of the relatively few risks associated with their use. Section 201(i) of the FDCA defines a "cosmetic" as:

1) an article intended to be rubbed, poured, sprinkled, or sprayed on, introduced into or otherwise applied to the human body or any part thereof for cleansing, beautifying, promoting attractiveness, or altering the appearance; and

2) an article intended for use as a component of any such article; except that such term shall not include soap.[1]

The FDCA prohibits the introduction into interstate commerce of any cosmetic that is "adulterated." Section 601 of the FDCA is very specific about what makes a cosmetic adulterated:

♦ if it bears or contains any poisonous or deleterious substance that may render it injurious to users under conditions of use prescribed in the labeling thereof, or under such conditions of use as are customary or usual;

♦ if it consists in whole or in part of any filthy, putrid or decomposed substance;

♦ if it has been prepared, packed or held under unsanitary conditions whereby it may have become contaminated with filth, or whereby it may have been rendered injurious to health;

♦ if its container is composed, in whole or part, of any poisonous or deleterious substance that may render the contents injurious to health; or

♦ if it is not a hair dye and it is, or it bears or contains, a color additive that is unsafe within the meaning of section 721(a).

FDA regulations provide that the presence of specified ingredients in the formulation render a cosmetic product adulterated.

Further, Food and Drug Administration (FDA) regulations provide that the presence of specified ingredients in the formulation render a cosmetic product adulterated. Examples of such ingredients include the antibacterial agent bithionol; mercury as an eye makeup preservative (except at strict limits); vinyl chloride included as a propellant in cosmetic aerosol products such as hairsprays; certain halogenated salicylanilides; zirconium in aerosol cosmetics; and specified cattle materials.

The FDCA also prohibits the sale of any cosmetic that is "misbranded." Under section 602 of the FDCA, a cosmetic is misbranded:

♦ if its labeling is false or misleading in any particular;

♦ if in package form unless it bears a label containing 1) the name and place of business of the manufacturer, packer or distributor; and 2) an accurate statement of the quantity of the contents in terms of weight, measure or numerical count: *Provided* That under the clause (2) of this paragraph reasonable variations shall be permitted, and exemptions as to small packages shall be established, by regulations prescribed by the Secretary.

♦ if any word, statement or other information required by the act to appear on the label or labeling is not prominently placed thereon with such conspicuousness (as compared to other words, statements, designs or devices in the labeling) and in such terms as to render it likely to be read and understood by the ordinary individual under customary conditions of purchase and use;

♦ if its containers are so made, formed or filled as to be misleading;

♦ if it is a color additive and its packaging and labeling are not in conformity with regulations issued under section 721 (this requirement does not apply to color additives marketed and intended for use only in or on hair dyes as defined in section 601(a)); or

♦ if its packaging or labeling is in violation of an applicable regulation issued pursuant to sections 3 or 4 of the Poison Prevention Packaging Act of 1970.

FDA regulations require that a manufacturer substantiate the safety of a finished cosmetic product and each of its ingredients. Because cosmetics are not required to be approved by FDA before marketing, FDA promulgated a labeling requirement for products where safety has not been substantiated before marketing. A product is considered misbranded if safety substantiation is not available, unless the following warning appears on the principal display panel: "*Warning* — The safety of this product has not been determined." (21 C.F.R. § 740.10(a)). FDA has made it clear that the safety substantiation requirement does not require that new testing be conducted in every case "where reasonable scientific opinion would regard the available data as adequate."

FDA regulations require that a manufacturer substantiate the safety of a finished cosmetic product and each of its ingredients. A product is considered misbranded if safety substantiation is not available, unless the following warning appears on the principal display panel: "Warning:—The safety of this product has not been determined."

COLOR ADDITIVES

The only cosmetic ingredients that must be pre-approved ("listed") by FDA to be used in a finished cosmetic product are color additives. Specified color additives also must be "certified," meaning each production batch must be approved by FDA.

FDA approves color additives specifically for use in a cosmetic, a drug, a device, or a food, or any combination of those products (e.g., D&C Green No. 5, FD&C Yellow No. 5). FDA also may put limitations on the cosmetic use of a color additive, such as where it may be used ("externally except eye area"), and may establish maximum allowable use levels (e.g., "Lip products (5% maximum)"). Use of an unapproved color in a cosmetic makes the product adulterated under the FDCA and subject to FDA seizure and other legal action. The requirement for pre-approval of color additives stems from the Color Additive Amendments of 1960.

These amendments prohibited use of a color additive unless a regulation permits the additive's use. The FDCA defines "color additive" as a "dye, pigment, or other substance [which] when added or applied to a food, drug or cosmetic, or to the human body or any part thereof, is capable (alone or through reaction with any other substance) of imparting color thereto . . . ."

The Delaney Clause imposes an absolute ban on any color "if, after tests which are appropriate for the evaluation of the safety of additives for such use, or after other relevant exposure of man or animal to such additive, it is found by the Secretary to induce cancer in man or animal."

The Color Additive Amendments also contain the "Delaney Clause," a provision named for its author, Congressman James Delaney (D-NY). This provision was intended to guard against cancer-causing ingredients and imposes an absolute ban on any color "if, after tests which are appropriate for the evaluation of the safety of additives for such use, or after other relevant exposure of man or animal to such additive, it is found by the Secretary to induce cancer in man or animal." (21 U.S.C. § 379e(b)(5)(B)). A court case concluded that Congress intended for FDA to deny approval of a color additive if it posed a risk, even a *de minimis* or trivial one, of inducing cancer in animals.

There is an exemption for coal tar-derived colors used in hair dyes. Section 601(a) of the FDCA states that a cosmetic is adulterated if it contains any deleterious substance that could harm the user when the product is used according to the labeling or customary use. This prohibition, however, does not apply to coal tar hair dyes if their labels bear the following statement:

> Caution This product contains ingredients, which may cause skin irritation on certain individuals, and a preliminary test according to accompanying directions should first be made. This product must not be used for dyeing the eyelashes or eyebrows; to do so may cause blindness.

In addition, the label should have adequate directions for preliminary testing such as patch test directions. If the label lacks the caution statement and patch test directions, FDA can take regulatory action. This exemption applies only to coal tar hair dyes and not to other coloring ingredients in hair dyes, or eyebrow and eyelash dye products.

FDA Enforcement Authority

The primary means for FDA to monitor the cosmetics industry is through random inspections of cosmetic facilities. FDA also checks imports at ports of entry and investigates consumer or competitor complaints about specific products. If FDA perceives a violation through information obtained during a facility inspection or an import inspection, it may send the company a "Warning Letter." The Warning Letter typically issues from FDA's district office, which oversees the facility or the place of import in the United States, but may occasionally come from the Center for Food Safety and Applied Nutrition at FDA headquarters.

FDA monitors the cosmetics industry through random inspection of cosmetic facilities, checks imports at ports of entry, and investigates complaints about specific products.

Inspection of cosmetic manufacturing establishments is one of FDA's primary means of cosmetic product oversight. FDA is not required to notify the facility in advance of inspection. The inspection usually is routine, but could be triggered by FDA's belief that a company's product(s) is being manufactured or marketed in violation of the law.

A Cosmetic Facility

FDA's authority during a cosmetic inspection is less comprehensive than for biologics or drugs, for example. A manufacturer is not legally required to provide FDA inspectors with master formula records, batch production records, products or ingredient analyses, safety testing data of any type and consumer complaint files or adverse experience data. Moreover, companies are not required to produce any financial data or other business records; however, if requested by an FDA inspector, companies are required to provide access to and copies of shipping records showing movement of cosmetics in interstate commerce.

The right of FDA inspectors to take photographs during an inspection is an area of continuing controversy among FDA, industry and the courts. In its *Inspections Operations Manual* (IOM), FDA takes the position that it has the authority to take photographs. The FDA IOM instructs inspectors not to request permission to take photographs but to take the camera into the firm and use it as necessary, as with any other inspectional equipment. Industry has taken the posture that it may deny inspectors the ability to take photographs, particularly when necessary to protect trade secrets regarding manufacturing equipment, formulations or processes.

In the course of cosmetic inspections, FDA inspectors frequently take samples of finished and unfinished materials and labeling. FDA frequently samples products to ensure that the cosmetic is using FD&C approved color additives.

FDA and Inspection of Cosmetic-Drugs Under FDAMA

The Food and Drug Administration Modernization Act of 1997 (FDAMA) changed FDA's inspection authority for drugs but *not for cosmetics*. Section 704 of the FDCA, however, as amended by FDAMA, allows facilities that manufacture products regulated both as cosmetics and drugs (such as skincare products containing sunscreen and antiperspirant/deodorant products) to be inspected to the same extent as prescription drug manufacturers. Under such circumstances, FDA has authority to request all records that could determine whether a cosmetic drug is adulterated or misbranded. The following records may be available under the OTC Drug Inspection Authority:

♦ Quantitative formulas, specifications for all active and inactive ingredients and all testing done to assure that ingredients met those specifications; all records relating to the manufacture of the drug, including batch records, validation records, stability testing data and all other types of records either required to be maintained under drug good manufacturing practice (GMP) regulations or that bear upon compliance with drug GMP regulations;

♦ all testing of ingredients and finished products relating to microbial content; all release specifications for finished product, all testing of finished products to determine compliance with release specifications, and all records relating to investigations of batches that in any way failed release specifications; all testing and other safety substantiation for inactive and active ingredients, and for finished products;

♦ all data relating to product packaging; all consumer complaints of any type relating to safety and effectiveness;

♦ all testing to support product claims of any type;

♦ all consumer complaints about product performance or other product attributes;

♦ formula records, manufacturing batch records, adverse reaction reports, and evidence of GMP compliance for cosmetic drugs.

This expanded inspection authority does not apply to cosmetic products that are not also drugs.

Labeling Deficiencies

FDA has issued Warning Letters to cosmetic companies in recent years alleging labeling deficiencies. These deficiencies fall into several basic categories. The largest category by far consists of labeling claims that, under the "intended use" doctrine, convert a cosmetic into a drug. FDA scrutinizes not only the claims and representations made about a product but also whether the mandatory labeling information is present (such as listing ingredients). Any resulting Warning Letter for labeling violations would allege that the product is "misbranded" under section 602 of the FDCA.

As with other FDA-regulated products, if FDA believes a cosmetic is adulterated or misbranded under the statute, the agency may opt to take several actions including seizure, refuse entry into the United States if it is a foreign product, go to federal district court to obtain a restraining order to prevent further shipments or initiate a criminal enforcement action. Examples of products seized as "adulterated" in the past include various eyebrow and eyelash dye products, and nail preparations containing methyl methacrylate.

In early 2011, FDA sent out a number of Warning Letters, possibly signaling an aggressive new approach by FDA to potential FDCA violations. In one recent example, FDA sent a Warning Letter to a manufacturer alleging that certain eyelash and eyebrow growth products were unapproved new drugs, in violation of sections 505(a) and 301(d) of the FDCA (21 U.S.C. §§ 355(a) and 331(d)), and misbranded drugs in violation of section 502 (21 U.S.C. § 352) of the FDCA. The Warning Letter also stated that, even if the eyelash and eyebrow growth products were not new drugs, they would still be adulterated and misbranded as cosmetics.

While it is too early to tell whether the increased number of Warning Letters represents a new phase of aggressive enforcement by FDA over the cosmetics industry, companies should be vigilant to avoid making "drug" claims about their cosmetic products.

Industry Self-Regulation

♦ **Cosmetic Ingredient Review**

In 1975, the cosmetic industry requested FDA establish a program to publicly substantiate the safety of cosmetic ingredients. Due to other resource commitments, FDA declined and suggested that the cosmetic industry establish its own program to evaluate cosmetic ingredient safety.

In response, the cosmetic industry developed and adopted a number of self-regulatory programs, with the Cosmetic Ingredient Review (CIR) becoming the cornerstone of the cosmetic industry's self-regulatory effort. This industry-funded body was established in 1976 by the Cosmetic, Toiletry, and Fragrance Association (CTFA) (now known as the Personal Care Products Council). The CIR

CIR was designed to help companies substantiate the safety of ingredients used in cosmetics and the final formulation without duplicating safety testing already done by others.

was designed to help companies substantiate the safety of ingredients used in cosmetics and the final formulation without duplicating safety testing already done by others.

As part of the ingredient safety assessment, the available scientific data on an ingredient is reviewed by a seven-member expert panel. Panel conclusions are publicly announced by CIR without private review or comment by the industry. The panel's scientists are nominated by consumer, scientific and clinical groups; government agencies; and industry. They are chosen from several scientific disciplines, such as dermatology and toxicology. The expert panel also has three nonvoting members representing a consumer group, industry and FDA.

The scientific review of each ingredient goes through several stages. The technical staff of CIR prepares a Scientific Literature Review summarizing known data gleaned from databases and industry studies. The Literature Review is made available for public comment with a request for any data, published or unpublished, that the review has not included. After 60 days, the comments received (including data submissions), are incorporated into the document for panel consideration. After a series of public meetings, the panel issues a Tentative Report.

The Tentative Report may reach any one of four tentative conclusions: safe as used, safe with certain qualifications, unsafe or insufficient data available to CIR to support safety. The Tentative Report is available for comment for 60 days. All comments are analyzed and a response developed. The CIR Final Report incorporates any changes based on public comment and is published in the peer-reviewed *Journal of the American College of Toxicology*. Final Reports on ingredient safety also appear in the *CIR Compendium*, published annually.

A primary goal of the Cosmetic Ingredient Review is to minimize duplication of ingredient safety testing.

A primary goal of CIR is to minimize duplication of ingredient safety testing; consequently CIR has deferred or excluded review of ingredients that are subject to other safety assessments. Examples include over-the-counter (OTC) drug active ingredients, fragrance ingredients (reviewed by the Research Institute for Fragrance Materials), ingredients in new drug applications, color additives reviewed by FDA under section 721 of the FDCA, and those subject to any final FDA regulation. The chemicals taken from CTFA's *International Cosmetic Ingredient Dictionary and Handbook* are ranked for priority according to potential biological activity, frequency of use, concentration of use, route of exposure (e.g., inhalation), area of exposure (e.g., the eyes) and any special group of users (e.g., infants).

♦ **Voluntary Registration and Reporting Programs**

Since the early1970s, the industry has participated in two voluntary programs administered by FDA that were established at the request of the cosmetics industry. One involves the voluntary registration of cosmetic facilities, including foreign facilities. Upon registering, a facility is assigned a registration number by FDA. The other program involves the voluntary registration of cosmetic product ingredient statements. FDA has developed an electronic database with industry input into which such information should be reported (and updated where necessary). The facility and formula information is entered into an FDA database that enables the agency to notify and investigate the appropriate entities in the event of an adverse incident involving a cosmetic product. The programs apply only to products sold at retail and exclude products sold for professional use.

♦ **Voluntary Industry Code of Practice**

In 2006, the Personal Care Products Council adopted a Consumer Commitment Code designed to reinforce industry practices already in place and to initiate additional actions intended to enhance cosmetic safety. The code incorporates existing practices such as the current reporting of manufacturing establishments and includes a new Safety Information Summary Program that provides FDA with relevant cosmetic product information and makes ingredient safety readily available upon request. The code went into effect on January 1, 2007, and is open to all members of the industry.

THE COSMETIC/DRUG DISTINCTION

In determining whether a product is a "cosmetic" or a "drug," it is important to examine the definitions for "cosmetic" and "drug" in the FDCA. As noted earlier, the term "cosmetic" means:

1) articles *intended* to be rubbed, poured, sprinkled, or sprayed on, introduced into or otherwise applied to the human body or any part thereof for cleansing, beautifying, promoting attractiveness, or altering the appearance, and

2) articles *intended* for use as a component of any such articles; except that such term shall not include soap. (emphasis added) (FDCA § 201(i); 21 U.S.C. § 321(i))

"Drug" means:

> articles *intended* for use in the diagnosis, cure, mitigation, treatment, or prevention of disease in man or other animal; and . . . articles (other than food) intended to affect the structure or any function of the body of man or other animals . . . ." (emphasis added) (FDCA § 201 (g)(1); 21 U.S.C. § 321(g)(1))

The key words in the cosmetic and drug definitions are "intended for use" and "intended to be."

The key words in the cosmetic and drug definitions are "intended for use" and "intended to be." The manufacturer's intent to market a "cosmetic" versus a "drug" is determined from the claims or representations made for the product in advertising or labeling. If the claims refer only to beautifying or promoting attractiveness, the product is a "cosmetic" and must be labeled in compliance with FDA regulations governing cosmetics.

The marketer can intend that products be both cosmetics *and* drugs if they contain both cosmetic and drug claims, such as an antiperspirant (drug)/deodorant (cosmetic) product. Cosmetic-drugs must comply with both the cosmetic and drug regulatory requirements for that product.

As cosmetic products become more sophisticated and offer greater benefits to consumers, FDA periodically has questioned whether the claims for some products cause them to become drugs, a category subject to more stringent regulation. The cosmetic/drug issue has been an occasional battleground between FDA and manufacturers. Three cases from the late 1960s remain the preeminent judicial guidance on when a "cosmetic" becomes a "drug." In one, the court held that claims associated with a product called "Sudden Change" (represented as giving a "face lift without surgery"; promising to "lift out puffs") were sufficient to make the product a "drug." In another case, the court held that claims for the product "Line Away" (such as "made in a pharmaceutical laboratory"; packaged under "biologically aseptic conditions"; creates a "tingling sensation" while "at work"; "tightening" facial skin; and "discouraging new wrinkles from forming") made this product a "drug." In a third case, involving a product called "Magic Secret," the court held that claims that the product was "pure protein" and that it caused an "astringent sensation" were *not* sufficient to cause consumers to conclude that the product would do anything more than alter their appearance, which was a cosmetic benefit.

These cases still provide guidance when determining whether a claim is a cosmetic or drug claim. Additionally, FDA issued regulatory letters to dozens of cosmetic manufacturers in 1987 challenging manufacturers' claims for skincare products as "drug" claims. While most of those matters were resolved privately,

FDA's response to a citizen petition arising out of one of those matters made it clear that the agency relies heavily on the decisions in *Sudden Change*, *Line Away* and *Magic Secret* when determining the "drug" or "cosmetic" status of a product. At the same time, FDA has declined to establish guidelines for cosmetic claims, stating that each claim or group of claims had to be viewed in context to determine whether it is a cosmetic or drug claim.

The agency has suggested, however, that the mere presence of an ingredient at levels that will "affect the structure or function of the body" may be sufficient to make the product a drug, regardless of the claims in advertising and labeling, a position that represents a divergence from its past practice. An example involves the presence of hormone ingredients in a topical preparation. FDA concluded that the mere inclusion of hormones, even in the absence of drug claims, made the products "cosmetic-drugs" subject to a monograph.[2] Later, however, it withdrew the proposed regulation that advanced this position with respect to a proposed ban on any hormone or estrogen ingredient in cosmetics.

LABELING REQUIREMENTS

FDA regulates cosmetics labeling under two federal laws—the FDCA and the Fair Packaging and Labeling Act (FPLA). FDA has issued labeling regulations under these laws in 21 C.F.R. Part 701. Labeling cannot be false or misleading, and label information must be prominent and conspicuous.

The FDCA requires that label information be placed on the immediate container of a cosmetic. If the retail package consists of an immediate container enclosed in an outside container (e.g., cologne bottle in a box), both the inner and outer containers must display the mandatory information. There are exceptions; for example, a product contained in a see-through transparent package or shrink-wrap would not have to be labeled if it surrounds a container otherwise properly labeled. If the information is easily legible through the outer container then the individual products inside the container can bear all the required labeling information.

Labeling:
The FDCA requires that label information be placed on the immediate container of a cosmetic. The FPLA only requires label information to appear on the outer container of a cosmetic.

A final concept affecting label placement under the FDCA is the distinction between "label" and "labeling." The FDCA defines "labeling" more broadly than "label":

> The term "labeling" means all labels and other written, printed, or graphic matter

(1) upon any article or any of its containers or wrappers, or

(2) accompanying such article.

Thus, the term "labeling" includes pamphlets, leaflets and other written material accompanying a cosmetic product, but not necessarily affixed to it.

Unlike the FDCA, the FPLA requires label information to appear only on the outer container of a cosmetic. Thus, if a retail package consists of an immediate container enclosed in an outside container (e.g., a jar of face cream in a box), the FPLA does not apply to the immediate (or inner) container label. It is sufficient to place the required information on the outer container only. If a cosmetic product is displayed for sale in its immediate container only (e.g., a deodorant in an aerosol can), however, the immediate container must comply with the FPLA.

These interpretations are consistent with the purpose of the FPLA, which is to provide purchasers with certain information at the point of retail sale so that they can compare ingredients in products and make value comparisons prior to purchase.

Only products intended to be displayed to retail purchasers are subject to the requirements of the FPLA. (A "consumer commodity is defined to include any food, drug, device or cosmetic sold at retail for use by the consumer in the home.") Therefore, shipping containers used to transport bulk quantities of a product need not comply with the FPLA. Similarly, cosmetics intended as free gifts or samples and not for sale, and products sold to salons for application to customers by professional cosmetologists, are not subject to these requirements.

The FPLA requires that specified information appear on the principal display panel (PDP). The PDP is defined as "that part of a label that is most likely to be displayed, presented, shown, or examined under normal and customary conditions of display for retail sale."

The label of a cosmetic must state the identity or name of the product. It is also permissible to include a common or usual name, an appropriately descriptive name, a fanciful name understood by the public or an appropriate illustration or vignette representing the intended cosmetic use. The statement of identity is required only to appear on the outer container. Most marketers, however, put it on both the inner and outer containers.

The purpose of the quantity statement is to allow consumers to make a value judgment about the products they are purchasing. The net quantity of contents tells the consumer how much of the cosmetic is in the container. The quantity statement must appear on both the inner and outer container under both the FDCA and the FPLA.

Under the 1992 amendments to the FPLA, the net quantity of contents in cosmetic labeling must be expressed in *both* the English and metric systems. The quantity declaration for "English" units is stated in avoirdupois pounds and ounces for weight or mass; and fluid ounces for fluid measure statements. The metric declaration of net contents must be stated in kilograms, grams or milligrams for solid, semisolid or viscous cosmetics, and liters or milliliters for liquid cosmetics.

Both the FDCA and FPLA require that the name and the place of business of the manufacturer, distributor or packer must appear on both the inner and outer cosmetic containers. The place of business must include the city, state and zip code. A street address is required only if it does not appear in a local telephone directory.

For products intended for retail sale, FDA requires ingredient labeling under the authority of the FPLA. Consequently, the ingredient declaration must appear on the outer container only. Cosmetic ingredients must be listed "in descending order of predominance" on "an appropriate information panel." For products not sold at retail and for free samples, ingredient statements are not mandatory.

For products not sold at retail and for free samples, ingredient statements are not mandatory.

There are two exceptions to the listing of all ingredient names. First, flavors and fragrances may be listed generically rather than by "name." As a result, the term "fragrance" or "flavor" may appear in the ingredient declaration in descending order of predominance. The second exception is when FDA has granted a manufacturer's petition for a trade secret exemption. If trade secret status is granted for the ingredient, the words "and other ingredient(s)" must appear at the end of the ingredient statement.

Ingredients must be listed by established name. FDA regulations identify a priority list of sources to determine the appropriate name for an individual cosmetic ingredient. Unless FDA has established a name by regulation, CTFA's *International Cosmetic Ingredient Dictionary and Handbook* is the primary source for an "adopted name." If an ingredient does not appear in the CTFA dictionary, alternative sources are listed in order of priority such as the U.S. Pharmacopoeia and others. Only if the ingredient does not appear in the recognized sources can the manufacturer choose to use a name generally recognized by consumers or, in the absence of that, a chemical or other technical name.

Warning statements on cosmetic labels are required under the authority of the FDCA "whenever necessary or appropriate to prevent a health hazard that may

Warning statements on cosmetic labels are required under the authority of the FDCA "whenever necessary or appropriate to prevent a health hazard that may be associated with the products."

be associated with the products." Warnings must appear on both the inner and outer containers, be prominent and conspicuous, and meet minimum type-size requirements. FDA regulations require warnings with specific language for cosmetics in self-pressurized containers (e.g., aerosols), feminine deodorant sprays, certain bubble baths and cosmetics that have not been substantiated adequately for safety. In addition, the FDCA requires a specific warning for coal tar hair dyes. FDA does not require specific flammability warnings for cosmetics, including aerosol or alcohol-based cosmetics, but many companies include such warnings voluntarily.

CONCLUSION

In sum, safety substantiation by cosmetic manufacturers of their ingredients and products and proper labeling remain the cornerstones of the regulatory scheme governing cosmetic products. These longstanding requirements, together with the voluntary industry reporting and registration programs, have rendered cosmetics the safest of all of the FDA-regulated product categories.

Endnotes

1. "Soaps" are not considered a cosmetic and, therefore, are exempt from all provisions of the FDCA. Soap products must, however, comply with the Federal Trade Commission's regulations issued under the Fair Packaging and Labeling Act (FPLA).
2. See 21 C.F.R. § 310.530 ("use of the word 'hormone' in the . . . ingredient statement is an implied drug claim").

Chapter 10

The Regulation of Foods and Food Additives

Daniel A. Kracov & Joshua M. Glasser, Arnold & Porter LLP, Washington, D.C.

Key Points

- Although the Food and Drug Administration (FDA) has primary authority over the regulation of most foods, the U.S. Department of Agriculture (USDA) regulates meat and poultry products, the Alcohol and Tobacco Tax and Trade Bureau regulates alcoholic beverages, and the Federal Trade Commission (FTC) has jurisdiction over food advertising.

- Adulteration is the central concept underlying FDA's regulation of the safety of food products. There are a number of statutory bases for a food to be adulterated, including the presence of poisonous or deleterious substances, insanitary practices in food processing or the use of unapproved food additives. The Food Safety Modernization Act, passed by Congress in December 2010, greatly expands FDA's authority over the safety and security of foods.

- Under the Food Quality Protection Act, a special regulatory framework applies to pesticides in food. The Environmental Protection Agency registers pesticide products and sets tolerances for the presence of pesticide residues in food products. These tolerances are then enforced by FDA.

- FDA applies its general regulatory authorities to products of food biotechnology. FDA asks developers of bioengineered foods to notify the agency of their intent to market a food from a bioengineered plant at least 120 days before marketing. Special labeling is required only when the use of biotechnology so alters a food's characteristics or composition that the information about the change is material and should be revealed to consumers.

- The concept of economic adulteration permits FDA to prevent consumer fraud. For example, the agency may ensure that damage to a food product is not concealed from the consumer, or that a food is not made to appear to be of greater value than it is, such as by the addition of unnecessary water to add weight.

- Misbranding is the statutory term for violations relating to the labels and labeling of food products, as opposed to actual composition and safety. The central standard in the Federal Food, Drug, and Cosmetic Act (FDCA) permits FDA to deem a product misbranded if its "labeling is false or misleading in any particular."

> ### Key Points, continued
>
> - FDA and USDA administer extensive regulations governing the labeling of food products, including the basic components of the label, mandatory nutrition labeling, and complex rules governing the nutrient content and health claims.
> - Dietary supplement products are regulated under the FDCA as amended by the Dietary Supplement Health and Education Act of 1994. Those amendments provide a separate definition for dietary supplements, as well as special rules governing the safety and labeling claims for such products.

INTRODUCTION

Foods represent the most basic of the Food and Drug Administration's (FDA's) public health responsibilities: ensuring that what is eaten on a daily basis is both wholesome and fairly represented to the public. This responsibility requires an understanding and careful balance of many factors, including chemical and biological safety risks, evolving information on nutrition and health, food marketing concerns and, more recently, food supply security—all within an increasingly complex statutory framework.

AGENCY JURISDICTION

An article is a "food" if it is used for human or animal food or drink, if it is a chewing gum or if it is used as a component of any food.

The Federal Food, Drug, and Cosmetic Act (FDCA) gives FDA jurisdiction to regulate most foods in interstate commerce. Under FDCA § 201(f), an article is a "food" if it is used for human or animal food or drink, if it is a chewing gum or if it is used as a component of any food. This is not necessarily a commonsense definition. For FDCA purposes, a food can include items that are not intended for consumption, such as seeds and rejected eggs. Raw, unprocessed food substances may or may not be foods. For example, although inedible green coffee beans were found to be a food within the statutory definition, *U.S. v. Green Coffee Beans*, 188 F.2d. 555 (2d Cir. 1951), the agency does not consider raw sugar to be a food because it contains certain impurities that can be removed only by the refining process. The agency also construes the term "food" to encompass substances migrating to food from food-contact articles such as containers and cutting surfaces.

In addition to the FDCA, there are other important food regulatory authorities at the federal level. The production and labeling of most meat and poultry products are regulated by the U.S. Department of Agriculture (USDA) under the Federal Meat Inspection Act and the Poultry Products Inspection Act. USDA exercises exclusive jurisdiction over the inspection of meat products until they leave a plant, but FDA and USDA have concurrent jurisdiction over misbranding and adulteration of meat products after inspection. Under an agreement between the agencies, FDA generally informs the USDA's Food Safety and Inspection Service (FSIS) when an apparent violation is encountered involving meat or poultry products, and usually will not initiate action against such products. USDA also regulates the production of eggs and egg products under the Egg Products Inspection Act. FDA has jurisdiction over game meats, such as deer and rabbit, as well as seafood products. FDA also regulates food products containing a relatively small proportion of meat—such as a dressing with bacon bits—interpreted as less than or equal to 3 percent meat.

FDA shares regulatory authority over alcoholic beverages with the Department of Treasury's Alcohol and Tobacco Tax and Trade Bureau (TTB). Although FDA may regulate ingredients used in alcoholic beverages, TTB generally is responsible for regulation of alcoholic beverage labeling, and has primary responsibility for recalls of alcoholic beverages.

The Federal Trade Commission (FTC) has primary responsibility over food advertising. The FTC frequently takes enforcement action in specific cases of deceptive food advertising, and routinely consults with FDA when such advertising raises issues of safety or nutrition.

FOOD SAFETY

The regulation of food safety under the FDCA centers around the legal definition of "adulteration." The term is defined by a range of acts specified in the FDCA that cause a food to be adulterated and, therefore, in violation of the statute.

Food safety, under the Federal Food, Drug, and Cosmetic Act, focuses on the legal definition of adulteration.

Poisonous or Deleterious Substances

The first adulteration provision under the FDCA is found in section 402(a)(1), which incorporates two standards under which a food may be deemed adulterated:

> If it bears or contains any poisonous or deleterious substance which may render it injurious to health; but in case the substance is not an added substance such food shall not be considered

adulterated under this clause if the quantity of such substance in such food does not ordinarily render it injurious to health.

This is the primary provision used by FDA to regulate the safety and purity of whole foods as opposed to the discrete ingredients added to foods.

The first part of the standard is much broader than it appears, for the term "added" can include the artificial introduction of a substance into a food by indirect means. Thus, in *United States v. Anderson Seafoods*, 622 F.2d 157 (5th Cir. 1980), the court determined that if a portion of the total amount of mercury found in swordfish resulted from industrial pollution, then all of the mercury in that product could be treated as an added substance subject to the "may render injurious" standard. Although the mere presence of an added poisonous or deleterious substance in a food does not satisfy the "may render" standard for proof of adulteration, FDA typically is given broad deference in its construction of the standard. *United States v. Lexington Mill & Elevator Co.*, 232 U.S. 399 (1914). Any "added" substance potentially could be subject to this standard, including microbial contamination.

The second part of section 402(a)(1), the "ordinarily render injurious to health" standard, is rather narrow in comparison. This provision applies to substances that are inherent in whole foods, such as toxins naturally present in fruits and vegetables. Such substances must be shown to be harmful before they result in food adulteration. As a result of the broad construction of the "may render" standard for "added" substances, this basis for adulteration is rarely invoked.

Unavoidable Contaminants

Under FDCA § 402(a)(2), a food is adulterated if it contains any avoidable added poisonous or deleterious substance that is "unsafe" within the meaning of FDCA § 406. An "unsafe" substance under section 406 is "any poisonous or deleterious substance added to any food, except where such substance is required in the production thereof or cannot be avoided by good manufacturing practice."

A food bearing or containing a poisonous substance is not considered adulterated if the quantity of the added substance is within an established tolerance level.

Section 406 permits FDA to establish tolerances for such "unavoidable contaminants." Such tolerances may limit the quantity of the substance in or on the food to the extent necessary for the protection of public health. If a tolerance is in effect, a food bearing or containing the poisonous substance is not considered adulterated if the quantity of the added substance is within the tolerance level. This tolerance provision permits the agency to take into account not just the presence of the poisonous or deleterious substance in the particular food in question, but the "other ways in which the consumer may be affected by the same or other deleterious substances."

Section 406 tolerances may be developed only through formal rulemaking, a time-consuming and resource-intensive process. As a result, the agency generally has adopted "action levels," which technically are nonbinding enforcement guidelines that identify levels of contamination above which FDA may bring an enforcement action. Both tolerances and action levels are based on the unavoidability of the added substances, and they do not establish a permissible level of contamination where the added substance is avoidable.

The agency also may establish "regulatory limits" through informal rulemaking, representing the level at which the agency would consider a food adulterated under section 402(a)(1). Such a regulatory limit may be appropriate where a substance cannot be avoided by current good manufacturing practices or there is insufficient information to establish a tolerance.

Filthy, Putrid or Decomposed Substances

A food may be considered adulterated under FDCA § 402(a)(3) "if it consists in whole or in part of any filthy, putrid, or decomposed substance." As a practical matter, virtually any natural food product will have some level of filth—whether mold or insect parts— that has little or no impact on its safety or quality. The courts have tried to give these statutory terms their "usual and ordinary meaning," but with little consistency. Thus, in *United States v. Tomato Paste*, 22 F. Supp. 515 (E.D. Pa 1938), the presence of worm fragments rendered tomato paste filthy, while in *United States v. Canned Tomato Paste*, 236 F.2d 208 (7th Cir. 1956), a paste that had a small number of insect fragments, fly eggs and rodent hairs was not adulterated.

Although FDA does not have authority to set tolerances for decomposition or filth in food, the agency has developed "defect action level" guidances.

The agency does not have authority to set tolerances for decomposition or filth. Nevertheless, to bring some consistency to this area, and based on its enforcement discretion under the FDCA, the agency has developed "defect action levels." Defect action levels are guidances that indicate levels of filth, mold and other contaminants that are not likely, taken alone, to result in an enforcement action, and can be achieved by applying cGMPs. It is important to note that a defect action level cannot be met by blending highly contaminated food with uncontaminated food, for FDA considers the finished product to be adulterated regardless of the net level of contamination.

Containers

Under FDCA § 402(a)(6), a food may also be adulterated if it is in a container that "is composed, in whole or in part, of any poisonous or deleterious substance which may render the contents injurious to health." This provision has rarely been invoked by FDA, which typically relies upon its other adulteration and indirect additive authorities.

Unfit for Food

A food may also be adulterated "if it is otherwise unfit for food" under FDCA § 402(a)(3). This provision describes a condition in which a food is in an inedible state, and does not necessarily depend upon the presence of filth or decomposition. The "unfit for food" adulteration provision is based on the perception of the average consumer. For example, in *United States v. Herring Roe*, 87 F. Supp. 826 (D. Me. 1949), the court found that in order for a fish roe to be unfit for food, it must be so tough and rubbery that the average consumer under ordinary conditions could not eat it. This statutory basis for adulteration is rarely used, largely because other adulteration provisions are less subjective and easier to prove.

Sanitation/Good Manufacturing Practices

One of the most important adulteration provisions is FDCA § 402(a)(4), which deems a food to be adulterated "if it has been prepared, packed, or held under insanitary conditions whereby it may have been contaminated with filth, or whereby it may have been rendered injurious to health." This provision does not require FDA to prove that a food product has been contaminated or rendered injurious to health. Rather, the mere presence of the insanitary conditions and the possibility that those insanitary conditions may have resulted in the adulteration is enough to bring the charge. Typically, the agency looks for evidence of rodent droppings, insect parts, unscreened windows or other insanitary practices where food is processed to bring a case under this provision.

FDA determined that one of the most effective ways to ensure sanitary conditions in food production was through controls on food manufacturing operations.

In 1967, FDA determined that one of the most effective ways to implement section 402, and thereby maintain a safe and sanitary food supply, would be through controls on manufacturing operations. That year, the agency published the first set of proposed food cGMP rules. After many revisions and several unsuccessful lawsuits challenging FDA's authority to promulgate the regulations, the cGMP rules have become an established condition of doing business in the food industry, and are found at 21 C.F.R. Part 110. Dietary supplements cGMP rules are found at 21 C.F.R. Part 111. As discussed in the next section, however, Congress recently passed a law that requires additional controls over food processing facilities—specifically, a requirement that food processors and other regulated facilities adopt a hazard-management and preventive controls plan. This requirement, when implemented, is expected to enhance, and not replace, the current food cGMPs.

The food cGMP regulations impose affirmative obligations on manufacturers to control the risk of chemical, microbiological and other contamination of food. The underlying theory is that effective sanitation requires careful planning and vigilance in every phase of production, and that manufacturers must carry the primary responsibility for maintaining a safe and sanitary food supply. FDA recognizes, however, that manufacturing operations can vary widely and still be safe and sanitary, and the umbrella cGMP rules allow for some flexibility in methods of compliance. The rules are couched in terms of a mandatory result, together with permissive guidelines for methods of compliance.

The umbrella cGMPs touch every aspect of food production, including raw material inspection, employee training, plant design, equipment specifications and cleaning, quality control testing and distribution of finished products. While recordkeeping requirements exist in other areas, FDA did not impose specific recordkeeping requirements in general food cGMPs. Daily production logs, manuals and other written records, however, provide proof to an FDA inspector that a company's compliance programs exist. The inspector then can verify that the written program reflects that company's actual, current practices.

"Umbrella" cGMP regulations address:
- *personnel practices*
- *plant design*
- *equipment specifications and cleaning*
- *production controls*
- *quality control testing*
- *product distribution*

The cGMP regulations require plant managers to take precautions to ensure that food products are not contaminated by employees. Four requirements are prescribed with regard to personnel practices: 1) any person with evidence of disease must be excluded from any operation where he or she may come into contact, either directly or indirectly, with food; 2) employees must maintain proper hygiene, including hand washing; 3) employees must be trained in sanitary practices; and 4) employees must be adequately supervised.

Under the food cGMPs, manufacturing facilities must be designed, constructed and maintained to protect against contamination of food. The regulations provide a partial checklist of points for plant managers to follow, setting forth requirements for the maintenance of grounds, construction of physical plants, adequate lighting and ventilation, pest control, use and storage of chemicals, water supply and plumbing, and waste removal.

The cGMP regulations also govern construction, cleaning and maintenance of equipment. Manufacturers must use only tools that can be properly cleaned and maintained, and must protect them from corrosion or contamination. Conveyor belts and other manufacturing systems, freezer and cold storage systems, compressed air cleaning systems, and instruments for measuring and regulating manufacturing conditions (e.q., temperature, acidity and water flow) must be well maintained.

Other cGMP provisions address production controls, including inspection of raw materials, in-process monitoring, and storage and transport. Manufacturers must adhere to adequate sanitation principles in all production procedures, including receiving, inspecting, transporting, preparing, manufacturing, packaging and storing foods. To meet the prescribed quality control standards, manufacturers must periodically test their products for chemical, microbial or extraneous material contamination, and either reject or reprocess any products that they determine to be contaminated. Similarly, raw materials must be inspected to ensure that they are clean and suitable for processing, and must be stored properly to avoid contamination and minimize deterioration. Moreover, manufacturers must monitor such factors as time, temperature, humidity and pH to ensure that mechanical breakdowns, delays and temperature fluctuations do not contribute to the decomposition or contamination of food. The rule also details specific techniques for preventing and minimizing microbiological contamination of batters and sauces, refrigerated foods, and acidified and dehydrated foods. Finished food must be transported and stored under conditions that will protect it against contamination and deterioration of the food and the container.

Recent Food Safety Measures

In recent years, FDA's existing framework for ensuring the safety of the nation's food supply has been called into question. A primary criticism of FDA's regulatory approach has been that it is primarily reactive and not sufficiently focused on the prevention of food-safety-related incidents. Several recent nationwide food recalls have only increased the public's attention on food safety issues and related FDA oversight.

Recent developments intended to improve the nation's food safety system include the creation of a Food Safety Working Group in March 2009 to advise the President on food safety issues.

Recent developments intended to improve the nation's food safety system include the creation of a Food Safety Working Group in March 2009 to advise the President on food safety issues. The Food Safety Working Group, which is chaired by the Secretary of Health and Human Services and the Secretary of Agriculture and includes participation from a range of federal agencies, has identified three core principles to guide the development of a modern, coordinated food safety system: 1) prioritizing prevention; 2) strengthening surveillance and enforcement; and 3) improving response and recovery.

In addition, FDA has made notable changes to its organizational structure for food regulation. In August 2009, Commissioner Margaret Hamburg created a new Office of Foods, which has oversight and authority over the two FDA centers that regulate food—the Center for Food Safety and Applied Nutrition and the Center for Veterinary Medicine. Among other things, the Office of Foods is tasked with responsibility for implementing recommendations of the Food Safety Working Group and new food safety authorities created by legislation.

A critical new law in this area is the Food Safety Modernization Act (FSMA) (Pub. L. No. 111-353), passed by Congress in December 2010, which is intended to reposition FDA as a proactive regulator focused on food safety prevention rather than remediation. FSMA greatly expands FDA's authority over the safety and security of regulated foods, and several aspects, such as enhanced registration requirements, an increased focus on inspections and food imports, and new mandatory recall authority, are discussed later in this chapter.

A key feature of FSMA is that food processing, shipping and other regulated facilities will be required to adopt a comprehensive hazard-management and preventive controls plan. See FDCA § 418. It is expected that this new requirement will not replace the "umbrella" food cGMPs discussed above; rather, FDA has stated that the food cGMPs likely will serve as the foundation for a preventive controls plan. FDA must issue implementing regulations within 18 months following enactment, establishing science-based minimum standards for preventive control plans.

A key feature of FSMA is that food processing, shipping and other regulated facilities will be required to adopt a comprehensive hazard-management and preventive controls plan.

The requirement for a preventive controls plan parallels Hazard Analysis and Critical Control Points (HACCP), which FDA currently requires of seafood processors (21 C.F.R. Part 123) and juice processors (21 C.F.R. Part 120), and which USDA's FSIS requires of meat and poultry processors. HACCP is a preventive strategy that is based on the development by the food producer of a plan that anticipates food safety hazards and identifies the specific critical points in the production process where a failure would likely result in a hazard being created or allowed to persist. Such critical control points are monitored systematically, and corrective action is taken when control over those points is lost.

Under FSMA, regulated facilities will be required to evaluate and prepare written analyses of known or reasonably foreseeable food safety hazards that could affect food manufactured, processed, packed, transported or held there (such as chemical hazards, pesticides, parasites and allergens, whether unintentionally or intentionally introduced) at least every three years or sooner, as appropriate. Facilities must then implement preventive controls to minimize or eliminate such hazards, monitor the effectiveness of such controls, take corrective action as needed and maintain documentation of the controls.

FSMA also imposes new requirements applicable to on-farm production. Historically, farms have been exempt from many FDA requirements (including facility registration and cGMP requirements) or otherwise subject to less intensive regulation. Instead, FDA mainly has relied on voluntary guidance documents to encourage good agricultural practices, such as the "Guide to Minimize Microbial Food Safety Hazards for Fresh Fruits and Vegetables" (October 1998) and the "Guide to Minimize Microbial Food Safety Hazards for Fresh Fruits and Vegetables" (February 2008).

This will change with FSMA, which requires FDA to issue regulations establishing science-based minimum standards for safe production and harvesting of fruits and vegetables (raw agricultural commodities) for which FDA determines such standards minimize the risk of serious adverse health consequences or death. See FDCA § 419. These produce safety standards must address growing, harvesting, sorting, storage, soil, hygiene, packaging, temperature controls, animal encroachment and water, and they would be enforced in the form of audit-based verification systems or inspections. Congress directs FDA to provide sufficient flexibility in its regulations to account for different scales and types of production, to coordinate with USDA and state agricultural agencies where appropriate, and to allow state or foreign governments to request a variance based on local growing conditions.

The Sanitary Food Transportation Act of 2005 gives broad authority to FDA to regulate the transportation of human and animal food products.

FDA is also taking steps to increase its regulatory oversight of food transportation activities by recently beginning the rulemaking process to implement the Sanitary Food Transportation Act of 2005 (SFTA), which shifted authority for the regulation of sanitary food transportation practice from the Department of Transportation to FDA. The SFTA gives broad authority to FDA to regulate the transportation of human and animal food products. See FDCA § 416. In April 2010, FDA issued an Advance Notice of Proposed Rulemaking requesting input from interested parties, 75 Fed. Reg. 22,713 (Apr. 30, 2010), and the agency issued a final guidance document, intended to apply while FDA develops regulations, that provides broadly applicable recommendations for controls to prevent of safety problems during food transport. "Guidance for Industry: Sanitary Transportation of Food" (Apr. 2010).

FOOD ADDITIVES

In the decades after the passage of the FDCA, the number of chemicals added to foods for functional purposes increased enormously, yet there was no mechanism for FDA premarket clearance based on a safety evaluation. To take action against an ingredient in the product, FDA could rely only on its evaluation of the product, already on the market, under its general adulteration standards for added substances. In 1954, congressional hearings before Congressman James Delaney (D-NY) focused on the safety of additives in the food supply, revealing that only 200 of the 1,400 chemicals known to be added to foods had been shown to be safe. This uncertainty suited neither FDA nor food companies, for there were no clear additive safety standards.

The consensus regarding the need for food additive regulation led to the passage of the Food Additives Amendment of 1958, in which Congress provided the agency with a framework for food additive regulation that mandated proof of safety prior to marketing. Under section 201(s) of the FDCA, the term "food additive"

The need for food additive regulation led to the passage of the Food Additives Amendment of 1958.

... means any substance the intended use of which results or may reasonably be expected to result, directly or indirectly, in its becoming a component or otherwise affecting the characteristics of any food (including any substance intended for use in producing, manufacturing, packing, processing, preparing, treating, packaging, transporting, or holding food; and including any source of radiation intended for any such use), if such substance is not generally recognized, among experts qualified by scientific training and experience to evaluate its safety, as having been adequately shown through scientific procedures (or, in a case of a substance used in food prior to January 1, 1958, through either scientific procedures or experience based on common use in food) to be safe under the conditions of its intended use.

This definition is quite broad, encompassing any substance that may reasonably be expected to directly or indirectly affect or become a part of a food. Such substances are presumed to be unsafe—and therefore adulterate a food—unless the additive has been the subject of a premarket approval by FDA.

There are significant exceptions to the food additive definition, most notably generally recognized as safe (GRAS) substances, pesticide chemical residues and dietary supplements. One additional, but relatively small, category of excepted uses of such substances are those that are subject to a "prior sanction." Prior sanctioned substances are those that were the subject of FDA or USDA safety opinions prior to 1958 and are "grandfathered" as part of the 1958 legislation. Such substances are still subject to the general adulteration standards and, in large part, have been eclipsed by the premarket approval and GRAS framework over time.

Any food that bears or contains any food additive that is unsafe within the meaning of FDCA § 409 (i.e., unapproved or used outside the parameters of an approval) is considered adulterated. Section 409 provides a formal petition process for the approval of food additives by the agency, which applies a science-based safety standard to review of food additive petitions. At a minimum, a food additive petition must include the name of the substance; its chemical identity and composition; the proposed conditions of its use; proposed labeling; physical effects data; technical effects (and levels) data; information on the manufacturing process, facilities and controls; methods of detecting and determining the quantity of the additive in the finished food; the results of safety investigations; and an environmental assessment. 21 C.F.R. Part 171.

Any food that bears or contains any food additive that is unsafe is considered adulterated.

The term "safe" for purposes of food additive approval means that there is a reasonable certainty in the minds of competent scientists that a substance is not harmful under its intended conditions of use. The agency considers the probable levels of consumption of the additive, and the cumulative effect of the additive and related substances in the diet in arriving at its determination. The toxicological testing requirements for food additives are the subject of a guidance document, known as the "Red Book." FDA will calculate the exposure to the additive based upon an estimated daily intake that is within an acceptable daily intake (ADI) derived from data on toxicological effects and the determination of a "no observable adverse effect level" to which an appropriate safety factor (typically 1/100) is applied. If FDA finds an additive to be safe, it issues a regulation specifying the conditions under which the additive may safely be used. See 21 C.F.R. Parts 172-178.

Although food additives are subject to a general safety standard, there is a significant exception. Section 409(c)(3)(a) of the FDCA contains what is commonly referred to as the "Delaney Clause," which provides that "[n]o additive shall be deemed to be safe if it is found to induce cancer when ingested by man or animal, or if it is found after tests which are appropriate for the evaluation of the safety of food additives, to induce cancer in man or animal."

Due to the absolute nature of the Delaney Clause, FDA has made significant efforts to avoid it by adopting policies of construction and interpretation. One statutory exception is the DES Proviso, which provides that the Delaney Clause does not prohibit the use of a compound if "no residue" of that compound administered to food-producing animals can be "found" in meat, milk or eggs by an approved analytical method. FDCA § 409(c)(3)(A). The agency also may make a scientific determination that a substance does not technically or directly "induce" cancer.

Under the Delaney Clause, no additive is deemed safe if it induces cancer when ingested by humans or animals, or is found after appropriate testing to induce cancer in humans or animals.

FDA interprets the term "additive" in the Delaney Clause to apply only to the additive as a whole and not its unavoidable, nonfunctional constituents. 47 Fed. Reg. 14,464 (Apr. 2, 1982). If carcinogenic constituents of an additive are detected, FDA conducts a risk assessment under the general safety standard for food additives. FDA first applied this "constituents policy" in its 1982 approval of the color additive D&C Green No. 6, which contains the carcinogenic contaminant n-toluene. The policy has been applied on numerous occasions since then, and has been challenged and upheld in court. Other efforts by FDA to avoid the Delaney Clause, however, such as the argument that it is too rigid and should be subject to a *de minimis* exception, have been rejected by the courts.

The Delaney Clause has consistently been criticized as outdated in light of current methods of assessing the risk of carcinogenicity. Nevertheless, although its applicability to pesticide residues was eliminated as part of the 1996 enactment of the Food Quality Protection Act (FQPA), the Delaney Clause remains in force in the food and color additive areas.

INDIRECT ADDITIVES/FOOD CONTACT SUBSTANCES

The food additive definition is extremely broad, extending beyond substances intentionally added for a functional purpose to include even nonedible items— such as adhesives, packaging and food contact surface materials—that "may reasonably be expected" to become a component or otherwise affect the characteristics of a food. These migrating indirect additives generally are subject to the same food additive and GRAS frameworks applicable to direct food additives.

FDA has established a process for determining when the likelihood or extent of migration to food of a substance used in a food contact article is so trivial as not to require food additive approval. This "threshold of regulation" exempts from food additive regulation those noncarcinogenic substances in food contact articles that result in a dietary concentration of the substance of 0.5 parts per billion (ppb) or less. Also exempted are regulated direct food additives when used in food contact articles at levels that result in a dietary exposure of 1 percent or less of the ADI for the additive as determined by the agency. 21 C.F.R. § 170.39. Such substances may not have a technical effect in the food, and must be the subject of a submission to FDA documenting eligibility for the terms of the threshold regulation, including an environmental assessment.

The 1997 Food and Drug Administration Modernization Act (FDAMA) created a new statutory classification to encompass indirect additives that does not require premarket approval. This class, referred to as "food contact substances," is defined as "any substance intended for use as a component of materials used in manufacturing, packing, packaging, transporting, or holding food if such use is not intended to have any technical effect in such food." Food contact substances typically consist of materials used in food packaging such as plastics, paper and adhesives, but can also include substances used in the manufacture of food.

FDAMA created a new statutory classification to encompass indirect additives that does not require premarket approval.

Section 409(a)(3) provides that a food additive will not be deemed unsafe if it is a food contact substance and the substance and its use have been approved in a food additive regulation like any other substance, or it is the subject of a notification that has become effective. Under section 409(h), manufacturers may file a notification with FDA regarding a food contact substance 120 days before its introduction into interstate commerce. The notification must identify the food contact substance and its intended use, as well as a description of the manufacturer's determination that the intended use is safe, including the information that forms the basis for that conclusion. All such information will be kept confidential by FDA for 120 days after receipt, at which time it will be available to the public, except for trade secrets or confidential commercial information.

In May 2002, FDA issued regulations governing this provision and a guidance document for industry on submitting food contact notifications (FCNs). 67 Fed. Reg. 35,724 (May 21, 2002) (codified at 21 C.F.R. Part 170, Subpart D); "Guidance for Industry: Preparation of Premarket Notifications" (May 2002). A manufacturer of a food contact substance is required to submit a FCN for new uses of food contact substances that are food additives. A notification is effective for the manufacturer that submitted the FCN—or anyone who can demonstrate that the food contact substance being marketed has been manufactured or supplied by the manufacturer—where the food contact substance is being used under the conditions that are the subject of the FCN. A notification becomes effective 120 days after receipt by FDA, at which time the food contact substance may be distributed in interstate commerce, unless FDA makes a determination that, based on the data and information before it, the use of the substance has not been shown to be safe and a food additive petition should be filed requesting that a regulation be issued.

GENERALLY RECOGNIZED AS SAFE SUBSTANCES

The general recognition of safety is not based on the opinion of the lay population—it is based on the views of experts qualified to evaluate the safety of foods.

In framing the food additive definition, Congress recognized that there was a range of food substances that should not be the subject of the petition requirement. Such substances are not merely safe, they are generally recognized as safe (GRAS). The burden of demonstrating such GRAS status falls upon the proponent of the GRAS use of an ingredient. Moreover, the general recognition of safety is not based on the opinion of the lay population—it is based on the views of experts qualified to evaluate the safety of foods. Although unanimity is not required, GRAS status must at least be a consensus opinion of qualified experts.

The passage of the Food Additives Amendment in 1958 presented a significant transitional problem. Many ingredients, including common foods such as vinegar, vegetable oil, salts, spices, flavors and gums, did not have a clear regulatory status. FDA clarified the status of those substances by publishing the "GRAS List" to which it subsequently added other categories of substances that the agency deemed to be subject to the GRAS exemption.

In 1970, as a result of banning cyclamate, an artificial sweetener previously considered to be GRAS, due to concern about carcinogenicity, the agency initiated a comprehensive study of substances presumed to be GRAS. In this "GRAS review," FDA evaluated a broad range of substances using contemporary scientific standards. It then issued regulations that affirmed the GRAS status of those ingredients where appropriate. FDA also promulgated a series of regulations setting forth the criteria for determining GRAS status, the category of food substances it considers eligible for GRAS status or GRAS affirmation, and the procedures for petitioning the agency to affirm the GRAS status of other substances. 21 C.F.R. §§ 170.30, 170.35.

Until recent years, a manufacturer could seek, through filing a GRAS affirmation petition, a formal determination from FDA that a given substance is GRAS and therefore appropriate for use in food without being approved as a food additive. See 21 C.F.R. Parts 184 and 186. This nonstatutory process generally proved interminable, and was a low priority for FDA's overburdened staff. FDA has long acknowledged, however, that GRAS status may be determined without formal FDA action (referred to as "self-determination of GRAS status"). Thus, the GRAS exception from the food additive definition creates a separate regulatory category for substances which, although intentionally added to food, are not subject to mandatory premarket review.

In making a GRAS self-determination, a company assumes a risk that FDA may not agree with its determination, and may seek withdrawal of the product through informal means or by resort to its seizure or injunctive authorities. This risk usually is minimized by having the product and its planned use(s) reviewed by independent scientific consultants and legal counsel.

The process of determining whether a substance is GRAS involves evaluation of the same safety issues as are raised with respect to food additives, as well as a determination that the terms for GRAS status have been satisfied. For substances used in food prior to January 1, 1958, GRAS status may be established through "experience based upon common use in food." For all other substances, GRAS status must be established through safety data collected by "scientific procedures"; i.e., studies. Experience data may serve, however, to confirm the findings of these studies, including information on use of the substance abroad.

The process of determining whether a substance is GRAS involves evaluation of the same safety issues as are raised with respect to food additives, as well as a determination that the terms for GRAS status have been satisfied.

"Scientific procedures" are defined by FDA to include "those human, animal, analytical, and other scientific studies, whether published or unpublished, appropriate to establish the safety of a substance." 21 C.F.R. § 170.3(h). The GRAS eligibility regulation further states that general recognition of safety through scientific procedures shall "require the same quantity and quality of evidence" as is required to obtain food additive approval and "shall ordinarily be based upon published studies which may be corroborated by unpublished studies and other data and information." 21 C.F.R. § 170.3(b).

It must be remembered, however, that the safety of a substance is evaluated within the context of its intended use. Thus, while a general purpose food ingredient may be deemed or affirmed as GRAS without any limitation on how it may be used, most GRAS determinations are made in the context of one or more specified uses. GRAS substances must comply with applicable specifications, must perform an appropriate function in the food, and must be present in the food at a level no higher than necessary to accomplish that purpose.

For a substance to be GRAS, the pertinent scientific community must be familiar with the substance and believe it to be safe. In other words, GRAS status depends on showing not only that a substance is safe, but also that it is widely viewed as such by experts in the field. FDA evaluates the qualifications of experts whose opinions are offered in support of GRAS status. The GRAS eligibility regulation repeats the statutory requirement that "general recognition of safety may be based only on the views of experts qualified by scientific training and experience to evaluate the safety of substances directly or indirectly added to food." 21 C.F.R. § 170.30(a). Thus, FDA effectively applies the concept of peer review to the scientist as well as to the science, and it relies on documented credentials as one factor in assessing the validity of studies and the integrity of other scientific evidence offered in support of GRAS status.

In April 1997, FDA proposed a new rule which, while not finalized, has largely replaced the prior GRAS petition framework. 62 Fed. Reg. 18,938 (Apr. 17, 1997). Under this notification procedure, a company has the option of notifying FDA of its GRAS self-determination. Rather than publishing a regulation with a finding of safety as it purports to do under the current system, FDA provides a response to the notice within 90 days, in which it either acknowledges the notifier's GRAS determination or identifies problems that it found in the submission.

The stated goal of the GRAS notification proposal is to increase the agency's awareness of private GRAS determinations, make the process by which FDA recognizes GRAS status more efficient, and reduce resources devoted to the nonstatutory GRAS affirmation process. While FDA's response to such notices does not carry the same weight as a GRAS determination by FDA, it enables manufacturers who make their own GRAS determinations to ascertain the agency's position on the matter quickly. Concurrently, the proposal has intensified commercial pressure on those marketing GRAS ingredients to submit notifications to FDA in lieu of private determinations of GRAS status.

Color Additives

Color additives are subject to a separate statutory approval framework under the FDCA. Section 201(t) defines a "color additive" as any material that, when added to food, is capable of imparting color, except those that the Secretary of Health and Human Services, by regulation, determines are used "solely for a purpose or purposes other than coloring." FDCA § 721 provides a framework for the listing and certification of color additives that is similar to the premarket approval process for food additives. Color additives must be shown with reasonable certainty to pose no risk to human health, to accomplish an intended effect and to not deceive consumers. Section 721 includes a Delaney Clause, although there is no exclusion for GRAS or prior sanctioned colors. Color additives may be subject to precise specifications, and FDA may subject color additives to batch certification to ensure that specifications are met.

Color additives must be shown with reasonable certainty to pose no risk to human health, to accomplish an intended effect and to not deceive consumers.

Pesticide Residues

Historically, pesticide residues have presented a major regulatory problem. Until the passage of the FQPA in 1996, the Environmental Protection Agency (EPA) was responsible for setting tolerances for pesticide residue on raw agricultural commodities under FDCA § 408, which incorporated a risk-benefit standard. Although a "flow-through" proviso permitted levels of pesticides in processed foods up to the level permitted in raw agricultural commodities under section 408, EPA also set tolerances for pesticide residues that concentrated in processed foods under section 409 (the food additive provision). Those residues, however, were subject to the food additive Delaney Clause. As a result of the judicial rejection of EPA's policy of applying a *de minimis* standard to these residues, *Les v. Reilly*, 968 F.2d 985 (9th Cir. 1993), a number of tolerances for important pesticides were subject to revocation.

The FQPA redefined "pesticide chemical" in FDCA § 201(q)(1) to include any substance that is a pesticide within the meaning of the Federal Insecticide, Fungicide, and Rodenticide Act (FIFRA), including active and inert ingredients in the pesticide. A "pesticide residue" is defined in section 201(q)(2) as a residue in or on a raw agricultural commodity or processed food of a pesticide chemical, or any other added substance that is primarily the result of the metabolism or other degradation of a pesticide chemical. These changes took all pesticide residues out of the food additive definition and the food additive Delaney Clause. Instead, all tolerances for pesticide residues in a food must be established on the basis of a single safety standard that requires a reasonable certainty that no harm will result from an aggregate exposure to the pesticide chemical residue,

All tolerances for pesticide residues in a food must be established on the basis of a single safety standard that requires a reasonable certainty that no harm will result from an aggregate exposure to the pesticide chemical residue, including all anticipated dietary exposures and all other exposures for which there is reasonable information.

including all anticipated dietary exposures and all other exposures for which there is reasonable information. FDCA § 408(b)(2)(A). Specific consideration also is given to exposures to infants and children, and the consideration of pesticide benefits in tolerance-setting is significantly limited to certain "eligible" residues.

The enforcement of tolerances for pesticide residues is now the responsibility of FDA, although EPA may initiate action if a violation of FIFRA is involved. The FQPA provides for civil penalties as an alternative method of taking enforcement action against the sale of a food that is adulterated by unsafe pesticide residues, although such penalties cannot be applied to farmers.

Food Biotechnology

The use of organisms to make food products, such as yogurt, represents one of the oldest of food technologies. A major scientific development in food science in the last decade, however, has been the application of new biotechnologies, including recombinant DNA techniques and cell fusion, to go beyond traditional methods and make direct genetic modifications to food sources. Food biotechnology, as well as animal cloning for agricultural purposes, has led to a great deal of discussion and inquiries to FDA, and there is a clear consensus that some form of FDA oversight is warranted.

Genetic Modification of Plant Varieties

In 1992, FDA issued a policy under which new plant varieties developed by application of genetic modification are regulated within the existing framework of the FDCA and FDA regulations. 57 Fed. Reg. 22,984 (May 29, 1992).

In general, FDA regulates foods derived from new plant varieties under the general adulteration standard, which requires the producer of a new food to evaluate its safety and ensure that FDA standards are met. FDA applies the food additive and GRAS frameworks to plant products derived from single gene transfers. Food additive petitions under section 409 of the FDCA are required in cases where the food differs in structure, function or composition so significantly as to raise safety questions that warrant formal premarket review to ensure public health protection.

Food additive petitions are required in cases where the food differs in structure, function or composition so significantly as to raise safety questions that warrant formal premarket review to ensure public health protection.

FDA has developed a decision tree approach that provides for the assessment of the new plant variety, the characteristics of the host and donor species, the nature of the genetic change, the identity and function of newly introduced substances, and unexpected or unintended effects that accompany genetic changes. Particular concerns that need to be assessed as part of this analysis include:

♦ toxins known to be characteristic of the host and donor species;

♦ the potential that food allergens would be transferred from one food source to another;

♦ the concentration and bioavailability of important nutrients for which a food crop is ordinarily consumed;

♦ the safety and nutritional value of newly introduced proteins; and

♦ the identity, composition, and nutritional value of modified carbohydrates, or fats and oils.

Originally, FDA administered a "voluntary" consultation system in which companies would decide whether to consult with the agency pursuant to the decision tree. FDA has since changed this approach, and companies must consult with the agency regarding their intent to market, at least 120 days before marketing. Based upon this notification FDA may determine that additional testing or labeling is necessary, or that a food additive filing may be required.

In 2006, FDA issued a guidance requesting that developers of new proteins in new plant varieties for food submit a safety evaluation to FDA prior to the stage of development where the protein could inadvertently enter the food supply. "Guidance for Industry: Recommendations for the Early Food Safety Evaluation of New Non-Pesticidal Proteins Produced by New Plant Varieties Intended for Food Use" (June, 2006). A safety evaluation need not be submitted where a protein has been previously reviewed as part of a consultation and no safety concerns were identified, or where a protein has been part of a previous safety evaluation with no identified safety concerns and is later introduced into another plant species.

A safety evaluation should focus on whether the new protein is an allergen or a toxin, and should contain information including a description of its purpose or intended technical effect and a list of any identities and sources of the introduced genetic material. The guidance document states that FDA should respond within 120 days with the results of the safety evaluation.

With respect to labeling of genetically modified foods, FDA applies its general analysis under section 403(i) of the FDCA, which requires that the producer of a food product describe the product by its common or usual name, or, in the absence thereof, an appropriately descriptive term. In addition, under section 201(n), all food product labeling must reveal facts that are material in light of representations made or suggested by labeling or with respect to consequences that may result from use. In other words, a new name or a label disclosure is only required when the application of biotechnology alters a food's characteristics or composition to such a degree as to create an important consumer expectation or safety concern. A good example would be the need to disclose the introduction of a peanut protein into a tomato that could result in an allergic reaction in a susceptible population.

Cloning in Animal Species Used for Food

FDA issued a draft assessment in 2006, and final risk assessment in January 2008, finding that meat and milk from clones of adult cattle, pigs and goats, and their offspring, are as safe to eat as food from conventionally bred animals.

Animal cloning has raised public concerns, and FDA has conducted an in-depth analysis of animal cloning in the last several years. In 2001, FDA requested that livestock producers and researchers not introduce food from animal clones or their offspring into the food supply until FDA evaluated potential risks to consumers. FDA issued a draft assessment in 2006, and final risk assessment in January 2008, finding that meat and milk from clones of adult cattle, pigs and goats, and their offspring, are as safe to eat as food from conventionally bred animals.

The result of the FDA risk assessment on animal cloning is that FDA has lifted the voluntary moratorium on products from the offspring of cloned animals. USDA has requested, however, that the voluntary moratorium remain in place temporarily for products from cloned animals (but not the offspring of cloned animals) to provide for an orderly introduction of such products into the food supply. Neither FDA nor USDA is requiring labeling or any other additional measures for food from cattle, swine and goat clones, or their offspring.

Genetically Engineered Animals Used for Food

In 2009, FDA issued a final guidance document addressing the regulation of genetically engineered (GE) animals. "Guidance for Industry: Regulation of Genetically Engineered Animals Containing Heritable Recombinant DNA Constructs" (Jan. 2009). The guidance applies to GE animals currently being developed for a number of uses based on the purpose of the genetic modification, one of which is to enhance food production or food quality traits (e.g., faster growing fish). In the guidance, FDA explains that a GE animal is an animal that contains an added recombinant DNA segment that is intended to alter the structure or function of the animal; as such, FDA has taken the position that GE animals contain a new animal drug and will be regulated under the new animal drug provisions of the FDCA.

The guidance explains that GE animals generally will require premarket approval by FDA prior to introduction to the marketplace, and developers must demonstrate that the proposed genetic modifications are safe for the health of the GE animal and, if they are food animals, for food consumption. In addition, FDA will be required to conduct an environmental assessment under the National Environmental Policy Act to assess environmental risk issues. The guidance also explains that food from GE animals approved for marketing will be subject to the same labeling requirements as other foods, and thus typically will not be required to be identified as coming from a GE animal. The one exception is where the food from a GE animal is materially different from that of its non-engineered counterpart, e.g., if the food from the GE animal has a different nutritional profile. USDA's FSIS, which regulates the labeling of most meat, poultry and egg products, has yet to take a position on the labeling of food from GE animals.

Genetically engineered animals generally will require premarket approval by FDA prior to introduction to the marketplace.

While FDA has yet to approve any GE animals for use in food, the agency is currently reviewing a premarket application for a GE Atlantic salmon developed by AquaBounty Technologies, Inc. In September 2010, FDA held two public meetings to consider this premarket application. As represented at these meetings, FDA concluded that the GE salmon were as safe to eat as food from conventional Atlantic salmon, and the GE salmon were not expected to have a significant environmental impact when raised as proposed in the application. There has been considerable opposition to this GE salmon application, and more generally to FDA's review process for GE animals as set forth in the guidance, from food safety advocates, environmental and consumer groups and commercial fisheries.

ECONOMIC ADULTERATION

The adulteration provisions of the FDCA are not limited to safety issues. "Economic" adulteration under section 402(b) can occur if:

♦ any valuable constituent has been in whole or in part omitted or abstracted; or

♦ any substance has been substituted wholly or in part; or

♦ damage or inferiority has been concealed in any manner; or

♦ any substance has been added or mixed or packed so as to increase its bulk or weight, or reduce its quality or strength, or make it appear better or greater value than it is.

Early cases in this area dealt with coloring foods in a manner that caused economic adulteration, such as the addition of pumpkin to bakery products to give the appearance of egg content. The addition of water to foods was—and remains—a popular approach to adulteration. Perhaps the most prominent example in recent years was the highly publicized case, *United States v. Beech-Nut Nutrition Corp.*, 871 F.2d 1181 (2d Cir. 1989), involving the economic adulteration of apple juice for babies with a substandard ingredient. In general, the economic adulteration provisions of the FDCA are used only when the agency cannot otherwise regulate nonsafety-related aspects of food formulation.

MISBRANDING

Misbranding is the statutory term for FDCA violations relating to the labels and the labeling of a food product, as opposed to its actual composition and safety.

Misbranding is the statutory term for FDCA violations relating to the labels and the labeling of a food product, as opposed to its actual composition and safety. The primary basis upon which a food may be deemed misbranded is if "its labeling is false or misleading in any particular" under section 403(a). A failure to reveal material facts under section 201(n) also can constitute misleading labeling under this standard. Other general bases on which FDA may make a misbranding finding include, in part:

- If a food is "offered for sale under the name of another food." FDCA § 403(b).

- "If it is an imitation of another food, unless its label bears, in type of uniform size and prominence, the word 'imitation' and, immediately thereafter, the name of the food imitated." FDCA § 403(c). See Standards of Identity, below.

- If "its container is so made, formed, or filled as to be misleading." FDCA § 403(d).

FOOD LABELING

The FDCA and the Fair Packaging and Labeling Act govern the regulation of food labeling.

Two primary statutory authorities—the FDCA and the Fair Packaging and Labeling Act (FPLA)—govern the regulation of food labeling. "Label" is defined under section 201(k) as a display of written, printed or graphic matter on the immediate container of any article. Under section 201(m), "labeling" is further defined to include all labels and other written, printed or graphic matter on any article or any of its containers or wrappers, or accompanying such article. Thus, the FDCA requires information appearing on the label to also be included on the outside container or wrapper of the retail package. In contrast, requirements imposed solely by the FPLA apply only to the outside container or wrapper of the retail package.

Basic Components of the Food Label

Over the years, FDA has developed regulations pertaining to virtually every aspect of food labeling, including specifications for both mandatory and voluntary information. Moreover, a number of exemptions have been recognized to accommodate special packaging and marketing issues, specific product categories and other attributes that may trigger specific labeling requirements. For example, products with nutrient content claims trigger specific referral and disclosure requirements. Drinks that purport to contain fruit juice must bear information regarding the percentage of juice in the product.

The regulations governing the basic components of the food label are found at 21 C.F.R. Part 101, Subpart A. These regulations specify two areas on a product's label where required information may appear: the Principal Display Panel (PDP) and the Information Panel (IP). The PDP is the part of the label most likely to be displayed, presented, shown or examined by the consumer under normal and customary conditions of display for retail sale. The IP is that part of the label that is immediately contiguous and to the right of the PDP as observed by the consumer facing the PDP. If there is more than one PDP, each must contain the mandatory label information. Only one IP is necessary, however, even if there is more than one PDP. An IP is not required if all required information is placed on a PDP.

In general, FDA regulations require certain information to appear on the PDP; other information may appear on either the PDP or the IP. For example, the identity and net content statements must appear on the PDP. If an IP is used, all necessary information except the identity and content statements may appear on the IP. If the IP is too small, the information may be split between the IP and the PDP. No one item, however, may be split between the two panels (e.g., part of an ingredient statement on each panel).

Each aspect of the food label is subject to specific requirements. The following are the basic parameters for major components of the food label:

♦ An **"identity statement"** is the standardized, common, or usual name of the food, or a fanciful name generally used by the public for the particular product. The identity statement should identify accurately or describe either the basic nature of the product or its characterizing properties or ingredients, using simple and direct terms. When the nature of the product is obvious, a fanciful name commonly used by the public may serve as the identity statement

♦ The **"net quantity of contents statement"** is the declaration in terms of weight, measure or numerical count of the unit container and, where carton labeling is necessary, the numerical count and the total package content. The statement should be placed in the bottom 30 percent of the PDP as a distinct item, in the most appropriate units of both the English and metric systems.

Major components of the food label:

- *identity statement*
- *net quantity of contents statement*
- *responsibility statement*
- *ingredient statement*
- *flavor labeling*
- *nutrition labeling*
- *nutrient content claims country of origin*

♦ The **"responsibility statement"** states the name, street address and zip code of the person who manufactures, packs or distributes the product. In the case of a corporation, the actual corporate name must appear. If the particular business address appears in a current city directory or telephone directory, the street address may be omitted but the zip code must be included. If the principal place of business differs from the place of manufacture, packing or distribution, only the principal place of business is required.

♦ The **"ingredient statement"** is a list of the product's ingredients by their common or usual name, in descending order of predominance by weight in the product (except for ingredients under 2 percent of the weight of the product).

♦ **"Flavor labeling"** details the type of flavoring of the product, including natural, artificial or a combination of the two. These labeling requirements are quite complex and require careful review. In general, if the label, labeling or advertisement of a food makes any direct or indirect representation regarding a primary recognizable flavor, or if the manufacturer or distributor wishes to designate the flavor of the food by any means other than through the statement of ingredients, that flavor becomes the "characterizing flavor" for the purposes of flavor labeling. The choice of which terms and wording to employ in the flavor labeling depend on the type and number of flavors a product contains. If a food contains any artificial flavor that simulates, resembles or reinforces the characterizing flavor, the name of the food must be accompanied by the name of the characterizing flavor, together with the word(s) "artificial" or "artificially flavored." Such labeling must precede or follow the characterizing flavor in the product, and is expressed as "artificial," "artificially flavored," etc., depending on the type of flavor(s) used, (e.g., artificially orange flavored). The disclosure should appear on the PDP with the identity statement.

♦ **Nutrition labeling** must appear by way of a prescribed format that provides detailed "Nutrition Facts" on the product. The nutrition labeling requirements are reviewed in detail below.

♦ If any **nutrient content claims** are made, a disclosure statement referring to nutrition labeling of a specific size relative to the claim must be included along with the claim if there are other food constituents present at certain disclosure levels. Nutrient content claims are subject to specific definitions and are reviewed in detail below.

♦ Every article of foreign origin must be marked in a conspicuous place to indicate the English name of the **country of origin**.

Ingredient Labeling

A food product is misbranded if the ingredients are not listed in descending order of predominance by weight, as such an ingredient statement is likely to confuse consumers. Ingredients that are present in amounts of 2 percent or less need not be listed in descending order if a qualifying statement such as "Contains _____ percent or less of _____" appears at the end of the ingredient statement, with the second blank filled in with the names of the ingredients present at less than 2 percent.

Each ingredient must be listed specifically by its common or usual name. Collective terms such as "artificial flavors," "natural flavors," "spices" and "artificial flavors," however, may be listed for those ingredients without further elaboration. FDA provides a definition for each of these terms, and lists those items that may be included under them in an ingredient statement. An ingredient statement for flavors is required in addition to any flavor labeling required in conjunction with the identity statement.

Each ingredient must be listed specifically by its common or usual name.

While flavors and spices may be listed generically in ingredient statements, certified colors must be identified individually. Certified colors added to foods are designated in the ingredient statement by a common or usual name (e.g., "FD&C Blue No. 1," "Blue 1," "Blue 1 Lake"). The terms "FD&C" and "No." may be omitted from the name of the color. A collective name, such as "artificial color" or "color added," may still be used to declare noncertified color additives, although many companies choose to list noncertified colors by their common or usual name (e.g., annatto, grape skin extract).

Preservatives must be identified in an ingredient statement, not only by the common or usual name of the preservative, but by a separate description of its function, e.g., "benzoate of soda—a preservative" or "stannous chloride to protect flavor." Incidental additives—those ingredients present in a food at insignificant levels and which do not have any technical or functional effect in the finished food—need not be included in the ingredient statement. There is a specific rule in the case of sulfites. If the sulfites have either a technical or functional effect on the product or are present in an amount greater than 10 parts per 1,000,000, then they are not considered incidental and must be included in the ingredient statement in the same manner as any other ingredient in the product.

The ingredient declaration may appear either on the PDP or the IP, but the entire statement must appear on a single panel.

Allergens

Under the Food Allergen Labeling and Consumer Protection Act (FALCPA) of 2004, all packaged foods labeled on or after January 1, 2006, also must comply with food allergen labeling requirements set forth in FDCA § 403(w). Specifically, a food that is not a raw agricultural commodity and contains a "major food allergen"—defined as milk, egg, fish, crustacean shellfish, tree nuts, wheat, peanuts and soybeans—is misbranded unless the label identifies, immediately after or adjacent to the list of ingredients, that the food "Contains" the food source from which the allergen is derived. These allergen labeling requirements apply to all foods regulated under the FDCA, including both domestically manufactured and imported products.

Nutrition Labeling

When Congress passed the Nutrition Labeling and Education Act (NLEA), the act reaffirmed the legal basis for FDA's labeling initiative and established an explicit timetable.

In 1990, Congress passed the Nutrition Labeling and Education Act (NLEA), Pub. L. No. 101-535, 104 Stat. 2353 (1990), to require uniform nutrition labeling on most FDA-regulated packaged food products. Extensive regulations are found at 21 C.F.R. § 101.9. USDA has adopted parallel nutrition labeling and nutrient content claims regulations. The statute and regulations provide a number of exemptions from nutrition labeling requirements, which can be lost if claims are made on the label or labeling. The exemptions include:

♦ food produced by certain small businesses;

♦ food served in restaurants and in other establishments for immediate consumption, such as schools, hospitals and airplanes (as discussed directly below, however, a new law, currently being implemented, will require nutrition labeling for certain foods served at "chain" restaurants and similar retail food establishments);

♦ ready-to-eat foods prepared primarily on-site (for example, at bakeries, delicatessens and candy stores);

♦ raw fruits, vegetables and fish;

♦ food shipped in bulk, provided that it is not sold in that form to consumers, and is used in the manufacture of foods at another site;

♦ foods that contain insignificant amounts of all nutrients and food components required to be declared on the nutrition label (for example, coffee beans and tea leaves);

♦ foods in small packages that have a total surface area of less than 12 square inches. Such foods are required to bear an address or telephone number that a consumer can use to obtain the required information. A modified label format is also provided for intermediate size packages (40 or less square inches), provided that these foods bear no nutrition claims or other nutrition information;

♦ medical foods;

♦ infant formulas; and

♦ dietary supplements (subject to separate labeling requirements).

As noted above, the Patient Protection and Affordable Care Act of 2010 (Pub. L. No. 111-148) amended the FDCA to require restaurants and similar retail food establishments that are part of a chain with 20 or more locations doing business under the same name (and offering for sale substantially the same menu items) to provide calorie and other nutrition information for standard menu items, including food on display and self-service food. See FDCA § 403(q)(5)(H). In April 2011, FDA issued a proposed rule to implement these new labeling requirements, 76 Fed. Reg. 19,192 (Apr. 6, 2011), in which the agency proposed to define the term "restaurant or similar retail food establishment" as an establishment that sells restaurant or restaurant-type food whose primary business activity is the sale of food to consumers. An establishment's primary business activity would be the sale of food to consumers if either: 1) it presents itself as a restaurant, or 2) it uses more than 50 percent of its total floor area for the sale of food.

Restaurants and similar retail food establishments that are part of a chain with 20 or more locations doing business under the same name (and offering for sale substantially the same menu items) will need to provide calorie and other nutrition information for standard menu items, including food on display and self-service food.

The nutrition labeling regulations found at 21 C.F.R. § 101.9 require manufacturers to include information about certain nutrients on product labels (mandatory nutrients). Information about certain other nutrients may be listed at the manufacturer's discretion (voluntary nutrients). If a claim is made about any of the voluntary nutrients, or if a food is fortified or enriched with any of them, information about that nutrient then becomes mandatory. The mandatory and voluntary nutrients enumerated in the regulations are the only ones permitted to appear on the nutrition panel. A revision to the mandatory nutrients information, implemented in 2006, requires that food labels list trans fatty acids ("trans fat") on a separate line immediately under the line for saturated fatty acids.

A revision to the mandatory nutrients information that was implemented in 2006 requires that food labels list trans fatty acids ("trans fat") on a separate line immediately under the line for saturated fatty acids.

Those mandatory nutrients (italicized) and the voluntary nutrients are listed below in the order in which they must appear on the label:

Mandatory Nutrients and Voluntary Nutrients	
Listed in the order in which they must appear on the label. Mandatory nutrients are italicized.	*total calories*
	calories from fat
	calories from saturated fat
	total fat
	saturated fat
	trans fat
	cholesterol
	sodium
	potassium
	total carbohydrate
	dietary fiber
	soluble fiber
	insoluble fiber
	sugars
	sugar alcohols
	other carbohydrate (the difference between total carbohydrate and the sum of dietary fiber, sugars, and sugar alcohol if declared)
	protein
	vitamin A
	vitamin C
	calcium
	iron
	other vitamins and minerals (see 21 C.F.R. § 101.9(c))

The regulations go into great detail on the methodology to be used in calculating nutrient content, and discuss specific analytical methods to be used to determine the amount of each dietary component present in foods. In most cases, a food manufacturer is free to use other methods. Where FDA contests the results found by the food manufacturer, however, the agency uses the analytical methods identified in the regulations.

When listing these nutrients, not only their absolute quantitative measure must be identified; the NLEA also requires that reference values for nutrients—the "Daily Value"—be included. The daily value is the average amount of a particular nutrient that an individual should consume in a day. A nutrition label must declare the daily value and, in some cases, the quantity by weight of all nutrients.

FDA has established a detailed format for the presentation of nutrition information on food products. The nutrient declarations are based upon serving size listed in "common household units" such as cups, tablespoons or teaspoons, except for beverages, which must be listed in fluid ounces. To determine the appropriate serving size for food product, a manufacturer must look to the reference amount in FDA's regulations for the relevant product category. 21 C.F.R. § 101.12. The reference amount customarily consumed (RACC) represents the amount of food from the product category that is customarily consumed per eating occasion. RACCs are not intended as dietary recommendations, but rather as guides to help manufacturers establish appropriate serving sizes. Manufacturers determine the serving size for a product by calculating what fraction of a sales unit equals the RACC. This is rarely an exact fit, so the regulations contain standards to convert RACCs to appropriate serving sizes. For example, if the sale unit of a product weighs at least 67 percent but less than 200 percent of the reference amount, the serving size of the product is one unit. Underneath the serving size is the "Number of Servings Per Container."

FDA has recognized that the levels of nutrients in food products generally will not calculate out as even, uniform numbers. The presentation of a wide array of numerical values, including fractions or decimal places, will render the nutrition label unnecessarily confusing to consumers, and make comparison of values among different products more difficult. Therefore, the regulations provide specific rules for rounding nutrient values on nutrition labels up or down, generally to increments of five or 10. The regulations establish different rounding parameters for different nutrients, and the level of adjustment made will vary for different ranges within individual nutrients (e.g., the different rules discussed above for rounding caloric values above or below 50).

If standard-size packages (those that have a total surface area available for labeling of more than 40 square inches) cannot fit the nutrition panel onto the information panel in the general tabular format, a modified, tabular format, which presents the information in a horizontal, side-by-side display, may be used. If the package lacks sufficient continuous vertical space to utilize even this modified vertical display, the regulations provide for a horizontal format. Small and intermediate-size packages (those which have a total surface area available for labeling of 40 square inches or less) are subject to looser requirements for the presentation of nutrition labeling. The Nutrition Facts label may appear on any label panel, not only the information panel. Moreover, if necessary for reasons of package space, the footnotes to the nutrition label may be omitted and replaced with an asterisked statement at the bottom of the label that percent daily values are based on a 2,000-calorie diet.

Small packages (those with a total surface area of 12 square inches or less available for labeling) are eligible for an even greater exception to the labeling format requirements. If necessary for reasons of space, small packages may

The nutrient declarations are based upon serving size listed in "common household units" such as cups, tablespoons or teaspoons, except for beverages, which must be listed in fluid ounces.

If necessary for reasons of space, small packages may omit the full nutrition labeling and instead merely list an address or telephone number through which to obtain nutrition information.

omit the full nutrition labeling and instead merely list an address or telephone number through which to obtain nutrition information. If a manufacturer uses the "telephone number exemption," it may not make any claims in the label as to the nutrient content of the product.

If a food contains insignificant amounts of seven or more of the mandatory nutrients and total calories, the manufacturer may use a simplified Nutrition Facts format that omits much of the information that appears in the standard display. "Insignificant amount" is defined as an amount that may be declared as zero under the nutrition labeling regulations, or for total carbohydrates, dietary fiber and protein, a declaration of "less than 1 g" (see the above discussion of rounding rules). Trans fat does not have to be included if the total fat in a food is less than 0.5 gram per serving and the label makes no claims about fat, fatty acids or cholesterol content. This simplified format contains information on total calories, total fat, total carbohydrate, protein and sodium only. These five nutrients must be declared, even if they are present in insignificant amounts. If the food product contains calories from fat and/or mandatory nutrients in greater than insignificant amounts, they must be declared on the label. Any nutrients added to the food must be declared as well.

The Nutrition Facts panel must appear on the principal display panel or the information panel. There are, however, exceptions to this requirement. For example, FDA gives packages that have a total surface area available for labeling greater than 40 square inches greater flexibility in displaying nutrition information. If the principal display panel and the information panel do not provide sufficient space to accommodate all of the required information, the manufacturer may use any alternate panel that can be seen readily by consumers for the nutrition label.

Nutrient Content Claims (Descriptors)

Nutrient content claims on food labels also are governed by NLEA. Manufacturers are permitted to place claims on a label regarding the level of a nutrient in a food, provided that they use only the descriptive terms that FDA has defined by regulation. This enables manufacturers to highlight particular nutritional attributes of their products through a uniform frame of reference.

FDA allows two types of nutrient content claims: absolute claims, which describe the level of a nutrient in a serving of a product, and relative claims, which compare the level of nutrient per serving in a product to that of a reference product.

FDA allows two types of nutrient content claims: absolute claims, which describe the level of a nutrient in a serving of a product, and relative claims, which compare the level of nutrient per serving in a product to that of a reference product. Absolute claims may utilize only the particular descriptive terms approved by FDA, which are listed and defined below. Relative claims only can compare products to appropriate classes of reference foods established by

FDA for use as the basis for relative claims. All nutrient content claims, whether absolute or relative, must be based on RACCs. Special rules apply to claims for foods with small RACCs.

Labels containing a relative claim must state, in immediate proximity to the claim, the identity of the reference product and the amount by which the reduced product differs from it, expressed as a percentage or a fraction, e.g., "30 percent fewer calories than regular _____." The label also must bear quantitative information comparing calories per serving to the reference product. This can be accomplished by a statement such as "calorie content of regular is 120 calories per 12 oz. serving; calorie content of diet is 2 calories per 12 oz. serving," or by a chart or graph display of the nutrient levels of the reference product, and the corresponding lower levels in the reduced product. This quantitative information must appear either next to the most prominent reduced calorie claim, or on the nutrition information panel.

If a product qualifies for a nutrient content claim, but contains a high level of certain other nutrients, a referral/disclosure statement is required. Specifically, if a food making a nutrient content claim contains more than 13 grams of fat, 4 grams of saturated fat, 60 milligrams of cholesterol or 480 milligrams of sodium per RACC, then the referral statement must read "See [appropriate panel] for information about [nutrient requiring disclosure] and other nutrients."

A table of FDA-approved nutrient content claims is found at the end of this chapter. The NLEA allows for the submission of petitions requesting that FDA promulgate definitions for new nutrient content claims or accept synonyms for defined terms, or allow the use of implied nutrient content claims in brand names.

Structure-Function Claims

Conventional foods may also bear "structure-function" claims—claims relating a food or food ingredients to an effect on the structure or function of the body. Such claims have been used on foods for many years, and include statements such as "calcium builds strong bones." One of the important distinctions between conventional foods and dietary supplements lies in this area: FDA takes the position that conventional food claims must be derived from the "nutritive value" of the food, an ambiguous concept that FDA regulations define as "a value in sustaining human existence by such processes as promoting growth, replacing loss of essential nutrients, or providing energy." 21 C.F.R. § 101.14(a)(3).

Health Claims

In addition to nutrient content claims, NLEA authorizes the use of health claims—defined as a statement that expressly or by implication characterizes the relationship of certain nutrients to a disease or health-related condition—on food labels. Health claims differ from nutrient content claims in that they focus not on the amount of a particular nutrient supplied by the food product in question, but rather on the potential health benefits of consumption of that nutrient, with the food product in question being but one source of that nutrient.

An "authorized health claim" is permitted only if FDA has promulgated regulation approving the claim and setting forth the conditions under which it may be used.

An "authorized health claim" is permitted only if FDA has promulgated a regulation approving the claim and setting forth the conditions under which it may be used. A food is misbranded, and may be considered an unapproved drug, if it bears any health claim other than those authorized by FDA, or if it fails to meet the requirements of the regulation authorizing its use. Food products are permitted to bear authorized health claims for certain relationships between a nutrient or a food and the risk of a disease or health-related condition.

FDA may issue an authorized health claim regulation on its own, or in response to a petition from manufacturers. Such a claim may be authorized if the agency determines, based on the totality of publicly available scientific evidence (including evidence from well-designed studies conducted in a manner consistent with generally recognized scientific procedures and principles), that the claim is supported by such evidence.

A "qualified health claim" is permitted where a claim is based on credible evidence, but the strength of the scientific evidence falls below the threshold for FDA to issue an authorized health claim regulation based on significant scientific agreement.

In addition, a "qualified health claim" is permitted where a claim is based on credible evidence, but the strength of the scientific evidence falls below the threshold for FDA to issue an authorized health claim regulation based on significant scientific agreement (the SSA standard). FDA established a review process for qualified health claims in response to several court decisions, including *Pearson v. Shalala*, 164 F.3d 650 (D.C. Cir. 1999), which ruled on First Amendment grounds that FDA may not reject a health claim found to be potentially misleading unless the agency also reasonably determines that no disclaimer would eliminate the potential deception.

In 2003, FDA established interim procedures for reviewing petitions for qualified health claims. "Guidance for Industry and FDA: Interim Procedures for Qualified Health Claims in the Labeling of Conventional Human Food and Human Dietary Supplements" (July 2003). Under this interim process, FDA reviews qualified health claim petitions on a case-by-case basis. FDA must respond by letter within 270 days notifying the petitioner whether FDA intends to exercise enforcement discretion with respect to a qualified health claim or to deny the petition. In a letter of enforcement discretion, FDA specifies the nature of the qualified health claim for which FDA has no objections. FDA has developed standardized qualifying language for qualified health claims subject to a letter of enforcement discretion, based on the three levels of support used in the evidence-based ranking system.

FDA posts on its website all petitions requesting a qualified health claim for a 60-day public comment period. FDA also posts on its website all letters of enforcement discretion and denial letters for qualified health claim petitions. The posted letters of enforcement discretion give notice to manufacturers regarding how FDA intends to exercise its enforcement discretion on the use of the qualified health claim.

In 2009, FDA issued a final guidance document that sets forth an evidence-based review system for the agency's evaluation of petitions submitted for SSA health claims or qualified health claims. "Guidance for Industry: Evidence-Based Review System for the Scientific Evaluation of Health Claims" (Jan. 2009). Thus, in contrast to previous practice, FDA is now using a single approach for evaluating SSA and qualified health claim petitions. Under this approach, FDA determines whether the scientific evidence meets the SSA standard or, if not, can support a qualified health claim that includes qualifying language that identifies limits to the level of scientific evidence. The guidance explains that the SSA standard is intended to be a strong standard that provides a high level of confidence in the validity of the substance/disease relationship. On the other hand, SSA does not require unanimous agreement within the relevant scientific community.

Per the guidance, FDA will observe the following steps when evaluating the scientific evidence for health claims: 1) identifying scientific studies that evaluate the substance/disease relationship; 2) identifying surrogate endpoints for disease risk; 3) evaluating human studies to determine if scientific conclusions can be made; 4) assessing the methodological quality of each human study; 5) evaluating the totality of the evidence; 6) assessing SSA; 7) analyzing the specificity of claim language for qualified health claims; and 8) reevaluating existing SSA or qualified health claims, as appropriate.

The FDCA, through the passage of FDAMA, also allows a class of health claims and nutrient content claims which are not required, prior to use, to be codified into a regulation as an authorized health claim or be the subject of letter of enforcement discretion as a qualified health claim. These claims, referred to as "authoritative statement" claims, are permitted if:

The FDCA, through the passage of FDAMA, allows a class of health claims and nutrient content claims which are not required, prior to use, to be codified into a regulation as an authorized health claim or be the subject of letter of enforcement discretion as a qualified health claim.

♦ a scientific body of the U.S. government with official responsibility for public health protection or research directly relating to human nutrition (e.g., the National Institutes of Health or the Centers for Disease Control and Prevention) or the National Academy of Sciences or any of its subdivisions, has published an authoritative statement, currently in effect, about the relationship between a nutrient and a disease or health-related condition to which the health claim refers, or which identifies the nutrient level to which the claim refers, as appropriate;

♦ the person intending to make the claim submits to FDA, 120 days before introducing the food into interstate commerce with such a claim, a notice of the claim, including: 1) the exact words to be used and a concise description of the basis for concluding that the authoritative statement relied upon has been made; 2) a copy of the authoritative statement relied upon; and 3) a balanced representation of the scientific literature relating to the relationship that is the subject of the health claim or nutrient content claim;

♦ the claim and the food for which it is made are in compliance with FDA regulations prohibiting claims on foods that contain nutrients in amounts that increase the risk of diet-related diseases or health conditions, and the general provisions on misbranding; and

♦ the claim is stated so that it accurately represents the authoritative statement on which it is based, and it enables the public to understand both the information provided and its relative significance in the context of the total daily diet.

During the 120-day period between notification to FDA and the introduction of the food bearing the claim into interstate commerce, FDA may inform the notifier that it has not submitted all of the information required by the act. As noted, a health claim or nutrient content claim based on an authoritative statement may be made without FDA approval. Such a claim may be continued until either: 1) FDA issues a regulation (and the regulation has become effective) prohibiting or modifying the claim, or finding that the requirements of the act for such a claim have not been met, including a finding that the notification did not include all of the information required; or 2) a federal court determines, in the context of an enforcement proceeding, that the statutory requirements have not been met.

Standards of Identity

Section 401 of the FDCA permits FDA to set a certain definition or standard for a food to "promote honesty and fair dealing in the interest of consumers." Such regulations may include establishing a common or usual name for a food, providing a reasonable definition and standard of identity, setting a reasonable standard of quality or reasonable standards of fill of container. See 21 C.F.R. Parts 102 (common or usual names for non-standardized foods), 103 (quality standards for foods with no identity standards), 104 (nutritional quality guidelines for foods) and 130-169 (general conditions for standards of identity, and specific standards). The development of standards for most products—to the extent developed at all—are subject to informal, notice-and-comment rule-making procedures rather than formal rulemaking.

To a large extent a standard of identity can be characterized as a recipe for a food that provides consumers with a consistent expectation as to composition and quality. A food may be considered misbranded if it is represented on its label as a food for which a definition and standard of identity has been established, yet fails to conform to that definition and standard even if it is wholesome and its label is otherwise truthful. See FDCA § 403.

A standard of identity can be characterized as a recipe for a food that provides consumers with a consistent expectation as to composition and quality.

Standards also may pertain to the quality of a food product. Products failing to meet a "standard of quality" must disclose the fact of substandard quality in a label statement. "Standards of fill" also commonly are used to protect against "slack fill" or products with excess water levels.

According to section 403(c) of the FDCA, a food is misbranded "[i]f it is an imitation of another food, unless its label bears, in type of uniform size and prominence, the word 'imitation' and, immediately thereafter, the name of the food imitated." FDA regulations further provide that "imitation labeling" is required if a food is a substitute for and resembles another food but is nutritionally inferior to that food. "Nutritional inferiority" is defined as any reduction in the content of the essential nutrient that is present at a measurable amount, not including caloric or fat content with a measurable amount considered to be 2 percent or more of the daily reference value for protein and potassium, and the referenced daily intake for specified vitamins and minerals. Rather than bearing the term "imitation"—which virtually ensures a food product's demise in the marketplace—products that resemble a standardized food but are not nutritionally inferior may bear an appropriate common or usual name, an appropriately descriptive term or a fanciful name that is not false and misleading.

Under 21 C.F.R § 130.10, a food may bear the name of a standardized food that does not meet the standard if the deviation from the standard is described by a nutrient content claim on the label. This regulation permits the development of healthful versions of standardized foods without requiring labeling that would prevent consumers from buying the product. Among a number of specific limitations, in order for a food product to comply with this "generic" standard of identity:

A food may bear the name of a standardized food that does not meet the standard if the deviation from the standard is described by a nutrient content claim on the label.

♦ nutrients may be added so that the product is not nutritionally inferior to the standardized food;

♦ the substitute food must possess the same or similar performance characteristics as the standardized food;

♦ deviations from the non-ingredient provisions of the standard are permitted if intended to produce the performance characteristics;

♦ deviations must be the minimum necessary to qualify for the nutrient content claim; and

♦ any significant deviations from the range of performance characteristics for the standardized food must be noted on the label, such as "not recommended for frying."

In May 2005, FDA and the USDA's FSIS, which regulates meat and poultry products standards of identity, issued a joint proposed rule to revise their respective food standards processes they employ. 70 Fed. Reg. 29,214 (May 20, 2005). The proposed rule establishes a set of criteria that both agencies would use to evaluate petitions to revise, eliminate or create a new standard of identity. The proposed rule also would give each agency the ability to propose, on its own initiative, to revise, eliminate or create a new standard of identity.

FOOD SECURITY/SAFETY

FDA has increasingly focused on issues of food security in the last several years.

FDA has increasingly focused on issues of food security in the last several years, which began in earnest in particular following the passage of the Public Health Security and Bioterrorism Preparedness Response Act (Bioterrorism Act) of 2002 (Pub. L. No. 107-88). In response to Title III of the Bioterrorism Act, "Protecting Safety and Security of Food and Drug Supply," FDA issued regulations governing facility registration (FDCA § 415), new food import requirements (FDCA § 801(m)), administrative detention authority (FDCA § 304(h)), and recordkeeping and access requirements (FDCA § 414). In addition, in response to the Food and Drug Administration Amendments Act of 2007 (Pub. L. No. 11085) (FDAAA), FDA established a reportable food registry through which food facility registrants must notify FDA about foods that may present a risk of serious adverse health consequences or death to humans or animals. See FDCA § 417.

Nevertheless, as previously discussed in this chapter, there have been continuing concerns about FDA's ability to ensure the safety of the nation's food supply. Responding to these concerns, Congress passed FSMA, which greatly expands FDA's authority over regulated foods. In addition to the new requirements discussed above (i.e., food facilities must adopt written preventive controls plans, and FDA must increase regulation over certain farm operations), FSMA includes various other provisions intended to bolster FDA's oversight and enforcement authorities, such as enhanced registration and recordkeeping requirements and administrative detention authority, increased FDA inspections, mandatory FDA recalls, and heightened scrutiny of food imports.

Food Facility Registration

In October 2003, FDA issued an interim final rule requiring domestic and foreign facilities that manufacture, process, pack or hold food for consumption by humans and animals in the United States to register with FDA by December 2003. 68 Fed. Reg. 58,894 (Oct. 10, 2003). In October 2005, FDA issued a final rule adopting the interim final rule requirements, set forth in 21 C.F.R. Part 1, Subpart H.

The current food facility regulations require that a food manufacturer separately register each facility once with FDA. The registration for foreign facilities also must include the name of the U.S. agent for the facility. FDA is required to compile and maintain an up-to-date list of registered facilities, which is available on its website.

Foreign facilities are not required to register with FDA where the manufactured food undergoes further processing or packaging at another facility outside the United States. In addition, manufacturers of food contact substances are not required to register with FDA. Other establishments excluded from the registration requirements include farms, restaurants and other retail food establishments, and nonprofit food establishments.

FSMA enhances the facility registration requirements in FDCA § 415 by requiring registration renewal every two years, and by granting FDA a significant new registration-related authority: suspension. Specifically, the FDA Commissioner can suspend a facility registration based on a determination that the food manufactured, processed, packed, received or held by the facility has a reasonable probability of causing serious adverse health consequences or death to humans or animals.

Prior Notice of Imported Food

In October 2003, FDA issued an interim final rule establishing prior notice regulations. In November 2008, FDA issued a final rule. 73 Fed. Reg. 66,294 (Nov. 8, 2008). The prior notice regulations are set forth in 21 C.F.R. Part 1, Subpart I. In 2009, FDA issued a compliance policy guide addressing prior notice requirements. Compliance Policy Guide, Guidance for FDA and CBP Staff (Sec. 110.310):

Prior notice must be given to FDA for all food for humans and animals imported or offered for import into the United States for use, storage or distribution in the United States.

Prior Notice of Imported Food Under the Public Health Security and Bioterrorism Preparedness and Response Act of 2002 (May 2009).

The prior notice regulations require that prior notice is given to FDA for all food for humans and animals imported or offered for import into the United States for use, storage or distribution in the United States. These requirements apply to food for trans-shipment through the United States to another country and food for future export, but are not applicable for foods that are imported and then exported without leaving the port of arrival until export. A prior notice may be submitted by any person with knowledge of the required information, and may be transmitted to FDA by a third party, such as a customer, on behalf of the submitter. Prior notices are submitted electronically to FDA through either 1) the U.S. Customs and Border Patrol (CBP) Automated Broker Interface of the Automated Commercial System (ABI/ACS) or 2) the FDA Prior Notice System Interface (PNSI). Prior notice submissions must contain detailed production, transportation and recipient information.

The time requirements for submission of prior notice, and confirmation by FDA for review, are as follows: 1) if the article of food is arriving by road, no less than two hours before arriving at the port of arrival; 2) if the article of food is arriving by rail, no less than four hours before arriving at the port of arrival; 3) if the article of food is arriving by air, no less than four hours before arriving at the port of arrival; or 4) if the article of food is arriving by water, no less than eight hours before arriving at the port of arrival. Except where a food is offered for import by international mail, a prior notice may not be submitted more than 15 calendar days before the anticipated date of arrival of the food for submissions through FDA's PNSI and not more than 30 calendar days before the anticipated date of arrival for submissions through CBP's ABI/ACS.

A food may be refused admission into the United States if the prior notice is inadequate—either due to no prior notice, inaccurate prior notice or untimely prior notice. A refused food must be exported (unless seized or administratively detained by CBP or FDA under other authority), or it must be held within the port of entry unless otherwise directed by CBP or FDA. A request may be made within five days for FDA to review whether a food refused admission is in fact subject to prior notice requirements or whether the information submitted in the prior notice is accurate. If FDA determines that the food is not subject to prior notice requirements or the prior notice submission is accurate, it will notify the requester that the food is no longer subject to refusal of admission.

In May 2011, FDA issued an interim final rule that amends the prior notice regulations as required by FSMA. 76 Fed. Reg. 25,542 (May 5, 2011). Under the interim final rule, a person submitting a prior notice of imported food is required to report the name of any country to which the article has been refused entry.

Administrative Detention

In June 2004, FDA issued a final rule establishing regulations, set forth in 21 C.F.R. Part 1, Subpart K, authorizing the detention of any food found during an inspection, examination or investigation conducted under the FDCA, when based on credible evidence or information indicating such food presents a threat of serious adverse health consequences or death to humans or animals. 69 Fed. Reg. 31,659 (June 4, 2004). FSMA gives FDA expanded authority in this area by lowering the standard for administrative detention provided in FDCA § 304(h). Under the new law, FDA may impose administrative detention of food if it has "reason to believe" that an article of food is adulterated or misbranded. In May 2011, FDA issued an interim final rule implementing its expanded detention authority. 76 Fed. Reg. 25,538 (May 5, 2011).

Under the new law, FDA may impose administrative detention of food if it has "reason to believe" that an article of food is adulterated or misbranded.

An officer or qualified employee of FDA may order an administrative detention, which must be approved by the Secretary or a designated official. The detention period must be reasonable and not exceed 30 calendar days. Any person entitled to claim the food if it were seized may appeal the detention order to the Secretary.

Records

In December 2004, FDA issued a final rule establishing regulations, set forth in 21 C.F.R. Part 1, Subpart J, requiring persons who manufacture, process, pack, transport, distribute, receive, hold or import food in the United States to maintain and allow FDA access to records. 69 Fed. Reg. 71,561 (Dec. 9, 2004). Records to be maintained by food firms relate to the identity of the immediate previous source of all food received and the immediate subsequent recipient of all food released, and records must be retained at or reasonably close to the establishment where the activities covered in the records occurred. The record retention period for human foods ranges from six months to two years depending on the food's shelf life, and the retention period for animal food is one year.

Persons who manufacture, process, pack, transport, distribute, receive, hold or import food in the United States must maintain and allow FDA access to records.

The following persons or facilities are not subject to the recordkeeping and access requirements: farms; restaurants; persons performing covered activities when the food is meat, poultry or egg products subject to exclusive USDA jurisdiction; and foreign persons, except those who transport food in the United States. The records requirements also do not extend to the following information: recipes for food; financial and pricing data, personnel data, research data or sales data (other than shipment data regarding sales). In addition, certain persons or facilities—including small retail food establishments and certain nonprofit food establishments—are not subject to the record establishment requirements, but are subject to the availability requirements for existing records.

FSMA moderately expands FDA's authority to inspect records at food facilities as provided in FDCA § 414. Currently, FDA must provide written notice before accessing records and must have a reasonable belief that an article of food is adulterated and presents a threat of serious adverse health consequences or death to humans or animals. FSMA removes the requirement that FDA must have a reasonable belief that the food is adulterated—if FDA reasonably believes the food will cause serious adverse health consequences or death. The requirement that FDA provide advance notice before accessing records remains in effect.

Reportable Food Registry

A reportable food is a food (other than a dietary supplement and infant formula) for which there is a reasonable probability that the use of, or exposure to, the food will cause serious adverse health consequences or death to humans or animals.

In September 2009, FDA established an electronic reportable food registry, as required by FDAAA. A reportable food is a food (other than a dietary supplement and infant formula) for which there is a reasonable probability that the use of, or exposure to, the food will cause serious adverse health consequences or death to humans or animals. A responsible party, defined as a person who submits a food facility registration to FDA for a facility where food is manufactured, processed, packed or held, is required to notify FDA through the reportable food registry within 24 hours after the party determines that a food is a reportable food.

The Food Safety Act enhances the reportable food registry system in FDCA § 417. Specifically, FDA is required to obtain consumer-oriented information about reportable foods, and to then prepare a one-page summary of the food that will be made available on the Internet and provided to grocery stores.

Inspections

FSMA requires FDA to increase the frequency of inspections of all domestic and foreign food facilities. In particular, FDA is required to identify and allocate resources to inspect "high-risk facilities," which will be identified based on a number of factors, including: known risks of the food, compliance history of the facility, and rigor and effectiveness of the facility's hazard analysis and risk-based preventive controls. See FDCA § 421. FDA must inspect all high-risk domestic facilities within five years of enactment of FSMA and no less than every three years thereafter, and must inspect all non-high-risk domestic facilities within seven years of enactment and no less than every five years thereafter.

With respect to foreign facilities, FSMA requires FDA to inspect at least 600 foreign facilities within one year of enactment, and to double those inspections every year for the next five years. FDCA § 421(a)(2)(D). The law provides that if a foreign facility registered with FDA refuses an inspection, its food cannot be imported into the United States. See FDCA § 807(b).

Mandatory Recall Authority

For the first time, FSMA grants FDA the authority to order mandatory recalls of food (other than infant formula, for which FDA previously had mandatory recall authority). See FDCA § 423. This new authority became effective on the date of enactment.

The law grants FDA mandatory recall over food if: 1) there is a reasonable probability that the food is adulterated or misbranded; 2) the use of or exposure to the food will cause serious adverse health consequences or death to humans or animals; and 3) the responsible party has refused to voluntarily cease distribution and recall the products. For any mandatory recall, or for a voluntary recall of food that will cause serious adverse health consequences or death to humans or animals, FDA must set up an incident command operation within 24 hours after initiation of the recall.

Food Imports

FSMA establishes a foreign supplier verification program (effective in January 2013), which requires each food importer to perform foreign supplier verification activities in accordance with FDA implementing regulations and guidance. See FDCA § 805. Each importer's program would be required to ensure that each of its foreign suppliers produces imported food employing processes and procedures that are documented in a written plan and designed to prevent adulteration and reduce hazards as required by other relevant provisions of the FDCA. Importers would maintain import-verification records for at least two years and make them available to FDA upon request.

FSMA also contains provisions that encourage coordination with foreign countries to ensure imported food safety. The law requires FDA, in consultation with other executive agencies and stakeholders, to develop a comprehensive plan to expand the technical, scientific and regulatory capacity of foreign governments and their respective food industries, from which foods are exported to the United States. FDA also is required to establish satellite offices in foreign countries to provide assistance to the appropriate foreign government entities in ensuring safety of food and other products regulated by FDA, including by directly conducting risk-based inspections of such articles and supporting inspections by foreign governmental entities.

MEDICAL FOODS

Medical foods are administered by physicians for dietary management of a specific disease or disorder.

Medical foods have always been a subject of confusion. Although the category was conceived as a special category of foods administered by physicians for dietary management of a specific disease or disorder, it was not until 1988, with the passage of the Orphan Drug Amendments, that a statutory definition was provided for medical foods:

> A food which is formulated to be consumed or administered internally under the supervision of a physician and which is intended for the specific dietary management of a disease or condition for which distinctive nutritional requirements based upon recognized scientific principles are established by medical evaluation.

Pub. L. No. 100-290, 102 Stat. 90 (1988) (codified at 21 U.S.C. § 301 note, 360; 42 U.S.C. § 236 note (1994)). This definition was later incorporated into the NLEA.

For many years, FDA discussed the establishment of regulations for medical foods. In 1996, FDA finally published an advance notice of proposed rulemaking (ANPR) to request comments on its approach to the "broad group of heterogeneous products that are marketed as medical foods." 61 Fed. Reg. 6066 (Nov. 29, 1996). Concerns were expressed about the "medical foods paradox"—while these products are intended for the specific dietary management of a disease or condition for which distinctive nutritional requirements had been established, they could be sold without any nutrition information on their label or labeling and could bear claims that were not evaluated by FDA. Additionally, no mechanism existed to ensure that the formulation of a medical food had been evaluated prior to sale to ensure that it was suitable for the intended patient population. The agency expressed specific concern that such a lack of scrutiny could have adverse public health consequences, especially if claims were not scientifically valid or if product labeling did not disclose information necessary for safe and effective use.

In the medical foods ANPR, FDA expressed the view that Congress did establish a strict standard for medical foods—"distinctive nutritional requirements based upon recognized scientific principles"—thus implicitly providing an expectation that the standard would be met. Accordingly, the agency will look to medical food marketers to provide substantiation of the nutritional efficacy of their medical foods.

Infant Formulas

Under FDCA § 201(z), the term "infant formula" means "a food which purports to be or is represented for special dietary use solely as a food for infants for reason of its simulation of human milk or its suitability as a complete or partial substitute for human milk." Special requirements for infant formula are provided under FDCA § 412, which deems an infant formula adulterated if it does not provide specific nutrients, does not meet quality requirements prescribed by the Secretary, or is not produced in compliance with applicable cGMPs and quality control procedures. Records development and retention requirements also apply to infant formula products, and FDA has the authority to review and copy all records containing microbiological testing results of raw materials used in infant formula powder and unfinished infant formula. FDA also maintains requirements for the labeling of infant formulas, including nutrient content, directions for preparation and use, and a "use by" date. Finally, special requirements also apply to procedures for processing consumer complaints relating to infant formulas.

An infant formula is deemed adulterated if it does not provide specific nutrients, does not meet quality requirements prescribed by the Secretary, or is not produced in compliance with applicable cGMPs and quality control procedures.

Under FDCA § 412(c), persons introducing any new infant formula into interstate commerce must submit a registration with FDA, at least 90 days before the marketing of a new infant formula, that includes the quantitative formulation of the new infant formula or description of any reformulation or change in processing of the formula. A "new infant formula" includes "an infant formula manufactured by a person which has not previously manufactured an infant formula, and .... an infant formula manufactured by a person who has previously manufactured infant formula and in which there is a major change, in processing or formulation, from a current or any previous formulation produced by such manufacturer." FDCA § 412(c)(2). Preparations for special uses, such as for infants with inborn errors of metabolism, low birth rate or other unusual medical or dietary problems, are exempt from the quality factors, quality control procedures and recordkeeping requirements, subject to terms and conditions established by FDA. Such deviations are based upon an appropriate rationale submitted to the agency that supports the deviation from the general requirements.

Persons introducing any new infant formula into interstate commerce must submit a registration with FDA, at least 90 days before the marketing of a new infant formula, that includes the quantitative formulation of the new infant formula or description of any reformulation or change in processing of the formula.

Conclusion

Food regulation continues to evolve as new challenges arise. The food law framework, particularly in the areas of food safety and security, has undergone considerable changes in recent years, and increased scrutiny of this framework likely will continue due to the risks of foodborne illness, food bioterrorism and as part of international harmonization efforts. Concurrently, the line between so-called "functional foods" and disease will continue to change historical notions as to the relative role of foods in the promotion and maintenance of health. Even in this era of increasing complexity, however, the traditional concerns that food must be wholesome and truthfully represented remain the central tenets of federal regulation of the food supply.

Approved Health Claims

Note: The model claim statements are examples. Certain regulations provide additional choices.

Approved Claims	Food Requirements	Claim Requirements	Model Claim Statements
Calcium and Osteoporosis, and Calcium, Vitamin D Osteoporosis § 101.72	For calcium and osteoporosis claim – high in calcium For calcium, vitamin D and osteoporosis claim – high in calcium and vitamin D Assimilable (bioavailable), supplements must disintegrate and dissolve, and phosphorus content cannot exceed calcium content	The claim makes clear the importance of adequate calcium intake, or when appropriate, adequate calcium and vitamin D intake, throughout life, in healthful diet, are essential to reduce osteoporosis risk. The claim does not imply that adequate calcium intake, or when appropriate, adequate calcium and vitamin D intake, is the only recognized risk factor for the development of osteoporosis. The claim does not attribute any degree of reduction in risk of osteoporosis to maintaining an adequate dietary calcium intake, or when appropriate, an adequate dietary calcium and vitamin D intake, throughout life.	Calcium and osteoporosis: – Adequate calcium throughout life, as part of a well-balanced diet, may reduce the risk of osteoporosis. – Adequate calcium as part of a healthful diet, along with physical activity, may reduce the risk of osteoporosis in later life. Calcium, vitamin D, and osteoporosis: – Adequate calcium and vitamin D throughout life, as part of a well-balanced diet, may reduce the risk of osteoporosis. – Adequate calcium and vitamin D as part of a healthful diet, along with physical activity, may reduce the risk of osteoporosis in later life.
Sodium and Hypertension § 101.74	Low Sodium	The claim states that diets low in sodium "may" or "might" reduce the risk of high blood pressure Required terms: "Sodium" "High blood pressure" Indicates that high blood pressure depends on many factors Includes physician statement (Individuals with high blood pressure should consult their physicians) if claim defines high or normal blood pressure	Diets low in sodium may reduce the risk of high blood pressure, a disease associated with many factors.
Dietary Fat and Cancer § 101.73	Low fat Fish & game meats: "Extra Lean"	The claim states that diets low in fat "may" or "might" reduce the risk of some cancer, without attributing any degree of reduction of risk Required terms: "Total Fat" or "Fat" "Some types of cancers" or "Some cancers" Indicates that the development of cancer depends on many factors Does not specify types of fats or fatty acids that may be related	Development of cancer depends on many factors. A diet low in total fat may reduce the risk of some cancers.

301

Approved Claims	Food Requirements	Claim Requirements	Model Claim Statements
Dietary Saturated Fat and Cholesterol and Risk of Coronary Heart Disease § 101.75	Low saturated fat Low cholesterol Low fat Fish & game meats: "Extra Lean"	The claim states that diets low in saturated fat and cholesterol "may" or "might" reduce the risk of heart disease, without attributing any degree of reduction of risk Required terms: "Saturated fat and cholesterol" "Coronary heart disease" or "Heart disease" Indicates that the development of heart disease depends on many factors Includes physician statement (Individuals with elevated blood total—or LDL—cholesterol should consult their physicians) if claim defines high or normal blood total and LDL-cholesterol	While many factors affect heart disease, diets low in saturated fat and cholesterol may reduce the risk of this disease.
Fiber-containing Grain Products, Fruits and Vegetables and Cancer § 101.76	A grain product, fruit or vegetable that contains dietary fiber, or a food that contains the above. Low fat, and good source of dietary fiber under § 101.54 (without fortification)	The claim states that diets low in fat and high in fiber-containing grain products, fruits and vegetables "may" or "might" reduce the risk of some cancers, without attributing any degree or reduction of risk Required terms: "Fiber," "Dietary fiber," or "Total dietary fiber" "Some types of cancer" or "Some cancers" Indicates that development of cancer depends on many factors Does not specify types of dietary fiber that may be related to risk of cancer	Low fat diets rich in fiber-containing grain products, fruits and vegetables may reduce the risk of some types of cancer, a disease associated with many factors.

Approved Claims	Food Requirements	Claim Requirements	Model Claim Statements
Fruits, Vegetables and Grain Products That Contain Fiber, Particularly Soluble Fiber, and Risk of Coronary Heart Disease § 101.77	A fruit, vegetable or grain product that contains fiber, low saturated fat, low cholesterol, low fat and at least 0.6 grams of soluble fiber per RACC (without fortification), and soluble fiber content provided on label	States that diets low in saturated fat and cholesterol and high in fruits, vegetables and grain products that contain fiber "may" or "might" reduce the risk of heart disease, without attributing any degree of reduction of risk. Required terms: "Fiber," "Dietary fiber," "Some types of dietary fiber," "Some dietary fibers," or "Some fibers" "Saturated fat" and "Cholesterol" "Heart disease" or "Coronary heart disease" Indicates that development of heart disease depends on many factors. Includes physician statement (Individuals with elevated blood total or LDL-cholesterol should consult their physicians) if claim defines high or normal blood total and LDL-cholesterol	Diets low in saturated fat and cholesterol and rich in fruits, vegetables and grain products that contain some types of dietary fiber, particularly soluble fiber, may reduce the risk of heart disease, a disease associated with many factors.
Fruits and Vegetables and Cancer § 101.78	A fruit or vegetable, low fat, and good source (without fortification) of at least one of the following: Vitamin A, Vitamin C or dietary fiber	States that diets low in fat and high in fruits and vegetables "may" or "might" reduce the risk of some cancers, without attributing any degree of reduction of risk. Required terms: "Fiber," "Dietary fiber," or "Total dietary fiber" "Total fat" or "Fat" "Some types of cancer" or "Some cancers" Characterizes fruits and vegetables as "Foods that are low in fat and may contain Vitamin A, Vitamin C, and dietary fiber" Characterizes specific food as a "Good source" of one or more of the following: Dietary fiber, Vitamin A, or Vitamin C	Low fat diets rich in fruits and vegetables (foods that are low in fat and may contain dietary fiber, Vitamin A, or Vitamin C) may reduce the risk of some types of cancer, a disease associated with many factors. OR Broccoli is high in vitamins A and C, and is a good source of dietary fiber.

Approved Claims	Food Requirements	Claim Requirements	Model Claim Statements
		Does not specify types of fats or fatty acids or types of dietary fiber that may be related to risk of cancer. Indicates that development of cancer depends on many factors.	
Folate and Neural Tube Defects § 101.79	"Good source" of folate (at least 40 mcg folate per serving) Dietary supplements, or foods in conventional food form that are naturally good sources of folate (i.e., only non-fortified food in conventional food form) The claim shall not be made on products that contain more than 100 percent of the RDI for Vitamin A as retinol or preformed vitamin A or vitamin D Dietary supplements shall meet USP standards for disintegration and dissolution or otherwise bioavailable Amount of folate required in Nutrition Label	States that daily consumption of adequate amounts of folate by a woman during childbearing years may reduce risk of spinal bifida or other neural tube defects, without attributing any degree of reduction of risk Required terms: Terms that specify the relationship (e.g., women who are capable of becoming pregnant and who consume adequate amounts of folate) "Folate," "Folic Acid," "Folacin," "Folate a B Vitamin," "Folic Acid, a B Vitamin," or "Folacin, a B Vitamin" "Neural tube defect," "birth defects, spinal bifida, or anencephaly," "birth defects of the brain or spinal cord anencephaly or spinal bifida," "spinal bifida or anencephaly, birth defects of the brain or spinal cord" Does not imply that folate intake is the only recognized risk factor for neural tube defects. Must also include information on the multifactorial nature and prevalence of neural tube defects, dietary sources of folate, and the safe upper limit of daily intake.	Healthful diets with adequate folate may reduce a woman's risk of having a child with a brain or spinal cord defect.

Approved Claims	Food Requirements	Claim Requirements	Model Claim Statements
Dietary Noncariogenic Carbohydrate Sweeteners and Dental Caries § 101.80	Sugar free, and when a fermentable carbohydrate is present, the food must not lower plaque pH below 5.7. The following are eligible substances: 1) sugar alcohol (xylitol, sorbitol, mannitol, maltitol, isomalt, lactitol, hydrogenated starch hydrolysates, hydrogenated glucose syrups, erythritol, or a combination of these); 2) sugar (D-tagatose and isomaltulose); and 3) non-nutritive sweetener (sucralose)	States that noncariogenic carbohydrate sweeteners do not promote dental caries, compared to other carbohydrates, without attributing any degree of reduction of risk. Required terms: "does not promote," "may reduce the risk of," "useful [or is useful] in not promoting," or "expressly [or is expressly] for not promoting" dental caries. "Sugar alcohol," "sugar alcohols," or the name of the sugar alcohols, or D-tagatose, or sucralose (note: D-tagatose may be identified as "tagatose") "Dental caries" or "tooth decay" When the substance that is the subject of the claim is a noncariogenic sugar (i.e., D-tagatose or isomaltulose), the claim shall identify the substance as a sugar that, unlike other sugars, does not promote the development of dental caries. Includes statement that frequent between meal consumption of foods high in sugars and starches can promote tooth decay. Packages with less than 15 square inches of surface area available for labeling may use a shortened claim.	Frequent between-meal consumption of foods high in sugars and starches promotes tooth decay. The sugar alcohols in [name of food] do not promote tooth decay. (Full claim) OR Does not promote tooth decay. (Short claim—on small packages only)

Approved Claims	Food Requirements	Claim Requirements	Model Claim Statements
Soluble Fiber from Certain Food and Risk of Coronary Heart Disease § 101.81	Meet requirements for low fat (unless due to fat content derived from listed whole oat sources), low saturated fat, and low cholesterol The food product must include one or more of the following whole oat or barley foods: 1) oat bran, 2) rolled oats, 3) whole oat flour, 4) whole grain barley or dry milled barley. The whole oat or barley foods must contain: 1) at least 0.75 g of soluble fiber per RACC of the food product; 2) Oatrim that contains at least 0.75 g of beta-glucan soluble per RACC of the food product; or 3) psyllium husk that contains at least 1.7 g of soluble fiber per RACC of food product. Beta-glucan soluble fiber from the following are eligible sources of soluble fiber: 1) oat bran; 2) rolled oats; 3) whole oat flour; 4) Oatrim; 5) whole grain barley and dry milled barley; 6) barley betafiber; and 7) soluble fiber from psyllium husk with purity of no less than 95%. The amount of soluble fiber per RACC must be declared in nutrition label	States that diets low in saturated fat and cholesterol that include soluble fiber from [source] "may" or "might" reduce the risk of heart disease, without attributing any degree of reduction of risk Does not imply that low saturated fat and cholesterol diets that include soluble fiber are the sole means of achieving a reduced risk of CHD Required terms: "Saturated fat" and "cholesterol" "Heart disease" or "coronary heart disease" In specifying the substance the claim uses the term "soluble fiber" qualified by the name of the eligible source of the soluble fiber, which is either whole oat or barley or psyllium seed husk. Claim specifies the daily dietary intake of the soluble fiber source necessary to reduce the risk of CHD Claim specifies the amount of soluble fiber in one serving of the product. For psyllium products — see potential warning/notice statement under 21 C.F.R. § 101.17(f)	Soluble fiber from foods such as [name of source] as part of a diet low in saturated fat and cholesterol may reduce the risk of heart disease. Diets low in saturated fat and cholesterol that include [_____ grams] soluble fiber per day from [source (can include name of food product)] may reduce the risk of heart disease. One serving of [*name of food*] provides___grams of this soluble fiber.
Soy Proteins and Risk of Coronary Heart Disease § 101.82	Meet requirements for low saturated fat, low cholesterol, and low fat (except that foods made from whole soybeans that contain no fat in addition to that inherent in the whole soybean are exempt from the "low fat" requirement) Shall contain at least 6.25 g of soy protein.	States diets that are low in saturated fat and cholesterol and that include soy protein "may" or "might" reduce risk of heart disease, without attributing any degree of reduction of risk. Required terms: "Heart disease" or "coronary heart disease" "Soy protein" "Saturated fat" and "cholesterol" Does not imply that consumption of soy is the only way to reduce risk of coronary heart disease. Claim specifies daily dietary intake levels of soy protein associated with reduced risk. Claim specifies amount of soy protein in a serving of food.	25 grams of soy protein a day, as part of a diet low in saturated fat and cholesterol, may reduce the risk of heart disease. A serving of [*name of food*] supplies_____grams of soy protein. Diets low in saturated fat and cholesterol that include 25 grams of soy protein a day may reduce the risk of heart disease. One serving of [*name of food*] provides_____grams of soy protein.

Approved Claims	Food Requirements	Claim Requirements	Model Claim Statements
Plant Sterol/Stanol Esters and Risk of Coronary Heart Disease § 101.83	Must meet requirements for low saturated fat and low cholesterol. Must contain at least 0.65 g of plant sterol esters per RACC of spreads or salad dressings, or at least 1.7 g of plant stanol esters per RACC of spreads, salad dressings, snack bars, and dietary supplements. Spreads and salad dressings that exceed 13 g fat per 50 g must bear the statement *"see nutrition information for fat content"* Salad dressings are exempted from the minimum 10% DV nutrient requirement	States diets low in saturated fat and cholesterol that include plant sterol/stanol esters may reduce the risk of coronary heart disease, without attributing any degree of reduction of risk. Required terms: "Heart disease" or "coronary heart disease" "Plant sterol esters" or "plant stanol esters;" except "vegetable oil" may replace the term "plant" if vegetable oil is the sole source of the sterol/stanol ester Claim specifies the daily dietary intake of plant sterol or stanol esters necessary to reduce CHD risk, and the amount provided per serving. Claim specifies that plant sterol or stanol esters should be consumed in two servings eaten at different times of the day with other foods.	Foods containing at least 0.65 gram per of vegetable oil sterol esters, eaten twice a day with meals for a daily total intake of least 1.3 grams, as part of a diet low in saturated fat and cholesterol, may reduce the risk of heart disease. A serving of [*name of food*] supplies_____ grams of vegetable oil sterol esters. Diets low in saturated fat and cholesterol that include two servings of foods that provide a daily total of at least 3.4 grams of plant stanol esters in two meals may reduce the risk of heart disease. A serving of [*name of food*] supplies_____ grams of plant stanol esters.

General criteria all health claims must meet:

Only information on the value that intake or reduced intake, as part of a total dietary pattern, may have on a disease or health-related condition

Enables public to understand information provided and significance of information in the context of a total daily diet

Complete, truthful, and not misleading

Food contains, without fortification, 10 percent or more of the Daily Value of one of six nutrients (dietary supplements excepted):

Nutrient	10%DV	Nutrient	10%DV
Vitamin A	500 IU	Calcium	100 mg
Vitamin C	6 mg	Protein	5 g
Iron	1.8 mg	Fiber	2.5 g

All information in one place without intervening material (Reference statement permitted)

Uses "may" or "might" to express relationship between substance and disease

Does not quantify any degree of risk reduction

Indicates disease depends on many factors

Disqualifying nutrients in foods contained at less than the levels specified:

Disqualifying Nutrient	Food	Main Dishes	Meal Products
Fat	13.0 g	19.5 g	26.0 g
Saturated Fat	4.0 g	6.0 g	8.0 g
Cholesterol	60 mg	90 mg	120 mg
Sodium	480 mg	720 mg	960 mg

Low Fat
Food: ≤ 3 g per RACC (and per 50 g if RACC is small)
Meals and main dishes: ≤ 3 g per 100 g and not more than 30% of calories from fat

Low Saturated Fat
Food: ≤ 1 g per RACC and ≤ 15% of calories from saturated fat
Meals and main dishes: ≤ 1 g per 100 g and < 10% of calories from saturated fat

Low Cholesterol
Food: < 20 mg per RACC (and per 50 g of food if RACC is small)
Meals and main dishes: < 20 mg per 100 g

Low Sodium
Food: ≤ 140 mg per RACC (and per 50 g if RACC is small)
Meals and main dishes: ≤ 140 mg per 100 g

"Extra Lean"
Seafood or game meat: < 5 g total fat and 2 g saturated fat and < 95 mg cholesterol per RACC and per 100 g
Meals and main dishes: < 5 g total fat and < 2 g saturated fat and < 95 mg cholesterol per 100 g and per LS

High in Calcium
Food: ≥ 200 mg per RACC
Meals and main dishes:
Contains food that is high in calcium and identifies the food

Good Source of Vitamin A
Food: ≥ 500 IU per RACC
Meals and main dishes: Contains food that is a good source of Vitamin A and identifies food

Good Source of Vitamin C
Food: ≥ 6 mg per RACC
Meals and main dishes: Contains food that is a good source of Vitamin C and identifies food

Good Source of Dietary Fiber
Food: ≥ 2.5 g per RACC
Meals and main dishes: Contains food that is a good source of dietary fiber and identifies food

ABBREVIATION: DV = Daily Value; **RACC** = Reference Amount Customarily Consumed per Eating Occasion; **LS** = Labeled Serving; **IU** = International Units; **RACC small** = ≤ 30 g or 2 tablespoons or less

To be labeled as "Healthy," a food must meet the definition of "Low" for fat and saturated fat, and neither cholesterol nor sodium may be present at a level exceeding the disclosure levels in 21 C.F.R. 101.13(h). In addition, the food must comply with definitions and declaration requirements for any specific nutrient content claims.

21 C.F.R. 101.65(d)(2)

Conditions for the Use of "Healthy"

Individual Food	Seafood or Game Meat[5/]	Meal or Main Dish
TOTAL FAT low fat	TOTAL FAT < 5 g fat /RACC & /100 g	TOTAL FAT low fat
SATURATED (sat) FAT low sat fat	SATURATED (sat) FAT < 2 g sat fat /RACC & /100g	SATURATED (sat) FAT low sat fat

SODIUM
  ≤ 480 mg /RACC and LS; or
  ≤ 480 mg /50 g, if RACC is small
	SODIUM
	  ≤ 480 mg /RACC and LS; or
	  ≤ 480 mg /50 g, if RACC is small
		SODIUM
		  ≤ 600 mg /LS

CHOLESTEROL
  ≤ disclosure level
	CHOLESTEROL
	  < 95 mg /RACC & /100 g
		CHOLESTEROL
		  ≤ 90 mg /LS

BENEFICIAL NUTRIENTS Contains at least 10% of DV/RACC for vitamins A, C, calcium, iron, protein, or fiber The following are excepted: 1) raw fruits and vegetables; 2) frozen or canned single ingredient fruits and vegetables (may include ingredients whose addition does not change the nutrient profile of the fruit or vegetable); 3) enriched cereal-grain products that conform to a standard of identity in 21 C.F.R. 136, 137, 139.	BENEFICIAL NUTRIENTS Contains at least 10% of DV / RACC for vitamins A, C, calcium, iron, protein, or fiber	BENEFICIAL NUTRIENTS Contains at least 10% of the DV /LS of two nutrients (for a main dish product) or of three nutrients (for a meal product) of vitamin A, vitamin C, calcium, iron, protein, or fiber.
FORTIFICATION Per 21 C.F.R. § 104.20	FORTIFICATION Per 21 C.F.R. § 104.20	FORTIFICATION Per 21 C.F.R. § 104.20

OTHER CLAIMS
Food complies with established definition and declaration requirements for any specific nutrient content claim

NOTE: RACC = Reference Amount Customarily Consumed per Eating Occasion, LS = Labeled Serving, DV = Daily Value
RACC small = 30 g or less or 2 tablespoons or less
5/ Raw, single ingredient seafood or game meat once processed becomes an individual food, meal or main dish.

Rounding Rules for Declaring Nutrients

Nutrient Serving	(M) or (V)*	Core Nutrient	Units	Increment Rounding**	Insignificant Amount	Other Relevant Information***
Calories	M	X	cal	< 5 cal express as zero < 50 cal express to nearest 5 cal increment > 50 cal express to nearest 10 cal increment	< 5 cal	§ 101.9(c)(1)
Calories from fat	M		cal	< 5 cal express as zero < 50 cal express to nearest 5 cal increment > 50 cal express to nearest 10 cal increment	< 5 cal	If < 0.5 g fat: "*cal from fat*" not required § 101.9(c)(1)(ii)
Calories from saturated fat	V		cal	< 5 cal express as zero < 50 cal express to nearest 5 cal increment > 50 cal express to nearest 10 cal increment	< 5 cal	§ 101.9(c)(1)(iii)
Total fat	M	X	g	< 0.5 g express as zero < 5 g express to nearest 0.5 g increment > 5 g express to nearest 1 g increment	< 0.5 g	§ 101.9(c)(2)
Saturated fat	M		g	< 0.5 g express as zero < 5 g express to nearest 0.5 g increment > 5 g express to nearest 1 g increment	< 0.5 g	§ 101.9(c)(2)(i)
Trans fat	M		g	< 0.5 g express as zero < 5 g express to nearest 0.5 g increment > 5 g express to nearest 1 g increment	< 0.5 g	§ 101.9(c)(2)(ii)
Polyunsaturated & Monosaturated fat	V		g	< 0.5 g express as zero < 5 g express to nearest 0.5 g increment > 5 g express to nearest 1 g increment	< 0.5 g	§ 101.9(c)(2)(iii) & (iv)
Cholesterol	M		mg	< 2 mg express as zero 2–5 mg express as "less than 5 mg" > 5 mg express to nearest 5 mg increment	< 2 mg	§ 101.9(c)(3)
Sodium	M	X	mg	< 5 mg express as zero 5–140 mg express to nearest 5 mg increment > 140 mg express to nearest 10 mg increment	< 5 mg	§ 101.9(c)(4)

Nutrient Serving	(M) or (V)*	Core Nutrient	Units	Increment Rounding**	Insignificant Amount	Other Relevant Information***
Potassium	V		mg	< 5 mg express as zero 5–140 mg express to nearest 5 mg increment > 140 mg express to nearest 10 mg increment	< 5 mg	§ 101.9(c)(5)
Total carbohydrate	M	X	g	< 0.5 g express as zero < 1 g express as "Contains less than 1 g" OR "less than 1 g" > 1 g express to nearest 1 g increment	< 1 g	§ 101.9(c)(6)
Dietary fiber	M		g	< 0.5 g express as zero < 1 g express as "Contains less than 1 g" OR "less than 1 g" > 1 g express to nearest 1 g increment	< 1 g	§ 101.9(c)(6)(i)
Soluble & Insoluble fiber	V		g	< 0.5 g express as zero < 1 g express as "Contains less than 1 g" OR "less than 1g" > 1 g express to nearest 1 g increment	< 0.5 g	§ 101.9(c)(6)(i)(A) & (B)
Sugars	M		g	< 0.5 g express as zero < 1 g express as "Contains less than 1 g" OR "less than 1g" > 1 g express to nearest 1 g increment	< 0.5 g	§ 101.9(c)(6)(ii)
Sugar alcohol	V		g	< 0.5 g express as zero < 1 g express as "Contains less than 1 g" OR "less than 1g" > 1 g express to nearest 1 g increment	< 0.5 g	§ 101.9(c)(6)(iii)
Other carbohydrate	V		g	< 0.5 g express as zero < 1 g express as "Contains less than 1 g" OR "less than 1g" > 1 g express to nearest 1 g increment	< 0.5 g	§ 101.9(c)(6)(iv)
Protein	M	X	g	< 0.5 g express as zero < 1 g express as "Contains less than 1 g" OR "less than 1 g" > 1 g express to nearest 1 g increment	< 1 g	§ 101.9(c)(7)

Nutrient Serving	(M) or (V)*	Core Nutrient	Units	Increment Rounding**	Insignificant Amount	Other Relevant Information***
When declaring nutrients other than vitamins and minerals that have RDIs as a % DV	M		% DV	express to nearest 1% DV increment	< 1% DV	
Vitamins & minerals (express as % DV)	M		% DV	< 2% of RDI may be expressed as: (1) 2% if actual amount is 1.0% or more (2) zero (3) an asterisk that refers to statement "Contains less than 2% of the Daily Value of this (these nutrients) (nutrients)".... (4) for Vit A, C, calcium, iron: statement "Not a significant source of_____(listing the vitamins or minerals omitted)" < 10% of RDI express to nearest 2% increment > 10% – < 50% of RDI express to nearest 5% increment > 50% of RDI express to nearest 10% increment	< 2% RDI	Vitamins and minerals other than Vit. A, C, calcium and iron, listed in (8)(iv), are mandatory if added as nutrient supplement in food or if claim is made § 101.9(c)(8)(iii) & (iv)
Beta-carotene (express as % DV)	V		% DV	≤ 10% of RDI for vitamin A express to nearest 2% DV increment > 10% – < 50% of RDI for vitamin A express to nearest 5% DV increment > 50% of RDI for vitamin A express to nearest 10% DV increment		§ 101.9(c)(8)(vi)

* (M) Mandatory and (V) Voluntary
** To express to the nearest 1 g increment, amounts exactly halfway between two whole numbers or higher (e.g., 2.50 to 2.99 g) round up (e.g., 3 g), and amounts less than halfway between two whole numbers (e.g., 2.01 to 2.49 g) round down (e.g., 2 g).
*** NOTES FOR ROUNDING % Daily Value (DV) for Total Fat, Saturated Fat, Cholesterol, Sodium, Total Carbohydrate, Fiber, and Protein:
(1) To calculate % DV, divide either the actual (unrounded) quantitative amount or the declared (rounded) amount by the appropriate RDI or DRV. Use whichever amount will provide the greatest consistency on the food label and prevent unnecessary consumer confusion (§ 101.9(d)(7)(ii)).
(2) When % DV values fall between two whole numbers, rounding shall be as follows:
    —for values exactly halfway between two whole numbers or higher (e.g., 2.50 to 2.99) the value shall round up (e.g., 3%)
    —for values less than halfway between two whole numbers (e.g., 2.01 to 2.49) the values shall round down (e.g., 2%).

Definitions of Nutrient Content Claims

NUTRIENTS*	FREE	LOW	REDUCED/LESS	COMMENTS[1]
	Synonyms for "Free": "Zero," "No," "Without," "Trivial Source of," "Negligible Source of," "Dietarily Insignificant Source of" Definitions for "Free" for meals and main dishes are the stated values per labeled serving	Synonyms for "Low": "Little," ("Few" for Calories), "Contains a Small Amount of," "Low Source of"	Synonyms for "Reduced/Less": "Lower" ("Fewer" for Calories) "Modified" may be used in statement of identity Definitions for meals and main dishes are same as for individual foods on a per 100 g basis	For "Free," "Very Low," or "Low," must indicate if food meets a definition without benefit of special processing, alteration, formulation or reformulation; e.g., "broccoli, a fat-free food" or "celery, a low calorie food"
Calories § 101.60(b)	Less than 5 calories per reference amount and per labeled serving Not defined for meals or main dishes	40 calories or less per reference amount consumed if reference amount is greater than 30 grams (and per 50 g if reference amount is smaller) Meals and main dishes: 120 cal or less per 100 g	At least 25% fewer calories per reference amount than an appropriate reference food (or for meals and main dishes, at least 25% fewer calories per 100 g) Reference food may not be "Low Calorie" Uses term "Fewer" rather than "Less"....	"Light" or "Lite": If 50% or more of the calories are from fat, fat must be reduced by at least 50% per reference amount. If less than 50% of calories are from fat, fat must be reduced at least 50% or calories reduced at least 1/3 per reference amount § 101.56 "Light" or "Lite" meal or main dish product meets definition for "Low Calorie" or "Low Fat" meal and is labeled to indicate which definition is met For dietary supplements: Calorie claims can only be made when the reference product is greater than 40 calories per serving

NUTRIENTS*	FREE	LOW	REDUCED/LESS	COMMENTS[1]
Total Fat § 101.62(b)	Less than 0.5 g per reference amount and per labeled serving (or for meals and main dishes, less than 0.5 g per labeled serving) No ingredient that is fat or understood to contain fat except as in note 2	3 g or less per reference amount (and per 50 g if reference amount is small) Meals and main dishes: 3 g or less per 100 g and not more than 30% of calories from fat	At least 25% less fat per reference amount than an appropriate reference food (or for meals and main dishes, at least 25% less fat per 100 g) Reference food may not be "Low Fat"	"_____% Fat Free": OK if food meets the requirements for "Low Fat" 100% Fat Free: Food must be "Fat Free" "Light": See above For dietary supplements: Fat claims cannot be made for products that are 40 calories or less per serving
Saturated Fat § 101.62	Less than 0.5 g saturated fat and less than 0.5 g trans fatty acids per reference amount and per labeled serving (or for meals and main dishes, less than 0.5 g saturated fat and less than 0.5 g trans fatty acid per labeled serving) No ingredient that is understood to contain saturated fat except as in note 2	1 g or less per reference amount and 15% or fewer calories from saturated fat Meals and main dishes: 1 g or less per 100 g and less than 10% of calories from saturated fat	At least 25% less saturated fat per reference amount than an appropriate reference food (or for meals and main dishes, at least 25% less saturated fat per 100 g) Reference food may not be "Low Saturated Fat"	Next to all saturated fat claims, must declare the amount of cholesterol if 2 mg or more per reference amount, and the amount of total fat if more than 3 g per reference amount (or 0.5 g or more of total fat for "Saturated Fat Free") (or for meals and main dishes, per labeled serving) For dietary supplements: Saturated fat claims cannot be made for products that are 40 calories or less per serving

NUTRIENTS*	FREE	LOW	REDUCED/LESS	COMMENTS[1]
Cholesterol § 101.62(d)	Less than 2 mg per reference amount and per labeled serving (or for meals and main dishes, less than 2 mg per labeled serving) No ingredient that contains cholesterol except as in note 2	20 mg or less per reference amount (and per 50 g of food if reference amount is small) Meals and main dishes: 20 mg or less per 100 g	At least 25% less cholesterol per reference amount than an appropriate reference food (or for meals and main dishes, at least 25% less cholesterol per 100 g) Reference food may not be "Low Cholesterol"	CHOLESTEROL CLAIMS ONLY ALLOWED WHEN FOOD CONTAINS 2 g OR LESS SATURATED FAT PER REFERENCE AMOUNT, OR FOR MEALS AND MAIN DISHES PRODUCTS, PER LABELED SERVING SIZE FOR "FREE" CLAIMS OR PER 100 g FOR "LOW" AND "REDUCED/ LESS" CLAIMS Must declare the amount of total fat next to cholesterol claim when fat exceeds 13 g per reference amount or labeled serving (or per 50 g of food if reference amount is small), or when the fat exceeds 19.5 g per labeled serving for main dishes or 26 g for meal products For dietary supplements: cholesterol claims cannot be made for products that are 40 calories or less per serving

NUTRIENTS*	FREE	LOW	REDUCED/LESS	COMMENTS[1]
Sodium § 101.61	Less than 5 mg per reference amount and per labeled serving (or for meals and main dishes, less than 5 mg per labeled serving) No ingredient that is sodium chloride or generally understood to contain sodium except as in note 2 "Salt Free" must meet criterion for "Sodium Free"	140 mg or less per reference amount (and per 50 g if reference amount is small) Meals and main dishes: 140 mg or less per 100 g "Very Low Sodium": 35 mg or less per reference amount (and per 50 g if reference amount is small). For meals and main dishes: 35 mg or less per 100 g	At least 25% less sodium per reference amount than an appropriate reference food Reference food may not be "Low Sodium"	"Light" (for sodium reduced products): If food is "Low Calorie" and "Low Fat" and sodium is reduced by at least 50% "Light in Sodium" If sodium is reduced by at least 50% per reference amount. For meals and main dishes, "Light in Sodium" meets definition for "Low in Sodium" "No Salt Added" and "Unsalted" must meet conditions of use and must declare "This is Not A Sodium Free Food" on information panel if food is not "Sodium Free" "Lightly Salted": 50% less sodium than normally added to reference food and if not "Low Sodium" so labeled on information panel
Sugars § 101.60(c)	"Sugar Free": Less than 0.5 g sugars per reference amount and per labeled serving (or for meals and main dishes, less than 0.5 g per labeled serving) No ingredient that is a sugar or generally understood to contain sugars except as in note 2 Disclose calorie profile (e.g., "Low Calorie")	Not defined. No basis for a recommended intake	At least 25% less sugars per reference amount than an appropriate reference food (or for meals and main dishes, at least 25% less sugar per 100 g) May not use this claim on dietary supplements of vitamins and minerals	"No Added Sugars" and "Without Added Sugars" are allowed if no sugar or sugar containing ingredient is added during processing. State if food is not "Low" or "Reduced Calorie" The terms "Unsweetened" and "No Added Sweeteners" remain as factual statements Claims about reducing dental caries are implied health claims "Sugars" do not include sugar alcohols

NOTES:

[1]Restaurant Foods that bear claims are exempt from certain accompanying information that must be provided by foods from other sources. See specific provisions for more information.

[2]Except if the ingredient listed in the ingredient statement has an asterisk that refers to the footnote (e.g., "adds a trivial amount of fat").

*"Small Reference Amount" reference amount of 30 g or less or 2 tablespoons or less (for dehydrated foods that are typically consumed when rehydrated with water or a diluent containing an insignificant amount, as defined in § 101.9(f)(1) of all nutrients per reference amount, the per 50 g criterion refers to the prepared form of the food).

Statement "See _____ panel for nutrition information" must accompany all content claims when levels exceed: 13 g Fat, 4 g Saturated Fat, 60 mg Cholesterol, or 480 mg Sodium per reference amount, per labeled serving or, for foods with small reference amounts, per 50 g, disclosure statement is required as part of claim (e.g., "See side panel for information on fat and other nutrients").

Other Nutrient Content Claims	
"Lean"	On seafood or game meat that contains 10 g total fat, 4.5 g or less saturated fat and 95 mg cholesterol per reference amount and per 100 g (for meals & main dishes, meets criteria per 100 g and per label serving). On mixed dishes not measurable with a cup (as defined in 21 C.F.R. 101.12(b) in table 2) that contain less than 8 g total fat, 3.5 g or less saturated fat and less than 80 mg cholesterol per reference amount.
"Extra Lean"	On seafood or game meat that contains 5 g total fat, 2 g or less saturated fat and 95 mg cholesterol per reference amount and per 100 g (for meals and main dishes, meets criteria per 100 g and per label serving)
"Good Source," "Contains," or "Provides"	Contains 10% or more of Daily Value (DV) to describe protein, vitamins, minerals, dietary fiber or potassium per reference amount May be used on meals or main dishes to indicate that product contains a food that meets definition but may not be used to describe meal or main dish itself May not be used for total carbohydrates
"High," "Rich in," or "Excellent Source of"[4]	Contains 20% or more of Daily Value (DV) to describe protein, vitamins, minerals, dietary fiber, or potassium per reference amount May be used on meals or main dishes to indicate that product contains a food that meets definition but may not be used to describe meal or main dish itself May not be used for total carbohydrates
"More," "fortified," "enriched," "added, "extra," or "plus"	10% or more of the DV per reference amount May only be used for vitamins, minerals, protein, dietary fiber and potassium
"High Potency"	May be used on foods to describe individual vitamins or minerals that are present at 100% or more of the RDI per RACC or on a multi-ingredient food product that contains 100% or more of the RDI for at least 2/3 of the vitamins and minerals with RDIs and that are present in the product at 2% or more of the RDI (e.g., "High potency multivitamin, multimineral dietary supplement tablets").
"Modified"	May be used in statement of identity that bears a relative claim, e.g., "Modified Fat Cheese Cake, Contains 35% Less Fat Than Other Regular Cheese Cake"
Any Fiber Claim	If claim is made and food is not low in total fat, must state level total fat per labeled serving.
Antioxidant Claims	Each nutrient for which a claim is made has recognized antioxidant activity (scientific evidence that after absorption from GI tract, the substance participates in physiological, biochemical or cellular processes that inactivate free radicals or prevent free radical-initiated chemical reactions) An RDI has been established for each antioxidant nutrient present

Other Nutrient Content Claims
Each antioxidant nutrient is present in amounts sufficient to qualify for a claim of "high," "good" or "more"
Beta-carotene may be the subject of an antioxidant claim when the level of vitamin A present as beta-carotene in the food is sufficient to qualify for the claim.
Claim must identify the particular nutrients for which it is made, and may not use terms such as "complete" or "antioxidant complex"

4 Dietary supplement of vitamins and minerals can not use these claims to describe any nutrient or ingredient (e.g., fiber protein, psyllium, bran) other than vitamins or minerals

Relative Claims

To bear a relative claim about the level of a nutrient, the amount of that nutrient in the food must be compared to an amount of nutrient in an appropriate reference food as specified below.

"Light"/"Lite"	(1) A food representative of the type of food bearing the claim, e.g., average value of top three brands for representative value from valid data base; and (2) A similar food (e.g., potato chips for potato chips)
"Reduced" and "Added" (or "Fortified" and "Enriched")	(1) An established regular product or average representative product and (2) A similar food
"More" and "Less" (or "Fewer")	(1) An established regular product or average representative product and (2) A dissimilar food in the same product category which may be generally substituted for labeled food (e.g., potato chips for pretzels) or a similar food

Accompanying Information for Relative (or Comparative) Claims

For all relative claims, percent (or fraction) of change and identity of reference food must be declared in immediate proximity to the most prominent claim. Quantitative comparison of the amount of the nutrient in the product per labeled serving with that in the reference food must be declared on the information panel. A relative claim for decreased levels of a nutrient may not be made if the nutrient content of the reference food meets the requirement for a "low" claim for that nutrient (e.g., 3 g fat or less).

Implied Claims

Claims about a food or ingredient that suggest that the nutrient or ingredient is absent or present in a certain amount or claims about a food that suggest a food may be useful in maintaining healthy dietary practices and which are made with an explicit claim (e.g., "healthy, contains 3 grams of fat") are implied claims and are prohibited unless provided for in a regulation by FDA. In addition, the agency has devised a petition system whereby specific additional claims may be considered.

Claims that a food contains or is made with an ingredient that is known to contain a particular nutrient may be made if the product is "Low" in or a "Good Source" of the Nutrient associated with the claim (e.g., "good source of oat bran").

Equivalence claims: "Contains as much [nutrients] as a [food]" may be made if both reference food and labeled food are a "Good Source" of the nutrient on a per serving basis (e.g., "Contains as much vitamin C as an 8 ounce glass of orange juice").

The following label statements are generally not considered implied claims unless they are made in a nutrition context: 1) avoidance claims for religious, food intolerance, or other non-nutrition related reasons (e.g., "100% milk free"); 2) statements about non-nutritive substances (e.g., "no artificial colors"); 3) added value statements (e.g., "made with real butter"); 4) statements of identity (e.g., "corn oil" or "corn oil margarine"); and 5) special dietary statements made in compliance with a specific Part 105 provision.

The term "healthy" and related terms ("health," "healthful," "healthfully," "healthfulness," "healthier," "healthiest," "healthily" and "healthiness") may be used if the food meets the requirements in 21 C.F.R. § 101.65(d)(2).

Claims on Food for Infants and Children Less Than 2 Years of Age

Nutrient content claims are not permitted on foods intended specifically for infants and children less than 2 years of age except:

1) Claims describing the percentage of vitamins and minerals in a food in relation to a Daily Value.

2) Claims on infant formulas provided for in Part 107.

3) The terms "Unsweetened" and "Unsalted" as taste claims.

4) "Sugar Free" and "No Added Sugar" claims on dietary supplements only.

Terms Covered That Are Not Nutrient Content Claims

"Fresh"	A raw food that has not been frozen, heat processed, or otherwise preserved
"Fresh Frozen"	Food that was quickly frozen while still fresh

Chapter 11

The Regulation of Dietary Supplements

Anthony L. Young & Jennifer A. Davidson, Kleinfeld, Kaplan and Becker, LLP, Washington, D.C.

Key Points

- Since enactment of the Dietary Supplement Health and Education Act in 1994, dietary supplements have had their own set of safety standards and labeling laws. Previously, they were regulated as either foods or drugs.

- The definition of "dietary supplement" turns on a product's formulation or delivery form, and by the definition of "dietary ingredients." Any "dietary ingredient" intended to supplement the diet may be a dietary supplement, so long as it meets other statutory and regulatory criteria.

- Regardless of the form of a dietary supplement, it may not be represented as a conventional food or for use as the sole item of a meal or of the diet.

- The first use of an ingredient determines its eligibility for use as a dietary supplement. If a product is first marketed as a dietary supplement and is later approved as a drug or biologic, it can continue to be marketed as a dietary supplement. If the ingredient is first marketed, however, as a drug or biologic, it is not normally eligible to be regulated as a dietary supplement.

- As a practical matter, safety substantiation for dietary supplements should be similar to that for foods. Careful written documentation by one or more qualified experts supporting the safety of the ingredient for its recommended use will help a manufacturer not only meet its regulatory obligations under the Federal Food, Drug, and Cosmetic Act, but also minimize the risk of product liability exposure in the event that something goes wrong.

- "New dietary ingredients" are those that have not been marketed in the United States before October 15, 1994. If a new dietary ingredient has not been present in the food supply as an article used for food in a form in which the food has not been chemically altered, then the marketer must submit a notification to the Food and Drug Administration (FDA) at least 75 days before marketing the product with information demonstrating that dietary supplements containing the ingredient will reasonably be expected to be safe.

- Comprehensive good manufacturing practice regulations for dietary supplements became effective in 2008, 2009 or 2010, depending on company size. They establish process controls to assure dietary supplement quality.

Key Points, continued

- A dietary supplement label must include: a) a statement of identity; b) an ingredient statement; c) nutrition information in the form of a Supplement Facts box; d) the name and place of business of the manufacturer, packer or distributor; and e) an accurate statement of the quantity of contents.

- Within 30 days of making a structure-function claim, the marketer must notify FDA that it has included such claim on the label or labeling of its dietary supplement and such claims must be linked to a statutorily required disclaimer.

- The Federal Trade Commission (FTC) regulates dietary supplement advertising. The FTC has published a guide to assist in understanding its rules, entitled "Dietary Supplements: An Advertising Guide for Industry."

INTRODUCTION

For many years, Food and Drug Administration (FDA)-related laws provided only two regulatory options for dietary supplements: they could be regulated as either "foods" or "drugs." Under most circumstances, vitamin and mineral supplements were regulated as foods. As a result, FDA took the position that ingredients in dietary supplements had to meet the same safety standards as ingredients added to foods—that is, they had to be "generally recognized as safe" (GRAS) or covered by a food additive regulation.

FDA also normally took the position that labeling claims for dietary supplements were governed by the same standards as those for foods. As a result, many health-related claims—even claims that, by today's standards, would be considered relatively benign claims about a dietary supplement's effect on the healthy structure or function of the body—could cause a supplement to be regulated as a drug. From shortly after the enactment of the Federal Food, Drug, and Cosmetic Act (FDCA), FDA brought actions against marketers of "dietary supplements" that made very frank drug claims as well as those making claims that would now be considered to be structure-function claims. These reported cases helped shape the rich history of our food and drug law.

In 1994, however, much of this rich history was reversed with the enactment of the Dietary Supplement Health and Education Act (DSHEA), an amendment to the FDCA. DSHEA adopted, for the first time, a legal definition for "dietary supplement" and included provisions specifically applicable to dietary supplements (related primarily to the safety, labeling and ingredients to be used in such products). As a result, dietary supplements now occupy a unique niche in the framework of food law.

Dietary supplements are still "foods" under the law, and many of the laws and regulations applicable to foods continue to apply. Dietary ingredients in dietary supplements, however, no longer need to be GRAS or covered by a food additive regulation to be legally marketed. In addition, there are some unique health-related claims that are permitted only for dietary supplements and not for conventional foods.

What Is a "Dietary Supplement"?

Statutory Definition

DSHEA codified a new definition for dietary supplements. A product is a "dietary supplement" only if it conforms to section 201(ff) of the FDCA, which establishes various criteria governing 1) ingredients, 2) formulation, 3) intended use and 4) relationship to drugs and biologics. These criteria are as follows:

A product is a "dietary supplement" only if it meets various criteria governing
- *ingredients*
- *formulation*
- *intended use*
- *relationship to drugs and biologics*

Ingredients. A dietary supplement must contain one or more of the following: 1) a vitamin, 2) a mineral, 3) an herb or other botanical, 4) an amino acid, 5) a dietary substance for use by man to supplement the diet by increasing the total dietary intake or 6) a concentrate, metabolite, constituent, extract or combination of any of the ingredients listed above. In addition, a dietary supplement may not be a tobacco product.

If this list of eligible ingredients seems almost all encompassing, it is because of the phrase in the fifth part of the definition. The phrase "dietary substance for use by man to supplement the diet by increasing the total dietary intake" might lead one to conclude that any new substance added to the diet through a dietary supplement would be covered by this phrase because it will increase the dietary intake of that substance to above zero. FDA, however, has interpreted "dietary substance" to mean a substance that is or has been in the diet and used for food, and not a substance that is for the first time intended for use to supplement the diet. The rationale for this position is straightforward; "dietary" means of, or pertaining to, the diet and one cannot increase the total dietary intake of a substance that is not presently in the diet.

Formulation. Dietary supplement ingredients may be formulated either into products that are intended for ingestion in capsule, tablet, liquid, powder, softgel or gelcap form, or into products that are in conventional food form (such as beverages or nutrition bars). Regardless of how they are formulated, however, a dietary supplement may not be represented as a conventional food or for use as a sole item of a meal or of the diet.

If a product looks, smells and tastes like a conventional food, can it be marketed as a dietary supplement? The answer would appear to be "yes," but only so long as the product is not "represented as" a conventional food. And there's the rub: at this time, from FDA's perspective, it does not take much to "represent" a product as a conventional food. For example, describing a product as a "shake in chocolate and vanilla flavors" or as a "good tasting and satisfying treat," may be enough to "represent" it as a conventional food and exclude it from dietary supplement status. It might even be possible to "represent" a product as a conventional food by marketing it in retail stores next to conventional foods, but FDA has never formally taken this position. As a general rule, if a product can be consumed primarily for its taste or aroma, or if it can be substituted for a conventional food in the diet, then there is a risk that FDA could regulate it as a conventional food and not a dietary supplement. While there have been no court decisions on this issue, FDA has publicly objected to the characterization of soup, yogurt snack products and candy bar-like products as dietary supplements. In addition, it should be noted that—as the statutory language provides—FDA takes the position that products represented as "meal replacements" are ineligible for dietary supplement status.

What does "intended for ingestion" mean? A court opinion states "The ordinary and plain meaning of the term 'ingestion' means to take into the stomach and gastrointestinal tract by means of enteral administration." *United States v. Ten Cartons Ener-B Nasal Gel*, 888 F. Supp. 381, 393-94 (E.D.N.Y.), aff'd, 72 F.3d 285 (2d Cir. 1995). As a result, FDA has taken the position that nasal products, topical skin products, sublingual tablets, sprayed products that are absorbed from the mouth, aromatherapy products, gargles and throat lozenges are ineligible for dietary supplement status because they are not "intended for ingestion." On the other hand, FDA has accepted sublingual and lozenge products that are labeled with directions to be held in the mouth or under the tongue and then swallowed (ingested).

A dietary supplement may not be intended for use as a conventional food.

Intended Use. A dietary supplement must be labeled as a dietary supplement and be intended to supplement the diet. As discussed above, it may not be intended for use as a conventional food. Also, it may not be intended for use as a drug; that is, it may not be intended for use in the diagnosis, cure, mitigation, treatment or prevention of disease. (A dietary supplement, however, is not a "drug" if it is labeled with an authorized health claim, even though that claim may refer to a disease. Health claims are described later in this chapter.)

Relationship to Drugs and Biologics. A dietary supplement may, under some circumstances, include substances that are approved or investigational drugs— if the substances were used first as foods or dietary supplements.

Approved Drugs. Under the statute, a product is eligible for regulation as a dietary supplement if it is or includes an article that was approved as a new drug or licensed as a biologic, so long as the article was marketed as a dietary supplement or as a food prior to the date it was approved as a drug or biologic (unless FDA has issued a regulation stating otherwise). If the article was not marketed as a dietary supplement or food prior to the approval date, then it is ineligible for dietary supplement status (unless, again, FDA has issued a regulation stating otherwise).

Investigational Drugs. If an article is authorized for use in substantial clinical investigations that have been instituted and the existence of which have been made public, and if the article was not marketed as a dietary supplement or food prior to the date when it was authorized for investigational use, then it is ineligible for dietary supplement status (unless FDA has issued a regulation stating otherwise).

In its "Draft Guidance for Industry: Dietary Supplements: New Dietary Ingredient Notifications and Related Issues (July 2011) (Contains Nonbinding Recommendations Draft-Not for Implementation)," FDA discusses these provisions in a question-and-answer format and this Draft Guidance should be consulted if there is any approved or investigational drug issue with respect to a dietary ingredient.

The Definition of "Article." The rules summarized in the two paragraphs above refer to "articles"; that is, if an "article" was marketed as a dietary supplement before being approved as a new drug, it is then eligible for dietary supplement status. But what exactly is an "article"? A court decision suggests that it is any substance that is intended to be in a dietary supplement. For example, if the dietary supplement is formulated to contain an ingredient that has been approved as a new drug, and if it is sold or promoted based on the presence of that ingredient, then that ingredient may be considered the relevant "article" for purposes of determining whether the product is eligible for dietary supplement status. This may be true even if the ingredient is a relatively minor constituent in the overall dietary supplement product.

An article marketed as a dietary supplement before being approved as a new drug is eligible for dietary supplement status.

The court decision dealt with a product containing red yeast rice, called "Cholestin," which was marketed as a dietary supplement for cholesterol reduction. FDA argued that the red yeast rice was manufactured purposely to contain high levels of lovastatin, an approved cholesterol-lowering drug that was not marketed as a food or dietary supplement prior to approval. FDA also argued that Cholestin was promoted for its lovastatin content. Therefore, FDA considered lovastatin to be the relevant "article" for purposes of determining whether Cholestin was eligible for dietary supplement status. The manufacturer argued that Cholestin simply contained red yeast rice, a traditional Asian product that happens to include some lovastatin as a minor constituent. It considered red yeast rice to be the relevant "article." The court found for FDA, concluding that, in this case, the relevant "article" was lovastatin.

The manufacturer in that case also argued that, even if lovastatin were the relevant "article," it was eligible for dietary supplement status because it had been marketed as a constituent of many traditional foods prior to its having been approved as a drug. The court rejected this argument, however, agreeing with FDA that, for lovastatin to have been marketed in foods prior to approval as a drug, the marketed foods must have been promoted for their lovastatin content, or the lovastatin must have been increased or optimized as a constituent. As a result, Cholestin was determined to be a drug, not a dietary supplement, because it contained lovastatin, an article that was not marketed as a dietary supplement or food before it was approved as a drug. *Pharmanex Inc. v. Shalala*, 35 F. Supp. 2d 1341 (D. Utah 1999), *rev'd and remanded*, 221 F.3d 1151 (10th Cir. 2000).

DIETARY SUPPLEMENT SAFETY

Under the law, all dietary supplements must be safe (i.e., not "adulterated").

Under the law, all dietary supplements must be safe.

♦ A dietary supplement is considered adulterated if either it, or any dietary ingredient contained in it, presents a "significant or unreasonable risk of illness or injury" under conditions of use recommended or suggested in labeling (or if no conditions of use are suggested or recommended in the labeling, under "ordinary" conditions of use).

♦ A dietary supplement also is considered adulterated if either it, or any dietary ingredient contained in it, bears or contains any poisonous or deleterious substance that may render it injurious to health.

There is a parallel between dietary supplements and GRAS food substances: the law leaves the initial determination of safety up to the manufacturer and FDA has no authority to review the safety of a product prior to marketing. Unlike GRAS food substances, however, there is no requirement that dietary supplements be "generally recognized" in the scientific community "as safe," or that safety be based on data and information that is published or otherwise generally available to the scientific community.

A comparison of the safety standards for dietary supplements and GRAS food substances is interesting. Whereas dietary supplements may not present a "significant or unreasonable risk of illness or injury," FDA has concluded that GRAS status must be based on "reasonable certainty that the substance is not harmful under the intended conditions of use." (62 Fed. Reg. 18,937 (Apr. 17, 1997).) It is possible that, to have some confidence that one's dietary supplement does not present a "significant or unreasonable risk of illness or injury," one would have to have a "reasonable certainty that the substance is not harmful"—but that is entering into the realm of speculation. Suffice it to say that the exact scope of the data needed to support safety has not been as clearly elucidated for dietary supplements as it has been for foods.

The exact scope of data needed to support safety has not been as clearly elucidated for dietary supplements as it has been for foods.

Accordingly, a manufacturer would be well advised to substantiate the safety of dietary supplements in a manner that would be recognized as adequate by the scientific community. As a practical matter, such substantiation would be not unlike that used for foods. For well-known dietary ingredients, it might be appropriate to rely on a conclusion based on a general recognition of safety supported by a long period of common use at the levels intended for the target population, or supported by adequate studies reported in the scientific literature. Where there is any question, however, about the safety of a particular ingredient or product, or about the interpretation of the scientific literature, it would be prudent to obtain the supporting opinion of qualified experts. Regardless of how a safety conclusion is reached, the company should document its conclusion in sufficient detail to substantiate that it has addressed the relevant safety issues. Careful documentation of the safety of a dietary supplement will help a manufacturer not only to meet its regulatory obligations under the FDCA but also to minimize product liability exposure in the event that something goes wrong.

It is particularly important that a dietary supplement manufacturer prepare labeling with clear conditions for use and warnings consistent with the safety profile of its dietary supplement. Under the statute, if labeling does not limit the conditions for use, then a dietary supplement may be considered adulterated if it presents a significant or unreasonable risk of illness or injury under all "ordinary" conditions of use—which can be a very broad category of uses. In most cases, then, it is prudent to limit the conditions of use recommended or suggested in labeling through the use of clear directions and warnings. For example, in March 2002, FDA issued a Consumer Advisory with respect to dietary supplements containing the botanical ingredient kava.[1] Following this advisory, many manufacturers and distributors of such products included cautionary information from the advisory on product labels.

DSHEA offers dietary supplement manufacturers two protections in the event of a legal action by FDA against the safety of a product. First, it specifies that FDA shall bear the burden of proof on each element to show that a dietary supplement is adulterated. Second, the manufacturer has the opportunity to present its views to FDA (i.e., to try to persuade FDA not to refer the case to a U.S. Attorney). The burden of proof on FDA to show that a dietary supplement is not safe was firmly established in 2006 when the Tenth Circuit Court of Appeals held that "Congress expressly placed the burden of proof on the government to determine whether a dietary supplement is adulterated" and further stated that: "The burden remains on the agency to show that the risks associated with a dietary supplement outweigh benefits and are, therefore, unreasonable." (*Nutraceutical Corporation v. von Eschenbach*, 459 F.3d 1033.)

FDA bears the burden of proof on each element to show that a dietary supplement is adulterated.

In reaching its decision, the court relied upon the standard of review for such FDA decisions that has evolved over the past 20 years: "The review of scientific literature is properly the province of the FDA, to which this Court grants deference based on its expertise" (459 F.3d at 1043). Using this standard, and its own review of the record, the court found that FDA had made its case by the "preponderance of the evidence" standard set out in DSHEA.

As a practical matter, the burden of proof provision of DSHEA, as applied by the court in *Nutraceutical Corporation*, means that FDA may, through rulemaking, deem a dietary supplement (or dietary ingredient) to be adulterated. In so doing, FDA has the burden to show by a preponderance of the evidence that the risks are either significant or outweigh the benefits and are, therefore, unreasonable. In such a rulemaking, FDA's review of scientific information would normally be given deference because of the agency's expertise.

New Dietary Ingredients

Manufacturers are responsible for determining whether their ingredients meet the "new dietary ingredient" definition.

If a dietary supplement contains a "new dietary ingredient," then: 1) it is subject to an additional safety requirement, and 2) information on the ingredient may need to be reported to FDA prior to marketing the product.

♦ **What is a "new dietary ingredient"?** Any dietary ingredient that was not marketed in the United States in a dietary supplement before October 15, 1994, is a new dietary ingredient. Manufacturers are responsible for determining whether their ingredients meet this definition of "new."

♦ **What additional safety requirements apply?** There is an additional standard for a "new dietary ingredient": If a dietary supplement is, or contains, a "new dietary ingredient" for which there is inadequate information to provide reasonable assurance that such ingredient does not present a significant or unreasonable risk of illness or injury, when used under the conditions recommended or suggested in the labeling of the dietary supplement then the product is considered adulterated. Therefore, manufacturers must ensure that their "new" ingredients are adequately substantiated as being safe when used under the conditions recommended or suggested in the labeling of the dietary supplement in which they are contained. (Of course, as discussed above, all dietary ingredients should be substantiated as being safe.)

♦ ***When does information need to be reported to FDA?*** If a dietary supplement contains a new dietary ingredient, but the ingredient has been present in the food supply as an article used for food in a form in which the food has not been chemically altered, then it need not be reported to FDA. A report, however, must be submitted if this is not the case; that is, if the ingredient has not been present in the food supply, or if its form has been chemically altered for use in a dietary supplement as compared with its form in the food supply (known as a "reportable new dietary ingredient" or "reportable NDI").

♦ For a reportable NDI, two requirements must be met. First, there must be a history of use or other evidence establishing that the dietary ingredient, when used under the conditions recommended or suggested in the labeling of the dietary supplement, will reasonably be expected to be safe. Second, at least 75 days before being introduced or delivered for introduction into interstate commerce, the manufacturer or distributor of the dietary ingredient or dietary supplement must submit information to FDA, including any citation to and copies of published articles or unpublished reports of safety studies, that is the basis on which the manufacturer or distributor has concluded that a dietary supplement containing such dietary ingredient will reasonably be expected to be safe. (Note that FDA will keep the 75-day notification confidential for 90 days after its receipt; after that time it becomes public, except for trade secrets or confidential commercial information.)

If these two conditions for a reportable NDI are not met, then the dietary supplement is deemed adulterated, and may be subject to FDA enforcement action if and when it is marketed.

In its "Draft Guidance for Industry: Dietary Supplements: New Dietary Ingredient Notifications and Related Issues (July 2011) (Contains Nonbinding Recommendations Draft-Not for Implementation)," which FDA distributed for comment purposes only, FDA discusses the NDI provision in detail.

A docket in which NDI notifications are filed has been established on Regulations.gov.[2] From this docket, it is possible to determine how FDA has addressed each NDI notification that it has received.

A petition process also is available for reportable NDIs: the FDCA permits a petition to be filed proposing the issuance of an order prescribing the conditions under which an NDI reasonably will be expected to be safe. FDA must make a decision on such a petition within 180 days of its filing.

Facility Registration

Under the Public Health Security and Bioterrorism Preparedness and Response Act of 2002, owners, operators or agents in charge of domestic or foreign facilities that manufacture, process, pack or hold food, including dietary supplements, for consumption in the United States are required to register the facility with FDA. Retail establishments are exempt from registration.

Foreign facilities that manufacture, process, pack or hold food, including ingredients intended for use in dietary supplements, or dietary supplements, also are required to register unless food from that facility undergoes further processing (including packaging) by another foreign facility before the food is exported to the United States. If the subsequent foreign facility performs only a minimal activity, however, such as putting on a label, both facilities are required to register.

All facilities are also subject to the recordkeeping requirements of the Bioterrorism Act.

cGMPs

A dietary supplement is adulterated if it has been prepared, packed or held under conditions that do not meet current good manufacturing practice (cGMP) regulations. FDA promulgated cGMP regulations for dietary supplements on June 25, 2007 (72 Fed. Reg. 34,751; 21 C.F.R. Part 111). FDA established three compliance dates for the regulations, allowing a longer period of time for the smallest companies. All three dates have now passed, meaning all companies should now be in compliance with the cGMP regulations. The focus of the regulations is the requirement for each manufacturer to implement a system of production and process controls that covers all stages of manufacturing, packaging, labeling and holding of the dietary supplement to ensure the quality of dietary supplements and that dietary supplements are packaged and labeled as specified in the master manufacturing record required for each product.

FDA did not propose to require expiration dating for dietary supplements because, while "there are current and generally available methods to determine the expiration date of some dietary ingredients, for example vitamin C, we are uncertain whether there are current and generally available methods to determine the expiration dating of other dietary ingredients, especially botanical dietary ingredients." (68 Fed. Reg. 12,157, 12,203-4 (Mar. 13, 2003).) In the final cGMP rule, FDA confirmed this decision. Nonetheless, as a practical matter, expiration dating, or shelf-life dating as it is sometimes called, is for the most part a market necessity. And FDA has made clear that "any expiration date that you place on a product label (including a 'best if used by' date) should be supported by data." (72 Fed. Reg. 34,855-6.)

FDA Warning Letters to dietary supplement companies regarding cGMP violations provide a rich source of information regarding FDA's interpretation of the cGMP regulations and enforcement observations and may be found on FDA's website.[3] Under the FDA Food Safety Modernization Act (FSMA), food facilities are required to develop Hazard Analysis and Risk-Based Preventive Controls programs to help ensure food safety. This requirement does not apply to a facility that manufactures, processes, packs or holds dietary supplements that are in compliance with the cGMP requirements and adverse event reporting requirements (described below). However, FDA could apply this requirement to the manufacture of ingredients in dietary supplements that are not dietary ingredients (e.g., food additives, GRAS substances or color additives that are used for their technical effect in the supplements). FSMA also requires importers of food to implement foreign supplier verification programs to ensure that imported products meet U.S. legal requirements. There is no exception for dietary supplement manufacturers to this provision of the law. Similarly, dietary supplement manufacturers are not exempted from FSMA's provision empowering FDA to order recalls if a company refuses to recall in situations where FDA has found a reasonable probability that the product will cause serious adverse health consequences or death to humans.

FDA Warning Letters to dietary supplement companies regarding cGMP violations provide a rich source of information regarding FDA's interpretation of the cGMP regulations and enforcement observations.

Third-Party Substantiation of Identity, Purity and Safety

Prior to the promulgation of cGMPs for dietary supplements, a number of organizations made efforts to establish voluntary criteria for the identity, purity and safety of dietary supplements. Industry trade associations established voluntary cGMP systems whereby manufacturers could submit to inspections in order to assure customers of the integrity of their facilities and processes. These voluntary programs form the basis for educating the dietary supplement industry with respect to compliance with the FDA cGMP. The U.S. Pharmacopoeia now publishes monographs for dietary supplement ingredients. In addition the National Institutes of Health (NIH), through the Office of Dietary Supplements, provides information on dietary supplements and the safety of ingredients.[4]

Products That Combine an OTC Drug with a Dietary Supplement

A number of companies have considered marketing a combination over-the-counter (OTC) drug and dietary supplement product. For example, a combination of low-dose aspirin and vitamin E, or an OTC cough suppressant and vitamin C, have been considered. In theory, such combination products should be "legal," provided: a) the "drug side" of the product falls under an OTC monograph and is labeled properly; b) the "dietary supplement side" of the product does not make drug claims; and c) the dietary supplement ingredients can be deemed safe and suitable inactive ingredients that do not cause the product to become a "new drug" requiring submission of a new drug application.

FDA advises against the marketing of combination over-the-counter drug and dietary supplement products.

FDA, however, has strongly advised against the marketing of such products in a series of letters to companies, noting "serious concerns about the marketing of any such combination product," and stating that it would take "appropriate measures" against such products. From FDA's perspective, these combination products raise several public health issues. For example:

- **Safety and Efficacy:** The addition of a new ingredient to a legally marketed drug product could affect/interact with the safety and efficacy of the drug component.

- **Potentially Misleading:** Consumers may potentially believe that both components have been subjected to the more stringent drug regulatory requirements, when, in fact, only the drug component may have been reviewed by the agency for safety and effectiveness.

- **Consumer Confusion:** It is uncertain under what circumstances the disclaimer required by DSHEA for certain dietary supplement claims (as discussed further below) could appear on a combination product without causing consumer confusion.

These policies remain in effect as FDA firmly seeks to maintain the boundaries between drugs and dietary supplements. FDA has issued Warning Letters to two major OTC drug manufacturers after those companies introduced OTC drug/dietary supplement combination products to the market.[5]

Postmarketing Surveillance and the Dietary Supplement and Nonprescription Drug Consumer Protection Act

In 1993, FDA initiated adverse event monitoring for special nutritional products, including dietary supplements. This database consisted of reports from FDA's MedWatch program; FDA's field offices; other federal, state and local public health agencies; and letters and phone calls from consumers and health professionals. In 2002, FDA announced that this system was limited and that the information in it was provided in a manner that made it difficult for users to appropriately interpret adverse events. Accordingly, FDA removed this information from its website and the Center for Food Safety and Applied Nutrition (CFSAN) then developed a new system for tracking and analyzing adverse event reports involving foods, cosmetics and dietary supplements.

As the dietary supplement industry matured, it came to understand that a mandatory system for adverse event reporting would benefit all its various "stakeholders"—industry, consumers, healthcare professionals and regulators. On December 22, 2006, the Dietary Supplement and Nonprescription Drug Consumer Protection Act was signed into law. This law requires adverse event reporting and recordkeeping for dietary supplements and nonprescription drugs marketed without an approved new drug application. Dietary supplement manufacturers, packers or distributors must report serious adverse events that may be associated with the use of their dietary supplements to FDA.

Manufacturers, packers, or distributors of dietary supplements are required to report serious adverse events that may be associated with use of their products to FDA.

The basic requirement of the law is that serious adverse events (those events that report death, a life-threatening experience, inpatient hospitalization, a persistent or significant disability or incapacity, or a congenital anomaly or birth defect; or require, based on reasonable medical judgment, a medical or surgical intervention to prevent a serious outcome) must be reported to FDA within 15 business days of receipt. These reports and records associated with these reports must be kept, along with all other reports of adverse events (i.e., nonserious adverse events), for six years, and made available to FDA inspectors upon request. As with all reports of adverse events to FDA, submission of the report is not regarded as an admission that the dietary supplement involved caused or contributed to the adverse event being reported.

To facilitate reporting of adverse events, the law also requires that manufacturers and distributors include a domestic telephone number or domestic address on the label of their products through which they may receive a report of an adverse event.

Dietary Supplement Labeling

Required Components of the Dietary Supplement Label

The basic required labeling components for conventional foods that are described in FDA regulations at 21 C.F.R. § 101, Subpart A are also applicable to dietary supplements. A dietary supplement label must include:

♦ a statement of identity (e.g., "dietary supplement" or " supplement" (with the name of the dietary ingredient in the blank));

♦ an ingredient statement;

♦ nutrition information;

♦ the name and place of business of the manufacturer, packer or distributor; and

♦ an accurate statement of the quantity of contents, in terms of weight, measure or numerical count.

If any of the above information does not appear in the correct format on a dietary supplement label, then the product will be considered misbranded and subject to FDA enforcement action (unless an exemption applies). Additionally, as with conventional food claims, any claims on dietary supplement labels or labeling must be truthful and not misleading in any aspect. False or misleading claims on dietary supplement labels will render the product misbranded.

In April 2005, FDA published a dietary supplement labeling guide that provides plain-language information regarding the labeling of dietary supplements.[6]

Nutrition Labeling

Following enactment of the Nutrition Labeling and Education Act (NLEA) some confusion existed as to the type of nutrition information to be included on dietary supplement labels. The NLEA Nutrition Facts box (required for foods) was not easily translated to dietary supplements. DSHEA subsequently clarified this point, requiring that dietary supplements bear nutrition labeling "in a manner appropriate" for these products.

To this end, FDA promulgated regulations set forth in 21 C.F.R. § 101.36 that specify the detailed nutritional labeling requirements for dietary supplements. The regulations require a Supplement Facts box that is similar in format and appearance to the Nutrition Facts box required for conventional foods. The Supplement Facts box and its contents must appear on the label in the precise format and type size set forth in the regulations. The box must state "Supplement Facts" across the top and must include information such as the serving size, servings per container (unless it appears as part of the net contents declaration), a listing of any dietary ingredients that have a reference daily intake (RDI) or a daily reference value (DRV) and their subcomponents (e.g., total calories, calories from fat, total fat, saturated fat, cholesterol, sodium, total carbohydrate, dietary fiber, sugars, protein, vitamin A, vitamin C, calcium and iron), and the amount per serving and percent daily value (if applicable) of such ingredients. These ingredients are referred to in the regulations as "(b)(2)-dietary ingredients" (based on the section of the regulations in which they are defined, section 101.36(b)(2)). Certain other listed nutrients may be declared with these ingredients, but they must be declared if a claim is made about them.

The regulations also discuss dietary ingredients for which RDIs and DRVs have not been established. In contrast to the (b)(2)-dietary ingredients, these ingredients are referred to as "other dietary ingredients," and if present in the dietary supplement, must be declared with their amounts in a separate section of the Supplement Facts box, just below the (b)(2)-dietary ingredients.

Proprietary blends and sources of dietary ingredients also must be declared consistent with the regulations. The regulations also specify how to declare ingredients for multivitamin and botanical products.

The following is an example of a Supplement Facts box for a dietary supplement containing dietary ingredients with RDIs and DRVs. Other examples are provided in the regulations at 21 C.F.R. § 101.36.

The Supplement Facts box required for dietary supplements is similar in format and appearance to the Nutrition Facts box required for conventional foods.

Supplement Facts
Serving Size 1 Tablet

	Amount Per Serving	% Daily Value
Vitamin A (as retinyl acetate and 50% as beta-carotene)	5000 IU	100%
Vitamin C (as ascorbic acid)	60 mg	100%
Vitamin D (as cholecalciferol)	400 IU	100%
Vitamin E (as dl-alpha tocopheryl acetate)	30 IU	100%
Thiamin (as thiamin mononitrate)	1.5 mg	100%
Riboflavin	1.7 mg	100%
Niacin (as niacinamide)	20 mg	100%
Vitamin B$_6$ (as pyridoxine hydrochloride)	2.0 mg	100%
Folate (as folic acid)	400 mcg	100%
Vitamin B$_{12}$ (as cyanocobalamin)	6 mcg	100%
Biotin	30 mcg	10%
Pantothenic Acid (as calcium pantothenate)	10 mg	100%

Other ingredients: Gelatin, lactose, magnesium stearate, microcrystalline cellulose, FD&C Yellow No. 6, propylene glycol, propylparaben, and sodium benzoate.

Ingredient Labeling

The declaration of ingredients on a dietary supplement label is required. Under some circumstances, ingredients may be declared in the Supplement Facts box as source ingredients (e.g., in the declaration "calcium (as calcium carbonate)" the source ingredient is calcium carbonate). Ingredients that are not declared in the Supplement Facts box should appear in a statement of ingredients immediately below the Supplement Facts box or, if there is insufficient space, immediately contiguous and to the right of the box. The detailed requirements for the declaration of ingredients on dietary supplement products can be found at 21 C.F.R. §§ 101.4(g), (h), and 101.36(d)

Optional Labeling Claims for Dietary Supplements

Three categories of optional claims can be made on dietary supplement labels and labeling:

- *structure-function claims*
- *health claims*
- *nutrient content claims*

There are three categories of optional claims that can be made on dietary supplement labels and labeling: 1) structure-function claims, 2) health claims and 3) nutrient content claims.

♦ **Structure-Function Claims**

DSHEA added section 403(r)(6) to the FDCA, which sets forth four types of optional claims for dietary supplements commonly referred to as "structure-function claims." A statement is a permissible structure-function claim if it:

- ♦ claims a benefit related to a classical nutrient deficiency disease (e.g., scurvy) and discloses the prevalence of such disease in the United States; or

- ♦ describes the role of a nutrient or dietary ingredient intended to affect the structure or function in humans (e.g., "calcium builds strong bones"); or

- ♦ characterizes the documented mechanism by which a nutrient or dietary ingredient acts to maintain such structure or function (e.g., "antioxidants maintain cell integrity"); or

- ♦ describes general well-being from consumption of a nutrient or dietary ingredient.

These claims are permitted on dietary supplement labels and labeling so long as certain conditions are met:

- ♦ **Substantiation.** The manufacturer making the claim must have substantiation that the claim is truthful and not misleading. This means that prior to making a claim, the manufacturer must have substantiation that provides a reasonable basis for the express or implied message being conveyed. FDA has published a guidance document entitled "Substantiation for Dietary

Supplement Claims Made Under Section 403(r)(6) of the Federal Food, Drug, and Cosmetic Act" that provides guidelines for proper claim substantiation.[7]

♦ **Notification.** Within 30 days of making a structure-function claim, the manufacturer, packer or distributor must notify FDA's Office of Nutritional Products, Labeling and Dietary Supplements that it has included such a statement on the label or labeling of its product. Details on the information to be included in this notification are set forth in FDA regulations at 21 C.F.R. § 101.93. If FDA objects to the claim, it will send a "Courtesy Letter" to the notifier, normally within 30 days, explaining why the claim is considered by FDA to be unlawful. This Courtesy Letter provides guidance so that the manufacturer or retailer will have fair warning of FDA's position with regard to the claim. If the notifier fails to remove the claim from its labeling following a Courtesy Letter, it may be considered by FDA to be operating in violation of the law; there is a risk that FDA will initiate official enforcement action against the notifier and/or the product in the future.

♦ **Disclaimer.** The following disclaimer in boldface type must accompany a structure-function claim: **"This statement has not been evaluated by the Food and Drug Administration. This product is not intended to diagnose, treat, cure, or prevent any disease."** FDA regulations at 21 C.F.R. § 101.93 require that the disclaimer either appear immediately adjacent to the statement or appear elsewhere on the same page as the statement and linked to it by a symbol (e.g., asterisk). If the statement is linked by a symbol, it must be set off in a box.

What is an appropriate structure-function claim?

In January 2000, FDA published a final regulation (21 C.F.R. §§ 101.93(f), (g)) in an attempt to define structure-function claims and to clarify how such claims can be distinguished from unapproved health claims or "disease" claims. Notably, a structure-function claim may not state or imply that the dietary supplement treats, cures, mitigates or prevents disease. If it does, then the product may be subject to enforcement action as a drug, and/or as a dietary supplement that is labeled with an unauthorized health claim. Prohibited disease claims include those that assert that the product:

A structure-function claim cannot state or imply that the dietary supplement treats, cures, mitigates or prevents disease.

♦ has an effect on a specific disease or class of diseases,

♦ has an effect on the characteristic signs or symptoms of a disease,

♦ has an effect on an abnormal condition associated with a natural state, if the condition is uncommon or can cause significant harm,

♦ has an effect on a disease as described by one or more of the following:

- the name of the product,
- a statement about an ingredient in the product that has been regulated by FDA as a drug,
- citation of a publication on the immediate product label so as to imply disease prevention or treatment,
- use of the term "disease" except in general statements that do not refer to a specific disease or product, or
- pictures, symbols or vignettes,

♦ belongs to a class of products that is intended to diagnose, mitigate, treat, cure or prevent disease,

♦ is a substitute for a product that is a therapy for disease,

♦ augments a therapy or drug action intended to diagnose, mitigate, treat, cure or prevent disease,

♦ has a role in the body's response to a disease,

♦ treats, prevents or mitigates adverse events associated with a disease therapy, or otherwise suggests an effect on a disease or diseases.

Distinguishing between structure-function claim and "disease" claims is one of the most troublesome issues confronting label-writers for dietary supplements. The difficulty in distinguishing such claims is evidenced by a few examples: "helps promote digestion" is a permissible structure-function claim whereas "relieves acid indigestion" is a disease claim, and "helps support cartilage and joint function" is a structure-function claim, whereas "maintains normal bone density in post-menopausal women" is an implied disease claim (implying treatment for osteoporosis). The preamble to FDA's January 2000 final rule (65 Fed. Reg. 1,000 (Jan. 6, 2000)) provides a good discussion of these issues. In addition, FDA has published a guidance document entitled "Structure/Function Claims Small Entity Compliance Guide" that provides simple, straightforward guidance for making these claims.[8]

♦ Health Claims

A health claim generally is not permitted unless FDA has issued a regulation stating the conditions for use of such claim, including the specific permissible language of the claim.

Health claims either expressly or by implication characterize the relationship of a conventional food or dietary supplement to a disease or health-related condition. Described in more detail in FDA regulations at 21 C.F.R. § 101.14, a health claim generally is not permitted unless FDA has promulgated a regulation setting forth the conditions for use of such claim, including the specific permissible language for the claim. An example of an approved health claim published in FDA regulations is as follows: "25 grams of soy protein a day, as part of a diet low in saturated fat and cholesterol, may reduce the risk of heart disease. 1 capsule provides X grams of soy protein." 21 C.F.R. § 101.82.

FDA may issue a health claim regulation on its own or in response to a petition from a manufacturer. When FDA receives a petition requesting approval of a new health claim, the claim may be authorized only if FDA determines that there is significant scientific agreement among experts qualified by scientific training and experience to evaluate such claims (based on the totality of scientific evidence), and that the claim is supported by such evidence.

FDA has grappled with the standard for substantiation of health claims (i.e., what represents "significant scientific agreement"). The current approach is described in a January 2009 final guidance entitled "Evidence-Based Review System for the Scientific Evaluation of Health Claims."[9]

FDA has accepted certain "qualified" health claims for use in dietary supplement labeling although these qualified health claims do not appear in FDA regulations and the process for the formal regulatory approval of such claims is still evolving.

"Qualified" health claims may be made for dietary supplements as well as conventional foods.

An example of a qualified claim negotiated by FDA and the industry is as follows: "As part of a well-balanced diet that is low in saturated fat and cholesterol, folic acid, vitamin B6 and vitamin B12 may reduce the risk of vascular disease." A disclaimer immediately adjacent to the claim in the same font size must appear: "FDA evaluated the above claim and found that, while it is known that diets low in saturated fat and cholesterol reduce the risk of heart disease and other vascular diseases, the evidence in support of the above claim is inconclusive."[10] Qualified health claims may also be made for conventional foods.

FDA has also provided a guidance to the industry with respect to submissions in support of qualified health claims entitled "Guidance for Industry: FDA's Implementation of "Qualified Health Claims": Questions and Answers; Final Guidance."[11] FDA publishes its evaluation of qualified health claims on its website.[12]

♦ **Nutrient Content Claims**

Nutrient content claims are used by manufacturers to highlight specific nutritional attributes of their products through a uniform frame of reference. Examples of such claims are "good source of Vitamin C" or "low in fat." The regulations pertaining to nutrient content claims are set forth at 21 C.F.R. § 101.13 and in Subpart D of Part 101. These regulations apply both to conventional foods and to dietary supplements and specify the types of nutrient content claims that are permissible and their requirements. Generally, to make such claims, the specific language used must be defined in the regulations. If not already defined, a manufacturer may submit a petition to FDA for approval and publication in the regulations.

Specific nutrient content claims also are permitted, provided the manufacturer provides notice to FDA at least 120 days prior to making the claim that an authoritative statement is supported by a scientific body of the U.S. government. FDA must then issue a regulation or seek a court order to prohibit the claim. This method was utilized with respect to nutrient claims for DHA, EPA, and ALA from fish oils. Several years after three petitions were filed with respect to these ingredients, FDA published a proposed regulation in early 2008 that would disallow all but one of the claims.

The primary difference between the regulation of nutrient content claims for conventional foods and dietary supplements is that, for claims about an ingredient that is not defined in the regulations or for which FDA has not established an RDI or DRV, dietary supplements may make nutrient content claims that characterize the percentage level of a dietary ingredient (e.g., "contains 200% of the lycopene in a tomato"). For conventional foods, any such claims cannot be made without approval by FDA through publication in a regulation or acceptance of an authoritative statement of a scientific government body.

INFORMATION ABOUT DIETARY SUPPLEMENTS THAT IS NOT REGULATED AS "LABELING" (THIRD-PARTY LITERATURE)

"Labeling" has been broadly interpreted by the Supreme Court and may include promotional materials.

The definition of labeling for all FDA-regulated products is found in section 201(m) of the FDCA. It includes "all labels and other written, printed, or graphic matter (1) upon any article or any of its containers or wrappers, or (2) accompanying such article." This definition is important because it means that "labeling" encompasses more than just the label, which is the written material appearing on the immediate product container. "Labeling" has been interpreted broadly by the Supreme Court and may include promotional materials, such as brochures, letters and videos, even if they don't physically accompany the product at the time of the sale. Therefore, claims found in these promotional vehicles are subject to FDA's jurisdiction. Websites, according to FDA, may be considered labeling, at least under some circumstances—although the Federal Trade Commission (FTC) also considers them to be advertising.

If a dietary supplement is promoted through its labeling to treat, diagnose, cure, mitigate or prevent disease, then FDA may consider the product to be a drug that cannot be marketed without prior approval of a new drug application. Prior to DSHEA, it was FDA's position that books and other publications disseminated by a dietary supplement manufacturer were labeling, even if they were written by third parties, if that literature discussed a dietary supplement product. DSHEA, however, exempts this type of literature from being regulated as labeling. This exemption often is referred to as the "third-party literature" exemption. It permits manufacturers, distributors and retailers to disseminate scientific literature, books and other publications so long as the criteria set forth in section 403B of the FDCA are met. Such a publication may be used in connection with the sale of a dietary supplement when it meets all of the following criteria:

♦ it is not false or misleading;

♦ it does not promote a particular manufacturer or brand of a dietary supplement;

♦ it presents a balanced view of the information;

♦ it is physically separate from the dietary supplements, if displayed in a store; and

♦ it does not have any information appended to it (e.g., a sticker with a company's name or logo).

As a result, marketers of dietary supplements are permitted to legally disseminate publications that refer to disease treatment and prevention, so long as the above criteria are met. Note that DSHEA's legislative history suggests that this exemption does not apply to a summary of a publication other than an official abstract of a peer-reviewed scientific publication. Significantly, the language of the law does not include this limitation. To date, the effect of the more restrictive language included in the legislative history, however, has not been established.

DIETARY SUPPLEMENT ADVERTISING

The FTC is the federal agency generally responsible for regulating product advertising. With respect to FDA-regulated products, the FTC and FDA have worked together under a longstanding agreement governing the division of responsibilities between the two agencies. FDA has primary responsibility for regulating claims in labeling and the FTC has primary responsibility for regulating claims in advertising. This means that dietary supplement claims found in traditional advertising media such as television, radio and print will be regulated and enforced primarily by the FTC, whereas claims found on dietary supplement labels and brochures will be regulated and enforced primarily by FDA. Claims found on the Internet and in promotional videos have been

The FTC regulates claims in dietary supplement advertising.

considered either advertising or labeling, and therefore both the FTC and FDA have taken enforcement action against false claims appearing in these promotional vehicles.

In 1998, the FTC published a guide, "Dietary Supplements: An Advertising Guide for Industry."[13] Throughout the guide, the FTC reiterates its basic common-sense principles used to regulate advertising for any product: 1) all advertising must be truthful and not misleading; and 2) before disseminating an advertisement, advertisers must have adequate substantiation for all claims (the Prior Substantiation Doctrine). The guide further explains that, just as with other product claims, claims for dietary supplements generally will require substantiation with "competent and reliable scientific evidence." This is defined as: "tests, analyses, research, studies, or other evidence based on the expertise of professionals in the relevant area that have been conducted and evaluated in an objective manner by persons qualified to do so, using procedures generally accepted in the profession to yield accurate and reliable results."

If the weight of the evidence does not support a claim, the claim should not be made, even if qualified.

While there is no fixed formula for the type and number of studies a manufacturer must have to substantiate its claims, in most cases if the weight of the evidence does not support the claim, it should not be made, even if qualified. Manufacturers and retailers must consider all relevant research relating to the claimed benefit of their dietary supplement and should not focus only on research that supports the effect, while discounting research that does not. To ensure compliance with the FTC guidelines, manufacturers and retailers should: 1) carefully draft advertising claims with particular attention as to how claims are qualified and what express or implied messages are actually conveyed; and 2) carefully review the support for a claim to make sure it is scientifically sound, adequate in the context of the surrounding body of evidence, and relevant to the specific product and claim advertised.

In recent years, the FTC has been quite active in taking enforcement action against dietary supplement manufacturers and retailers making false, misleading or unsubstantiated claims about their products. As a result, some dietary supplement marketers have been required to pay consumer redress of up to $20 million, or more, due to false or misleading advertising claims made in advertising materials challenged by the FTC. In seeking redress, it is the FTC's position that sellers must return all "ill-gotten gains" to consumers. This means the value of the sales to consumers, not the net profits. In the usual case, the FTC requires the production of detailed financial information to track "ill-gotten gains" to assure that they are accounted for. In more than one recent case, the FTC has required the sale of company owners' homes, cars and boats as part of the resolution of the case.

In addition to the FTC, state attorneys general are also active from time to time in enforcing against false or misleading dietary supplement claims, and such actions often result in the payment of extensive monetary damages.

THE FUTURE OF DIETARY SUPPLEMENT REGULATION

Over the almost 15 years since DSHEA was passed, the regulatory scheme for dietary supplements has matured with regulations covering labeling, cGMP and a law that mandates the reporting of serious adverse events and the retention in company files of all adverse events. At the same time, FDA enforcement resources have been stretched and strained as more and more products regulated by the agency come from sources outside the United States. Against this background, the future of the dietary supplement industry may, in the main, be under the control of the industry itself. Over the next decade, the industry will come into compliance with cGMP through a learning process as FDA inspectors and manufacturers interact over the nuances of these regulations. At the same time, there will be a body of adverse event information that will be developed that will provide signals to both the industry and to regulators regarding dietary supplement safety.

The future of the dietary supplement industry is in its own hands.

The dietary supplement industry is still perceived by many healthcare professionals, the media and legislators as "unregulated." This is probably because the products come mainly in pill form, which gives them the appearance of drugs, but the products are not approved by FDA prior to marketing. While ephedrine alkaloid-containing dietary supplements remained on the market, the industry was barraged with bad publicity, usually associated with serious adverse events alleged to be associated with the use of products containing this ingredient. That publicity adversely affected the entire product category while often spiking ephedra sales upward. If the industry were to market another product alleged to cause serious adverse events at a level approaching what was reported with ephedra, legislative action to change the present regulatory structure would be a likely consequence. Accordingly, the future of the dietary supplement industry is in its own hands.

CONCLUSION

FDA's promulgation of cGMPs for dietary supplement manufacture and distribution, and legislation mandating adverse events reporting, have taken the dietary supplement category to a higher level of regulation.

The Dietary Supplement Health and Education Act of 1994 created a new regulatory scheme for dietary supplements. Since enactment, FDA has promulgated regulations implementing the law. Two recent events, the promulgation by FDA of cGMPs for dietary supplement manufacture and distribution, and the enactment of legislation mandating the reporting of serious adverse events associated with the use of dietary supplements, have taken this relatively newly created product category to another, higher, level of regulation.

Endnotes

1. See http://www.fda.gov/Food/ResourcesForYou/Consumers/ucm085482.htm.
2. See Docket FDA-1995-S-0039, *available at* http://www.regulations.gov/#!docketDetail;dct= FR%252BPR%252BN%252BO%252BSR;rpp=10;po=0;D=FDA-1995-S-0039.
3. http://www.fda.gov/ICECI/EnforcementActions/WarningLetters/default.htm.
4. See http://ods.od.nih.gov/.
5. http://www.fda.gov/ICECI/EnforcementActions/WarningLetters/2008/ucm1048456.htm; http://www.fda.gov/ICECI/EnforcementActions/WarningLetters/2008/ucm1048083.htm. http://www.fda.gov/ICECI/EnforcementActions/WarningLetters/2009/ucm188361.htm.
6. See http://www.fda.gov/Food/GuidanceComplianceRegulatoryInformation/Guidance Documents/DietarySupplements/DietarySupplementlabelingguide/default.htm.
7. See http://www.fda.gov/Food/GuidanceComplianceRegulatoryInformation/Guidance Documents/DietarySupplements/ucm073200.htm.
8. See http://www.fda.gov/Food/GuidanceComplianceRegulatoryInformation/Guidance Documents/DietarySupplements/ucm103340.htm.
9. See http://www.fda.gov/Food/GuidanceComplianceRegulatoryInformation/Guidance Documents/FoodLabelingNutrition/ucm073332.htm.
10. http://www.fda.gov/Food/LabelingNutrition/LabelClaims/QualifiedHealthClaims/ ucm072855.htm.
11. See http://www.fda.gov/Food/GuidanceComplianceRegulatoryInformation/Guidance Documents/FoodLabelingNutrition/ucm053843.htm.
12. FDA's determinations may be found at http://www.fda.gov/Food/LabelingNutrition/ LabelClaims/QualifiedHealthClaims/ucm073992.htm.
13. http://business.ftc.gov/documents/bus09-dietary-supplements-advertising-guide-industry.

Chapter 12

Introduction to Tobacco Product Regulation by FDA

Joseph A. Page, Georgetown University Law Center, Washington, D.C.

Key Points

- The Family Smoking Prevention and Tobacco Control Act (Tobacco Act or FSPTCA) subjects the manufacture, labeling, marketing and distribution of tobacco products to comprehensive federal regulation.
- The Tobacco Act created a new Chapter IX within the Federal Food, Drug, and Cosmetic Act.
- Cigarettes, cigarette tobacco, roll-your-own tobacco and smokeless tobacco fall within the definition of tobacco product.
- The Tobacco Act explicitly exempts from regulation raw tobacco and those who produce it.
- Adulteration and misbranding are among the many acts prohibited by the FSPTCA.
- Tobacco product manufacturers are required to report registration information, health-related information, records and reports, and test data to the Food and Drug Administration.
- The Tobacco Act regulates the production of modified risk tobacco products, which are sold for the purpose of reducing the dangers associated with the consumption of commercially available tobacco products.

INTRODUCTION

In 2009, four and a half decades after the publication of a U.S. Surgeon General's Report recognizing a causal connection between cigarette smoking and cancer, Congress enacted the Family Smoking Prevention and Tobacco Control Act (the Tobacco Act or FSPTCA), which for the first time subjected the manufacture, labeling, marketing and distribution of tobacco products to comprehensive federal regulation. The new law gave the U.S. Food and Drug Administration (FDA) authority to carry out its directives, most of which have become part of the Federal Food, Drug, and Cosmetic Act (FDCA).

A Brief History of Tobacco Product Regulation in the U.S.

The effort to bring the number-one cause of preventable deaths in the United States under legal control has been of epic dimensions. In the 1950s, scientific studies began to link cigarette smoking and cancer, which in turn incentivized personal-injury lawyers to launch tort suits against tobacco companies on behalf of cigarette consumers claiming that they had suffered smoking-related harm. In the early 1960s, a second front against the industry opened. The Federal Trade Commission (FTC), which has authority to promulgate trade regulation rules aimed at preventing deceptive commercial practices such as the dissemination of false advertising, began to give serious thought to the regulation of the labeling and promotion of cigarettes. The commission's initiative received a considerable boost from the publication of the Surgeon General's Report, which gave powerful support to FTC's argument that the failure to inform consumers of the health hazards associated with smoking amounted to a deceptive practice. Shortly thereafter, the Federal Communications Commission (FCC) opened a third front. Utilizing its so-called "fairness doctrine," which obligated broadcasters to provide free time for the airing of opposing views on matters of public controversy, the agency promulgated a rule that required television and radio stations accepting cigarette commercials to balance them by furnishing free time for anti-smoking messages, and an appellate court upheld the commission. FDA, however, remained on the sidelines, as it hewed to the view it had always taken—that so long as manufacturers made no disease-prevention claims, cigarettes escaped the embrace of the legal definition of "drug," and hence the agency had no authority to regulate them.

While the Federal Trade Commission and the Federal Communications Commission took action with regard to cigarettes, FDA remained of the view that so long as manufacturers made no disease-prevention claims, cigarettes escaped the legal definition of "drug," and hence the agency had no authority to regulate them.

In response to the initiatives of FTC and FCC, the tobacco industry helped persuade Congress in 1965 to enact a statute that required a specified health warning on cigarette packs,[1] and four years later, a law that both strengthened the warning and banned all electronic advertising of cigarettes.[2] This legislation also limited the FTC rulemaking, and brought to an end the need for FCC-mandated radio and TV counter-advertising.

The tobacco companies succeeded in warding off the "first wave" of personal-injury suits. Adopting a no-settlement approach and contesting each claim with all the considerable resources at their disposal, they wore down their opponents by forcing plaintiffs in each case to offer proof that the defendants knew or should have known of the hazards of smoking (or that cancer-causing cigarettes were not reasonably fit for their intended use), that cigarette smoking might cause cancer, and that smoking caused the harm suffered by individual claimants. Defendants also argued that smokers assumed the risks of smoking, which would amount to a complete defense. By requiring warnings, the 1965 and 1969 statutes made the latter defense even more robust, and in addition contained preemption provisions that companies could use as a shield against claims that they should have included additional, more stringent warnings on cigarette labels. Their strategy proved effective in the short run, as regulatory efforts waned and plaintiffs in tort suits continued to come up empty-handed.

The multifaceted campaign against the tobacco industry, however, did not wane as the annual body count attributable to cigarette smoking remained at high levels and additional diseases were linked to tobacco consumption. Congress passed a law that made the warning labels required on cigarette packs even more stark and explicit.[3] In addition, personal-injury lawyers seeking to take advantage of the evolving rule of strict liability in tort for defective products mounted a second wave of lawsuits. However, an emerging general consensus among courts and commentators posited that the new doctrine would not apply to goods that contained inherent, unavoidable risks. In addition, the United States Supreme Court ruled that the 1969 statute preempted many claims against the tobacco companies.[4]

In the 1990s, a third wave of suits began, as states filed legal actions seeking reimbursement from the tobacco industry for Medicaid expenses they had incurred for providing health benefits to citizens suffering ill health because of smoking, and plaintiffs in tort suits sought to utilize various techniques of claims aggregation. These lawsuits in their discovery phase began to produce documentary evidence that tobacco industry officials not only had long been fully aware of the addictive properties of nicotine, but they manipulated nicotine levels in order to keep cigarette smokers smoking.

In the 1990s states began filing lawsuits seeking reimbursement from the tobacco industry for Medicaid expenses they had incurred for providing health benefits to citizens suffering ill health because of smoking.

The issue soon attracted the attention of David Kessler, Commissioner of FDA, and further investigation by the agency convinced him to reverse FDA's hands-off position vis-à-vis tobacco products. After a lengthy rulemaking process, the agency published regulations based on a finding that cigarettes are medical devices designed and intended to deliver a drug—nicotine —into the human body, and put a number of restrictions on the marketing of these products to minors.[5] The industry then sought judicial review of the rules. A lower court upheld FDA's jurisdiction but invalidated, on statutory-construction grounds, the limits FDA sought to place on cigarette advertising and promotion. The latter ruling became moot in 2000. In *Food and Drug Administration v. Brown & Williamson Tobacco Corporation*,[6] the United States Supreme Court set aside the entire initiative on the ground that Congress never meant to include cigarettes within the meaning of the statutory terms "drug" or "medical device," unless their manufacturers made disease-prevention claims, and hence FDA had no authority to regulate them.

The failure of a subsequent attempt to revive the FDA regulations by making them part of a law that would settle claims being asserted against the tobacco companies by the states brought matters to a temporary halt on the legislative front. However, the states and a group of tobacco companies signed a so-called Master Settlement Agreement (MSA) that did not require approval by Congress. It required defendants to pay more than $200 billion to the states over the next quarter century, plus additional sums thereafter. It also imposed restrictions, like bans on promotional techniques aimed at minors. In 1999, the federal government opened a new judicial assault by filing a civil suit against the major tobacco companies under the Racketeer Influenced and Corrupt Organizations Act (RICO), asking for $280 billion in damages representing the disgorgement of ill-gotten gains, as well as injunctive relief, and early efforts by defendants to have the case dismissed met with denial.

In the end, pressure on Congress to take some action in response to the enormous damage being caused by tobacco products prevailed. Moreover, in a crucial turn of events, Philip Morris suddenly switched positions and came out in favor of a federal bill. The company provided important political support and participated actively in the drafting process. As a result, in 2009 Congress finally enacted comprehensive legislation that gave FDA legal authority to regulate tobacco products.

A PRELIMINARY LOOK AT THE TOBACCO ACT

The same enforcement mechanisms the government might use against manufacturers of food, drugs, cosmetics, medical devices and dietary supplements will for the most part be available in proceedings against the makers of tobacco products.

The statute eventually signed into law by President Barack Obama brought all tobacco products within the purview of the FDCA and gave administrative responsibility over them to FDA, on the ground that the agency was the most logical choice within the existing federal regulatory universe. This meant that the same enforcement mechanisms the government might use against manufacturers of food, drugs, cosmetics, medical devices and dietary supplements would for the most part be available in proceedings against the makers of tobacco products.

The Tobacco Act, which bristles with detail, created a new Chapter IX within the FDCA. It constructed a regulatory regime with elements that are in part novel and in part borrowed from pre-existing statutory language applicable to other products, and it incorporated elements of FDA's proposed 1996 rules as well.

The Preamble to the Tobacco Act

The Tobacco Act comprises the first of two divisions of Public Law 111-31. The initial six sections of the act amount to a preamble and include factual findings, a statement of purposes, and limitations on scope and effect, as well as a severability provision and modifications of deadlines that other sections of the statute impose on FDA.

The Tobacco Act does not incorporate any of these preliminary provisions into the text of the FDCA. Language in a statute's preamble cannot be used to contradict directive parts of a statute that are expressed clearly, but may be of help in construing ambiguities.

Language in a statute's preamble cannot be used to contradict directive parts of a statute that are expressed clearly, but may be of help in construing ambiguities.

Findings

The findings listed in section 2 are lengthy and detailed. Several themes emerge. Subsections (1) to (29) spell out the scope and dimensions of the health problems caused by tobacco products, and do so in a way that amounts to an understated yet unmistakable indictment of the behavior of the tobacco industry, especially in purposefully addicting minors to nicotine. Subsections (30) to (32) give reasons why the restrictions the act places on the advertising and promotion of tobacco products do not violate the free-speech guarantee of the First Amendment to the Constitution. Subsections (33) to (35) insert miscellaneous facts, such as the chronic nature of tobacco dependence, the need to achieve smoking cessation because it is the only safe alternative to smoking, and the link between the illicit trade of tobacco products and both organized crime and terrorist activity. Subsections (36) to (43) stress the importance of risk reduction as a goal of the regulation of tobacco products. Subsections (44) and (45) indicate why Congress decided to give FDA the task of administering the Tobacco Act. Subsection (46) explains why manufacturers should not be allowed to include in labeling or advertising any statement to the effect that FDA regulates the product. The last three subsections (47, 48 and 49) return to the backdrop of industry blameworthiness and cite findings of fact made in an exhaustive 2006 opinion by a United States District Court judge, to the effect that tobacco companies had not stopped targeting young people as potential smokers, and that they "designed their cigarettes to precisely control nicotine delivery levels and provide doses of nicotine sufficient to create and sustain addiction while also concealing much of their nicotine-related research."[7]

Purposes

The Tobacco Act's purposes, set out in section 3, justify the selection of FDA to take charge of regulating tobacco products and the creation of "new and flexible enforcement authority" to enable the agency to perform its duties. At the same time, they betray traces of internal inconsistency, with subsection (9) calling for the promotion of the cessation of smoking and subsection (7) directing FDA to continue to allow adults to purchase tobacco products. Subsection (6) speaks to a need to inform consumers about the ill effects that flow from the use of tobacco products, a goal that would not seem to have any impact on persons so helplessly addicted to nicotine that they are in no position to make free choices. Accurate information would be useful only to non-addicted adults willing and able to stop using tobacco products or non-users capable of making a choice about whether or not to begin using a tobacco product. Perhaps what Congress had in mind was the preservation of a libertarian value, the right of competent adults to decide to engage or continue to engage in risky conduct that endangers no one but themselves. However, neither the stated findings nor the goals make this point nor do they take account of how what some have termed massive market manipulation on the part of the tobacco industry may dilute individual freedom.

Scope and Effect

Section 4, dealing with the statute's scope and effect, places certain broad limits on the reach of the Tobacco Act. Subsection (a)(1) is somewhat enigmatic, stating that the act is not to be "construed to ... establish a precedent with regard to any other industry, situation, circumstance, or legal action." Statutes, of course, cannot take on the force of precedent that binds the legislative branch, since lawmakers, subject only to constitutional constraints, are free to borrow from or ignore existing statutes when they enact new laws. Hence, this language would seem to be directed at the courts. Yet it does not clearly indicate what kind of statutory interpretations are meant to fall under the "no-precedent" rule it purports to establish.

Nothing in the Tobacco Act affects any authority currently exercised by the Secretary of Agriculture over raw tobacco.

Section 4 also declares that nothing in the act affects any authority currently exercised by the Secretary of Agriculture over raw tobacco. This prevents FDA from imposing any health-related restrictions over tobacco until it leaves the control of the farmers who grew it or on the domain of the Internal Revenue Service with respect to excise taxes levied on tobacco products.

Broad Limitations on FDA Authority

The FSPTCA particularizes the scope of FDA's new regulatory authority by both detailing the powers delegated to the agency and by placing express limitations on them. On a broad level, Congress subjected FDA to two important restrictions. First, the Tobacco Act defines terms in ways that limit the scope of the statute. Second, the act excludes from FDA's regulatory reach certain entities engaged in tobacco-related activity.

Definitions

"Tobacco Product." Section 201(rr) of the FDCA spells out the meaning of the key phrase "tobacco product." The term encompasses "any product made or derived from tobacco that is intended for human consumption, including any component, part, or accessory of a tobacco product (except for raw materials other than tobacco used in manufacturing a component, part, or accessory of a tobacco product)."

Section 901(b) provides that Chapter IX applies to cigarettes, cigarette tobacco, roll-your-own tobacco and smokeless tobacco. Thus, these items fall automatically within the definition of "tobacco product." The subsection goes on to give FDA authority to promulgate regulations that include other items within the definition of "tobacco products." To make sense of this cryptic language, one must imagine a tobacco product that does not meet the definitions of one of the four products mentioned by name in section 901(b). For example, suppose that a dissolvable nicotine lozenge does not consist of cut, ground, powdered or leaf tobacco, and hence does not meet the statutory definition of "smokeless tobacco," but it is still a product that is "made or derived from tobacco," and therefore falls within the definition of "tobacco product." Section 901(b) seems to be a barrier that blocks FDA from regulating these kinds of lozenges under Chapter IX until the agency first goes through the administrative process of promulgating a regulation that deems them to be "tobacco products." An item that would otherwise fall within the definition of "tobacco product" is excluded from that category if it also falls within the definition of "drug" or "medical device," a proviso that eliminates the possibility of dual classification. In addition, once an item is by definition a "tobacco product," it cannot legally be sold in combination with any other product regulated under the FDCA.

An item that would otherwise fall within the definition of "tobacco product" is excluded from that category if it also falls within the definition of "drug" or "medical device."

"Additive." The definition of "additive" in section 900(1) is identical to the first part of the statutory definition of "food additive," and includes a similar specific parenthetical inclusion of materials intended for use in producing, manufacturing, packing, processing, preparing, treating, packaging, transporting, or holding. It does not replicate the food additive exclusion for substances generally recognized as safe, but it does exclude "tobacco or a pesticide chemical residue in or on raw tobacco or a pesticide chemical." Falling within the definition of tobacco "additive," however, does not carry with it the same consequences as classification as a "food additive." In the latter instance, the additive could not be marketed without premarket approval by FDA. There is no similar requirement for tobacco "additives."

"Smokeless Tobacco." Section 900(18) defines "smokeless tobacco" as "any tobacco product that consists of cut, ground, powdered, or leaf tobacco, and that is intended to be placed in the oral or nasal cavity." Products that fall squarely within this definitional category include snuff and chewing tobacco.

FDA has issued a statement asserting its authority to potentially regulate dissolvable tobacco products, such as nicotine lozenges, as "smokeless tobacco."

FDA has issued a statement asserting its authority to regulate dissolvable tobacco products as "smokeless tobacco." These items would include nicotine lozenges meant to be placed in the mouth, where they gradually dissolve, allowing the ingestion of nicotine. To meet the definition, such products would also need to consist of "cut, ground, powdered, or leaf tobacco," which seems to be the case with most of these items since they are made from compressed tobacco. The broad requirement that they be "intended to be placed in the oral cavity" would logically encompass pellets designed to dissolve in the mouth. However, in response to a section 911 Modified Risk Tobacco Product Application filed by Star Scientific, Inc. for its "Ariva-BDL" and "Stonewall-BDL" dissolvable tobacco lozenges, in March 2011, FDA sent the company a letter stating that it determined that its products are not tobacco products currently regulated by the Tobacco Act (i.e., FDA determined that Star Scientific's products did not fall within meaning of cigarettes, cigarette tobacco, smokeless tobacco or roll-your-own tobacco). The reasoning behind FDA's decision regarding Star Scientific's dissolvable tobacco lozenges is not publicly available. To the extent that dissolvable tobacco lozenges contain extracted tobacco to the exclusion of cut, ground, powdered or leaf tobacco, such products would not fall within the meaning of smokeless tobacco.

Similarly, another potential class of tobacco products that could fall within the meaning of smokeless tobacco are heatless, smoke-free tobacco inhalers that contain cut, ground, powdered or leaf tobacco, provided that such a product, or a component, part, or accessory thereof (e.g., a mouthpiece), must be placed in the oral or nasal cavity for such product to be consumed.

Exclusion for Raw Tobacco

The FSPTCA explicitly exempts raw tobacco and those who produce it. The definition of "tobacco product" in section 201(rr)(1) embraces "any product made or derived from tobacco," which would not logically include the raw tobacco itself. Section 901(c)(2)(A), moreover, removes from the scope of Chapter IX "tobacco leaf that is not in the possession of a manufacturer of tobacco products," as well as "the producers of tobacco leaf, including tobacco growers, tobacco warehouses, and tobacco grower cooperatives …." Reflecting an awareness of FDA's occasional forays into overly creative interpretation, Congress added section 901(c)(2)(C), which declares that no exercise of statutory construction should permit the agency "to promulgate regulations on any matter that involves the production of tobacco leaf or a producer thereof, other than activities by a manufacturer affecting production."

PROHIBITED ACTS

Adulteration

The Tobacco Act sets out eight distinct ways by which FDA might deem a tobacco product to have been adulterated. Three of them relate to actual or potential contamination caused by a direct exposure to a harmful substance or condition. Four relate to what might be termed indirect adulteration caused by the failure to conform to regulatory requirements designed to protect against actual or potential contamination. One has very little, if anything, to do with contamination.

The Tobacco Act sets out eight distinct ways by which FDA might deem a tobacco product to be adulterated.

Actual or Potential Contamination. Section 902(1) of the FDCA provides that a tobacco product is adulterated if "it consists in whole or in part of any filthy, putrid, or decomposed substance, or is otherwise contaminated by any added poisonous or added deleterious substance that may render the product injurious to health." The first clause is copied verbatim from section 501(a)(1), dealing with adulterated drugs and devices. The second is less straightforward, taken from the "may-render-injurious" standard for added substances in food. Neither the courts nor FDA have elaborated on the meaning of this language, mainly because of the multitude of special provisions Congress has inserted into the FDCA to regulate specific added substances. The adverb "otherwise" suggests that the harmful effect from an added substance must result from a causative factor other than filth, putrescence or decomposition. This section seems to deal with health risks that are marginal, certainly when compared to the inherent dangers posed by tobacco products, so that FDA is not likely to assign a high priority to its enforcement.

Subsections (2) and (3), dealing with insanitary conditions and packaging composed of poisonous or deleterious substances, copy verbatim the standards for the adulteration of drugs and medical devices.

Indirect Adulteration. The Tobacco Act authorizes FDA to set tobacco product standards, review certain tobacco products before they can be marketed, promulgate rules that specify good manufacturing practices and regulate modified risk tobacco products. These provisions aim in part to prevent tobacco products that might carry with them risks even greater than the hazards inherent in them from entering the stream of commerce. Section 902 classifies as adulterated any tobacco products that have been marketed but do not comply with regulations designed to protect consumers from these additional risks, without regard to whether the products in question were actually harmful, or had been exposed to actual insanitary conditions, or had come into contact with any actual or potentially harmful substance.

Technical Adulteration. Section 902(4) deals with tobacco products whose manufacturer has violated provisions of section 919 requiring the payment of user fees. The link between user fees and the factual contaminating of a product is highly tenuous, perhaps based on the supposition that a manufacturer's refusal to pay the fees might in some way hinder FDA in its efforts to prevent the marketing of tobacco products that subject consumers to the risk of adulteration.

Misbranding

Section 903 takes a multi-pronged approach to misbranding, which, like adulteration, is a prohibited act. First, it contains a general prohibition against false or misleading labeling or advertising of a tobacco product. Second, the section specifically lists certain information that must appear on the labels of tobacco products, and provides that a label not bearing this information will be deemed misbranded. Third, with respect to advertising as well as labeling, the section categorizes as misbranding failures to conform to certain of the act's requirements identifying information that must be conveyed to potential consumers and customers.

A tobacco product can be deemed misbranded due to:

- *false or misleading labeling or advertising*
- *failure to list certain factual information on the labeling*
- *failure to include required identifying information with respect to both labeling and advertising*

In addition to the substantive requirements that certain information appear on labels and labeling, section 903 speaks to the method by which this information is to be conveyed. Subsection (a)(3) provides that mandated information must be prominent and conspicuous and must be comprehensible to the ordinary consumer under ordinary conditions of purchase and use; if not, the product may be deemed misbranded.

General Prohibition Against False or Misleading Statements. Section 903(a)(1) begins with a general proposition, found elsewhere in the FDCA, to the effect that the labeling of a tobacco product is misbranded if it is "false or misleading in any particular." Section 903(a)(8) applies this rule to advertising as well.

The supplementary language in section 201(n), to the effect that the failure to reveal material facts may be relevant in determining whether labeling or advertising is false or misleading in any particular, is also applicable to tobacco products. Hence, the prohibition against misbranding covers not only untrue affirmations but also omissions that create misimpressions.

The prohibition against misbranding covers not only untrue affirmations but also omissions that create misimpressions.

As a general proposition, FDA may use its informal rulemaking authority to declare as misleading the failure to disclose information not specifically required by other sections of Chapter IX. The extensive jurisprudence that section 201(n) has generated in cases involving other product categories may be relevant in cases involving tobacco products. However, the Tobacco Act contains so many particularized disclosure requirements that FDA is unlikely to make frequent or significant use of section 903(a)(1).

Specific Requirements Contained in Section 903. Section 903(a)(2) requires that the labels of tobacco products in package form bear certain factual information, such as the name and place of business of the manufacturer. Section 903(a)(8) imposes a similar mandate for advertisements.

Specific Requirements Contained in Other Sections. Section 903 puts teeth into provisions found in other sections of the Tobacco Act and requires that specific information designated either by those provisions or by FDA regulations appear on the labeling or advertisements of tobacco products. These include sections 920(a) (origin labeling for tobacco products other than cigarettes), 905 (registration information) and 907 (labeling required by a tobacco product standard).

In addition, section 903 designates as misbranding the failure to comply with certain statutory or regulatory requirements imposed elsewhere in Chapter IX of the act and having nothing to do with the communication of information to consumers. These mandates encompass restrictions on the sale and distribution of tobacco products, the failure to comply with requirements to furnish health information to FDA, the failure to comply with FDA orders that notices of risks be given or recalls undertaken, and the failure to keep required records and reports and provide them to FDA when requested.

Other Prohibited Acts

In addition to applying the concepts of adulteration and misbranding to the manufacture and marketing of tobacco products, the FSPTCA adds a number of particularized items to the long list of prohibited acts in section 301 of the FDCA. These include: failure to comply with recordkeeping and reporting requirements mandated by sections 909 and 920; failure to furnish health information, as required by section 904; and failure to comply with substantive obligations as they relate to labeling (section 903(b)), tobacco product standards (section 907), notification (section 908), modified risk tobacco products (section 911) and advertising (section 913). Other miscellaneous prohibitions relate to the shipping of a detained product, the sale of tobacco products in violation of a no-sale order, the counterfeiting of tobacco products, their charitable distribution, and the failure on the part of a manufacturer or distributor to report knowledge of the illegal trade of tobacco products.

Finally, section 301(tt) contains an explicit prohibition against any representation in the labeling or advertising of tobacco products to the effect that FDA approves or endorses them, or considers them safe, or that tobacco products are safe and less harmful because they are regulated by FDA. To the extent that such representations are false or misleading, they would also constitute misbranding. However, the advantage of this section is that it dispenses with the need for the government to prove that such statements amount to deception.

There is an explicit prohibition in the FDCA against any representation in the labeling or advertising of tobacco products to the effect that FDA approves or endorses them, or considers them safe, or that tobacco products are safe and less harmful because they are regulated by FDA.

Enforcement

The enforcement options that the government can invoke against the commission of prohibited acts relating to tobacco products fall into three categories: 1) they may be identical to mechanisms applicable to food, drugs, medical devices and cosmetics; 2) they may be identical to mechanisms applicable only to certain products regulated by the FDCA; and 3) they may be unique to tobacco products.

Common Mechanisms. The rules that govern criminal penalties and injunctions in enforcement actions dealing with food, drugs, cosmetics and medical devices also apply to tobacco products. This means that the case law and rules interpreting the imposition of these mechanisms in proceedings involving these products will also govern proceedings affecting tobacco products. Moreover, tobacco establishments registered with FDA are subject to mandatory biennial inspections governed by section 704, which also authorizes inspections of food, drug, medical device and cosmetics establishments. Finally, the provision of the FDCA giving FDA authority to generate publicity also applies to tobacco products.

Selective Mechanisms. Also applicable to tobacco products are the substantive and procedural rules governing judicial actions to seize medical devices and administrative proceedings to detain them. Moreover, section 303(f)(5), containing procedural rules for the imposition of civil penalties, applies to all products, including tobacco products, implicated in statutory violations for which these sanctions might be imposed.

Unique Mechanisms. The Tobacco Act creates a special section authorizing the assessment of civil penalties for statutory violations in cases involving tobacco products. This provision specifies the amounts of penalties that may be awarded, and the effect of a defendant's efforts to correct a violation.

The Tobacco Act also permits the government to impose a no-tobacco-sale order on retail outlets found to have committed repeated violations of regulations promulgated under section 906(d), dealing with restrictions on the sale and distribution of tobacco products.

REPORTING REQUIREMENTS

The Tobacco Act requires all tobacco product manufacturers to report certain information to FDA. These mandates help the agency accomplish a principal goal of the act, "to impose appropriate regulatory controls on the tobacco industry," a task that will require FDA access to data that only the industry can provide. The statute itself particularizes some of these reporting requirements. In other instances, it authorizes FDA to promulgate rules mandating the submission of additional information.

All tobacco product manufacturers are required to report certain information to FDA so as to allow the agency "to impose appropriate regulatory controls on the tobacco industry."

Section 905 calls for the annual registration of entities engaged in the manufacture of tobacco products. Section 904 obliges the submission of health-related information to FDA. Section 909 authorizes FDA to issue regulations requiring the maintenance of records and the submission of reports deemed necessary for assuring that tobacco products are not adulterated or misbranded, and for otherwise protecting the public health. Section 915 directs FDA to finalize rules requiring tests and the disclosure of test results when the agency deems this necessary to safeguard the public.

The act also places limitations on reporting requirements, in order to protect the tobacco industry from data requests that are either quantitatively or qualitatively unreasonable. Moreover, some reporting obligations apply only to certain tobacco products, such as those intended to modify risks.

Registration

Section 905, dealing with annual registration, applies to existing domestic manufacturers, new domestic manufacturers and foreign manufacturers whose tobacco products will be imported into the United States. Domestic manufacturers must report their names, places of business and all other tobacco-related establishments they operate. Foreign establishments will be subject to registration requirements established by FDA regulations.

Registration requirements for tobacco product manufacturers closely track the language of FDCA § 510, which sets out the registration requirements for producers of drugs and devices.

These mandates closely track the language of section 510, which sets out the requirements for the registration of producers of drugs and devices. Thus, subsection 905(b) copies section 510(b) by requiring the registration of all establishments engaged in "manufacture, preparation, compounding or processing"; in language taken directly from sections 510(a) and (b), section 905(a) includes repackagers, and subsection (b) requires that in the case of partnerships the "name" include each partner, and in the case of corporations, the "name" include each corporate officer, director and the state of incorporation.

The information that must accompany registration includes not only names and places of business, but also "a copy of all consumer information and other labeling" and a sample of advertisements for the product. The act does not define the somewhat vague term "consumer information." Its linkage to the phrase "other labeling" suggests strongly that it incorporates information that has the same characteristics as labeling. Hence, it would seem to embrace any material that a tobacco company communicates to consumers, even if it does not fall within the sweep of the terms "labeling" and "advertising."

Health-Related Information

Section 904(a) obligates tobacco companies to submit to FDA a list of all ingredients in their products, as well as a description of the content, delivery and form of nicotine contained therein, a list of all product constituents determined by FDA to be hazardous, and all documents concerning the health, toxicological, behavioral or physiological effects of their tobacco products.

Section 904(b) expands even further the duty to report health-related information. It gives FDA authority to promulgate regulations requiring the submission of all documents incorporating research done, supported by or in the possession of tobacco companies and relating to the health, toxicological, behavioral or physiological effects of tobacco products, or relating to the existence of technology that might reduce health risks associated with tobacco products, and all documents relating to marketing research and its effectiveness.

Records and Reports

Section 909(a) gives FDA broad authority to issue regulations requiring the maintenance of records and the making of reports deemed necessary to protect the public health. The only example specifically provided targets "information that reasonably suggests that … marketed tobacco products may have caused or contributed to a serious unexpected adverse experience associated with the use of the product or any significant increase in the frequency of a serious, expected adverse product experience."

The Tobacco Act does not explain the meaning of the term "serious adverse experience," a curious omission because the expression "serious adverse drug experience" is defined in Chapter V of the FDCA. Since the ordinary use of tobacco products can cause death or certain kinds of serious bodily harm, the term must refer to other types of serious bodily harm, or an increase in the rate of death or serious bodily harm normally caused by these products.

Subsection 909(a) requires FDA to provide reasons for the reporting rules it is imposing. It also contains some specific limitations on FDA's authority to promulgate regulations dealing with records and reports. For example, they must not be "unduly burdensome," and FDA must balance the cost of complying with them against the health benefits they are expected to produce. Curiously, this is the only Tobacco Act provision that directs FDA to take into account financial burdens that a regulation might impose on tobacco companies.

FDA must provide reasons for the reporting rules it imposes.

A further reporting requirement is contained in section 909(b), which calls on FDA to issue regulations mandating that the agency be notified whenever a tobacco producer takes corrective action on its own to remove a tobacco product from the market in order to reduce a health risk or because the product violates some provision of Chapter IX.

Test Data

Section 915(b) directs FDA to finalize regulations that will require the tobacco industry to test product ingredients and additives by brand and sub-brand and to report the results; and to make public disclosures of the results of tests on tar, nicotine and other constituents as determined by the agency. Section 915(c) permits FDA to conduct or to require tests on constituents, including constituents of smoke, and to require the public disclosure of results.

Tobacco Product Standards

Although section 907 bears the title "Tobacco Product Standards," it in fact conflates the concepts of standards and bans by authorizing (or barring) the prohibition of certain types of tobacco products while at the same time legalizing the regulatory imposition of requirements relating to their composition, design, labeling or marketing. Thus, the section gives FDA authority to set the latter type of standard, and at the same time creates self-executing rules prohibiting the inclusion of certain flavors as the characterizing ingredients in cigarettes and certain pesticide residues in tobacco. Violations of these rules and standards would amount to prohibited acts.

Special Rules

Consistent with a major purpose of the Tobacco Act—the protection of minors from the perils of cigarette smoke—section 907(a)(1)(A) prohibits the inclusion of flavors, herbs and spices as constituents or additives amounting to ingredients that characterize cigarettes. They may be artificial or natural, and might include strawberry, grape, orange, clove, cinnamon, pineapple, vanilla, coconut, licorice, cocoa, cherry or coffee—all flavors that might be appealing to young people. FDA may use this version of its standard-setting authority to set rules for artificial or natural flavors, herbs or spices not enumerated in section 907(a)(1)(A). Tobacco flavor receives a permanent exemption from this ban.

A flavor given special treatment is menthol because of its special appeal to African-American smokers, more than three-quarters of whom use cigarettes spiced with it and because of increased risks of harm associated with them. Section 907(a)(1)(A) permits FDA to ban menthol cigarettes, but only after first obtaining a report and recommendation from its Tobacco Products Scientific Advisory Committee and then promulgating a regulation under section 907(a)(3). On March 25, 2011, the committee recommended that FDA take appropriate action to remove menthol cigarettes from the marketplace.

The special rules in FDCA § 907(a)(1)(A) apply only to cigarettes and their component parts.

The special rules in section 907(a)(1)(A) apply only to cigarettes and their component parts. Thus, a manufacturer might be able to circumvent the ban by converting its flavored cigarettes into flavored cigars. FDA would then have to go through the process for setting a tobacco product standard that would extend the flavor ban beyond cigarettes.

Promulgation of Standards for Tobacco Products

In addition to creating the special, self-executing rules in subsection (a)(1), section 907 gives FDA the power to develop tobacco product standards. The act spells out with considerable detail the types of standards that might be adopted, the factors FDA must take into account in promulgating a standard, and the procedure the agency must use.

Types of Standards. Although the act nowhere defines the term "tobacco product standard," section 907(a)(4) gives a number of examples of standards that might be appropriate for the safeguarding of the public health. They all relate to the composition, design, testing and marketing of tobacco products, and hence cover broad ground. Thus, standards may set levels of nicotine yields or lessen or eliminate the presence of other constituents. They also may affect the construction, components, ingredients, additives, constituents and properties of a tobacco product. Finally, standards may impose requirements for testing, sale and distribution, and labeling necessary to assure the proper use of the product.

Section 907(d)(3) places an important limitation on FDA's authority to set standards. It prohibits FDA from issuing a regulation that bans cigarettes, smokeless tobacco products, cigars, pipe tobacco and roll-your-own tobacco products, or that reduces nicotine yields to zero. The reason given is the importance of such a regulation, most likely in the sense that it implicates the sort of policy decision that should be left to the legislative and executive branches, given the public health, cultural and law-enforcement ramifications that a total prohibition might produce.

FDA is prohibited from issuing a regulation that bans cigarettes, smokeless tobacco products, cigars, pipe tobacco and roll-your-own tobacco products, or that reduces nicotine yields to zero.

Considerations. In order to justify the setting of a tobacco product standard, FDA must make a finding that it would be "appropriate for the protection of the public health." Section 907(a)(3)(B)(i) requires the agency to take into account scientific evidence establishing the risks and benefits of the standard to both consumers and affected third parties; any increase or decrease in the odds that current consumers will stop using the tobacco product involved; and any increase or decrease in the danger that non-consumers will begin to use it.

Noticeably absent here is any express mandate that FDA take into account the extent of any economic burden with which a standard might saddle the tobacco industry. Other consumer protection statutes explicitly require the consideration of the costs of compliance with standards. Moreover, an executive order issued by the Office of Management and Budget (OMB) directs federal agencies to consider the costs and the benefits of all possible regulatory options and to choose regulatory options that maximize societal benefits. Since the act forbids

FDA from banning cigarettes and other tobacco products, it seems clear that FDA could not promulgate a standard that would impose such heavy costs that it would amount to a *de facto* ban.

In addition to determining the appropriateness of a proposed standard in terms of public health, FDA must also consider whether compliance with the standard is technologically achievable and whether the standard might have any countervailing (or negative) effects on the health of young users, adult users and non-users.

Standard-Setting Procedure. Section 907(c) sets out the procedures FDA must follow when proposing to set, amend or revoke a tobacco product standard. They generally track the informal processes the agency normally utilizes in promulgating regulations under section 701(a), except that here the statute specifies certain requirements, such as the providing of a justification to support the necessary finding that the standard will appropriately protect the public health, an invitation to interested parties that they submit a competing proposal for a standard, and consultation with the Secretary of Agriculture.

Section 907(d) provides for the promulgation of a final rule, along with the findings that subsection (c) directs FDA to make. It also requires the consideration of a number of factors relevant to the establishment of an effective date for the regulation. These include the technical feasibility of complying, the existence of patents that might make compliance impossible and alterations in the methods of growing tobacco domestically.

Appellate Review. Section 912(a) provides for judicial review of the establishment, amendment or revocation of a tobacco product standard by a United States Court of Appeals in accordance with section 706(2)(a) of the Administrative Procedure Act, which directs the setting aside of agency actions if they are "arbitrary, capricious, an abuse of discretion, or otherwise not in accordance with the law." In this respect, tobacco product standards differ from medical-device performance standards, motor vehicle safety standards and consumer product safety standards, all of which must be justified by substantial evidence in the record as a whole.

Tobacco product standards differ from medical device performance standards, motor vehicle safety standards and consumer product safety standards, all of which must be justified by substantial evidence in the record as a whole.

On the other hand, as has been demonstrated, the act spells out in great detail the numerous findings FDA must make in support of standards the agency promulgates. Compliance with these requirements will not only strain FDA resources but may also heighten judicial scrutiny. Given the relatively recent reduction in the deference courts have traditionally paid to FDA expertise, there exists a very real possibility that the standard setting might turn out to be so exacting and so burdensome that FDA will rarely engage in it.

Will History Repeat Itself? In this regard, it is useful to recall that in the past, federal agencies have faced such enormous difficulties in setting product-safety standards that they have all but abandoned the process. Take, for example, the performances of the National Highway Traffic Safety Administration in promulgating motor vehicle safety standards under the National Traffic and Motor Vehicle Safety Act; the Consumer Product Safety Commission setting consumer product safety standards under the Consumer Product Safety Act; and FDA itself in finalizing performance standards for medical devices under the FDCA. In each instance, procedural as well as substantive obstacles in enabling statutes made the standard-setting process so time- and resource-consuming, and the development of a sufficient factual predicate so difficult, that the agencies opted to concentrate on other regulatory mechanisms, such as recalls.

SUBSTANTIVE LABELING REQUIREMENTS

The Tobacco Act uses the misbranding provision to require manufacturers to place a considerable amount of factual information on the labeling of tobacco products. Normally, labeling conveys directions for the safe use of a product, as well as hazard-related communications that enable both actual and potential consumers to make informed choices about whether or not to expose themselves to risks attributable to the use of a product. What makes tobacco product regulation unique is that the most widely marketed items, such as cigarettes and smokeless tobacco, are inherently dangerous, and there is no way to consume them in a safe way. Moreover, the deadly risks to which they expose consumers, when compared to the benefits they provide, would seem to suggest only one rational choice—non-consumption.

The Tobacco Act uses the misbranding provisions to require manufacturers to place a considerable amount of factual information on the labeling of tobacco products.

REGULATION OF ADVERTISING

The Tobacco Act makes applicable to cigarette and smokeless-cigarette advertisements the warnings requirements applicable to the labels of those products. Secondly, it directs FDA to promulgate a final rule that incorporates regulations the agency issued in 1996, with some limitations. In addition, it more broadly authorizes FDA to develop regulatory restrictions on the advertisement of any tobacco product upon a finding that "such regulation would be appropriate for the protection of the public health." With respect to advertisements and other descriptive printed material issued by the manufacturer, packer or distributor, section 903(a)(8) mandates the inclusion of certain specific information. Finally, section 903(a)(7)(A) provides that a tobacco product is misbranded if its advertising is false or misleading in any particular.

DISTRIBUTION CONTROLS

One reason for FDA's original choice to regulate cigarettes as medical devices was the availability of existing statutory provisions that empowered the agency to regulate distribution of devices, authority FDA would not have enjoyed if it had classified cigarettes as "drugs." Moreover, the 1996 rules were meant to protect minors, which would have been very difficult to do without restricting how these products might get into the hands of underage consumers.

The Tobacco Act requires FDA to develop new regulations governing non-face-to-face contacts between retailers and consumers.

The Tobacco Act shares this goal, and hence places limitations on the distributors and retailers who form the links between manufacturers and consumers. The act does so in four ways. First, as in the case of advertising, it directs FDA to promulgate the distribution requirements and restrictions that the 1996 regulations would have imposed. Second, it puts limitations on the distribution of free samples. Third, it authorizes FDA to promulgate additional restrictions on the sale and distribution of tobacco products. Finally, it requires FDA to develop new regulations governing non-face-to-face contacts between retailers and consumers.

NEW TOBACCO PRODUCTS

When Congress imposed new rules on the manufacturers of new drugs and certain medical devices, by requiring premarket approval for efficacy in the case of the former and premarket clearance for both safety and efficacy for certain devices, it also made these obligations apply retroactively. This served to provide consumers with the benefit of demonstrated efficacy with respect to both older and newer drugs.

Another reason for this was to allow manufacturers of new drugs and risk-generating devices introduced into the marketplace after the effective date of the new rules to compete on a level playing field with marketers of new drugs and potentially hazardous devices already in the stream of commerce. However, the same concern clearly does not animate provisions in the FSPTCA dealing with new tobacco products, which must surmount restrictions that do not apply to tobacco products marketed before February 15, 2007. This may reflect a recognition on the part of Congress that except in the case of modified risk tobacco products, there are no persuasive policy reasons to encourage the development of new products with serious inherent risks and questionable benefits by putting them on an equal footing with competitors, or it may reflect a political trade-off to help secure the enactment of the bill.

The Tobacco Act defines what constitutes a "new tobacco product," and directs FDA to grant or deny premarket approval to tobacco products deemed "new" in accordance with specified standards and procedures.

Definition of a "New Tobacco Product"

Section 910(a)(1) defines a "new tobacco product" as a tobacco product either not commercially available in the United States before February 15, 2007, or a tobacco product marketed before that date and subject to modification after that date. Examples of modification include any change in overall design, the change of a component, part or constituent, a change in the content, delivery or form of nicotine, or any other additive or ingredient. How FDA will interpret the term "modification" will be of critical import because of the onerous regulatory obligations that the law imposes on "new tobacco products."

A "new tobacco product" is defined as a tobacco product either not commercially available in the United States before February 15, 2007, or a tobacco product marketed before that date and subject to modification after that date.

Exemptions from Requirement of Premarket Approval

There are two ways by which a manufacturer can avoid having to secure premarket approval of a "new tobacco product." First, it can make a showing that the product is substantially equivalent to a tobacco product marketed before February 15, 2007. This approach is modeled after the system of premarket notification in the medical device section of the act. Second, the manufacturer can demonstrate that the product falls within a special exemption.

Substantial Equivalence. Under section 905(j), a manufacturer wishing to market a new tobacco product deemed substantially similar to a tobacco product in commercial distribution before February 15, 2007, must submit to FDA a report explaining the basis for that determination. Section 910(a)(3)(A) defines the latter term as requiring the possession of the same characteristics as the predicate tobacco product, that is, the product to which the new tobacco product is substantially similar. Subsection (B) defines "characteristics" as "materials, ingredients, design, composition, heating source, or other features of a tobacco product." If the product characteristics are different, substantial equivalence may still be found if the new tobacco product does not raise questions of public health that are different from those raised by the predicate product. Section 910(a)(3)(C) bars a finding of substantial equivalence if FDA had removed the predicate tobacco product from the market, or if a court decision had found it to be adulterated or misbranded.

Special Exemption. Section 905(j)(3) authorizes FDA to exempt from the premarket approval requirements a tobacco product modified by the adding or deleting of a tobacco additive, or the changing of the amount of an existing additive, on findings that the modification was minor, filing a report under this section would not be necessary to establish that allowing the product onto the market would be appropriate for safeguarding the public health, and an exemption would otherwise be appropriate. The minor-modification exemption has the potential to become a major gateway, if FDA defines the term broadly.

Premarket Approval

Given the difficulty and cost of complying with the new premarket approval rules, it seems likely that they will see infrequent use.

If a manufacturer of a new tobacco product cannot establish the requisite substantial equivalence and cannot qualify for an exemption, the only remaining recourse is to apply to FDA for premarket approval. Given the difficulty and cost of compliance with the new rules, it seems likely that they will see infrequent use.

What an Application Must Include. Section 910(b)(1) mandates the submission of an application containing full reports of information showing the health risks linked to the product and an indication that these risks are less serious than those attributable to other tobacco products; a full description of the components, ingredients, additives and properties of the new tobacco product and a description of how it operates; a full account of how it is manufactured, processed and, if relevant, packed and installed; a reference to any applicable tobacco product standard and information to demonstrate that either the new product conforms to it or why any deviation from the standard is justifiable; product samples; and any other information FDA might request.

Standards for Denial. Under section 910(b)(2), FDA must deny the application if there is no proof that letting the product on the market would be appropriate for the protection of the public health; if the methods used to manufacture, process or pack the product do not conform to the good manufacturing practice requirements of section 906(e); if the proposed labeling is false or misleading in any particular; or if the new product does not meet an applicable product standard.

Given the inherent riskiness of tobacco products, the only health advantage a new product might bring with it is hazard reduction, which would seemingly subject it to regulation as a modified risk product.

Meaning of "Appropriate for the Protection of the Public Health." The critical part of the standard for the approval for new tobacco products is the meaning of the phrase "appropriate for the protection of the public health." This is the same test FDA must meet in order to justify regulations placing restrictions on the advertising, promotion and distribution of tobacco products under section 906(d)(1), and when promulgating tobacco product standards under section 907(a)(3). The agency must consider whether existing users of tobacco products will stop using those products, and that non-consumers will begin to use them. The phrase is somewhat awkward, since it suggests that a new product must somehow bring about a positive degree of protection to the public at large. Given the inherent riskiness of tobacco products, the only health advantage a new product might bring with it is hazard reduction, which would seemingly subject it to regulation as a modified risk product.

Procedures for Withdrawal. Section 910(d) sets out procedures for the withdrawal or temporary suspension of new tobacco products previously approved by FDA. The agency must first submit the issue to the Tobacco Products Scientific Advisory Committee, and then provide an opportunity for an informal hearing. On the basis of the facts before it, including the recommendation of the Advisory Committee and any additional information and argumentation that surfaced at the hearing, FDA will then make its determination.

Standards for Withdrawal. FDA may then withdraw its approval order if the agency can conclude that keeping the product on the market would no longer be appropriate to protect the public health; the application contained an untrue statement of a material fact; the applicant's conduct fell below standards set out elsewhere in the act; or that certain new information has surfaced, justifying the withdrawal.

Temporary Suspension. Section 910(d)(3) enables FDA, after giving an opportunity for an informal hearing, to suspend on a temporary basis a premarket approval order, if the continued marketing of the product "would cause serious adverse health consequences or death, that is greater than ordinarily caused by tobacco products on the market."

Modified Risk Tobacco Products

Amid the lengthy list of findings of fact in the FSPTCA are eight findings that express serious congressional concern about the marketing of tobacco products for which manufacturers make assertions that they reduce risks or exposures to risks inherent in similar products and about the harm this can cause to the public health if the claims made for them do not come to fruition or consumers misunderstand them. Thus, it should come as no surprise that the act includes a set of comprehensive, richly detailed directives that create a system of premarket approval for what are termed "modified risk tobacco products."

Premarket Approval

The act first defines "modified risk tobacco products," to which the requirement of premarket approval will apply. It then sets out the procedures that applicants and FDA must follow and the substantive standards the agency must apply in passing judgment on the application. Finally, it establishes a special exception applicable to certain modified risk products.

Definition. Section 911(b)(1) defines a "modified risk tobacco product" as one that is "sold or distributed for use to reduce harm or the risk of tobacco-related disease associated with commercially marketed tobacco products." Subsection (b)(2) then refines the definition by limiting it to situations in which the manufacturer represents that the product presents a lesser risk of a tobacco-related disease or is less harmful than one or more commercially available tobacco products, or presents a reduced exposure to or does not contain a substance or substances. The representation may be made through a label, labeling, advertising or, after the enactment of the FSPTCA, by any other action directed by the manufacturer to consumers. In addition, the definition would apply if the label, labeling or advertising uses the descriptive terms "light," "mild," "low" or a similar adjective.

FDCA § 911(b)(1) defines a "modified risk tobacco product" as one that is "sold or distributed for use to reduce harm or the risk of tobacco-related disease associated with commercially marketed tobacco products."

Application Process. Section 911(d) mandates submissions of applications that contain a description of the product and the proposed labeling and advertising; the conditions for its use; its formulation; sample labels and labeling; all health-related documents (favorable or unfavorable, and including scientific data) relating to the capacity of the product to reduce risk or exposure and relating to human health; data concerning how consumers actually use the product; and any other information FDA may require. The agency must make this information available to the public, subject to protections normally afforded trade secrets and otherwise confidential commercial information, and solicit comments about this material and about the label, labeling and advertising samples included in the application. FDA must also submit the application to the Tobacco Products Scientific Advisory Committee for review and recommendation.

Standard for Approval. The test FDA must use to determine whether or not to approve an application to market a modified risk tobacco product is whether it will "significantly reduce harm and the risk of tobacco-related disease to individual tobacco users," and will "benefit the health of the population as a whole taking into account both users of tobacco products and persons who do not currently use tobacco products." The burden of proof here falls on the applicant.

Special Rules for Certain Products. Section 911(g)(2) creates an exception for applicants unable to meet the requirements for modified risk tobacco products. To qualify, four conditions must be met: FDA must determine: 1) that an approval order would promote the public health; 2) that what makes the label, labeling and advertising qualify the product for modified risk treatment arises from explicit or implicit representations that the product or its smoke does not contain, or contains a reduced level of, a substance or presents a reduced exposure to a substance in tobacco smoke; 3) that the only available evidence to show this would have to derive from long-term epidemiological studies; and 4) that the only other scientific evidence available indicates that "a measurable and substantial reduction in morbidity or mortality among individual users is reasonably likely in subsequent studies."

Conditions of Marketing for Special Cases. Section 911(g)(2)(C) provides that approval under these special rules will last only for a five-year term, subject to renewal; and the applicant must conduct postmarket surveillance and studies, and submit results of them to FDA annually.

Additional Conditions for Marketing All Modified Risk Products. Section 911(h) spells out additional preconditions for the marketing of modified risk tobacco products. They include proof that the advertising and labeling of the product will enable the public to understand the information conveyed about modified risk and the relative importance of this information in relation both to overall health and the tobacco-related diseases and conditions. In addition, FDA may exercise regulatory oversight over comparative claims and quantitative comparisons, and require additional label disclosures and labeling about conditions of use.

Postmarket Obligations. Under section 911(i), FDA must require postmarket surveillance and studies, and annual submissions of results. The required focus here is on consumer perception, behavior and health, for the purpose of enabling FDA to review the soundness of its premarket approval.

FDA must require postmarket surveillance and studies, and annual submissions of results, for modified risk tobacco products.

Withdrawal of Authorization. If FDA determines that it has grounds to withdraw its approval of an application to make modified risk claims, section 911(j) provides that it must first give the applicant the opportunity for an informal hearing. The agency must then decide whether to take the product off the market. The grounds for withdrawal are: new information indicating that FDA can no longer make the findings it had to make under section 911(g); the subsequent discovery of the absence of material information, or the inclusion of any untrue statement of a material fact, in the application; a finding that a representation that the product reduces risk or exposure is no longer valid; or the applicant's failure to conduct required postmarket surveillance or submit results of it or of any other required studies.

DRUGS INTENDED TO TREAT TOBACCO DEPENDENCE

Section 918 directs FDA to consider classifying new drug products for smoking cessation, including nicotine-replacement products, as fast-track research and approval products within the scope of section 506. It also mandates that FDA give thought to authorizing the prolonged use of nicotine-replacement products, such as patches, gums and lozenges, for the treatment of tobacco dependence and of evidence for additional indications for nicotine-replacement products, such as for relief of craving and relapse avoidance. Finally, it calls on FDA to prepare and submit to Congress a report on how best to regulate, promote and spur the development of innovative products and treatment to achieve total abstinence from tobacco use, reductions in tobacco consumption and reductions in the harm caused by continued tobacco use.

FDCA § 918 directs FDA to consider classifying new drug products for smoking cessation, including nicotine replacement products, as fast-track research and approval products.

POSTMARKETING CONTROLS

The Tobacco Act creates two types of postmarketing controls that FDA might exercise over all tobacco products. Section 908 permits the agency to notify the public of a risk discovered after a tobacco product has entered the stream of commerce or to order a recall of the product. Section 909 requires manufacturers and importers to notify FDA about adverse reactions that they have discovered after the products linked to them entered the marketplace. In addition, section 911 imposes extra postmarketing mandates on manufacturers of modified risk tobacco products.

Notice Requirements

Section 908(a) mirrors language in section 518(a) dealing with medical devices. It enables FDA to order the issuance of warnings relating to product-related risks that have come to light after the initial marketing of the product. FDA must make two factual findings: the product must "present an unreasonable risk of substantial harm to the public" and notification must be both "necessary" and "the most practicable means" for eliminating that risk. Once the agency has made these determinations, it may then require that notification be given "in an appropriate form by the persons and means best suited under the circumstances involved, to all persons who should properly receive such notification in order to eliminate such risk." One method of notice is specifically mentioned as an option—public service announcements.

Recalls

As in the case of notification, the Tobacco Act borrows liberally from the medical device section of the FDCA to give FDA authority to mandate recalls of tobacco products. The agency must first make a finding that "serious adverse health consequences or death" would with reasonable probability result from "a manufacturing or other defect not ordinarily contained in tobacco products on the market." An order based on this finding must target an "appropriate person (including the manufacturers, importers, distributors, or retailers of the tobacco product)," and must call for an immediate cessation of distribution. The act then gives any person subject to the order an opportunity for an informal hearing within 10 days of the issuance of the directive. At issue in the hearing would be whether the actions required by the order are appropriate and whether the order should be amended to include a recall.

The Tobacco Act borrows liberally from the medical device section of the FDCA to give FDA authority to mandate recalls of tobacco products.

If FDA opts to go ahead with a recall, the agency must develop a timetable and require progress reports. Recalls may not reach down to the level of individual purchasers and must include notification to persons put at risk by the use of the product. If these individuals cannot be found, FDA is authorized to contact them through the use of its authority to generate publicity, as spelled out in section 705(b), which contains a further limitation to the effect that the product put consumers in "imminent danger to health."

Miscellaneous Provisions

Good Manufacturing Practice Requirements

Section 906(a) directs FDA to promulgate regulations that require manufacturers of tobacco products to conform to current good manufacturing practice (GMP) or hazard analysis and critical control point (HACCP) methodology. Affected parties may apply for permanent or temporary exemptions or variances. The agency must solicit input from the Tobacco Products Scientific Advisory Committee in the drafting stage of GMP rules, and on whether or not to grant an exemption or variance. Interested parties must be given an opportunity for an oral hearing before a GMP regulation is promulgated as a final rule, and petitioners for exemptions or variances must be given an opportunity for an informal hearing after issuing an order either approving or denying the petition.

Tobacco Products Scientific Advisory Committee

Section 917 directs FDA to set up a 12-member entity to be known as the Tobacco Products Scientific Advisory Committee. The responsibilities of the committee are to furnish FDA with advice, recommendations and information as specifically provided for in the act, on the effects of reducing nicotine levels in tobacco products, on the possibility of finding a nicotine level that will not produce tobacco dependence, and on any other issues as requested by FDA. Members of the committee must have technical qualifications relating to tobacco products and represent various specified interest groups. They are subject to the conflict-of-interest rules in section 712.

The provisions of the act that call for input from the committee include sections 906(e)(1)(B)(i) (good manufacturing practice requirements), 907(d)(1) and (5) (tobacco product standards), 907(e)(1) (menthol cigarettes), 910(b)(2) (new tobacco products) and 911(f) (modified risk tobacco products).

User Fees

Failure to pay user fees will cause a manufacturer's or importer's products to be considered adulterated under FDCA § 902(4).

Section 919 establishes a schedule of user fees to be assessed against the manufacturers and importers of tobacco products. According to subsection (b)(3), fees are to be calculated according to the type of product being made or imported and the percentage of market share based on the total volume of domestic sales of the class of product during the fiscal year. Failure to pay user fees will cause a manufacturer's or importer's products to be considered adulterated under section 902(4).

Prevention of Illicit Trade

Although the Tobacco Act explicitly bars FDA from banning cigarettes and other specific tobacco products and from mandating that nicotine yields of a tobacco product be reduced to zero, the act does prohibit the sale of many kinds of flavored cigarettes. It also imposes on manufacturers a number of obligations that will increase the costs of production, which could in turn cause them to discontinue the marketing of certain tobacco products or to increase prices; in the latter instance, some consumers may no longer be able to afford these items. Both unavailability and unaffordability could give rise to illegal commerce. To deal with this possibility, the Tobacco Act includes several provisions aimed at discouraging the illegal trade of tobacco products.

Origin Labeling. Section 902(a) requires that all tobacco products bear on their labels, packaging and shipping containers the legend "sale only allowed in the United States." The purpose of this obligation is to facilitate the detection of tobacco products manufactured abroad and then sold illegally in this country.

Recordkeeping. Section 920(b) directs FDA to promulgate recordkeeping regulations that will make it easier to monitor the commercial movement of tobacco products in order to aid in the suppression of illicit trade. These rules may include the requiring of label codes. The agency's authority here is limited to "the establishment and maintenance of records by any person," which suggests that it may be directed at an individual rather than on an industry-wide basis. Another limitation, aimed at protecting the privacy of individual purchasers, prohibits FDA from mandating the production of records of individual purchases for personal consumption.

Inspection of Records. Section 920(c) gives FDA access to certain records if the agency has a reasonable belief that a tobacco product is part of an illegal trade or smuggling operation or is a counterfeit. The language of the section contains a troublesome ambiguity since it does not limit this access to persons involved in the manufacture or marketing of the specific tobacco products suspected of being involved in an illicit operation. However, logic would seem to dictate the implication of this constraint. Records inspections must take place "at reasonable times and within reasonable limits and in a reasonable manner, upon presentation of appropriate credentials and a written notice." The refusal to permit access to or the copying of any record as required by section 920(c) is a prohibited act under section 301(e).

FDCA § 920(c) gives FDA access to certain records if the agency has a reasonable belief that a tobacco product is part of an illegal trade or smuggling operation or is a counterfeit.

Awareness of Illegal Transactions. Under section 920(d), manufacturers and distributors of tobacco products have an obligation to notify the Attorney General or the Secretary of the Treasury promptly if they have reason to know that one of their products that has left their control is being marketed by a person who is not paying the required duties or taxes or is involved in an illicit sales operation. The requisite state of mind here is either actual knowledge or "the knowledge which a reasonable person would have had under like circumstances or which would have been obtained upon the exercise of due care." The latter amounts to a negligence test. The failure to make a report as required by this section is a prohibited act under section 301(e).

CONSTITUTIONAL CHALLENGES

When the Commonwealth of Massachusetts attempted to limit both outdoor and indoor advertisements of smokeless tobacco and cigars, the United States Supreme Court ruled that the promotional materials under scrutiny amounted to constitutionally protected commercial speech.[8] A majority of the Court found that the limitations Massachusetts sought to impose on billboards and outdoor advertising constituted an undue infringement on the right of defendants to communicate with adult smokers. Given this backdrop, it came as no surprise that elements of the tobacco industry have raised constitutional objections to both the new law and FDA regulations issued under its authority.

Attack on Marketing Restrictions

Shortly after the FSPTCA became law, a group of cigarette manufacturers sued the federal government to prevent FDA from implementing several of the marketing provisions of the act, on the ground that they violated the Constitution. A U.S. District Court ruled in plaintiffs' favor on several counts.[9] In *Discount Tobacco City & Lottery Inc. v. United States of America*,[10] a three-judge panel of the Court of Appeals for the Sixth Circuit affirmed several rulings of the District Court and reversed several others.

Cigarette Package Warnings. Section 201 of the Tobacco Act updates the warnings cigarette packs must bear, specifies their size and location, and authorizes FDA to mandate additional, graphic warnings. The Sixth Circuit rejected the companies' claim that consumers are already aware of smoking risks and in fact overestimate them. By a 2-1 vote, the panel also ruled that FDA's authority to require graphic images was not in itself unconstitutional, since they can convey factual information reasonably related to the act's goal of preventing consumer deception.

Ban on Color and Imagery in Advertisements. Plaintiffs challenged the act's requirement that labeling and advertising use only black text on a white background, with no imagery, as well as the narrowness of the exceptions to the rule. The Court rejected the government's claim that all uses of color and imagery are likely to attract minors, and held that to avoid invalidation on constitutional grounds, restrictions should confine themselves to speech necessary to carry out the goal of protecting young people. In the Court's view, the act's ban on color and imagery is "vastly overbroad," and hence violates plaintiff's commercial-speech rights.

Brand-Name Event Sponsorship and Merchandise. On the other hand, the panel upheld the regulatory ban on the use of brand names to sponsor events to which children might be exposed, or to distribute items such as caps and T-shirts or corporate logos, on the ground that it was not more than necessary to reduce youth exposure to brand names or possession of branded merchandise.

Premarket Review of Risk-Reduction Claims. Plaintiffs also took aim at the statutory requirement that harm-reduction claims made by a modified risk tobacco product be subject to premarket review by FDA, so that a manufacturer who made such claims before FDA preclearance would violate the act. The companies asserted that this would prevent them from participating in public health debates about tobacco-harm reduction, and hence would infringe upon their right to free speech. The Court, however, ruled that the act sought to prohibit only commercial speech embodied in the labeling and advertising of specific products, a restriction justified by the industry's long history of using misleading health claims to market reduced-risk cigarettes; the prohibition would not apply to non-commercial speech in any public health debate.

Attack on FDA Labeling Regulations

In *R.J. Reynolds Tobacco Company v. United States Food and Drug Administration*,[11] five cigarette manufacturers sued to invalidate FDA's final regulations requiring graphic images and new textual warning to appear on cigarette packages, as authorized by sections 201 and 202 of the Tobacco Act. A United States District Court judge, ruling in favor of the plaintiffs, held that the FDA rules violated the companies' First Amendment free-speech guarantee.

"Compelled Speech." The Court accepted the tobacco companies' argument that the FSPTCA's size-and-placement rules for warnings, as well as the graphic images and additional warnings mandated by FDA, amounted to "compelled speech" meant to influence a "public debate." As such, they would not fall into the category of commercial speech, which is subject to a looser standard of constitutional protection, but instead they would be evaluated under a strict-scrutiny standard.

The only exception to the application of strict scrutiny for compelled speech would apply if the disclosures involved purely factual or uncontroversial information, and were not unjustified or excessively burdensome. The Court concluded that the graphic images were not purely factual, but instead were meant to elicit emotional responses. Moreover, if considered in conjunction with the newly required warnings statements, the images sought to encourage smoking cessation, which in the Court's view remains a matter of opinion.

Strict Scrutiny. Under the strict-scrutiny rule, FDA would have to show that it had tailored its regulations narrowly, to meet a compelling government interest. The Court found that the agency had failed to do this, because its purpose was not to inform or educate, but rather to advocate non-smoking. Moreover, the government has other less onerous methods to pursue its agenda. These include less emotional and more factually oriented images for cigarette packages, higher taxes on the products, the intensification of its public relations campaigning against smoking, and imposing further restrictions on cigarette sales to minors.

Endnotes

1.   The Federal Cigarette Labeling and Advertising Act, Pub. L. No. 89-92, 79 Stat. 282 (1965).
2.   The Public Health Cigarette Smoking Act, Pub. L. No. 91-222, 84 Stat. 87 (1969).
3.   The Comprehensive Smoking Education Act, Pub. L. No. 98-474, 98 Stat. 2200 (1984).
4.   Cipollone v. Liggett Group, Inc., 505 U.S. 504 (1992).
5.   *See* Food and Drug Administration, Regulations Restricting the Sale and Distribution of Cigarettes and Smokeless Tobacco to Protect Children and Adolescents, 61 Fed. Reg. 44,396 (Aug. 28, 1996).
6.   529 U.S. 120 (2000).
7.   United States of America v. Philip Morris, USA, Inc., 449 F. Supp. 2d 1 (D.D.C. 2006).
8.   Lorillard Tobacco Co. v. Reilly, 533 U.S. 525 (2001). The Court used the test it had adopted in *Central Hudson Gas & Elec. Corp. v. Public Serv. Comm'n of New York*, 447 U.S. 557 (1980), which applies to speech that is neither false nor misleading. To restrict it, the government must show that it has a substantial interest in doing so, that the restriction directly advances that interest, and that it is not more extensive that would be necessary to promote the interest.
9.   678 F. Supp. 2d 512 (W.D. Ky. 2010).
10.   Civil Case Nos. 10-5234/5235, United States Ct. of App, 6th Cir., Mar. 19, 2012.
11.   Civil Case No. 11-1482, United States Dist. Ct., D.C., Feb. 29, 2012.

Chapter 13

Regulation of Promotion and Distribution

Wayne L. Pines, APCO Worldwide Inc., Washington, D.C.

Key Points

- The promotion of medical products is central to their proper use. The Food and Drug Administration (FDA) regulates promotional materials for medical products, including advertising as well as other materials that are product-specific and that are issued by a company or an agent of that company.
- A few basic principles apply to FDA's regulation of advertising and promotion: materials must be truthful and not misleading, must contain a fair balance of benefits and risks, and must provide for full disclosure of prescribing (drugs) or usage (devices) information.
- FDA is especially concerned about the promotion of off-label uses for approved drugs and devices, the pre-approval promotion of new medical products, the lack of fair balance and adequate risk information, and comparative claims of superiority.
- FDA does not prohibit any communication techniques from being used to promote medical products, but there are nuances of policy that apply to each technique.
- FDA generally enforces the law by issuing letters to companies in violation. The letters cite the alleged violation and seek remedy. Most enforcement actions stem from FDA's review of materials submitted by companies or from complaints from competitors or physicians.
- Other statutes also apply to marketing medical products.
- Settlements under the False Claims Act and anti-kickback statute have changed the way that pharmaceutical and medical device companies market their products.

OVERVIEW

The promotion of medical products is central to their success and optimum use. Promotion encompasses a variety of objectives: informing consumers about new and existing products that may be of value in improving their health; educating healthcare providers about new and existing products and how to use them; providing information needed by those who finance or pay directly for medical products, such as managed care organizations or hospitals; and positioning products to differentiate them from those of competitors.

There also is the need to keep other audiences informed about research and new products. The public demands such information; everyone wants to know about medical progress. Investment capital for new companies is dependent on understanding research progress, as well as the potential market value of new products. Maintaining investment community interest in a company hinges upon focused communications. Healthcare providers need to know, on a continuing basis, what kinds of advances are being made in their specialty areas.

These forms of communication, when initiated by a medical products company or by one of its agents (e.g., an advertising or public relations agency), are regulated by the Food and Drug Administration (FDA). Promotional materials issued by medical products companies or their agents are among the most regulated of all forms of communication in the United States. FDA's concerns about product communications that are controlled (directly as well as indirectly) by drug or device companies center primarily upon communications that promote the products for "off- label" uses, make claims that are false and/or misleading, make unsupported comparisons with other products, and/or overstate efficacy or minimize risk.

"Off-label," in particular, has become a controversial term. Basically it means that the claims made in the promotional materials or statements are not included in or are not consistent with the officially approved labeling for the product. FDA's underlying concern with "off- label" promotional efforts is that they may result in patients being prescribed unproven therapies or ones that may be less effective or more risky than therapies approved for that use by FDA. The agency also is concerned that "off-label" promotion can undermine companies' incentive to conduct additional studies that will establish safety and efficacy for the new use.

FDA concern about off-label promotion raises First Amendment issues.

One of the issues that arises in most debates is FDA's reliance on the product labeling as the basis of what can be communicated. There are arguments that information that is generally accepted as being medically truthful and not misleading should be permitted to be communicated by companies, even if that information is not included in the official FDA-approved labeling or does not meet FDA's definition of "substantial evidence." Denying the right of companies to communicate truthful and nonmisleading information, many contend, is in fact contrary to the interests of patients and the public health in general.

Others argue that advertising and promotion should be regulated more aggressively. Some contend that physicians should receive medical information primarily from traditional scientific sources, such as peer-reviewed medical journals, not from drug or device companies with an interest in selling a product. Abuses of promotion and marketing efforts by companies over the years have reinforced this view.

Concerns also have been raised about the extent of FDA's jurisdiction. FDA has assumed regulation of all product-specific communications by a medical products company, even before the product is approved and available. FDA also assumes jurisdiction over conversations that take place between a company's sales representative and a physician, and the sales information provided to an accountant at a managed care organization. FDA also regulates what is said by a practicing or academic physician who receives compensation from a drug or device company to promote a product, even when the physician is describing his or her own research or clinical experiences.

One ambiguous facet of the issue is that FDA does accept the need for and value of communicating legitimate and accurate product information in the period before a product or new use is approved and there is no labeling to provide parameters. FDA's own regulations establish the legitimacy of "scientific exchange"—the well-recognized need for scientists to communicate with each other about research findings, and for companies to communicate research information. It is when such "exchange" crosses over into "commercialization"—and FDA has never defined that line with precision—that FDA regulators become concerned.

"Scientific exchange" has never been defined with precision.

In its enforcement actions, FDA also seems to draw a distinction based on who within the company is involved in the communication of "non-promotional," scientific information. The basis for FDA enforcement actions is generally the content of what is said, not who says it. FDA has indicated, however, that it is less suspicious when medical personnel deal with "off-label" information. At the same time, it must be recognized that medical personnel who use the opportunity to promote a product "off-label" or before approval are subject to the same restrictions as all other company employees.

Because of these issues, the regulation of promotional materials is one of the most challenging areas of FDA regulation. The agency's approach is continually evolving to meet new communications technologies and creative programming by marketing staffs. At the same time, medical products companies generally have learned to work within the agency's regulatory framework. Larger companies have full-time regulatory staffs dedicated to assuring compliance with FDA promotional requirements. Smaller companies often rely on consultants to keep them up to date on FDA policies.

Drawing a line between violative and permitted activities usually requires experienced judgment. Within companies, FDA promotional policies often are a source of conflict between the marketing and public relations staffs on the one hand, and regulatory and legal staffs on the other. The marketing and public relations teams want their companies to be appropriately aggressive based on their understanding of the rules; regulatory and legal staffs want to make sure the company is in compliance, even when the rules are vague and evolving. Each company's management must decide its own policies and internal processes in designing and implementing marketing and communications programs, and whether to seek FDA review in advance for certain materials.

WHAT THE LAW REQUIRES

The legal basis for FDA's authority to regulate medical product communications dates from the 1962 Drug Amendments. Before 1962, promotional activities for prescription drugs were regulated by the Federal Trade Commission (FTC). The 1962 amendments gave FDA authority over prescription drug advertising after Congress heard testimony of alleged abuses by pharmaceutical companies in seeking to market their products to physicians. The concern about marketing abuses by medical products companies has been a recurring theme and frequently has been the subject of hearings before Congress or media stories.

The pharmaceutical advertising section of the Federal Food, Drug, and Cosmetic Act (FDCA), as enacted in 1962, consists of a single paragraph in the section of the law that defines a "misbranded" product (FDCA § 502(n); 21 U.S.C. § 352(n)). It requires that the generic name of the drug appear "prominently" in promotional materials, that the drug's formula appear and that a "brief summary" relating to side effects, contraindications and effectiveness appear in all advertising. It also prohibits FDA from requiring that advertising materials be approved in advance, except in "extraordinary circumstances." FDA issued detailed regulations in the 1960s and 1970s to establish specific requirements for paid advertising for prescription drugs.

Further, similar requirements for medical devices (FDCA § 502(r); 21 U.S.C. § 352(r)) have evolved from the requirements of the 1962 Drug Amendments, as well as guidances and enforcement actions that affect the marketing of all FDA-regulated medical products—human drugs and biologicals, veterinary drugs and medical devices.

FDA regulations that apply to the promotion of medical products are contained in several sections of the *Code of Federal Regulations* (Title 21). Among the applicable sections are Part 200 and, most particularly, Part 202 for pharmaceutical promotion, Part 510 for veterinary drugs, Part 601 for biological products and Part 801 for medical devices. The sections that deal with human prescription drugs generally set the policies for prescription veterinary drugs.

Since 1962, there have been dramatic changes in how medical products are marketed, in the audiences that need and want to know about them and in communications technology generally. No longer are medical products promoted just to healthcare providers. No longer is the printed medical journal or the visit by the company's sales representative the primary vehicle of communicating product information. FDA has adapted to this continuously evolving environment.

FDA regulation has adapted to the changing environment.

The formal FDA regulations provide only a small measure of the information needed to comply with FDA requirements. The regulations are most helpful when it comes to understanding the requirements for traditional paid advertising directed at physicians—the oldest form of marketing now being practiced and the regulatory objective of the 1962 amendments. For more recently introduced communications methods, FDA policy is set forth in other FDA documents, most prominently in guidances and enforcement action letters issued by the agency. To keep up with evolving policies, careful attention must be paid to the Warning Letters and other correspondence that involve specific companies or products. Further, policies have been elucidated in the meetings and symposia where FDA regulators speak.

It's Basic!
A few basic principles underlie all of FDA's regulation of promotion and advertising.

UNDERLYING PRINCIPLES

A few basic principles underlie FDA's regulations, guidances and regulatory actions regarding promotion and advertising. Essentially, any medical product that fails to adhere to these principles in its promotional practices could be viewed as "misbranded" by FDA and subject to an enforcement action. The basic principles that underlie FDA's advertising and promotion policies, and that apply to all medical products categories, are:

♦ **Product-specific promotional information issued by medical products companies is regulated.** While the 1962 amendments envisioned that FDA primarily would regulate advertising directed at physicians, because that was the principal means of promoting prescription drugs at the time, over the years FDA has expanded the horizons of its jurisdiction to include all promotional information. While some attorneys dispute FDA's expanded view of its jurisdiction, as a practical matter FDA does regulate, to varying degrees, not just prescription drug advertising but also sales materials, information directed at consumers, press materials, information provided to the investment community, sales materials for managed care organizations and hospitals, and oral statements made by any company employee or representative that discuss a specific product.

♦ **FDA regards promotional materials issued by drug companies as either "advertising" or "labeling."** "Advertising" consists of traditional paid advertising (e.g., when a company pays to place an advertisement). "Labeling," or more precisely "promotional labeling," to distinguish the term from being confused with the package insert, includes everything else (e.g., brochures, booklets, direct mail pieces, press releases, letters to formulary committees, slide kits and audio- visual materials). "Advertising" and "promotional labeling" must meet the same general standards for truthfulness, accuracy, and balance.

There is one disclosure requirement that differentiates "advertising" and "promotional labeling." When paid advertising appears, the risk disclosure requirements can be met with the inclusion of a "brief summary" of risk information, whereas materials classified as "promotional labeling" generally must be accompanied by the full package insert.

Sometimes materials issued by or on behalf of a medical products company that do not mention a specific product, such as information about a disease, may be regarded as "labeling" or "promotional labeling" if the materials are intended to be used in conjunction with the promotion of a product or if a reasonable person would be able to identify the product based on the implicit claim.

All information in promotional materials issued by or on behalf of a drug or device company must be truthful and not false and/or misleading.

♦ **Under FDA's regulations, all information in promotional materials issued by or on behalf of a drug or device company must be truthful and not false and/or misleading.** FDA, however, imposes requirements above and beyond simple accuracy and truthfulness. For example, a press release may accurately and truthfully describe new research on an unapproved use of an approved product, but if it also does not include a "fair balance" of risk factors and provide for "full disclosure" of risk information, then it could be regarded by FDA as violative. Further, if the issuance contains information inconsistent with FDA-approved labeling, even if that information is medically accurate, truthful and well accepted by experts in the medical field, that information may be regarded by FDA as violative.

♦ **Information must be fairly balanced with risk information.** FDA defines "fair balance" as a "balanced presentation of benefits and risks." This means that, in an advertisement, to the extent that a particular benefit is described, the medical risks associated with that benefit also must be described. In a press release, when benefits are described, FDA expects that the major adverse experiences and side effects also will be described. "Fair balance" also may mean that a product's limitations must be delineated. "Fair balance" is hard to define with any better precision because it differs for each individual product.

Television advertising that is product-specific must also meet the "fair balance" requirement by including risk information within the advertising itself. Further, television advertising must also meet the "brief summary" requirement. It does so by making "adequate provision" for the recipient of the information to obtain prescribing information.

"Adequate provision" for television advertising directed to a consumer audience can be met through mechanisms set forth by FDA (initially in an August 1997 draft guidance, and then again two years later in a final guidance). It was this guidance that basically opened the door to product-specific direct-to-consumer (DTC) television advertising. FDA stated that the "adequate provision" requirement could be met for television by including in the commercial an 800 number that the consumer can call to ask for further information to be mailed, faxed or read; a referral to an Internet site; a referral to information in an advertisement in a current issue of a print publication that included the brief summary; or provision of information that healthcare professionals can provide to patients.

The "net impression" of a promotional piece is a major consideration for FDA in evaluating its compliance. In May 2009 FDA issued a draft guidance entitled "Presenting Risk Information in Prescription Drug and Medical Device Promotion" which set forth the factors that FDA reviewers look for in deciding whether a particular promotional piece has adequate risk disclosure. In this document, the agency said: "It is important to emphasize that when FDA evaluates the risk communication in a promotional piece, FDA looks not just at specific risk-related statements, but at the net impression—i.e., the message communicated by all elements of the piece as a whole. The purpose of the evaluation is to determine whether the piece as a whole conveys an accurate and non-misleading impression of the benefits and risks of the promoted product. Manufacturers should therefore focus not just on individual claims or presentations, but on the promotional piece as a whole. A promotional communication that conveys a deceptive net impression of the product could be misleading, even if specific individual claims or presentations are not misleading."

♦ **Companies may make therapeutic claims for products in advertising and promotional labeling only when that claim is consistent with the FDA-approved labeling or, in some cases when the labeling is not up to date, based on "substantial evidence" or "substantial clinical experience."** (As a practical enforcement matter, FDA generally does not permit claims to be made solely on the basis of "substantial clinical experience," but this language remains in the FDA regulations.) This requirement has been very controversial. Even if information is well accepted in the medical community, it may not, in FDA's view, be used in company promotional material if it is not included in FDA-approved labeling or based on what FDA regards as "substantial evidence."

FDA's rationale in restricting the use of "off-label" information in company promotional materials is that it could mislead healthcare providers and consumers into believing a product is effective for a use when it has not been shown effective to FDA's satisfaction. Further, FDA believes that if companies are permitted to disseminate off-label information, it will remove any incentive they have to conduct needed research on that use. Congress addressed this issue in 1997 legislation, the Food and Drug Administration Modernization Act (FDAMA). This matter also has been addressed in litigation (the Washington Legal Foundation case) and is central to ongoing debates about FDA's policies and its exercise of its enforcement discretion.

♦ **Material facts about the product must be disclosed in company promotional materials.** If an advertisement or promotional piece fails to mention a material fact that would influence the prescribing, use or purchase of a product, then the piece could be regarded by FDA as being violative.

The rules governing advertising and promotional labeling apply to any product-specific information issued or caused to be issued by a company, either directly or through any agent.

♦ **The rules governing advertising and "promotional labeling" apply to any product-specific information issued or caused to be issued by a company, *either directly or through any agent*.** FDA has made clear that third parties hired by a company to speak publicly about a product in a promotional context must keep the remarks within approved labeling and otherwise comply with the same rules that apply to company employees.

The same principle applies to an advertising or public relations agency hired by a medical products company to promote a product, and it further applies when a company provides money to a third-party organization to issue information on behalf of one of its products. The indictment in the spring of 2006 by the U.S. Attorney in the Eastern District of New York of a physician for alleging promoting "off-label" uses on behalf of a pharmaceutical company underscores the government's concern with off-label promotion. (The physician pleaded guilty to a misdemeanor).

Off-label promotion
FDA believes that promoting a marketed product for an unapproved use could pose a significant potential threat to the public health.

SPECIFIC FDA POLICIES

In the view of FDA, promoting a marketed product for an unapproved use could pose a significant potential threat to the public health or could reduce a manufacturer's incentive to perform the studies and research necessary to obtain FDA approval of such indications.

FDA rules and enforcement policy seek to discourage drug and device companies from disseminating information about "off-label" uses. This policy is controversial, as the argument has been made that the standard for dissemination of "off-label" information in a nonpromotional context should be whether the claim itself is medically justified and supported, even if it has not been incorporated into the official FDA labeling. The argument is premised on the fact that FDA labeling lags behind science, and drug and medical device companies should be entitled to provide truthful and nonmisleading information.

Some of the specific kinds of "off-label" promotional activities that FDA objects to are: implying in an advertisement that a drug is useful for a particular use when it has not been shown to be (for example, FDA objected to a photograph in an advertisement for a drug that depicted a young woman, when the drug was indicated for older women); posting information on the Internet that indicates that a medical device is useful for a broad range of procedures when it was approved under a 510(k) application only for a limited type of procedure; or suggesting that a drug is useful as first-line therapy when it was approved only as second-line therapy.

One particular issue that companies have grappled with is the issuance of articles that appeared in the peer-reviewed medical literature and that contain, even in minor references, information that is off-label. In January 2009, FDA issued a guidance that set forth its criteria for when companies could distribute peer-reviewed medical journal articles. Many companies use the provisions in the "reprint guidance" to provide reprints of peer-reviewed medical journal articles to healthcare professionals, with full disclosure that the reprint contains off-label information.

The commercialization of a product before approval is another issue. The agency's view was set forth in 1994 correspondence which expressed its interpretation of section 312.7 ("scientific exchange") of the regulations:

> Prior to approval, promotional materials provided by the sponsor are often inaccurate with respect to the indications and risk information that ultimately appear in the approved product labeling. This inaccuracy occurs because the sponsor does not know what indications and other information the final product labeling will contain. Additionally, the sponsor's assessment of the drug may be overly optimistic, exaggerating efficacy while minimizing risk. Thus, the sponsor's biases may be incorporated into the promotional materials it provides prior to approval of final product labeling. Such promotional materials do not fulfill the needs of healthcare providers or benefits managers to obtain balanced, accurate information about new drugs, but instead disseminate misinformation and create potential risk and misuse.

Investigational products may not be commercialized, but can be discussed as "scientific exchange."

FDA has a somewhat different policy for medical devices in the pre-approval stage, recognizing that purchasers need to commit large sums of money to buy certain devices. Medical device companies may notify potential customers about a new product whose 510(k) application is still being reviewed by FDA, but may make no conclusory claims with regard to effectiveness or safety, and may not take orders for the product.

Another principal concern of FDA is comparative claims made by companies for their products. In an environment in which competition in the medical products industries is intense, all companies seek to differentiate their products, and all want to claim that their product is superior. Examples of comparative claims are "drug of choice," "unsurpassed," or "more effective."

Comparative claims
FDA requires that any claim of superiority for a prescription drug be supported by "substantial evidence" and not be based solely on a comparison of labeling information.

FDA requires that any claim of superiority for a prescription drug be supported by "substantial evidence," usually two adequate and well-controlled studies or in some cases a single large multicenter trial. The studies must be "head-to-head" (i.e., they must be designed prospectively to directly compare the products). Generally, the agency wants two such studies, but it will permit a limited claim (e.g., our product is better absorbed, or works faster or is more easily swallowed by patients) to be made on the basis of a single study. FDA prohibits a claim of superiority based solely on a comparison of data in the two products' labeling.

In addition, if a comparative claim is made, it cannot be false or misleading and cannot leave out other measurements by which the company's product is inferior to its competitor.

Two kinds of comparative claims that companies have increasingly been making involve cost-effectiveness (our product is more cost-effective than our competitor's) or quality-of-life claims (our product helps patients obtain a high quality of life, either in absolute terms or in comparison with our competitor's product). FDA generally requires that any such claims be proven by studies. Quality-of-life claims must report not just positive findings but also negative ones found in the study.

With regard to cost-effectiveness claims, in the 1997 FDAMA, Congress recognized the need of companies to provide such information to medical products purchasers (as contrasted with prescribers). The law said that cost-effectiveness information could be supplied to managed care organizations, but only to such organizations, if the information is "competent and reliable." The legal history of FDAMA made clear that the same information that is provided to product purchasers based on "competent and reliable" data may not also be provided to consumers or even to healthcare providers in their capacity as prescribers.

Communications Techniques

In the modern world, there are many ways for information to be communicated. FDA does not object to the use of any specific format mode of communication for medical products information. Medical information can be provided to healthcare providers, consumers, managed care purchasers or anyone else in various formats, and with whatever communication mechanisms exist: electronic or print, television commercials or journal advertising, Internet or CD/DVD. What FDA is concerned about is the content of these materials and whether it is false or misleading in any way.

Requirements that apply to specific formats and methods of communication are as follows:

- **Reminder ads:** FDA regulations permit companies to sponsor advertising that does not mention the indications or uses for a product, but that is intended to "remind" readers or viewers of the name. Such advertising may state the name (including the generic name); the ingredients; the dosage form; and the name and address of the manufacturer, packager or distributor. The advertisement, however, may not mention what the product is used for, and may not make a safety or efficacy claim or any other representation, including a graphic representation, about the use of the product. Such advertising is exempt from the requirement for a "brief summary." "Reminder ads" may not appear for drugs for which there is a "boxed" warning in the FDA-approved labeling, or, in the case of older drugs, whose efficacy has not been reaffirmed by FDA.

  Reminder ads are exempt from risk summaries.

- **Press releases:** FDA does not have a specific regulation or guidance applying to press releases, but does regulate product-specific releases as "promotional labeling." While some attorneys dispute whether FDA has the authority to regulate press releases, as a practical matter both the drug and devices industry generally accede to FDA's authority. Based on FDA expectations (as derived from various enforcement actions and statements by FDA), the agency expects promotional press releases to contain "fair balance" within the release itself. Because they are regarded by FDA as "promotional labeling" rather than advertising, FDA expects that press releases be accompanied by the full package insert, not just a "brief summary" of risks.

- Press releases often contain disclaimers that help put the product into regulatory context (e.g., in a research announcement for a product not yet approved, it is best to make clear that the product is not approved or that an application is pending before FDA, if that is the case). Press releases issued before product approval must avoid saying that the product has been shown to be safe and effective, and should avoid any statements that might be construed as promotional, such as using words like "promising" or "breakthrough."

♦ **Video news releases:** These 90-second electronic versions of press releases are regarded by FDA as "promotional labeling," and therefore under FDA policy must contain balanced information if they are product-specific.

♦ **Materials for investors:** Investor-directed press releases and other materials, such as annual reports, are subject to the same regulatory requirements, according to FDA policy. FDA, however, recognizes that these materials are not intended to be used in a product promotion context and that the primary audience is not prescribers. FDA's enforcement policies are geared accordingly. For example, an annual report handed out at a medical meeting might be regarded as promotional if it contains certain information about new uses for approved products, and FDA might consider taking enforcement action if the report is disseminated for promotional purposes. The same report issued only to investors is not likely to raise the same concerns. FDA does not require annual reports issued to investors that mention ongoing research or newly approved products in this context to include the labeling as an attachment. FDA has a formal working relationship with the Securities and Exchange Commission in regulating investor materials.

♦ **Scientific meetings:** The sponsorship by companies of medical and other meetings has been controversial. The concern by FDA and other government agencies is that companies will use the meetings to promote off-label uses of their products, or that companies will exert control over meetings that are depicted as independent.

Any scientific meeting that is under the content control of a company and that is product-specific must meet all criteria for fair balance and full disclosure. FDA, however, does not regulate the content of legitimate continuing medical education (CME) funded by medical products companies, as long as the CME grant is provided to a third party and the CME is conducted independently of the company.

CME is not regulated by FDA if it is independently conducted.

Companies that fund CME generally have standard contracts with providers that set forth a specific relationship that is intended to ensure independence of the program, the presenters and the derivative material, such as monographs or publications. In evaluating whether a CME program is truly independent, FDA looks at about a dozen factors, most particularly who controls the program agenda and speaker selection. The Accreditation Council for Continuing Medical Education accredits CME programs and has issued rules to assure a high level of independence from commercial interests.

♦ **Internet:** FDA does not have a formal Internet or social media policy, but does actively regulate information on the Internet sponsored by medical product companies. For the most part, information about approved products may be posted as long as the information is consistent with labeling and provides ready and easy access to product labeling.

The regulatory challenges arise with the failure to balance promotional claims with risk information, with links to other Internet sites that contain off-label information, or with chat rooms where off-label information may be discussed. Generally companies do not sponsor such links or chat rooms. Another issue is how to regulate information that emanates from overseas affiliates, especially if it relates to products also sold in the United States. In such cases, companies generally indicate clearly which part of the website is intended for U.S. audiences as contrasted with audiences in countries where the product may be approved for uses not approved in the United States.

♦ **Homemade materials:** Company personnel in the field may seek to create their own promotional materials to provide to healthcare professionals. Homemade materials can contain misleading claims and/or lack risk information. FDA discourages this practice, and most companies have specific policies prohibiting the creation of homemade materials. These policies generally state that sales representatives who want to distribute their own materials must go through the company's approval process.

Companies prohibit "homemade" materials as a matter of policy.

♦ **Requests for information:** FDA issued a draft guidance in December 2011 on how companies can respond to unsolicited requests for product information that is outside of labeling. Under the draft guidance, companies are not permitted to encourage or solicit requests for off-label information. The draft guidance said there are two categories of unsolicited requests— those that are received "privately," that is, one-on-one, and those that are received publicly, for example at a public meeting. A "private request," the draft guidance said, should be handled by the company's medical or scientific staff, which should be independent from the sales or marketing department. The response should be accompanied by labeling, references for the information and a clear statement that the use described in the response is not approved or cleared by FDA. Records should be kept of the request and response.

For "public" requests, the draft guidance said, companies should respond only when one of its products is mentioned. The response should convey that the question pertains to an unapproved or uncleared use. No substantive off-label information should be provided to the group; rather, the individual asking the question should be invited to follow up with the company's medical or scientific affairs department. Further, the draft guidance said, company representatives must clearly disclose their involvement with the company and the response may not be promotional.

♦ **Direct-to-consumer promotion:** Most countries, including those in the European Union, do not permit companies to advertise prescription drug promotional information directly to consumers. The United States is the only country other than New Zealand that permits DTC advertising of prescription products. Companies in the United States also target other promotional materials directly to the consumer, such as materials that may be distributed in a physician's waiting room.

FDA requires that all consumer-directed information must meet the same criteria for accuracy, truthfulness, fair balance and full disclosure as materials intended for healthcare professionals. Print advertising must fairly present the risks as well as benefits, and also must include the "brief summary" or a consumer version of it.

Under a policy announced by FDA in August 1997, and reiterated in August 1999, advertising of prescription drugs on commercial television also is permitted, but it must make "adequate provision" for the consumer to obtain further information via the Internet, a toll-free number or some other means. FDA encourages disease-oriented or "help-seeking" advertising to consumers that does not mention any product name, but that identifies a disease condition and urges consumers to see their doctors.

Advertising of prescription drugs on commercial television is permitted, but it must make "adequate provision" for consumers to obtain further information.

WASHINGTON LEGAL FOUNDATION CASE

A celebrated legal case involving the promotion of medical products was brought by the Washington Legal Foundation (WLF). In 1993, WLF filed a citizen's petition with FDA objecting to the agency's policies restricting the ability of pharmaceutical companies to provide scientific information to healthcare professionals that is truthful and nonmisleading but not consistent with FDA-approved labeling for the product. This case evolved into protracted litigation that lasted until 2000.

The case focused on the right of pharmaceutical companies to provide healthcare professionals with truthful and nonmisleading scientific information, including reprints of peer-reviewed materials and sponsorship of CME programs. WLF took the view that the criteria for such communication should be whether the information itself was truthful, not whether the information was consistent with the FDA-approved labeling.

On July 30, 1998, the court enjoined FDA from seeking to limit any pharmaceutical manufacturer's ability to disseminate to healthcare professionals any off-label information published in a peer-reviewed journal, to disseminate bona fide textbooks or suggest content or speakers for an independent CME program, even when off-label uses are to be discussed. This decision was later vacated.

In 2000, during oral argument on appeal, FDA stated that it viewed its CME guidance as establishing a "safe harbor" for pharmaceutical company sponsorship of medical education, and would take enforcement action against companies that provided peer-reviewed articles to healthcare professionals only if the information itself was false and/or misleading or contrary to the public health. In March 2000, FDA published a notice in the *Federal Register* that reiterated its "safe harbor" position.

FDA's articulation of its policy did not resolve the uncertainty. WLF returned to court to seek clarity, but on November 30, 2000, the district court denied the request. The court criticized FDA for failing to resolve the issue: "After six years' worth of briefs, motions, opinions, congressional acts and more opinions, the issue remains 100% unresolved, and the country's drug manufacturers are still without clear guidance as to the permissibility of this conduct." *Washington Legal Foundation v. Henney*, 128 F. Supp. 2d 11, 15 (D.D.C. 2000).

ENFORCEMENT

FDA cannot mandate, but does expect, companies to have written policies and procedures for reviewing promotional materials and programs, including an internal review process. The agency also cannot mandate, but does expect, regular training for staff, including the sales force, on regulatory requirements. Training has become a major focus for many companies that want to be sure that everyone in the company, from top management to the sales force, is aware of the company's philosophy toward FDA's rules, especially with regard to how the sales force conducts its activities on a day-to-day basis. Training also is required under corporate integrity agreements (CIAs) signed by companies that settle cases under the False Claims Act or anti-kickback statute (see below).

Submission to FDA
Promotional materials for drugs and biological products, but not devices, must be submitted to FDA at time of first use.

For pharmaceuticals and biological products, FDA regulations require that all product-specific promotional materials must be submitted to FDA at the time of their first use. Promotional pieces for pharmaceuticals are submitted to the FDA Office of Prescription Drug Promotion (OPDP, formerly known as the Division of Drug Marketing, Advertising and Communications) in the Center for Drug Evaluation and Research, and for biologics to the Advertising and Promotional Labeling Staff in the Center for Biologics Evaluation and Research. Medical device and veterinary medicine manufacturers have no requirements for routine submission of promotional materials.

FDA enforcement actions generally are premised on its review of materials submitted at the time of their first use by companies and on its own surveillance of the marketplace. Many actions, however, also are based on competitor complaints (i.e., complaints filed by one company against another, or by healthcare professionals). Such complaints often are submitted formally, in writing, to the FDA division responsible for regulating the advertising and promotion of the product. Many companies encourage their employees to gather intelligence about their competitors' promotional activities to assure that regulation is even-handed. In addition, FDA initiated what became known as its "Bad Ad" campaign in which it proactively encouraged physicians to report what they regarded as illegal or inappropriate promotion.

Typically, when FDA detects a violation, it sends the offending company either an "untitled" letter or a warning letter. Both identify FDA's concern and seek remedial action, such as discontinuation of the promotional piece at issue. The letters indicate that the agency has concluded that a legal violation has occurred and remedial action is required, such as withdrawal of the violative materials. FDA also may request that a "Dear Health Professional" letter be disseminated. It also can seek other corrective measures, such as employee training or preclearance of any new promotional materials for a period of time.

Enforcement letters usually provide 10 to 15 days for the company to respond and present a plan of action. Companies often seek a meeting or teleconference with FDA to discuss the appropriateness of the remedial action. Enforcement letters are made public upon issuance by FDA, and thus become a potential source of negative publicity, as well as a potent enforcement tool. FDA posts warning and untitled letters on its Internet site (www.fda.gov), along with the violative materials.

FDA has other enforcement options. FDA has the option to seek a seizure, injunction or criminal action (misdemeanor or felony) against violative companies or activities. FDA usually includes in its "untitled" letters, and always in its Warning Letters, the possibility of more stringent action but as a practical matter a seizure, injunction or criminal prosecution is unlikely.

OVER-THE-COUNTER PRODUCTS

The FTC has authority over the advertising and promotion of nonprescription drugs and nonrestricted devices, as well as foods and cosmetics. The FTC's authority, which predates FDA's, stems from section 5 of the Federal Trade Commission Act, which gives the commission authority to prevent companies from "using unfair methods of competition . . . and unfair or deceptive acts or practices in or affecting commerce." (The FTC technically retains some legal jurisdiction over prescription drug advertising, but as a practical matter defers to FDA.)

The FTC regulates the advertising and promotion of nonprescription drugs, nonrestricted devices, foods and cosmetics.

FDA and the FTC work together in cases involving medical products because the FTC does not have a medical staff and any FTC action must be based on FDA-approved labeling of over-the-counter (OTC) drugs or nonrestricted devices. FDA and the FTC operate under a 1971 Memorandum of Understanding that sets forth how the relationship between the two agencies will work. FTC procedures permit companies to engage in formal discussions with staff before any matter is resolved. The usual resolution of an FTC investigation is the signing of a consent decree in which the company admits no wrongdoing but agrees never to repeat the activity to which the FTC has objected. The FTC also has the authority to seek a temporary restraining order or an injunction.

PRESCRIPTION DRUG MARKETING ACT

The use of drug samples—small quantities of a product that are provided free of charge to a physician so that he or she may provide them free to a patient as a "starter"—is addressed in specific legislation, the Prescription Drug Marketing Act (PDMA), a section of the FDCA. The law addressed concern that control over samples was not sufficient to preclude their diversion into commercial channels or, more important, that samples of drugs subject to potential abuse might be readily diverted.

PDMA prohibits the diversion of prescription drugs or biological products into illegitimate commercial channels. It also prohibits the sale of drug samples. The law provides that companies must obtain the signature of a physician for all drug samples. The law also requires recordkeeping and careful storage of samples. Whenever a manufacturer discovers any diversion, it must report this to FDA.

FDCA prohibits sale and diversion of drug samples.

FALSE CLAIMS ACT

The federal False Claims Act was originally passed during the Civil War to prevent vendors from defrauding the government. The law was amended in 1986, and a dozen years later the government started using the law to bring actions against the pharmaceutical and medical devices industries.

The basic allegation in the cases was that if a drug or device company promoted a product "off-label," and if, as a consequence, the product cost was reimbursed by the government, then that constitutes fraud against the government. The law provides that whistle-blowers can initiate such cases, and the vast majority of cases brought against the drug and device industries have been brought by whistle-blowers, often current or former company employees, who under the law can collect 15 to 30 percent of the fine. These are known as *"qui tam"* cases.

Several dozen such cases have been brought against pharmaceutical and medical device companies, resulting in fines that often are in the hundreds of millions or billions of dollars. The cases also resulted in companies signing Corporate Integrity Agreements (CIAs) with the government. The cases are brought by the Department of Justice in conjunction with the Office of the Inspector General of the Department of Health and Human Services (OIG HHS), which usually is intimately involved in negotiating the settlements.

HHS's interest and authority in this area comes from the fact that it administers the Medicaid and Medicare programs, and the OIG HHS is responsible for preventing fraud and abuse in these programs. (Medicaid is a joint state/federal healthcare reimbursement program for people who cannot afford treatment, while Medicare is a federal program that reimburses for healthcare for the elderly and disabled.)

Many states also have their own false claims statutes and state attorneys general also have brought cases and have shared in the settlements.

In one settlement, three corporate officials pleaded guilty to misdemeanors and paid substantial fines for their roles in promotional activities. This reflected the government's interest in pursuing individual liability.

The OIG sets standards for internal compliance programs.

In 2003, OIG HHS issued a guidance explaining what it expects from pharmaceutical companies to avoid making false claims under the False Claims Act. The guidelines, published in the *Federal Register* on May 5, 2003, set forth standards for internal compliance programs for pharmaceutical manufacturers. The guidance contained both broad principles for compliance, such as encouraging a corporate culture of compliance, as well as specific policies that companies are expected to adopt and follow.

The guidance set forth seven elements "that have been widely recognized as fundamental to an effective compliance program." The seven elements constitute the basis for much of the contents of CIAs. The seven elements are:

- ♦ **Implementing written policies and procedures:** The written policies should "verbalize" the company's commitment to compliance and address specific areas of fraud and abuse, such as the reporting of pricing and rebate information, and sales and marketing practices.

- ♦ **Designating a compliance officer and committee:** The compliance officer and committee are responsible for developing and monitoring the compliance program and should report directly to the board of directors or president/chief executive officer of the company.

- **Conducting effective training and education:** All affected employees should be trained substantively at regular intervals.

- **Developing effective lines of communication:** There should be effective communication between the compliance officer and all employees. Companies should establish a telephone hotline for reporting internal complaints. This safeguards the anonymity of complainants and protects whistle-blowers from retaliation.

- **Conducting internal monitoring and auditing:** There regularly should be audits or other risk evaluation techniques to monitor compliance or identify problem areas.

- **Enforcing standards through well-publicized disciplinary guidelines:** Companies should develop policies and procedures to preclude the employment of individuals or companies excluded from participating in federal healthcare programs and to enforce disciplinary action against employees or contractors who have violated the rules.

- **Responding promptly to detected problems and undertaking corrective action:** Firms should implement policies and procedures for identifying and investigating any instances of noncompliance or misconduct.

ANTI-KICKBACK

Another federal law that applies to marketing medical products is the "anti-kickback" law (42 U.S.C. § 1320a-7b). This law, which dates from 1972, is not part of either the FDCA or the False Claims Act; instead, it relates to the Medicaid and Medicare statutes.

The anti-kickback law relates to the Medicaid and Medicare statutes.

The anti-kickback statutes are intended to prevent overuse of and overcharging for medical products that are subject to government reimbursement under either Medicaid or Medicare (or other government-reimbursed healthcare programs). They prohibit any activity in which a medical products company may try to persuade, other than with sound therapeutic arguments, a physician or another healthcare provider or facility to use a particular product.

Specifically, the law, which is enforced by the OIG HHS, prohibits a company from offering "any remuneration (including any kickback, bribe or rebate) directly or indirectly, overtly or covertly, in cash or in kind" to anyone to induce them to purchase a product or service for which reimbursement may be sought under Medicaid or Medicare. The regulations do provide certain exceptions, also known as "safe harbors," which do permit some marketing activities.

A number of settlements with pharmaceutical and medical device companies have been signed under the anti-kickback law. The cases have entailed significant fines and the signing of CIAs.

PhRMA and AdvaMed Codes

In 2002, the Pharmaceutical Research and Manufacturers of America (PhRMA)—the trade association of research-oriented drug companies—adopted a Code on Interactions with Healthcare Professionals. It attempted to redefine the relationship between healthcare professionals and the pharmaceutical industry. It was adopted by the PhRMA Board of Directors and became effective in 2002, and was later updated effective January 2009. The code is voluntary but has been adopted by most companies and become the standard of conduct for drug companies.

In January 2004, AdvaMed, the trade association representing large medical device companies, issued its own code. It was similar to the PhRMA code except in those areas in which pharmaceutical marketing differs from medical device marketing, such as the ability of device companies to promote their products before approval (but not make any claims or take orders).

Specific provisions of the codes include:

♦ **Informational presentations:** Presentations by industry representatives and others speaking on behalf of a company are encouraged. Occasional meals (but no entertainment or recreational events) may be offered as long as the meals: 1) are modest as judged by local standards; 2) occur in a venue and manner conducive to informational communication; and 3) take place in conjunction with activities that provide scientific or educational value.

♦ **Medical education:** Financial support from companies for scientific and educational conferences or professional meetings is permissible provided no strings are attached. Such financial support should be given to the conference's sponsor through a grant.

♦ **Consultants:** Consultants who provide legitimate services to companies may be offered compensation at fair market value as well as reimbursement for travel, lodging and meal expenses. Token consulting should not be used. It is not appropriate to pay honoraria, travel or lodging expenses to nonfaculty and nonconsultant attendees at company-sponsored meetings.

♦ **Grants:** No grants, scholarships, subsidies, support, consulting contracts or educational or practice-related items or other remuneration should be provided or offered to a healthcare professional in exchange for prescribing products. Nothing should be offered or provided in a manner or under conditions that would influence or interfere with the independence of a doctor's prescribing practices.

♦ **Gifts:** Gifts to physicians are not permitted under the PhRMA code unless they are of an educational nature. This provision eliminated pens, pads and other items provided by drug companies, as well as items for display in medical offices.

In January 2006, another PhRMA code, setting forth principles for DTC advertising, took effect. This is a voluntary code with which most major pharmaceutical companies have agreed to comply. It states that "all DTC information should be accurate and not misleading, should make claims only when supported by substantial evidence, should reflect balance between risks and benefits, and should be consistent with FDA approved labeling."

Further, these principles also state that "DTC television and print advertising for prescription drugs should clearly indicate that the medicine is a prescription drug, to distinguish such advertising from other advertising for non-prescription products." Companies should "spend an appropriate amount of time to educate health professionals about a new medicine or a new therapeutic indication before commencing the first DTC advertising campaign" and "should submit all new DTC television advertisements to the FDA before releasing these advertisements for broadcast. . . . DTC television and print advertising should include information about the availability of other options such as diet and lifestyle changes where appropriate for the advertised condition" and "DTC television and print advertisements should be targeted to avoid audiences that are not age appropriate for the messages involved."

The adoption of the PhRMA principles led to a significant increase in the number of DTC advertising campaigns for prescription drugs submitted to the agency for an advisory opinion.

There has been a significant increase in the number of DTC advertising campaigns for prescription drugs submitted to the agency for an advisory opinion.

CONCLUSION

FDA's regulation of marketing practices by medical products companies—specifically their promotional programs—has become a highly specialized and especially dynamic field within food and drug law. The rules are set forth in a variety of ways—in FDA regulations, in guidances and in enforcement actions—but are constantly refined in public discussions by regulators. The policies and their nuances continue to evolve as new products are introduced and new means of communications become available.

In essence, however, the key principles underlying FDA regulation have been constant. Programs and materials must be truthful, they must prominently disclose risk information, "scientific exchange" but no commercialization may take place before a product is approved and there may be no efforts by medical products manufacturers to persuade or induce healthcare providers to use products for uses not approved by FDA.

Chapter 14

Review of FDA Inspections and Related Regulations

Ronald F. Tetzlaff, Ph.D. & David L. Chesney, PAREXEL Consulting, Duluth, GA and Lowell, MA

Key Points

- FDA inspections are administrative investigations to determine whether the inspected company is in compliance with the Federal Food, Drug, and Cosmetic Act (FDCA) or other laws enforced by the Food and Drug Administration (FDA).
- Inspectors' actions must comply with general statutory standards of reasonableness (time, limits, manner) and specific procedures as provided by law.
- Inspections may be initiated for routine purposes, for cause or as a follow-up to prior adverse findings. This chapter explains the more common reasons for inspections, with a focus on good manufacturing practices (GMP) inspections.
- FDA employees who conduct inspections have a wide variety of backgrounds. Inspections are conducted by FDA investigators, chemists, microbiologists, engineers and various scientists having specialized education and training.
- Effective preparation and management of FDA inspections may significantly influence the outcome.
- FDA has put in place a variety of policies, procedures and forms with a bearing on inspections. These are public documents and companies are well advised to be familiar with their content and purpose.
- Companies may facilitate FDA inspections by following general guidelines for effective communication and interaction with inspectors and other agency officials.
- A trained person should act as escort for FDA during the course of the inspection.
- A conference room or office should be set aside for FDA's use during the inspection. A separate conference room should serve as the company's command post for the inspection.

INTRODUCTION

One of the principal functions of the Food and Drug Administration (FDA) is to conduct inspections of facilities that manufacture, process, pack or hold foods, drugs, medical devices, biologicals, cosmetics and other products that are subject to FDA regulation. The purpose of FDA inspections is to determine whether regulated products have been processed, packed or held under conditions that may result in such products being adulterated or misbranded within the meaning of the Federal Food, Drug, and Cosmetic Act (FDCA), or whether products lacking FDA approval (where approval is required) are being sold and shipped. FDA inspections conducted within the United States and its territories are usually unannounced (foreign inspections, with very rare exceptions, are pre-announced), and may include examination of manufacturing sites, contract laboratories, warehouses and quality control laboratories for evidence of violations, including reviews of production and laboratory control records to determine if conditions and practices are in compliance with applicable laws and regulations.

FDA inspections are usually unannounced, and may include examination of manufacturing sites, contract laboratories, warehouses and quality control laboratories for evidence of violations.

Inspections are also conducted under what FDA terms its "bioresearch monitoring" inspections program. These inspections are done at sponsors' clinical trials sites, Contract Research Organizations (CROs) and/or sites where clinical investigations are conducted to determine compliance with applicable regulations, commitments made in relevant submissions (e.g., investigational new drug (IND) applications and investigational device exemption (IDE) applications), and to assess data integrity. Under FDA-approved INDs or IDEs, sponsors are permitted to use investigational drugs and devices to obtain safety and effectiveness data needed to support new drug applications (NDAs) and premarket approval (PMA) applications. In addition, under the bioresearch monitoring program, FDA inspects Institutional Review Boards (IRBs) for compliance with 21 C.F.R. Parts 50 and 56, nonclinical (animal safety testing) laboratories for compliance with the Good Laboratory Practice (GLP) regulations (21 C.F.R. Part 58), and bioanalytical laboratories that support bioequivalence and bioavailability testing of generic drugs, for compliance with 21 C.F.R. Part 320.

Specially trained investigators and laboratory personnel conduct FDA inspections. FDA inspection approaches vary for each of the different types of products regulated. For example, most inspections of food-manufacturing facilities and warehouses are intended to determine if products have been processed, packed or held under insanitary conditions whereby they may have been contaminated with filth, rendered injurious to health or are otherwise unfit for consumption. For drugs, medical devices and biologicals, FDA inspections evaluate the adequacy of controls used to ensure the identity, strength, quality or purity of such products, and to verify that they are in conformance with applicable compendia.

When FDA detects violative conditions or practices during its inspections, evidence is collected to support recommendations for regulatory sanctions against individuals, companies and/or products, when deemed necessary.

Evidence may be in the form of direct observations by investigators, copies of production and control records, and reports to prove violations of laws and regulations, as well as shipping records to prove the connection with interstate commerce necessary to establish federal jurisdiction. Sometimes, samples of products or extraneous material are collected for analysis to support inspection findings.

Inspections that detect significant violations, such as insanitary conditions or noncompliance with current good manufacturing practice (cGMP) regulations, may lead FDA to initiate legal proceedings to effect corrective actions, or to punish responsible persons. Before proceeding to litigation, however, FDA frequently (but not necessarily) will issue a Warning Letter to advise management of the nature of the violations and the applicable sections of the law that the agency is prepared to invoke against the company or individual. When such warnings are ineffective, or if conditions are egregious or pose imminent health hazards, FDA may initiate formal administrative or judicial actions such as seizures, criminal prosecutions or civil monetary penalties, temporary restraining orders or permanent injunctions to prevent continued distribution of violative products in interstate commerce.

FDA authority to conduct inspections is derived from section 704 of the FDCA (21 U.S.C. § 374), which defines the conditions under which FDA may conduct its inspections. Inspections may extend to a factory, warehouse, laboratory or other establishment that manufactures, processes, packs or holds foods, drugs, devices and cosmetics. Inspections may encompass facilities, records, finished or unfinished products, files, papers, records and other documents. Regulations that are relevant to FDA inspections or cGMPs include, but are not limited to, the following:

FDA authority to conduct inspections is derived from the FDCA, which defines the conditions under which FDA may conduct its inspections.

♦ food-related regulations, including infant formulas (21 C.F.R. Part 106);

♦ low-acid canned food (21 C.F.R. Part 113) and food (GMPs) (21 C.F.R. Part 110);

♦ human and veterinary finished pharmaceuticals, including GMP regulations (21 C.F.R. Parts 210 and 211) and medicated animal feeds and premixes (21 C.F.R. Parts 225 and 226);

♦ medical devices (21 C.F.R. Part 820) and quality system regulations; and

♦ biologicals, such as biological products (21 C.F.R. Part 600) and blood and blood components (21 C.F.R. Part 606).

GMP regulations for drugs, biologics and devices are binding, and have the force and effect of law. The general food GMPs found at 21 C.F.R. Part 110 are interpretive and serve as guidance to the food industry. FDA has not promulgated GMPs for the cosmetics industry.

FDA INSPECTION AUTHORITY

Federal Food, Drug, and Cosmetic Act

FDAMA amended the provisions of the FDCA and the biological provisions of the Public Health Service Act, including a number of sections that deal with FDA inspection authority.

The FDCA is the principal law that provides FDA authority to conduct factory inspections. It provides FDA with the authority to inspect any factory, warehouse or establishment in which foods, drugs, devices or cosmetics are manufactured, processed, packed or held for introduction into interstate commerce (or after such introduction) or any vehicle being used to transport or hold such food, drugs, devices or cosmetics in interstate commerce. The FDCA also defines prohibited acts and provides for regulatory and administrative sanctions that enable FDA to bring noncomplying companies or persons into compliance with the law. The Food and Drug Administration Modernization Act of 1997 (FDAMA) amended the provisions of the FDCA and the biological provisions of the Public Health Service Act, including a number of sections that deal with FDA inspection authority (such as new provisions that extended FDA's authority to have access to records for over-the-counter (OTC) drugs).

The following chapters of the FDCA are relevant to the FDA inspection process:

Chapter	Topic
III	Defines what acts are prohibited and provides for certain administrative and criminal sanctions (penalties)
IV	Provides the basic definition of what constitutes adulteration and misbranding for foods
V	Defines adulteration and misbranding for drugs
VI	Defines adulteration and misbranding for cosmetics
VII	Establishes FDA authority to conduct inspections
VIII	Provides requirements for imports and exports

FDA's General Inspection Authority

Chapter VII of the FDCA confers general inspection authority on FDA. It authorizes duly accredited FDA personnel to enter and inspect certain types of regulated facilities at ". . .reasonable times, and within reasonable limits and in a reasonable manner. . .." The specifics of what constitutes a "reasonable time" are not defined in the statute, but precedents exist that establish that a "reasonable time" is any time regulated activities are being conducted. Other specifics of the "reasonableness standard" have been the subject of debate for many years, such as whether the agency has statutory authority to take photographs during inspections.

In 1952, the Supreme Court ruled that the factory inspection provisions of the 1938 FDCA were too vague to be enforced as criminal law (*United States v. Cardiff*). As a result, Congress passed the Factory Inspection Amendments in 1953 to provide clarification to the 1938 act. These amendments provided for FDA to present manufacturers with a written notice of inspection at the beginning of an inspection, and written reports of observations at the conclusion of the inspection. The amendments also required FDA to provide written receipts for samples, as well as reports of analysis for certain types of samples (FDCA § 704). The provision for a written report of observations at the conclusion of an inspection forms the basis for today's Form FDA-483.

Upon initiating an inspection, FDA personnel must display appropriate credentials and give the owner, operator or agent in charge a written notice of inspection.

Upon initiating an inspection, FDA personnel must display appropriate credentials and give to ". . .the owner, operator or agent in charge. . ." a written notice of inspection. For this purpose, the agency uses the Notice of Inspection, Form FDA-482.

Section 704 of the FDCA confers to FDA specific authority to conduct inspections of any factory, warehouse or establishment where food, drugs, devices or cosmetics are manufactured, processed, packed or held for introduction into interstate commerce (or after such introduction). For prescription and OTC drugs and restricted medical devices the inspection authority generally extends to all things having a bearing on whether the products have been manufactured, processed, packed or held under conditions whereby they may become adulterated or misbranded within the meaning of the law. The statutory authority includes the following language:

> . . . In the case of any factory, warehouse, establishment, or consulting laboratory in which prescription drugs, nonprescription drugs intended for human use, or restricted devices are manufactured, processed, packed, or held, the inspection shall extend to all things therein (including records, files, papers, processes, controls, and facilities) bearing on whether prescription drugs, nonprescription drugs intended for human use, or restricted devices which are adulterated or misbranded within the meaning of this Act, or which may not be manufactured, introduced into interstate commerce, or sold, or offered for sale by reason of any provision of this Act, have been or are being manufactured, processed, packed, transported, or held in any such place, or otherwise bearing on violation of this Act. No inspection authorized by the preceding sentence or by paragraph (3) shall extend to financial data, sales data other than shipment data, pricing data, personnel data (other than data as to qualifications of technical and professional personnel performing functions subject to this Act), and research

data (other than data relating to new drugs, antibiotic drugs, and devices and subject to reporting and inspection under regulations lawfully issued pursuant to section 505(i) or (k)[*] section 519, or 520(g), and data relating to other drugs or devices which in the case of a new drug would be subject to reporting or inspection under lawful regulations issued pursuant to section 505(j)). . . .

For this special category of products, the law grants access to all things therein that have a bearing on adulteration or misbranding. The act specifically exempts from FDA inspection certain types of information including financial, sales and pricing (other than shipment data), research data and certain personnel data unless such information directly has a bearing on whether a product may be adulterated, misbranded or otherwise in violation of applicable laws or regulations. Notably, this exception does not apply to research data relating to new drugs that are subject to reporting and inspection under regulations issued pursuant to the new drug provisions of the FDCA, such as under sections 505(i) or (k), 507(d), and others.

For new drugs and medical devices and for licensed biological products, FDA must act on requests for regulatory approvals (including but not limited to NDAs, abbreviated new drug applications (ANDAs), PMAs for devices, biologic license applications (BLAs), and other similar submissions). FDA decisions are based upon information and data contained in applications submitted by sponsors. To verify the accuracy and completeness (integrity) of such information and data relative to pending or approved applications, FDA has authority to access both facilities (on-site inspections) and records. Failure to allow access to records to which FDA is entitled is a prohibited act under section 301 of the FDCA. A refusal may cause the agency to seek an administrative inspection warrant to compel such access. An administrative inspection warrant affirms FDA's existing statutory authority and may interpret certain aspects in more specific terms than provided by statute. However, an administrative inspection warrant is not a search warrant and does not broaden FDA's authority beyond existing statutory limits. For example, an administrative inspection warrant may be sought to compel a company to allow FDA to take photographs during an inspection (subsequent to a refusal to permit photography) on the grounds that photographs are sometimes necessary to a "reasonable" inspection. This specific use of administrative inspection warrants is not common. When it does occur, it may be controversial, but serves to illustrate the potential use of such warrants for situations that are less egregious than outright refusal to permit entry.

With the FDA pre-approval inspection program, FDA investigators routinely request access to new drug and biologic development records. The same is true for medical device design history files, which are mandated by the Quality

System Regulation (QSR). FDA investigators expect access to records that are retained by personnel with "research" functions or responsibilities if the data support product applications. FDA generally will not be persuaded that access is not permitted because testing performed represents "discovery" rather than "developmental" research, after a submission has been filed based on the development data.

There are exemptions from inspection that are provided by statute. Section 704(a)(2) of the FDCA states that FDA authority does not include access to records and facilities that manufacture prescription drugs and restricted devices in four specific instances: 1) pharmacies that are in conformance with local laws (provided their activities are limited to dispensing and selling drugs or devices at retail); 2) practitioners who are licensed by law to prescribe or administer drugs (or use devices) if the manufacture or processing is for use in the course of their professional practice; 3) persons who manufacture such products solely for use in teaching, research or chemical analysis where such products are not for sale; and 4) any other classes of person as designated by FDA by regulation to be exempt upon finding that inspection is not necessary for the protection of public health.

Section 704(b) requires that FDA, upon completion of an inspection, leave with the owner, operator or agent in charge a written report that identifies any conditions or practices observed by the employee

Upon completion of an inspection, FDA personnel must leave a written report with the owner, operator or agent in charge.

> . . .which, in his judgment, indicate that any food, drug, device, tobacco product, or cosmetic in such establishment (1) consists in whole or part of any filthy, putrid or decomposed substance, or (2) has been prepared, packed, or held under insanitary conditions whereby it may have become contaminated with filth or whereby it may have been rendered injurious to health. . .

FDA generally records its observations on a form known as an FDA-483 (List of Inspectional Observations). While the statute itself only mandates that a report be issued for adulteration-related observations, FDA has for many years included other inspection-related observations on the form as a matter of policy. Certain exceptions are described in Chapter 5 of FDA's *Investigations Operations Manual*, which is available at http://www.fda.gov.

When FDA collects a physical sample during the course of an inspection, a written receipt for samples must be provided to the owner, operator or agent in charge. Such receipt (FDA Form FDA-484) must be issued upon completion of the inspection, and prior to before leaving the premises. In the case of food samples collected during an inspection, FDA is required by section 704(d) to provide a written report on any sample analyzed for evidence of being filthy, putrid or decomposed. This provision applies only to foods and does not extend to samples of drugs, devices or cosmetics that are collected during FDA inspections, nor does it apply to results of food analysis other than ascertaining if food consists in whole or part of any filthy, putrid or decomposed substance or is otherwise unfit for food.

FDA employees authorized to conduct inspections, while acting in the course of their official duties, are authorized to possess controlled substances as per 21 C.F.R. § 1301.24(a)(1) and other sections; e.g., 21 C.F.R. § 1309.26(a)(1). This permits FDA investigators to collect samples of controlled substances during inspections and other special assignments. The Form FDA-484 prepared by the FDA investigator, however, must contain FDA's Drug Enforcement Administration (DEA) Registration Number and that of the establishment from which the products are obtained. All other inventory controls required by DEA regulations apply to FDA and to anyone providing samples of controlled substances to an FDA investigator.

While there may be some "gray areas" between "pure research" and new drug development activities, firms should expect FDA to routinely request access to the records supporting process validity.

For many years, controversies have persisted about the legal requirements for process validation in the GMPs, and their application to research and development activities. While there may be some "gray areas" between "pure research" and new drug development activities, firms should expect FDA to routinely request access to the records supporting process validity. While some firms have been reluctant to provide FDA access to drug development records based on the erroneous assumption that FDA is not entitled to "research" data, the FDCA provides FDA with authority to access and copy records and reports required under the new drug provisions. Drug development involves a continuum from "pure" research activities (i.e., discovery related) through transition phases where the activities clearly have a bearing on GMP or validation issues. Therefore, the statutory exemption from access to research data should be considered applicable only until the point when the data is intended to be used in support of an application for FDA approval to permit use of the new drug or medical device in clinical trials (and beyond). At that stage in the development process, the research data that forms the basis of claims made in the relevant submission may be subject to review during FDA inspections. Correspondingly, research data that is not relevant to any current submission to the agency would be considered exempt from inspection, because it has no bearing on the status of any marketed product or on the validity of any submission to FDA.

For drug manufacturers located outside the United States, there is no specific statutory authority for FDA to conduct factory inspections. FDA has an active international inspection program, and inspections are conducted routinely in various parts of the world. While strictly speaking, foreign inspections are voluntary, firms that refuse to allow FDA inspection may find that FDA will invoke advisory or administrative sanctions, such as preventing the importation of the company's products into the United States under provisions of section 801. Another potential sanction is the withholding of NDA or ANDA approvals, as well as withholding approval of other regulatory submissions that have been made by that firm or by a sponsor who lists the firm in their application(s). When FDA inspections of drug or device manufacturers reveal insanitary conditions or practices that do not conform to current GMP or QSR regulations, FDA may invoke administrative sanctions that result in refusal to permit entry into the United States.

CURRENT GOOD MANUFACTURING PRACTICES CONCEPTS

The 1962 Drug Amendments added two important sections that are relevant to FDA inspections. FDA was granted authority to promulgate regulations and a provision was added that required companies to comply with "current good manufacturing practices" (FDCA § 501(a)(2)(B)). Although the law did not define what constituted "current good manufacturing practices," the FDCA was amended to allow FDA to publish regulations to define its requirements and expectations. FDA published its interpretation of cGMPs in 1963 (currently 21 C.F.R. Parts 210, 211 for human and veterinary drug products, and 21 C.F.R. Parts 225, 226 for medicated premixes and medicated feeds for animals).

The 1962 Drug Amendments granted FDA authority to promulgate regulations and added a provision that required companies to comply with "current good manufacturing practices."

The following are examples of the key regulations that have been promulgated to define cGMPs for specific commodities. It should be noted, however, that the term "current good manufacturing practice" is limited to drugs and medical devices in the statute. Conceptually, the idea of cGMP has been extended to include regulations governing food manufacturing, but the statutory basis of cGMP is derived from the drug and device adulteration provision of the FDCA as cited above.

- *Foods*—The low-acid canned food regulations (21 C.F.R. Part 113) and the companion rules for acidified food (21 C.F.R. Part 114) were issued as a consequence of a number of botulism outbreaks that occurred during the 1960s and 1970s involving food products packaged in hermetically sealed containers. These regulations define the minimum requirements and controls necessary to ensure such products are processed in a manner that ensures they are safe.

- *Devices*—The Quality System Regulation (QSR) (21 C.F.R. Part 820) defines cGMP for medical device facilities. The QSR applies to the methods, facilities and controls that are used during the design and manufacture (including packaging, labeling, storage, installation and servicing).

♦ *cGMPs for Finished Pharmaceuticals*—These were promulgated in 1963 and have been updated a number of times over the years (usually in reaction to incidents or problems) (21 C.F.R. Part 211). In 2007, FDA issued a Direct Final Rule to amend the drug GMPs in an effort to modernize the requirements and to better harmonize with regulatory authorities in foreign countries. The cGMPs describe the minimum FDA requirements for conforming to the cGMP requirements of the FDCA.

FDA published the cGMP regulations as being legally binding requirements; i.e., they define the minimum cGMP that must be followed for the production and control of finished pharmaceuticals. The cGMPs describe the minimum FDA requirements for conforming to the current good manufacturing practices that are cited in the FDCA. Although the cGMPs are substantive, they do not spell out in detail how firms are expected to satisfy the requirements. The cGMPs require that firms have in place standard operating procedures (SOPs) that provide the additional detail needed to apply the regulations to a specific site, and that such SOPs be followed. This is the manner in which the cGMPs are made relevant to specific local circumstances

The cGMPs are considered broad "umbrella" regulations in that they apply to all finished pharmaceuticals for humans and animals.

The cGMPs included within 21 C.F.R. 211 are considered broad "umbrella" regulations in that they apply to all finished pharmaceuticals for humans and animals. The language of the regulation is broad enough to describe the requirements for all dosage forms (tablets, capsules, oral liquids, topicals, transdermals, parenterals, etc.), and the requirements apply to both prescription and OTC drugs. Because they apply across the board to all finished drug products, the regulation contains ample use of subjective terms (such as adequate, appropriate, sufficient and others). (Conceptually, the same is true for the cGMP regulations for medicated animal feeds and premixes; see, at 21 C.F.R. 225 and 226.)

♦ *Drug Regulations* (21 C.F.R. Parts 300-499)—FDA has promulgated extensive regulations covering many of the administrative details concerning procedures that must be followed when submitting NDAs and ANDAs to FDA. These sections contain detailed requirements for filing NDAs and ANDAs, as well as the requirements for various drug products. The requirements for submissions for postapproval change have been effected directly by FDAMA, which added section 506A to the FDCA. The major effects of this section on FDA inspections are the statutory requirement to validate postapproval changes, and the subdivision of supplements into four principal types: Pre-approval supplement; Changes Being Effected (30 days); Changes Being Effected (immediate) and Annual Report submissions. This is quite similar to the previous scheme except for the addition of the Changes Being Effected (30 days) provision. Manufacturers filing this type of submission must wait 30 days before implementing the change, to allow FDA an opportunity to review the change and comment (or object).

New drugs that are intended to be administered to humans or animals must be manufactured in accordance with the cGMP regulations, and the NDAs must certify conformance. If production is done in laboratory research facilities or pilot plant production facilities, the procedures may be different from those used in full-scale production facilities. NDAs must include detailed descriptions of manufacturing and control procedures. If changes are made from NDA commitments, it may be necessary to obtain prior approval from FDA or to notify FDA following the change.

♦ *Applications for FDA Approval to Market a New Drug or Antibiotic* (21 C.F.R. Part 314)—This section describes requirements for NDAs and various administrative actions followed by the agency for reviewing and approving applications.

♦ *Other Postmarketing Reports* (21 C.F.R. § 314.81)—FDA inspections frequently are triggered as a result of firms filing an NDA Field Alert Report (FAR) as provided for by this section. Applicants are required to submit, within three working days of receipt, information about products that: 1) involve any incident that causes a drug product or its labeling to be mistaken for another (e.g., label mix-up), 2) failure of a distributed product to meet specifications listed in applications, or 3) significant change or deterioration of the drug product (such as physicochemical deterioration or microbiological contamination). NOTE: Licensed biologics that are also drugs are not covered by this regulation, but rather, by the Biological Product Deviation Reporting (BPDR) requirements at 21 C.F.R. 600.14. While similar in many ways to the requirements for FARs, a key difference in the BPDR regulation is that the report must be submitted within 45 working days rather than three days as is the case for FARs.

♦ *Annual Report* (21 C.F.R. § 314.81)—Sponsors holding approved NDAs must file annual reports. During postapproval inspections, FDA inspection teams review the content of NDAs and the annual reports to compare actual conditions at the facility against commitments. FDA investigators will verify that annual reports have been filed, and that information contained in them is accurate and complete for significant new Information. Such information includes summaries about any matter that may affect the safety, efficacy or labeling including summaries of actions taken in response to new information or intentions to take actions such as supplements, new warnings or initiate new studies. FDA may verify that annual reports contain distribution data showing the quantity of the drug

During postapproval inspections, FDA inspection teams review the content of NDAs and the annual reports to compare actual conditions at the facility against commitments.

product distributed and summary of labeling changes made, as well as copies of representative package labels, inserts, etc. FDA will be alert for the presence or absence of reports of new information about experiences, investigations, studies or tests that involve physical, chemical or micro-biological properties that may affect FDA conclusions about the safety or effectiveness of the drug. Finally, FDA will review documentation about any changes to manufacturing and controls that do not require submis-sions of supplements under Part 314.70 and the various other summaries that are related to nonclinical and clinical studies.

♦ *Drug Master Files* (21 C.F.R. § 314.420)—A Drug Master File (DMF) is a submission to FDA that may be used to provide confidential detailed information about facilities, processes or articles used in the manufactur-ing, processing, packaging and storing of one or more human drugs. The submission of a DMF is not required by law or FDA regulation, and a DMF is not a substitute for an IND application, NDA, ANDA or export applica-tion. There is no process whereby a DMF is "approved" or disapproved by FDA. During the conduct of pre-approval inspections FDA inspection teams frequently review copies of applicable DMFs that relate to contain-ers, closures and facilities. FDA will carefully compare commitments made in DMFs (such as specifications, test methods, release limits and the like) against the corresponding specifications, methods or release limits that are in place at the user firm. If discrepancies are noted, this may result in an FDA citation.

Five DMFs and the rules for submitting them are listed in 21 C.F.R. § 314.420:

♦ Type I (now rescinded), see below

♦ Type II covers drug substances, drug substance intermediates and material used in their preparation.

♦ Type III covers packaging material, including toxicological data on these materials, if such data is not otherwise available.

♦ Type IV covers excipients, colorants, flavors, essences or materials used in their preparation, including toxicological data.

♦ Type V covers "accepted reference information," which does not fit any of the above categories. FDA actively discourages this type of DMF. If a firm desires to submit one, prior consultation with FDA is required.

In January 2000, FDA announced a revision of the regulation governing DMFs. FDA removed the provision for submitting Type I DMFs (which formerly covered facilities, operating procedures and personnel) and the agency no longer permits information submitted in a Type I DMF to be incorporated by reference in IND applications, NDAs, ANDAs or amendments or supplements to any of these. FDA's stated intention is to eliminate submissions of information that is not needed for FDA to conduct its inspections of manufacturing facilities or is not needed for its review on the chemistry, manufacturing and controls sections of applications (such as INDs, NDAs and ANDAs). The effective date of this change was July 10, 2000.

♦ *Bioavailability and Bioequivalence* (21 C.F.R. Part 320)—This section describes FDA expectations and procedures for determining the bioavailability or bioequivalence of drug products. Companies submitting full or abbreviated NDAs are required to submit evidence demonstrating bioavailability of the drug product or to request a waiver from the bioavailability requirement. The regulation describes changes reported in supplements for which bioavailability studies may be required, such as changes in manufacturing process that alter product formulation or strength beyond variations permitted in the approved application, or labeling changes, or the establishment of a new dosage regimen. This section also describes FDA requirements for requesting a waiver from bioavailability or bioequivalence testing requirements.

♦ *Biological Product Regulations* (21 C.F.R. Parts 600-680)—Used by FDA for the enforcement of section 351 of the Public Health Service Act, these regulations are similar in content to the drug GMP regulations. Licensing provisions and procedures for Establishment License Applications (ELAs) and Product License Applications (PLAs) are described as are the establishment standards for manufacturing whole blood for transfusions, blood components and blood derivatives. It is important to note that all biological products are by definition also drugs or medical devices as defined in the FDCA, and thus are subject to both statutes. Therapeutic biologicals are most commonly drugs, though some exceptions exist that are devices. Most biological devices are in vitro diagnostic products such as monoclonal antibody test kits, and certain reagents used in blood grouping and typing.

Biological product regulations are similar in content to the drug GMP regulations.

PREPARING FOR AN INSPECTION

Inspections are conducted generally by FDA investigators, most of who are assigned to one of FDA's district offices. Investigators may be assisted by laboratory analysts, engineers, microbiologists, FDA headquarters technical experts and other specialists. Each district office bears responsibility for inspecting the regulated companies located within its geographic boundaries. FDA also

Inspections are conducted generally by FDA investigators, most of who are assigned to one of FDA's district offices.

performs inspections abroad for products that are intended to be shipped into the United States. Some investigators are members of the Commissioned Corps of the U.S. Public Health Services, assigned to FDA. These employees are distinguished by the fact that they use military rank titles such as Lieutenant Commander, and often wear military-style uniforms while on duty. For practical purposes, these employees are no different than any other FDA investigator in terms of the operations they conduct.

Each district office maintains files of previous inspection reports, communications with industry and the results of sample testing. Before performing an inspection, the FDA team usually will review these records to determine whether previous inspections have encountered significant discrepancies or violations. If previous inspections have found problems, the follow-up inspection will assess the adequacy of corrective actions. For pharmaceutical, biologic and medical device inspections, preparation also may include the review of product approval applications to determine compliance with commitments made to the agency. Previously issued FDA-483s are usually reviewed prior to each inspection, as are the associated narrative Establishment Inspection Reports (EIRs). The inspection team will be alert for patterns and trends that reflect evidence of continuing noncompliance, and/or issues that may suggest potential problems in areas not covered previously.

FDA inspection team members also will review appropriate regulatory standards for the facility to be inspected. For example, the team may utilize applicable compendia, such as the U.S. Pharmacopoeia or National Formulary; relevant trade association guidelines; documents that may constitute industry standards; the *Investigations Operations Manual,* which guides the investigators in procedural matters; and the *Compliance Program Guidance Manual,* which contains several hundred documents that describe inspection procedures for particular industries. While FDA investigators may use industry guidelines and standards as references, they are not permitted to impose them as legal requirements.

When preparing for an FDA inspection of a company that has multiple sites, FDA offices often will coordinate their activities to determine whether violations suggest a larger systemic problem. When FDA finds repeated violations at multiple sites for a single company, the agency may consider taking stronger, corporate-wide measures, including the issuance of injunctions.

FDA Inspection Techniques

During a typical FDA inspection, one or more FDA investigators arrive unannounced at a facility. (One exception is domestic inspections of firms as sponsors of clinical investigations, which by policy are routinely pre-announced, no more than 10 days prior to the inspection. Other exceptions to the unannounced inspection policy may be made at the agency's discretion.) FDA inspections may be as short as a few hours or last several weeks or months depending on the purpose. A typical inspection of a food-processing facility may last for a few days and a complex inspection of a pharmaceutical manufacturer may require more than two weeks. If FDA detects significant objectionable conditions, the inspection may be extended as necessary.

FDA inspections may be as short as a few hours or last several weeks or months depending on the purpose.

FDA inspection approaches vary considerably depending on the type of product manufactured at the facility. Typically inspections of food manufacturers concentrate on basic sanitation and employee practices. For example, FDA will examine warehouse areas for evidence of rodents, insects or other vermin, and will observe manufacturing equipment and employee practices for evidence of inadequate cleaning or insanitary employee practices. FDA also is alert for conditions that may lead to food safety issues, such as conditions that may promote microbiological growth in food products, or unsafe handling of insecticides, cleaning agents and other hazardous materials.

The scope of an inspection of a pharmaceutical manufacturer will depend upon the purpose of the inspection, the type of product (which determines the applicable regulations), any special concerns such as current complaints and other factors. For example, FDA inspections of pharmaceutical manufacturers usually include examinations of the facilities and personnel for basic sanitation. In addition, FDA will examine manufacturing and control records to verify conformance with applicable GMPs. Drug products must be manufactured according to manufacturing instructions that have been reviewed and double-checked by at least two persons. The weighing and addition of ingredients must be verified by at least two persons, and personnel must record each significant step in the manufacturing and control operations. Appropriate "in-process" inspections and tests are required to ensure products meet specifications, and before any batch can be released, it must be tested against predetermined specifications. The GMP regulations specify the types of records that must be maintained and the document retention requirements. FDA investigators will examine laboratory facilities and laboratory control records to ensure that appropriate records are being maintained and that test methods are suitable for the intended use. Before any batch can be released it must be tested according to an approved method, and if a product is covered by an official compendial monograph (such as the U.S. Pharmacopoeia), it must be tested to confirm conformance to this standard.

The scope of the inspection will depend upon the purpose of the inspection, the type of product, any special concerns such as current complaints and other factors.

415

A major focus of recent FDA drug and device inspections has been the review of product process validation, as well as the activities surrounding the development of drug formulations and the design of medical devices. FDA expects firms to provide adequate assurances that drugs have the identity, strength, quality and purity characteristics that they purport or are represented to possess. When pre-approval inspections detect application integrity problems or noncompliance with GMPs, FDA may withhold approval of pending product applications.

During FDA inspections, the team will review records covering the manufacturing and testing of any or all batches made to date, and the documents that establish the firm is capable of consistently producing a product that meets predetermined specifications (i.e., verify that processes are validated). If early development activities are found by FDA to be deficient or not well documented, firms may not be in a position to justify the validity of their conclusions about the safety and effectiveness of their drug product.

Recent Inspection Trends

For many years, FDA inspectors have adopted a "quality system" approach, as opposed to the more traditional facility or product-oriented approach. FDA has an established methodology for use of this approach in medical device inspections, known as the Quality System Inspection Technique (QSIT). The QSIT approach is now standard for medical device inspections that focus on compliance with the Quality System Regulation, 21 C.F.R. Part 820.

FDA applies a quality system approach—as opposed to the more traditional facility or product-oriented approach—to medical device, pharmaceutical and biologic inspections.

Since 2002, FDA has also applied a quality system approach to pharmaceutical and biologic inspections. FDA has adopted a six-system definition for purposes of inspection as follows:

1. The *Quality System* includes a wide variety of areas that involve how the company manages its quality operations. Included here are nonconformance investigations, the responsibilities and authority of the Quality Unit, the requirement for annual review of product quality performance and other overall quality management functions.
2. The *Facilities and Equipment System*, which, as the name implies, involves evaluation of the adequacy of the environment and equipment used to produce drugs and biologics.
3. The *Materials System*, which includes evaluation of components, containers and closures, packaging and finishing materials, etc.
4. The *Production System*, which includes review of the controls used to keep manufacturing operations running in compliance with GMP.
5. The *Packaging and Labeling System*, which again as the name implies, involves evaluation of controls to assure that products are properly packaged and carry the correct labels and associated labeling.

6. The *Laboratory Controls System*, which involves evaluation of the procedures, controls and methods used in the laboratory for the analysis of materials, in process and finished products.

Associated training, change control, and records pertinent to each of the systems are reviewed within the context of the systems themselves.

The quality system approach currently used by FDA differs slightly depending on whether the product is a drug (generally regulated by the Center for Drug Evaluation and Research (CDER)) or a biologic (generally regulated by the Center for Biologics Evaluation and Research (CBER)). Both CDER and CBER have issued compliance programs to FDA Field Offices describing how the quality system approach is to be used for the products they regulate. Both compliance programs (7356.002, "Drug Manufacturing Inspections" and 7345.848, "Inspection of Biological Drug Products") provide for either an abbreviated or comprehensive approach, depending on the history of the company, current concerns and findings of the inspection. The reader is referred to the cited compliance programs, available at http://www.fda.gov, for further details.

Due to the increasing globalization of the pharmaceutical industry and the increased importance of supply chain integrity, FDA has expanded its presence in foreign countries, establishing local offices in China, India, Central America, South Africa, Europe and other locations. While FDA personnel assigned to these offices do conduct some inspections, a primary purpose of these offices is to establish working relationships with counterpart agencies in the various nations, and to gain firsthand intelligence about the state of the industry in each locale. Foreign inspections continue to be supported by staff based in the United States, including a dedicated Foreign Inspection Cadre of approximately 15 investigators whose job is limited to foreign inspections. Other District Office based personnel, National Expert level Investigators, and personnel from the Centers continue to support foreign inspections as in the past.

TWO CONTROVERSIAL INSPECTION ISSUES: PHOTOGRAPHY AND AFFIDAVITS

Photography During Inspections

FDA has for many years taken the position that photography is sometimes necessary to a reasonable inspection, and therefore is "just another evidence-gathering tool" authorized under the general "reasonableness" standard of section 704 of the FDCA. However, industry lawyers often take the position that

FDA has for many years taken the position that photography is sometimes necessary to a reasonable inspection.

because the law does not specifically authorize photography, FDA has no right to take photographs, and some companies have policies or procedures that state that FDA personnel will not be allowed to take photographs.

FDA's *Investigations Operations Manual* provides the following instructions to investigators in the event they need to take photographs:

> Do not request permission from management to take photo-graphs during an inspection. Take your camera into the firm and use it as necessary just as you use other inspectional equipment. If management objects to taking photographs, explain that pho-tos are an integral part of an inspection and present an accurate picture of plant conditions. Advise management the U. S. Courts have held that photographs may lawfully be taken as part of an inspection.

The reference goes on to cite two court cases in support of the agency's posi-tion. Nevertheless, the question of whether or not FDA has the right to take photographs during an inspection remains a subject of debate. Opinions in the industry and the legal community vary, and some disagree with the agency's position on the matter.

In practice, FDA rarely takes photographs except during food inspections, most commonly to show gross insanitary conditions.

In practice, FDA rarely takes photographs except during food inspections, most commonly to show gross insanitary conditions. However, it is possible during any inspection (including pharmaceutical and medical device facilities) that the agency may proceed to take photographs. If companies refuse to permit photography, there is a risk that FDA may go to court (ex parte) to seek an administrative inspection warrant to compel the inspected company to allow photography. FDA has been successful in obtaining such warrants, and has also included provisions mandating photography during inspections in consent decree settlements.

An approach used by some companies is to allow limited photography, provided the agency personnel are willing to wait for the company to obtain a camera so that identical photos can be taken by company personnel. Cir-cumstances under which the authors believe companies may have legitimate reasons for prohibiting photography include the presence of volatile vapors that might explode in the presence of electrostatic discharge, instances where camera flashes might create a hazard to operators of dangerous equipment, or situations where the presence of a camera may pose a risk of malfunction of sensors or controllers on equipment or instruments in the facility. The final deci-sion as to whether to allow photography during an inspection should be made in concert with legal counsel.

Affidavits

FDA investigators are trained to prepare affidavits to link evidence collected to documents that establish the connection with interstate commerce that is necessary for FDA to establish jurisdiction. Such affidavits may be written and provided to company personnel with a request that personnel sign them. There is no statutory mandate requiring company personnel to sign these affidavits. Here again, the decision whether to sign is one best made by legal counsel after consideration of all the facts. In the experience of the authors, however, many if not most, pharmaceutical companies have policies that require company personnel not to read, agree to or to sign affidavits that are prepared by FDA personnel during inspections. FDA personnel are familiar with policies and are not likely to be upset by company personnel refusals to sign.

The majority of companies have policies that require company personnel not to read, agree to or sign affidavits prepared by FDA personnel during inspections.

FDA-483s

The stated purpose of the List of Inspectional Observations (Form FDA-483) is to cite observations concerning filth, insanitary conditions or danger to health. In practice, however, FDA reports a wide variety of inspectional observations on the FDA-483, including deviations from approved protocols in clinical trials, recordkeeping problems, deviations from GMPs and many other general observations related to inspection findings.

The reverse side of the FDA-483 states a dual purpose: 1) for the purposes required by statute and 2) to assist firms to comply with the provisions of the act. The latter category accounts for the majority of FDA-483 observations. Following each inspection, the FDA team prepares an EIR that describes observations made during the inspection and includes exhibits to support findings (including photographs, production and control documents, records of interstate commerce, etc.). The EIR is reviewed and endorsed by district personnel. Reports that are endorsed as violative are referred to district management for a decision about appropriate compliance action(s). When necessary the case is forwarded to the appropriate FDA headquarters center for final review and disposition.

Hosting FDA Inspections

This section describes some of the important points that companies should consider when hosting inspections conducted by FDA employees. It includes information about the types of FDA employees who usually conduct inspections and the logistical issues associated with hosting an inspection. Also described are some common sense etiquette issues (i.e., "do's and don'ts"), as well as methods to deal with requests that are outside the scope of FDA's inspection authority.

Types of Employees Who Conduct FDA Inspections

Inspections are conducted by FDA investigators, chemists, microbiologists, engineers and various scientists having specialized education and training.

FDA employees who conduct inspections have a wide variety of backgrounds. Inspections are conducted by FDA investigators, chemists, microbiologists, engineers and various scientists having specialized education and training. Every employee who participates in an inspection must possess official FDA credentials and must properly display them to an appropriate official of the company at the beginning of each inspection. Each FDA employee is required by law to present a written notice to the owner, operator or agent in charge before beginning an inspection. FDA uses the "Notice of Inspection" (Form FDA-482) to provide this notice. However, a Form FDA-482 is not normally issued for foreign inspections.

The titles of FDA employees who conduct inspections may vary. Each of the more common titles, with a brief description of the duties, follows:

♦ *Consumer Safety Officer (CSO)*—This is an official job title for personnel management purposes within FDA, and some employees may identify themselves using the CSO job title. The employees who identify themselves as "investigators" are usually CSOs, although several other specialized positions exist in the CSO job series. For example, also included are the following "functional" titles: Investigator, Compliance Officer, Reviewer, Program Analyst, Small Business Representative, Interstate Travel Sanitation Specialist, Sanitarian, Shellfish Specialist, Food Service Specialist and others. Various FDA headquarters-based personnel who sometimes participate in inspections are also included in the CSO job series.

♦ *Commissioned Corps Officers*—Commissioned officers of the U.S. Public Health Service are on assignment to the agency in a variety of positions, including as investigators. These employees may provide one of the titles given above for CSO positions, or may use their military title as a member of the commissioned corps, such as Commander, Captain, etc. Commissioned corps officers hold the same status and authority as civil service FDA employees.

♦ *Consumer Safety Inspector (CSI)*—The CSI is a para-professional level position. CSIs carry out such activities as collecting samples and inspecting warehouses. Many CSIs operate exclusively in import related activities, mainly collecting samples of products offered for importation at the point of entry into U.S. commerce. CSIs usually identify themselves by that title, but may use the title of "Inspector."

♦ *Analyst*—An analyst normally works in FDA laboratories, but occasionally may participate in on-site inspections. Functional job titles include chemist, microbiologist, biologist or entomologist. Infrequently, certain para-professional laboratory personnel, such as physical science technicians, may assist on inspections. Laboratory personnel occasionally conduct inspections alone, but normally they are present to assist the investigators with laboratory portions of more complex inspections.

♦ *Special Agent, Office of Criminal Investigations (OCI)*—Special Agents rarely take part in regulatory inspections. If a special agent from OCI is participating in an FDA inspection, his or her presence would provide a signal that the inspection has a special or unusual purpose. Companies that are visited by special agents should consider this to be highly unusual, and should consider seeking the advice and assistance of legal counsel. Special agents have full police powers, including the right to carry firearms and make arrests. A special agent, however, may be assigned to accompany an investigator on an inspection as part of his or her on-the-job training or orientation to agency operations. Companies should ask for and expect to be provided with a full and complete explanation about the purpose of a special agent's presence during a regulatory inspection.

Logistics While an Inspection Is in Progress

A trained person should act as escort for FDA personnel during the course of the inspection. For complex industries, it is advisable to have multiple persons who can fill this role. There may be multiple FDA staff present for the inspection, and an escort should be available for each FDA employee. One or more persons should be designated to act as scribe to maintain an accurate transcript of questions, answers, and any significant discussions about issues, concerns, or corrective actions reported to FDA.

There may be multiple FDA staff present for the inspection, and an escort should be available for each FDA employee.

The person(s) serving as scribe should not be the designated escort. The escort should not be burdened by trying to take notes while meeting the needs of FDA personnel (such as monitoring FDA activities and responding to requests from the investigators). Written policies or procedures should be prepared in advance, describing how inspections are to be handled by the firm. The policy or procedure should include, but not be limited to, the company's position on such matters as access to areas of the company, photography, affidavits, collection of samples, providing copies of documents and granting FDA requests for interviews with company employees.

A conference room or office should be set aside for FDA's use during the inspection, as needed. This facilitates review of the large number of documents that may be requested by FDA. The location of the conference room may be near document storage areas, photocopying resources or production areas depending on the inspection objectives. For lengthy inspections (several weeks or longer) companies may wish to consider dedicated clerical support for the FDA team during the inspection.

A separate conference room should be available to serve as the company's command post for the inspection. This room should be near, but not too near, the room dedicated to FDA's use. It should be located in an area of the company not subject to inspection by FDA, such as administrative office space, to enable frank discussions to take place without risk of them being overheard by the investigators.

Companies are encouraged to have daily debriefing of all company personnel who were involved with FDA during the course of an inspection. Debriefings should include key issues covered by FDA, topics discussed, information provided, any allegations of violations made by the investigators, corrective actions taken or promised, and any other significant issues.

After the inspection, the company should prepare its own final report, providing a permanent record of the inspection. The record furnishes the company's perspectives and is supported by original notes taken by company personnel during the inspection. Each company should establish a policy as to whether to keep permanent copies of the notes taken during an inspection. If notes are maintained, procedures should define how they are to be identified (signed and dated), how they will be preserved and by whom. The benefits of having the notes available in the event of litigation must be weighed against any possible adverse consequences of maintaining potentially problematic information. The final decision on retention of original notes should be determined with advice of legal counsel.

Managing the Exit Discussion

At the conclusion of an inspection and prior to leaving the premises, FDA will issue a Form FDA-483, List of Inspectional Observations if FDA has found conditions or practices in the facility which in the judgment of the inspection team may cause a food, drug or device to become adulterated under the provisions of the FDCA. As a matter of FDA policy, the inspection team will afford the personnel of the inspected company to have an opportunity to present their views and ask questions during the exit discussion.

While most companies will discuss the List of Observations with the FDA inspection team to better understand the basis for each observation, some companies elect not to comment during the exit discussion, preferring to comment only in writing and after the fact. Each company must decide the best strategy in this regard. Ultimately the decision whether or not to hold an exit discussion may depend on the advice of counsel. Opting not to have the exit discussion precludes an important opportunity to ensure FDA understands the company's position, and to ensure that the company understands the basis for FDA's findings. Even if the company does not agree, understanding FDA's position is critical for preparation of an appropriate response.

Some companies elect not to comment during the exit discussion, preferring to comment only in writing and after the fact.

If a decision is made to participate in an exit discussion, among the objectives of the discussion should be the following, at a minimum:

♦ ensure a correct understanding of FDA's reason for citing items on the 483 (even if the company disagrees, a clear understanding will be essential to a good response);

♦ ensure that the facts stated on the 483 are accurate;

♦ ensure that the wording of the 483 is complete and not misleading (for instance, inadvertent omission of a word like "not" from a sentence may change the entire meaning); and

♦ request that FDA delete items from the 483 if the inspection team agrees they are inaccurate or erroneous. (FDA policy is to delete items that can be shown to be in error or not factually correct.)

Ensure that the right people are present for the discussion. Generally, this means senior management and subject matter experts for topics that were covered during the inspection. It is best to avoid having large numbers of people present who will not be contributing substantively to the discussion and those who have little or no authority to make commitments for the company.

It is important to decide in advance who will control the discussion from the company's perspective, and who will speak for the company regarding actions in response to the 483 and who may offer time lines for corrections. Care should be taken to avoid characterizing FDA's observations as "violations" or "deviations," instead simply refer to them as FDA-483 "items" or "citations."

The decision of whether or not to have counsel present for the exit discussion is best determined on a case-by-case basis. In the experience of the authors, most companies elect not to have counsel present unless there appears to be an imminent risk of enforcement action, or a significant dispute has arisen over FDA authority. The ultimate decision is best left to senior management in collaboration with counsel.

Responding in Writing to the FDA-483

While there is no statutory requirement that requires a company to respond either orally or in writing to the FDA-483, such responses are a nearly universal practice in all segments of the FDA-regulated industry. Failing to promptly respond in writing is likely to be perceived negatively by FDA enforcement personnel. In the *Federal Register*, Vol. 74, No. 153, Tuesday, August 11, 2009, FDA published a statement of policy that establishes a 15-business day time frame to respond to an FDA-483. As a matter of policy, when FDA is considering whether to escalate an enforcement action to a Warning Letter or more serious step following an inspection, FDA will not take into consideration a company's response that has been submitted more than 15 business days after the inspection was completed. Therefore, if a company wants FDA to consider its viewpoint, it is prudent to timely submit the response to the FDA-483 within the 15 business-day time frame.

Etiquette Points for Dealing with FDA Investigators

Utmost care should be taken by the company to avoid any offer to FDA inspectors that could be construed as a bribe or gratuity.

The etiquette for dealing with FDA staff is fairly straightforward and is based on an understanding of FDA inspection authority, FDA policy for the conduct of inspections, the company's policy and an understanding of FDA's ethical restrictions. FDA staff work under a very restrictive standard of ethical conduct, which is repeatedly and strongly reinforced over the course of their employment with the agency. The standard is one of avoidance of even an appearance of a conflict of interest. Therefore, it is inadvisable to offer anything of more than nominal value. Refreshments such as coffee, tea or soft drinks are generally acceptable and will not be seen as inappropriate. The utmost care should be taken to avoid any offer that could be construed as a bribe or gratuity.

Requests Outside the Scope of FDA Authority

Historically, FDA has taken the position that during an inspection it may ask for any type of information, but will insist upon access only to statutorily mandated areas and information.

Historically, FDA has taken the position that during an inspection it may ask for any type of information, but will insist upon access only to statutorily mandated areas and information. In practice, FDA investigators will routinely request whatever information they believe they need, and will not, as a rule, take the initiative to explain to the company being inspected just which types of information must be provided versus information requested on a purely consensual basis. Historically, FDA has taken the position that it is the company's responsibility to know the difference.

For these reasons, FDA investigators may sometimes request access to areas or information that are outside the scope of the general inspection authority under section 704. The investigators usually will answer questions from the company if asked whether release of the information or access to the area is within the scope of section 704. Since it may be assumed, however, that the investigator's interests are served by obtaining the information on a consensual basis, caution and careful consideration are required before a company accedes to a request that is outside FDA's statutory authority.

There are cases where a company may decide to agree to such a request. For example, if an investigator asks about a company's annual volume of business (a common question), and such information is already a matter of public record, a company may decide that answering will serve to promote goodwill and honest communication while not disclosing information of a proprietary or damaging nature. The factors to be considered in deciding whether to supply information to FDA when the company is not legally required to do so include, among others:

♦ understanding the reason for FDA's request;

♦ an assessment of the potential adverse consequences of disclosure;

♦ an assessment of the benefits of cooperating with the inspector's request versus not cooperating; and

♦ an assessment of the ease with which the agency may be able to obtain the information from alternative sources, and whether the procedure of obtaining the information in that way might expose the company to questions at suppliers, customers, or others.

Note: There is no statutory requirement or precedent that requires FDA to inform a company (or individual persons) of their rights during the context of an FDA inspection. While companies have argued that FDA investigators should provide Miranda warnings or similar warnings to company officials (especially when the agency develops an awareness that the matter under investigation may be referred for criminal prosecution), courts have consistently found that Miranda warnings are not required in the context of an FDA inspection. The FDA *Investigations Operations Manual* instructs investigators to provide Miranda warnings only when the person being interviewed is in custody or under detention, and therefore is not free to leave.

> *There is no statutory requirement or precedent that requires FDA to inform a company (or individual persons) of their rights during the context of an FDA inspection.*

Forms Commonly Used during FDA Inspections

FDA uses several forms for a wide variety of purposes during regulatory inspections. The forms are commonly referred to by either their name or their number. For example, the Notice of Inspection may be referred to as the "Notice of Inspection," the "Notice," the "FDA-482" or simply the "482." FDA employees and industry representatives use the terms interchangeably. The forms FDA-482, FDA-483 and FDA-484 are designed to comply with statutory requirements imposed on FDA by section 704 of the FDCA (see details below). The majority of the current content of section 704 of the FDCA was established through the Factory Inspection Amendments to the FDCA in 1953, with some subsequent modification by the 1997 FDAMA.

Form FDA-482 cites authorities granted by other laws enforced by FDA, and therefore it is used for all inspections, regardless of which law is being enforced.

FDA-482, Notice of Inspection

This form is issued to the "owner, operator or agent in charge" of a facility at the beginning of an inspection. Its purpose is to comply with the provisions of section 704(a) of the FDCA that require that written notice be given before an inspection is undertaken. The form lists the name and address of the facility being inspected, and bears the signature(s) and typed or printed name(s) of the FDA employee(s) conducting the inspection. The form cites the sections of the law that grant inspection authority. In addition to the FDCA, the form cites authorities granted by other laws enforced by FDA, and therefore it is used for all inspections, regardless of which law is being enforced. This is convenient for the agency, because in many cases the inspection is in fact being conducted under authority granted by more than one statute. For example, an inspection of a licensed blood bank may be conducted under both the FDCA and section 351 of the Public Health Service Act.

FDA-483, Inspectional Observations

This form is issued at the conclusion of the inspection in accordance with section 704(b) of the act. By law, the investigators must list those observations which, in their judgment, may indicate that a food, drug, medical device or cosmetic processed, packed or held on the inspected premises consists in whole or in part of a filthy, putrid or decomposed substance, or has been prepared, packed or held under insanitary conditions whereby it may have become contaminated. As previously described, the agency uses this form to cite a wide variety of observations, far beyond the scope of what is required by statute. Generally speaking, the form is used to list all potential violations that can be directly observed by the investigators. Certain exceptions exist for issues that generally involve suspected violations that cannot be easily established through inspection observations, such as the adequacy of label claims, status of a drug as a new drug and other issues. The *Investigations Operations Manual,* Chapter 5, lists these exceptions.

This form is also used to list recordkeeping violations, GMP deviations, discrepancies noted in the review of clinical trial records and a host of other conditions and practices that range far from its statutorily mandated use. If the FDA employee(s) believe it is necessary to re-initiate any part of the inspection after the FDA-483 has been issued, they will issue a new FDA-482 and another inspection will officially commence.

FDA-484, Receipt for Samples

This form is used to account for any physical evidence removed from the premises being inspected. Product samples (raw materials, in-process goods and finished products) are listed on the FDA-484, as are samples of extraneous material that may be taken to document conditions observed during the inspection. Extraneous material may include live or dead insects, rodent filth, foreign material, spillage, residues, bacterial swabs and so forth. Documentary evidence such as labels, copies of production records, invoices and shipping records are not listed on the FDA-484.

Practices may vary as to the timing of issuance of the FDA-484. Some investigators will issue the form each day when samples are collected. Others will wait until the conclusion of the inspection and issue the form then, to cover all samples collected during the inspection. While firms are undergoing an inspection, it is advisable to request that the form be issued daily when samples are collected, to keep management fully apprised of any materials leaving the premises. The inspected firm also may elect to charge FDA for the materials taken, as they sometimes amount to a considerable value.

Firms undergoing inspection should request that Form FDA-484 be issued daily when samples are collected, to keep management fully apprised of any materials leaving the premises.

Controlled substances present a special case. FDA investigators and special agents are authorized to collect samples of controlled substances under DEA regulations. In these cases immediate completion of all required paperwork, including the FDA-484, is essential.

FDA-463, Affidavit

This form is often prepared by the inspecting FDA employee at the conclusion of an inspection. This form historically has been used primarily to document the connection with interstate commerce necessary to establish jurisdiction, but in recent years its use has expanded to serve as a vehicle to also document individual responsibility. The FDA employee may represent that the statements related to the individual employee job responsibility are intended to qualify the individual to make the statements that follow on the affidavit. Many FDA employees will refer to such statements to bolster other evidence of individual responsibility that has been gathered during the inspection.

Affidavits come in several forms, with individual form numbers. All have basically the same purpose. There are several fill-in-the-blank affidavits that are intended to serve common purposes, such as a "Dealer's Statement," "Warehouseman's Statement," affidavits for use with United Parcel Service shipments and so forth. The FDA-463 is the most common one, however, and is simply a blank page with the necessary introductory wording preprinted on it with a space for the affiant's name and the name of the FDA employee taking the statement.

In regulatory inspections, FDA uses affidavits principally to establish linkage between evidence that is collected by investigators and the element of interstate commerce.

In regulatory inspections, FDA uses affidavits principally to establish linkage between evidence that is collected by investigators and the element of interstate commerce. Should the inspection lead to legal action and a trial, the agency's lawyers will subpoena the original records and call the affiant to testify, using the affidavit as a record of his or her prior statements.

Because company attorneys often advise their clients not to sign FDA affidavits, investigators are trained to read the affidavit out loud and ask if the statements are true. When a verbal affirmation is received, the investigator will so annotate the affidavit, and will secure a witnesses' signature if possible. The investigator will ask the proposed affiant why he or she is not willing to sign, and also will annotate the reason given. For this reason, many attorneys advise their clients not to read or listen to the content of FDA affidavits. The decision of whether to read, sign or verbally affirm an affidavit should be made based on advice of legal counsel. Experienced FDA investigators are accustomed to this response and will generally not press the matter further when they encounter refusals to sign or listen to the content of affidavits.

Other Forms

Other forms for special purposes may come into play during a regulatory inspection. Examples include facsimile forms used to make manual "true copies" of invoices or shipping documents; consumer complaint forms used by the agency to record complaints; the FDA-472, a special form of the FDA-484 issued to truck drivers or operators of other interstate conveyances; and various other special purpose forms such as checklists used to record inspectional observations.

FDA POLICIES AND ADMINISTRATIVE PROCEDURES

The actions of FDA employees are directed by a variety of internal policies, procedures, guidelines and guidance documents that are issued by FDA headquarters units.

The *Investigations Operations Manual* contains a wide range of information, from administrative matters to detailed instructions for preparing and routing of inspection reports. Instructions found in its chapters include instructions for filling out FDA forms and expense reports, and policies and guidance for how to effectively interact with company managers. This manual contains basic reference information that is used on a day-to-day basis by investigators.

The manual is of primary importance during litigation involving FDA inspections, because it defines the standard of conduct and procedures that FDA personnel are expected to follow during their day-to-day activities. The manual provides the basis of the presumption of official regularity in the performance of duty. Investigators are expected to justify and obtain approval for any deviation from established procedures outlined in the manual.

The *Compliance Program Guidance Manual* is a compilation of specific instructions for directed inspections of segments of the industries regulated by FDA. The manual is divided into chapters by industry. It serves as the primary document that guides the conduct of most inspections. Most compliance programs are now available from FDA's Internet website and are valuable references for use in preparing for particular types of FDA inspections.

Most compliance programs are now available from FDA's Internet website and are valuable references for use in preparing for particular types of FDA inspections.

FDA *Compliance Policy Guides* (CPGs) are internal policy documents. FDA describes issues and responses in simple policy statements, which field personnel use during their inspections to support their findings. Many CPGs establish informal internal action levels for analytical findings on regulatory samples. Others establish "direct reference" procedures, where the local FDA office can expedite the processing of regulatory actions by eliminating the need for technical or policy reviews by headquarters staff. If "direct reference" criteria are met, the district may initiate legal proceedings without the need for concurrence and prior approval by some of the usual reviewing offices in FDA headquarters. CPGs are not enforceable documents, because they have not been subjected to notice-and-comment rulemaking.

The *Regulatory Procedures Manual* is maintained by the Office of Enforcement within the Office of Regulatory Affairs (ORA). It addresses policies and procedures for processing regulatory actions by the field force. It also establishes standard format and provides certain standardized templates with language for pleadings in criminal and civil cases. In addition, the manual provides regulatory guidance in certain other non-litigation matters, such as product recalls.

The *Investigations Training Manual* consists of a series of outlines used during the initial orientation/basic training program for new investigators. This manual provides training in the basic provisions of the FDCA and other laws enforced by FDA, and orientation to the major reference documents, programs and procedures used by field personnel. The manual is used heavily by new investigators during their initial months on the job, but usually is not often referred to following completion of basic training.

FDA *Field Management Directives* (FMDs) are documents that address administrative and compliance matters dealt with by the field force. Most of the topics in these documents are of limited significance for inspections. Exceptions include FMDs on recall management, consumer complaints and the classification of EIRs.

FDA *Staff Manual Guides* are issued at the highest level of the agency, and are mainly human resources and financial management documents. They also contain formal delegations of authority, establish position names, describe procedures for the issuance of official credentials and state policies involving ethical conduct and other matters that have bearing on regulatory inspections.

Inspection Technical Guides are short, focused technical references on topics relevant to inspections.

Inspection Technical Guides and their earlier versions known as Inspection Bulletins are produced and distributed by ORA. These documents are short, focused technical references on topics relevant to inspections.

All of the aforementioned manuals and publications are accessible from FDA's Internet website, http://www.fda.gov.

PRODUCT RECALLS AND MARKET WITHDRAWALS

Recall is an effective method of removing or correcting consumer products that are in violation of laws administered by FDA.

With few exceptions, a product recall is a voluntary action to remove a product from channels of distribution. Manufacturers and distributors initiate recalls to protect the public from products that represent a risk of injury or gross deception, or are otherwise defective. A market withdrawal is removal of a product from the market where the violation is not severe enough to result in regulatory action by FDA if the product is not withdrawn. Product recalls and market withdrawals may frequently trigger inspections, or, if discovered for the first time during an inspection for another purpose, companies can expect FDA to direct significant attention to these activities. Therefore, an understanding of FDA's view of recall activities is a necessary predicate to good inspection management.

The FDCA authorizes FDA to order recalls of medical devices, under certain circumstances and subject to certain controls, but there is no similar authority for drugs or cosmetics.

The Food Safety Modernization Act provides FDA with the authority to order a recall of a food product that is deemed to be unsafe, if the company refuses to do so voluntarily after being requested to do so by FDA. Under the infant formula regulations, 21 C.F.R. 107, "When the Food and Drug Administration determines that an adulterated or misbranded infant formula presents a risk to human health, a manufacturer shall immediately take all actions necessary to recall that formula, extending to and including the retail level..."

FDA-directed recalls, however, are relatively rare. The agency may request a product recall if the firm is not willing to remove dangerous products from the market without FDA's written request. Only when a medical device, human tissue products, foods and infant formula pose a risk to human health the law specifically authorizes FDA to prescribe a recall and to rule on the scope and extent of the same. In situations involving serious hazards to health, however, FDA often does request firms to take a recall action. Typically, in these instances, the request will be made under the signature of the Associate Commissioner for Regulatory Affairs and often will be hand delivered to a responsible official of the company, to underscore the agency's concern. If a company fails to respond to FDA's request for a recall, the agency must then rely on other measures, such as multiple seizure actions or injunctions, to remove the product from the market.

FDA's general policy about recalls is in 21 C.F.R. §§ 7.3 and 7.40-7.59. Removal of a product from channels of distribution is deemed to be a "recall" when 1) the product is not under the control of the recalling firm and 2) it is in violation of law to the extent that FDA would take action to remove it from distribution channels if it was not recalled. In most cases, firms will recall products voluntarily when these conditions are met. FDA classifies recalls as Class I, Class II or Class III. The criteria for these classifications reflect the agency's assessment of the relative degree of health hazard represented by the reason for recall. The definitions of the three classification levels are as follows:

- Class I is a situation in which there is a reasonable probability that the use of, or exposure to, a violative product will cause serious adverse health consequences or death.

- Class II is a situation in which use of, or exposure to, a violative product may cause temporary or medically reversible adverse health consequences or where the probability of serious adverse health consequences is remote.

♦ Class III is a situation in which use of, or exposure to, a violative product is not likely to cause adverse health consequences.

The agency monitors to ensure that recalls are carried out effectively. The degree of monitoring activities and their nature (i.e., telephone calls, visits by investigators and so forth) is dictated by the classification assigned to each recall, the product involved and the steps necessary to ensure effectiveness of the recall. For example, a Class III recall of a food product might receive little or no monitoring, while a Class I recall of a contaminated drug product might require a visit by an investigator to 100% of the locations that should have been notified of the recall, to make certain that the notification was received and instructions were properly followed.

FDA sometimes requests the court to direct a company to recall products by seeking a court order called an "injunction."

FDA sometimes requests the court to direct the company to recall products by seeking a court order called an "injunction." Where FDA has no explicit statutory authority to order a recall, courts must decide that the agency's general injunctive powers, granted under section 302, are sufficiently broad to allow the court to issue an injunction. In some cases, the court has in fact ordered the company to recall. In other cases, the court has found that the lack of explicit authority to order a company to carry out a recall prevents the court from ordering a recall in connection with an injunction action.

FDA authority to mandate medical device recalls is set forth in 21 C.F.R. 810. The authority for infant formula recalls is found at 21 C.F.R. 107.

Endnotes

[*] So in law. A comma probably should appear after "section 505(i) or (k)". See the amendment made by section 125(b)(2)(L) of Pub. L. No. 105-115 (111 Stat. 2326).

Chapter 15

FDA Enforcement: How It Works

Arthur N. Levine, Retired Partner, Arnold & Porter LLP, Washington, D.C.

Key Points

- The Food and Drug Administration (FDA) has broad discretion to decide which violations of law it will take action against, and what kind of action it will take.
- The primary objective of FDA's enforcement program is to promote compliance with the Federal Food, Drug, and Cosmetic Act (FDCA), and with FDA regulations promulgated under authority of that act. By promoting compliance, FDA also deters regulated companies and individuals from conducting their businesses in ways that create substantial risks of noncompliance.
- Some enforcement actions may be brought directly by FDA against products, individuals or companies. Other enforcement actions must be brought by the Department of Justice (DOJ) on behalf of FDA. In either setting, the evidence for these actions almost always arises from FDA inspections and/or investigations by FDA.
- The enforcement action that FDA uses most frequently is a 483 list issued at the conclusion of an FDA inspection. This tool has been effective in promoting compliance through corrective action. Where FDA believes that a company's response to a 483 has been inadequate, it may issue a Warning Letter seeking more robust or comprehensive corrective action.
- The issuance of adverse publicity is a form of FDA enforcement tool that can have a dramatic and immediate effect on a company or a product.
- Seizure actions are brought to remove a violative product from commerce. Such products may be seized without any notice to the company or prior judicial hearing.
- FDA may recommend, and DOJ may bring, injunction cases to prevent a company from continuing to manufacture and market products in a way that does not comply with FDA regulations.
- DOJ may file criminal charges against individuals and companies for violations of either the FDCA or other federal criminal laws, or both. An individual may be prosecuted for violating the FDCA even if he or she did not know of or participate in the events that led directly to the violation. It is enough if the individual had the power and authority to prevent or correct the violation but failed to do so. The existence of this doctrine of "strict liability" has been an important underpinning of FDA enforcement for more than 60 years, although few of such cases have been brought in the past decade.

INTRODUCTION

The Food and Drug Administration (FDA) is a law enforcement organization. It enforces the law through a variety of administrative actions and, with the approval and assistance of the Department of Justice (DOJ), through judicial actions. The agency can take action against products, companies and individuals. FDA has broad discretion to decide which violations it will take enforcement action against; what kind of action to take; and which products, companies or individuals to bring the action against. FDA takes enforcement actions to remove violative products from the market or prevent their distribution in the first place, to obtain compliance with FDA requirements, to punish persons responsible for causing violations and to deter others from violating FDA requirements in the same or similar ways.

The Source of FDA's Enforcement Powers

FDA's enforcement power comes primarily from the Federal Food, Drug, and Cosmetic Act.

FDA's enforcement power comes primarily from the Federal Food, Drug, and Cosmetic Act (FDCA). FDA is empowered to take enforcement action against products that are either "adulterated" or "misbranded" as defined in the FDCA, and against companies and individuals who cause products to become adulterated or misbranded. FDA also can prevent the marketing of products that are required to be approved by the agency but that do not have approval.

The FDCA is not static; it has been amended by Congress repeatedly since it was first enacted in 1938. Many of the amendments expand FDA's enforcement powers by defining conduct that constitutes a crime or authorizing FDA to take an ever-enlarging array of enforcement actions. In 2009, Congress amended the FDCA to give FDA new regulatory authority over an entire industry—tobacco products.

In addition to the violations defined in the FDCA, FDA can define and establish requirements that are "binding" and have "the full force and effect of law." FDA does this by promulgating regulations—all of which are codified in Title 21 of the U.S. Code of Federal Regulations (C.F.R.). For this reason, when FDA promulgates a regulation, interpreting some requirement in the FDCA, it is establishing a new, more specific, legal requirement. Then FDA can take an enforcement action against a noncompliance with that requirement.

FDA also promotes compliance by issuing informal guidance documents that announce its interpretation of the FDCA and FDA regulations. These guidance documents are not legally binding on either FDA or on the industries regulated by it. They influence how companies act, however, because FDA usually will not take enforcement action if a company is operating consistent with its advice.

FDA's Enforcement Philosophy

A primary guiding principle in FDA's enforcement policy is to use all appropriate legal means to secure compliance with FDA laws and regulations.

♦ FDA encourages and expects compliance with the laws and regulations it enforces.

♦ FDA conducts inspections and investigations over the industries it regulates to continuously assess compliance and discover noncompliance.

♦ FDA protects the public health by using its enforcement tools, both administrative and judicial, according to the seriousness of the violation and the impact and consequences of that violation.

Historically, FDA has made decisions regarding enforcement action by weighing six factors:

♦ the seriousness of the violation,

♦ the number of people affected by the violative conduct or product,

♦ the extent to which people would be affected,

♦ the strength of the evidence of violation,

♦ the likelihood of success of the enforcement action, and

♦ the need for FDA to resolve the problem.

How FDA Brings Enforcement Actions

For the most part, enforcement actions are built on evidence of noncompliance with FDA requirements that is gathered by FDA investigators from the district offices during FDA inspections or by agents in FDA's Office of Criminal Investigations (OCI), supplemented by information obtained from other sources. The agency also may rely on information that a company submits to meet FDA requirements (such as adverse reaction reports) or that a company submits voluntarily (such as information about product recalls).

Enforcement actions are built on evidence of noncompliance with FDA requirements.

For most administrative and civil judicial actions, compliance officers in the district office evaluate the evidence. The district office makes an initial decision about whether a violation exists, its significance, the need for enforcement action and the kind of action that seems appropriate. In some situations, the power to initiate an enforcement action rests with the district office and no further review within FDA is required. In other situations, a summary of the evidence and a recommendation for enforcement action is sent to the Office of Compliance in the FDA center that has jurisdiction over the product. That office may either authorize the action or, if required by FDA internal procedures, obtain further review and concurrence of the proposed action from either FDA's Office of Regulatory Affairs or its Office of the Chief Counsel (OCC), or both. For criminal enforcement, the evidence is most often reviewed and assessed by OCI.

As a general matter, either the center compliance office or OCC must review and approve administrative and civil enforcement actions that could have a significant impact upon a company or FDA policy. Regardless of the review process, there is usually a district compliance officer who has primary responsibility for supporting every enforcement action and monitoring the action to resolution.

Types of Enforcement

FDA may bring enforcement actions through either administrative or judicial procedures.

FDA may bring enforcement actions through either administrative or judicial procedures. Administrative enforcement may be brought by the agency itself; it does not need either approval from DOJ to initiate the action or an order from a federal court to impose a sanction. As a result, administrative enforcement can be resource efficient for FDA. Individuals and companies that are the subject of FDA administrative enforcement actions may challenge those actions in court but, in most instances, a court will not intervene in FDA's decision to initiate an administrative action until there is a final action. For some administrative actions, FDA regulations or established practice require the agency to provide an opportunity for a hearing, or an informal meeting, before FDA makes its decision.

Judicial enforcement actions involve DOJ and the federal courts. FDA does not have the power to go to court itself to obtain an order against a product, company or individuals. Rather, the agency may recommend to DOJ that an action be filed on its behalf. The department may either accept FDA's recommendation, modify it (by revising the alleged violations, naming different products or persons as defendants, or changing the type of action to be sought), or decline the recommendation altogether. Enforcement of the FDCA is brought in federal court in the state in which the products are located, the facility in which the products were manufactured is located, or where the company or individuals who may have been responsible for the violation do business.

These two types of enforcement action—administrative and judicial—are not mutually exclusive. First, FDA repeatedly has announced that it is free to use either or both to accomplish its enforcement objectives. Second, FDA's inability to resolve a problem administratively often will be used to justify a subsequent request to DOJ for judicial enforcement. Finally, the mere threat of judicial enforcement, particularly prosecution, provides FDA with significant leverage in discussions with potential defendants to obtain a lesser administrative sanction. Both types of enforcement actions have two predictable consequences. They lead to greater FDA scrutiny of the responsible companies in the future and they decrease FDA's confidence in the companies and individuals against whom enforcement actions have been brought.

Enforcement Trends

Over the past decade, FDA has altered significantly its approach to enforcement actions. The agency has developed compliance policies and procedures that are more varied, more resource-efficient and swifter than many of the traditional enforcement actions. As a result, FDA's current enforcement approach relies more heavily on administrative (rather than judicial) enforcement actions; greater coordination between district offices and the relevant FDA offices of compliance and of product evaluation; greater coordination with state enforcement authorities, and with professional and trade associations; greater use of adverse publicity; greater reliance on rulemaking to promote compliance; and the use of informal policy guidance documents to leverage companies to meet FDA's compliance expectations even if those expectations are not legally binding. In the area of judicial enforcement, FDA has focused on cases involving fraud, intentional or knowing violations of the FDCA, and on cases involving product defects with significant consequences for users.

Recent enforcement trends reflect FDA's efforts to maintain a robust and credible enforcement program in an era of limited resources. While there have been fewer FDA seizure and injunction cases in the past decade, the number of criminal convictions has increased. In addition, FDA has cooperated with DOJ in its review of evidence and initiation of actions under the False Claims Act. These cases usually involve both criminal and civil dispositions and are based on off-label promotion, including charges of misbranding under the FDCA.

While there have been fewer FDA seizure and injunction cases in the past decade, the number of criminal convictions involving fraud and intentional offenses has increased.

Congressional expansion of FDA's regulatory authority is not always matched by a commensurate increase in the agency's budget. Thus, FDA continuously re-evaluates its enforcement programs to identify ways to maintain deterrence and promote compliance with the resources it has. One agency strategy is to focus on enforcement actions that will have a substantial impact, and to pursue those actions vigorously. It has been persistent in obtaining full compliance in those circumstances where it has taken action. In this regard, FDA enforcement is both opportunistic and unpredictable.

ADMINISTRATIVE ENFORCEMENT

FDA has a wide variety of administrative enforcement powers. Many are informal; they can be imposed without significant review within the agency. Others are brought only after extensive review. Many of FDA's administrative enforcement powers apply to all FDA-regulated products; some apply only to certain products.

List of Inspectional Observations

The core of FDA's enforcement programs has been, and remains, the inspections conducted by FDA investigators. These inspections gather the evidence of noncompliance that supports the agency's enforcement actions. During the period 2008-2010, FDA has conducted, on average, about 16,500 inspections per year of manufacturing and related facilities in the United States. During this same period, FDA has increased its inspections of facilities outside this country that make products for sale in the United States (from about 950 in 2008 to about 1,700 in 2010, and near 1,900 projected for 2011).

During the period 2008-2010, FDA has conducted, on average, about 16,500 inspections per year of manufacturing and related facilities in the United States.

At the conclusion of an FDA inspection, the FDA investigators may issue a List of Inspectional Observations (FDA Form 483). This form—provided to a company following a facility inspection—identifies those observations that, in the opinion of the investigator, are deviations from FDA requirements. FDA investigators issue 483 Lists of Observations in about 40 percent of all inspections. A 483 should be viewed not only as part of an FDA inspection but also as an FDA enforcement action because, almost without exception, it results in corrective action by a company to achieve compliance with FDA requirements. FDA expects that the company's corrective actions not only address the investigator's specific observations but also will address the systems, procedures or organizational structure that may, unless changed, permit a recurrence of the noncompliances or similar deficiencies to those listed in the 483.

In most circumstances, a company's response to the 483 will resolve the noncompliance and no further enforcement action will be sought. A company can, however, expect a follow-up inspection during which FDA will look to verify that corrective measures described in the 483 response have been effectively implemented.

Warning Letters

An FDA Warning Letter is just that: a written warning from FDA that a company is, in the agency's view, not operating in compliance with FDA requirements. The primary purpose of the letter is to achieve compliance by threatening judicial enforcement if the company's noncompliance is not remedied.

In the late 1980s and early 1990s, Warning Letters became the most prominent type of FDA enforcement action. Even after that peak, during the period from 1993 to 2002, FDA issued, on average, about 1,200 Warning Letters per year. However, from 2003 through 2010, that number had fallen to, on average, about 550 per year.

Whether a Warning Letter is initiated by the district or the center, a Warning Letter represents a formal declaration by the agency that the operations and conditions at a facility do not comply with FDA requirements and that products manufactured in that facility will continue to be either adulterated or misbranded unless the company changes its systems, policies, procedures or performance.

In most cases, a Warning Letter is based on the results of an FDA inspection that the agency believes has demonstrated reasonably significant deviations from FDA requirements. Therefore, the noncompliant circumstances described in the Warning Letter closely parallel the key items in the 483. In most cases, but not all, if a company has made an adequate and sufficiently comprehensive response to the 483, FDA will not issue a Warning Letter. An adequate response to the 483, however, does not mean that a Warning Letter will not be issued anyway.

In most cases, a Warning Letter is based on the results of an FDA inspection that the agency believes has demonstrated reasonably significant deviations from FDA requirements.

The basic elements of a Warning Letter are fairly straightforward. The letter summarizes the facts or circumstances found during an FDA inspection, labeling review, adverse reaction report, recall or some other underlying event. The letter asserts that those facts or circumstances cause the recipient's products to be adulterated or misbranded, and describes the facts giving rise to a finding of noncompliance. The letter provides the recipient with 15 working days to notify the agency of the corrective actions that the company has taken or intends to take. Finally, the letter notifies the recipient that a failure to make an adequate response may lead to a product seizure, an injunction or some other enforcement action.

A Warning Letter may, in some circumstances, be more than a warning. In many settings, the issuance of a Warning Letter results in the facility that is the subject of the letter being put on "compliance hold." As a result, FDA may not approve a pending product application or re-issue an export certificate for a product manufactured at that facility until the issues raised in the letter are resolved to FDA's satisfaction.

Typically, Warning Letters will advise the recipient that the instance(s) of non-compliance described in the letter should not be read as a comprehensive list, and that the recipient has an obligation to consider the issues raised by the

Warning Letter as they may apply to other of the company's products or activities. This standard language reflects FDA's effort to maximize the degree of corrective action obtained from issuing the Warning Letter. It also underscores the need for companies to review the significance of the letter beyond the particular instances of noncompliance described in it.

The legal authority for a Warning Letter is found in that section of the FDCA that allows FDA to issue "a suitable written notice or warning" when it believes that a violation exists but has chosen not to pursue a judicial sanction, at least initially. While the issuance of a warning is authorized, it is not required. In addition, FDA is under no obligation to issue a Warning Letter before recommending a judicial enforcement action. FDA has found Warning Letters to be effective in obtaining compliance and has chosen to use them in numerous situations where, in earlier years, it may have recommended a seizure action or an injunction.

Warning Letters are public information.

Like 483s, Warning Letters are public information. Many Warning Letters are automatically made available by FDA to the public and press, without the need for a formal Freedom of Information request. Therefore, once issued, they stand as a public accusation by FDA that a company's operation does not meet FDA standards and that the company's product(s) violate the law. Moreover, FDA routinely sends a copy of Warning Letters to federal procurement agencies, such as the Department of Defense and the Veterans Administration. These referrals can lead to a decision to terminate federal government contracts to purchase products implicated in the Warning Letter. These are a few of the many reasons why, as a practical matter, a company almost always will provide a comprehensive written response to a Warning Letter.

The primary objective when responding to a Warning Letter is to demonstrate a serious and significant effort by the company to address the allegations of noncompliance. FDA expects, and most companies provide, a response that goes beyond any particular examples or circumstances of noncompliance referenced in the letter to include a comprehensive, "systemic" solution designed to preclude a recurrence of the problems. While some deficiencies may be amenable to specific corrections, many can be addressed only through new or revised company policies and procedures, organizational restructuring, employee training and/or other broad-based activities. Nevertheless, companies generally do not promise more than they can or are willing to deliver. Therefore, most companies try to describe their corrective actions as precisely as possible, often including particular targeted completion dates or implementation schedules.

If FDA discovers that commitments made in a response to a Warning Letter have not been met and there is no compelling explanation, the recipient can anticipate a significant escalation of FDA enforcement action. Accordingly, commitments that are made in response to a Warning Letter cannot be made lightly; well-counseled companies assess realistically what changes they are prepared to make, in what amount of time and how broadly the changes will be applied throughout the company. In considering the extent of its commitments for corrective action, companies generally keep in mind that FDA views a Warning Letter as a "second bite at the apple" (because the company's response to the underlying 483 is seen as inadequate). Thus, in most circumstances, companies will significantly "up the ante" in undertaking corrective actions beyond those described in their 483 response.

If a company disagrees with the alleged instances of noncompliance discussed in the Warning Letter, it may decide to explain why a change is unnecessary or would create even greater problems. In some circumstances, a company that disagrees with the agency may choose to make a change anyway because the company believes that it is unlikely that it will be able to convince FDA that its present processes and procedures are adequate. Often, a company will express its disagreement with FDA and explain its position, but implement changes anyway.

As is apparent, a Warning Letter can result in a significant amount of corrective action by a company. While these corrections are the principal objective in FDA issuing the letter, it serves another important FDA enforcement purpose: a Warning Letter documents that the company, and the particular person to whom it is addressed, has received formal notice that the company's operations are not satisfactory. If the same or similar noncompliances continue, the existence of this "prior notice" or "prior warning" may be a significant element in FDA persuading DOJ to bring either an injunction action or a criminal prosecution.

A Warning Letter documents that the company, and the particular person to whom it is addressed, has received formal notice that the company's operations are not satisfactory.

Because a Warning Letter can result in nearly as much corrective action as can be obtained through a judicial injunction action, and because injunctions are resource intensive for FDA and require approval by DOJ, FDA is much more likely to issue a Warning Letter than it is to seek an injunction where it believes that a company's policies, processes and procedures need to be changed in order to prevent continued noncompliance.

Adverse Publicity

The FDCA authorizes FDA to issue publicity to warn the public about possible adverse consequences associated with the use of the products it regulates. This statutory authority provides FDA with a broad platform to not only issue public advisories but also to publicize significant enforcement actions.

Generally, FDA does not routinely issue press announcements of its enforcement actions. There is no assurance, however, that FDA will refrain from seeking publicity about these actions.

As a matter of general practice, FDA does not routinely issue press announcements of its enforcement actions, such as the issuance of a Warning Letter, the institution of a seizure, the signing of a consent decree of injunction or even a criminal conviction. There can be no assurance, however, that FDA will refrain from seeking publicity about any of these events. Because the effects of FDA-initiated adverse publicity can be devastating to a product or company, the agency's ability to issue such publicity cannot be taken lightly. Indeed, an FDA press release about a public health problem with a product can be the most immediate and effective form of enforcement action—it can end the product's marketability. FDA has significant media and public credibility, particularly when it comes to product-specific safety concerns.

While FDA may be willing to provide notice to a company that publicity about it or one of its products is about to issue, it generally does not negotiate with the company about the text of the FDA announcement. Nor will FDA share the text of a press communication with a company in advance. Thus, a company can try to contain the potential adverse effects of FDA publicity by issuing its own, preemptive statement. Ultimately, however, there is relatively little a company can do in most circumstances to significantly diminish the effect of an agency adverse press release.

Although FDA does not routinely issue press releases for enforcement actions, it is more likely to issue a press release to announce a criminal prosecution, an enforcement action against a large corporation or an enforcement action that involves a well-recognized product or brand. Where FDA has initiated judicial enforcement, a press release may be issued by the U.S. Attorney's Office that is responsible for handling the case. Many U.S. Attorneys' Offices routinely issue press releases on criminal cases.

Adverse publicity issued by either FDA or DOJ may be reported in the local media and, in many circumstances, may become a national story. Any adverse publicity issued by FDA will be reported by the food, drug and device trade press, and often by the investment community press. The "news" or other story may also be spread by the various social networks.

FDA may publicize the results of its enforcement action by means other than a standard "press release."

FDA may publicize the results of its enforcement action by means other than a standard "press release." These include interviews with the press; appearances on television and radio talk shows; speeches at consumer programs, medical and professional association meetings, and professional conferences; descriptions of the enforcement action in congressional testimony; or providing information to be released during a congressional hearing.

While FDA seeks publicity only when it deems it necessary, it routinely publishes lists of violative products that have been recalled or have been the subject of other enforcement action in its enforcement report. Some of these reports are repeated or summarized in the trade press, including trade publications that report on specific types of FDA enforcement actions, such as Warning Letters and inspectional observations.

Of course, adverse publicity based on an FDA enforcement action can result merely because the action is public. Indictments in criminal cases, complaints in injunction and seizure cases, Warning Letters, 483s and other FDA enforcement initiatives are all public documents. Copies of these documents can be obtained from a court, from FDA and, in many cases, through the Internet. Copies of these documents also can be obtained from FDA under the Freedom of Information Act, either in the name of the requestor or anonymously by obtaining copies through a requesting service.

Recalls

With very few exceptions, product recalls by companies are voluntary. As a result, FDA is often unaware of the recall until it has begun. When a company recalls a product because it is adulterated or misbranded, FDA counts that as an enforcement action even though it is undertaken voluntarily.

With very few exceptions, product recalls by companies are voluntary.

Although companies are not required by law to report recalls to FDA, recalls of FDA-regulated products are reported to the agency regularly by companies in deference to FDA's request that it be advised. Because a recall involves the removal from the market of a product that is adulterated or misbranded within the meaning of the FDCA, companies report their recalls so that FDA knows that the products are already being removed from commerce and, therefore, an enforcement action is unnecessary. Companies also report their recalls to FDA to maintain a good relationship with the agency, and to demonstrate that they have the capacity to identify their own noncompliances and the willingness to take action without being forced to do so.

From 1998 to 2007, companies increased the number of recalls from approximately 3,500 per year to more than 5,500 in 2007. During 2008-2009, FDA recorded approximately 2,700 "recall events" involving about 5,800 products. In 2010, FDA recorded approximately 3,800 recall events involving about 9,300 products. Each recall may affect one particular manufactured lot of a product or all of a product made during a substantial period of time. Some recalls involve many products.

There are, of course, many reasons for a company to recall a product quite apart from FDA; these include a desire that customers not receive an inferior product, a desire to limit exposure to liability litigation if a user were injured as a result of use of a product (a use that could have been avoided by a recall), a desire to avoid adverse publicity associated with the distribution of a defective or inferior product, and a desire to maintain the reputation of the company or of the product/brand.

Most companies that decide to recall a product adhere to FDA's recall guidelines. These guidelines advise companies to follow a recall strategy that addresses the depth of the recall (to the wholesale or retail level); the need for a public warning; a communication plan to notify wholesalers, retailers, hospitals and others being asked to return the product; and a process for checking the effectiveness of the recall.

A recall strategy addresses:
- *the depth of a recall,*
- *the need for a public warning,*
- *a communication plan, and*
- *a process for checking the effectiveness of the recall.*

The agency can and often does request that a company conduct a recall. When FDA learns about the distribution of a product that it believes presents a significant public health risk or a gross fraud, and where a company has not taken action to remove the product from the market, FDA may contact the company directly and request that the company conduct a recall.

If a company does not respond to such a request, FDA in effect can initiate the recall on its own by contacting the company's accounts—distributors, warehousers, hospitals or individuals—and advising them directly of FDA's conclusion that the product is adulterated or misbranded and should not be used. During these FDA-initiated recalls, the agency may request that the product be returned to the manufacturer. FDA has initiated a recall in this way very rarely, and there is no direct statutory authority for such a recall. The basis for an FDA-initiated recall would appear to be FDA's authority to notify the public of any dangers associated with the use of FDA-regulated products together with its authority to seek adverse publicity. While companies may complain about FDA initiating a recall, the agency will do so when it concludes that a significant public health problem exists, that other enforcement actions may be inefficient or burdensome and that the company has not itself taken adequate action. Although FDA lacks general authority to order a product recall, Congress specifically has provided FDA with that authority in five product areas:

◆ Medical Devices: FDA may order a company to conduct a recall if it finds "a reasonable probability that a device intended for human use could cause serious adverse health consequences or death." Before ordering a recall of a dangerous medical device, FDA must provide the company with an opportunity for an informal hearing to discuss whether a recall is necessary. FDA can exercise this authority even if the company already has voluntarily recalled some of the product.

♦ Biologics: FDA can order the recall of a licensed biological product if it presents "an imminent or substantial hazard to the public health."

♦ Tobacco Products: FDA may order the immediate cessation of distribution, and subsequently a recall of a tobacco product where FDA has found that there is a "reasonable probability that the tobacco product contains a manufacturing or other defect not ordinarily contained in tobacco products on the market that would cause serious adverse health consequences or death." The responsible person has an opportunity for an informal hearing within 10 days of FDA's order.

♦ Infant Formula Products: FDA can order the recall of infant formula products that lack the required nutrients or are otherwise adulterated or misbranded.

♦ Foods: Where FDA determines that there is a reasonable probability of adulteration or misbranding of a food and that "the use of or exposure to [the food] will cause serious adverse health consequences or death" to humans or animals. FDA may, initially, order the cessation of distribution of the food. Before ordering a recall, FDA must give the responsible company an opportunity to take a recall voluntarily.

Enforcement Concerning Product Approvals

Many FDA-regulated products can be sold only if FDA approves an application for marketing. By the same token, the FDCA provides that FDA may withdraw its approval in a number of circumstances, including noncompliance with good manufacturing practice (GMP) requirements, false or misleading labeling, new evidence that the product is no longer safe or effective, or the submission of false statements to FDA.

The FDCA provides that FDA may withdraw its product approval.

To withdraw a product approval, FDA must publish a notice in the *Federal Register* of its intention to withdraw and invite comments from the company holding the approval as well as others. Next, the agency must publish a notice of an administrative hearing to decide whether the approval should be withdrawn. In most circumstances, however, no hearing is held. Rather, FDA and the company marketing the product settle the dispute, usually by agreeing to an orderly withdrawal of the product from the market or by agreeing on a labeling change.

When a public health hazard exists, FDA may temporarily suspend its approval of certain product applications without any prior notice or opportunity for an administrative hearing. FDA approvals of new drug and new animal drug applications may be suspended summarily if FDA finds that the product creates an "imminent hazard" to the public health. An approved biologics license can be summarily suspended if continued distribution would create a danger to health.

FDA may revoke a permit to make thermally processed foods in hermetically sealed containers if the manufacturer is not in compliance with FDA's low-acid canned foods regulations.

FDA may temporarily suspend the approval of the premarket application for a medical device, but only after providing an opportunity for an informal hearing. If there is reasonable probability that the continued distribution of the device would cause serious adverse health consequences or death, the agency may order the temporary suspension of the distribution of drugs covered by an approved abbreviated new drug application (ANDA) but only after it has provided an opportunity for a hearing on any disputed facts. The suspension of distribution of an ANDA drug is authorized if FDA finds that the applicant has engaged in bribery or submitted false statements, or has engaged in flagrant and repeated material violations of the drug GMP requirements so that such violations undermine the safety of the drugs and have not been corrected within a reasonable period of time.

FDA may refuse to review a product application if the agency concludes that the data in the pending application is unreliable and possibly fraudulent.

In addition to withdrawing or temporarily suspending product approvals, FDA may refuse to review one or more of a company's product applications, even if they contain the required evidence of safety and effectiveness, if FDA concludes that data in the pending application is unreliable and possibly fraudulent. This deferral of review is one element of FDA's "Applications Integrity Policy." When FDA questions the reliability of data in a pending product application and invokes this policy, the company that submitted the application must do four things for FDA to proceed with its review:

♦ cooperate with FDA in looking for the cause of any wrongdoing that has resulted in the submission of false or unreliable data;

♦ identify to FDA those individuals who were or may have been associated with any wrongdoing, and remove them from positions of authority on FDA matters;

♦ conduct a comprehensive internal review to assess the integrity of its product development and application processes; and

♦ provide a written commitment to FDA to develop a corrective action plan.

In addition, FDA may conduct its own "validity assessment" to ensure that any potential causes of unreliable or false data have been identified and remedied. These activities can take a long time, depending on the apparent source and scope of the data integrity problem. Some companies have had FDA review of their product applications deferred for one to three years while they undertook the prescribed corrective program.

Enforcement Against Imported Products

FDA, working with U.S. Customs and Border Protection (Customs), has authority to prevent products from entering U.S. commerce if those products appear to be adulterated or misbranded, or otherwise violate the FDCA.

When a product is identified by an importer as an FDA-regulated product, that declaration is communicated to FDA by an electronic link between Customs and the agency. If FDA requests, Customs will hold the product for FDA examination or sampling. In fact, FDA examines only a very small portion of the FDA-regulated products that are offered for importation each year—less than 2 percent. This reflects the enormous volume of import entries of FDA-regulated products each year and the lack of FDA resources available. If FDA decides to take an enforcement action against an import, however, its powers are significant.

FDA examines only a small portion of the FDA-regulated products that are offered for importation each year.

First, the standard for taking enforcement action is relatively low. FDA may refuse entry into U.S. commerce if the product merely "appears" to be violative. Second, FDA's interference with an import can have a significant economic impact, particularly for perishable products or products with short shelf lives. Thus, even the temporary detention of an import for examination pending a final decision on entry often leads to "voluntary" corrective action by the importer without the issuance of a formal refusal of entry. Finally, FDA may block importations of products by placing an automatic detention on all products that meet the detention criteria. For example, if FDA has evidence demonstrating that a certain product made in a particular country has regularly been shown to be contaminated, FDA can issue, on the basis of that historical data, an automatic detention to preclude the importation of all entries of that product from that country.

Because products can be refused entry on the basis of examination, sampling or "otherwise," and because importation of products from outside the United States traditionally has been considered a privilege, not a right, FDA's significant authority to control the importation of violative products has been generally sustained. A few courts, however, have questioned whether such FDA detention criteria are individual enforcement actions that the agency may pursue at its discretion, or whether they are "rules" that FDA can impose only after rule-making. Notwithstanding this unresolved legal issue, FDA has established an effective, even if very selective, enforcement process for those imports that the agency has resources to assess.

The issue of FDA's ability to effectively "guard the border" against noncompliant products has been seriously assessed in the past few years.

The issue of FDA's ability to effectively "guard the border" against noncompliant products has been seriously assessed in the past few years. FDA has observed that the nation increasingly relies on other countries to produce the food, drugs, devices and cosmetics that are consumed here. Ten to 15 percent of all foods, nearly two-thirds of fruits and vegetables, half the medical devices, about 40 percent of finished drug products and about 80 percent of active pharmaceutical ingredients used to make finished drug products for sale in the U.S. are manufactured abroad. In 2011, it is estimated that 24 million shipments of FDA-regulated products will be imported into the country. To address this situation, FDA plans, among other strategies, to establish foreign offices in China, India, Europe, Latin America and the Middle East. It also plans to increase its inspection of foreign establishments to approximately 1,900 per year. In addition to its import entry authority, FDA has begun to issue Warning Letters to foreign manufacturing facilities.

FDA is authorized to detain any food offered for import into the U.S. if the agency has "credible evidence" that the food presents a threat of "serious adverse health consequences or death" to humans or animals.

As a result of congressional action to prevent acts of bioterrorism by the use of poisonous food, FDA is authorized to detain any food offered for import into the U.S. if the agency has "credible evidence" that the food presents a threat of "serious adverse health consequences or death" to humans or animals. The importer or owner of the food may appeal FDA's decision. In addition, food establishments must register with FDA and FDA is authorized to hold any imported food if the foreign manufacturing facility is not registered. To allow FDA to exercise its regulatory powers over imported food, companies must give FDA notice of their intent to import foods into the United States prior to its arrival at an American port. Moreover, under the FDA Food Safety Modernization Act (FSMA), signed into law in January 2011, FDA is authorized to require importers to perform supplier verification activities and to obtain certifications that imported foods comply with safety requirements.

Civil Money Penalties

For certain products, Congress has authorized the agency to obtain a civil money penalty. A civil money penalty is a fine that is assessed against a company, an individual or both. FDA has civil money penalty authority in 10 program areas. In most of them, FDA has been authorized to impose the penalty itself, administratively. In a few areas, only federal courts have the authority to impose the penalty.

FDA has the authority to impose a civil money penalty for most violations of FDA requirements applicable to medical devices. FDA can impose these fines administratively; it does not need the approval of DOJ or an order from a court. For many violations, FDA can assess a penalty only if the violation is "significant" or "knowing," or a company can avoid a fine by showing that, notwithstanding the violation, it has operated in "substantial compliance" or that there have been no product defects or significant adverse consequences as a result of the violation. FDA may impose a civil money penalty of up to $15,000 for each violation or up to $1,000,000 for all violations involved in a single civil money penalty proceeding. A company or an individual that has been fined by FDA may appeal the fine to a federal court of appeals.

FDA also may seek a civil money penalty against companies or individuals for violating provisions of the FDCA covering radiation-emitting products. Violations that could lead to a fine include the manufacture or distribution of an electronic product that does not meet applicable federal standards, issuing false certificates of compliance with standards, or the failure to permit an FDA inspection or make an FDA-required report. For radiation-emitting products, FDA cannot impose a civil money penalty administratively. Therefore, FDA must request that DOJ file a complaint for a penalty in a federal court.

Under the Prescription Drug Marketing Act (PDMA), FDA is authorized to seek civil money penalties but only against companies, not individuals. A company can be assessed a fine if a representative of the company has been convicted of selling drug samples or if the company fails to report to FDA the fact that any of its representatives have been convicted of such violation. Under certain circumstances, a company can avoid a civil money penalty by demonstrating that it could not reasonably have been expected to have detected the violation, notwithstanding its having an internal audit system to detect possible wrongdoing by its employees. The fines that may be imposed range from $50,000 to $1,000,000, depending on the number of violations, the similarity of violations if more than one company representative is involved and the number of violations that have occurred within a certain time period. FDA has asserted its authority to impose penalties in this area administratively, although the PDMA refers only to the assessment of a civil money penalty by a federal court.

Under the PDMA FDA is authorized to seek civil money penalties only against companies, not individuals.

FDA also may impose a civil money penalty against a company that has failed to comply with an FDA order to recall a defective biological product. The penalty is not imposed for the distribution of the product but for failing to comply with FDA's recall order. Thus, this penalty resembles a fine for contempt and, accordingly, is based on each day of continued noncompliance with the FDA recall order, up to $100,000 per day.

The Generic Drug Enforcement Act of 1992 gave FDA authority to impose civil money penalties administratively for a number of prescribed violations involving ANDAs. Civil penalties may be assessed against companies or individuals for making false statements, failing to disclose a material fact, destroying evidence, obstructing an FDA investigation or bribing or attempting to bribe an FDA employee. In addition, a company may be assessed a civil money penalty if it uses the services of an individual who has been debarred by FDA from work on drug products. The maximum fine is $250,000 for an individual and $1,000,000 for a company, for each violation.

FDA also may impose a penalty under the National Childhood Vaccine Injury Act of 1986 (for destroying, altering or falsifying documents submitted by a vaccine manufacturer under the childhood compensation program) and under the Mammography Quality Standards Act of 1992 (for a testing facility's failure to obtain the required certificate for operation or for failing to comply with applicable standards). In addition, the Food Quality Protection Act of 1996 authorized civil money penalties for introducing into interstate commerce a food that contains an unsafe pesticide.

The Food and Drug Administration Amendments Act (FDAAA), enacted in 2007, authorized FDA to impose a civil money penalty if a company fails to comply with FDA requirements to register clinical trials and their results in the National Institutes of Health registry or submits registration or study data information that is false or misleading. A penalty of $10,000 may be imposed; violations that are not corrected within 30 days are subject to a civil penalty of up to $10,000 per day until the violation is corrected. The FDAAA also requires drug companies to develop risk evaluation and mitigation strategies and established new postapproval safety labeling requirements. The new amendments also authorized civil money penalties against companies that issue false or misleading direct-to-consumer advertisements, up to $500,000 if violations recur.

Most recently, in the Family Smoking Prevention and Tobacco Control Act (FSPTCA), signed into law in June 2009, Congress authorized FDA to impose administratively civil money penalties against any person or company that "violates a requirement of this Act." The law authorizes penalties in the range of $250,000 per violation to $1,000,000 for all violations adjudicated together, as well as up to $10,000,000 for violations that continue after FDA notice. Separately, the act authorizes civil money penalties in the range of $250 to $10,000 against retailers who sell tobacco products in violation of the act or the restrictions on sales in FDA regulations.

Except where explicitly required by the statute, FDA can impose a civil money penalty without a showing of knowing, willful or intentional conduct by the person who is fined.

FDA has established procedures for imposing civil money penalties. Under these procedures, the penalty process is initiated by filing a "complaint" alleging the violations on which the proposed penalty is based. If a defendant does not want to challenge the allegations in a complaint, a penalty can be assessed without any further proceedings. If the company or an individual challenges the complaint, FDA and the defendant may settle the case and agree upon a fine, or, if they are unable to reach agreement, the case will go forward. Either there will be a hearing or the hearing officer may decide that there are no genuine issues of material fact justifying a hearing, and he or she may issue a decision on the basis of stipulated facts and other documentation presented by both sides. In a civil money penalty proceeding, subpoenas can be issued by FDA and by the defendant. There is no right to issue subpoenas, however; the hearing officer may accept or reject a request for the issuance of a subpoena by either party.

FDA has used its civil money penalty authorities infrequently. Part of the reason is that some of these authorities are relatively new. Another reason is that developing a penalty case is resource intensive and may not be as attractive as other enforcement actions because the penalty itself does not correct the problem and FDA does not gain control over the operation of the company as it does by an injunction.

Referral to State Authorities

Nearly all states have adopted food, drug and device laws nearly identical to the FDCA. Most of those states amend their laws to incorporate significant new amendments to the FDCA. More than 20 states have provisions in their laws by which amendments to the FDCA are automatically adopted into and become part of the state law. Given the common definitions of adulteration and misbranding between federal and state laws, and a significant degree of similarity in enforcement authorities, FDA has the option of asking the state authorities to take an enforcement action. The state authorities may take enforcement action against any product manufactured or distributed within their state that violates state law.

Given the common definitions of adulteration and misbranding between federal and state laws, and a significant degree of similarity in enforcement authorities, FDA has the option of asking the state authorities to take an enforcement action.

To foster cooperation and coordination between FDA and the states, the agency works cooperatively with the National Association of Attorneys General. In recent years, the states' Attorneys General have had a particular interest in bringing enforcement actions involving consumer fraud. Once one state has initiated an action, the Attorneys General in other states often will file or threaten to initiate enforcement actions in their states. This strategy has often resulted in an "agreement" between the company and the Attorneys General for many states in which a company undertakes corrective action, such as stopping certain promotional claims and issuing "corrective advertising."

The states' Attorneys General have often worked with both the DOJ and FDA's OCI in the development of cases for alleged healthcare fraud involving state Medicaid programs, and the states often receive a portion of the disposition of the False Claims Act case when the federal settlement is reached.

In addition to enforcement tools similar to those of FDA, state health officials have two additional tools. First, state officials usually can suspend the license of a manufacturer, distributor or retailer to practice within the state. (Almost all businesses must obtain a state license to operate.) Second, in all states but one, health officials have the authority to embargo violative products on the spot.

In addition to referring certain noncompliant conduct for state enforcement action, FDA may commission state health officials to gather evidence for the agency to use in its federal enforcement action under the FDCA.

Debarment

In limited settings, FDA has the power to debar either a company or an individual.

In limited settings, FDA has the power to debar either a company or an individual. FDA's debarment authority applies to ANDAs, may implicate other drugs and, under the bioterrorism laws, applies to food importation.

An individual who has been debarred may not provide any services to a company that has any FDA approved or pending drug product applications. Thus, when a company submits a drug product application, it must certify to FDA that it has not used the services of any debarred individual in developing or submitting the application.

An individual may be debarred if he or she has been convicted of a felony under federal law for illegal conduct relating to the development or approval of any drug product. An individual also may be debarred if that individual has been convicted of a felony relating to the regulation of any drug, not just activity concerning approval. Debarment may be based on the fact that the individual has been convicted of any one of a number of other federal or state crimes, or "materially participated" in any conduct that was the basis of a conviction, even though that individual was not convicted. Finally, FDA may debar an officer or director of a company or some other "high managerial agent" if that person knew that others at the company were engaging in criminal conduct but did not report that conduct to FDA or the appropriate compliance official within the company.

When a drug company has been debarred, FDA will not accept or review any ANDA submitted by that company. In other words, during the period a company is debarred, FDA will not approve any new ANDAs for that company, although the company may continue to submit and FDA may continue to approve other product applications, and the company may continue to manufacture and distribute any drugs for which it already obtained FDA marketing approval. A company may be debarred if it has been convicted of a felony relating to the development or approval of any ANDA or if that company has been convicted of certain specified federal crimes or state law. FDA may not debar either an individual or a company until it has provided an opportunity for a hearing on any disputed issues of material fact.

The names of individuals and companies that have been debarred are published in the *Federal Register*. Because companies can be debarred only if they have been convicted of a crime, FDA is somewhat limited in its ability to exercise this power because it must await action by DOJ or by a State Attorney General to file criminal charges against a company and obtain a conviction. From the beginning of the debarment program in 1993 to the end of 2010, FDA has permanently debarred over 80 individuals and over 20 other individuals have been debarred for designated periods of time, most often three to five years. FDA has not yet debarred any company.

Congress has authorized FDA to debar persons who are convicted of a felony relating to food importation or who have engaged in a pattern of offering for import adulterated food that presents a threat of serious adverse health consequences or death to humans or animals.

Additional Enforcement Powers

Congress has amended the FDCA numerous times since its initial passage in 1938. Many of the amendments have established new or elevated requirements for market entry, addressed specific operational functions of FDA, enhanced the agency's inspection powers or provided new enforcement authority. Three amendments enacted over the past 20 years have and are likely to have a significant impact on FDA's enforcement powers and their role in protecting the public health—the Safe Medical Devices Act (SMDA), FSPTCA and, most recently, FSMA.

Medical Devices

In addition to its standard enforcement tools for regulated products, the agency has additional specific enforcement powers regarding medical devices. These authorities were provided by Congress primarily in the SMDA.

For medical devices, an FDA investigator has the power, during an inspection, to order that a device be detained if the investigator has reason to believe that it is adulterated or misbranded. The detention may last only 20 days and is designed to provide FDA with an opportunity to decide whether to bring a seizure action against the product or to obtain an injunction against the company. If FDA decides that it needs more time to consider its next step, however, the period of detention may be extended an additional 10 days.

Because companies can be debarred only if they have been convicted of a crime, FDA is somewhat limited in its ability to exercise this power because it must await action by DOJ or by a State Attorney General to file criminal charges against a company and obtain a conviction.

The Safe Medical Devices Act provides for additional enforcement authorities against noncompliant medical devices.

FDA also may order that a device manufacturer issue a notification to distributors, retailers, doctors or users of a device if the agency has concluded that the device presents an unreasonable risk of substantial harm to the public and that notification is necessary to eliminate that risk. The only prerequisite to FDA invoking this authority is to "consult with the persons who are to give the notice." In effect, this provision authorizes FDA to mandate that a manufacturer distribute adverse information about its product, which is likely to result in modification of the conditions under which the device is used, cessation of the use of the device due to anxiety associated with the notification or the return of the device by those who believe that it is no longer safe.

FDA may order a device manufacturer to "immediately cease distribution" of a device and to "immediately notify health professionals and device user facilities... to cease use" of it. FDA may invoke this authority if it finds that there is a reasonable probability that the device would cause serious adverse health consequences or death. FDA may make that finding on its own and issue a cease distribution order without giving the company an opportunity for any hearing. FDA must provide an opportunity for such a hearing, however, within 10 days after issuing its order. At that time, the agency may withdraw or modify the order, or it may amend the order to require the company to recall the device. In other words, this statutory provision gives FDA the authority to issue both an injunction and a mandatory recall administratively.

Finally, FDA may declare a device to be restricted in its sale, distribution or use. In invoking these restrictions, FDA may require either that the device be made available only on prescription or may impose "such other conditions" as it believes are necessary to provide a reasonable assurance that the product can be used safely and effectively. If FDA declares a device to be restricted—which it may do only by regulation—it also gains control over certain aspects of the advertising of that device. A restricted device is the only kind of device over which FDA has any authority over advertising.

Tobacco Products

The FSPTCA was, to a substantial degree, modeled after the FDA regulatory regime for medical devices.

The FSPTCA was, to a substantial degree, modeled after the FDA regulatory regime for medical devices. As a result, as with devices, FDA has its standard administrative and judicial enforcement tools as well as product detention, manufacturer notification and the ability of FDA to order the immediate cessation of distribution, followed by mandatory recall. In addition, as with devices, there are various restrictions on the sale and advertising of tobacco products. Indeed, because FDCA amendments reflect Congress's resolution of product-specific issues, the FSPTCA contains a number of prohibitions and limitations that, if not complied with, result in a tobacco product being adulterated, misbranded or otherwise violative. For example, under the FSPTCA and the regulations that it created, tobacco product promotional materials may be only in black and white (not color); may not be sold with descriptors such as "light" or "low"; packs must contain new, large warning statements on the negative health effects of smoking; and cigarettes may not be flavored. FDA may also issue regulations that establish standards for, and limitations on, the ingredients and characteristics of tobacco products, including reducing the levels of addictive nicotine.

Food

Under FSMA, the agency may now order the cessation of distribution of food, and its recall from the market, if the requisite criteria are met. Importers are required to perform supplier verification and obtain certification that food imports meet safety standards. FSMA also authorizes enhanced FDA inspectional access to food facility records and establishes new recordkeeping requirements for foods designated as high risk.

JUDICIAL ENFORCEMENT

The FDCA authorizes three types of judicial enforcement: product seizure, injunction and prosecution. The first two are civil sanctions; the last is criminal.

Three types of judicial enforcement:
- *seizure*
- *injunction*
- *prosecution*

Seizure

Under section 304 of the FDCA, a product that is adulterated or misbranded is subject to seizure. Products may be seized in a manufacturing facility, a warehouse or distribution facility; from a truck or other carrier of the product; from a retail store; from a hospital or doctor's office; or from a consumer. In most cases, seizures are made at the facility where the products were made, or from the warehouse or distribution center where they are held.

At one time, FDA pursued more than 200 seizures each year. During the past several years, FDA has used seizure actions very infrequently—only six in 2007, eight in 2008, six in 2009 and 10 in 2010.

FDA can recommend a seizure to the U.S. Attorney in the state where the products are located. If the U.S. Attorney agrees to initiate the seizure action, he or she will file a "complaint" in the federal court. The complaint identifies the products and describes the ways in which they are adulterated or misbranded, or both. After the complaint is filed, the clerk of the court issues a warrant for the "arrest" (the seizure) of the products. Usually, a Deputy U.S. Marshal will make the seizure. In nearly all situations, products are seized where they are found ("in place"), and cannot be moved or handled without the court's permission.

There is no judicial hearing before the products are seized, so once the seizure is accomplished, FDA has—temporarily—won the case. After that, the court will condemn the products or it can find that the allegations in the complaint have not been proven and release the products from seizure.

Recently, FDA has used seizures in three settings: seizures designed to remove from the market products that FDA believes present a serious public health risk, seizures of products that violate the law in a way that FDA wants to publicly highlight and "mass seizures." FDA may recommend a "mass seizure" of all products that have been manufactured or are being warehoused under violative conditions. Typically, a mass seizure will be brought where the products are alleged to be adulterated because they have not been manufactured in compliance with GMP regulations, or they have been manufactured or held under insanitary conditions. Where such manufacturing or storage conditions exist, all of the products are adulterated. A mass seizure can significantly disrupt normal business operations. As a result, there is often a prompt resolution.

In the vast majority of seizure cases, the products are condemned either by default or consent.

In the vast majority of seizure cases, the products are condemned either by default or consent. One reason for this success rate is that FDA usually does not recommend a seizure action unless it has reasonably strong evidence that the products are adulterated or misbranded. Another is the absence of a judicial hearing before the seizure is accomplished—the owner of the seized products is at a substantial disadvantage because the products remain under seizure during the lengthy judicial process. Thus, it is often in the owner's best business interest to resolve the seizure promptly.

In many seizures, the owner or manufacturer allows the products to be condemned by "default." When this occurs, the court usually will order that they be destroyed. In other situations, the manufacturer will file a claim to the seized products and enter a consent decree agreeing that the court may condemn them. Where products are condemned as part of a consent decree, the decree usually gives the owner or manufacturer an opportunity to recondition them— by relabeling, sorting, cleaning or similar procedures—in order to salvage as many of them as possible for distribution. Under typical FDA consent decrees, FDA decides whether the products have been reconditioned successfully. Once they have been reconditioned and FDA has released them, the products may be distributed just like any other product because they are no longer in violation of the FDCA. Condemned products that cannot be reconditioned to FDA's satisfaction will be destroyed.

In recent years, FDA has been able to settle a seizure action through a consent decree that not only resolves the seizure but also includes injunctive language designed to address the underlying causes of the violations. In this way, FDA uses the seizure as leverage to obtain manufacturer agreement to an even broader decree—one that is frequently more rigorous than FDA would have otherwise secured.

On a few occasions, the owner or manufacturer not only believes that the seized products are not adulterated or misbranded but also that FDA-supervised reconditioning is not acceptable. In those cases, the owner or manufacturer will contest the seizure with the hope of demonstrating to the court that the products are not violative and should be released for distribution as is. At trial, the government has the burden of showing, by a preponderance of evidence, that the seized products are violative.

Injunction

Through an injunction FDA hopes to force a company to make significant changes in its operations. An injunction is a court order that the company cease manufacture and distribution of products unless and until the company complies with FDA requirements. A court will issue an injunction if it believes that, without an injunction, violations are likely to recur. The injunction is designed to prevent such recurrence. Usually FDA will seek injunctive relief only after other enforcement actions have been unsuccessful in bringing about corrective action. Most often, FDA will seek injunctive relief for persistent violations of its GMP regulations, or for repeated noncompliance with FDA requirements for labeling and promotion.

An injunction is a court order that the company cease manufacture and distribution of products unless and until the company complies with FDA requirements.

FDA recommends injunction actions to the Office of Consumer Protection Litigation, the part of DOJ assigned to review FDA cases. Typically, the complaint for injunction proposed by FDA will identify, in substantial detail, those practices that FDA believes do not comply with its regulations. It is FDA's hope that after reading the lengthy complaint a judge would be inclined to enter an order of injunction against the defendants.

It is FDA's policy that an injunction case should be brought not only against the company but also against company officials who have the most direct responsibility for the alleged violations. Thus, for example, an injunction might include as defendants the company president, the vice president for operations, the director of quality assurance and, possibly, the plant manager. It has been FDA's experience that by naming corporate individuals as defendants it obtains the maximum amount of cooperation in achieving compliance, as well as the maximum amount of deterrence against other corporate officials who have similar responsibilities in their companies.

There are three types or phases of an injunction. If the alleged violations create a significant and immediate public health risk, FDA will request that DOJ seek a temporary restraining order (TRO). If a court enters a TRO, it will prevent the company from shipping violative products for up to 20 days until there can be a further judicial hearing. A TRO can be entered without a formal hearing before the court. In most cases, however, a court will not enter a TRO without some informal opportunity for a company to appear and offer either an explanation or some assurance about the operations of the company. A court can enter a TRO, however, without any representative from the company being present.

Most FDA injunctions include a request for preliminary relief.

Whether or not a TRO is sought, most FDA injunctions include a request for "preliminary" relief. A preliminary injunction usually prevents the defendants from making or distributing products until the noncompliant procedures and practices are corrected, and until there can be a full judicial hearing on a permanent injunction. In many cases, however, a preliminary injunction may be in effect for several weeks. During that time, a company may negotiate with DOJ to settle the case. A preliminary injunction may be entered only after a judicial hearing.

If neither a TRO nor a preliminary injunction has been entered, the company may continue to operate until a full hearing on a permanent injunction is held and the court has ruled. Usually, FDA seeks both a preliminary and a permanent injunction. In some cases, however, where violations have persisted over a long time but the consequences are not particularly significant, FDA may seek only a permanent injunction.

FDA has pursued injunctive relief somewhat selectively in recent years.

FDA has pursued injunctive relief somewhat selectively in recent years. In the years 2003 to 2010, FDA recommended approximately 115 actions to DOJ—on average, about 15 per year. Most of these injunction cases are based on alleged violations of FDA's GMP regulations for drugs and devices. As a result, resolution of most GMP injunctions are very burdensome on the defendant company.

Most injunction actions filed on behalf of FDA are resolved through the entry of a consent decree of permanent injunction that has been negotiated between DOJ and the defendants. This often occurs because the defendants decide that FDA has sufficient evidence to win an injunction after judicial hearing or they want to resolve the dispute with FDA as quickly as possible. A consent decree may be agreed to even before the complaint for injunction is filed. This occurs when the DOJ attorney provides the potential defendants (through their lawyers) with a copy of the complaint that DOJ intends to file in court and a copy of a proposed consent decree of permanent injunction. Most consent decrees of injunction contain four standard provisions:

♦ First, the defendants must cease manufacture and distribution "unless and until" they make a number of corrections in their policies and procedures, which are specified in the consent decree itself. In some cases, a consent decree may allow the company to continue to manufacture and ship its products—or most of them—while it is implementing corrective action and undergoing verification of such action by external audit. Such "going for-ward" decrees are less disruptive for companies although the required reme-dial programs are usually comprehensive, very burdensome and can take years to be fully implemented. Consent decrees may permit the enjoined company to continue to make and distribute medically necessary products.

♦ Second, the defendants must submit a written report to FDA describing the corrections they have implemented or intend to implement to achieve compliance. The corrective actions are often developed with the assistance of outside GMP experts.

♦ Third, the defendants must retain an independent expert consultant to review their operation and to report to the defendants, and certify to FDA, that the company is in compliance. Based on the consultant's report, the defendants also must certify to FDA that they are in compliance.

♦ Finally, FDA will make an inspection, at the defendants' expense, to verify that the company is operating in compliance with the FDCA, and that the corrections are adequate and have been fully implemented.

In addition, the defendants usually must agree to hold all the products in their possession or under their control on the date the consent decree is entered until FDA determines that the products are suitable for release or until the prod-ucts are reconditioned to FDA's satisfaction. In this way, nearly every injunction action contains within it a mass seizure. As is apparent, meeting the terms of a consent decree of injunction is resource intensive for the defendant company. It is time consuming and expensive and may involve significant changes in the way the company operates.

The terms of the consent decree will generally reflect the specific underlying nature of noncompliance with FDA requirements alleged in the complaint, as well as the significance of the noncompliance, the type of product, the conse-quences for users if the product is not in compliance, and the regulatory history of the company and the individual defendants. It will also reflect DOJ's assess-ment of the defendants' ability to demonstrate that effective corrective actions have already been implemented, and that the likelihood that the violations will recur is significantly reduced. Finally, the terms of the consent decree will reflect the "give and take" of the negotiation processes.

A consent decree may impose requirements or give FDA additional powers not conferred by the FDCA itself.

459

As a result, a consent decree may impose requirements or give FDA additional powers not conferred by the FDCA itself. For example, companies often are required to have their operations audited routinely by an independent expert and to submit the audit reports to FDA even after they are allowed to resume operations under the consent decree. Some consent decrees require the defendants to conduct ongoing employee training programs. Under some decrees, FDA is authorized to order recalls of the defendants' products. In a consent decree based on allegations of unsubstantiated advertising, the defendants may be required to recall and destroy all material that promotes a product for an unapproved use, submit new promotional material to FDA for advance approval and conduct a corrective advertising program including issuance of "Dear Doctor" letters and corrective advertisements to appear in journals named by FDA. In some recent consent decrees, the defendants have agreed to pay FDA's costs in investigating and bringing the injunction action, or they have been required to set aside an amount of money to ensure adequate funds for process improvements even after the resumption of operations under the consent decree.

Two recent appellate courts have upheld FDA's position that the government can obtain equitable monetary relief—restitution or disgorgement—as part of an injunction under the FDCA. The theory of this relief is that companies should not be allowed to retain the profits they have made from the sale of violative products before the injunction was entered. So far, FDA has sought this additional relief selectively and important legal issues about its imposition remain.

Complaints for injunction and consent decrees are public documents. Injunction actions are widely reported by FDA trade press and, depending upon the nature of the problem and the size of the defendants, often are reported in the lay press.

Because a consent decree is a court order, any knowing violation of it constitutes a contempt of court.

Even though a consent decree is agreed to by both FDA and the defendants, it is a court order just as if it had been entered by the court after the defendants had challenged the injunction and lost. Because a consent decree is a court order, any knowing violation of it constitutes a contempt of court. The power of the court to hold individuals in contempt undoubtedly is designed to encourage compliance with the decree.

Developing injunction cases is time consuming for FDA. In addition, there is no guarantee that DOJ will agree to file an injunction that FDA recommends, although in most cases the department accepts FDA's recommendation. While the primary burdens of a consent decree fall upon the defendants, FDA has certain obligations to monitor and supervise the defendants' compliance activities. Thus, an injunction is not completely a one-way street. For these reasons, FDA does not recommend injunction cases lightly. It usually reserves this type of enforcement for companies that have failed repeatedly, after notice from the agency, to adequately correct significant noncompliance with FDA requirements.

Criminal Prosecution

While the FDCA identifies numerous "prohibited acts," most criminal cases are based on either the shipment of adulterated or misbranded products in interstate commerce or the manufacture of a product under conditions that cause it to be adulterated or misbranded. Any individual or company that engages in those prohibited acts or causes any such violation may be punished, criminally. FDA's policy is to recommend criminal charges against individuals as well as companies. FDA believes that criminal charges against the company alone, without individual defendants, does not provide adequate deterrent or adequate punishment.

The most fundamental feature of FDA criminal law is that an individual can be prosecuted even without knowing about the violative conduct or without intent to violate the law. Rather, the prosecution is based on the individual's responsibility for the conduct that results in the violation, as reflected in the individual's power and authority in the company. This "strict liability" basis for criminal prosecution is based upon two Supreme Court decisions. The first, *United States v. Dotterweich*, was decided in 1943. In that case, the Supreme Court said that a violation of the FDCA is committed by all company officials who are "responsible" for the violative conduct.

Under FDA criminal law an individual can be prosecuted even without knowing about the violative conduct or without intent to violate the law.

More than 30 years later, the Supreme Court reaffirmed and amplified the standard of criminal strict liability under the FDCA in its decision in *United States v. Park*. The Court described the standard for criminal liability under the FDCA this way:

> The Act imposes not only a positive duty to seek out and remedy violations when they occur but also, and primarily, a duty to imple-ment measures that will ensure that violations will not occur. The requirements of foresight and vigilance imposed on responsible corporate agents are beyond question demanding and even onerous but they are no more stringent than the public has the right to expect of those who voluntarily assume positions of authority in business enterprises whose services and products affect the health and well being of the public that supports them. . . . [It is enough if the] defendant had, by reason of his position in the corporation, responsibility and authority either to prevent in

> the first instance or promptly to correct the violation complained of, and that he failed to do so. . . . We are satisfied that the Act imposes the highest standard of care and permits conviction of responsible corporate officials, who in light of this standard of care, have the power to prevent or correct violations.

The Court also observed that

> . . . those corporate agents vested with the responsibility, and power commensurate with that responsibility, to devise whatever measures are necessary to ensure compliance with the Act bear a "responsible relationship" to, or have a "responsible share" in, violations.

The strict liability basis for criminal prosecution is based upon two Supreme Court decisions.

Under the strict liability standard of the "*Park* doctrine," a person who has a responsible relationship to the violations may be prosecuted for a failure to detect, prevent or correct the violations. The only legal defense under the *Park* doctrine is a showing that the violation occurred notwithstanding "extraordinary" efforts to prevent it. In such a circumstance, the courts have held that compliance is, in effect, impossible. Of course, any individual defendant may show that he or she did not stand in a responsible relationship to the violative conduct because the defendant lacked the necessary power or authority. For that reason, the individual would try to demonstrate that he or she was powerless to prevent the violation and cannot be convicted for what was impossible.

The ability to recommend a criminal prosecution based on the *Park* doctrine provides FDA with a substantial amount of discretion in choosing targets for criminal action. In recent years, however, FDA recommendations for prosecution under the *Park* doctrine have become few and far between. Since 2000, FDA has referred only a handful of *Park*, strict liability criminal cases to DOJ. In addition, DOJ has hesitated to file criminal charges against individuals based only on the *Park* doctrine. Rather, it has preferred to bring criminal charges against individuals who have intentionally or fraudulently violated the law or who have been grossly negligent or have recklessly disregarded the FDCA.

In 2010 FDA began to take steps to revive the *Park* doctrine. It revised its criteria—nonbinding considerations—for recommending strict liability criminal cases and in 2011 published them in its *Regulatory Procedures Manual*. The criteria are not novel; they reflect the potential defendants' authority to prevent or correct a violation, as well as actual knowledge of the circumstances resulting in a violation. In addition, FDA will consider whether the violation involves harm to the public, is serious or widespread, whether the issue or product defect was obvious or whether it reflects a failure to respond to prior notice or warnings. It is yet to be seen if in fact FDA will begin to refer such prosecution cases to DOJ and whether DOJ will accept such recommendations.

Whatever the outcome of FDA's renewed focus on criminal strict liability cases, the recent focus of criminal enforcement has been on knowing or intentional violations of the FDCA or other cases involving fraud. These cases are usually investigated by FDA's Office of Criminal Investigations. In the five years between 2003-2007, OCI accounted for approximately 1,500 criminal convictions. In 2007, OCI reported nearly 350 convictions; in each of 2008 and 2009, it reported 370 convictions, and in 2010 it reported just under 270 convictions.

The Park *doctrine has been a valuable part of FDA's criminal enforcement but most criminal cases brought in recent years involve intentional violations.*

OCI investigates cases concerning willful misconduct involving FDA-regulated products, obstruction of justice, submitting false information to FDA, mail fraud, wire fraud, racketeering, criminal conspiracy and product tampering.

Most of these violations are defined by the federal criminal laws, not the FDCA. In some of these cases, while the investigation has focused on federal, non-FDCA felonies, the defendants may resolve the investigation by agreeing to plead guilty to FDCA *Park* violation. Even where a plea bargain may involve a conviction for an FDCA violation, the penalties associated with these cases often include fines of several million dollars and periods of incarceration for some defendants.

With the assistance of the DOJ, OCI investigators often use evidence-gathering tools that are not available to FDA. These include grand jury subpoenas for evidence, grants of immunity to individuals in exchange for their cooperation against targets of the investigation and electronic surveillance (wiretapping). OCI investigators often work with agents from the Federal Bureau of Investigation (FBI) and other federal law enforcement investigative agencies to develop these cases.

In recent years, a new area of law enforcement has become the primary context in which most FDA criminal charges are included. These are cases brought to enforce the False Claims Act (FCA), which establishes penalties against companies that "cause" doctors and hospitals to submit claims for Medicare and Medicaid reimbursement, claims that are considered false because the medication for which payment is sought is for an unapproved, off-label use. These "healthcare fraud" cases are usually based on whistleblower reports and are investigated and developed by the HHS Inspector General's office, FDA's OCI and the FBI. Because nearly all of these cases involve off-label promotion of drugs, allegations of criminal misbranding under the FDCA are usually brought and the settlement of the majority of these cases includes companies or individuals pleading guilty to FDCA criminal misbranding charges, including felony violations. While the largest portion of the fines accessed in these settlements are civil penalties under the FCA and payments to states, some of the fines are based on the criminal FDCA violations, as well as criminal violations of other, related laws, such as the anti-kickback laws and various fraud statutes. Penalties for violations of the FDCA and other criminal statutes in these cases have often included companies being required to enter into corporate integrity agreements—aggressive remediation programs much like those imposed under an FDA injunction—and have resulted in terms of imprisonment for some individuals. Conviction for healthcare fraud can also result in corporate and individual exclusion from federal healthcare programs. These FCA/misbranding cases have been most noteworthy for their very substantial fines, in excess of $2 billion in one recent settlement. It has been reported that in the past decade, fines and penalties from settlement of cases alleging off-label promotion have totaled more than $10 billion.

Conviction for healthcare fraud can result in corporate and individual exclusion from federal healthcare programs.

The vast majority of criminal cases involving FDA are resolved by conviction of the defendants as part of a plea bargain. For a corporate defendant, the plea bargain may involve not only the payment of a fine but also an agreement to establish a corporate compliance program or corporate integrity agreement that contains many elements of an FDA injunction. For individuals, a plea bargain may involve not only a recommendation regarding a fine or against imprisonment but also may involve an agreement by the defendant not to participate in certain FDA-regulated activities.

Violations of the FDCA under the Park *doctrine are misdemeanors.*

Violations of the FDCA under the *Park* doctrine are misdemeanors. Violations of the FDCA with intent to defraud or mislead and most violations of the federal criminal laws are felonies. The distinction between misdemeanors and felonies, however, has been significantly affected as a result of federal fines and sentencing laws and the U.S. Sentencing Guidelines under which fines against corporations and periods of incarcerations of individuals may be calculated under a complex scheme that considers various factors outside of the misdemeanor/felony distinction. In addition, a company can be placed on corporate probation, a sentence that has some of the characteristics of an FDA injunction. Under the Guidelines, a company can reduce the level of its fine if it can demonstrate that, notwithstanding the violations, it had an effective corporate compliance program designed to detect and prevent violations of law.

CONCLUSION

FDA enforcement has been an effective deterrent in promoting compliance among FDA-regulated companies. FDA has a variety of effective enforcement tools available to it and broad discretion in deciding which tools to use to remedy violations of the FDCA. FDA has the greatest flexibility and control in taking administrative enforcement actions. These are often as effective as judicial enforcement and do not require the concurrence of DOJ. However, recent enforcement actions based on collaborative FDA/DOJ investigations have resulted in penalties that have significantly enhanced the deterrent effect of enforcement.

Chapter 16

Being Prepared

William Vodra, Retired Partner, Arnold & Porter LLP, Washington, D.C.

Key Points

- A crisis for a company regulated by the Food and Drug Administration (FDA) may take many forms, but usually it involves public allegations of legal violations that endanger consumers, resulting in multiple legal proceedings and negative publicity that can threaten the company's reputation and even its survival.
- The crisis generally will be based on either an apparent risk to the public health or a plausible charge of fraud.
- Although every crisis has acute phases that must be properly managed, the company facing the crisis will have to make a prolonged and steady commitment of resources. Endurance and patience are essential.
- Five principles of crisis management are:
  - o Recognize a possible crisis early and act accordingly.
  - o Get ahead of the potential crisis by anticipating its possible scope.
  - o Staff the crisis adequately.
  - o Ensure truth and consistency in public statements.
  - o Deal effectively with FDA and other constituencies.
- Not all crises can be prevented, but good crisis management programs contribute to limiting and resolving the unavoidable crisis.

CHARACTERISTICS OF A CRISIS FOR A FDA-REGULATED FIRM

Anyone working in the food and drug field will meet the greatest challenges during a "regulatory crisis." Every business tries hard to prevent a disaster, but despite the best of these efforts, one still may be encountered. For firms that are regulated by the Food and Drug Administration (FDA), the nature of the product means that crises inevitably will occur. It is essential to keep in mind the motto of the Boy Scouts: "Be Prepared."

Crises pose unusual and unique demands on a company. Important steps should be taken early during a crisis to manage it as well as possible. Crisis prevention activities may assist in containing the unavoidable crisis.

The characteristics of a regulatory crisis include:

♦ allegations of violations of FDA law endangering consumers;

♦ public awareness of these allegations;

♦ multiple legal proceedings involving parties other than the company and FDA that influence and complicate the interactions between the regulators and the regulated; and

♦ significant threats to the company's reputation or products, and perhaps to the organization and key employees as well.

A "regulatory crisis" is not a normal confrontation with FDA. Any business regulated by FDA has numerous and diverse opportunities to run afoul of regulations. Indeed, given an intensive audit by the agency, any company on any particular day could be found in violation of some legal requirement. These "routine" violations generally do not trigger any formal FDA action. The agency looks at whether a business is substantially in compliance with legal requirements, determined in part by whether the firm has control of its operating processes and systems. If FDA believes the systems generally are under control, the agency usually will bring the "routine" violations to the company's attention and recommend voluntary remedial action.

In a regulatory crisis, the alleged violations plausibly create an immediate and significant danger to consumers.

In a regulatory crisis, the alleged violations plausibly create an immediate and significant danger to consumers. The injury would result from one or more of three common elements:

♦ a product is unsafe as made, labeled, used or promoted;

♦ consumers are being defrauded; or

♦ the government is failing to protect the public because it was misled by the company.

If no risk of serious harm to users of the product is perceived, a confrontation between FDA and a company over the alleged violations will rarely develop into a "crisis."

A regulatory crisis inevitably involves public awareness. Normally, "routine" violations result in a relatively private dialogue between the regulatory agency and the regulated firm. When news media make the public aware of the alleged misconduct, however, a regulatory crisis can explode. Perceptions about the business and its products are always at the core of the situation. Firms supplying foods, drugs, medical devices, cosmetics and other FDA-regulated items must maintain a high degree of consumer and healthcare professional confidence. In 2003, manufacturers of certain antidepressants warned of potential increased risk of suicide in children and adolescents, amidst charges that these risks had been concealed previously. Shortly thereafter, prescription rates for these drugs fell by 18 percent. In a regulatory crisis, therefore, a firm is challenged to maintain the trust of the consuming public in its products and in its corporate image.

During a regulatory crisis, parties other than the company and FDA inevitably become active players. Furthermore, important events and pressures emerge in many arenas at the same time. For example, a company may be faced simultaneously with different lawsuits asserting claims for product liability, securities law violations, wrongful discharge of employees, unfair trade practices or denial of insurance coverage. Inquiries can be initiated by congressional committees, corporate directors and federal agencies in addition to FDA. Investigative news reporters can start a search for scandal. Similar regulatory activities, litigation and investigations may erupt in other countries where the product is marketed or the firm does business.

A regulatory crisis could result in:
- *plummeting sales,*
- *share values falling,*
- *cumulative sanctions, or*
- *civil and criminal liability.*

A regulatory crisis is marked also by enormous stresses within a company. Sales of individual products may plummet. The sales force, operating on a commission basis, immediately loses personal income. Workers in production and distribution areas may be laid off if sales soon do not recover. Even employees not directly responsible for the involved products may worry about the company's ability to respond to the emergency. In short, morale is put in jeopardy throughout the organization.

Second, if the company's securities are publicly traded, values of shares of stock may fall. In May 2007, after the *New England Journal of Medicine* published a study purporting to show that Avandia (rosiglitazone) increased the risk of heart attacks in diabetic patients, the manufacturer's stock price dropped more than 10 percent in days, wiping out $15 billion in market value. Such precipitous declines expose firms to litigation for alleged failure to disclose risks (thus overvaluing the stock), as well as hostile takeover bids. Even without these dire consequences, management remains answerable to existing shareholders for loss in market value. In the short term, a crisis will require senior executives to devote significant energy to responding to Wall Street analysts.

Third, the potential exposure of the company to cumulative sanctions—criminal prosecution, civil fines and penalties, disgorgement of profits or restitution to consumers, debarment from government procurement programs, and punitive damages in private litigation—can be staggering. Bankruptcy is not unheard of; it was the fate of Able Laboratories following a crisis involving the reliability of generic drug products. Managing these risks can demand resources for years after the immediate crisis has passed.

Finally, individuals within the company may be exposed to civil and criminal liability, as well as debarment from further employment in the industry. The ability of law-respecting "white collar" employees faced with allegations of criminal wrongdoing to bear up under investigations, hearings, depositions and media coverage is highly variable. This personal element frequently is overlooked in the heat of activities, but can be critical to the firm's ability to survive the crisis intact.

These stresses give a regulatory crisis another dimension that often is not appreciated until it is experienced. Within the company during a crisis, profound interpersonal tensions can emerge. Resources previously committed to future projects are diverted to addressing the problems at hand. Root cause assessments may turn individuals and operating units against each other. Employees begin to consider new career opportunities. The more serious and prolonged the crisis, the more intense becomes the pressure on the company to find a quick and decisive resolution. Management's ability to keep the organization functioning can be severely challenged.

Although a regulatory confrontation may originate between a company and FDA at any time, it becomes a regulatory crisis when it spreads into the public domain and invites other parties to become involved. Preparedness may not prevent a crisis, but it is critical to weathering it successfully.

EVOLUTION OF A CRISIS

Major crises tend to fall into two patterns: the public health crisis and the fraud crisis.

Major crises tend to fall into two patterns: the "public health" crisis and the "fraud" crisis.

The preponderance of the most serious FDA regulatory crises have begun with a real or perceived danger to the public health associated with a marketed product. In some circumstances, the questions relate to product quality and alleged contamination of a product, whether by diethylene glycol in toothpaste, melamine in pet food, oversulfated chrondroitin sulfate in heparin, or *E. coli* on spinach. Other situations emerge from new discoveries questioning the safety of an established product. Newspapers routinely break stories about possible links between products and terrifying hazards, even when the underlying studies are preliminary and inconclusive. In recent years, American society has been buffeted by scares such as whether antidepressants cause patients to commit suicide, whether preservatives in childhood vaccines produce autism, whether a widely used class of anti-arthritis drug triggers heart attacks and whether drug-coated coronary stents are more dangerous than earlier "bare-metal" stents. In response to intense criticism for failing to disclose data on potential product safety issues, FDA now regularly publicizes early notices about unconfirmed reports of possible risks. These situations seem to explode with little prior warning.

When a food, drug, device or cosmetic in active use is discovered—or merely alleged—to present a significant risk of illness, injury or death, both the company and FDA must deal with urgent health questions:

♦ Should the product be temporarily or permanently removed from the market?

♦ Should new warnings or risk minimization controls restrict use of the product?

♦ Should consumers be advised to get medical care?

These issues must be addressed promptly and with a public conclusion—even if that conclusion is no more than a conscious choice to defer any action until more information is available.

A public health crisis need not present any actual dangers to the public.

A public health crisis need not present any actual dangers to the public. Consumer advocacy groups, scientific researchers, investigative journalists, members of Congress and even organizations with political agendas unrelated to FDA regulation can make widely publicized accusations that specific products or classes of products are endangering the public health. In every case, Congress and the public expect FDA to review the data dispassionately and to reach a reasoned conclusion about the merits of the allegations. Even though the allegations ultimately prove baseless, the mere fact that they were made can have long-term adverse consequences for the product. For example, public attacks linking Bendectin, a drug for morning sickness during pregnancy, with birth defects were unequivocally rejected by FDA as unsupported by any scientific evidence; nevertheless, continued product liability litigation and hostile publicity led the manufacturer to remove the product from the market.

After any immediate remedial actions are taken to address a public health crisis, FDA almost always will investigate whether the firm either could have prevented the problem or actively concealed it. The search is always looking to answer the critical pair of questions: what did the company know and when did the company know it?

Allegations that company officials knew a product was dangerous but hid that information from the public and regulators make great headlines and can profoundly influence future events. To illustrate, each of the most prominent criminal prosecutions of pharmaceutical manufacturers in the 1980s (Eli Lilly & Co. for Oraflex, Smith Kline & French for Selacryn and Hoescht AG for Merital) followed public claims that the drug firm had evidence that its product could cause a fatal side effect prior to marketing, failed to disclose that evidence adequately to FDA during premarket review and, as a result, was able to sell the product with insufficient warnings.

A "fraud crisis" also may emerge independent of any prior public health crisis. In this situation, it is alleged that the firm committed fraud on someone—FDA, other government bodies or the public—in connection with obtaining approval of or marketing a product. The assertions may relate to misrepresentations in or omissions from applications submitted to FDA, to misleading promotional claims or to inconsistent statements made to other bodies or to investors. The public accountability of FDA and the agency's concern for the integrity of its processes require these allegations to be pursued diligently. For example, FDA recently brought a successful prosecution against a company and its chief executive officer, based on charges that it knowingly and deceptively marketed an approved product for sterilizing reusable surgical devices.

Many of the examples just discussed first appeared to be "public health" crises, with widespread stories of illness or deaths linked to the products. But in each case, as well as the other examples, the crisis evolved into a "fraud" crisis where the company was under a lengthy investigation for misconduct.

DURATION OF A CRISIS

A fraud crisis attracts episodic attention:

- *when allegations are first exposed*
- *whenever there are important subsequent revelations*
- *if litigation results, when cases are tried*

To most outsiders, a crisis seems like a bomb explosion: noisy and brief. The public perceives crisis activities as short-lived or episodic. The situations flare, attract considerable attention and soon become forgotten. The public health problem, for example, is addressed promptly: the product is removed, relabeled or given a "clean bill of health." A fraud crisis attracts attention episodically: when the allegations are first exposed; whenever there are important subsequent revelations; and, if litigation results, when cases are brought or tried.

This image is deceptive for those actually involved in a FDA regulatory crisis. For a business, management of the problems can require resources for many months or years. The company still must respond to the potential litigations and investigations that are spun off by the initial controversy. Probably it will engage in its own internal investigation and analysis of "what went wrong" and "how could we do better." And it may need to implement changes in personnel and procedures as a result of the crisis.

The litigation surrounding the diet drugs fenfluramine and dexfenfluramine (aka "Phen/Fen Litigation") illustrate the amount of time resolution of these problems can take. In 1997, medical reports linked these drugs with cardiac disease; they were withdrawn from the market almost immediately. The products became the target of product liability lawsuits, which resulted in a class action settlement and an adjudication procedure for processing claims. Claimants could nevertheless litigate if certain conditions were met. Over a decade later, individual cases were still in the courts.

Understanding how long a crisis might last is important for a company. The problems will divert resources for extended periods and require recurring management attention. As patience wears thin, the desire for a "quick fix" will intensify.

PREPARING FOR A CRISIS IN TODAY'S BUSINESS WORLD

In today's downsized corporation, different crisis management strategies are needed.

The common recommendation for crisis management involves having designated teams available, written procedures, training exercises and mock rehearsals. There is great merit in this approach, but in the downsized corporation of today, other strategies are needed. Many firms no longer have the capacity for training and rehearsing. Moreover, given regular personnel turnover, the potential benefits from developing and maintaining a state of readiness may not appear to managers and directors to be worth the investment.

Thus, additional ways must be found to prepare for managing the future regulatory crisis.

Contemporary crisis management requires at least five elements:	
1	Recognize a possible crisis early and act accordingly.
2	Get ahead of the potential crisis by anticipating its possible scope.
3	Staff the crisis adequately.
4	Ensure truth and consistency in public statements.
5	Deal effectively with FDA and other constituencies.

The first challenge is to recognize a potential crisis early so that appropriate steps can be taken. This step is perhaps the most difficult to take. Most firms and individuals in a potential—or actual—crisis situation cannot accept easily the possibility that something terrible might happen. Not only does the potential for a crisis suggest that the lives of many people will be disrupted; it implies some failure or error on the part of someone in the organization. By the same token, being the bearer of bad news is neither welcomed nor honored. Consequently, the natural human incentives always work against thinking the unthinkable. This tendency toward complacency frequently can lead a company into giving insufficient attention to an emerging issue until too late.

Firms must attempt to get ahead of any potential crisis. To anticipate the possible scope of problems that may have to be addressed, the company must assume a "worst case" scenario. As with warnings about possible crises, this unpleasant exercise is not welcomed and may be greeted with criticisms of "doom-saying." While it might be hoped that such prognostications at least would soften the shocks when things go from bad to worse, it should not be a surprise that—when predicted scenarios come to pass—people will complain they were not really warned about this or that possibility.

Firms must attempt to get ahead of any potential crisis. To anticipate the possible scope of problems that may have to be addressed, the company must assume a "worst case" scenario.

Legal advisers need to assess the company's potential vulnerabilities so that immediate actions can take them into account. These vulnerabilities include potential exposure to enforcement action by FDA or other governmental agencies; claims for damages from consumers, customers and vendors, third-party insurers, employees and stockholders; and investigations from legislative bodies. Nonlawyers must be involved also, for many of the most pressing demands for rapid response from the company will arise from media and business considerations, not simply legal obligations. Interested and indirectly affected constituencies may include shareholders (particularly major investors and securities analysts); suppliers and distributors; employees and their unions; insurance carriers; and federal, local and foreign government agencies. These constituencies cannot be overlooked when focusing on the ultimate consumers of the product, lay media or regulators such as FDA.

Once the potential or emerging crisis is identified and its dimensions are sketched out, the company must promptly allocate adequate and qualified resources. Two groups of inside employees are essential to handling the situation: those who will be responsible for corporate management of the crisis and those who uniquely possess the factual background essential to support the crisis management effort. These indispensable people must be made available, even if it means that other assignments do not get accomplished. To help them focus on the crisis, these individuals should have job priorities adjusted promptly.

Beyond these essential persons, the company should ensure that adequate numbers of people with knowledge, skills or experience appropriate to the demands of the crisis are located and assigned. Transferring people will not be easy, as it necessitates a painful process of choosing priorities among competing needs of the business. Here lies the importance of understanding the potential extended duration of a crisis: projects potentially could be postponed not merely for a few weeks, but indefinitely unless other resources are found.

A further staffing consideration is the ability of each individual to function under prolonged stress. Most scientists, regulatory affairs, marketing and business management people are not trained to—nor do they wish to—work in the adversarial circumstances of, for example, a criminal investigation by FDA or extended civil litigation. Thus, the composition of a crisis management team should take into account the long-term demands on its members. For a variety of reasons, bringing in outside resources is almost always prudent and necessary. They probably have more experience in crises, particularly if the company and its current management have been fortunate enough to have avoided any FDA crisis in recent memory. They also are not being pulled from other corporate commitments. Finally, they usually are more accustomed to a stressful and adversarial environment. Companies should avoid a natural tendency to attempt to manage the situation using only internal resources; a delay in bringing in the appropriate resources can be costly.

For a variety of reasons, bringing in outside resources is almost always prudent and necessary. They probably have more experience in crises, particularly if the company and its current management have been fortunate enough to have avoided any FDA crisis in recent memory.

During a crisis, it is imperative to ensure the truth and consistency of public statements. A regulatory crisis generally involves allegations that a product appears to endanger the public health. These allegations will become public through news reports. Consequently, the business is pressured to respond to public inquiries and attacks. Carefully managing the media is critical, particularly in the early stages of a crisis. In addition, if there are parallel proceedings—such as lawsuits, congressional hearings, or inquiries from other government agencies and/or governments—the company will be making statements in those arenas..

These pressures can be the most difficult for lawyers or regulatory affairs officials. These individuals often prefer to have matters resolved quietly, out of the spotlight, as much as possible. In a regulatory crisis, however, this approach does not serve the company's interests well. The business must maintain consumer and public trust. It may be compelled to undertake remedial actions and self-correction activities to reassure the public. If company officials are so worried about future liabilities that these immediate priorities are ignored, the business will hurt itself for both the short- and the long-term.

All public statements must be accurate and truthful, and be capable of being proven so, for they likely will be closely scrutinized in the future in many different circumstances.

All public statements must be accurate and truthful, and be capable of being proven so, for they likely will be closely scrutinized in the future in many different circumstances. The company must avoid injuring itself through its public statements. In an era of "spin doctors" the tendency to rebut an allegation with a plausible tale or statement of principle may make the company briefly look good. But if the assertion cannot be substantiated—or worse, later can be proven wrong—the statement will haunt the company for a long time. In dealing with press communications, despite the best public relations effort, no company is going to be able to control media coverage. At most, the story can be influenced toward accuracy and balance. Thus, the value of an unsubstantiated assertion is limited, while the risks are not.

Another common tendency of companies is to make sweeping promises of corrective or remedial actions, in an effort to forestall FDA regulatory activity. It is critical to ensure that any promises to government regulators both can be kept and will be kept. FDA has seen firms pledge to undertake changes in manufacturing processes, for example, that were technologically impossible. Such promises undermine credibility and certainly do not deter an FDA enforcement action. Similarly, failure to fulfill a commitment made in the urgency of the hour must be explained later. The explanation that the cost of the commitment proved unacceptable to corporate management will not be favorably received by FDA. The company also should be careful to avoid any inference that the failure to have previously implemented a particular step or activity represents an admission of past legal violations. FDA has been known to interpret an unqualified pledge to take corrective steps as an admission of prior noncompliance.

Companies should avoid the following when making public statements:

- *unsubstantiated assertions*
- *sweeping promises of corrective or remedial actions*
- *inconsistent statements*

A third dimension of public statements involves assuring consistency among statements. Given the potential breadth and duration of a regulatory crisis, the company must ensure adequate coordination and communication among those who are making statements on behalf of the firm. A few years ago, one firm was embarrassed (and worse) when a spokesperson in a European country defended the safety of its product on the basis of a particular study; it turned out that the company had previously advised FDA that it could not establish the integrity of that study. The challenge of assuring consistency is especially important with respect to assertions made under oath or under legal rules proscribing false statements. Once a firm makes a sworn statement of fact to one government body, it cannot readily deny the truth of the statement before another agency or in court. To be sure, as information changes, prior statements no longer may be fully accurate, but the burden will be on the firm to demonstrate that its information evolved.

The last principle in contemporary management of a FDA crisis is to deal with FDA effectively. As with attempts to control the media during a crisis, efforts to control the actions and responses of FDA generally are doomed to failure. The agency has been mandated by Congress to protect the public and to ensure the integrity of its own processes, by independent investigation and evaluation of the underlying facts. FDA automatically fails in this duty if it accepts a company's story uncritically and without scrutiny. The more serious the alleged threat to the public, the more egregious the alleged fraud on the agency or the consumer, or the more public the allegations become, the greater will be the likelihood that FDA will conduct its own investigation, notwithstanding the statements and promises from the regulated firm.

Complicating the situation is the fact that FDA has two distinct roles, one seeking to protect the public health, the other charged with enforcing the law. In the first capacity, there is no inherent conflict between the agency and the company, which has no interest in injuring its customers. In a metaphorical sense, the marketer sits side-by-side with FDA confronting the public health issue with the best science and medicine both can bring to bear. Cooperation and candor assist both in resolving the safety issues.

But when the question is "What did the company know and when did it know it?", FDA and the firm are in an adversarial mode. In this situation, cooperation and candor may result in facilitating a criminal prosecution. Because the Federal Food, Drug, and Cosmetic Act (FDCA) contains strict criminal liability penalties, the intent or good faith of the firm and its officers is irrelevant to conviction. This fact infuses interactions between the company and FDA with inherent tensions and problems for lawyers, regulatory affairs personnel and business managers.

Because of the strict liability provisions of the FDCA, voluntary disclosure of any violation is tantamount to an admission of criminal wrongdoing.

To complicate the situation further, FDA has no voluntary disclosure program analogous to those of the Department of Defense or Environmental Protection Agency. These programs provide incentives to companies to reveal instances of violations in exchange for a commitment by the government not to impose the most severe sanctions legally available. Because of the strict liability provisions of the FDCA, voluntary disclosure of any violation is tantamount to an admission of criminal wrongdoing.

Despite these special burdens, the regulated business must communicate with FDA throughout a regulatory crisis. In doing so, it should avoid unnecessary confrontations, recognizing the high levels of stress already present. These interactions are not occasions for company employees to vent their past frustrations with regulatory processes at FDA. Nor should irrelevant agendas be incorporated into the situation.

The most sensitive and difficult communication between a company and FDA during a crisis involves "bad news." For the reasons just outlined, the natural tendency is to say nothing. If FDA is likely to learn the bad news eventually, however, the firm should be the first to tell the agency. This process permits the company to put the information into context and offer appropriate explanations. Disclosure also may enhance the credibility of the company with the agency.

The problems that can occur when others convey the bad news first are illustrated by the history of silicone breast implant regulation in the early 1990s. FDA had completed an interim review and concluded that the implants could continue to be marketed. During the same time, plaintiffs' counsel in product liability litigation identified internal corporate documents suggesting unanswered safety issues with the implants. These documents were supplied to FDA and apparently surprised officials, leading the agency to reverse its policy and suspend product marketing immediately. A subsequent investigation, however, led both FDA and the Department of Justice to conclude that the documents did not contain any material safety information not previously known to the agency. But by then the damage was done.

Dealing with FDA during a crisis involves complex and difficult choices. Handling the interactions effectively will never guarantee an outcome that the company might consider optimal. Unnecessary confrontations and a loss of credibility, however, will increase the probability of an undesirable outcome from the firm's perspective.

CRISIS PREVENTION

Strong crisis prevention programs can

- *limit the scope of a crisis*
- *reduce the duration of a crisis*
- *lessen the potential for a subsequent fraud crisis*

Some crises cannot be prevented, so preparation to deal with the inevitable crisis is important. Crisis prevention, however, remains a useful exercise. To the extent that prevention succeeds, it is all to the good. But even if a crisis occurs, strong crisis prevention programs can limit the scope and duration of any public health crisis and reduce the potential for a subsequent fraud crisis.

FDA is interested in knowing whether a firm has control of its operating systems and processes. FDA looks at two key factors: the "closed-loop" design of each system and the documentation of the critical decisions.

From the perspective of FDA, every regulated activity is or should be governed by a system. Each system should contain five fundamental elements:	
1	Written specifications or performance goals that the activity is to attain,
2	Written operating procedures by which the activity is to be conducted in order to meet the specifications or goals,
3	Training employees in the procedures,
4	Monitoring activity to detect failures to meet the specifications or goals, and
5	A self-correcting mechanism to identify the cause of each failure and institute appropriate remedial action.

The fifth element gives the system its "closed-loop" nature. Once the system has identified a failure, in theory it can identify what corrective action is needed. In somewhat oversimplified terms, the problem arose because:

♦ the specifications did not include all of the necessary targets for the system to attain; or

♦ the specifications were adequate but the operating procedures were deficient in assuring the correct conduct of the activity; or

♦ the specifications and procedures were both adequate, but employees were insufficiently trained to follow the procedures; or

♦ the specifications, procedures and training were adequate, but adherence to the training and procedures was insufficiently ensured.

The effort to identify the source of the failure, sometimes termed a "root cause analysis," not only permits the system to restore itself to compliance; it is also an essential prerequisite to meaningful corrective action.

FDA believes that these five elements should exist for all aspects of FDA-regulated activities, from the manufacture of individual products, to the development of labeling and promotional material, to the research and development process for new products, to the identification and reporting of adverse events. Good crisis prevention programs will ensure that each regulated operating system or activity has all five elements in place and functioning.

The primary contribution of these crisis prevention programs to crisis management lies in providing the company an opportunity to identify the situation early and to initiate steps to limit the scope and duration of any public health crisis. Secondarily, the existence of strong internal closed-loop systems may lead FDA to conclude that enforcement actions are not needed to bring about compliance from the company. Many of the elaborate and intrusive consent decrees obtained by the agency against individual firms reflect a sense that FDA had lost confidence in each firm's ability to get its own house in order and under control.

Documentation of internal decisions represents the second major crisis prevention activity of importance to FDA. The agency recognizes that its investigations have 20/20 hindsight accuracy. What is ultimately pivotal to initiating enforcement action against the firm is the agency's assessment of how the company performed when making the decisions that are now under FDA review. Successful prosecutions are less likely if the firm's actions were not unreasonable; the fact that a decision proved wrong does not make it unreasonable, even in hindsight.

Nevertheless, an action that looks reasonable in *post hoc* argument may not prevent enforcement actions. What the agency is looking for is a conscious decision, not inadvertent actions. Hence, FDA will look for documentation that shows the company made a decision that was:

♦ reasonable,

♦ reasoned,.

♦ timely, in that it occurred within the applicable time limits (e.g., by FDA reporting regulations or prior to product release in accordance with good manufacturing practices), and

♦ documented contemporaneously.

The last three items avoid *post hoc* arguments to defend actions that might have been reasonable.

Documentation leading to a company's reasoned decision can defuse and resolve questions about the company's conduct.

The benefit of such documentation to crisis management is that it can defuse and resolve questions about the company's conduct. If a firm can demonstrate through memoranda or other papers generated at the time decisions were being made that it promptly reached a reasoned decision, taking into account what was known and what the law required, all that FDA—or any private litigant—can argue in a court is that a different decision would have been more reasonable. Because the law generally recognizes that reasonable persons can disagree, these documents provide an important defense.

CONCLUSION

An FDA regulatory crisis may not be avoidable. If and when it strikes, a firm that is prepared to respond early and effectively will have an enormous advantage. The company that is not faces serious threats to its reputation, financial health and potentially, its viability.

Chapter 17

Research and the FDA

Gary L. Yingling, J.D., B.S.Pharm., M.S., & Ann M. Begley, J.D., B.S.N., K&L Gates LLP, Washington, D.C.

Key Points

- Each of the Food and Drug Administration's (FDA's) six substantive centers has its own requirements for research.

- Experimental animal research is regulated closely by both the U.S. Public Health Service and the U.S. Department of Agriculture to ensure the humane treatment of laboratory animals.

- In clinical research, the essential purpose of an Institutional Review Board is to review research to assure it meets the ethical obligations of a clinical study, whereas the principal investigator controls the integrity of the research and manages the other professionals conducting the research and the sponsor must monitor the study and the principal investigator's research to assure compliance.

- To assure that persons involved as subjects in a clinical study are properly informed, FDA requires that investigators obtain written informed consent from study subjects.

- When submitting data to FDA for review, a major consideration will be the integrity of the data.

INTRODUCTION

Research is central to the mission of the Food and Drug Administration (FDA)—not just research that FDA itself does, but more particularly the research that companies must submit to gain approval to market their products in the United States. This chapter provides an overview of the regulatory framework for research required by the centers for the various products regulated by FDA.

Each of FDA's six substantive centers has its own requirements for research. The centers require research studies to gain approval or marketing authorization for at least some of the products subject to their jurisdiction. The Center for Drug Evaluation and Research (CDER), the Center for Biologics Evaluation and Research (CBER), and the Center for Devices and Radiological Health (CDRH) each have statutory, regulatory and guidance documents creating standards and expectations of how the research is to be conducted. The Center for Veterinary

Medicine (CVM) has a similar expectation but not as detailed, and the Center for Food Safety and Applied Nutrition (CFSAN) and the Center for Tobacco Products (CTP) are evolving but there are expectations nonetheless.

FDA's research requirements and expectations have significant impact on how research is conducted in the United States and, to some degree, in other countries. These regulatory standards continue to develop as new methodologies and technologies emerge.

ANIMAL RESEARCH

A number of years ago, animal research was not the subject of government regulation and there was little dialogue relative to the ethical treatment of animals. Not so today. While not the subject of significant regulation by FDA, experimental animal research is regulated closely by both the U.S. Public Health Service (PHS) and the U.S. Department of Agriculture (USDA). Both PHS and USDA have established rules and standards governing the humane treatment of laboratory animals. Of particular relevance to those conducting preclinical research are USDA's Animal Welfare Regulations, which include provisions covering the licensing and registration of research facilities, as well as attending veterinarians; standards for adequate veterinary care; recordkeeping requirements; compliance quality standards; and various other research practices (see 9 C.F.R. Chapter 1, Subchapter A, Parts 1-3). These regulations require all animal research laboratory facilities to register and submit to federal inspection. Also, researchers are required to adhere to Good Laboratory Practices (GLPs) when conducting animal experiments (21 C.F.R. Part 58) if the collected research data is going to be submitted to FDA in support of a product application.

Each facility is required to establish and maintain an Institutional Animal Care and Use Committee to review and approve study protocols for proposed research involving the use of animals and to monitor ongoing animal studies.

Additionally, each facility is required to establish and maintain an Institutional Animal Care and Use Committee (IACUC) to review and approve study protocols for proposed research involving the use of animals and to monitor ongoing animal studies. Under this system, there are instances when an IACUC will not allow an experiment because it is considered torture to the animal. For example, 20 years ago one could remove both of a rat's kidneys making the animal uremic as part of an experimental design (bilateral nephrectomy). Today, it would be unethical to approve such a study design and an IACUC would most likely approve no greater than 5/6 removal. While such limitations on experimental design do create challenges, most can be overcome without compromising the objectives of the proposed study.

CLINICAL RESEARCH

FDA expects that all clinical trials will be conducted in accordance with good clinical practice (GCP) standards which, in essence, are intended to represent current best practices in the conduct of human subject research in terms of design, conduct, performance, monitoring, auditing, recording, analyses and reporting of clinical trials or studies. The purpose of GCP is to provide a level of public confidence that the rights, safety and well being of subjects are protected and the data collected meets expected standards of quality, reliability and integrity.

Institutional Review Board

Regulatory controls on clinical research start with the Institutional Review Board (IRB). Research involving human subjects that raises questions of safety cannot be undertaken without having the proposed experiment, protocol and informed consent reviewed by an IRB. An IRB is responsible for ensuring that the health and rights of human test subjects are adequately protected in a clinical research setting.

The origin of the IRB dates back to 1964, when the Declaration of Helsinki was adopted by the World Medical Assembly and one of the recommendations was that research be reviewed by an independent committee. The Department of Health, Education and Welfare issued a policy in 1971 governing federally funded studies that required that research be reviewed by "an appropriate institutional committee" charged with determining whether the rights and welfare of subjects are protected. The Belmont Report, a 1979 document issued by the National Commission for the Protection of Human Subjects of Biomedical and Behavioral Research, stated that an ethical review of research was necessary to protect human subjects. The federal policy resulted in two different sets of regulations governing human subject protection. Fifteen agencies have codified by separate regulation the "common rule," which covers most federally funded research. An example of the common rule is set forth in the Department of Health and Human Services (HHS) regulation. 45 C.F.R. Part 46. FDA's human subject protection regulation is similar to the "common rule" but takes into account FDA's unique authority as it relates to investigational products. 21 C.F.R. Part 56.

FDA and the Office for Human Research Protections (OHRP) (within the HHS) have specific regulations governing the various types of IRBs that may be established, their responsibilities and membership, and the need for minutes reflecting their decision making. The essential purpose of an IRB is to review research to assure it meets the ethical obligations of a clinical study. The IRB

The essential purpose of an IRB is to review research to assure it meets the ethical obligations of a clinical study.

can be an academic IRB, organized within an academic institution such as a university; an IRB organized by a clinical site that is conducting studies; or an independent IRB that acts as an IRB for clinical investigators or others who do not wish to undertake the obligation of creating an IRB organization. Additional information regarding FDA's regulation of the IRB and the board's composition and responsibilities can be found in Chapter 5 of this book.

In the drug and device area, both FDA and OHRP exercise inspectional jurisdiction. FDA's inspection is normally done as part of an on-site inspection by an FDA bioresearch monitoring professional, while most of OHRP's are done by correspondence and conference call. While the styles may be different, the objectives are the same. Each agency wants to assure that the IRB is fulfilling its ethical obligations to protect the human subject in clinical research.

Informed Consent

To assure that persons involved as subjects in a clinical study are properly informed, FDA requires that investigators obtain written informed consent from study subjects for "all clinical investigations regulated by FDA" that support product applications (21 C.F.R. Part 50). The informed consent statement/form, simply stated, must explain to the person who is considering whether to become a clinical subject, the following: the purpose of the study; its potential benefits, if any; and the risks that are potentially associated with participation in the study. The objective is to provide sufficient information so the person can make an informed decision on whether to participate in the study.

FDA has created regulations that specifically address the information that must be included in the informed consent document.

FDA has created regulations that specifically address the information that must be included in the informed consent document. Some of the required elements of informed consent include descriptions of: reasonably foreseeable risks, benefits that may be reasonably expected, the duration of the research activity and who to contact with questions about the research or a subject's rights during the study. The informed consent must be written using language understandable to the subject (fifth-grade level; translated); it must be reviewed and approved by the IRB; it must provide the subject with sufficient opportunity to consider whether or not to participate in the study; and the informed consent must be signed by the subject or the subject's legal representative to confirm the patient was informed (see 21 C.F.R. § 50.25).

It really does not matter whether the study concerns a food ingredient, a drug, cosmetic or device; the expectation is that a person being asked to participate in a research study should be provided with complete and understandable disclosure of the benefits and risks of study participation and provide his or her informed consent on a form examined and approved by an IRB. During its inspection of a clinical study, one of the main focus points of an FDA bio-research monitoring inspection or an OHRP audit will be whether the written informed consent that was signed by the study subject or representative fulfills the FDA or HHS regulation of fully and properly informing the subject. Failure to inform has often been the basis for FDA to disallow data or OHRP to question a research institution's compliance.

The Sponsor/Sponsor-Investigator

The sponsor is the person or organization who takes responsibility for and initiates a clinical investigation. Among other things, the sponsor is responsible for monitoring the conduct of the study being conducted by the principal investigator (PI) to assure compliance, ensuring that FDA and all participating investigators are notified about new adverse effects or risks associated with the investigative drug, and for the collection and analysis of the study data. The sponsor may be a pharmaceutical company, a private or academic organization or an individual. The sponsor-investigator, however, is an individual who both initiates and conducts a clinical investigation and under whose immediate direction the investigative drug is being administered and dispensed. It is the sponsor or sponsor-investigator who generally seeks FDA approval before beginning a clinical study. A relatively new requirement for clinical study sponsors is the need to list most studies on the National Institutes of Health's (NIH's) website (www.clinicaltrials.gov) before the enrollment of the first subject. The sponsor must submit to FDA a certification of compliance with the NIH testing requirement when it submits its investigational product application.

Principal Investigator

When one considers clinical research performed for the purpose of making a scientific data submission to FDA, careful attention should be paid to the PI because that person has primary responsibility for the FDA clinical research process. It is the PI who controls the integrity of the research and manages the other professionals conducting the research. FDA, by requiring the drug/biologic investigator to sign a Form 1572, places the ultimate responsibility for the clinical investigation on the PI. A Form 1572 is a "Statement of Investigator" Form. No investigator may participate in an investigation until he/she provides the sponsor with a completed and signed Form 1572 (21 C.F.R. § 312.53(c)). By signing the form, the investigator agrees, among other things, to conduct the investigation according to the approved protocol, to personally conduct or supervise the described investigation, to inform patients that drugs are being used for investigational purposes, to ensure that requirements related to informed consent and IRBs are met, to report any adverse events that occur in the course of the investigation to the sponsor, to report to the IRB unanticipated

The principal investigator has primary responsibility for the FDA clinical research process.

problems involving risks to the subjects and others, and to ensure compliance with all other applicable FDA regulations.

In the device process, the PI must sign an agreement with the sponsor which will include language that commits the PI to following the FDA regulations governing device studies.

Whether the investigational product is a drug or a device, the PI is responsible to several different parties in the research process. For example, when the study protocol is not followed, FDA holds the PI absolutely responsible. The IRB looks to the PI to advise it of unanticipated problems and to properly perform the informed consent process. When a Contract Research Organization (CRO) is employed, the CRO will expect the PI to follow the procedures for coordinating the research and enrolling patients. Finally, the sponsor will expect the PI to enroll patients, provide accurate and complete case report forms, submit adverse event reports and follow the protocol. The data collected by the PI are a critical part of the drug/device application process. As can be seen from these expectations, the PI is the foundation on which all studies are based.

Clinical research is first and foremost data collection, and the clinical site is only as good as its data collection process.

The most significant challenge for sponsors and FDA is that few physicians doing their first clinical study as a PI understand that clinical research is not clinical medical practice. Clinical research is first and foremost data collection, and the clinical site is only as good as its data collection process. The average medical professional who agrees to perform a clinical study and signs a 1572 or device letter agreement may have little understanding of the time and effort that will be required of the staff or the investigator personally. The PIs remain ultimately responsible if there are problems at the study site. The obligation is significant because the investigator can face criminal and civil sanctions should the staff fail to fill out the case report forms correctly. Unfortunately, many PIs do not fully appreciate the level of responsibility they have assumed and fail to properly educate themselves or their staff. (See FDA Guidance for Industry—Protecting the Rights, Safety, and Welfare of Study Subjects—Supervisory Responsibilities of Investigators, available at www.fda.gov/cder/guidance/index.htm.)

CENTER FOR FOOD SAFETY AND APPLIED NUTRITION

Food additives, color additives and Food Contact Notifications require the submission of scientific studies and data to support marketing.

Almost all of the studies are focused on safety and involve the use of various animal models and some tissue testing. Parties are expected to submit both supportive and other data when making submissions to FDA (i.e., provide FDA with information supporting approval of their submission, as well as information of which they are aware that does not necessarily support approval of their submission).

When submitting data to FDA for review, a major consideration will be whether the collected data is statistically significant. For example, were enough animals placed in the study to provide a statistically significant result? Most submissions also require a statement certifying that the study was conducted in accordance with GLPs. GLPs for nonclinical laboratory studies are discussed at 21 C.F.R. Part 58. These regulations include requirements pertaining to organization and personnel, facilities, testing, test and control articles, study protocols and recordkeeping among other things. While one might think that all laboratories practice GLPs, in fact this is not the case; many laboratories have not adopted the procedures necessary to satisfy GLP standards. Data from a laboratory that does not practice GLPs will, in all likelihood, be rejected by FDA. As to studies in humans being submitted to FDA, they are very rare so the center has no formal policy or procedure for submitting an application. One area in foods that often does include human testing is taste panels, but normally a taste test falls outside the definition of "research." Moreover, such testing is rarely submitted to FDA.

CENTER FOR VETERINARY MEDICINE

The CVM is concerned with both pharmaceutical and food testing in that the center is charged with approval of animal feeds, animal drugs and the level of drug that may be present in the animal tissue to be eaten by humans. This creates a unique situation not found in any of the other centers; CVM has oversight responsibility relative not only to animal feeds, but also with respect to the pharmaceuticals given to animals and the level of the pharmaceutical given the animal that can be present in the animal tissue at the time of slaughter.

CVM has oversight responsibility relative not only to animal feeds, but also with respect to the pharmaceuticals given to animals and the level of the pharmaceutical given the animal that can be present in the animal tissue at the time of slaughter.

For the most part, testing in animals is similar to safety testing for human foods in that it requires no pretesting submission to FDA. CVM, however, is increasingly focused upon the potential implications associated with the presence of residual levels of drugs that remain in animal tissue of food products ingested by humans. Where the drug is being tested in a food-producing animal and the intent is to use the tissue from that animal for human food, CVM will require research testing that evaluates not only the effect of the drug on the animal, but also the level of residue of the drug in the animal tissue to be eaten by human consumers.

Where questions of animal and consumer safety are involved, an investigational new animal drug (INAD) application (referred to in the regulations as a "Notice of Claimed Investigational Exemption for a New Animal Drug") must be filed with FDA before shipping the test article in interstate commerce. Studies evaluating the impact of such drug residues on human health will likely be required (21 U.S.C. § 512(j)). The legal requirements for conducting studies, tests and investigations under an INAD exemption are located at 21 C.F.R. Part 511. Among other things, these include labeling the product as investigational, ensuring that the test product is used for tests only in animals and not humans, maintaining adequate shipment records, and actually filing the INAD application. Usually this responsibility lies with the sponsor. Trials using the investigational drug may commence at any time following the submission of the INAD to FDA so long as the regulatory requirements mentioned above are satisfied. Additionally, animals treated with the investigational product may not be used for food until expressly authorized by FDA. Before conducting a study, drug sponsors are encouraged to consult with the agency on study design.

New animal drugs used for tests in vitro and in laboratory research animals are less strictly regulated and covered by the provisions of 21 C.F.R. § 511.1(a). Generally, if the animal tissue is not going to be used as a human food, then submission of an application prior to testing is not required.

CENTER FOR DRUG EVALUATION AND RESEARCH AND CENTER FOR BIOLOGICS EVALUATION AND RESEARCH

Unlike preclinical research, clinical drug research with human subjects requires FDA notification and involves more active FDA oversight. This is meant to protect the safety and general well-being of the human test subjects participating in the study and to ensure the integrity of the collected test data.

Before a clinical trial can begin, FDA must be notified to ensure that the research will be useful and not result in a study that would expose subjects to the risk of research without providing data that would be useful in a drug approval.

Before a clinical trial can begin, FDA must be notified to be sure the proposed test/experiment/research will be useful and not result in a study that would expose subjects to the risk of research without providing data that would be useful in a drug approval. To be sure the research will be of value, a well-designed and IRB-approved protocol should be used that includes appropriate controls such as informed consent and study monitoring. FDA requires that an investigational new drug (IND) application be submitted to the agency at least 30 days before the drug or biologic is shipped and administered to a test subject. Among other things, the IND should be accompanied by a copy of the IRB-approved protocol and any preclinical laboratory data supporting the proposed investigation. An FDA Form 1571 should be submitted, which identifies the phase of the study and specifies the sponsor's commitment to follow regulatory requirements.

An FDA Form 1572 signed by the PI should also be filed with the IND. By signing the FDA Form 1572, the PI commits to conducting the study in accordance with FDA regulations, including properly obtaining informed consent from each study participant, following the protocol, accurately recording all collected data, and ensuring that all of the investigational product is accounted for. In addition, the PI may work with sub-investigators who also must be listed in the filing with FDA so that the agency knows who is involved in conducting the study. During the 30-day period before the study is allowed to start, FDA will review the IND to assure that research is appropriate and the subjects will not be subjected to unreasonable risk. If the agency does not place a clinical hold on the IND within 30 days, then the IND becomes effective and the sponsor can begin the clinical trial. As a practical matter, the sponsor will generally seek some type of assurance from FDA that the sponsor can proceed with the study before actually starting; there have been times when FDA has delayed beyond 30 days in providing its view and the study has been placed on clinical hold.

Once the IND has been at the agency for 30 days and assuming that a clinical hold has not been placed on the IND, the sponsor/CRO can notify the PI that the PI can then enroll subjects into the study provided they meet the inclusion/exclusion criteria of the protocol and are properly consented into the study. During the study, the PI or the staff collect data from the subject and record it in the patient's clinical records and the case report forms (CRFs) for forwarding to the CRO or sponsor for review and analysis.

During the clinical study, it is likely that the PI will be monitored by the sponsor/CRO to assure that the PI is following the protocol and fully understands the study. If problems are identified at the clinical site, the monitor may try to educate the PI or the site may be closed because the quality of the research is such that it cannot be relied on to support any study conclusions. If the monitoring visit goes well, the PI will continue to enroll patients until the enrollment criteria have been met or the study is stopped. At that point, the PI will submit any data (CRFs) not already submitted and either destroy or return any unused drug. The PI's assignment is then concluded. Now the sponsor takes over the leadership role, analyzing the data from various PIs and conducting a statistical evaluation to see if the data supports a conclusion that the drug is better than a placebo.

Center for Devices and Radiological Health

Many devices can be proven to be effective based on nonclinical data.

Clinical research in the medical device area is only a little different from that performed in the area of drugs. As noted earlier, the PI does not sign a 1572, but instead agrees in a letter to the sponsor to follow FDA's medical device regulations. The center also does not require as much clinical research; many devices can be proven to be effective based on nonclinical data, including various physical measurements or animal data.

CDRH also does not require a pre-submission for almost all clinical studies. The center has concluded that there are two types of clinical studies with medical devices. The first type involves a study in which the clinical risk associated with the device is considered not serious, and is called a "Non-Significant Risk" study. In those cases, FDA has concluded that there is no real need in having an investigational device exemption (IDE) application formally submitted to FDA for review. Instead, the agency relies on the IRB to make the risk determination. If the IRB says there is no significant risk and approves the study, the sponsor/CRO does not need to file an IDE and the study may begin immediately (see 21 C.F.R. § 812.150). If, however, the IRB says the device does present a significant risk, then the sponsor/CRO must submit an IDE 30 days before the first patient is enrolled.

The IDE submission for the significant risk device is similar to the IND and is governed by 21 C.F.R. Part 812. In the case of an IDE submission, FDA has 30 days to make a decision on the application, and the sponsor must have FDA approval prior to sending the device to the PI. The PI can then seek to enroll patients who meet the study criteria and complete the informed consent process. Once the study is complete, any devices not used are to be returned to sponsor.

Center for Tobacco Products

As the newest center at FDA, the CTP's regulation of tobacco-related research is evolving. Under the Family Smoking Prevention and Tobacco Control Act of 2009, a company must submit a premarket tobacco product application (PTPA) to FDA to seek marketing authorization for "new tobacco products." In late 2011, FDA issued draft guidance describing its expectations as to the PTPA content, including content reporting human and nonclinical testing. Under the act, the PTPA must include information that establishes that the new tobacco product is "appropriate for the protection of the public health," which FDA understands to require an analysis of whether there is an increased or decreased likelihood that existing users will stop using such products, or that non-users will start using such products.

FDA plans to issue regulations providing conditions under which new tobacco products can be investigated in humans, but until that time, it is exercising discretion in enforcing the PTPA review requirements. In the meantime, however, it states that clinical studies must be designed to evaluate health risks of the new tobacco product, and that compliance with 21 C.F.R Parts 50 and 56 is recommended. FDA recommends that parties planning to conduct clinical research contact the FDA to discuss such plans.

The FDA guidance also describes its expectations as to nonclinical studies; specifically, they should evaluate the new tobacco product for toxicity, abuse liability, and carcinogenicity.

CONCLUSION

As noted, FDA's centers for drugs, biologics and medical devices have specific statutory and regulatory requirements governing the practice of preclinical and clinical research. Several of these requirements, such as the approval of the study by an IRB, and obtaining the informed consent of study participants, are required for all studies submitted to FDA. It is important for PIs and sub-investigators to fully appreciate their responsibility to ensure that the patient is properly informed, the recordkeeping is accurate and there is adherence to GCPs.

CVM focuses primarily on pharmaceutical research in food-producing animals while the CFSAN focuses on nonclinical research, and CTP rules on research conduct are evolving. Each of the centers is concerned with the quality of the research.

Chapter 18

International Regulation

Richard Kingham, Covington & Burling LLP, Washington, D.C.

Key Points

- Nearly every industrialized nation maintains regulatory systems comparable to the Food and Drug Administration's (FDA's), although those systems are not always based on the U.S. model.
- Food and drug law is not a recognized specialty outside of North America because most developed countries have not established agencies like FDA.
- Most advanced regulatory systems are in the European Union (EU), Canada, Australia and Japan.
- EU legislation governing foods, drugs and similar products is drafted by the European Commission.
- The first European medicines directive required member states to establish premarket approval systems. Today, requirements for marketing authorization applications are harmonized.
- Medical device directives in Europe rely on a new approach to harmonization, developed by the EU.
- Cosmetics legislation in Europe provides for ingredient declarations, use of common European nomenclature and requires manufacturers to maintain product dossiers.
- The EU has issued numerous directives, regulations and decisions affecting food regulation.
- The Health Products and Food Branch is the primary federal regulator in Canada.
- In Australia, drugs, devices and similar products are regulated by the Therapeutics Goods Administration; foods are regulated by several agencies.
- The Ministry of Health, Labor, and Welfare conducts food and drug regulation in Japan.
- The State Food and Drug Administration is the responsible national agency in China.
- The United States is unusual in the high degree to which it seeks to regulate exports.
- Efforts to coordinate international food and drug regulation and reduce obstacles to trade take three forms: international cooperation, harmonization of regulations and standards, and mutual recognition. Only the last of these actually eliminates duplicative approval requirements, but it has proved the most difficult to achieve.

INTRODUCTION

Nearly every industrialized nation maintains regulatory systems comparable to the Food and Drug Administration's (FDA's), although those systems are not always based on the U.S. model. In recent years, the United States has borrowed ideas from other countries, and there is a growing trend toward international harmonization of food and drug regulation.

It is thus essential to have at least a general understanding of international food and drug regulation. This chapter focuses on three topics: regulatory systems outside the United States, FDA regulation of exports and other matters affecting international trade, and international harmonization initiatives.

FOREIGN REGULATORY SYSTEMS

"Food and Drug Law" is not a recognized specialty outside North America for the simple reason that most developed countries in Europe and elsewhere have not established agencies like FDA. Instead, regulation of products under FDA's jurisdiction is commonly entrusted to several agencies, often in different ministries or departments. Within product categories, enforcement is sometimes divorced from policymaking and product-approval functions.

Many countries are now looking to the EU as an alternative to the FDA model.

The most advanced regulatory systems are in the European Union (EU), Canada, Australia and Japan. The regulatory system in China is less well developed, but is increasingly relevant because of the importance of the Chinese market to U.S. manufacturers. Perhaps the most important jurisdiction is the EU, which is now the biggest unified market in the industrialized world. As of 2012, the EU comprised 27 member states with a total population of 502 million, compared to 314 million in the United States. The EU's efforts to harmonize national regulation of consumer products provide a lesson in what can reasonably be expected from such initiatives. Many countries are now looking to the EU as an alternative to the FDA model.

European Union

The Legal Framework

♦ Sources of EU Food and Drug Law

There are two main sources of food and drug regulation in the EU: judicial decisions under provisions of the EU Treaty that correspond roughly to the Interstate Commerce Clause of the U.S. Constitution, and harmonizing legislation issued by the EU.

♦ Free Movement of Goods

The EU Treaty guarantees free movement of goods among the member states, and regulations that create obstacles to free movement may be struck down by the courts if they are not justified on specific grounds identified in the treaty (e.g., protecting the health and safety of consumers), or are not "proportional" to the public interests that justify them. The European courts have developed a substantial body of case law relating to national rules on foods, drugs, cosmetics, and other consumer products. Decisions have rendered unenforceable, for example, a French law defining "cassis de Dijon" and a 16th-century German beer-purity law that prohibited use of additives.

♦ Harmonization Measures

Beginning in the 1960s, the EU issued a series of measures aimed at harmonizing national regulations of consumer goods so that products are assured free movement and requirements for duplicative national approvals are minimized. The pace was accelerated greatly in 1985, when the EU set the deadline of December 31, 1992, for the issuance of more than 300 measures required to complete the "internal market." Amendments in 1986 to the EU Treaty furthered this "EC-92" initiative by eliminating provisions that allowed individual member states to veto harmonization measures.

Beginning in the 1960s, the EU issued a series of measures aimed at harmonizing national regulations of consumer goods.

Today, the EU maintains comprehensive systems of measures governing foods, drugs and similar products. The extent of actual harmonization, however, varies greatly among product categories. The following is a brief summary of the major measures.

Medicines

◆ Medicines

The first medicines directive, issued in 1965, required member states to establish premarket approval systems based on proof of efficacy, safety and quality. Today, requirements for marketing authorization applications are harmonized, as are provisions for labeling, advertising, regulation of wholesalers, good clinical practice, good laboratory practice (GLP), good manufacturing practice (GMP) and other matters.

Until 1995, marketing authorizations for medicines were granted country-by-country, and divergent decisions were common. Efforts to establish a coordinated "multistate procedure" (an early version of mutual recognition) were largely ineffective, because there was no mechanism to enforce harmonized decisions.

◆ The European Medicines Agency

Since 1995, a London-based independent agency, the European Medicines Agency, has been responsible for coordinating EU drug approval procedures.

Since 1995, a London-based independent agency, the European Medicines Agency (EMA), has been responsible for coordinating EU drug-approval procedures. Marketing authorization applications for new biotechnology products and many new chemical entities must be submitted to the EMA, and applications for certain other innovative products may be submitted on an optional basis. An expert body (the Committee for Medicinal Products for Human Use) reviews applications and renders opinions to the European Commission (the executive branch of the EU), which issues approvals that are effective throughout the EU.

For other products, national approvals also are available. Products that are intended to be marketed in more than one member state, however, must be submitted through mandatory mutual recognition or "decentralized" procedures that are backed up by a binding arbitration process administered by the EMA.

◆ Current Issues

A directive on clinical trials, which took effect in 2004, established requirements similar to those for investigational new drugs in the United States, although separate approvals or notifications are required in each member state where trials are conducted. An orphan drug regulation provides a 10-year period of marketing exclusivity, and there are incentives for investment in research on medicines for pediatric use.

EU law provides periods of data exclusivity after new drugs are approved, during which "generic" marketing authorization applications (the EU equivalent of abbreviated new drug applications) cannot be submitted. Under legislation that took effect in 2005 (which applies to innovative products for which marketing authorization applications were submitted after the effective date), the EU recognizes a uniform protection period that is often referred to as "8 + 2 + 1." Generic applications cannot be filed until eight years after the reference product is approved, and generic products cannot enter the market until the end of the tenth year, but this period can be extended to 11 years if a medically significant new use is authorized within the first eight years after the reference product is approved. A special system has been established for approval of follow-on biological products (referred to as similar biological medicinal products, or biosimilars).

Medical Devices

Separate directives establish uniform regulatory requirements for marketing active implantable medical devices (e.g., pacemakers), medical devices and in vitro diagnostics. All of these directives rely on a "new approach" to harmonization developed by the EU to facilitate the EC-92 initiative. The directives establish relatively general "essential requirements." Products that comply with those requirements are labeled with a mark of conformity (the CE mark) and are entitled to move freely throughout the EU, subject to a "safeguard clause" allowing national enforcement actions in extraordinary circumstances. Essential requirements are supplemented by standards issued by the European standard-setting bodies. Conformity to standards is not mandatory, but constitutes presumptive evidence of compliance with essential requirements.

Manufacturers are legally responsible for determining whether their products conform to essential requirements and thus may bear the CE mark. Conformity assessment procedures depend on the risk classification of a device, which is determined by principles in the medical device directives. For the lowest risk devices, conformity assessments may be performed by manufacturers without any intervention by third parties. Manufacturers must notify member state governments when such products are introduced to the EU market.

Manufacturers are legally responsible for determining whether their products conform to essential requirements.

Conformity assessments for higher-risk devices require interaction with "notified bodies" (quasi-governmental entities designated by member state governments). This may consist of product-specific design reviews or certification of quality systems, or both. Quality systems certifications are based on a European version of the International Organization for Standardization (ISO) 9000 series of standards, with modifications specific to medical devices. A recast of the medical device legislation is currently under consideration, but it is likely that the general regulatory approach will remain intact.

Cosmetics

A directive first issued in 1976 establishes a general safety requirement for cosmetics; sets harmonized labeling requirements; prohibits or restricts certain ingredients; and requires affirmative listing of specified categories of ingredients (ultra violet filters, preservatives and color additives). The European Commission, working with a scientific committee and the member state governments, periodically revises the ingredient lists.

The directive provides for ingredient declarations, using a common European nomenclature, and requires manufacturers to maintain product dossiers. The dossiers must include reports of safety evaluations, which are subject to inspection by member state governments. Manufacturers must submit notifications when products are introduced in the EU. The directive also includes a ban on testing of cosmetic products and new cosmetic ingredients in animals.

The EU has adopted a cosmetics regulation that will supersede the directive and apply directly in the member states. There will be requirements for premarket notification (but not premarket approval) through a centralized system for finished products containing nanomaterials, reporting of serious, undesirable effects to government authorities, and other enhanced regulatory responsibilities. The basic framework will, however, remain the same, and enforcement will continue to be the responsibility of the member states.

Foods

◆ Harmonizing Measures

The EU has issued numerous directives, regulations and decisions affecting food regulation.

The EU has issued numerous directives, regulations and decisions affecting food regulation. These include "horizontal" measures on labeling, additives, contaminants, hygiene and food-contact materials, and "vertical" measures establishing standards for particular foods (e.g., chocolate, fruit juices, mineral waters and sugars). The European Food Safety Authority, which has replaced the Scientific Committee on Food, advises the European Commission on all matters with a direct or indirect impact on food safety, and other technical issues relating to food legislation. Not all aspects of food regulation are harmonized, however, and there is still scope for national variations.

◆ Free-Movement Principle

A 1989 EU "communication" seeks to prevent member states from enforcing national requirements that create obstacles to free movement unless there is a clear public health or consumer protection benefit, and requires member states to establish expedited procedures for approving imports from other EU countries that comply with food regulations in the country of origin.

OTHER JURISDICTIONS

Canada

♦ Laws and Agencies

The principal federal statute is the Food and Drugs Act (passed in 1953, but with predecessor legislation dating back to 1860), supplemented by the Food and Drug Regulations and numerous guidance documents. The Health Products and Food Branch (HPFB) in "Health Canada" (the Department of Health) is the primary federal regulator, although certain aspects of food regulation are entrusted to Agriculture and Agri-Food Canada, other federal departments, and a Canadian Food Inspection Agency established in 1997.

The principal federal statute in Canada is the Food and Drugs Act (passed in 1953, but with predecessor legislation dating back to 1860), supplemented by the Food and Drug Regulations and numerous guidance documents.

The HPFB maintains a system of premarket approval for new drugs, for which applicants submit new drug submissions and obtain notices of compliance. A procedure for abbreviated new drug submissions provides for an eight-year data exclusivity period to protect innovators, with provision for linkage to patent expiry. A separate system governs medicines containing old active ingredients, for which submissions are required to obtain drug information numbers or GP numbers.

For many years, Canada maintained a relatively simple notification system for most medical devices, with more elaborate requirements for safety substantiation of specified products. The HPFB has established a premarket screening procedure, in which the level of scrutiny depends on relative risk based on classification principles similar to those used in the EU. The ISO 9000 series of standards for quality systems also plays a role.

The Food and Drug Regulations contain requirements for labeling of cosmetics and for notifications of new products, and the HPFB has issued guidelines on permissible claims. Drug/cosmetic products are permitted, but must be registered as proprietary medicines and meet other requirements for drugs (e.g., GMP).

Food additives require prior approval, and the Food and Drug Regulations establish requirements for labeling. The HPFB has issued numerous informal guidelines, including detailed guidance on health-related claims for foods.

Australia

Drugs, devices, and similar products are regulated by the Therapeutic Goods Administration (TGA) in the Commonwealth Department of Health and Ageing. Foods are regulated by several federal and state agencies, with many requirements established by Food Standards Australia New Zealand. Cosmetics that are not classified as drugs are subject only to general regulations for consumer products. The TGA has entered into a mutual recognition agreement with the EU concerning medical device regulation.

In Japan, drugs, devices, foods and cosmetics are regulated at the national level by the Ministry of Health, Labor, and Welfare. The Pharmaceutical Affairs Law of 1960 governs drugs, devices and cosmetics, while the Food Sanitation Law of 1947 governs foods.

Japan

Drugs, devices, foods and cosmetics are regulated at the national level by the Ministry of Health, Labor, and Welfare (MHLW). The Pharmaceutical Affairs Law governs drugs, devices and cosmetics, while the Food Sanitation Law governs foods.

Drugs ordinarily require a manufacturing or import license (*kyoka*) and a product license (*shonin*). Data requirements for marketing authorization applications are set out in guidelines issued by the MHLW. New chemical entities are subject to a period of postmarket "re-examination," during which abridged applications for generic copies are not accepted. There are simplified procedures for approval of products containing established active ingredients.

Medical device regulation was revised in 1995, and the current system assigns devices to several classes based on relative risk. Product approvals are no longer required for the lowest risk devices, but quality standards apply.

Cosmetic products require premarket approval. Applications for products containing novel active ingredients require safety data, as do those for "quasi-drugs," a category that includes many products regulated as ordinary cosmetics in Europe and the United States.

Food imports require prior notification. Detailed labeling requirements apply, and there is a system of premarket approval of food additives, with different requirements for "chemical compound additives" and substances of natural origin.

China

Drugs, devices, foods and cosmetics are regulated at the national level by the State Food and Drug Administration, with significant responsibilities also entrusted to authorities in the provinces, autonomous regions and municipalities. Drug manufacturing and distribution are subject to license requirements, as are clinical trials. Separate systems have been established for licensing imported drug products, with provision for a six-year period of data exclusivity for new chemical entities. There are special licensing systems for traditional Chinese medicines and ethnomedicines, vaccines, blood products and diagnostic reagents. In addition, licensing requirements apply to medical devices, cosmetics and many food products.

FDA REGULATION OF FOREIGN TRADE

General Controls on Exports

Every developed country regulates imports of foods, drugs and similar products, but the United States is unusual in the degree to which it seeks to regulate exports. Section 801 of the Federal Food, Drug, and Cosmetic Act (FDCA) permits exports of foods, drugs and other articles that are adulterated or misbranded under U.S. law if they conform to the specifications of foreign purchasers, do not conflict with foreign law, and meet certain other requirements. FDA has narrowly interpreted the exemption provisions of the section to restrict exports of banned color additives, aflatoxin-contaminated feedstuffs and similar products. The agency has asserted that exporters bear the burden of proving compliance with foreign law and has demanded proof of compliance, including letters from foreign government officials.

The United States is unusual in the degree to which it seeks to regulate exports.

Exports of Unapproved Drugs and Devices

◆ Historical Background

Unapproved drugs (and, since 1976, unapproved devices) have presented the most difficult problem. By a quirk of legislative drafting in 1938, the new drug application requirement was not linked to the adulteration and misbranding provisions of the FDCA. As a result, the export exemption in section 801 was ineffective for unapproved new drugs. It is unclear whether Congress intended this result, because it chose seven years later (without discussion) to regulate penicillin, and later other antibiotics, under the adulteration provisions and thus make them eligible for the export exemption.

◆ FDA Enforcement Policy

In the decades following 1938, FDA consistently took the position that exports of unapproved new drugs were prohibited. The agency extended the ban not only to finished products but also to bulk pharmaceuticals, applied the export restriction to foreign trade zones, and prohibited import of unapproved products intended solely for re-export.

The agency permitted exports of "chemical intermediates" used to manufacture drug substances, on the theory that they were not new drugs, but refused to apply a similar policy to precursors of biological products.

◆ The 1968 and 1976 Amendments

By the 1960s, the U.S. ban on exports of unapproved drugs, whatever its historical origins, had become a matter of political significance. Consumer groups drew attention to the "dumping" of unsafe and ineffective medicines in developing countries and urged the United States to provide moral leadership to the industrialized world. When it enacted the Animal Drug Amendments of 1968 and the Medical Device Amendments of 1976, Congress specifically incorporated special procedures for FDA approval of exports of banned or unapproved devices in a conscious effort to drastically deter such exports.

◆ The 1986 Export Amendments

By the 1980s, the political climate had changed. There was increased concern about the competitiveness of U.S. businesses in world markets, and manufacturers argued that U.S. export controls served mainly to encourage companies to locate research and manufacturing facilities abroad.

In 1984, FDA issued regulations permitting exports of unapproved drugs for clinical trials, subject to permits. In 1986, Congress enacted amendments that allowed exports of unapproved drugs to any of 21 listed countries, subject to specified conditions, including FDA permits. The legislation included special provisions for unfinished biologics and drugs for tropical diseases.

◆ Current Law

The FDA Export Reform and Enhancement Act of 1996, among other things, lifted the import-re-export ban.

The FDA Export Reform and Enhancement Act of 1996 lifted the import/re-export ban, allowed exports of unapproved drugs and premarket approval devices to any country if they were approved in one of several designated jurisdictions, permitted exports for clinical trials in the listed jurisdictions and eliminated the requirement for prior approval of most exports (although a simple notification was still required). The legislation also authorized FDA to expand the list of designated countries and to permit, on a case-by-case basis, exports of products not approved in listed countries.

INTERNATIONAL INITIATIVES

Efforts to coordinate international food and drug regulation and reduce obstacles to trade take three forms: international cooperation, harmonization of regulations and standards, and mutual recognition. Only the last of these actually eliminates duplicative approval requirements, but it has proved the most difficult to achieve.

Efforts to coordinate international regulation and reduce obstacles take three forms:
* *international cooperation,*
* *harmonization of regulations and standards, and*
* *mutual recognition.*

Cooperative Agreements

♦ **General**

Information exchanges and other cooperative efforts among government agencies have existed for many years. FDA, for example, began "tri-partite" meetings with drug regulators in the United Kingdom and Canada more than 25 years ago, and the World Health Organization (WHO) has long maintained an international clearing house for information on adverse drug reactions. FDA officials now meet periodically with their counterparts in the European Commission.

More recently, FDA has entered into formal information-sharing agreements with the EU and Japanese authorities relating to drug approvals, inspections and safety reporting. FDA and the EMA have also agreed to procedures for providing joint scientific advice to pharmaceutical companies on develop-ment of new drug products.

Responding to public concern about imports of contaminated drugs, cosmet-ics and other products, FDA has established inspection posts in countries that export significant quantities of products to the United States.

♦ **Memoranda of Understanding**

FDA's more formal cooperative agreements with foreign regulatory agencies are commonly set out in memoranda of understanding (MOUs), exchanges of letters and similar documents. Typically, these are signed by FDA and its coun-terparts in foreign countries, but approval by the U.S. Secretary of State may also be required. Agreements cover a wide range of topics, from information exchanges to mutual acceptance of inspections and product standards.

The precise legal status of these agreements has never been entirely clear. They are not treaties within the meaning of the U.S. Constitution, and they cannot supersede FDA's obligations under U.S. statutes or regulations. Some FDA officials have expressed concern that such agreements might impermissibly delegate FDA enforcement functions to foreign governments. Nevertheless, MOUs and similar agreements have great practical importance for the industrial sectors affected.

International efforts to harmonize food and drug regulatory standards have proliferated.

Harmonization

In recent years, international efforts to harmonize food and drug regulatory standards have proliferated. WHO, the Organization for Economic Cooperation and Development (OECD), international standard-setting bodies (especially the ISO), and numerous sectoral and regional organizations have played a role in the process. The Uruguay Round amendments to the General Agreement on Tariffs and Trade (GATT), signed in 1994, enhanced the significance of these initiatives, because signatory countries now may be required to justify failure to implement agreed-upon international standards.

◆ Major Initiatives

Codex Alimentarius

Among the oldest efforts is the Codex Alimentarius Commission, established by the United Nations Food and Agriculture Organization and the WHO in 1962 to develop international standards for foods. The Codex Commission, whose members include representatives of more than 150 countries, aims to protect the health of consumers and ensure fair international trade in food. Major areas of activity include food labeling, food additives and contaminants, food hygiene, pesticide residues, veterinary drug residues, analytical methods and food inspection. The Codex Commission is advised by expert committees, such as the Joint Expert Committee on Food Additives and the Joint Meeting on Pesticide Residues.

Although the United States has long participated in Codex activities, it has given a relatively low priority to implementing Codex standards.

International Conference on Harmonization

The International Conference on Harmonization of Technical Requirements for Registration of Pharmaceuticals for Human Use (ICH), established in 1989, has been an extraordinarily productive initiative. Sponsors include FDA; the

Japanese MHLW; the European Commission; and the national trade associations of the pharmaceutical industries in the United States, the EU and Japan, with coordination from the International Federation of Pharmaceutical Manufacturers & Associations. Other governments and international entities participate as observers.

From its inception, the ICH decided not to seek mutual recognition, but to focus instead on harmonization of technical requirements for product registration. Activities have been undertaken in the areas of safety (e.g., toxicology testing), efficacy (clinical testing) and quality (manufacturing and chemistry). The result has been a series of consensus documents that participants transpose into guidelines or regulations. The volume of documents has been considerable. In some cases, however, full implementation requires issuance of new regulations or other legislation; this has proved difficult to accomplish, especially in the United States. The ICH has also developed a "common technical document" to help harmonize marketing authorization applications.

Medical Devices

A Global Harmonization Task Force, with participants from the United States, Canada, the EU, Japan and other countries, is seeking to duplicate the accomplishments of the ICH for medical devices. One of the greatest forces for international harmonization of medical device regulation has been the ISO 9000 series of quality systems standards, which can be used as the basis for external certification of companies' systems for controlling the design, testing, production and distribution of any product or service. The EU's decision to use modified versions of ISO 9001 and 9002, coupled with notified-body certifications, as one means of compliance with its medical device directives greatly enhanced the significance of the standards, as did FDA's decision to incorporate major elements of the standards in its regulations governing GMPs for devices.

A Global Harmonization Task Force, with participants from the United States, Canada, the EU, Japan and other countries, is seeking to duplicate the accomplishments of the ICH for medical devices.

♦ Effect of GATT and Other Agreements

International agreements aimed at eliminating nontariff barriers to trade lend increased importance to harmonization initiatives. Much attention has been devoted to the North American Free Trade Agreement (NAFTA), but GATT is potentially more significant, because it includes an effective enforcement mechanism.

Under GATT, measures that might affect international trade must not be stricter than necessary for protection of human, animal or plant health; must not be maintained without sufficient scientific evidence; and must be based on scientific principles. The World Trade Organization has been established to enforce these requirements.

Mutual Recognition

FDA maintains agreements with many countries on shellfish sanitation inspections.

FDA traditionally has been reluctant to enter into broad mutual recognition agreements with foreign countries, and such agreements have often been confined to narrow sectors or areas of regulation. For example, the existence of OECD guidelines for GLP, based in large measure on the U.S. GLP regulations, made it possible for FDA to enter into MOUs with several countries for mutual acceptance of GLP inspections. FDA maintains agreements with many countries on shellfish sanitation inspections. Mutual recognition, however, has proved much more difficult to accomplish for product sectors that are subject to premarket approvals and similar controls. A 1997 U.S./EU Mutual Recognition Agreement, which covered six product sectors (including drugs and medical devices), proved much less useful than was hoped. In particular, an arrangement for mutual recognition of GMP inspections for pharmaceuticals was never put in operation, largely due to FDA's reluctance to accept the results of inspections by certain national authorities in the EU.

Index

P

Pandemic and All-Hazards Preparedness Act of
2006, 58
"paper NDA," 150
Park doctrine, 462, 464
patents
        biologics, 168-169
        patent certification, 154-156
        patent extension, 146
Patient Protection and Affordable Care Act, 60-
61, 283
Pearson v. Shalala, 288
pediatric exclusivity, 52, 148
Pediatric Research Equity Act of 2003, 56, 138
Personal Care Products Council, 249, 251
pesticides
        Federal Insecticide, Fungicide, and
           Rodenticide Act (FIFRA), 109,
           273
        residues, 273-274
        tolerance setting, 39, 109
pet food, 59
Pfizer, 170
Pharmaceutical Research and Manufacturers of
America (PhRMA), 398
pharmacovigilance
        adverse drug experience, 175
        adverse event reporting, 175
        reporting requirements, 175
        report types, 176-183
        safety signals, 182
        supplemental applications, 183-185
        unexpected drug experience, 176
Pharmanex Inc. v. Shalala, 328
photography, 247, 417-418
Poison Prevention Packaging Act of 1970, 43
police power, 3
postmarketing
        adverse reaction reporting, 144
        change being effected supplement,
           142-143
        label changes, 143-144
        Phase IV studies, 145
        withdrawal, 144
postmarketing controls
        tobacco products, 372-373
postmarketing surveillance
        dietary supplements, 335
practice of medicine, 75-78
preemption, 4-5, 8, 50, 118, 349
premarket approval (PMA)
        annual reports, 221
        contents of, 214-217

device modifications, 220-221
        postapproval requirements, 218-219
        postmarket surveillance, 219-220
        review process, 217-218
premarket notification (510(k))
        Abbreviated 510(k),
           contents of, 205-207
        device modifications, 207-208
        New 510(k) Paradigm, 208
        overview, 204-205
        PMA approval process comparison,
           212-213
        Special 510(k): device modification,
        review process, 208-209
        third-party review, 210
premarket review
        philosophy of, 70-71
Prescription Drug Import Fairness Act of 2000,
53
Prescription Drug Marketing Act of 1987, 47,
449
Prescription Drug User Fee Act of 1992, 49
press releases, 389
primary mode of action, 228-230
principal investigator, 487-488
privileged information, 12-13
Product Development Protocol, 222
Project BioShield Act of 2004, 57
promotion. *See also* advertising; promotional
material
        advertising v. labeling, 384
        communications techniques, 389-392
        comparative claims, 388
        direct-to-consumer advertising,
           391-392
        drug samples, 395
        enforcement, 393-397
        fair balance, 384-385
        FDA regulation, 382-383
        material fact disclosure, 386
        off-label use, 395-397
        regulation by FDA, 379-400
        sales force training, 393
        third parties, 386
        truthfulness, 384
        voluntary conduct codes, 398-399
Public Health Security and Bioterrorism
Preparedness and Response Act of 2002,
54-55, 292
public statements, 475, 476
Pure Food and Drugs Act of 1906, 25-29

Waxman-Hatch Act. *See* Drug Price Competition
  and Patent Term Restoration Act
Weinberger v. Bentex Pharm., Inc., 157
Weinberger v. Hynson, Westcott & Dunning, Inc.,
  157
whistle-blowers, 55, 71, 403, 405, 471
Wiley, Harvey W., 25, 63-64